Introducing Microsoft® Office InfoPath™ 2003

Roger Jennings

PUBLISHED BY
Microsoft Press
A Division of Microsoft Corporation
One Microsoft Way
Redmond, Washington 98052-6399

Library of Congress Cataloging-in-Publication Data
Jennings, Roger.
Introducing Microsoft Office InfoPath 2003 / Roger Jennings.
p. cm.
Includes index.
ISBN 0-7356-1952-2
1. Microsoft InfoPath. 2. Business--Forms--Computer programs. I. Title.

HF5371.J46 2004
005.36--dc22 2004045751

Printed and bound in the United States of America.

2 3 4 5 6 7 8 9 QWT 9 8 7 6 5 4

Distributed in Canada by H.B. Fenn and Company Ltd.

A CIP catalogue record for this book is available from the British Library.

Microsoft Press books are available through booksellers and distributors worldwide. For further information about international editions, contact your local Microsoft Corporation office or contact Microsoft Press International directly at fax (425) 936-7329. Visit our Web site at www.microsoft.com/learning/. Send comments to *mspinput@microsoft.com.*

Acquisitions Editor: Juliana Aldous Atkinson
Project Editor: Dick Brown
Vendor: Studioserv, Steve Sagman
Technical Editor: Chris Russo
Copy Editors: Jennifer Harris, Teri Bucknell
Indexer: Caroline Parks, Indexcellence

Body Part No. X10-09367

This book is dedicated to my wife, Alexandra.

Contents At a Glance

Contents

Foreword

This book is an excellent hands-on introduction to Microsoft Office InfoPath, which represents a revolutionary leap in XML editing technologies and a new paradigm for gathering business-critical information. A wide variety of audiences will appreciate the information provided in this book: Information workers will learn how to fill out forms. Managers will learn how to approve or establish requirements for new or modified InfoPath form designs. Form designers will learn how to create or modify forms for their organization as well as use customer-defined XML schemas, and form developers will learn how to add custom business logic to their forms.

I was delighted when I learned that Roger Jennings, an experienced and talented author with more than a million copies of books in print on Microsoft productivity applications and XML Web services, had decided to write a book on InfoPath. Roger's book helps to fulfill a dream I and many of my colleagues in the XML community have had for over 15 years—bringing XML to the masses.

What is interesting and unique about InfoPath is the type of information it allows users to gather. It lets companies design and edit "semi-structured" documents, or documents that blend contexts or regions of meaning (the kind of meaning that columns in a database have, for example). Although InfoPath provides great design and editing capabilities within traditional forms such as purchase orders and equipment requests, it also targets information that historically has been more difficult to capture, such as business-critical data contained in sales reports, inventory updates, project memos, travel itineraries, and performance reviews.

I think of InfoPath as a hybrid tool because it combines the best of a traditional document editing experience, such as a word processor or an e-mail program, with the rigorous data-capture capabilities of forms. With InfoPath, form designers can easily design their own document templates that contain customer-specific schema for gathering information. What this means is that the customer defines the overall structure of the information that will be gathered from an InfoPath template and the type of content each data element will contain. Being able to define your own schema is a critical business advantage because no one knows what kind of information your company needs to gather better than you do.

Most mission-critical data isn't typically entered into forms. Think about a typical status report that a salesperson compiles: it contains customer information, sales information, and perhaps information about particular customer problems and promised remedies. Such a report is usually created in a traditional document editing application, but it often contains data that will be used over and over, not only by the salesperson who filed the report but also by coworkers and managers. If the salesperson had created the report in a basic forms application, it could have been spell-checked or formatted. But because forms applications don't have the familiar editing environment that traditional document editing applications provide, they can be hard to use, and so salespersons often don't use them as often as they should, meaning that valuable information can be lost. Another drawback to using a form for this type of document is that classic forms are static on the page; that is, they can't expand. Such a restriction becomes a big problem when data is constantly changing and the amount of it is growing. Not being able to provide added information—say, an optional executive summary—makes it difficult, if not impossible, to convey the full context of the data. The result is that people end up using multiple tools to get their jobs done, and they often lose half the data they collect.

InfoPath is similar to a forms package in that it provides all the functionality you could imagine from forms, such as the ability to structure and validate the data, but it lets you do much more. It is a tool that gives people the best of both worlds—the ease of use of word processing and the rigor of forms, all within the familiar Microsoft Office environment.

The XML community has been trying to build a tool like InfoPath for a long time. XML is about creating documents in which the content is delimited, or set apart, by tags that explain the meaning of each piece of content. With XML, documents can become a source of information as rich as a database, enabling search, processing, and reuse.

InfoPath has been built from the ground up to understand XML. The underlying structure of the information in an InfoPath template is described using a *schema*. A schema describes how the data is constructed, in the same way that a blueprint describes how a building is constructed. Because InfoPath understands XML, customers can define their own business-specific schema using the latest XML standards. Native support of XML also means that InfoPath can send data using customer-defined schemas to back-end systems via XML Web services. InfoPath is the first tool that can gather and send, or receive and read, XML data from a Web service without having to first translate the data to the .xml file format. The benefits of this innovation are enormous. Because XML is the native file format of all the information that is gathered in an InfoPath template, there are no translation errors, and custom programming is unnecessary, which means that both development time and costs are reduced. This level of support in InfoPath also lowers the cost of developing new solutions that use this data because the data is represented and structured the way you need it from the beginning.

Many of the features in InfoPath are the result of a key architectural design decision to adhere to the XML paradigm of separating the data in a document from the formatting. InfoPath associates "editing views" with abstract data structures, providing users with familiar Office functionality such as rich text formatting, table and picture support, and AutoCorrect. It also lets users save forms to their computers so that they can work on them at their convenience, even offline. In addition, industry-standard XML schema validation and business logic validation in InfoPath prevent costly data errors. For forms designers, InfoPath provides the same, integrated What You See Is What You Get (WYSIWYG) design environment. So a form designer starts with a custom-defined schema and builds a template around it. InfoPath also includes a built-in set of controls that make it easy to lay out forms as well as a set of 25 ready-to-use sample forms.

Microsoft's long-term vision for InfoPath is really the vision behind Microsoft's overall Web services strategy: to make it easy to create, access, and share XML data between different systems on a network. InfoPath is the first end-user product that gives information workers the capability to exploit XML and Web services. Enjoy the book!

Jean Paoli
XML Architect, Office Productivity Group, Microsoft Corporation
Co-creator of the W3C XML 1.0 Recommendation
Co-creator of Microsoft Office InfoPath

Acknowledgments

Thanks to Jean Paoli, Microsoft's XML Architect for the Office Productivity Group. Jean is the co-creator of InfoPath 2003 and the co-creator of the World Wide Web Consortium's XML 1.0 Recommendation, so he provides a unique perspective on InfoPath's objectives and features and its role as a member of Microsoft Office System 2003.

Producing a book of this scope is a team effort. Juliana Aldous Atkinson, program manager for Microsoft Press, managed the acquisition and scheduling process. Dick Brown was the initial project editor; Sally Stickney took over when Dick retired during the closing moments of the editing process. Tess MacMillan produced the CD that accompanies the book, and Charlotte Bowden handled the CD's quality control tests. Acey Bunch, now a documentation manager with the Microsoft SQL Server User Education group, prepared the original table of contents and chapter outlines for Parts I through III of the book.

Steve Sagman and his Studioserv team–Chris Russo, technical editor, Jennifer Harris and Teri Bicknell, copy editors, and Sharon Bell, layout artist–handled the book's production. Chris's sharp eyes caught many errors of omission and commission; those that remain are solely my responsibility. Jennifer and Teri corrected my grammar and style mistakes. Steve and Sharon are responsible for what I consider to be a very attractive book.

I couldn't have provided accurate descriptions and examples of new InfoPath 2003 SP-1 features without assistance from Microsoft's InfoPath development and support team. Boris Rivers-Moore, Paul Lorimer, Kamaljit Bath, Claudio Caldato, Miladin Pavlicic, Silviu Ifrim, Joel Alley, David Fries, Rodrigo Lode, Nora Selim, and Vani Mandava answered my numerous questions about SP-1 features. Vani also peer-reviewed most of the book's chapters for technical accuracy. Special thanks go to Alessandro Catorcini for clarifying Chapter 17's description of InfoPath SP-1 security levels.

Roger Jennings
http://www.oakleaf.ws/InfoPath/
Oakland, California, USA
May, 2004

Introduction

Microsoft Office InfoPath 2003 is a new and unique Microsoft Office System 2003 application that enables information workers to capture and edit information in dynamic, easy-to-complete forms and then store the resulting data in industry-standard Extensible Markup Language (XML) files. InfoPath increases information workers' productivity by letting them share forms and data with other team members, accept group contributions to a common form, merge multiple form files, and repurpose–if necessary–the XML data for incorporation in workflow processes.

InfoPath's use of the World Wide Web Consortium (W3C) XML and related standards–XML Schema, Extensible Stylesheet Language Transformations (XSLT), and XML Path Language (XPath)–enables integrating InfoPath data with a wide range of XML-enabled applications, including Web services and databases. Users can export InfoPath data to Microsoft Office Word, Excel, and Access 2003; import or copy data from these and other sources; route forms by e-mail with Microsoft Outlook 2003; and share InfoPath forms and files from Microsoft Windows SharePoint Services form libraries. E-mailing or uploading to a Web site a static version of an InfoPath form makes a read-only copy available to those who don't have InfoPath installed.

Introducing Microsoft Office InfoPath 2003 is more than an introduction to this versatile data gathering, sharing, and collaboration application. This book's examples and procedures teach you how to fill out basic types of InfoPath forms, such as a sample project status report. Step-by-step procedures lead you through the process of designing forms to generate customized XML data files, retrieve and update data from Microsoft Access and Microsoft SQL Server 2000 databases, and communicate with Web services. You can design very useful and sophisticated InfoPath forms without adding any programming code. If you need complex business logic that you can't implement with InfoPath SP-1's design features, *Introducing Microsoft Office InfoPath 2003* shows you how to program forms with Visual Basic .NET.

This book is intended for the following audiences:

- **Information workers** Those who fill out forms and route InfoPath data to others by e-mail, shared folders, Web servers, Windows SharePoint Services form libraries, or workflow applications–such as Microsoft BizTalk Server–for review, approval, or consolidation. Information workers often become designers of workgroup-level or department-level forms.

- **Supervisors and managers** Those who review, approve, and consolidate InfoPath data as appropriate to the type of form and its stage in the organization's workflow process. Supervisors and managers commonly establish requirements for new or modified InfoPath form designs.
- **Form designers** Those who create new or modified forms from their organization's or customer-defined XML schemas, from sample XML data documents, or by defining a new custom data structure in InfoPath. Form designers graduate to developer status if they program InfoPath forms with script or, preferably, Microsoft Visual Basic .NET or Microsoft Visual C#.
- **Form developers** Those who implement custom business logic by adding programming code that interacts with the InfoPath Object Model. Form developers commonly serve double-duty as form designers.

InfoPath 2003 Service Pack 1

This book's examples and procedures require installing Microsoft Office Service Pack 1 (SP-1), which performs a major upgrade to InfoPath 2003's initial version. SP-1 adds a host of new features to improve the efficiency and versatility of InfoPath forms. If you're an early InfoPath adopter, you'll appreciate the following form capabilities that SP-1 enables:

- The new Fill Out A Form dialog box that opens when users launch InfoPath from the Start menu or a desktop shortcut simplifies opening a recently used form, working with one of InfoPath's 25 sample forms, or designing a new form.
- The Form Conflict dialog box appears when users have two versions of the same form open and lets them select which version to use.
- Microsoft Office's AutoSave feature automatically saves form copies at specified intervals. AutoRecover opens a task pane if a user with a form open suffers a power outage or system failure and gives the choice of using the AutoSave copy or reverting to an earlier version, if one is available.
- The Data Connection Wizard, which replaces the Data Source Setup Wizard, simplifies the creation of new InfoPath forms from sample XML data documents, XML schemas, database tables, and Web services.

- User roles lets form designers assign specific Windows user accounts and security groups to custom-named roles, which you can use to enable or disable changes to the data document and the editing controls on forms.
- Digital signatures, which previously applied to an entire form only, now can authenticate individual parts of a data document. Digital signatures apply independently, or can be used to cosign or countersign information.
- Event-based rules display messages, change data values, use a specified data connection to request data from or send data to a database or Web service, or open a new form to complete when the form's content and user role satisfy a specific set of conditions.
- Developers who need a high level of security–called *full trust*–for their forms can substitute use of a code signing certificate for the task of creating and deploying custom-installed InfoPath solution files–called *form templates*. Digitally signed templates lets users share fully trusted forms from Web servers, shared folders, or Windows SharePoint Services sites.
- InfoPath 2003 SP-1 enables installation and use of the Microsoft Office InfoPath 2003 Toolkit for Visual Studio .NET, which lets you program forms with Visual Basic .NET or Visual C#.

The preceding list of new SP-1 features is far from complete, but the examples and procedures in this book show you how to take full advantage of all InfoPath 2003 SP-1 enhancements, except choice and repeating recursive section controls.

Managed Code Behind InfoPath Forms

Form developers using any edition of Microsoft Visual Studio .NET 2003 and the Microsoft Office InfoPath 2003 Toolkit for Visual Studio .NET together, create *InfoPath form projects*. InfoPath form projects let form developers substitute Visual Basic .NET or Visual C# managed code for Microsoft Visual Basic Scripting Edition (VBScript) or Microsoft JScript. The Microsoft .NET Framework 1.1 and managed code, together with Visual Studio .NET's integrated development environment (IDE), enables Microsoft IntelliSense statement completion and parameter lists to simplify coding and greatly improves the debugging process for complex business logic code. An InfoPath form project incorporates an assembly .dll file in the form template file and doesn't expose your source code to unauthorized modification by others. You can create an InfoPath form project for a new form design or base the project on a copy of an existing InfoPath 1 or SP-1 template file.

This book's form developer examples and procedures use Visual Basic .NET because most Office System developers find that migrating from Microsoft Visual Basic Applications Edition to Visual Basic .NET is more efficient than adopting Visual C#. There's no difference in the performance of projects written in either Visual Basic .NET or Visual C#, because both generate the same Microsoft Intermediate Language (MSIL) assembly code for InfoPath form project classes.

How This Book Is Organized

This book is divided into four parts of increasing technical depth and form complexity:

- **Part I, "Introducing Microsoft Office InfoPath 2003 SP-1"** Covers InfoPath basics–an overview of the benefits of InfoPath and XML for information exchange, a description of filling out a sample form, and a description of the XML technologies that InfoPath uses. The chapters in Part I are intended for information workers, form designers, and form developers who are new to InfoPath 2003.
- **Part II, "Designing InfoPath Forms"** Runs the gamut of form design techniques, including creating simple forms from a sample XML document, form layout and formatting, InfoPath's basic and advanced HTML controls, data validation and conditional formatting, adding form views, digitally signing data documents and form templates, and publishing forms to shared folders, intranet sites, and Windows SharePoint Services form libraries. Part II is intended primarily for form designers, but information workers will learn how to add digital signatures to InfoPath data documents. Form developers will gain an understanding of a codeless form's capabilities and limitations and will learn how to determine when programming code is necessary to accomplish the form's objectives.
- **Part III, "Working with Databases and Web Services"** Shows form designers and developers how to use the Data Connection Wizard to create InfoPath data sources that retrieve, display, update, insert, and delete records in Microsoft Access and Microsoft SQL Server 2000 Desktop Edition (MSDE) tables. You'll also learn how to design InfoPath forms that connect to a real-world Microsoft ASP.NET XML Web service and retrieve or update information in a remote database.

- **Part IV, "Programming InfoPath Forms"** Instructs form developers who have at least some experience with Visual Basic .NET programming how to create InfoPath form projects from scratch or copies of existing templates. The chapters' coverage ranges from writing simple event handlers to creating forms that generate custom-formatted XML documents and validate them against a third-party schema. Developers familiar with ASP.NET programming learn how to duplicate Part III's Web service and publish the Web service on a local computer.

Chapter Contents

Each chapter contains the following sections:

- **In this chapter you will learn to** A list of the tasks that you'll learn how to perform in the chapter.
- **To work through these sections** A sidebar at the beginning of each chapter that describes the skills and knowledge you need to understand the chapter's topics and gain maximum benefit from the examples and exercises.
- **For more information** A list of references to chapters that cover topics related to those in the current chapter and, in some cases, to external Web resources.
- **Hands-on procedures** Detailed, step-by-step instructions for performing specific form completion, design, or programming tasks to accomplish the objectives of the chapter.
- **Chapter Summary** A brief description at the end of each chapter of the chapter's contents and what you learned by completing it.
- **Q&A** A list at the end of each chapter of related questions and answers about the chapter's topics.
- **On Your Own** Hands-on exercises at the end of each chapter whose purpose is to demonstrate your grasp of that chapter's topics by presenting more challenging extensions of the chapter's procedures.

Sample InfoPath Forms

InfoPath 2003 comes with 25 "out of the box" sample forms that Microsoft Office System 2003 SP-1 upgrades to the new version. You use one of these forms–Status Report–as an example in the chapters in Part I. The chapters in Parts II, III, and IV use one or more derivations of three sample forms on the companion CD—Contacts, Rss2, and NWOrders—in examples and step-by-step procedures:

- **Contacts** A simple template with sample InfoPath data documents that contain names, addresses, and other information for fictitious faculty members of an equally fictitious Oakmont University in Texas. This form demonstrates basic InfoPath design techniques with very simple XML documents and schemas.
- **Rss2** A series of forms that create Really Simple Syndication (RSS) 2.0 files to demonstrate design and programming techniques for text-based forms. You start with a basic form and progressively add formatting, data validation, and other InfoPath features as you progress through Parts II and III. The Rss2Production project you create in Part IV is a full-fledged production InfoPath application for generating validated RSS 2 rss.xml files, which you can use for Web site content syndication.
- **NWOrders** A series of forms based on the Northwind.mdb (Jet) and NorthwindCS (MSDE) sample databases of Microsoft Access 2002 and 2003 to demonstrate InfoPath forms that participate in a business workflow process, work with numeric values, use multiple views, and require advanced data validation methods. You start the design of the NWOrders series from a sample XML data document, adapt the form to a live Jet and MSDE database, and then repurpose the form to an InfoPath Web service client that connects to a public ASP.NET XML Web service running on a demonstration Web server.

The sample files for each chapter's procedures include the starting version of the form and the final result after you complete the exercises.

About the Companion CD

This book's companion CD contains the template and data document files you need to complete each chapter's procedures. Much of the content of the companion CD requires Microsoft Internet Explorer 5.5 or later. InfoPath SP-1 requires Internet Explorer 6, which Microsoft Office System 2003 SP-1 installs if necessary.

Inserting the companion CD in the disk drive opens a licensing agreement that you must agree to before you can install the CD's files. If AutoRun is disabled, double-click the StartCD.exe file in the CD's root folder.

CD Content

Here's a list of the menu links on the CD that accompanies this book:

- **Readme** Opens the Readme.txt file, which offers additional information about installing the companion CD files.
- **Browse CD** Opens Windows Explorer and displays the CD's files and folders.
- **InfoPath Extras** Installs the InfoPath templates and XML data documents described in the section "Sample InfoPath Forms," earlier in this introduction. The next section provides instructions for installing the sample files.
- **Trial Version of InfoPath** Opens the Microsoft InfoPath 2003 Trial Software page from which you can download a trial version of InfoPath 2003 SP-1, the InfoPath 2003 Software Development Kit (SDK), and Microsoft Learning Support.
- **Software Development Kit** Opens the Microsoft Office InfoPath 2003 Developer Resources Kit page where you can order the InfoPath 2003 Developer Resources Kit DVD and Trial Software CD. The DVD includes the InfoPath 2003 Software Development Kit.
- **Microsoft Learning Support** Opens the Microsoft Learning Support page.
- **eBook** Contains the fully searchable content of *Introducing Microsoft Office InfoPath 2003* as an eBook in Adobe Systems' PDF format, which requires the Adobe Reader.
- **Adobe Reader** Opens the Adobe Systems Incorporated home page from which you can download the current version of Adobe Reader.

Installing and Using the Sample Files

To install the book's sample files, click the CD menu's InfoPath Extras link, click Next, accept the License Agreement, and click Next. By default, the sample files are copied to the C:\Microsoft Press\Introducing InfoPath 2003 folder and its subfolders, if your operating system boots from drive C. If your operating system boots from a different logical drive, click Change, change the drive letter to **C**, and click OK to return to the Custom Setup screen. Click Next and click Install to create and copy the files to the destination folders, and click Finish to dismiss the InstallShield Wizard. Each chapter has its own Chapter## subfolder, and most Chapter## folders have subfolders containing multiple form versions. Each exercise identifies the full path to the required and optional sample files.

Sample forms must be installed to the C:\ logical drive

You *must* permit the installer to copy the sample files to your C:\ drive and the default folder structure. If you install the sample files to a different logical drive or alter other parts of the path, you must re-save the sample form templates and you won't be able to open the sample InfoPath XML documents. InfoPath form templates and XML data files contain internal references to the appropriate C:\Microsoft Press\Introducing InfoPath 2003\Chapter## folder or its subfolders.

System Requirements

Working with this book's sample files adds the following system requirements, which are in addition to the basic system requirements for InfoPath published at *www.microsoft.com/office/infopath/prodinfo/sysreq.mspx:*

- The Microsoft Visual Basic .NET Standard edition of Visual Studio .NET 2003 or higher and the Microsoft Office InfoPath 2003 Toolkit for Visual Studio .NET for Part IV's InfoPath form project examples. Visual Studio .NET requires 900 MB of free disk space, and installing the complete MSDN Library documentation needs another 1.9 GB. The Microsoft Office InfoPath 2003 Toolkit for Visual Studio .NET consumes about 30 MB.
- A few of this book's procedures require Microsoft Office Excel, Word, or Outlook 2003 to be installed on the computer running InfoPath 2003 SP-1. The procedures in Chapter 13, "Connecting Forms to Databases," and later chapters require you to install the MSDE and have local access to the Northwind.mdb sample database, which are included with Microsoft Office Professional Edition 2002 and 2003. Chapter 12, "Publishing Form Templates," needs access to a Windows SharePoint Services site.
- Most examples in Chapter 11, "Setting Form Template and Digital Signing Options," require a digital signing certificate issued by a recognized public certificate authority (CA) or by your organization's private CA.

Support Information

Every effort has been made to ensure the accuracy of this book and the contents of the companion CD. To provide feedback on the book's content or the companion CD, you can contact the author at *Roger_Jennings@compuserve.com*, send e-mail to *mspinput@microsoft.com*, or write to the author in care of the following address:

Introducing Microsoft Office InfoPath 2003 Author
Microsoft Press/Microsoft Learning
One Microsoft Way
Redmond, WA 98052

Microsoft Press provides corrections for books through the World Wide Web at *www.microsoft.com/learning/support/*. To connect directly to the Microsoft Press Knowledge Base and enter a query regarding a question or issue that you might have, go to *www.microsoft.com/learning/support/search.asp*. For support information regarding Microsoft Office InfoPath 2003 SP-1, you can connect to Microsoft Technical Support on the Web at *support.microsoft.com/*.

PART I

Introducing Microsoft Office InfoPath 2003 SP-1

Part I's chapters explain the primary roles of InfoPath 2003 SP-1—capturing, editing, and sharing structured or semi-structured information that's contained in industry-standard XML files. You begin by exploring InfoPath's data entry and form design modes, progress to filling out sample InfoPath forms, and gain a basic understanding of the World Wide Web Consortium's XML recommendations that apply to InfoPath forms.

CHAPTER 1

Presenting InfoPath 2003 SP-1

In this chapter, you will learn how to:

- **Describe what you can accomplish with InfoPath**
- **Describe how InfoPath works in general**
- **Describe how InfoPath interacts with other Microsoft Office applications**
- **Start InfoPath and open a sample form in data entry mode**
- **Switch between InfoPath data entry and design modes**
- **Open the Microsoft Script Editor and view JScript form programming code.**
- **Describe how the Microsoft Office InfoPath 2003 Toolkit for Visual Studio .NET enables programming forms with Visual Basic .NET or Visual C#**

The original purpose of Extensible Markup Language (XML) was to define new text-based document formats for the World Wide Web. Subsequently, XML evolved into a language for describing almost any type of data so it's been responsible for an information-processing revolution. XML's capability to represent common data types–such as rows from a database or cells in a spreadsheet–as plain-text, human-readable documents has so dramatically increased its use in the information technology industry that it's become the world-wide standard for exchanging data between software applications running on all popular operating systems. As a testament to XML's popularity, searching Google.com for "XML" returned more than 30 million hits when this book was written.

Today's most common use of XML is behind the scenes–transferring data between servers and, to a lesser extent, between servers and client PC applications. XML provides the foundation for new and rapidly growing software markets, such as Web services, weblogs, and workflow automation.

To work through this chapter:

- You should be competent in managing Microsoft Windows XP Home or Professional Edition or Microsoft Windows 2000 Professional.
- You should have experience using recent versions of Microsoft Office applications, such as Microsoft Word and Microsoft Excel. Familiarity with Microsoft Office System 2003 applications is helpful but not essential.
- You should have Microsoft Office InfoPath 2003 Service Pack 1 (SP-1) installed on your computer. For more information about SP-1, go to www.microsoft.com/infopath. Prior to installing SP-1, you must have installed the InfoPath 2003 release version from a network installation folder or the retail packaged version.
- Optionally for this chapter, you should have the sample files from the CD that accompanies this book installed in your C:\Microsoft Press\Introducing InfoPath 2003\Chapter## folders. The section "About the Companion CD" in the Introduction describes the sample file installation process.

XML isn't dependent on a specific computer language or operating system. Almost all recent commercial software applications and development platforms support at least basic XML processing, but very few information workers have manipulated an XML document in its original format. Most PC users encounter their first .xml file or one of the other "x-files" (.xsd, .xsl, and the like) by opening the file in Internet Explorer, often accidentally. Making sense of complex XML documents is a formidable challenge for XML neophytes.

The objective of Microsoft Office InfoPath 2003 is to make creating and editing XML document files on the desktop or laptop as common as working with Microsoft Word, Excel, Outlook, and Access. InfoPath is certain to cause a dramatic increase in the use of XML by information workers and, as a consequence, their overall productivity.

The Benefits of InfoPath

InfoPath 2003 is a new member of the Microsoft Office System that enables ordinary PC users to collect information by typing data or making selections in an easily designed, simple-to-use, HTML-based form and save the information in a XML document file that any other XML-enabled application can process. Your first reaction to this understatement might be: "So what? There are plenty of HTML form design programs available, including Microsoft FrontPage, and I can create data entry forms in Microsoft Access, Excel, and Word."

Here's the key to InfoPath's success: Microsoft designed InfoPath for capturing semi-structured data in an intuitive form with the familiar Office-standard user interface (UI). *Semi-structured* means that the XML data that you create or edit doesn't need to adhere to a rigid data model, such as the row-column organization of an Excel worksheet or the relational data structure of an Access or Microsoft SQL Server database. If you design your own XML data document, you can choose to add or omit optional information, include text that's formatted with HTML tags, and specify whether parts of your form represent single or multiple information items. InfoPath forms ensure that the XML data file you save complies with XML formatting rules.

Imposing structure with predefined documents

If you base your form on someone else's XML data document design for a typical paper business form, such as a purchase order or invoice, you probably won't have the freedom to alter the document's design or apply HTML tags to the data. In this case, the XML data is called a (fully) *structured document*

InfoPath's capability to capture semi-structured data lets you combine in a single form related data that you or your coworkers presently might collect from a combination of Microsoft Outlook e-mail messages, Word documents, Excel worksheets, Access or SQL Server 2000 queries, HTML pages, and text files. InfoPath increases productivity by eliminating multiple cut-and-paste operations and time-consuming, error-prone data retyping. You can send the XML document as an e-mail attachment to InfoPath-equipped coworkers, who add and edit data or approve the data and then return the document to you for final processing. Figure 1-1 illustrates a sample InfoPath form opened in Outlook 2003. If the recipient has InfoPath installed and network access to the form's file, clicking the ChangeOrder1.xml file Attachments link opens the form for editing.

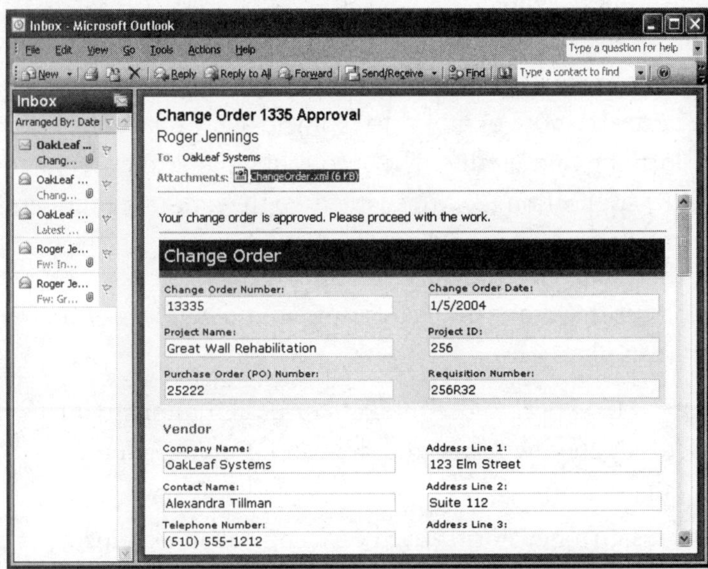

Figure 1-1 E-mailing a form as an attachment to a manager or customer for approval is a common InfoPath scenario.

InfoPath's ability to route data documents makes it easy to set up formal, multistep workflow processes without writing any programming code. As an example, assume that you're supervising a new product-development team and must send a comprehensive monthly status report to management. You maintain budget data in an Access database. Team members send you Excel worksheets with their time and cost expenditures, which you integrate into a master worksheet. You receive e-mail messages from team members that contain brief narratives of progress during the month, list issues outstanding, and provide the percentage completion of individual tasks. You have a Microsoft Word template into which you copy and paste data from Access queries, the master worksheet, and parts of e-mail messages; edit the content;

and send the .doc file as an e-mail attachment to your manager and the accounting department. It takes you five hours or more to assemble and edit the incoming mélange of data.

An InfoPath form, such as the sample Status Report form you open in this chapter's later section "Touring InfoPath" and fill out in Chapter 2, lets individual team members do *all* the work. You e-mail the form to the first team member, who contributes her status information to the form, and then passes it on to the next person to add his data, and so on. Each team member can see previous members' contributions, which avoids data duplication. You receive the final version, look it over, and e-mail it to management.

Signing Forms with Digital Certificates

To assure your form's authenticity, you can add a digital signature to the entire form or to specific elements of the form called data blocks. Team members can sign the data they contribute, and you can co-sign or countersign the content they add. Chapter 11, "Setting Form Template and Digital Signing Options," shows you how to add digital signatures to forms and code-signing certificates to templates. If someone tampers with the form you sign, InfoPath notifies the form's recipient that its digital signatures are invalid.

InfoPath reduces your five hours or more of monthly agony to a few minutes of checking numbers and performing minor edits. The accounting department's enterprise resource planning (ERP) application is XML-enabled, so the monthly numbers go directly to the general ledger without manual intervention.

Here are a few additional features that make InfoPath a unique and highly productive form design and data capture application:

- You don't need to be an XML expert to use InfoPath or design InfoPath forms. The familiar Office UI, task panes, wizards, and drag-and-drop design tools shorten your learning curve.
- It's a simple process to design a new form based on a copy of an existing XML document or the design specification for a document, which is called an *XML schema*. Most of this book's sample forms are based on sample XML documents. If you don't have an XML schema for the document, InfoPath generates one for you automatically.
- The Data Connection Wizard guides you through the steps of generating data entry forms from Access (Jet) and SQL Server database tables. Alternatively, you can receive data from and submit data to XML Web services.
- You can quickly define the structure of a new XML document in a graphical task pane and then design the form based on the XML schema that InfoPath creates for you.
- InfoPath forms validate data that users enter before saving the underlying XML document. By default, InfoPath checks the data against the document's design

as defined by its schema. You can highlight incorrect entries with conditional formatting and apply custom data validation rules without writing programming code.

- It's easy to post a static version of a form to a Web site by exporting it in .mht (Single-File Web Page) format. The .mht file doesn't include the XML document, so the recipient can't edit the form.
- Most applications that understand XML can process the XML documents you create or edit in an InfoPath form. The XML standard isn't tied to any programming language or operating system.
- You don't need to be a programmer to design and deploy useful InfoPath forms. However, form programming lets you implement many advanced form features and add custom business logic to forms.

See Also **Part II, "Designing InfoPath Forms," provides detailed explanations of the form design process and step-by-step instructions for designing simple and complex InfoPath forms. Part III, "Working with Databases and Web services," illustrates use of the Data Connection Wizard. Part IV, "Programming InfoPath Forms," covers customizing advanced forms with Microsoft Visual Studio .NET 2003 or Microsoft Visual Basic .NET Standard Edition 2003 and the Visual Basic .NET programming language.**

Understanding How InfoPath Works

Defining forms, templates, data documents, and views

InfoPath's documentation doesn't always distinguish between forms, templates, data documents, and views. This book uses the term form to mean a combination of an XML data document, which you save as an .xml file, and an editing template (.xsn file). Form also refers to the static version sent as an e-mail attachment (refer to Figure 1-1) or exported in .mht format. A view is the HTML representation of a form; all forms have a default view. Chapter 3 describes the files used by an InfoPath form and how InfoPath creates views. Chapter 12 shows you how to send static and dynamic forms by e-mail.

The original goal of the developers of XML was to provide a way of separating content (data in XML format) from presentation (HTML text and formatting code) in Web documents. This distinction enables displaying the same data in multiple presentation formats–typically browsers running on conventional PCs, handheld organizers, and cell phones. InfoPath forms follow the principle of separation of data and presentation. An InfoPath form combines an XML data document and a *template*; the template defines the presentation of the data for editing, messaging, and printing.

Another benefit of presentation independence is the ability to provide different views of the data in a single form. One form view might display summary data for multiple document parts, whereas an alternative view might show detailed information for a selected part. You also can design views that are optimized for different devices, such as Pocket PCs or even cell phones.

Previewing a Sample InfoPath Form

InfoPath's UI is quite similar to those of other Microsoft Office System 2003 applications, which makes working with forms a familiar process. Figure 1-2 shows a simple contact form in data entry mode, also called edit mode or "fill out a form" mode.

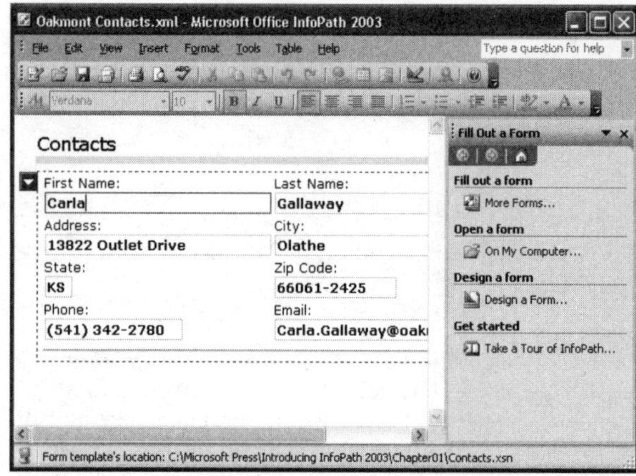

Figure 1-2 This simple InfoPath form enables capturing contact data.

Here's a list of the similarities and differences between the InfoPath 2003 and Word 2003 primary UI elements:

- The InfoPath 2003 menu bar is almost identical to that of Word 2003; only Word's Window menu option is missing.
- Most buttons on the InfoPath 2003 Standard toolbar correspond to those on the Word 2003 Standard toolbar. InfoPath SP-1 has additional Design and Format Painter buttons borrowed from Microsoft Office Access 2003.
- InfoPath and Word use the standard Windows shortcut keys, such as Ctrl+O to open a form and Ctrl+P to print a form.
- Three InfoPath task panes–Search Results, Help, and Clip Art–are common to other Office System 2003 applications. The others–Find, Replace, Font, and Bullets And Numbering–assist users with InfoPath data entry operations.
- The InfoPath work area is an HTML-based form. The simple Contacts example form shown in Figure 1-2 uses text boxes inside table cells for data entry. InfoPath offers many other HTML control types, such as option (radio) buttons, check boxes, ordered and unordered lists, and a special rich text box control to which you add HTML-formatted text.
- The status bar at the bottom of the Contacts form differs from Word by showing the path to the form's template.

Saving Data as XML Files

When you open an empty InfoPath form, you're opening the default view of a form template and an in-memory (cached) XML document that contains no data. As you enter data in the form, InfoPath adds the information to the cached document. Saving the form as DataDocName.xml writes the cached information to a disk file in a folder (My Documents, by default). Alternatively or additionally, you can store the XML file in a shared folder of a file server, POST it to a Web site, or add it to a Windows SharePoint Services form library. InfoPath SP-1's AutoSave/AutoRecover features prevent losing a data document in the event of a power failure or hardware problem.

Listing 1-1 shows the Oakmont Contacts.xml file with the data entered in Figure 1-2. The first line is called the XML declaration and is present in all InfoPath and most other XML documents. The listing excludes XML content (called processing instructions) that's specific to InfoPath.

```
<?xml version="1.0" encoding="UTF-8"?>
<contacts>
  <contact>
    <firstName>Carla</firstName>
    <lastName>Gallaway</lastName>
    <address>13822 Outlet Drive</address>
    <city>Olathe</city>
    <state>KS</state>
    <zipCode>66061-2425</zipCode>
    <phone>(541) 342-2780</phone>
    <eMail>Carla.Gallaway@oakmont.edu</eMail>
  </contact>
</contacts>
```

Listing 1-1 The XML content of a contacts list with a single contact entry.

XML files are text-based files that you can open and edit in Notepad or read in Internet Explorer. Figure 1-3 shows a slightly modified version of Figure 1-2's XML data document open in Internet Explorer 6.0. Applications other than InfoPath disregard the processing instructions (PIs), which begin with *<?mso-infoPathSolution* and end with ?>. This means that almost every XML-enabled application running under any computer operating system can process an InfoPath data document.

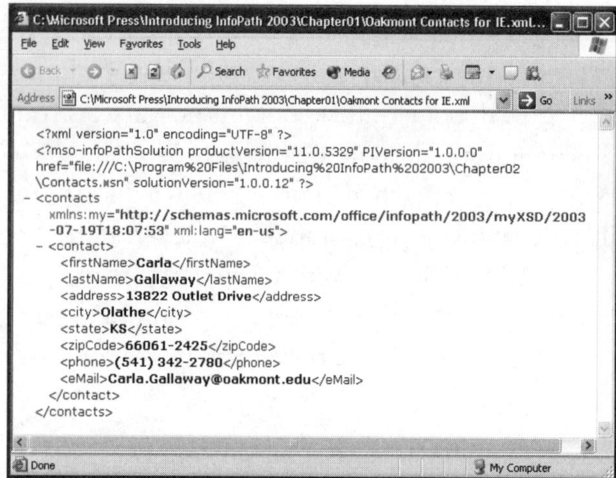

Figure 1-3 Internet Explorer 6.0 will display an InfoPath XML data document if it's modified to prevent InfoPath from opening it automatically.

XML content consists of pairs of start and end tags, such as *<lastName>* and *</lastName>*, to describe the content between the tag pairs, which define XML document elements. Tag pairs that contain text information only are called *leaf elements* or *leaf nodes*; the *<firstName>* through *<eMail>* nodes are leaf nodes. The capability to choose your own descriptive tag names for your data is what makes XML extensible and—more importantly—*self-describing*. Unlike HTML, which is very forgiving of missing tags, XML requires each start tag to have a corresponding end tag or use the shorthand version of an empty tag: *<tagName />*. As an example, HTML allows a stand-alone *
* (break) tag, XML requires empty *
* or *
 tags*. XML tag names are case-sensitive, so a *<lastName>* start tag won't match a *<LastName>* end tag.

Viewing InfoPath XML files in Internet Explorer

InfoPath XML data files open in InfoPath when you choose Open With, Internet Explorer from the file's shortcut menu. Installing the sample files creates original and modified versions of Oakmont Contacts.xml in your C:\Microsoft Press\Introducing InfoPath 2003\Chapter01 folder. The modified version will open in Internet Explorer.

See Also Chapter 3 describes in detail XML 1.0 data documents and the related XML dialects that InfoPath uses to define templates and views and how InfoPath interprets processing instructions.

Integrating InfoPath with Other Applications

InfoPath's use of XML as its data exchange format means that XML-enabled applications, such as Microsoft Word 2003 and Excel 2003, can import and edit InfoPath data files. You also can view, update, and save information stored in databases or retrieved from XML Web services. The following sections provide brief descriptions of InfoPath's most important interoperability features.

Working with Office Excel and Word 2003

You can import simple InfoPath XML data documents to Excel 2003 Professional Edition workbooks and assign XML leaf element text to worksheet list columns automatically. Assigning individual elements to columns is called *mapping*. You must make minor changes to Excel's default mapping to enable exporting the XML data. Figure 1-4 shows a longer version of the Oakmont Contacts.xml file mapped to an Excel 2003 list.

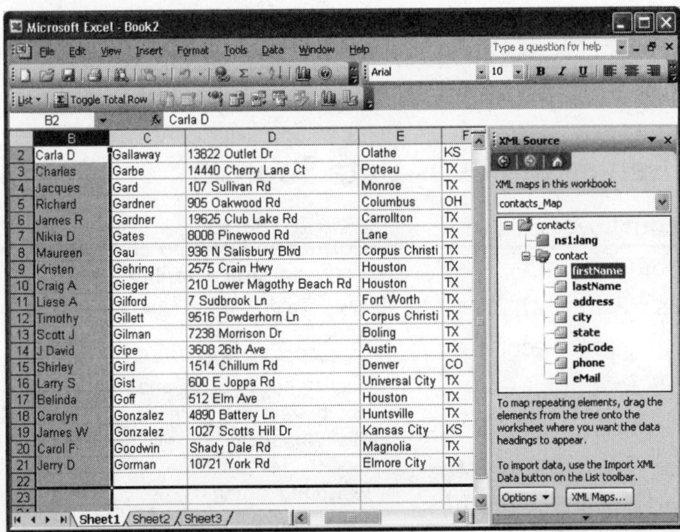

Figure 1-4 This is an InfoPath XML data document imported to an Excel 2003 Professional list.

XML files that you modify in Excel and save as XML Data (.xml) won't open in InfoPath automatically, because Excel strips the processing information from the file.

Opening the same Contacts.xml file in Word 2003 Professional Edition generates the XML document view shown in Figure 1-5. Unlike Excel, saving an edited Word XML document doesn't remove the PIs, so the saved document opens in its original InfoPath template.

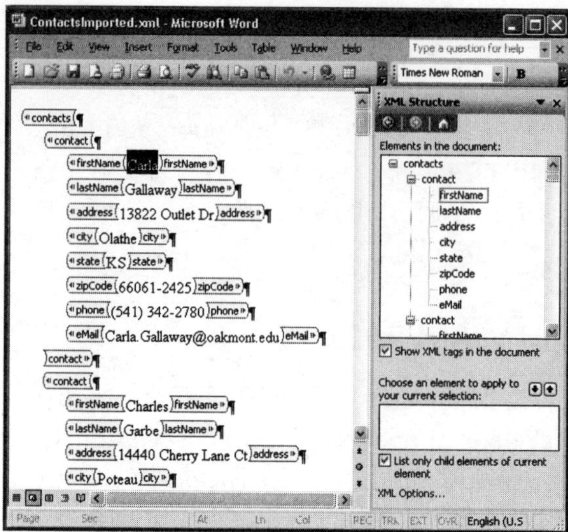

Figure 1-5 This InfoPath XML data document has been imported to Word 2003.

Alternatively, you can import an InfoPath schema file (Schema.xsd) into Word's Schema Library and add data to elements you select from the XML Structure task pane. Word 2003 XML documents you create from scratch with imported schemas and save as .xml files don't include InfoPath PIs.

Using Access or SQL Server Tables as Data Sources

InfoPath forms aren't a fully qualified substitute for Access data entry forms, but they offer unique advantages. You can save an XML data document that you route to others for action or approval, or you can send the document to a workflow management application, such as Microsoft BizTalk Server 2004. Integration with BizTalk Server 2004 is beyond the scope of this book, but you can learn more about this new Windows Server System application at *www.microsoft.com/biztalk/*.

> **Cutting and pasting elements between Office applications**
>
> You can copy formatted text and tables in InfoPath rich text boxes and paste these elements into Microsoft Word version 2000 and later documents, and vice versa. Copying and pasting cells from Excel version 2000 and later worksheets into rich text box tables (and the reverse) also works. The extent to which formatting is preserved depends on the version of Word or Excel you use. The section "Adding Tables to Rich Text Boxes," in Chapter 2, describes the cut-and-paste process in detail.

InfoPath's Data Connection Wizard lets you select tables from Access (Jet), Microsoft SQL Server Desktop Engine (MSDE) 2000, or other SQL Server 2000 editions to create forms for selecting, adding, editing, and deleting records. The Data Connection Wizard lets you specify the relationships between related tables to generate forms that emulate Access forms and subforms. Clicking Finish in the last Data Source Setup Wizard screen generates an empty template with a combined query and data entry view.

Figure 1-6 illustrates a sample data entry and editing form for Access 2003's NorthwindCS MSDE database. Entering a valid value in the Order ID text box and clicking the Get Order Data button displays an Orders record and its related Order Details records at the bottom of the form. Clicking the New Order button lets you add a new Orders record and multiple Order Details records. InfoPath handles updates to records with SQL Server identity or Jet autonumber columns without a hitch. This feat might surprise database developers who've worked extensively with identity or autonumber fields.

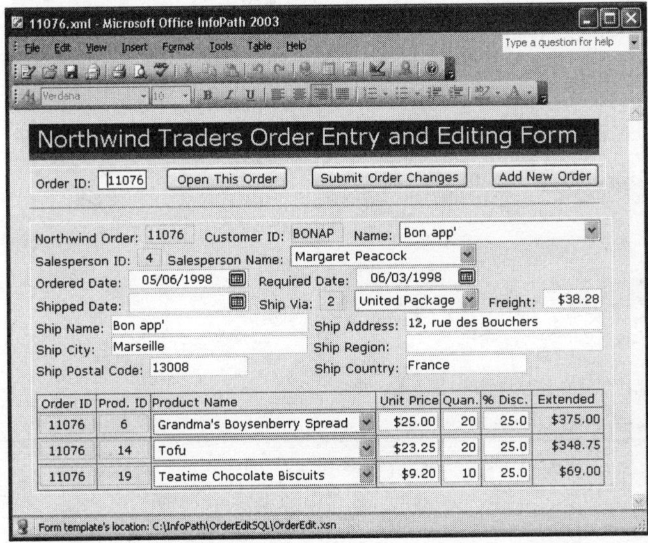

Figure 1-6 This InfoPath form emulates an Access form-subform combination.

The Northwind Traders Order Entry And Editing Form template introduces four InfoPath controls that don't appear on the Contacts form:

- **Date pickers** Adjacent to the three date text boxes. When you click the date picker button a calendar opens to let you select a date.
- **Drop-down list boxes** In this form, display data based on adjacent primary key values, such as a customer name from the customer code. Drop-down list boxes let you select from value/display-name pairs.
- **Expression boxes** In this form, calculate the Extended line item values. Expression boxes most commonly perform calculations with numerical values, but also can manipulate character values.
- **Buttons** Used for initiating built-in or custom InfoPath actions. The form's buttons execute built-in Run Query, Submit, and New Record actions.

Here's the most interesting fact about this data entry form, which also implements InfoPath's data validation features: it doesn't require a single line of programming code.

See Also Chapter 6, "Adding Basic Controls and Lists," describes how to take advantage of InfoPath's repertoire of "smart" HTML controls. Chapter 8, "Validating Form Data," shows you how to implement data validation. Chapter 13, "Connecting Forms to Databases," explains how to use tables as a form's primary data source and populate drop-down list boxes from secondary data sources.

Adding Data Documents to a SharePoint Form Library

If you have access to a Windows SharePoint Services site running under Windows 2003 Server, you can publish your InfoPath template and its associated XML data documents to a form library. Figure 1-7 shows a sample form library, which contains data files for seven NorthwindCS orders. A SharePoint site is the most convenient way to make an InfoPath form accessible to coworkers and group the form's XML data documents in a single shared location.

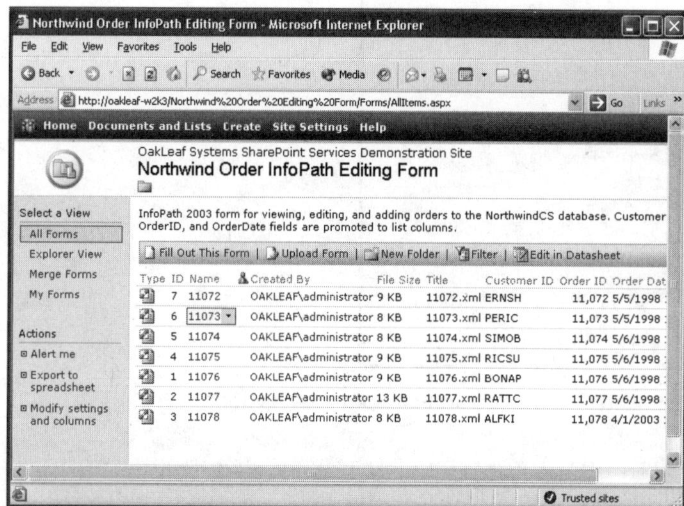

Figure 1-7 This demonstration Windows SharePoint Services form library lists InfoPath data documents for sample orders.

The form library is the default location for saving new and edited data files. You can also save copies of the data files to a shared folder on a file server or on your own computer.

See Also The section "Publishing Templates to Windows SharePoint Services Form Libraries," in Chapter 11, gives you step-by-step instructions for creating a new form library and publishing a form to the library. Visit *www.microsoft.com/sharepoint/* for more information about Windows SharePoint Services, the successor to SharePoint Team Services.

Connecting Forms to XML Web Services

Web services have recently become a major contributor to the widespread adoption of XML technologies. Web services deliver an open standards approach to transferring data between networked computers running different operating systems and programming environments. For example, a properly designed ASP.NET Web service created with Microsoft Visual Studio .NET and running under Windows 2000 or later can interoperate with Java-based Web services or Web service clients running under various UNIX flavors, and vice versa. Every major player in the software development platform, database management system, and enterprise-scale application businesses now supports Web services technologies at varying levels of sophistication.

One of Microsoft's objectives for InfoPath 2003 was to make it easy to connect to and collect data from XML Web services. InfoPath's Data Connection Wizard offers the option of connecting to a Web service and creating an InfoPath schema from it. Creating a form with a Web service connection is very similar to using database tables as the form's data source. Figure 1-8 is the Web service version of the form shown in Figure 1-6. Chapter 14, "Designing InfoPath Web Service Clients," and Chapter 17, "Writing Advanced Event Handlers," show you how to design forms that connect to an ASP.NET Web service to retrieve and update information in an SQL Server or MSDE 2000 database.

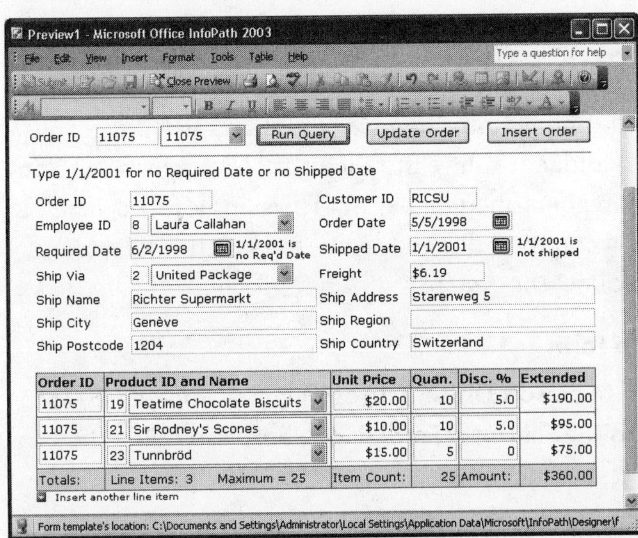

Figure 1-8 This InfoPath XML Web service client that you develop in Chapter 17 emulates Figure 1-6's form and adds an expression box to display the running sum of the Extended column.

Touring InfoPath

The preceding examples of InfoPath forms demonstrate what you'll be able to do with InfoPath after working your way through the design-related chapters in Part II and Part III. Now it's time to launch InfoPath and give it a test drive with one of InfoPath's sample forms.

InfoPath's Guided Tour

To watch an animated (Macromedia Flash) preview of how InfoPath works, you can take the Microsoft Office InfoPath 2003 Tour by following these steps:

1. Choose Start, (All) Programs, Microsoft Office, Microsoft Office InfoPath 2003 to open the Fill Out a Form dialog box.
2. Click the Take A Tour Of InfoPath link at the lower right of the dialog box to open the first tour page. Download the Macromedia Flash Player, if necessary, and then click the Start Tour button. The Flash presentation eventually displays the What Is InfoPath? page.
3. Click Continue twice to display the InfoPath Tour Contents page. You can return to the Contents page at any time by clicking the Contents button at the top of a page.
4. Click the Filling Out Forms link, which leads to a page of the same name.
5. Click the Play button to start an animated segment.
6. When the segment completes its animation cycle, click the Return link and then the Continue link. Filling Out Forms, for example, has 7 animated segments. The Designing Your Own Forms topic has 10 segments.

Opening a Sample InfoPath Form

Installing InfoPath 2003 adds 25 sample forms to your \Program Files\Microsoft Office\Office11\InfForms\1033 folder, if you've installed the U.S. English version. (The locale code differs for other regions and languages.) The sample forms emulate paper business forms and share a common design theme. To launch InfoPath and open one of the simpler forms, follow these steps.

▶ **Launch InfoPath and open a form**

1. **Choose Start, (All) Programs, Microsoft Office, Microsoft Office InfoPath 2003 to launch InfoPath, which opens the Fill Out A Form dialog box, also called the dashboard.**
2. **Click the Sample Forms link under the Form Categories heading to display icons for the 25 sample "out-of-the-box" forms, as shown on the next page.**

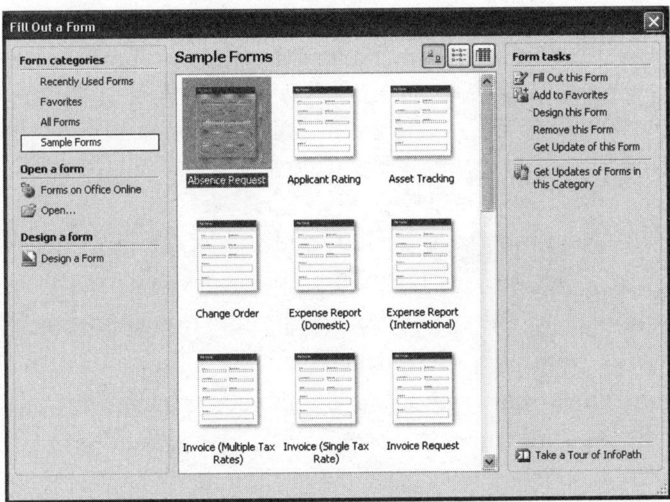

3. Scroll to the end of the list, double-click the Status Report item to close the Fill Out A Form dialog box and display the form in InfoPath's work area, with the default Standard and Formatting toolbars visible. JScript code in the form's template automatically sets the date picker's value to your system date.
4. Maximize the window, if necessary, to display the topmost elements of the form. The sample forms are designed to fill an 800-by-600-pixel window with the task pane visible.
5. If the task pane isn't open, press Ctrl+F1. Click inside the rich text box under the Summary heading to enable the Formatting toolbar's buttons, as shown here:

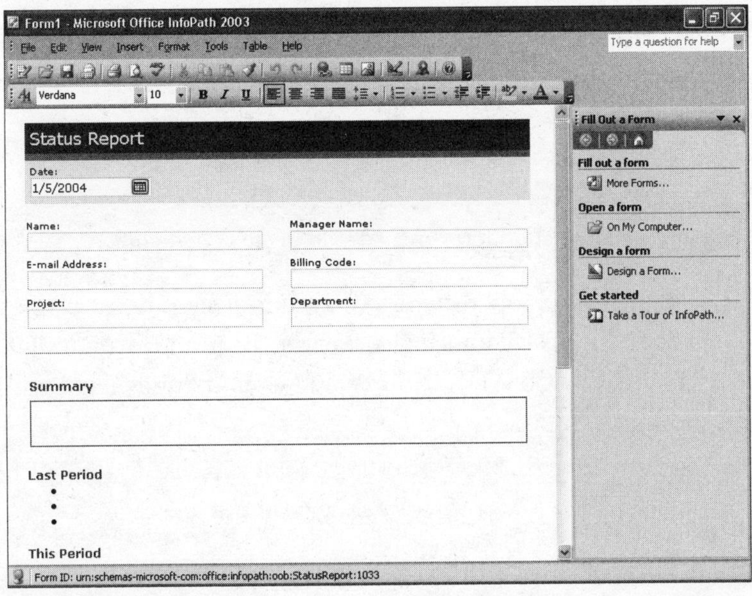

6. **In data entry mode, the Formatting toolbar is fully enabled only for data entry in rich text boxes. Rich text boxes also enable three buttons of the Standard toolbar: Insert Hyperlink, Insert Table, and Insert Picture.**

Using Design Mode to Create or Modify Forms

To display the sample Status Report form in design mode, click the Design This Form button, or choose Tools, Design This Form. If you've worked with Microsoft Access, you'll notice that InfoPath's design mode corresponds to Access data page design view. In design mode, InfoPath's Standard toolbar gains Preview Form and Design Tasks buttons, and the Formatting toolbar is enabled, as shown in Figure 1-9. When you open a sample form in design mode, the default template name is Template1.

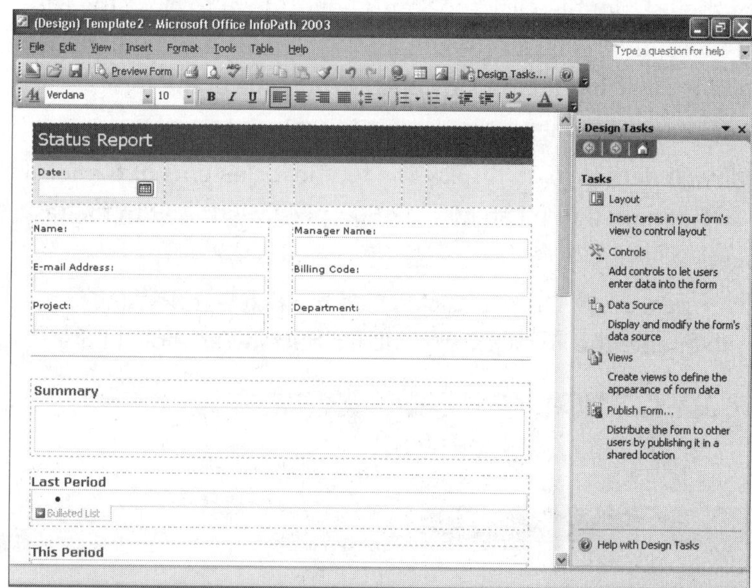

Figure 1-9 This is the sample Status Report form opened in InfoPath's design mode.

The Design Tasks task pane, which opens when you enter design mode, displays links to other task panes and a wizard for the five basic steps in the form design and deployment process: Layout, Controls, Data Source, Views, and Publish. In Part II, an entire chapter is devoted to each task.

Programming Forms with VBScript or JScript

Most Office System applications use Microsoft Visual Basic for Applications (VBA) as their application programming language. Office's Visual Basic Editor (VBE) makes it easy to add or modify macros or, in the case of Access, code behind forms or in modules. InfoPath 2003 departs from this norm by using Microsoft JScript or Microsoft Visual Basic Scripting Edition (VBScript) and the Microsoft Script Editor (MSE) as the default code editing tool to customize the behavior of forms. JScript is InfoPath's default scripting language, but you can change the default to VBScript. The next section, "Programming Forms with Visual Basic .NET Code" describes this book's preferred alternative to scripting InfoPath forms. Fortunately, you don't need to write custom code to create useful InfoPath forms, as demonstrated by the database and XML Web service examples in the section "Integrating InfoPath with Other Applications," earlier in this chapter.

If you're a competent VBA programmer, adapting to VBScript, which is a subset of VBA, is reasonably easy. However, the sample forms and most InfoPath programming examples use JScript, Microsoft's implementation of ECMAScript–originally known as Netscape JavaScript. You need basic JScript skills to understand the code behind the sample forms and take advantage of their array of standard functions in the script that you add to your forms. Moving from VBA and the VBE to JScript and MSE isn't a piece of cake, and debugging complex script is difficult at best.

With the Status Report form open in design mode, choose Tools, Script, Microsoft Script Editor or press Alt+Shift+F11 to open MSE and display the JScript functions behind the form in a new window. Figure 1-15 shows MSE with the Project Explorer and Properties windows hidden to expose more of the JScript code.

Form events, such as opening a form, execute JScript functions called *event handlers*. The Document Outline window lists all event handlers and other functions for the template. The *function XDocument::OnLoad(oEvent)* event handler corresponds to VBA's *Private Sub Form_Load* event handler. This function inserts the system date in the date picker control at the top of the form.

At this point, close the MSE window to make InfoPath's design window active, and then close the design window to return to the Status Report form in data entry mode. Don't save any accidental changes.

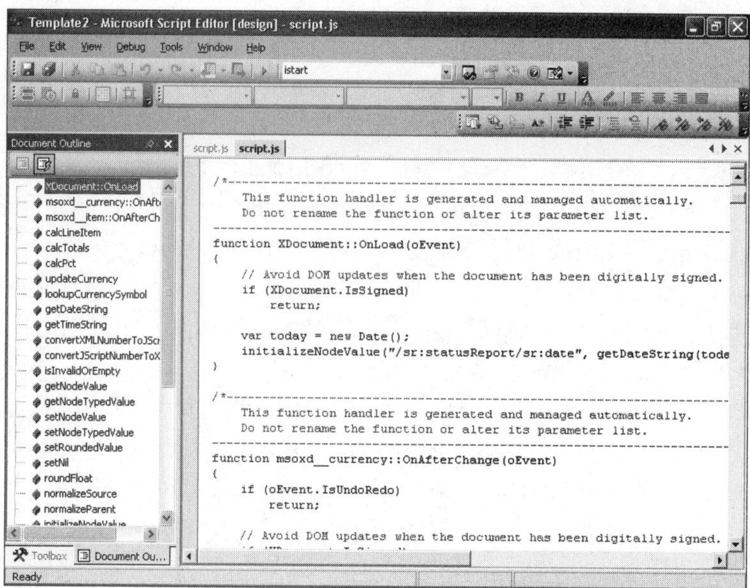

Figure 1-10 MSE displays only a small part of the code behind the sample Status Report form in this window.

Programming Forms with Visual Basic .NET Code

One of InfoPath SP-1's most important new features is the ability to create InfoPath Form Projects, which substitute managed Visual Basic .NET or Visual C# code behind forms for VBScript or JScript. It's probably easier for most Office developers and Visual Basic 6.0 coders to adapt to Visual Basic .NET than learn JScript. Your expenditure of time and energy learning Visual Basic .NET will deliver a much higher return on investment than a transition to JScript or downlevel VBScript, which some analysts call "Microsoft's forgotten language."

To take advantage of InfoPath Form Projects, you must have Microsoft Visual Studio .NET 2003 Professional edition or higher, or the $99 (estimated retail price) Visual Basic .NET 2003 Standard Edition, and the Microsoft Office InfoPath 2003 Toolkit for Visual Studio .NET installed on your development computer. You can download the Toolkit from a link on the InfoPath page at *msdn.microsoft.com/office/understanding/infopath/*. Users of forms with managed code must have the Microsoft .NET Framework 1.1 runtime version, available at no charge, installed on their computer.

Installing the Toolkit adds a Microsoft Office InfoPath Project node to Visual Studio .NET's New Project dialog box, and a Visual Basic Projects subnode with an InfoPath Form Template icon in the Templates folder. If you have the Visual Studio .NET Professional edition or higher, you'll also see a Visual C# subnode, as shown in Figure 1-11.

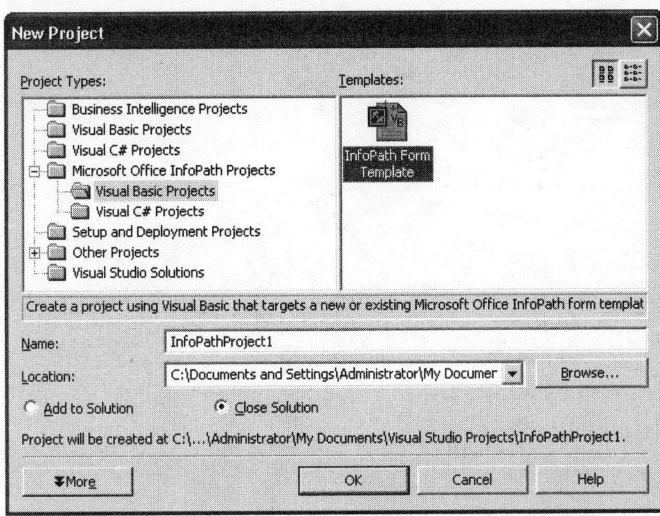

Figure 1-11 Installing the Microsoft Office InfoPath 2003 Toolkit for Visual Studio .NET adds these nodes and an InfoPath Form Template icon in the New Projects dialog box.

Chapter 15, "Introducing InfoPath Form Template Projects," describes the Toolkit installation process and how to write simple event-handling procedures with Visual Basic .NET. The remaining two chapters of Part IV demonstrate increasingly complex coding techniques. Figure 1-12 shows the FormCode.vb window of the NWOrdersWSProject example, which Chapter 17, "Writing Advanced Event Handlers," describes in detail. InfoPath automatically generates event-handling procedures with starting code for you. In most cases, you can import VBScript event-handling code into the event handlers and run the project with very few, minor changes.

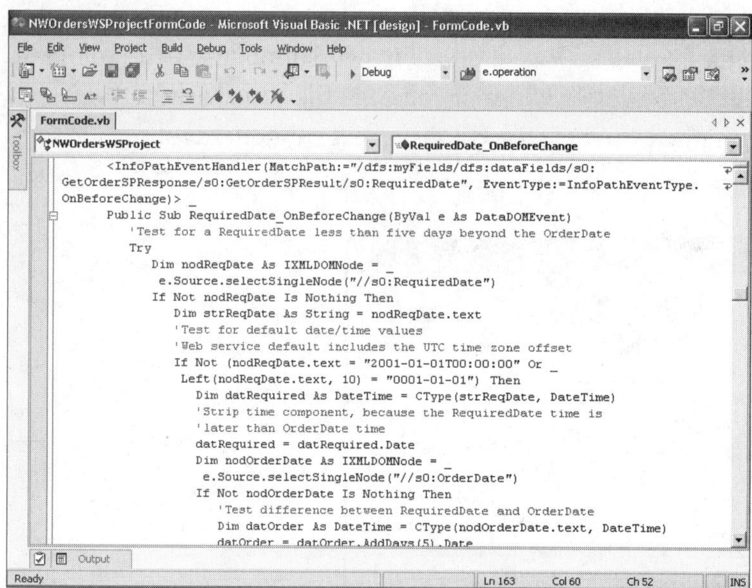

Figure 1-12 This Visual Studio .NET 2003 FormCode.vb window displays part of the Visual Basic .NET code for the sample XML Web service client of Figure 1-8.

Chapter Summary

Microsoft Office InfoPath 2003 SP-1 is the newest member of the Microsoft Office System 2003. The primary purpose of InfoPath is to create forms for capturing and saving semi-structured or fully structured data in the open-standard XML 1.0 format. InfoPath's user interface is very similar to that of Word 2003; InfoPath shares many features that are common to all Office 2003 applications, such as task panes and AutoSave/AutoRecover.

An InfoPath form has two components: a *template* that defines the design of a form and an *XML data document* that contains the information you capture. You can e-mail forms with Microsoft Outlook, export the XML data to an Excel worksheet, and import the XML data into an Excel 2003 list or an XML view of a Word 2003 document.

InfoPath has two basic operating modes: *data entry* for filling out and saving forms and *design* for creating or modifying and saving form templates. The Fill Out A Form dialog box, which opens automatically when you launch InfoPath, makes it easy to open a recently used form or one of the 25 InfoPath sample forms. In addition to form creation, InfoPath includes functionality for Windows SharePoint Services integration, connecting to Access (Jet) and SQL Server databases or XML Web services, offline form editing, form merging, and digital signatures.

You can design and deploy production InfoPath forms without programming, but you might find that you must add code to implement specialized business logic. You add JScript or VBScript code to forms in the Microsoft Script Editor. The sample forms use JScript, which is InfoPath's default programming language. InfoPath SP-1 and the Microsoft Office InfoPath 2003 Toolkit for Visual Studio .NET enable programming forms with Visual Basic .NET or Visual C#.

Q&A

Q. Must everyone who needs to fill out forms have a valid InfoPath 2003 license?

A. Yes. There is no "reader" program that can be used to read and fill out a form; you must have InfoPath installed to do that. However, InfoPath does support exporting to the Single-File Web Page (.mht) format, also called Web-Archive (Single File), so you can create a static view of a form that can be viewed in a Web browser.

Q. Can people who don't have Office System 2003 licenses use InfoPath?

A. Yes. You can purchase the retail, packaged version of InfoPath 2003 from any authorized Microsoft distributor or retail software outlet and upgrade it to SP-1. You can download and install the Microsoft Office InfoPath 2003 Toolkit for Visual Studio .NET from the Microsoft Web site after you install the SP-1 upgrade.

Q. Will InfoPath 2003 run on Tablet PCs?

A. Yes. InfoPath 2003 includes a special ink control for hand-signing forms.

Q. Is a version of InfoPath available for Pocket PCs?

A. Not at this time.

Q. Do I need experience writing VBA code to program custom InfoPath forms?

A. Not if you're a JScript programmer or have VBScript experience. You need competency with VBA, Visual Basic 6.0, or, preferably, Visual Basic .NET to add managed code to InfoPath forms. Visual C# is an alternative, but moving from VBA or Visual Basic 6.0 to Visual Basic .NET is a more practical choice for most Office System developers.

On Your Own

Here's an additional exercise for opening an InfoPath form and navigating between data entry and design mode, including previewing the form in design mode:

1. Close and reopen InfoPath 2003.
2. Use the Fill Out A Form dialog box to open one of the InfoPath sample forms as Form1.
3. Use the Standard toolbar's Design This Form button to switch to design mode.
4. In design mode, choose Tools, Script, Microsoft Script Editor to open MSE.
5. Explore a few of the supporting JScript functions below the three event-handling functions. (Most sample templates have JScript code.)
6. Close MSE to return to design mode.
7. Click the Preview Form button on the Standard toolbar to open the form for previewing.
8. Click the Close Preview button.
9. Close the Template1 window.
10. Close the Form1 window to exit InfoPath without saving changes.

CHAPTER 2

Filling Out Forms

In this chapter, you will learn how to:

- **Open and fill in a moderately complex InfoPath form**
- **Test InfoPath's conditional formatting and data validation features**
- **Save, preview, and print the data document you filled in**
- **Relate the data you enter in a form to the content of its XML data document**
- **Merge two or more data documents to produce a summary form**

For more information:

- **Refer to the section "Opening a Sample InfoPath Form," in Chapter 1.**
- **Refer to the section "Getting Help with InfoPath," in Chapter 1.**

InfoPath's primary objective is capturing data and saving it as an XML data document, so most InfoPath users will–or at least should–run InfoPath in data entry mode only. This chapter's primary objective is to show you how InfoPath's intuitive, Microsoft Office–based UI makes it easy for users to fill in moderately complex forms that emulate paper business documents.

As you progress through this chapter, you'll gain expertise in using InfoPath's repertoire of basic controls and lists, and learn the special techniques that InfoPath uses to capture semi-structured data. A working knowledge of the data entry process is essential before you begin designing your own forms in Part II.

To work through this chapter:

- You should be familiar with Microsoft InfoPath's user interface (UI), which is described in Chapter 1, "Presenting InfoPath 2003 SP-1."
- You should be familiar with basic HTML 4.01 *FORM* elements, such as *INPUT* and its control types.
- You should have installed in your C:\Microsoft Press\Introducing InfoPath 2003\Chapter## folders the sample files from the CD that accompanies this book. The "Using the Accompanying CD" section in the Introduction describes the sample file installation.

Filling Out the Status Report Form

The Status Report form you opened in Chapter 1 is only one of the 25 sample forms included with InfoPath 2003. Status Report includes examples of most basic data entry controls–contained in tables, optional sections, and repeating tables–making it a good candidate for a detailed demonstration of InfoPath's data entry process.

To open the Status Report form for this data entry exercise, follow these steps.

▶ Open the Status Report form

1. **Launch InfoPath, if it isn't running, which opens the Fill Out A Form dialog box. If InfoPath is running and the Fill Out A Form task pane isn't visible, open the task pane's drop-down menu, select Fill Out A Form, and click the More Forms link to open the Fill Out A Form dialog box with the Recently Used Forms list active.**
2. **If you opened the Status Report form in the section "Opening a Sample InfoPath Form," in Chapter 1, the More Forms list includes the Status Report form. In this case, you can double-click the Status Report icon, and skip the following step.**
3. **Click the Sample Forms link under the Form Categories heading to display the Sample Forms list, scroll to the bottom of the list, and double-click the Status Report icon.**

InfoPath loads the StatusReport.xsn template, and creates an empty Form1 XML data document in memory. Now you're ready to begin entering data.

Working with the Date Picker Control

The date picker control is a text box that displays dates in the Short Date format that's set in Control Panel's Regional And Language Options tool. The date picker control is in the left cell of the uppermost table of the form. As mentioned in Chapter 1, Microsoft JScript code behind the Status Report template sets the default value of the date picker control to your computer's system date.

To change the date, click the button that shows the calendar icon to the right of the Date text box to open the pop-up calendar. Click a different day of the month, as shown in Figure 2-1, to close the calendar. Alternatively, change the month by clicking one of the two arrow buttons in the calendar and then clicking the date.

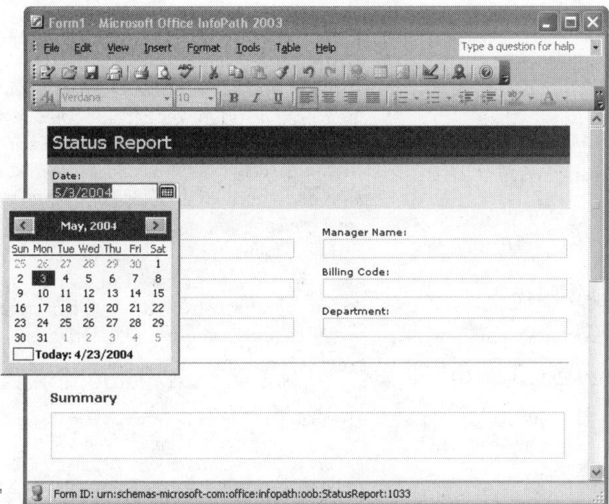

Figure 2-1 You can use the date picker control to postdate a report.

Entering Data in Text Boxes

Text boxes are InfoPath's most widely used control. Following are the most important data entry characteristics of text boxes:

- A text box bound to a string field can contain letters, numbers, symbols, and punctuation.
- A text box bound to an *integer* numeric field can contain only numbers and plus signs or minus signs. You can add decimal points, digit grouping symbols, and currency symbols to a *double* numeric field.
- Digit grouping and currency symbols are permitted only when the template applies special number formatting the text box.
- You can't apply character formatting–such as boldface or italic attributes–to a text box's contents.

Typing data in a standard (string) text box is a no-brainer, so fill the six text boxes (Name, Manager Name, E-mail Address, and so on) in the second table with sample text. Moving the mouse pointer into a text box or rich text box changes the pointer from a selection arrow to an I-beam. The text box's default light gray outline changes to dark gray, which indicates that the control is enabled for text entry. When you click or tab into the box to enter text, the border changes to blue, indicating that the control has the focus.

The default tab order for controls in tables is top-to-bottom, left-to-right. Pressing the Tab key repeatedly sets the focus to each active control on the form. When you reach the end of the form, the focus cycles to the topmost control—in this case, the date picker.

Entering sample text in all fields is important

Add text and other entries to every control on the form, including repeating tables contained in optional sections, which you will encounter later in this chapter. Doing this creates an XML data document with fields (elements) that have content you can relate to your original entries. Making entries in all fields, with the exception of an optional Task List, also is necessary to demonstrate the fields of data documents that will be merged when you reach the section "Merging Forms," later in this chapter.

Inserting Symbols and Special Characters

InfoPath's Insert menu has a simplified version of Microsoft Word's Symbols dialog box. To add a special symbol, such as ©, follow these steps.

▶ Insert a special symbol

1. **Choose Insert, Symbol to open the Symbol dialog box.**
2. **Select Verdana, InfoPath's default font for most languages, from the Font list.**
3. **Many commonly used symbols appear by default in the Recently Used Symbols group, as shown here. If you don't see the symbol you want in this group, scroll up or down in the main symbol list until you do.**
4. **Select the symbol as shown here:**

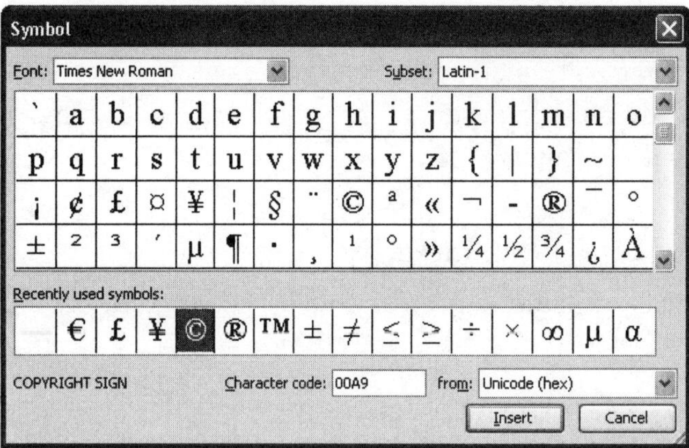

5. **Click Insert or double-click the symbol to add it to the text box, and click Close to close the dialog box.**

Testing the Office Spelling Checker

Deliberately misspell a word in the Project or Department text box to verify that the Office spelling checker is operational, which is indicated by a wavy red line under the misspelled word. (The spelling checker is disabled for the other four text boxes.) Press F7 or choose Tools, Spelling to display the Spelling task pane, which offers suggestions for correcting the error, as shown in Figure 2-2. Select the appropriate suggestion and click Change to correct the typo.

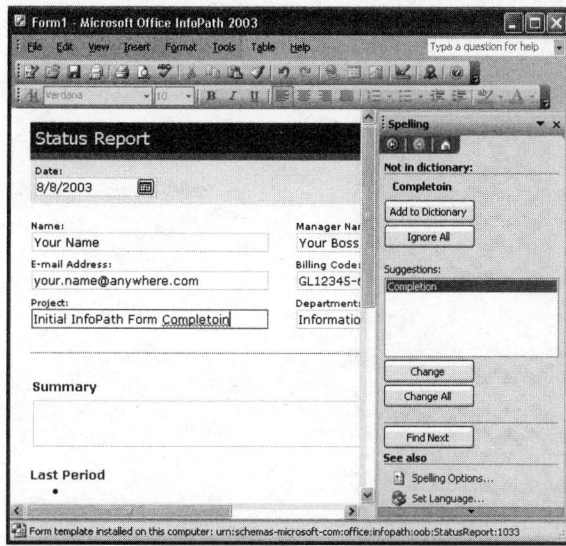

Figure 2-2 The Spelling task pane suggests a correction for a typo in a text box.

Setting Spelling, Language, and AutoComplete Options

The Spelling task pane has links to the Options and Set Language dialog boxes. Click the Spelling Options link to open the Options dialog box, or choose Tools, Options and click the Spelling tab. Figure 2-3 shows InfoPath's default spelling options. You might want to select the Ignore Words In UPPERCASE check box to skip checking acronyms and abbreviations, such as XSD (for XML Schema Definition).

Click the Set Language link or choose Tools, Set Language to open the Language dialog box, as shown in Figure 2-4.

InfoPath's AutoComplete feature is linked to an Internet Explorer setting, which might be disabled on your computer. If you clear one of the text boxes, tab out and back in to it, and then type the initial letter of a previous entry, AutoComplete for forms opens a drop-down list of prior entries beginning with the same letter, as shown in Figure 2-5. If this doesn't work for you, AutoComplete probably is disabled.

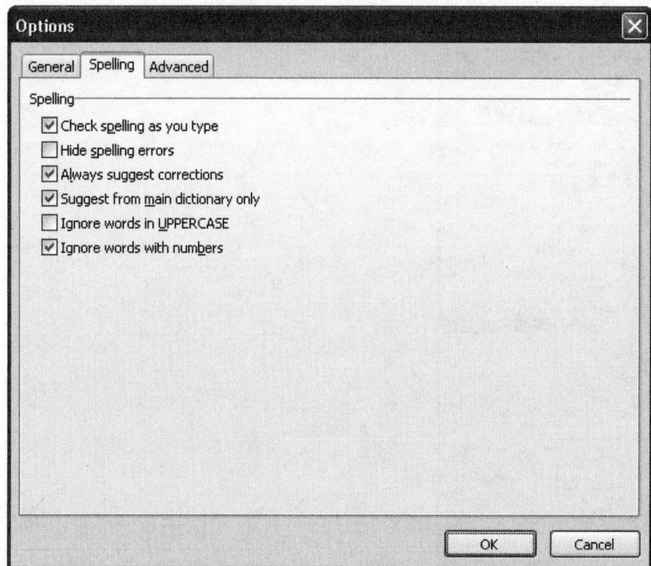

Figure 2-3 The Spelling tab of the Options dialog displays InfoPath's default spelling checker options.

Figure 2-4 Change the spelling checker's default language in this dialog box.

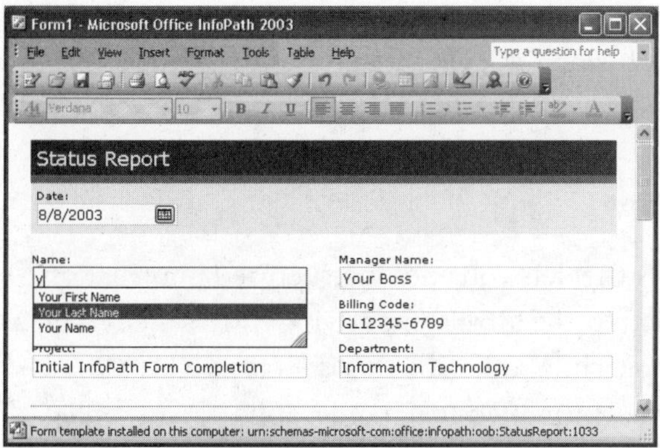

Figure 2-5 The AutoComplete feature displays a list of previous values that start with the first letter you type in the text box.

The AutoComplete options are buried in Internet Explorer's Internet Options dialog box. AutoComplete remembers URLs for Web pages you visited recently, data you've entered in HTML forms, and user names and passwords for forms. InfoPath uses the data in forms feature only. Any AutoComplete changes you make are applied to InfoPath and to all your future Internet Explorer sessions. To enable AutoComplete for forms, follow these steps.

▶ Enable AutoComplete for forms

1. **Choose Tools, Options, and select the General tab in the Options dialog box.**
2. **Click the Internet Options button to open Internet Explorer's Internet Properties dialog box, select the Content tab, and then click the AutoComplete button to open the AutoComplete Settings dialog box, shown here:**

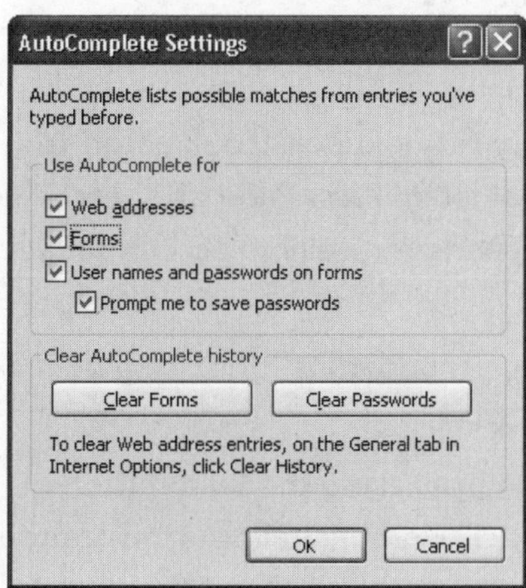

3. **Enable AutoComplete for InfoPath by selecting the Form check box. To disable AutoComplete, clear all the check boxes. Click OK three times to return to filling out your form.**

Formatting Rich Text Data

The Summary control is a rich text box that lets you add unstructured information to a form. *Unstructured data* isn't governed by the form's underlying XML schema rules, as indicated by its official *any* data type. (InfoPath calls this data type XHTML.) Almost anything goes in a rich text box–formatted text, paragraphs, tables, bulleted and numbered lists, hyperlinks, and graphics images.

As mentioned in the section "Opening a Sample Form," in Chapter 1, giving the focus to a rich text box control enables the Office-standard Formatting toolbar's buttons. The process of formatting a rich text box's content is almost identical to formatting the text of Microsoft Word version 2000 and later documents. Compatibility with Word documents extends to Clipboard operations also. You can copy and paste formatted rich text box content into a Word document and vice versa. Depending on the version of Microsoft Word you're using, a few formatting features–such as paragraph indentation–might disappear.

Displaying formatting shortcut keys

Most Office users are familiar with shortcut keys for boldface, italic, and underline text formatting. InfoPath has additional shortcut keys for text alignment, indenting, and outdenting. To display the shortcut key in the ScreenTip for toolbar buttons that have shortcut keys, choose Tools, Customize, select the Options tab, and select the Show Shortcut Keys In ScreenTips check box.

The following two procedures demonstrate the character and paragraph formatting capabilities of the rich text box's XHTML editor.

▶ **Format text characters**

1. **Type about six lines of text into the Summary rich text box. (Look ahead to Figure 2-4 for suggested text that you format later.) Press Enter after each line to generate paragraph breaks. The text box expands vertically to accommodate the added content.**
2. **Select a word or phrase in the first line, and apply underline formatting by clicking the toolbar's Underline button or pressing Ctrl+U.**
3. **Repeat step 2, but apply boldface formatting by clicking the Bold button or pressing Ctrl+B, and add italic formatting by clicking the Italic button or pressing Ctrl+I.**
4. **Select another word or phrase, and click the Highlight button to add a yellow (or other color you choose) background to some text.**

5. **Repeat step 4, but click the arrow to the right of the Font Color button and choose a color to apply to the selected text.**
6. **In the second line, select a word or two, and change the font size from the default 10 points to 12 points. Select another couple of words, and change the font family from the default Verdana to Times New Roman.**

▶ **Format paragraphs**

1. **Position the insertion point in the second line, and click the Increase Indent button or press Ctrl+M to indent the paragraph.**
2. **Position the insertion point in the third line, and click the Numbering button, which has no shortcut key, to start a numbered (ordered) list.**
3. **Move to the next line, and click the Bullets button or press Ctrl+Shift+L to start a bulleted (unordered) list.**
4. **Select the next line, and click the Center button or press Ctrl+E to center the text.**
5. **Select the last line, and click the Left button or press Ctrl+R to right-align the line.**

At this point, your Summary rich text box should appear similar to that shown in Figure 2-6.

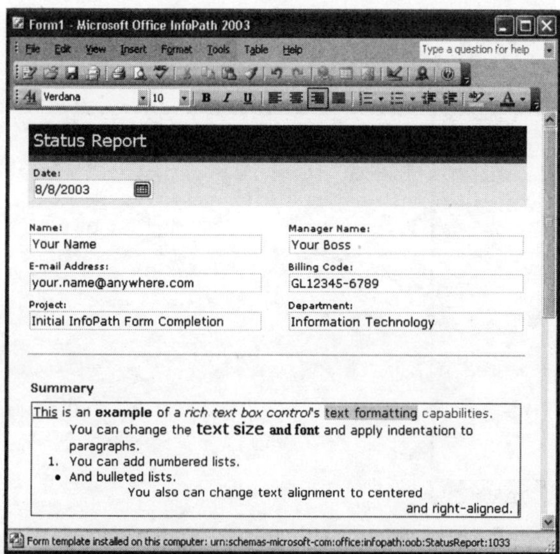

Figure 2-6 Your Summary rich text box should now contain formatted text and paragraphs similar to those shown here.

Working with Bulleted and Numbered List Controls

InfoPath's bulleted lists correspond to HTML unordered lists, but save their content in a repeating section of the data document. InfoPath handles the formatting of bulleted lists. The Status Report form doesn't demonstrate a numbered list, but numbered lists behave identically to bulleted lists. Plain lists omit the bullet or number. You can do the following with bulleted, numbered, and plain lists:

- ✦ Add to the list by selecting (giving the focus to) an item and pressing Enter to add the empty item below the selected item.
- ✦ Delete an item by selecting it and pressing Delete. Lists must contain at least one item, but the item can be empty. If you want a single list item, delete all other blank list items before entering text in the remaining item.
- ✦ Format selected characters with boldface, italic, and underline attributes.
- ✦ Change the font family and font size of all or part of the text.
- ✦ Apply highlighting to, and change the font color of, selected characters.

Figure 2-5 shows the Last Period, This Period, and Issues lists in the Status Report form with deleted and added items and character formatting applied. Use the techniques you learned in the earlier section "Format text characters" to duplicate the list item formatting shown in Figure 2-7.

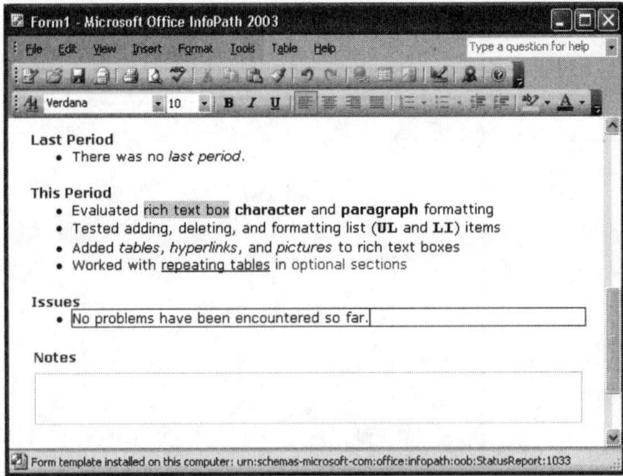

Figure 2-7 This Status Report document has three bulleted lists with deleted, added, and formatted items.

Adding Tables to Rich Text Boxes

The Notes control is the Status Report's second rich text box control. You use this control to experiment with adding and formatting HTML tables, copying and pasting tables to and from other Office applications, and adding hyperlinks and pictures. Manipulating tables inside rich text boxes is similar to working with Word tables, as you'll discover in the three following procedures.

▶ Insert and modify an empty table

1. **Give the Notes rich text box the focus by clicking it, and choose Insert, Table to open the Insert Table dialog box, which defaults to 5 columns and 2 rows, as shown here:**

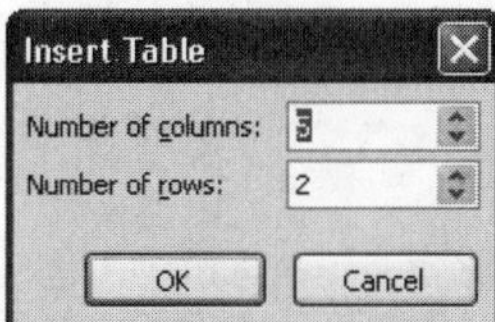

2. **Change the number of columns to 2, and click OK to add the table, which opens with the insertion point in the first cell of the top row and all Formatting toolbar buttons enabled. Active tables have a rectangular selection button in the upper left corner.**
3. **Choose View, Toolbars, Tables to display the Tables toolbar.**
4. **Click and drag the right edge of the table to reduce its width as much as possible, and then click and drag the vertical divider to create columns of approximately equal width.**
5. **Drag the mouse pointer across the top row to select the two columns, and click the Merge Cells button on the Tables toolbar or choose Table, Merge cells to create a single cell in the top row.**
6. **Type some text, such as Inserted Table, in the top cell, press Ctrl+E to center the text, select the text, and press Ctrl+B to apply the boldface attribute.**
7. **Enter 1000 and 2000 in the bottom row's cells. Position the insertion point in each cell, and press Ctrl+R to right-align the numbers.**

> **Drawing tables**
>
> Drawing tables using a pencil cursor is an alternative to inserting tables with a specified number of rows and columns. To draw a table, choose View, Toolbars, and select the Tables toolbar. Click the Draw Table button on the Tables toolbar and add cells to the table with the pencil cursor. You'll probably find, though, that inserting tables is easier than drawing them.

At this point, your added table appears as shown in Figure 2-8.

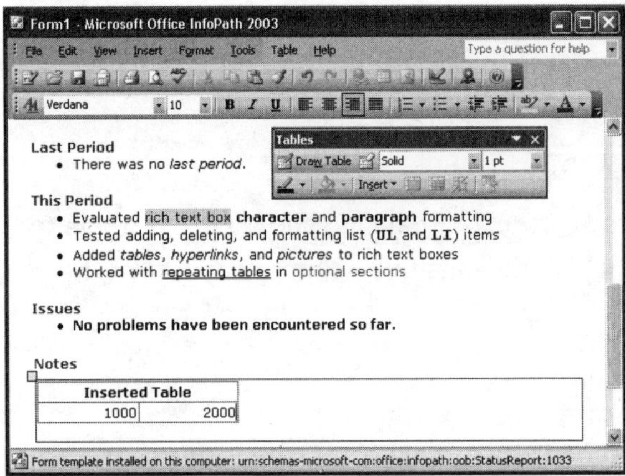

Figure 2-8 When you insert a table into a rich text box, its selection button appears at the table's top left corner.

▶ Modify table properties

1. **Click the table's selection handle to select all cells, and then click the Table Properties button on the Tables toolbar or choose Table, Table Properties to open the Table Properties dialog box, which opens with the Table tab selected. InfoPath's Table Properties dialog box is a downsized version of Word 2003's implementation.**
2. **Accept the default Left Horizontal Alignment option, or click the Center or Right Horizontal Alignment button. Center is shown selected here. If you change the alignment, click Apply.**

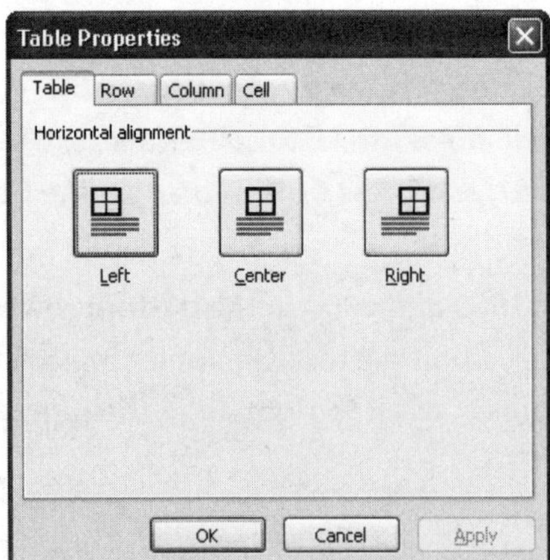

3. Select the Row tab, and accept the default minimum row height, or select the Automatically Set Row Height option, as shown here, to adjust the row height of the selected row or rows to accommodate their contents. You can select px (pixels), in (inches), cm (centimeters), or pt (points) as the unit of measurement when you specify a minimum row height. Click the Next Row button to change the row heights of successive rows. If you make a change, click Apply.

4. Select the Column tab, and optionally, change the width of the columns (A and B for this example), as shown here. Click Apply.

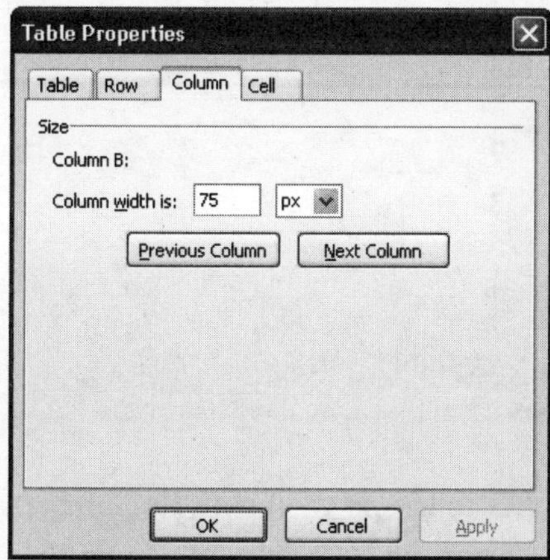

5. Select the Cell tab to change the vertical alignment and padding of the *selected* cells only, as shown on the next page. (*Padding* is the distance between the edge of the cell and the text or other element contained in the cell.) Click Apply, and then click OK to close the dialog box.

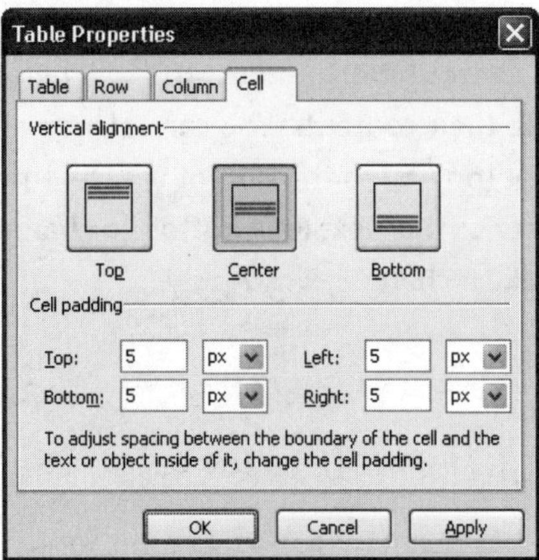

Figure 2-9 shows the effect of horizontally centering the table, changing the column widths to 75 pixels, vertically centering the cells, and changing all cell padding values to 5 pixels.

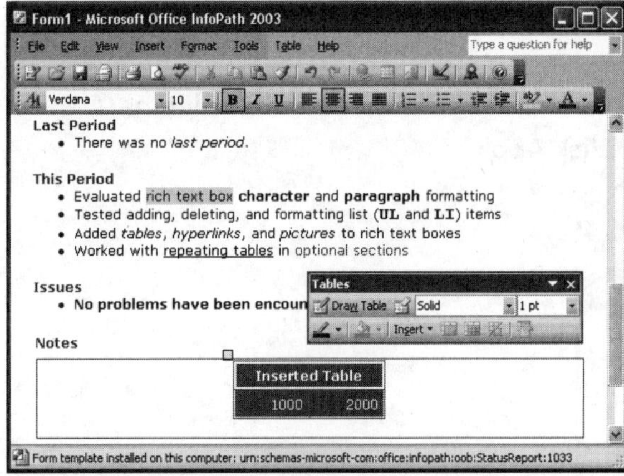

Figure 2-9 This table is the modified version of the table from Figure 2-6.

▶ Modify table borders and shading

1. **Click the table's selection button to select all cells, and then click the Borders And Shading button on the Tables toolbar or choose Table, Borders And Shading to open the Borders And Shading dialog box with the Borders tab selected. Like the Table Properties dialog box, InfoPath's Borders And Shading dialog box exhibits a Word 2003 heritage.**
2. **You can't change the table's border style, width, or color, but you can remove the default borders by clicking the buttons in the Border section, as shown here. The buttons toggle the associated border on and off.**

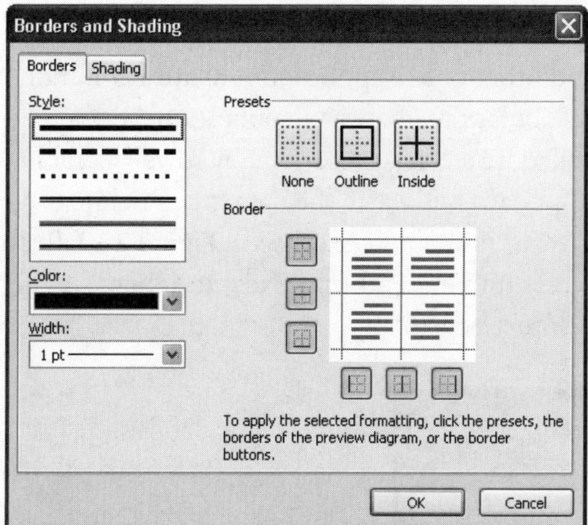

3. Select the Shading tab, and then click the Color option button to add a background color to the selected table cells. At the top of the color picker, you can select one of the six standard colors of the form's color scheme—Blue for all sample forms—as shown here, or you can click More Colors to define a custom background color.

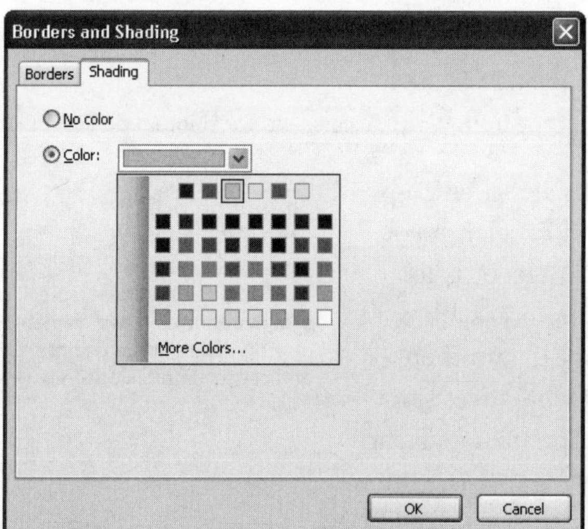

See Also You'll learn more about the use of tables in InfoPath's design mode in Chapter 5, "Laying Out Forms," and about color schemes in Chapter 7, "Formatting Forms."

Copying Tables from and to Other Office Applications

Microsoft Word, Excel, Access, and other Office applications share a common Clipboard format for transferring tabular data between applications. If you have Access version 2000 or later installed, you can select and copy rows of a table or query in Datasheet view to the Clipboard and paste the data into a rich text box. The same process also works for Word tables and Excel cells. Figure 2-10 illustrates copying and pasting data from Access into InfoPath and Excel and then copying and pasting the Excel data into the rich text box.

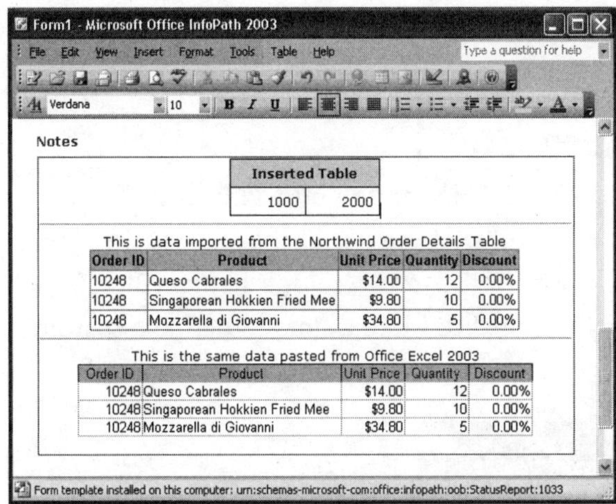

Figure 2-10 You can paste tables you copy from Word, Access, and Excel into a rich text box.

You can select InfoPath table cells and then copy and paste the cells into Word and Excel, but you can't use Edit, Paste Append to add records to an Access table. To add records to an Access table, copy the cells to an Excel worksheet, and then choose Paste Append to add the worksheet's rows to an Access table with the appropriate data structure. In most cases, you can safely ignore the Import Errors message.

> **Separating rich text data with horizontal lines**
> Figure 2-10 shows two horizontal separator lines between the three tables. To add a separator between two elements, position the insertion point at the end of the first element, and choose Insert, Horizontal Line.

Adding Hyperlinks

Rich text boxes can contain hyperlink controls. To add a hyperlink to a rich text box, position the insertion point where you want the text, and choose Insert, Hyperlink to open the Insert Hyperlink dialog box. Type the URL for the site in the Link To text box and the site's description in the Display This Text text box, as shown in Figure 2-11, and then click OK to add the link.

Figure 2-11 Type the hyperlink's URL in the Link To text box and the link text in the Display This Text box.

InfoPath embedded hyperlinks don't behave the same as hyperlinks in Web pages or the hyperlink controls you learn about in Chapter 6, "Adding Basic Controls and Lists." You must right-click the embedded link and choose Open Hyperlink from the shortcut menu, as shown in Figure 2-12, to open the destination page.

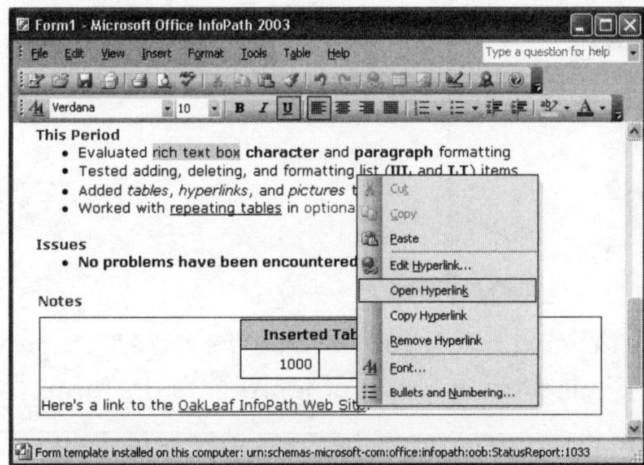

Figure 2-12 You use the shortcut menu to navigate to the Web site specified by the hyperlink control.

Inserting Pictures into Rich Text Boxes

Placing images in tables

If you want to add text adjacent to an image, insert a one-row, two-column table, and place the picture in one of the cells. Use the Borders And Shading dialog box to remove the cell borders and the Table Properties dialog box to adjust cell padding.

Another use for rich text boxes is displaying graphics images from local files or clip art from the Microsoft Office Clip Art and Media gallery. Inserting images increases the size of your XML data document greatly. For example, the simple Windows Metafile (.wmf) image you add in the following procedure increases the size of the XML file from 7.2 KB to 14 KB at this point in the completion process. You'll see the reason for the file size increase when you examine the saved file later in this chapter.

▶ **Add a picture from a local file**

1. Position the insertion point where you want the picture to appear, and choose Insert, Picture, From File to open the Insert Picture dialog box with My Pictures as the default folder. If you have a logo or other image file that's less than 15 KB or so in this folder, select it, and skip the next step.
2. Navigate to a folder containing image files, such as \Program Files\Microsoft Office\Media\Cagcat10. Vector-based files (.wmf, .emf, .eps) are the best bet because they scale better than bit-mapped graphics (.gif or .jpg) files. Select the thumbnail for the image you would like to insert, as shown here:

3. Click Insert to add the image to the rich text box. If you selected the clip art image shown in the preceding figure, its original size is out of proportion to the form.
4. Right-click the image, choose Format Picture to open the Format Picture dialog box, and select the Size tab.
5. With the Maintain Proportions check box selected, type a reasonable size—such as **80 px**—in the Height text box, as shown here:

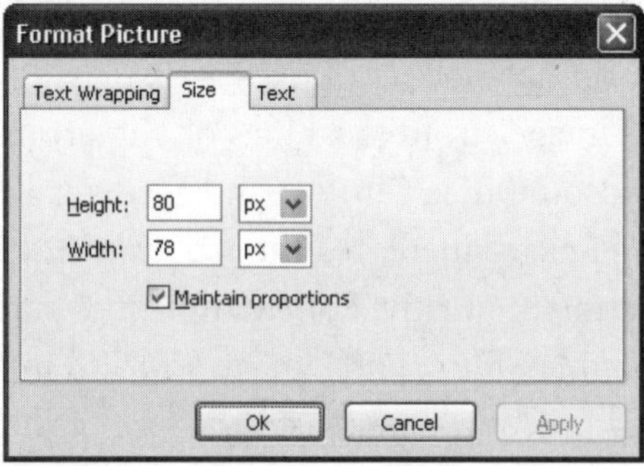

6. Click OK to close the dialog box and shrink the image, as shown here:

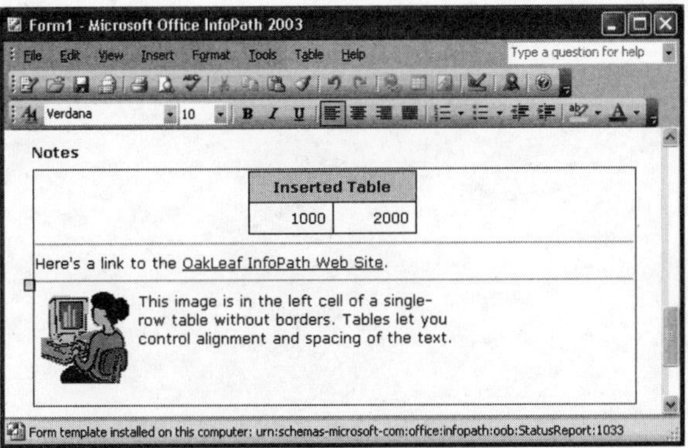

If you don't have a suitable image file available, you can select from thousands of royalty-free clip art images that Microsoft provides for Office System users. To add an image from the Office Clip Art gallery, follow these steps:

▶ Insert an image from the Clip Art task pane

1. **Position the insertion point where you want to add the image, and choose Insert, Picture, Clip Art to display the Clip Art task pane.**
2. **Type a subject keyword in the Search For text box, and click Go. By default, images in your \Program Files\Microsoft Office\Media\Cagcat10 folder appear first.**
3. **Open the Search In list to restrict the search to clip art collections you create with the Microsoft Clip Art Organizer, the Office Collections installed on your computer by Office or InfoPath, or the Microsoft Office Clip Art and Media gallery. You can restrict the file type to clip art by opening the Results Should Be list and clearing all check boxes except Clip Art.**
4. **Scroll the thumbnail list to download additional clip art from the Microsoft Office Clip Art and Media gallery, as shown on the next page.**
5. **Click the thumbnail image to insert the image at the insertion point location.**
6. **Resize and format the image as described in the preceding procedure.**

Adding and Filling Out Optional Sections

Optional sections are another feature that distinguishes InfoPath forms from those of structured forms-based applications, such as Microsoft Access and Microsoft Visual Basic. If you don't add an optional section, its elements don't appear in the form's XML data document; InfoPath disregards the section. The ability to add or omit optional sections is the basis for defining InfoPath as a *semi-structured* XML document generator and editor. Optional sections can contain tables, individual controls, sections, nested optional sections, and nested repeating tables.

The Status Report form has three optional sections–Time Report, Budget Report, and Task List–that contain repeating tables. An icon–a small orange circle with a right-pointing arrow–and a text instruction line act as a placeholder for an empty optional section. Clicking the Time Report placeholder opens a repeating table embedded in an optional section, as shown in Figure 2-13.

The Time Report repeating table has a static header, a single row for data, and a footer. The data row contains text boxes for the Description, Time Allotted, and Time Spent columns. The % Spent column is a read-only text box that displays the ratio of Time Spent to Time Allotted (multiplied by 100) and formats the value as a percentage. The footer contains read-only text box controls that calculate total Time Allotted and Time Spent values, and the average % Spent value.

To add the optional Time Report section and enter data in the repeating table, follow these steps:

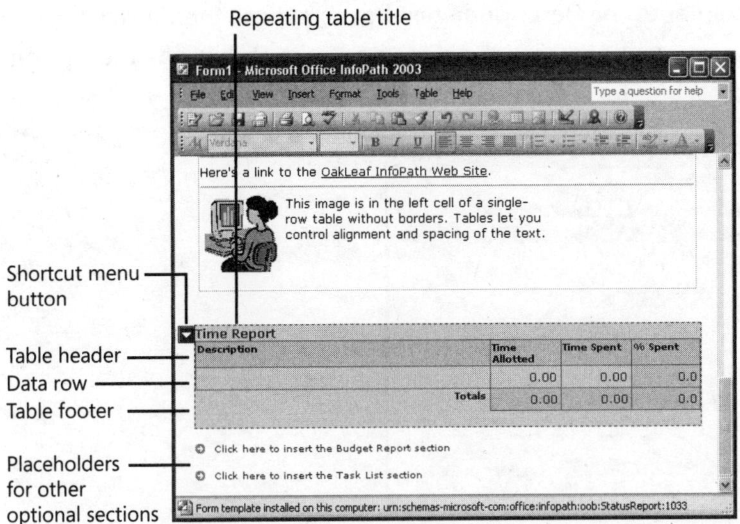

Figure 2-13 The Status Report form has optional sections that contain empty repeating tables.

▶ Add and fill out an optional section

1. Click the Click Here To Insert The Time Report Section placeholder in the Status Report Form to display the optional section and its repeating table.
2. Press Tab to move to the Description text box, and type a brief description of an activity, such as **Read "Introducing InfoPath 2003" Chapter 1**.
3. Press Tab to move to the Time Allotted text box, type **2**, press Tab to move to the Time Spent column, and type **1.5**.
4. Press Tab to calculate the % Spent and Totals values, as shown here:

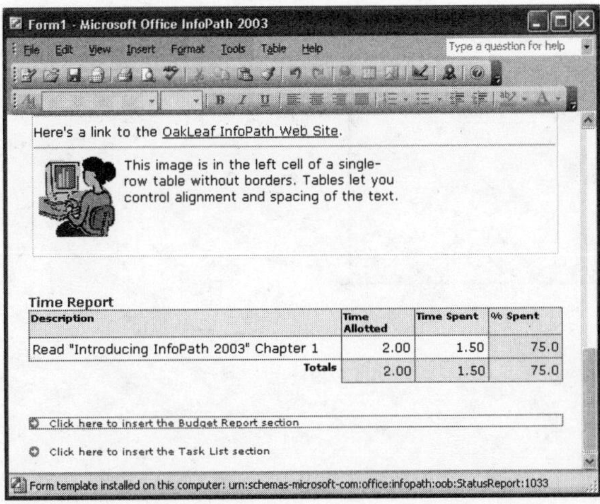

5. Move the mouse pointer to the Description text box to expose the shortcut menu button with the down arrow, and click the button or right-click inside the section to open the shortcut menu for repeating tables, as shown here:

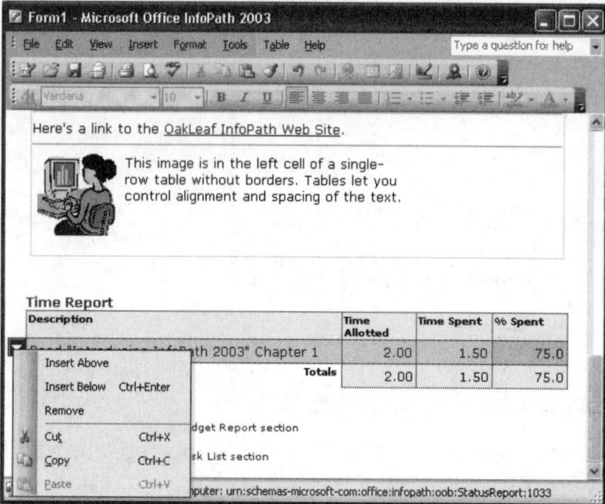

6. Choose Insert Below to add a new data row below your first entry.
7. Repeat steps 2 through 4 with different Description and numeric values, as shown here:

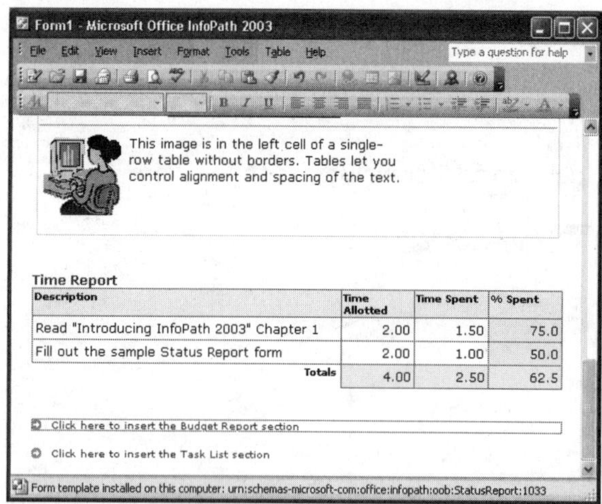

The optional section's shortcut menu and shortcut keys do the following:

- **Remove Time Report** Deletes the entire Time Report section. If you remove the section accidentally, press Ctrl+Z to undo the operation.
- **Copy (Ctrl+C)** Copies the section's contents to the Clipboard.
- **Cut (Ctrl+X)** Copies the section to the Clipboard and then deletes the original.
- **Paste (Ctrl+V)** Overwrites the contents of the section or inserts the section elements into an added empty section from a Clipboard copy. If you cut the section accidentally, open a new section and paste the Clipboard copy.

Sorting a repeating table's rows
To reorganize the sequence of a repeating table's rows, cut the row to be moved, insert a new row at the desired location, and paste the Clipboard copy into the new empty row. InfoPath doesn't offer a command to sort rows of repeating tables.

Following are the actions you can take with the repeating table's shortcut menu and shortcut keys:

- **Insert Above** Adds a new empty data row above the selected row.
- **Insert Below (Ctrl+Enter)** Adds a new, empty data row below the selected row.
- **Remove** Deletes the selected row. You can recover from an accidental selection by pressing Ctrl+Z.
- **Copy (Ctrl+C)** Copies the selected row to the Clipboard.
- **Cut (Ctrl+X)** Copies the selected row to the Clipboard and then deletes the original.
- **Paste (Ctrl+V)** Overwrites the contents of the selected row with a Clipboard copy of a row.

Understanding InfoPath's Drop-Down Lists

The optional Budget Report section's repeating table includes a drop-down list control that lets you choose one of 91 currencies for budgeted and spent amounts, as partially shown in Figure 2-14. All sample InfoPath forms that have currency-formatted text boxes incorporate this drop-down list. U.S. dollars–USD ($)–is the default currency for the 1033 (U.S. English) locale.

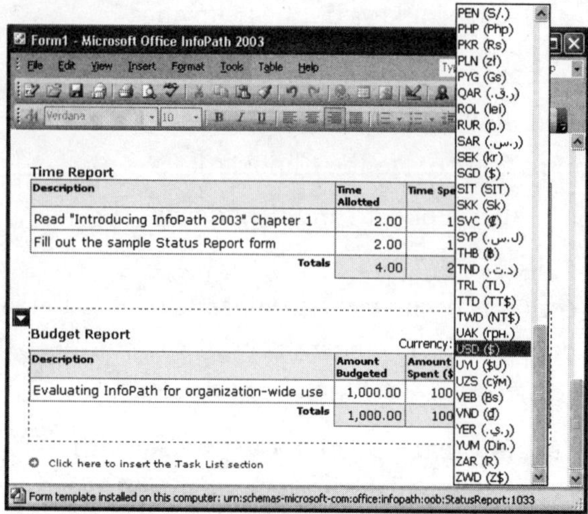

Figure 2-14 The Currency drop-down list lets you select the currency used by the Budget Report's Amount Budgeted and Amount Spent columns.

A drop-down or conventional list control requires a data source to provide its items collection. The data source can be an XML file that you specify as a secondary data source, a manually typed list of entries, or a repeating section in the form's data document. The data source for the Currency list is a secondary data source that's created from an XML data document (currencies.xml) that has three child (sub) elements–*name*, *symbol*, and *display*. The name and symbol fields bind to the XML data document's *name* and *symbol* child elements of the *currency* element. The *display* child element provides the parenthetical currency symbol ($) for the Amount Spent column.

Handling Data-Entry Errors

The data you collect and save in XML format is only as valuable as its consistency and accuracy. InfoPath includes several features for detecting data inconsistency errors, such as omitting required values or typing letters instead of numbers in controls that specify a numeric data type. InfoPath's name for the process of detecting and prompting users to correct data entry errors is *data validation*. If you've applied Access's field and table validation rules, you'll find InfoPath's data validation process to behave similarly.

InfoPath validates the data you enter in a form with the following conformance tests:

- **Data structure conforms to the form's XML schema.** The form's schema may have constraints, such as the minimum and maximum number of elements in a repeating section. For example, attempting to add more than the maximum number of rows specified for a section that's bound to a repeating table opens an error message.

- **Presence of data conforms to the form's XML schema.** If the schema specifies that a field must have a value (a required field) and the bound control is empty, InfoPath flags the control as having an error by adding a red asterisk to the control. By default, all numeric and date fields require a value.
- **Data type conforms to the schema.** If you type letters instead of numbers in a numeric field or an invalid date–such as 13/13/2003–in a date field, the field is marked with an error flag and a dashed red border.
- **Data values comply with declarative validation rules.** InfoPath's design mode includes dialog boxes for establishing data validation rules for controls. *Declarative* refers to operations that you can specify in InfoPath's design UI. Data that fails validation tests are marked with a dashed red border.

Comparing schema conformance and validation rule compliance

XML documents are valid only if they conform to their associated XML schema. For this reason, InfoPath tests schema conformance—a process called *document validation*—before performing declarative data validation tests, which aren't specified by schemas that InfoPath creates for you or from which you create the form design.

- **Data values comply with data validation programming code.** If declarative validation rules alone can't handle the data value test, programming code is usually required to handle validation.

The Status Report form doesn't make extensive use of data validation, but data validation is important when you customize a form for your organization's use. For example, Date, Name, E-Mail Address, Project, and Billing Code aren't required fields, but most organizations would require this information to be provided. As another example, you can enter negative numbers in Time Allotted and Time Spent text boxes, as well as the Amount Budgeted text box in the Budget Report's repeating table. Negative numbers make little or no sense for these field values.

See Also Chapter 6 shows you how to specify required field values in design mode, and Chapter 8, "Validating Form Data," explains in detail the declarative validation process. Part IV, "Programming InfoPath Forms," introduces you to adding code behind forms with Visual Basic .NET.

InfoPath has two validation menu choices: Tools, Go To Next Error (Ctrl+Shift+E) and Show Error Message (Ctrl+Shift+S). You'll learn how to use these commands in the procedure that follows.

To test InfoPath's data validation features with the Status Report form, follow these steps.

▶ Test data validation features

1. **Select the value in the Time Allotted text box of the Time Report table's first row, and press Delete. A red asterisk appears in the cell because a null value violates the schema's requirement for a numeric field value, and the % Spent value changes to 100.0.**
2. **Add a minus sign to the Time Spent value, which is an obvious mistake that doesn't cause a validation error.**
3. **Type abcd or other letters in the second row's Time Allotted text box. The cell's border changes from blue to a dashed red line as a result of a data type conflict with the schema's number specification for this field (double).**
4. **If you haven't done so already, add an optional Budget Report section.**
5. **Specify -1000.00 as the Amount Budgeted value and 100 as the Amount Spent value. You don't generate a data validation error, but the % Spent value's format changes from normal, black to boldface, red. A declarative *conditional formatting (pctSpent > 1)* expression causes the format change shown here:**

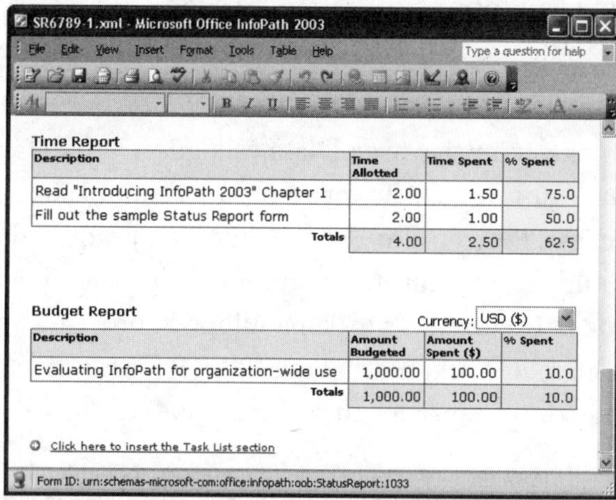

6. **Click inside the Summary rich text box to give it the focus.**
7. **Choose Tools, Go To Next Error or press Ctrl+Shift+E to give the empty Time Allotted text box the focus and enable the Show Error Message item on the Tools menu.**

8. **Click Tools, Show Error Message to display the strangely dimensioned message box shown here:**

9. **Click OK to close the message box and fix the error.**
10. **Repeat steps 7 through 9.**
11. **Press Ctrl+Z repeatedly until the changes you made in the preceding steps return to original values.**

Conditional formatting is related to data validation, but values detected as out of range by conditional formatting don't set error flags. Chapter 7 describes how to apply in design mode conditional formatting to the basic controls that support this feature.

Saving, Previewing, and Printing Forms

After you complete the data entry process, it's time to save your form. Like most other Microsoft Office applications, InfoPath has an AutoRecover feature that automatically saves a current copy of the form. The default AutoRecover interval is 10 minutes. To change the interval, choose Tools, Options to open the Options dialog box, click the Advanced tab, and change the number of minutes in the spin box.

InfoPath is intended to replace printed forms but, like other Microsoft Office applications, InfoPath offers Print Preview and Print dialog boxes. The following sections describe how to save, preview, and print a completed form.

Saving Data Documents

Saving a form's data document is similar to saving any other Office document: press Ctrl+S or choose File, Save or Save As, give the form a name–InfoPath automatically adds the .xml extension–and click Save. The basic rule is "save early and often," despite the AutoRecover safety net.

Looking for the File, Properties dialog box?
Most other Office applications, such as Word, Excel, and Access, save documents in compound document files (DocFiles), which include a properties element for adding information about the file. InfoPath generates plain-text XML files that don't include file properties data. Thus, you won't find a Properties item the File menu. XML, after all, is intended to be self-describing.

The primary issue when saving forms is how to name and where to locate them; InfoPath's defaults are Form1.xml in your My Documents folder. Unlike other Office applications, InfoPath's Options dialog box doesn't offer a default file folder setting. Collecting all your files in subfolders of My Documents is a recommended practice. Most network administrators back up each client PC's My Documents folder and its subfolders nightly to a file server, and a single My Documents folder simplifies migrating to a new or repaired computer. If you follow this recommendation, create an InfoPath subfolder with sub-subfolder names by template, such as \My Documents\InfoPath\StatusReport.

InfoPath's developers could have set the default form name to *TemplateName*1.xml or *TemplateNameYYYYMMDD*.xml, where *YYYYMMDD* is the date, but they didn't. The Status Report form doesn't have a project number field, so for example you might choose a part of a Billing Code that represents the project number–6789 for this form. A file name such as SR6789-1.xml makes sense for a project's first status report, as shown in Figure 2-15. The choice is up to you, but *be consistent* when naming data document files.

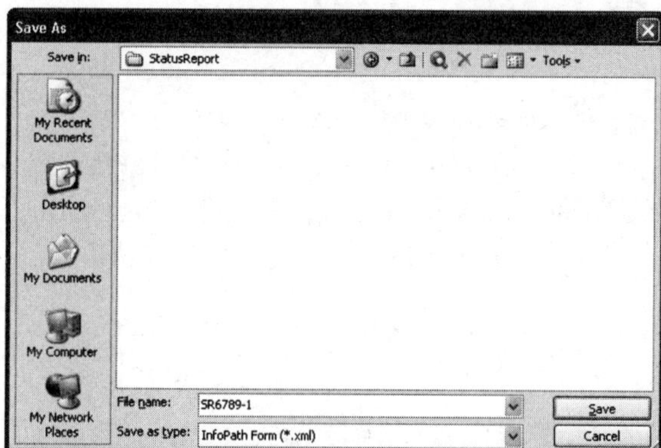

Figure 2-15 Save completed sample InfoPath data documents in your \My Documents\InfoPath\ StatusReport folder.

Previewing and Printing Forms

The 25 InfoPath sample forms are designed to resemble their paper business form counterparts, and many sample forms have signature blocks at the bottom. The sample form designers apparently don't believe that InfoPath will bring about the elusive "paperless office"–at least not in the near future.

InfoPath shares Office-standard print preview and printing features. The default printing margins, which you set in the Page Setup tab of the View Properties dialog box, are 0.75 inch on all sides for English measurement units. To open the View

Properties dialog box, choose File, Page Setup. Chapter 10, "Adding Views to a Template," shows you how to apply printer settings to individual views of a form. The Status Report form has only a single (default) view.

Choosing File, Print Preview or pressing Ctrl+F2 opens the Print Preview window, shown in Figure 2-16. InfoPath doesn't print form background colors, such as those applied to Status Report's top (heading) table.

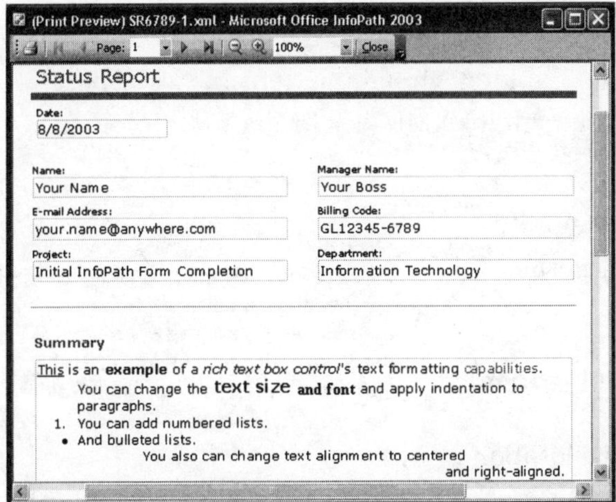

Figure 2-16 InfoPath's Print Preview window is similar to those of other Microsoft Office applications.

Choosing File, Print or pressing Ctrl+P opens a simplified version of the Office Print dialog box, which offers Print Page Range and Copies settings only. Click Print to print the form.

Closing the Form

To close the current form but leave InfoPath open in startup mode with the working area empty, choose File, Close. To close the form and InfoPath at the same time, choose File, Exit.

Exploring XML Data Documents

The Status Report form's XML data document is much larger and more complex than the simple Contacts.xml file you opened in the section "Saving Data as XML Files," in Chapter 1. Status Report data documents have many more elements than

Contacts.xml, and the form you completed in the preceding sections includes elements that contain XHTML-formatted data and a picture. The Status Report form doesn't have controls bound to most XML elements that are specified by the document's schema. A few other sample forms add values to elements that Status Report doesn't use.

Modifying Data Documents for Display in Internet Explorer

You can view InfoPath data documents in Notepad and, with a minor modification to the file, in Internet Explorer. Internet Explorer's built-in Extensible Stylesheet Language Transformations (XSLT) document for XML files formats the InfoPath document as HTML for easier reading.

To open SR6789-1.xml in Notepad and modify it to create a copy that you can open in Internet Explorer, follow these steps

On the CD

If you've installed the sample files from the CD that accompanies this book, you can skip the following steps and open the C:\Microsoft Press\Introducing InfoPath 2003\Chapter02\SR6789-1 for IE.xml in Internet Explorer.

▶ Modify a document for display in Internet Explorer

1. **In Windows Explorer, navigate to the location where you saved SR6789-1.xml, right-click the file item, and choose Open With, Notepad. If Notepad doesn't appear on the Open With menu, click Choose Program to display the Open With dialog box, click Notepad in the Program list, and click OK. (Don't select the Always Use The Selected Program To Open This Kind Of File check box.)**
2. **If text extends past the right edge of Notepad's window, choose Format, Word Wrap to turn on wordwrap.**
3. **Select the *<?mso-application progid="InfoPath.Document"?>* element, as shown here, which causes the document to open in InfoPath, and press Delete to remove it. (Be careful not to delete more or less than this element.)**

SR6789-1.xml - Notepad

File Edit Format View Help

```
<?xml version="1.0" encoding="UTF-8"?><?mso-infoPathSolution
PIVersion="1.0.0.0"
name="urn:schemas-microsoft-com:office:infopath:oob:StatusReport:1033"
solutionVersion="1.0.0.1" productVersion="11.0.6250"
?><?mso-application progid="InfoPath.Document"?><sr:statusReport
xmlns:sr="http://schemas.microsoft.com/office/infopath/2003/sample/Sta
tusReport"
xmlns:my="http://schemas.microsoft.com/office/infopath/2003/myXSD"
xmlns:xhtml="http://www.w3.org/1999/xhtml" xml:lang="en-us">
	<sr:date
xmlns:xsi="http://www.w3.org/2001/XMLSchema-instance">
		2003-08-08
	</sr:date>
	<sr:employee>
		<sr:name>
			<sr:prefix></sr:prefix>
			<sr:givenName></sr:givenName>
			<sr:middleName></sr:middleName>
			<sr:surname></sr:surname>
			<sr:suffix></sr:suffix>
			<sr:singleName>Your Name</sr:singleName>
		</sr:name>
		<sr:address>
			<sr:line1></sr:line1>
			<sr:line2></sr:line2>
			<sr:line3></sr:line3>
			<sr:line4></sr:line4>
```

4. **Choose File, Save As to open the Save As dialog box, and change the file name to SR6789-1 for IE.xml.**
5. **Select All Files in the Files Of Type list. (If you don't do this, Notepad appends .txt to the file name.)**
6. **If UTF-8 isn't specified in the Encoding list, select it.**
7. **Click Save to save the copy and close Notepad.**

Viewing the Status Report Document in Internet Explorer

Follow these steps to view elements to which you assigned values earlier in the chapter:

▶ View Status Report in Internet Explorer

1. **In Windows Explorer, double-click SR6789-1 for IE.xml to open it in Internet Explorer.**
2. **If the document opens in an application other than Internet Explorer, close the application, right-click the file name, and choose Open With, Internet Explorer.**
3. **Scroll down to display the *<sr:date ...>* and *<sr:employee>* elements. *sr:* is the XML namespace prefix for the Status Report form. Most elements are empty, as shown on the next page.**

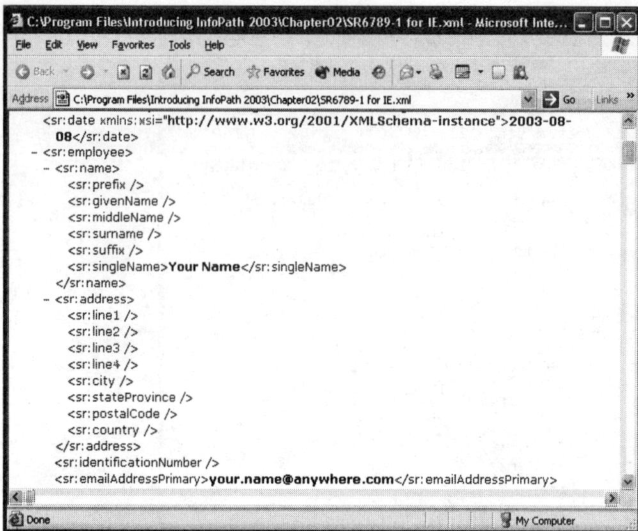

4. **Continue to scroll until the *<sr:billingCode>* element is at the top of the Internet Explorer window. The *<sr:summary>* element bound to the Summary rich text box control contains XHTML-formatted text, as shown here:**

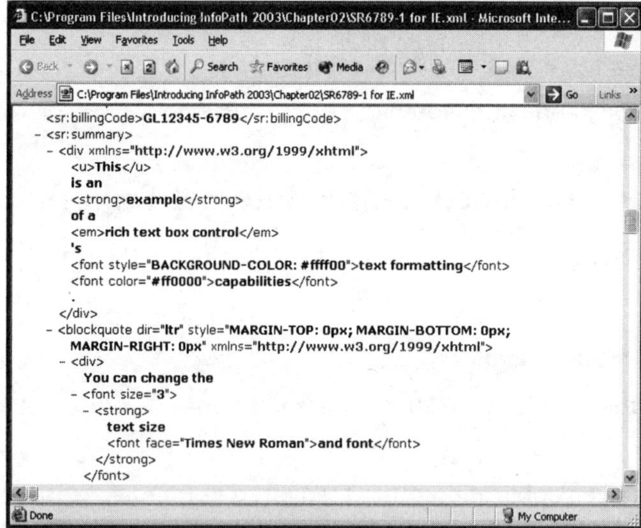

5. **Continue scrolling past the *<sr:lastPeriod>* and *<sr:thisPeriod>* bulleted lists, which also contain XHTML-formatted text, to the *<sr:notes>* element and its tables.**

6. **Scroll down until you reach the *<img ...>* element for the picture control you added to the Notes rich text box. The *xd:inline="R0lGODlhvQDAAH ..."* attribute, shown here, contains the data to generate the picture's bitmap. The data is**

encoded in *base64 format*, which is required to include binary data in an XML document. The "Incorporating Pictures" section of Chapter 6 explains how base64 encoding works.

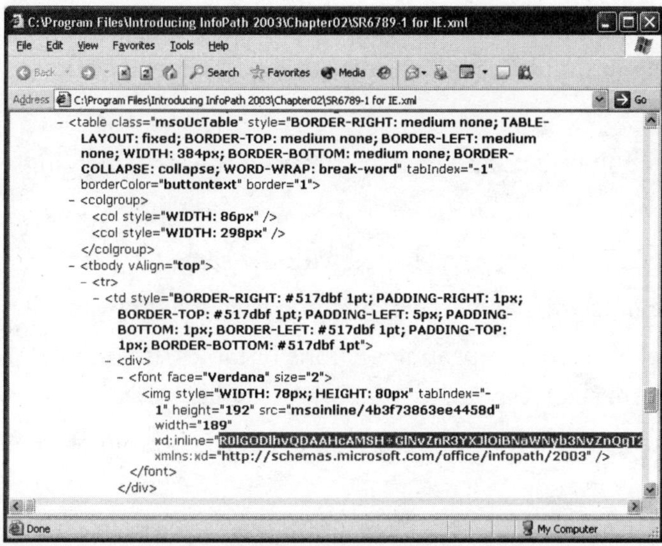

7. **Scroll to the right to see how many characters (5,784) are required to encode the small bitmap. You might need to click the encoded data a few times to make all of it visible as you scroll.**
8. **Finally, scroll past the *<timeReport>* and *<budgetReport>* elements to the end of the file. Notice that there's no optional *<taskList>* element, unless you added one, and then close Internet Explorer.**

> **Conducting business electronically with XML**
>
> Automating business transactions by exchanging XML documents, such as purchase orders, shipping notices, and invoices, is becoming a common practice. Electronic Business XML (ebXML) is an example of a standard XML vocabulary for global e-business information exchange. The tag overhead of XML documents hasn't been and won't be a barrier to XML's widespread adoption. The benefits of an open-standard, self-describing messaging format far outweigh the size penalty of XML "tag bloat." For more information about ebXML, visit *www.oasis-open.org*.

Examining the XML data document for a relatively complex form demonstrates InfoPath's data capture prowess. The procedure also gives you an indication of the verbosity of the XML format–the size of SR6789-1.xml is 15,722 bytes. The "no-frills" version of SR6789-1.xml that you use in the next section doesn't have a bitmap or a table but weighs in at 5,487 bytes to deliver 900 bytes of data, which includes XHTML formatting tags. Eliminating the XHTML tags reduces the data size to 559 bytes–approximately 10 percent of the XML document's total size. However, XML continues to thrive as a data interchange format despite its substantial overhead.

Merging Forms

Another unique InfoPath feature is the ability to merge multiple forms into a single summary form. As an example, a manager might want to see a summary of all status reports for a single project with total time consumed and funds expended to date. The form merging process is simple; even managers can merge forms without help desk assistance.

Following are the basic requirements and characteristics of the form merging process:

- The forms you merge must have been created with the same template.
- The form's template must enable merging; merging is enabled by default.
- Data in repeating fields, such as repeating sections or tables, is added at the bottom of the first form's corresponding sections or tables.
- Data in plain, bulleted, and numbered lists is added at the bottom of the corresponding list.
- Merging adds a separator line to rich text boxes and then adds the data from the merged form below the separator.
- Data in text boxes that aren't contained in repeating form elements doesn't merge. If you merge multiple forms into an empty form, text boxes in nonrepeating elements are empty.
- Date picker controls that aren't incorporated in repeating sections display the date of the initial form, not that of the latest merged form. Hopefully, this oversight will be corrected in a future InfoPath version.
- Custom merge operations let you alter the merging process with programming code.

Merging forms with the sample files

The sample files in your C:\Microsoft Press\Introducing InfoPath 2003\Chapter02 folder include SR6789-2.xml, a file intended for demonstrating merging with SR6789-1.xml, which is included in this folder. You can merge SR6789-2.xml with the SR6789-1.xml file you created earlier in this chapter or from the sample files folder.

The Status Report form uses a custom merge operation that adds the value of the *Name* element to identify merged elements in rich text boxes and doesn't add separator lines between the XHTML content of merged forms.

To give the merge process a test drive with two Status Report forms, follow these steps.

▶ Test the merge process

1. **With the SR6789-1.xml file open in InfoPath, choose File, Merge Forms to open the Merge Forms dialog box.**
2. **Navigate to the C:\Microsoft Press\Introducing InfoPath 2003\Chapter02 folder, and select SR6789-2.xml, as shown here:**

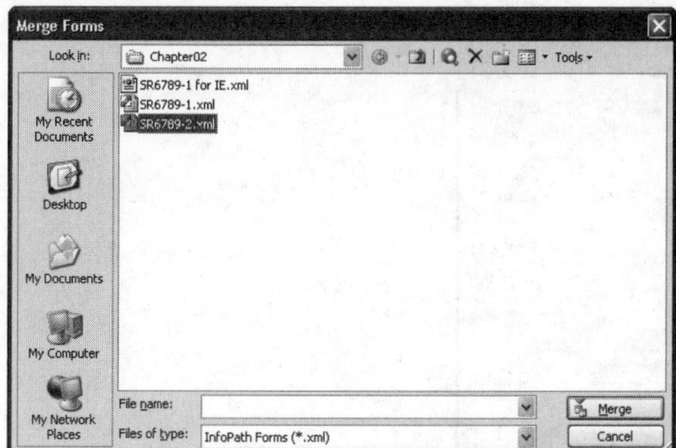

3. **Click Merge to close the dialog box and complete the merging process.**
4. **Choose File, Save As, and save the merged form as SR6789-1&2.xml.**

Figure 2-17 shows the Summary rich text box and two of the bulleted lists with elements added from the merged forms.

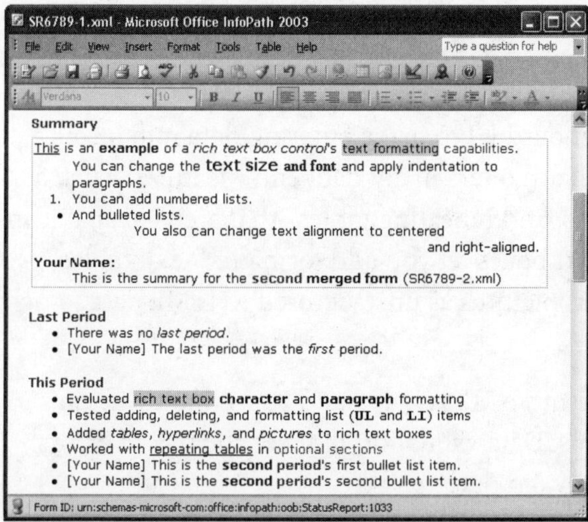

SR6789-1.xml - Microsoft Office InfoPath 2003
File Edit View Insert Format Tools Table Help
Type a question for help
Verdana 10
Summary
This is an example of a rich text box control's text formatting capabilities.
You can change the text size and font and apply indentation to paragraphs.
1. You can add numbered lists.
• And bulleted lists.
You also can change text alignment to centered
and right-aligned.
Your Name:
This is the summary for the second merged form (SR6789-2.xml)
Last Period
• There was no last period.
• [Your Name] The last period was the first period.
This Period
• Evaluated rich text box character and paragraph formatting
• Tested adding, deleting, and formatting list (UL and LI) items
• Added tables, hyperlinks, and pictures to rich text boxes
• Worked with repeating tables in optional sections
• [Your Name] This is the second period's first bullet list item.
• [Your Name] This is the second period's second bullet list item.
Form ID: urn:schemas-microsoft-com:office:infopath:oob:StatusReport:1033

Figure 2-17 The merged form's content adds to the Summary rich text box, and Last Period and This Period lists.

Figure 2-18 shows additions to the Time Report and Budget Report repeating tables. It's clear from the merged Budget Report values that Amount Budgeted values should represent a budget detail amount, not the total budget for the project. The merged form adds the Task List item, which wasn't present in SR6789-1.xml.

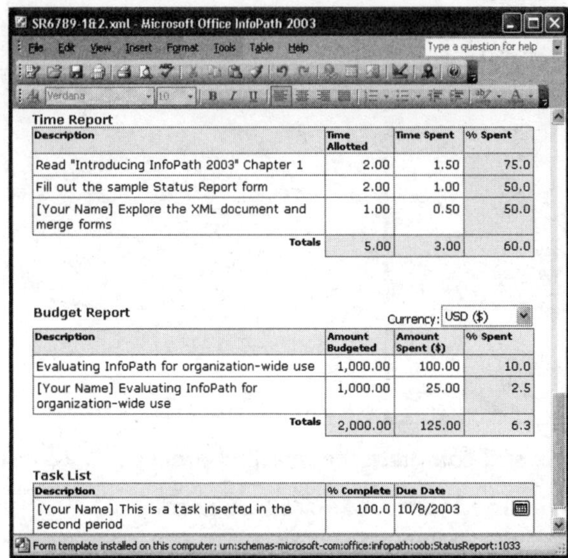

SR6789-1&2.xml - Microsoft Office InfoPath 2003

File Edit View Insert Format Tools Table Help — Type a question for help

Time Report

Description	Time Allotted	Time Spent	% Spent
Read "Introducing InfoPath 2003" Chapter 1	2.00	1.50	75.0
Fill out the sample Status Report form	2.00	1.00	50.0
[Your Name] Explore the XML document and merge forms	1.00	0.50	50.0
Totals	5.00	3.00	60.0

Budget Report — Currency: USD ($)

Description	Amount Budgeted	Amount Spent ($)	% Spent
Evaluating InfoPath for organization-wide use	1,000.00	100.00	10.0
[Your Name] Evaluating InfoPath for organization-wide use	1,000.00	25.00	2.5
Totals	2,000.00	125.00	6.3

Task List

Description	% Complete	Due Date
[Your Name] This is a task inserted in the second period	100.0	10/8/2003

Form template installed on this computer: urn:schemas-microsoft-com:office:infopath:oob:StatusReport:1033

Figure 2-18 Merging Status Report forms totals the Time Report and Budget Report summary values.

Chapter Summary

InfoPath 2003 provides an Office-standard UI to make entering data into forms a familiar process for Office users. InfoPath offers many data entry features–such as date picker controls, optional sections, and repeating tables–that aren't available in ordinary HTML-based forms. Rich text boxes let you add formatted text; tables; plain, bulleted, or numbered lists; and pictures as unstructured XHTML data to rich text boxes.

InfoPath validates data against the form's XML schema and rules that the form's designer applies to individual controls. Data validation reduces the risk of errors resulting from incomplete forms or invalid data.

Saving and printing forms follows the Office model closely. Exploring the saved XML data document gives you insight into the relationship between the document's elements and the form's control values. Merging forms, which is one of InfoPath's most powerful features, combines data from rich text boxes and repeating sections or tables of multiple forms that are based on the same InfoPath template.

Q&A

Q. Can I work on multiple forms at one time?

A. Certainly. InfoPath supports working on many different forms at one time, each of which can be opened in one of the different InfoPath modes. You can open a form in data entry, design, and programming modes simultaneously; each mode has its own window.

Q. Don't rich text boxes that contain a variety of objects not defined in the form's schema conflict with the goal of creating semi-structured, self-describing XML documents?

A. Not necessarily. Some widely used XML specifications permit unstructured XHTML content in optional elements. An example is the Really Simple Syndication (RSS) 2.0 format, which you'll learn about in Chapter 4. In general, use rich text boxes sparingly and only when the applications that consume your data documents specifically support XHTML.

Q. Can I save a form that has validation errors?

A. Yes, but you won't be able to submit the form to a database or Web service, merge it with another form, or digitally sign it.

Q. Can I save an InfoPath data document to a network share so that others can use it?

A. Absolutely. Saving a form's data document is just like saving any other type of Office System file or document. When the Save As dialog box opens, navigate to the network share, and save the .xml file there. Alternatively, use Windows Explorer to copy the .xml file from your disk to the network share.

Q. Do other users need the template to open data documents created from it?

A. Yes. Users need network access to or a local copy of the template (.xsn) file to open or edit the document. You set up templates for shared access by *publishing* them to a server share. (Chapter 12, "Publishing Form Templates," describes the publishing process.) A copied template must be in a folder with exactly the same path as the original template, such as C:\Program Files\InfoPath*TemplateName**TemplateName*.xsn. In most cases, copying a template to a subfolder of another user's My Documents folder won't work because individual users' My Documents paths differ. Unmodified InfoPath sample forms are an exception; all InfoPath users have these templates if they chose a full InfoPath installation. The sample templates are called *fully trusted forms* and use registry entries to specify the templates' location. Chapter 12 shows you how to deliver fully trusted forms to InfoPath users.

On Your Own

Here's an additional exercise for opening an InfoPath sample form, completing it, changing form views, and then merging it with another form:

1. Start InfoPath, and open the sample Resume form.
2. Fill in some test data, and then save the form to \My Documents\InfoPath\Resume\Resume1.xml.
3. Use the View menu to switch between different views of the Resume1 form.
4. Use the Fill Out A Form task pane to complete a new sample Resume form.
5. Add different test data, and then save the form as Resume2.xml in the same folder.
6. Open Resume1.xml, and merge it with Resume2.xml.
7. Examine the results of the merge, and optionally, save the merged form as Resume1&2.xml.
8. Exit InfoPath.

CHAPTER 3

Understanding Form Technologies

In this chapter, you will learn how to:

- **Describe the files that InfoPath requires to define a form template and data document, and describe how InfoPath uses XPath to navigate a data document**
- **Relate the files in an InfoPath template to their corresponding World Wide Web Consortium (W3C) XML recommendations and use Internet Explorer 6.0 to test whether XML documents are well-formed**
- **Read a schema for a simple data document and validate a data document against its schema with the Microsoft XML Schema Definition (XSD) Validator tool**
- **Apply a custom XSLT transform to a modified data document and display it in Internet Explorer 6, and describe where and how InfoPath uses XHTML**

For more information:

- **Refer to the section "Modifying Data Documents for Display in Internet Explorer," in Chapter 2, which describes how to remove the processing instruction that causes InfoPath data files to open in Internet Explorer instead of InfoPath.**
- **Refer to the section "Viewing the Status Report Document in Internet Explorer," in Chapter 2, which shows examples of Extensible Hypertext Markup Language (XHTML) formatting of rich text box content.**
- **Refer to Chapter 10, "Adding Views to a Template," which describes adding multiple transforms to an InfoPath form.**

To work through this chapter:

- You should have a basic understanding of HTML. (You don't need to be a Web page designer.)
- You should have the sample files from the CD that accompanies this book installed in your C:\Microsoft Press\Introducing InfoPath 2003\Chapter## folders.

Bill Gates introduced the concept of a "universal canvas" at the Forum 2000 conference, held on June 22, 2000, at Microsoft Corporation's Redmond campus. Gates envisioned the universal canvas as a single browser-based UI for common computing activities: gathering information, generating documents, and managing time. All data flowing to and from the universal canvas–numbers, text, graphics images, and other complex data types–is contained in XML documents, defined by XML schemas, and transformed into HTML by XML style sheets. The universal canvas has not yet arrived, but InfoPath represents an initial step toward achieving Gates's goal. InfoPath uses the XML technologies that will implement the universal canvas.

It's not essential that you master InfoPath's underlying XML technologies, but you need a basic understanding of the W3C XML 1.0 and related recommendations before you begin designing InfoPath forms to accomplish specific data gathering tasks. Knowing how InfoPath handles XML namespaces, interprets or infers XML schemas, and renders XML data documents to HTML prevents false starts and radical form redesigns. By the time you reach the end of this chapter, you'll be able to impress your boss and astonish your colleagues with your newfound knowledge of InfoPath's XML technologies.

Relating InfoPath's Components

You learned in the preceding two chapters that an InfoPath form consists of an InfoPath form *template file*–also called a *solution file*–and an XML data document. The template file is a cabinet file with a .xsn extension, similar to a .zip archive file, that contains compressed versions of the files required to define and render InfoPath data documents. WinZip version 8 or later can't create or extract CAB files, but WinZip can display the contents of a template file, as illustrated by Figure 3-1. When you open the *FormName*.xsn template file in design mode, InfoPath extracts the files, uncompresses them, and caches their contents in memory automatically. When you save your design changes, InfoPath updates the individual files and reincorporates them in the .xsn file.

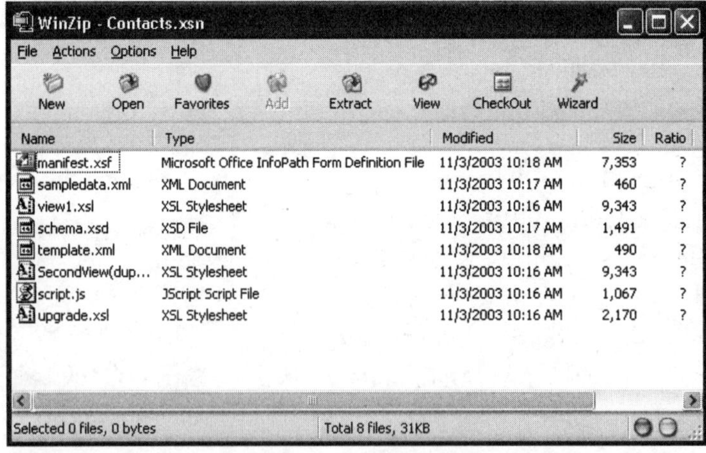

Figure 3-1 WinZip 8.1 SR-1 displays the contents of a simple template file.

Following are the names and descriptions of the files contained in a basic InfoPath template (.xsn) file:

- **manifest.xsf** The form definition file, which contains a list of all files in the template file, also called the *package*; global properties of the form, such as language and default view width; view properties; and application parameters, including the last form view you opened. The manifest.xsf file contains all the information needed to generate or re-create the .xsn file.

- **sampledata.xml** A data document that provides sample data for a form. Unless you specify use of sample data when you create a new form from an XML document, all sample leaf elements are empty.
- **schema.xsd** The XML schema for the form. The .xsd extension is an abbreviation of XML Schema Definition. The schema specifies the hierarchical structure of the form's data document and the data types of its leaf elements. When you create a form based on a data document instead of a schema, myschema.xsd replaces schema.xsd.
- **script.js** The file that contains the Microsoft JScript event-handling code for the form, unless Microsoft Visual Basic Scripting Edition (VBScript) was specified as the template's scripting language, in which case the file name is script.vbs. The default script.js or script.vbs file contains a single *XDocument.DOM.setProperty* expression. *XDocument* is InfoPath's data document class (called the InfoPath Object Model), and *DOM* is an acronym for the Microsoft XML Core Services (MSXML) Document Object Model. Chapter 16, "Navigating the InfoPath Object Model," describes the *XDocument.DOM object and its properties and methods.*
- **template.xml** The XML data document that InfoPath uses to create a new, data document in memory. Form sections and HTML controls bind to the cached document's elements.
- **view1.xsl** The XSLT document that generates the HTML code for the default view. InfoPath renders the resulting HTML code to display the form in InfoPath's working area. Some InfoPath sample forms use view_1.xsl as the default view file name.
- ***ViewName*.xsl** The XSLT transforms that generate additional form views. *ViewName* is the name, with spaces removed, assigned in design mode to the additional view.
- **internal.js** The file that contains JScript code to change views of a form. This file is present only if the form was created in the original InfoPath release version and has more than one view. Like script.js, this file is named internal.vbs if VBScript is the form's default programming language.

Figure 3-2 illustrates the relationships between *TemplateName*.xsn, *FormName*.xml (a saved data document), and the files described in the preceding list. Files and relationships in gray apply only if the form has a second view. The script.js file isn't included in this diagram, because it's only meaningful if the design includes custom script code.

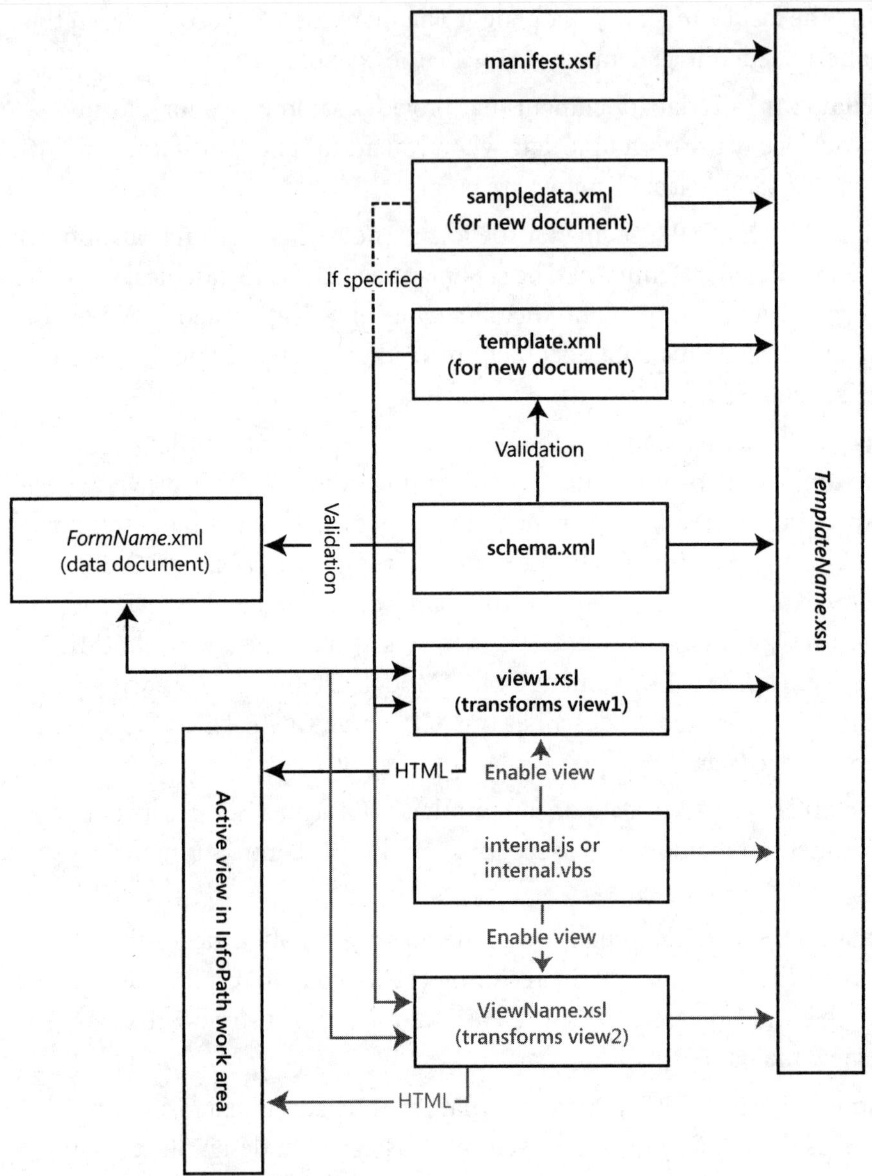

Figure 3-2 This diagram shows the primary files contained in an InfoPath template file and their relationships.

All files except the .js or .vbs scripts are XML 1.0 documents. The W3C recommendations don't specify the .xsd and .xsl file extensions for schema and transform documents, but these extensions have become standardized by common usage. You might see an .xslt extension for transform files occasionally. InfoPath projects include TemplateName.dll (a .NET 1.1 assembly file) and, when you build a form in debug mode, TemplateName.pdb (a debug symbols file.)

Exploring the sample files for this chapter

Installing the sample files from the CD that accompanies this book adds a complete set of files for the simple Contacts form you explored in Chapter 1 to your C:\Microsoft Press\Introducing InfoPath 2003\Chapter03\Contacts folder. The C:\Microsoft Press\Introducing InfoPath 2003\Chapter03\StatusReport folder contains template and data document files created from the Status Report form you completed in Chapter 2 that you use to complete the exercise in the "On Your Own" section at the end of this chapter. The C:\Microsoft Press\Introducing InfoPath 2003\Chapter03\XMLDocs folder has a set of XML documents that you'll explore in this chapter's later sections. The C:\Microsoft Press\Introducing InfoPath 2003\Chapter03\XSLT folder contains examples of simple transforms and XML source documents.

Spelunking the manifest.xsf File

This chapter uses the Contacts form from Chapter 1 for many examples, because Contacts.xsn contains very simple schema and moderately complex transform files. Changes to the manifest.xsf file structure for complex forms, such as Chapter 2's Status Report, are minor, as you'll discover when you reach this chapter's "On Your Own" section.

To open and explore the Contacts form's manifest.xsf file in Internet Explorer 6.0, follow these steps.

▶ **Open the manifest.xsf file in Internet Explorer 6.0**

1. **Start Microsoft Windows Explorer, and navigate to the C:\Microsoft Press\ Introducing InfoPath 2003\Chapter03\ Contacts folder.**
2. **Right-click the manifest.xsf item, and choose Open With, Internet Explorer.**
3. **If Internet Explorer doesn't appear as an Open With menu item, click Choose Program, select Internet Explorer in the Programs list, and click OK.**

Figure 3-3 shows the beginning of manifest.xsf in Internet Explorer 6.0. Like all other InfoPath XML documents, the first line of manifest.xsf is the XML 1.0 declaration. All but a few element names in the file carry the *xsf:* namespace prefix, which is defined by the *xmlns:xsf="http://schemas.microsoft.com/office/infopath/2003/solutionDefinition"* namespace declaration. Only one of the other namespaces declared (*xd:* for *XDocument*) is used in this sample document. The section "Understanding XML Namespaces," later in this chapter, explains how InfoPath uses XML namespaces.

Child elements of the *<xsf:files>* node define the file names and properties of the other files contained in the .xsn file. (This book uses *node* as a synonym for *element.*) Scrolling to the *<xsf:views ...>* node shows the properties of the two identical views and the Insert menu items that are defined for this version of the Contacts form. The *<xsf:fragmentToInsert>* node defines the empty element to add to the form when you choose Insert Contact from the repeating section's drop-down menu, as shown in Figure 3-4.

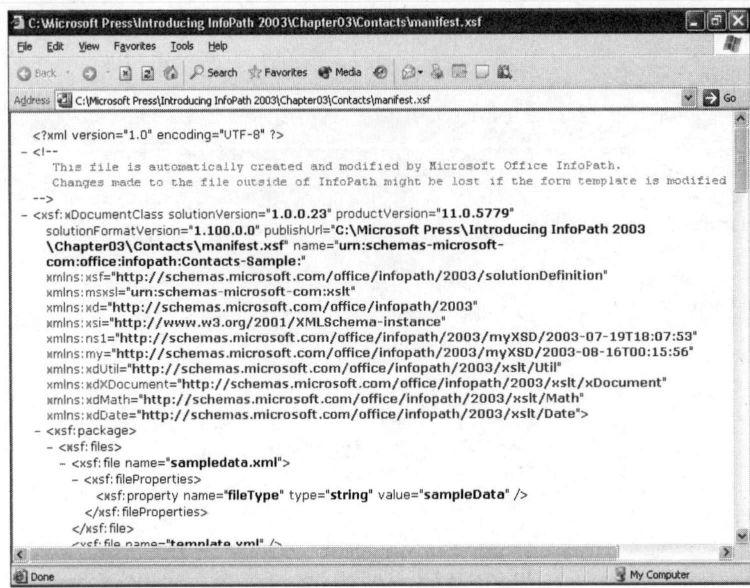

C:\Microsoft Press\Introducing InfoPath 2003\Chapter03\Contacts\manifest.xsf
File Edit View Favorites Tools Help
Back Search Favorites Media
Address C:\Microsoft Press\Introducing InfoPath 2003\Chapter03\Contacts\manifest.xsf
Go
<?xml version="1.0" encoding="UTF-8" ?>
- <!--
This file is automatically created and modified by Microsoft Office InfoPath.
Changes made to the file outside of InfoPath might be lost if the form template is modified
-->
- <xsf:xDocumentClass solutionVersion="1.0.0.23" productVersion="11.0.5779"
solutionFormatVersion="1.100.0.0" publishUrl="C:\Microsoft Press\Introducing InfoPath 2003
\Chapter03\Contacts\manifest.xsf" name="urn:schemas-microsoft-
com:office:infopath:Contacts-Sample:"
xmlns:xsf="http://schemas.microsoft.com/office/infopath/2003/solutionDefinition"
xmlns:msxsl="urn:schemas-microsoft-com:xslt"
xmlns:xd="http://schemas.microsoft.com/office/infopath/2003"
xmlns:xsi="http://www.w3.org/2001/XMLSchema-instance"
xmlns:ns1="http://schemas.microsoft.com/office/infopath/2003/myXSD/2003-07-19T18:07:53"
xmlns:my="http://schemas.microsoft.com/office/infopath/2003/myXSD/2003-08-16T00:15:56"
xmlns:xdUtil="http://schemas.microsoft.com/office/infopath/2003/xslt/Util"
xmlns:xdXDocument="http://schemas.microsoft.com/office/infopath/2003/xslt/xDocument"
xmlns:xdMath="http://schemas.microsoft.com/office/infopath/2003/xslt/Math"
xmlns:xdDate="http://schemas.microsoft.com/office/infopath/2003/xslt/Date">
- <xsf:package>
- <xsf:files>
- <xsf:file name="sampledata.xml">
- <xsf:fileProperties>
<xsf:property name="fileType" type="string" value="sampleData" />
</xsf:fileProperties>
</xsf:file>
Done
My Computer

Figure 3-3 Internet Explorer 6.0 displays the beginning of the manifest.xsf file for the Contacts template.

As you continue to scroll through the file's contents, you encounter *<xsf:menuArea ...>* nodes that define the drop-down menu's items for the repeating section and the View menu's first two items–First View and Second View (Duplicate) for this example, as shown in Figure 3-5.

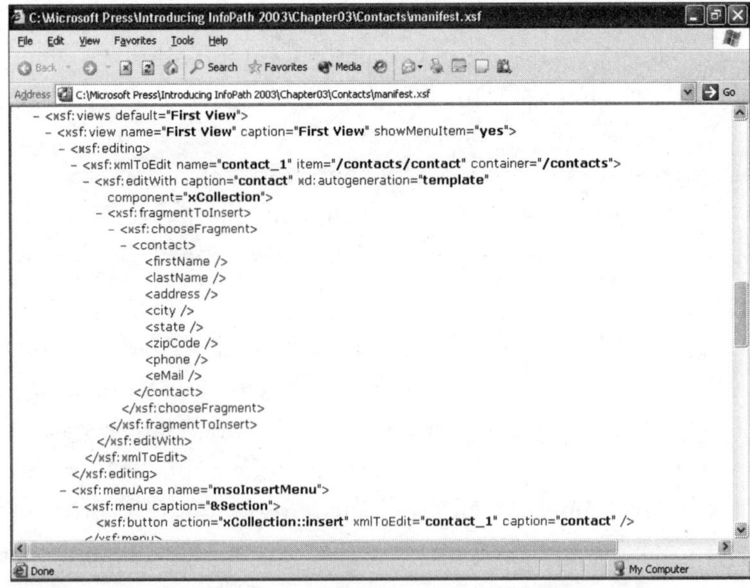

Figure 3-4 These are the initial nodes of manifest.xsf that define the available views of the form.

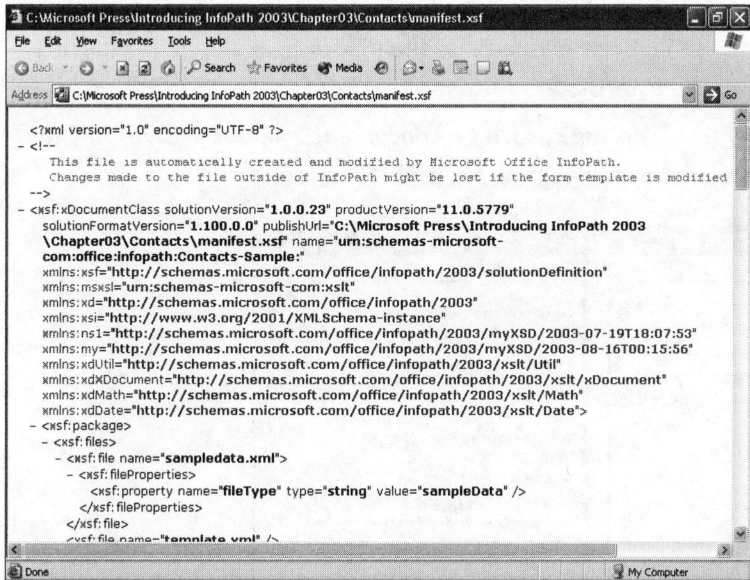

Figure 3-5 These nodes specify Insert and View menu items, the namespace for fields you add to the form, the file used for new forms, and the name of the schema file.

The remaining nodes specify the transform file for the second view, the namespace for elements you add to the schema (the same as the *xmlns:my* namespace at the top of the file), the empty template.xml file for new Contacts data documents, and the data document schema. Figure 3-4 doesn't include the last node, which specifies the default script language (JScript) and, for this example, internal.js for changing views.

Learning More About manifest.xsf

InfoPath's online help system contains an InfoPath XSF Reference book that expands to display several XSF-related chapters and topics, which probably tell you more than you want to know about form definition files.

To open an XSF diagram and display the help topic for an XSF element, follow these steps.

▶ **Open an XSF diagram and display the help topic for an XSF element**

1. **Open InfoPath with or without an active form, and press F1 to display the InfoPath Help task pane.**
2. **Click the Table Of Contents link to open the Table Of Contents, and click InfoPath Developer's Reference to display its contents.**

3. **Click to expand the InfoPath XSF Reference book, and click the InfoPath XSF Diagram to display the first few elements of the diagram, as shown in Figure 3-6 (left). Elements with red asterisks are optional.**
4. **Click an element with a help topic, such as *<documentSchemas>*, to display the associated help file, as shown in Figure 3-6 (right).**

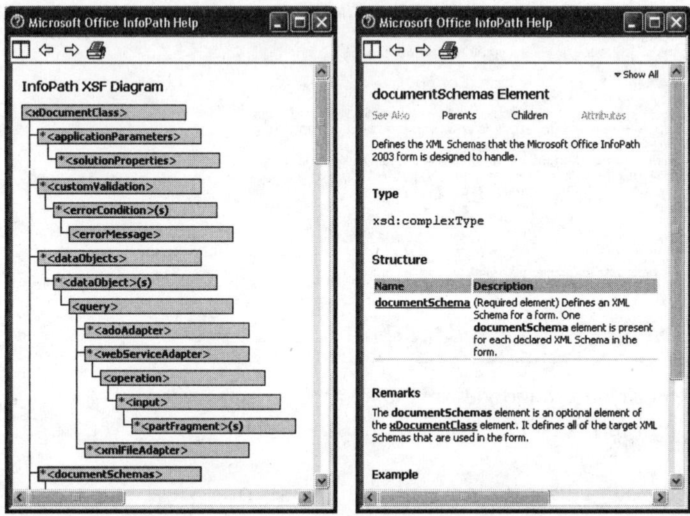

Figure 3-6 The first 16 elements of the InfoPath XSF Diagram are shown on the left, and the help topic for the *<documentSchemas>* element is shown on the right.

The XSF Diagram lists child elements of the root *<xDocumentClass>* node in alphabetical order. The position of the *<documentSchemas>* node is near the end of the .xsf file (refer to Figure 3-5). The relative position of nonleaf elements of the .xsf file isn't significant.

XSF help topics have Parents and Children links to open help files for elements higher and lower in the document's hierarchy. The *<documentSchemas>* node has only one child element (*<documentSchemas>*) and a single parent node (*<xDocumentClass>*). Most elements have several child nodes, and some, such as *<query>*, appear under multiple parent nodes. Links to child nodes also appear under the Structure heading. The Example section displays a sample node's contents.

Standardizing on XML Data Documents

Chapter 1 explained the benefits of a nonproprietary, open standard document format for exchanging information between desktop applications, local server-based systems or software components, remote servers, or all three. One of the primary advantages of text-based documents is their ability to emulate HTML traffic delivered by the HTTP to TCP port 80. Almost all corporate and personal firewalls permit unlimited two-way, HTTP transfer of text that's encoded as ordinary ASCII characters or their Unicode UTF-8 and UTF-16 counterparts. Firewalls that block port-80 traffic would prevent users with network connections behind the firewall from accessing the Internet.

Blocking XML traffic

It's possible to block or divert XML traffic with a firewall that detects XML's text/xml or application/xml Multipurpose Internet Mail Extensions (MIME) media subtypes in the HTTP header. A few special firewalls divert XML Web service traffic to dedicated servers, but these firewalls usually exempt ordinary XML documents. For more information about XML media subtypes, go to *www.ietf.org/rfc/rfc2376.txt*.

Encoding Text

Encoding the world's alphabets and pictograms into standardized, computer-compatible binary data has been and still is an enormous task. XML is self-describing, but the *encoding="..."* attribute in the XML declaration line isn't. Following are the most common text encoding methods in use today, in the approximate order of their development:

- ASCII Abbreviation for the American Standard Code for Information Interchange, which uses seven binary bits to define 128 characters, including uppercase and lowercase letters of the English alphabet, numbers, punctuation symbols, and special control characters, such as horizontal tab, linefeed, and carriage return. The XML encoding attribute for ASCII is *encoding="us-ascii"*, but specifying ASCII encoding of XML documents isn't a common practice. Internet Explorer versions 5.5 and earlier don't recognize this encoding; you receive a *System does not support the specified encoding* error message when you attempt to open the document; Internet Explorer 6.0 fixed this problem.
- EBCDIC Abbreviation for IBM's Extended Binary Coded Decimal Interchange Code for its mainframe computers. EBCDIC is an 8-bit encoding scheme that's related to but differs greatly from ASCII encoding. One of the objectives of the pending XML 1.1 recommendation is to permit use of EBCDIC-specific characters in XML documents. Translation between ASCII and EBCDIC is tricky, at best. EBCDIC isn't used for XML text encoding.
- ANSI Abbreviation for the American National Standards Institute. ANSI defines 128 additional characters based on—but not identical to—the ISO Latin-1 character set that's the default for Web browsers. The last four rows of the Microsoft Windows 95 and 98 CharMap applet display the ANSI extensions. You can specify ANSI (Windows) encoding for 14 alphabets in the Microsoft Windows 2000 and later and Windows XP CharMap applet by selecting the Advanced View check box and making a selection

from the Character Set list. The encoding attribute for Windows: Western European is *encoding="widows-1252"*; ISO Latin-1 uses *encoding="ISO-8859-1"*.

- Unicode Text-encoding system based on the Universal Character Set (UCS). UCS is an international standard—ISO/IEC 1046-1—for a multibyte (more correctly, *multi-octet*) encoding scheme that can handle most writing systems in use through the world. Unicode—now quite mature at version 4.0—is a registered trademark of the Unicode Organization (*www.unicode.org*), whose members include most major software vendors. Unicode, which is the default text encoding method for Windows 2000 and later, Windows NT, and Windows XP, uses 16 bits to represent 63,000 different characters.
- UTF Abbreviation for Unicode (or UCS) Transformation Formats. Most, but not all, XML documents use one of the following UTF encoding formats:
- UTF-8 Encodes the standard 128 ASCII characters as single bytes, which makes UTF-8 and ASCII encoding compatible. Non-ASCII characters are encoded in 1-byte to 4-byte sequences or blocks. UTF-8 is becoming a more common format for encoding Web pages, especially those that use Extensible HTML (XHTML), and is the most common encoding scheme for XML documents. The encoding attribute for UTF-8 is, not surprisingly, encoding="UTF-8", although you sometimes see encoding="utf-8".
- UTF-16 A Unicode variant that extends to about 1 million the maximum number of different encoded characters. UTF-16 is less common than UTF-8 as a Web page and XML encoding format. A byte-order mark (BOM) at the beginning of a file distinguishes UTF-16 from UTF-8 encoding. If the BOM is missing or not understood, the encoding attribute for UTF-16, encoding="UTF-16", usually handles the problem.

The Internet Explorer versions 5.0 and later View, Encoding menu item lets you specify the encoding scheme, but it's better to turn on Auto-Select and let Internet Explorer determine the encoding. If Internet Explorer displays an encoding error message when opening an XML document, verify that the Auto-Select option is selected.

See Also **You can learn more about Unicode, UTF-8, UTF-16, and the new UTF-32 encoding formats at *www.unicode.org/faq/*. The Internet Engineering Taskforce (IETF) has an Internet Note on the relationship between UTF-8 and UCS encoding at *www.ietf.org/rfc/rfc2279.txt*.**

Testing for Well-Formed Data Documents

XML documents that serve as InfoPath data sources must be *well-formed*. When you design a new form, an easy method for creating the new form's data source is to modify an existing XML document or write a new one from scratch. Doing this requires that you know the definition of a well-formed document.

The Extensible Markup Language (XML) 1.0 (Second Edition) recommendation, paraphrased here, defines a well-formed XML document as having the following basic characteristics:

- The document must contain one or more elements. An element is defined by a start tag and an end tag or, for empty elements, the empty element tag.

- The names of an element's start tag and end tag must match.
- The document must contain a single root element, which also is known as the top-level element.
- All other document elements are descendants (children), of the root element. Child elements must be properly nested with matching start tags and end tags or employ empty tags.
- Processing instructions (PIs) are instructions to applications that process the document, and are not considered elements. Technically, PIs aren't part of the document's character data.

Comparing well-formed and malformed documents

Your C:\Microsoft Press\Introducing InfoPath 2003\Chapter03\XMLDocs folder contains a collection of Contacts-*.xml files, which illustrate well-formed and malformed documents. The files contain an extended version of Chapter 1's Contacts.xml document.

The XML 1.0 specification contains many other requirements for well-formed documents, such as restrictions on the attributes of an element, but the preceding list contains the most important requirements for elements.

Internet Explorer performs a test for well-formed XML documents prior to applying its built-in XSLT formatting code. Figure 3-7 shows Contacts-WellFormed.xml open in Internet Explorer 6.0. You can collapse elements by clicking the minus sign prefix; when an element is collapsed, clicking the plus sign prefix expands it.

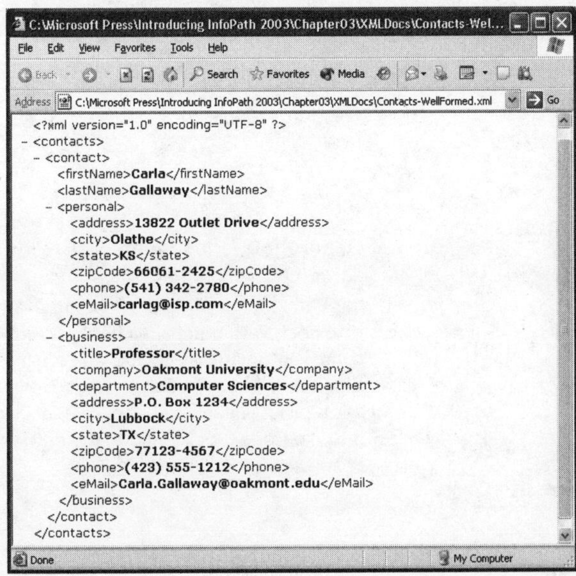


```
  <?xml version="1.0" encoding="UTF-8" ?>
- <contacts>
  - <contact>
      <firstName>Carla</firstName>
      <lastName>Gallaway</lastName>
    - <personal>
        <address>13822 Outlet Drive</address>
        <city>Olathe</city>
        <state>KS</state>
        <zipCode>66061-2425</zipCode>
        <phone>(541) 342-2780</phone>
        <eMail>carlag@isp.com</eMail>
      </personal>
    - <business>
        <title>Professor</title>
        <company>Oakmont University</company>
        <department>Computer Sciences</department>
        <address>P.O. Box 1234</address>
        <city>Lubbock</city>
        <state>TX</state>
        <zipCode>77123-4567</zipCode>
        <phone>(423) 555-1212</phone>
        <eMail>Carla.Gallaway@oakmont.edu</eMail>
      </business>
    </contact>
  </contacts>
```

Figure 3-7 This is a well-formed XML document open in Internet Explorer 6.0.

The document's root, or top-level element is <*contacts*>; <*contact*> is a child element of the root, and has four child elements of its own: <*firstName*>, <*lastName*>, <*personal*>, and <*business*>. It's common practice to refer to these elements as grandchildren and their child elements as great-grandchildren of the root element. The <*firstName*>, <*lastName*>, and great-grandchildren elements are leaf nodes in this example. The four grandchild elements are called *siblings*, as are the three sets of leaf nodes.

The Zoology of Element Names

You've probably noticed that the tag names used in InfoPath's sample forms and many of this book's examples begin with a lowercase word or prefix. If the names have two or more words, these words are internal caps, as in *orderLineItems*. Tag names must begin with a letter or an underscore and can't contain spaces or other common punctuation symbols, other than a colon (:), hyphen (-), underscore (_), or period (.). The colon is reserved for separating namespace prefixes from element names. Using internal caps to identify multiple words makes tag names more legible, although using the underscore as a word separator also solves the readability problem.

The common term for the *lowercaseInternalCaps* tag name format is *camelCase*, although there is some controversy as to the format's rules, as a visit to *http://c2.com/cgi/wiki?CamelCase* demonstrates. Some folks argue that camelCase should allow only one capitalized letter (which might be better named dromedaryCase, because a dromedary has one hump).

Lowercasing the initial word or abbreviation might have originated from naming conventions for C-language variables, called *Hungarian notation*, in which a lowercase prefix specifies the variable's data type, as in *lpszLongPointerToAStringZeroTerminated*. (The term *Hungarian notation* might have originated from the use of *sz* in the prefix, or from the birthplace—Budapest—of the notation's originator, Charles Simonyi.) There's no official standard for case in tag names, but remember to be consistent. XML, unlike Microsoft Visual Basic and Visual Basic for Applications (VBA), is *case-sensitive*.

Troubleshooting Malformed Documents

If a document is malformed, Internet Explorer displays an error message to indicate the type of problem and its location. To learn how Internet Explorer handles malformed XML documents, follow these steps.

Generating "friendly names" from camelCase

InfoPath detects camelCase and generates text box labels with friendly names from field names automatically, as you'll discover in Chapter 4, "Creating Forms." <*firstName*> adds a First Name label, and <*zipCode*> turns into Zip Code (not ZIP Code, the official U.S. Postal Service trademark.

▶ View a malformed XML document in Internet Explorer

1. **Start Windows Explorer, and navigate to the C:\Microsoft Press\Introducing InfoPath 2003\Chapter03\XMLDocs folder.**

2. **Double-click the Contacts-NoRoot.xml item to display it in Internet Explorer, which displays an *Only one top-level element is allowed in an XML document* error message and opens a message box.**
3. **Click the Show Details button to expand the dialog box and display the line and character numbers to pinpoint where the error occurred, as shown here:**

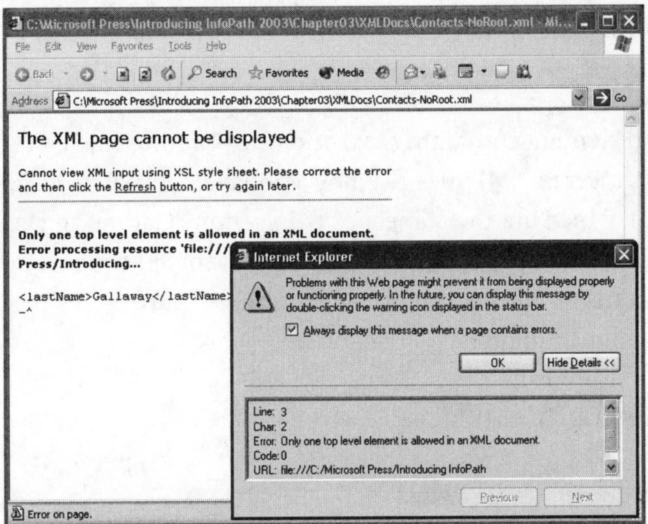

4. **Choose View, Source to open a temporary text copy of the errant document in Notepad, as shown here, with the line highlighted:**

Contacts-NoRoot.xml - Notepad

File Edit Format View Help

```
<?xml version="1.0" encoding="UTF-8"?>
<firstName>Carla</firstName>
<lastName>Gallaway</lastName>
<personal>
	<address>13822 Outlet Drive</address>
	<city>Olathe</city>
	<state>KS</state>
	<zipCode>66061-2425</zipCode>
	<phone>(541) 342-2780</phone>
	<eMail>carlag@isp.com</eMail>
</personal>
<business>
	<title>Professor</title>
	<company>Oakmont University</company>
	<department>Computer Sciences</department>
	<address>P.O. Box 1234</address>
	<city>Lubbock</city>
	<state>TX</state>
	<zipCode>77123-4567</zipCode>
	<phone>(423) 555-1212</phone>
	<eMail>Carla.Gallaway@oakmont.edu</eMail>
</business>
```

5. **Close Notepad, and repeat steps 2 through 4 for the Contacts-BadEndTag.xml and Contents-Mis-Nested.xml files. Use the line and character numbers to identify the error in the Notepad copy.**

The errors in the three deliberately malformed documents are obvious, but tracking problems in long, complex documents isn't easy without Internet Explorer's assistance. When authoring InfoPath data source documents, give them a pass through Internet Explorer before attempting to create the form.

Uncovering hidden malformations
When testing if very long documents are well-formed, be sure to scroll to the end of the document. In some cases, such as after the error message box has been disabled, the error message doesn't appear until you reach the approximate location of the error in the document.

Avoiding Mixed Content

Mixed content consists of an element containing text and one or more child elements. Mixed content is quite common in XML files used by publishers, but not in XML Information Sets (infosets), which are the subject of the section "Gathering Data into XML Infosets," later in this chapter. Figure 3-8 illustrates mixed content in the *<contact>* element of the Contacts-Mixed.xml file; the highlight emphasizes the added text that creates the mixed content.

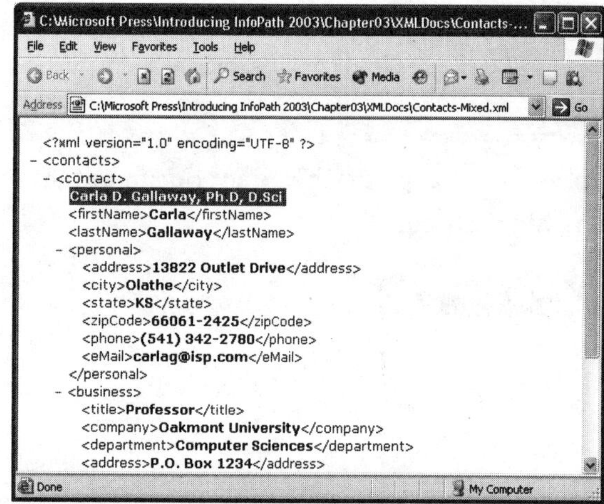

Figure 3-8 This member of the sample Contacts-*.xml documents contains mixed content.

InfoPath disregards mixed content when you create a data source from an XML document or an XML schema that specifies *mixed="true"* in the element's definition. If the text of a mixed content element is important, add an element to contain the text, such as *<fullName> ... </fullName>* for this example.

Understanding XML Namespaces

Gaining a full understanding of XML namespaces and how to use them properly in an XML document isn't a walk in the park. The purpose of XML namespaces is to prevent *namespace collisions*–situations in which two software modules share the same tag name but interpret it differently. The W3C Namespaces in the XML recommendation (at *www.w3.org/TR/REC-xml-names/*) lists query processors, style-sheet-driven rendering engines, and schema-driven validators as typical *software modules*. InfoPath performs all three functions.

The W3C recommendation requires that namespaces be specified by a Universal Resource Identifier (URI), which takes the form of a unique URL, such as *http://schema.oakleaf.ws/infopath/contacts*, or a Universal Resource Name (URN) in the form *urn:schemas-oakleaf-ws:infopath:contacts*. Namespace names based on registered domain names, such as *oakleaf.ws*, can be made unique by extensions managed by the domain name's owner.

InfoPath uses URLs and URNs as namespace names in the manifest.xsf file, as illustrated by the following lines in the <*xsf:xDocumentClass* ... > root element tag that have an *xmlns:* namespace prefix:

```
<xsf:xDocumentClass solutionVersion="1.0.0.23" productVersion="11.0.5531"
solutionFormatVersion="1.0.0.0"
xmlns:xsf="http://schemas.microsoft.com/office/infopath/2003/solutionDefinition"
xmlns:msxsl="urn:schemas-microsoft-com:xslt"
xmlns:xd="http://schemas.microsoft.com/office/infopath/2003"
xmlns:xsi="http://www.w3.org/2001/XMLSchema-instance"
xmlns:my="http://schemas.microsoft.com/office/infopath/2003/myXSD/2003-07-
19T18:07:53">
```

Opening namespace pages from URLs
URIs in URL format don't need to point to a live Web site and default page. The namespaces beginning with *schemas.microsoft.com* and *schemas.oakleaf.ws* return an HTTP 404 error. Many W3C namespace names, such as *http://www.w3.org/2001/XMLSchema-instance*, have a corresponding page, but some cause Internet Explorer to display error messages. *http://www.w3.org/2001/XMLSchema* has a viewable page.

Figure 3-9 shows a modified version of the Contacts-WellFormed.xml file (Contacts-Namespace1.xml) with a *default namespace* declaration: *xmlns="http://schemas.oakleaf.ws/infopath/contacts"*. The default namespace applies to all elements of the document that don't have local namespace declarations. The <*personal*> and <*business*> elements have local namespace declarations, which apply to these elements and their children. In this example, the default namespace applies only to the root <*contacts*> node, its <*contact*> child node, and the <*firstName*> and <*lastName*> leaf nodes.

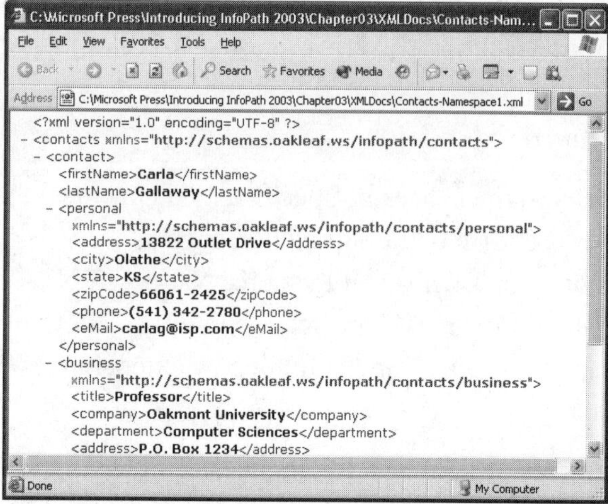

Figure 3-9 This XML document shows examples of default and local namespace declarations.

The more common method of defining namespaces is that used by InfoPath's .xsf files. In this case, you declare all namespaces as attributes of the root element and designate a namespace prefix in this format: *xmlns:tns="This-NameSpace-URI"*, where *tns* is the prefix. You add the namespace prefix (also called a *namespace qualifier*) with a colon separator to the element name, which becomes the *local name*. The Contacts-Namespace2.xml file, shown in Figure 3-10, takes this approach.

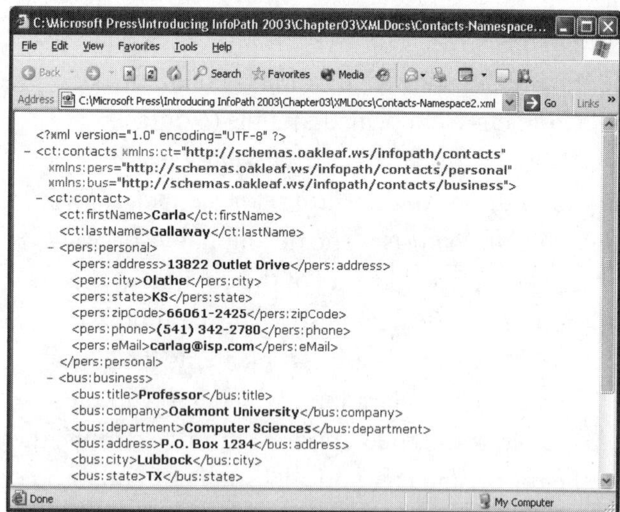

Figure 3-10 This document declares and assigns XML namespaces with namespace prefixes.

Using namespace prefixes minimizes ambiguities when a document contains elements from several different namespaces. When you create an InfoPath form from an XML document that uses either of the approaches described here, the resulting XML data documents reproduce the namespace assignments faithfully.

InfoPath makes extensive use of XML namespaces in its manifest, view, and schema files, but there's no absolute requirement that the XML documents you use as source documents for your forms use namespaces. If you expect to base your InfoPath form designs on documents that rely on namespaces, it's comforting to know that InfoPath provides full namespace support.

Gathering Data into XML Infosets

XML was used primarily for delivering the content of text documents, such as Web pages, when the W3C approved the original XML 1.0 recommendation in February 1998. Since then, it's become a common practice to use XML for representing a wide range of other data types, such as information extracted from databases and spreadsheets. The W3C XML Information Set (infoset) recommendation (at *www.w3.org/TR/xml-infoset/*) defines a formal *information model* for XML documents. Many XML purists consider the infoset to be the "real XML" and the XML 1.0 specification as a "character-based syntax" for XML infosets.

The infoset recommendation comprises a set of definitions for information items, which the editors describe as "an abstract description of some part of an XML document: each information item has a set of associated named *properties*." The recommendation also specifies allowable properties for each information item. For example, the XML 1.0 specification allows element names to contain colons without defining how colons are used; a colon in an infoset element name is restricted to acting as a separator for namespace prefixes and local names.

A detailed analysis of the infoset recommendation is beyond the scope of this book. Simply put, InfoPath adheres to the infoset information model, so the XML data documents your forms produce are "real XML."

Validating Documents with XML Schemas

XML is a simplified subset of the Standard Generalized Markup Language (SGML), which is an international standard document publishing format. SGML originated in the late 1980s and remains widely used for publishing complex documents, such as commercial aircraft maintenance manuals. The U.S. Government Printing Office uses SGML to publish the Federal Register and other official documents. SGML requires document type definitions (DTDs) to define the tags used for specifying the content and formatting of documents. One of the purposes of a DTD is to validate documents; *validation* means testing the contents of a document for conformance to a set of rules expressed in the DTD. A software module called a *parser* performs the validation.

The XML 1.0 specification adopted a simplified version of SGML DTDs to define the elements, attributes, and entities of a document. The most common example of entities is HTML's named entities, which substitute for characters, such as *&* for the ampersand (&). Early XML developers wanted a simpler DTD version that could be expressed as an XML document. (The text format of a DTD doesn't comply with the XML 1.0 recommendation.) The result was W3C's three-part XML Schema recommendation, which turned out to be much more complex than XML DTDs. The moral of this story is: "Be careful what you wish for, especially from a technical standards committee."

See Also **If you're interested in learning more about XML DTDs, the four-part DTD Tutorial at *www.javacommerce.com/tutorial/xmlj/dtd.htm* explains the DTD and its element, attribute, and entity definitions in detail.**

Constraining Element and Attribute Data Types and Values with XML Schemas

One of the primary benefits of XML schemas is their capability to define data type constraints for element contents and attribute values. DTDs assume that XML documents represent only textual information. An XML schema lets you select from a wide range of built-in data types, such as *string* (text), *integer*, *decimal*, *date*, *dateTime*, and many others–you can even define your own custom data types. You can restrict the range of numeric values and string formats also. Listing 3-1, which is adapted from an example in the XML Schema Part 0: Primer recommendation, illustrates data type, value, and format constraints.

```
<xsd:schema xmlns:xsd="http://www.w3.org/2001/XMLSchema">

<!-- Several definitions omitted for brevity -->

<xsd:complexType name="Items">
  <xsd:sequence>
   <xsd:element name="item" minOccurs="0" maxOccurs="unbounded">
    <xsd:complexType>
     <xsd:sequence>
      <xsd:element name="productName" type="xsd:string"/>
      <xsd:element name="quantity">
       <xsd:simpleType>
        <xsd:restriction base="xsd:positiveInteger">
         <xsd:maxExclusive value="100"/>
        </xsd:restriction>
       </xsd:simpleType>
      </xsd:element>
      <xsd:element name="USPrice"  type="xsd:decimal"/>
      <xsd:element ref="comment"   minOccurs="0"/>
      <xsd:element name="shipDate" type="xsd:date" minOccurs="0"/>
     </xsd:sequence>
     <xsd:attribute name="partNum" type="SKU" use="required"/>
    </xsd:complexType>
   </xsd:element>
  </xsd:sequence>
 </xsd:complexType>
 <!-- Stock Keeping Unit, a code for identifying products -->
 <xsd:simpleType name="SKU">
  <xsd:restriction base="xsd:string">
   <xsd:pattern value="\d{3}-[A-Z]{2}"/>
  </xsd:restriction>
 </xsd:simpleType>
</xsd:schema>
```

Listing 3-1 Part of an XML schema for a purchase order (from the W3C XML Schema Part 0: Primer recommendation).

The *<xsd:restriction base="xsd:positiveInteger">* tag restricts the values of the *<quantity>* element to positive values, and *<xsd:maxExclusive value="100"/>* specifies 100 as its maximum value. The *<xsd:pattern value="\d{3}-[A-Z]{2}" />* regular expression restricts the user-defined *SKU* type for the *partNum* attribute value to a combination of three digits, a hyphen, and two capital letters. The ability of an XML schema to define data type constraints makes XML practical as a messaging format for database content, as you'll learn in Chapter 13.

See Also You can view the data document (po.xml) and read a more detailed description of the purchase order schema (po.xsd) at *www.w3.org/TR/xmlschema-0/*. The other two parts of the recommendation, XML Schema Part 1: Structures and XML Schema Part 2: Datatypes, are at *www.w3.org/TR/xmlschema-1/* and *www.w3.org/TR/xmlschema-2/*.

Viewing a Simple InfoPath Schema

The schema for Chapter 1's Contacts form is simpler than the W3C purchase order schema, because the data document contains non-numeric data and imposes no restrictions on the text content or format. XML schemas are well-formed XML documents, so Internet Explorer displays them with its built-in transform. Figure 3-11 shows part of the schema.xsd file in your C:\Microsoft Press\Introducing InfoPath 2003\Chapter03\Contacts folder displayed in Internet Explorer 6.0. To get the most out of the following brief discussion of the file's contents, open schema.xsd in Internet Explorer.

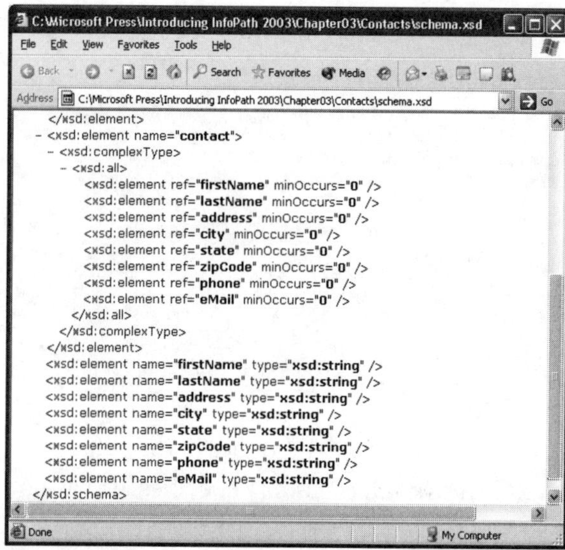

Figure 3-11 These are the last lines of the XML schema for the Contacts.xsn template's data documents.

InfoPath schemas define elements by their names and data types, as in *<xsd:element name="firstName" type="xsd:string"/>* and refer in *complexType* elements to the element definition, as in *<xsd:element ref="firstName" minOccurs="0"/>*. (A *complexType* element has more than one subelement.) The *minOccurs="0"* attribute indicates that the element is optional and infers that, if present, it can occur only once. Scrolling to the top of the schema exposes the *<xsd:element ref="contact" minOccurs="0" maxOccurs="unbounded"/>* definition for multiple *<contact>* subelements. Elements having the *maxOccurs="unbounded"* attribute bind to InfoPath repeating sections or tables.

Validating an XML Document to an InfoPath Schema

Internet Explorer tests for well-formed XML documents, but it doesn't validate them against a schema. Microsoft's GotDotNet site at *www.gotdotnet.com* offers an online validating parser that validates XML documents against XML schemas that reside on your PC.

To give the XSD Schema Validator a test drive, follow these steps

▶ Test the XSD Schema Validator

1. **Start Internet Explorer, and open the XSD Schema Validator, at *http://apps.gotdotnet.com/xmltools/xsdvalidator/*.**
2. **Click the Schema Document's Browse button to open the Choose File dialog box.**
3. **Navigate to C:\Microsoft Press\Introducing Infopath 2003\Chapter03\Contacts, and double-click schema.xsd to close the dialog box.**
4. **Leave the Namespace URI text box empty, because Contacts.xsd and Contacts.xml don't have a namespace declaration. Technically speaking, Contacts.xml's elements don't belong to a namespace.**
5. **Click the Browse button next to the XML Document field, and double-click Contacts.xml.**
6. **Click the Submit button to validate Contacts.xml against its schema, as shown on the next page.**

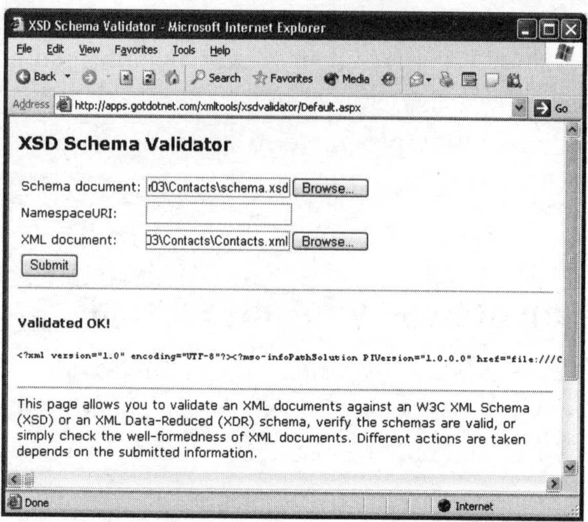

7. **Repeat steps 3 through 6, but substitute Contacts-Invalid.xml for Contacts.xml in step 5. You receive a *Validation error* message because the first contact substitutes *<givenName>* for *<firstName>* and *<familyName>* for *<lastName>*. Red text describes the errors and gives their locations by line and character number.**
8. **Double-click Contacts-Invalid.xml in Windows Explorer to attempt opening it in InfoPath. You'll get the error message shown here when you click the Show Details button. InfoPath shows the first error only and doesn't provide the row and character location of the error.**

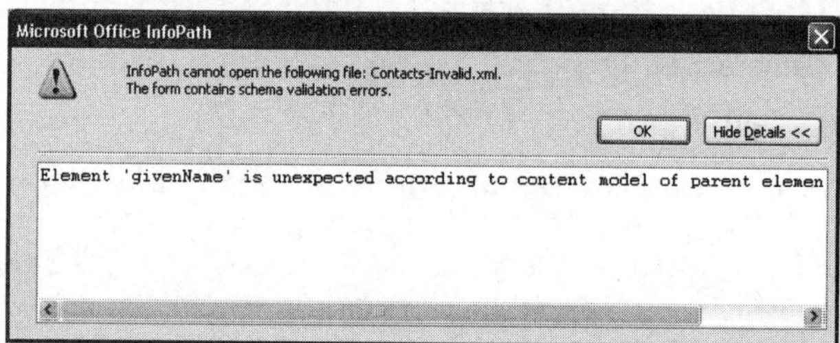

You'll find the XSD Schema Validator tool handy when you modify data documents or schemas manually for use in creating your own forms. It's a good practice to validate a data document against its schema–or vice versa–before basing a form design on either file.

Navigating Documents with XPath

InfoPath uses XPath 1.0 to locate specific nodes of a document, return node values, manipulate text, and perform calculations on numeric values. XPath is InfoPath's only XML technology that isn't represented by XML documents; XSLT form views use XPath expressions to select the XML data document's element and attribute values to appear in HTML controls. The declarative conditional formatting and data validation rules you add to forms generate XPath expressions to perform the tests.

See Also The Microsoft XML Core Services (MSXML) 3.0 parser was the first version to support XSLT 1.0 and XPath 1.0. Installing Microsoft Office System 2003 or InfoPath installs MSXML 5.0. To learn more about XPath, search for "XPath Developer" (with the quotation marks) at *msdn.microsoft.com* to find the latest version of the XPath Developer's Guide. The W3C XML Path Language (XPath) 1.0 specification, at *www.w3.org/TR/xpath*, describes XPath syntax in turgid detail. XPath 2.0 (*www.w3.org/TR/xpath20/*) was in the working draft stage when this book was written.

Your introduction to XPath in Chapter 6, "Adding Basic Controls and Lists," will involve writing XPath expressions to calculate expression box values. The OrderEdit.xsn template that you create in Chapter 13, Connecting Forms to Databases," uses the XPath expression shown in Figure 3-12 to calculate the extended values of order line items.

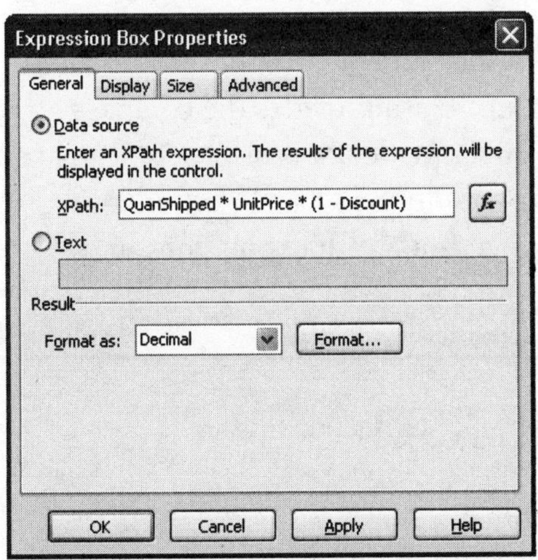

Figure 3-12 An XPath expression for calculating order line items totals.

XPath's *@name* expression returns the value of an attribute; omitting @ returns the value of an element. If the value is a number, you can specify XPath's numeric operators–such as +, -, *, and *div*–to return calculated values. The *@Quantity * @UnitPrice * (1 - @Discount)* expression in Figure 3-12 calculates the total net amount of each line item of an order in Microsoft Access's NorthwindCS sample database and displays it in the Extended column's expression boxes, as illustrated by Figure 3-13. Fortunately, you don't need a full understanding of XPath syntax to create formulas. InfoPath's Insert Formula dialog box generates XPath statements from combinations of field names, operators, and functions that you select from lists or type in a text box.

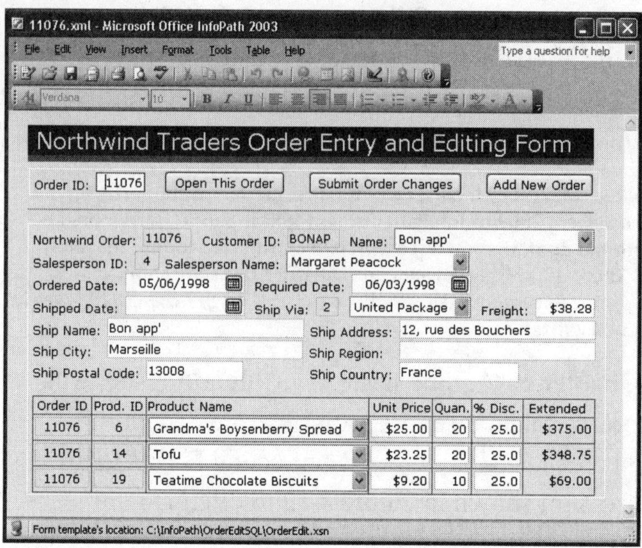

Figure 3-13 The extended line item values are calculated by the XPath expression in Figure 3-12.

At this point, you need to be aware only that XPath is integrated with XSLT and is an important element of InfoPath form development. XPath provides the compass for navigating InfoPath's XML DOM with JScript, VBScript, Visual Basic .NET, or Visual C# .NET code. InfoPath's sample forms and the examples in Part IV of this book, "Programming InfoPath Forms," make extensive use of XPath expressions in programming code.

Presenting Form Views with XSLT

XSLT is a language for transforming an XML document (called the *source tree*) into another document (the *result tree*). The most common use of XSLT is transforming XML documents into HTML or XHTML Web pages, but XSLT also can transform XML documents into other XML documents, plain text, and comma-separated values. XSLT is a declarative language, not a procedural language like VBA, Visual Basic .NET, JScript, or VBScript. You define rules for the transformation, and the XSLT processor (MSXML5 for InfoPath) establishes the sequence of operations required to complete the task. A template contains the transformation rules, which use XPath expressions to specify values that the transform assigns to the output document.

Working with a Simplified Style Sheet

InfoPath's default view1.xsl template is a forbiddingly complex document, even for the very rudimentary Contacts form. A simple transform is the best approach to gaining a basic understanding of how XSLT works. Fortunately, XSLT has an abbreviated syntax to make writing style sheets easier for XSLT beginners who have basic HTML authoring skills. Listing 3-2 is the abbreviated XSLT template to transform a modified version of Contacts.xml (Contacts-Simplified.xml) to a formatted HTML table that's sorted by ZIP Code.

```
<?xml version="1.0" encoding="UTF-8"?>
<html xmlns:xsl="http://www.w3.org/1999/XSL/Transform" xsl:version = "1.0" >
   <head>
      <title>Oakmont Contacts</title>
      <link rel="stylesheet" href="Contacts.css" type="text/css" />
        </head>
   <body>
      <table>
         <th colspan="6">Oakmont Contacts Sorted by Zip Code</th>
         <xsl:for-each select="//contact">
         <xsl:sort select="zipCode" />
         <tr>
            <td><xsl:value-of select="firstName" /></td>
            <td><xsl:value-of select="lastName" /></td>
            <td><xsl:value-of select="address" /></td>
            <td><xsl:value-of select="city" /></td>
            <td><xsl:value-of select="state" /></td>
            <td><xsl:value-of select="zipCode" /></td>
         </tr>
         </xsl:for-each>
      </table>
   </body>
</html>
```

Listing 3-2 This simplified transform syntax renders an XML document as a formatted XHTML table.

The *<html xmlns:xsl="http://www.w3.org/1999/XSL/Transform" xsl:version = "1.0" >* namespace declaration in the root element designates all elements with the *xsl:* prefix as XSLT template rules. The transform copies the HTML tags and their contents to the HTML document.

Here's a brief explanation of the purpose of the template rules in Listing 3-2:

- The *<xsl:for-each select="//contact">* rule instructs the processor to inspect each descendant node of the root node. (// is XPath shorthand for children of the current node, which is the root node by default.)
- The *<xsl:sort select="zipCode" />* instruction sorts the resulting document by ZIP Code.

- The *<td><xsl:value-of select="elementName" /></td>* instructions insert the value of the specified element in the corresponding cell of the table.

Internet Explorer 6.0 uses MSXML's XSLT processor to apply transforms to XML data documents and display the resulting document. To specify the appropriate .xsl file, you add this XSLT PI immediately after the document's XML declaration: *<?xml:stylesheet type="text/xsl" href="Filename.xsl"?>*. (The *href="Filename.xsl"* attribute value assumes that the .xml and .xls files are in the same folder. If not, prefix the file name with its full path or specify a URL to a Web-accessible template.) Figure 3-14 shows the Contacts-SimplifiedSS.xml file transformed by SimplifiedSS.xsl, which applies Contacts.css–a cascading style sheet (CSS) file–to format the table. All three files are in your C:\Microsoft Press\Introducing InfoPath 2003 \Chapter03\XSLT folder; double-click Contacts-SimplifiedSS.xml to open the files in Internet Explorer.

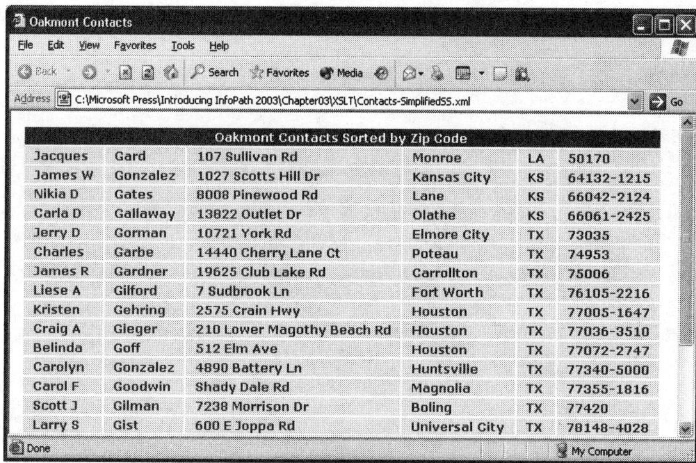

Oakmont Contacts Sorted by Zip Code					
Jacques	Gard	107 Sullivan Rd	Monroe	LA	50170
James W	Gonzalez	1027 Scotts Hill Dr	Kansas City	KS	64132-1215
Nikia D	Gates	8008 Pinewood Rd	Lane	KS	66042-2124
Carla D	Gallaway	13822 Outlet Dr	Olathe	KS	66061-2425
Jerry D	Gorman	10721 York Rd	Elmore City	TX	73035
Charles	Garbe	14440 Cherry Lane Ct	Poteau	TX	74953
James R	Gardner	19625 Club Lake Rd	Carrollton	TX	75006
Liese A	Gilford	7 Sudbrook Ln	Fort Worth	TX	76105-2216
Kristen	Gehring	2575 Crain Hwy	Houston	TX	77005-1647
Craig A	Gieger	210 Lower Magothy Beach Rd	Houston	TX	77036-3510
Belinda	Goff	512 Elm Ave	Houston	TX	77072-2747
Carolyn	Gonzalez	4890 Battery Ln	Huntsville	TX	77340-5000
Carol F	Goodwin	Shady Dale Rd	Magnolia	TX	77355-1816
Scott J	Gilman	7238 Morrison Dr	Boling	TX	77420
Larry S	Gist	600 E Joppa Rd	Universal City	TX	78148-4028

Figure 3-14 This formatted HTML table was generated by transforming the sample XML file with the simplified style sheet from Listing 3-2.

See Also **The W3C XSL Transform 1.0 specification at *www.w3.org/TR/xpath* describes XPATH documents in prose that's best described as a "sure cure for insomnia." For a more readable explanation of XSLT techniques, search for "XSLT Developer" at *msdn.microsoft.com* to find the current version of the XSLT Developer's Guide.**

Upgrading to Conventional Style Sheets

Simplified style sheets have limitations, which makes them suitable only for basic transformation tasks. InfoPath uses conventional style sheets, which include *<xsl:stylesheet>* and *<xsl:template match="/">* or *<xsl:template match="rootName">* elements. Listing 3-3 shows the standard version of the style sheet in Listing 3-2, with a sort on *<lastName>*, and the *<firstName>* and *<lastName>* elements combined with the XPath *concat* string concatenation function. The *<xsl:output method="html" indent="yes" />* line is optional, but adding it is a good XSLT programming practice.

```
<?xml version="1.0" encoding="UTF-8"?>
<xsl:stylesheet xmlns:xsl="http://www.w3.org/1999/XSL/Transform" version = "1.0" >
<xsl:output method="html" indent="yes" />
   <xsl:template match="/">
   <html>
      <head>
         <title>Oakmont Contacts</title>
         <link rel="stylesheet" href="Contacts.css" type="text/css" />
           </head>
      <body>
         <table>
             <th colspan="5">Oakmont Contacts Sorted by Last Name</th>
            <xsl:for-each select="//contact">
            <xsl:sort select="lastName" />
            <tr>
               <td><xsl:value-of select="concat(firstName, ' ', lastName)" /></td>
               <td><xsl:value-of select="address" /></td>
               <td><xsl:value-of select="city" /></td>
               <td><xsl:value-of select="state" /></td>
            <td><xsl:value-of select="zipCode" /></td>
            </tr>
            </xsl:for-each>
         </table>
      </body>
   </html>
   </xsl:template>
</xsl:stylesheet>
```

To see the effect of the *<td><xsl:value-of select="concat(firstName, ' ', lastName)" /></td>* rule on the HTML table design, double-click the Contacts-StandardSS.xml document item.

Displaying a Document with an InfoPath Transform

The Contacts-InfoPathSS.xml file in your C:\Microsoft Press\Introducing InfoPath 2003\Chapter03\XSLT folder uses a copy of the view1.xsl transform from the ...\Contacts folder. Double-click Contacts-InfoPathSS.xml to display a static version of the Contacts form in Internet Explorer 6.0, as shown in Figure 3-15. This version is identical to the exported Contacts_FirstView.mht file in the ...\Contacts folder–a whopping 126 KB of inscrutable HTML code.

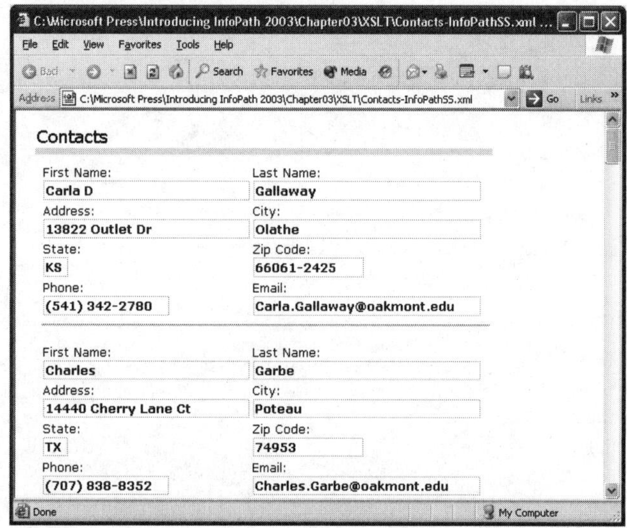

Figure 3-15 Applying the view1 transform to the Contacts-InfoPathSS.xml data document generates a 126-KB inanimate clone of InfoPath's version of the form.

Transforming an XML data document with the corresponding InfoPath view's transform applies the form's styles to the HTML rendition, but not the behavior of the HTML controls. Double-click view1.xsl to see why a detailed explanation of InfoPath's template rules would require more than the number of pages in this chapter.

See Also The Microsoft Office InfoPath 2003 Software Development Kit (SDK) installs a Downlevel command-line tool that you can use to automate generation of static HTML versions of forms.

Displaying Rich Text as XHTML

The section "Formatting Rich Text Data," in Chapter 2, introduced you to XHTML. The W3C XHTML 1.0 The Extensible HyperText Markup Language (Second Edition) recommendation calls XHTML "a reformulation of HTML 4 as an XML 1.0 application." The XHTML specification imposes a set of rules for expressing HTML

4.01 content as a well-formed XML document. The most evident XHTML rule is this: HTML element and attribute tag names must be all lowercase (not camelCase). There is a growing trend among Web page authors to replace traditional capitalized tag names with lowercase versions in anticipation of moving to XHTML 1.0 or a later version.

See Also **The W3C XHTML 1.0 recommendation, at *www.w3.org/TR/xhtml1/*, is an XHTML document that conforms to the XHTML 1.0 Strict requirements. Open the document in Internet Explorer, and choose View, Source to display its contents in Notepad. There are several W3C XHTML recommendations; visit *www.w3.org/MarkUp/* for a list of—and links to—the other recommendations.**

InfoPath's transforms don't generate XHTML to render forms; InfoPath uses XHTML to apply formatting to rich text box contents only. The section "Viewing the Status Report Document in Internet Explorer," in Chapter 2, shows part of the XHTML content of the Status Report form's *<sr:summary>* and *<sr:notes>* elements. XHTML embedded in XML data documents requires a local *xmlns="http://www.w3.org/1999/xhtml"* namespace declaration and embedded CSS for formatting.

Chapter Summary

InfoPath forms are created from an InfoPath template file (.xsn), which contains compressed versions of the files required to define the form's design, render the form in InfoPath's work area, and validate XML data documents. The manifest.xsf file contains a list of the files required by the template, which include the schema for the data document (schema.xsd or myschema.xsd), at least one XSLT file to define the default form view (view1.xsl), XML files used when opening an empty form (template.xml and sampledata.xml), and script files (script.js and, in some instances, internal.js).

InfoPath forms are based on W3C standards that were current when Microsoft first released InfoPath 2003 in October 2003. All files, except programming script (.js or .vbs) files, conform to the XML 1.0 specification. Schemas for validating data documents meet the requirements of parts 0, 1, and 2 of the W3C XML Schema recommendation. Transforms for views comply with the XSLT 1.0 and XPath 1.0 recommendations. InfoPath uses XHTML 1.0 syntax to format the content of rich text box controls. Contrary to a few computer press analysts' reports, InfoPath does *not* use Microsoft-proprietary schemas to generate XML data documents. You can define your own data documents with almost any schema you create yourself or obtain from someone else. The basic requirement is that the schema conform to the W3C XML Schema recommendation.

Q&A

Q. Do I need to know XPath and XSLT syntax to design InfoPath forms?

A. No. InfoPath interactively builds the XSLT transform body with the required XPath expressions as you add sections, tables, HTML controls, and validation rules to views in design mode. The XPath expressions you use to calculate expression box values are simple—they resemble ordinary math notation (except *div* for division). Customizing forms with JScript or VBScript requires some familiarity—but not expertise—with XPath.

Q. Is a data document opened in Internet Explorer with an InfoPath transform an exact duplicate of the exported .mht version?

A. Almost. The primary difference is that pictures you add to rich text boxes are missing, as you'll see when you complete the following "On Your Own" section.

Q. Does a data document that I modify to open in Internet Explorer with an InfoPath transform PI enable users without InfoPath to edit the document?

A. No. Users must have InfoPath installed on their computers to create new documents or edit existing documents. Adding the PI for the transform prevents InfoPath from opening the form.

Q. I've heard of a W3C proposed recommendation called XForms. Does InfoPath support XForms?

A. No. XForms share many of the objectives of InfoPath, such as separation of form presentation and form data, which XForms calls *instance data*, and data validation. InfoPath relies on the XML Schema and XSLT standards to create form views that contain HTML-based controls. XForms are intended primarily for browser-based data capture applications from a variety of devices. InfoPath is a conventional, "thick-client" Windows application, similar to the other Microsoft Office applications. For more information about XForms, go to *www.w3.org/MarkUp/Forms/*.

Q. Can I modify an InfoPath style sheet to customize a view?

A. Yes, but it's much easier and less error-prone to customize views in InfoPath's design mode, which is the subject of Chapter 5, "Laying Out Forms"; Chapter 7, "Formatting Forms"; and Chapter 10, "Adding Views to a Template." You also lose the changes you make to the style sheet when you redesign a view. Chapter 17, "Writing Advanced Event Handlers," shows you how to preserve the template changes you must make to display in expression boxes values that you calculate with Visual Basic .NET code.

On Your Own

Here's an additional exercise to learn more about the XML technologies described in this chapter:

1. Navigate to your C:\Microsoft Press\Introducing InfoPath 2003\Chapter03\StatusReport folder.
2. Right-click StatusReport.xsn, and choose Design from the shortcut menu to open the template in design mode.
3. Choose File, Extract Form Files to open the Browse For Folder dialog box.
4. Accept the default location (the current folder), and click OK to extract and decompress the files, which include a secondary data source file (currencies.xml) and its schema (currencies.xsd), and a custom aggregation template (agg.xsl) for merging Status Report data documents.
5. Double-click currencies.xml to display it in Internet Explorer. The currency file provides the data source for the Currency drop-down list.
6. Open currencies.xsd to view the very simple schema for currencies.xml.
7. Double-click SR6789-1.xml, which has been modified to apply the view_1.xsl transform in Internet Explorer rather than in InfoPath.
8. Right-click SR6789-1.xml, and choose Microsoft Office InfoPath to attempt to open the modified document in InfoPath. You'll receive a error message as a result of the modifications.
9. Scroll to the Notes rich text box, which is missing the image you added in Chapter 2. Displaying embedded images outside of InfoPath requires you to export the form in Web Archive Single-File (.mht) format.
10. Open and explore the other files you extracted from StatusReport.xsn in Internet Explorer or Notepad. Use Notepad to open the script.js file, which contains several event-handling functions and many other functions for calculating dates and values.
11. Close InfoPath, and proceed to Chapter 4.

PART II

Designing InfoPath Forms

Part II covers all aspects of InfoPath 2003 SP-1 form design and deployment, ranging from creating simple forms to deploying form templates to server shares, Web sites, and Windows SharePoint Services. You learn how to lay out and format InfoPath templates, use conditional formatting and data validation to govern user data input, create multiple form views, and add attachments and digital signatures to XML data documents. You also learn how to dissuade or prevent users from changing your form designs.

CHAPTER 4

Creating Forms

In this chapter, you will learn how to:

- **Describe InfoPath's form design process**
- **Create and modify a copy of an InfoPath sample form in a new folder**
- **Create an InfoPath template and data document from a new blank form**
- **Generate a schema and template from an existing XML data document**
- **Create a template and XML data document from an existing XML schema**
- **Modify an existing XML data document for use with an altered or a relocated template**
- **Modify a form's schema to remove or change the default *my:* namespace declaration**

For more information:

- **Refer to Chapter 3, which explains element and attribute naming conventions, XML namespaces, and document validation with XML schema.**
- **See Chapter 7, "Formatting Forms," which describes how to apply conditional formatting to text boxes.**
- **Refer to Chapter 8, "Validating Form Data," which explains how to ensure that users enter required data and that entries have reasonable values.**
- **See the "Designing Forms" topics listed in the table of contents of InfoPath's online help.**

This chapter is the first step in your InfoPath form creation journey. The remaining chapters of this book cover one or more specific aspects of the form design process. As Chapter 1, "Presenting InfoPath 2003 SP-1," points out, you don't need to be an XML guru or a programming wiz to modify an existing InfoPath sample template or create a new template that's based on an existing XML document or schema. InfoPath's Microsoft Office–standard interface and wizards minimize the time and effort needed to develop, test, and deploy a new form to its user community. Thus, InfoPath forms have the potential to deliver a very high return on investment (ROI), which is the primary business justification for new IT projects.

To work through this chapter:

- You'll need the Microsoft InfoPath data entry skills that you acquired in Chapter 2, "Filling Out Forms."
- You should be familiar with InfoPath terminology, Extensible Markup Language (XML) data documents and schema, and the components of template files, as described in Chapter 3, "Understanding Form Technologies."
- You should have the sample files from the CD that accompanies this book installed in your C:\Microsoft Press\Introducing InfoPath 2003\Chapter04 folder. You'll use these XML data document and schema files for most of the example forms you create in this chapter.

Understanding the Form Design Process

InfoPath's Design A Form task pane lists five basic design tasks–Layout, Controls, Data Source, Views, and Publish. Why InfoPath's developers didn't put the Data Source topic at the top of this list is a mystery; the form's data source is the key to the entire design process. Even more important than the data source, however, is up-front planning and requirements analysis for production forms before you begin their design. In the overall form design process, *why* is as important as *how*.

Following are the basic design steps and some advice for creating a successful InfoPath form:

1. **Clarify the business need for and objectives of the form.** As an example, the initial objective for an expense report form might be to replace a complex expense worksheet that has proven difficult for users to complete accurately or that the accounting department has discovered won't integrate with its new accounting software. A possible secondary objective is enhancing workflow by e-mailing expense reports for management approval and routing approved reports to the accounting department. Bear in mind that the purpose of the form is to generate a return on the organization's investment in your time to learn InfoPath, design and test the form, and roll it out for use by your coworkers.
2. **Determine the scope of the form's use within your organization.** If you work for a large organization, don't expect the entire enterprise to adapt its modus operandi to your new form and its XML data documents. Start small–at the team, group, or department level–and demonstrate the new form's ROI to management.
3. **Get user input early and often in the form design process.** You don't need a design review committee to shepherd a modest InfoPath project, but bear in mind that you're creating the form for coworkers to complete. If potential users find your form design cumbersome to use, incomplete, or subject to data entry errors, your design is doomed from the start.
4. **Define the data source for the form carefully.** If your organization has an XML infrastructure in place or under development, you'll probably use an existing XML schema or data document as the data source for the form. In this case, don't reinvent the wheel by creating your own XML document design. Changes to the data document structure after you design, format, and publish a form can wreak havoc on your form development budget.

5. **Beautify the form after the initial usability tests.** Don't squander your design budget on adding logos, background colors, and other frills until you've proven that the basic design meets user *and* business needs. Chapters 5 and 7 describe techniques for conforming your design to your organization's graphics standards.
6. **Validate data entry where possible.** InfoPath's conditional formatting and declarative data validation rules are easy to implement. Take advantage of them to ensure that users enter required data, don't enter numeric values outside reasonable minimum and maximum limits, and don't make other mistakes that you can trap with a validation expression. Chapters 7 and 8 cover InfoPath's conditional data formatting and validation features. Part IV, "Programming InfoPath Forms," shows you how to write Microsoft Visual Basic .NET managed code to validate dates and other element or attribute values that declarative validation can't handle.

Creating a real-world form
This is an introductory chapter on form design, but one of the templates (Rss2v1.xsn) that you create in this chapter and enhance in later chapters is a form that many organizations can use immediately. Taking advantage of Rss2v1.xsn and its successive versions doesn't require XML workflow expertise or other XML-enabled applications.

Modifying an Existing Template

The quickest and easiest way to become familiar with InfoPath form design techniques is to customize one of the 25 sample forms. You're already familiar with the Status Report form, so it's a good candidate for a design change. The following sections show you how to make changes to the form's sections and controls by adding new fields and removing unneeded fields. You also learn how to provide default values for text box controls.

Creating a Copy of a Sample Template

InfoPath makes it easy to modify any of its included sample forms. To create a copy of the Status Report form for modification, follow these steps.

▶ **Make a copy of the Status Report sample form**

1. **Start InfoPath. In the Fill Out A Form dialog box, click the Sample Forms link under the Form Categories heading, select the Status Report form, and click the**

Design This Form link under the Form Tasks heading. The Status Report form opens in design mode as the default Template1 with the Design Tasks task pane active.

2. Press Ctrl+S or choose File, Save to open a message box that gives you the option of saving or publishing your form, as shown here:

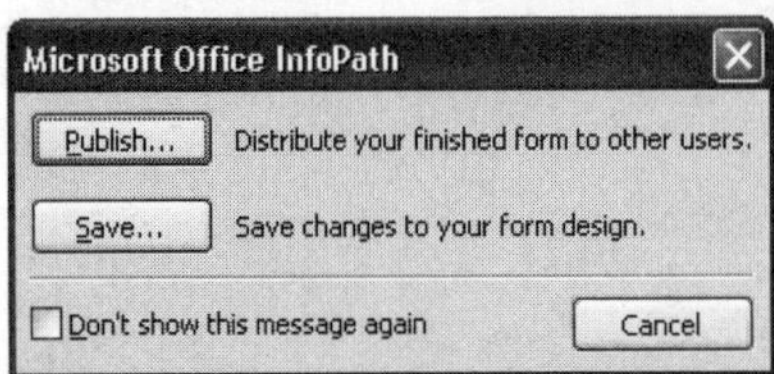

3. Click Save to open the Save As dialog box, which defaults to your My Documents folder.
4. If you didn't create an InfoPath subfolder in Chapter 2, click the Create New Folder toolbar button to open the New Folder input box, name the new folder **InfoPath**, and click OK to create the folder.
5. Create a subfolder of \My Documents\InfoPath named **StatusReportV1.**
6. Change the file name from Template1.xsn to **StatusReportV1**. InfoPath adds the .xsn extension automatically. Click Save.

7. Choose File, Properties to open the Form Properties dialog box, and change the template's name to **Custom Status Report**, as shown here:

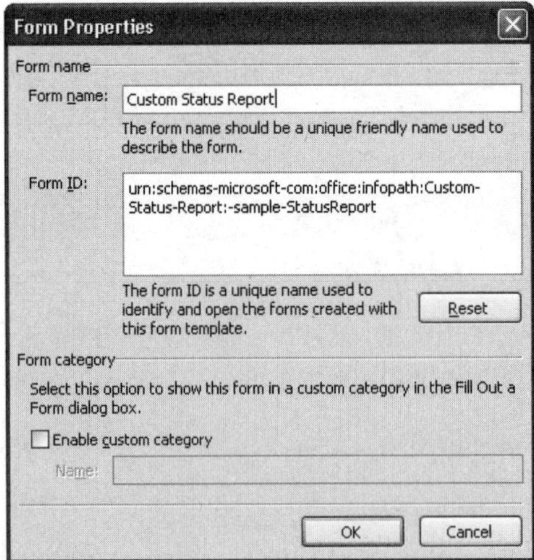

As you change the form name, the Form ID values changes, substituting hyphens for spaces.

8. **Click OK to close the Form Properties dialog box.**
9. **In the form, click the Status Report label, press the Home key, add the word Custom to the label text, and close the Design Tasks task pane. The only text you see in design mode at this point is in labels; you can edit all form labels by clicking their text and adding or deleting characters.**
10. **Press Ctrl+S to save your design change.**

Adding and Relocating Controls

Learning to add controls introduces you to InfoPath's Data Source task pane and drag-and-drop addition of text boxes bound to the data source's fields. A useful addition to the Status Report form is the manager's e-mail address, which you must alter to conform to the layout of the other text boxes in the second layout table on the form. The term *layout table* distinguishes tables whose cells contain manually added labels and controls from the repeating tables that InfoPath generates for you automatically. You can drag controls to relocate them, but you must cut and paste labels. Remove controls and labels by selecting them and pressing the Delete key.

▶ **Add a manager's e-mail text box to a layout table**

1. **Press Ctrl+F1 to open the Design Tasks task pane, if it isn't open, and click the Data Source link to make the Data Source task pane active.**
2. **Click the plus sign (+) in front of the manager field in the Data Source list to display the standard subelements for individuals. All sample InfoPath forms share a common set of fields to specify personal properties.**
3. **Pass the mouse pointer over the E-Mail Address field on the form to display an icon that identifies the element for storing the employee's e-mail address, *emailAddressPrimary*, as shown on the next page:**

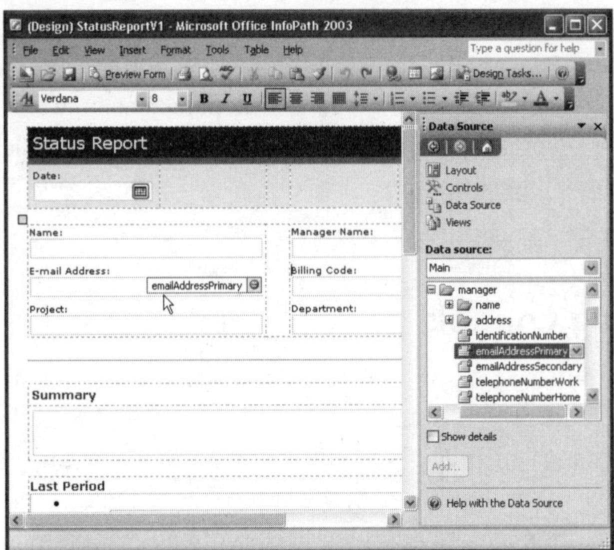

4. The manager's e-mail address should use the same element name as the employee's, so select the manager's emailAddressPrimary field in the Data Source list, hold down the left mouse button, and drag the insertion point to the left of the Billing Code label, just before the B. Releasing the mouse button adds a new field and a "friendly name" label above the Billing Code label, as shown here:

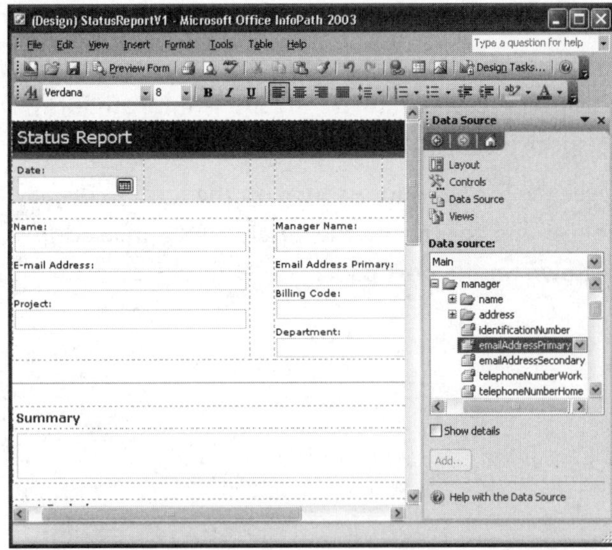

5. **Click the label, and change its name to Manager E-mail Address.**
6. **Press Ctrl+S to save your changes.**

Generating friendly names

InfoPath capitalizes the first letter of the field name and adds spaces before uppercase letters of element names that use camelCase conventions. The sidebar "The Zoology of wsElement Names," in Chapter 3, explains InfoPath's use of camelCase for element and attribute names.

▶ Change a text box's height and margins

1. **To conform the height of the text box and maintain the same spacing as other text boxes in the table, right-click the Manager Name text box, and choose Text Box Properties to open the eponymous dialog box.**
2. **Click the Size tab to determine the height and bottom margin of a typical text box. The Auto setting for height doesn't shed much light on the correct setting, which is 20 px. The Bottom margin setting (7 px) applies to all text boxes in the table. Click OK to close the dialog box,**
3. **Right-click the Manager E-Mail Address text box, choose Text Box Properties, and click the Size tab. Type 20 in the Height text box, select px (pixels) from the adjacent list, and type 7 in the Bottom text box in the Margins section, as shown here:**

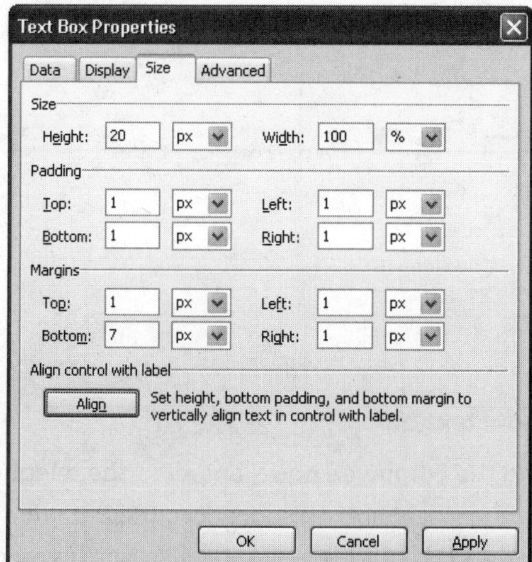

The Align button formats the text box so that its contents align vertically with the text of an adjacent label. This text box doesn't have an adjacent label, so vertical alignment isn't required.

4. **Click OK to close the dialog box, and press Ctrl+S to save your changes.**

▶ Relocate a text box and its label

1. Select the Project text box, and drag it to a position after the *N* in the Name label. (It's a bit tricky to position the insertion point before a label's first character, and positioning it after the first letter adds space for the label you add later.)
2. Use the mouse pointer to select the Project label, cut the label, and paste it in front of the N.
3. Delete the trailing *N* and add an N to the Name label.
4. Add a 7 px bottom margin to the Project text box, as you did in step 3 of the preceding procedure. This text box doesn't have a bottom margin because it was originally at the bottom of the table. Notice that the Data Source list's selection corresponds to the selected control on the form, as shown here:

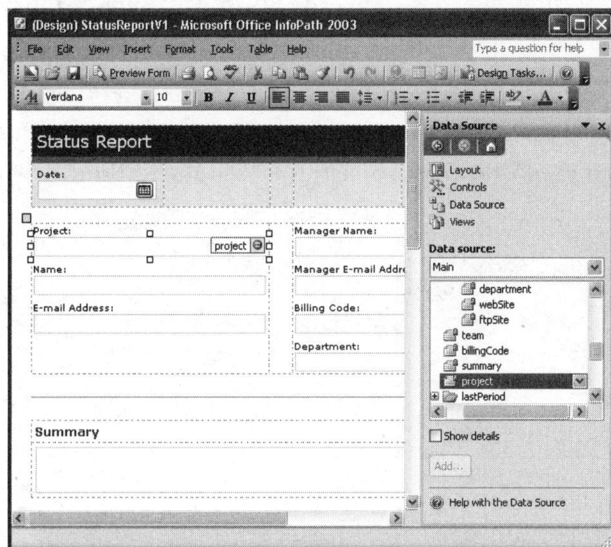

5. Press Ctrl+S to save your changes.

▶ Change the font size of a label and a text box

1. In the Data Source task pane, expand the Employee node, and drag the telephone-NumberWork node to the bottom of the table. At this location, the default auto-generated label font size is 10 points and the text box height is 20 px. (If you drag the node immediately below the E-Mail Address field, the label font size is 8 points and the text box has a height less than 20 px. In this case, press Ctrl+Z to undo the change, and repeat this step.)
2. Select the entire label, and select 8 from the toolbar's Font Size list to match the size of the other labels.

3. **Position the insertion point above the label, and delete the empty line.**
4. **Change the label to Work Telephone Number:**
5. **Change the font size of the Manager E-Mail Address text box from 8 points to 10 points by selecting the text box and then selecting 10 from the toolbar's Font Size list.**
6. **Press Ctrl+S to save your changes.**

Setting Default Control Values and Adding Placeholders

Supplying default values for text boxes saves users time when filling out the form and minimizes formatting and data entry errors. Placeholders consist of text that disappears when a user types the first character in a text box; a placeholder prompt is especially useful if a text box requires a particular format. Follow these steps to add default values for text boxes.

▶ **Add default text box values**

1. **Right-click the Work Telephone Number text box, and choose Text Box Properties from the shortcut menu to open the Properties dialog box with the default Data tab active.**
2. **Type the default text to display in the form for the text box by entering the desired text into the Value field in the Default Value area. For this example, enter (707) 425- , as shown here.**

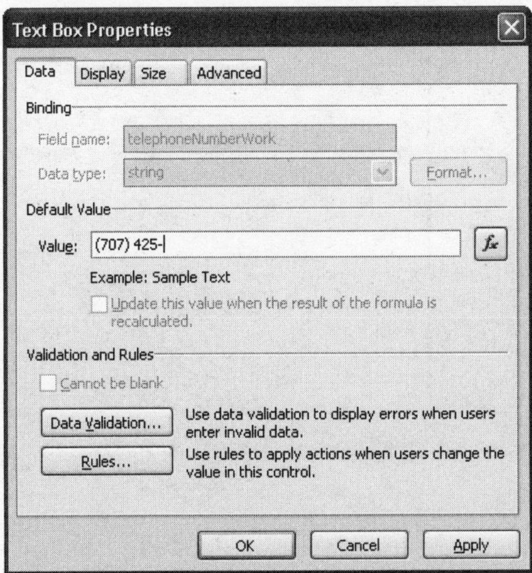

3. **Click OK to close the dialog box and display the default text in the text box.**
4. **Add default values to other fields in the form, such as the prefix for the billing code, the department name, and the domain name for the two e-mail addresses.**

Follow these steps to add placeholder text to text boxes.

▶ **Add text box placeholders**

1. **Right-click the Project text box and select Text Box Properties from the shortcut menu.**

2. **On the Display tab, type the placeholder prompt in the Placeholder text box—in this case, Type the full name of the project. You can specify whether to use the spelling checker, AutoComplete, or both. (Selecting the Paragraph Breaks check box or selecting the Wrap Text check box and specifying a Scrolling option lets you add a multiline text box, which isn't appropriate for this field.)**

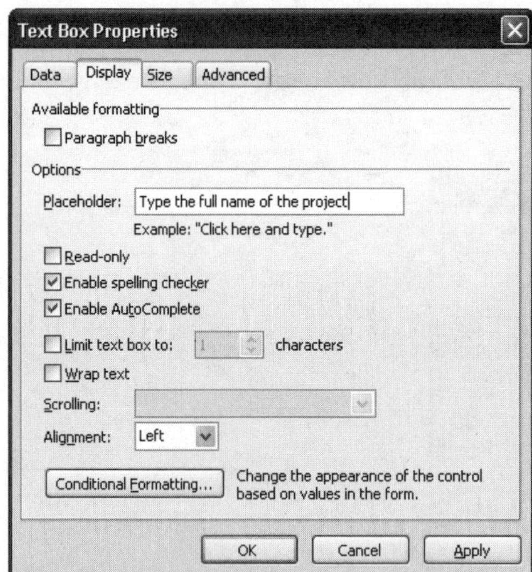

3. **Click OK to apply your changes, and press Ctrl+S to save them. Your form in design view appears as shown here:**

Understanding disabled controls in the Text Box Properties dialog box

The Field Name and Data Type text boxes on the Data tab of the Text Box Properties dialog box are disabled because these values are set when you add a text box control to the form. The Status Report's XML schema determines the data type and whether you can specify that the field can't be blank (empty). You can, however, add a data validation rule to prevent users from leaving required fields empty. Chapter 8 shows you how to add text box data validation rules.

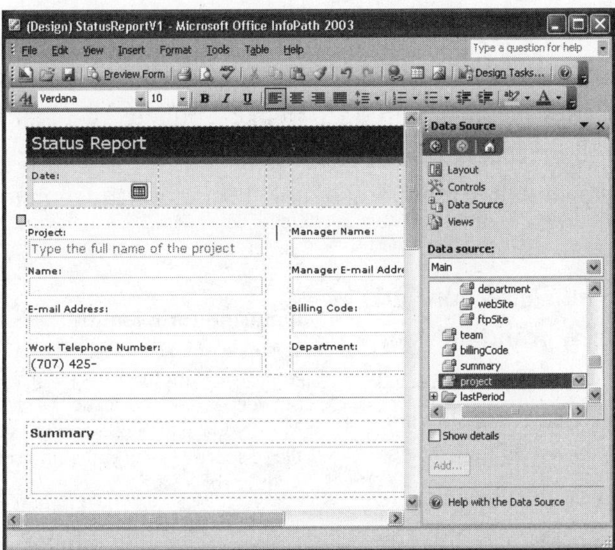

Restricting Formatting of Rich Text Boxes

You can limit users' unbridled authority to add ransom-note-formatted text, family or pet pictures, and other "creative" elements to rich text boxes. To do so, right-click a rich text box, such as the Summary field in the Status Report form, choose Rich Text Box Properties from the shortcut menu, select the Display tab in the Properties dialog box, and set appropriate restrictions, as shown in Figure 4-1. You can specify text box scroll bar appearance and behavior by selecting an option in the Scrolling drop-down list.

Previewing the form as you work

Click the Preview Form button each time you make a significant change to the form.

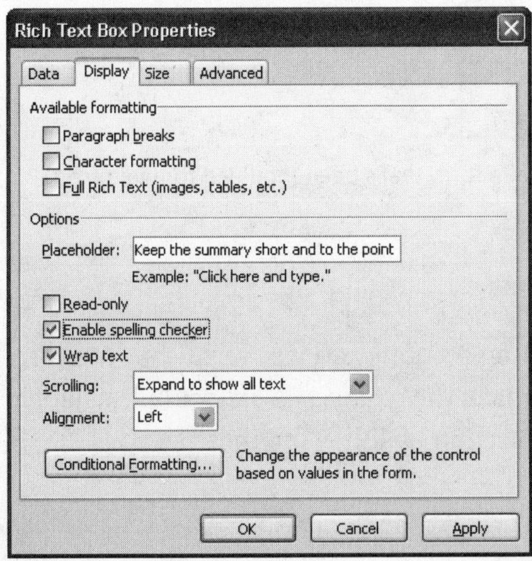

Figure 4-1 You can remove users' rich text box formatting options by changing settings in the Rich Text Box Properties dialog box.

Removing Unneeded Elements and Sections

You can delete individual elements, such as entire plain, bulleted, or numbered lists, that the forms schema doesn't specify as required. To delete a bulleted list inside a layout table, such as Last Period, select the table and press Delete to remove the table and its contents. Press Delete again after removing a table to remove the remaining empty line.

Similarly, you can delete an optional section and its contents by selecting the section and pressing Delete. The Time Report section is a good candidate for deletion if your forms' users are salaried rather than hourly workers. Figure 4-2 shows a preview of the customized form with several elements deleted, all empty lines removed, and the Formatting and Tables toolbars hidden.

Reducing form length

To create more compact forms and save paper when you print them, delete the extra lines between tables and sections in the sample forms you customize. Some lines have a couple of spaces, which you also must delete to remove the lines.

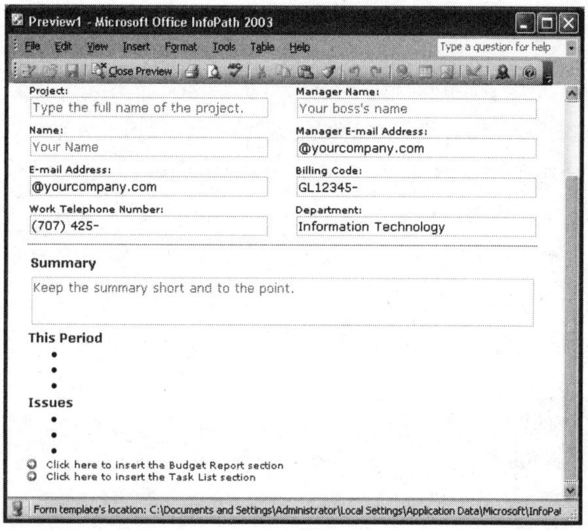

Figure 4-2 This preview shows the working area of a form that's been modified to minimize its length.

Changing a Section's Type

You can change a repeating table to a repeating section—and vice versa—but you lose the fields in the section or table when you make the change. As an example, change the Task List repeating table to a repeating section by following these steps.

▶ **Change the Task List repeating table to a repeating section**

1. **Right-click the Task List's Repeating Table tab to select the table (not the Optional Section), and choose Change To, Repeating Section. The contents of the table will disappear.**
2. **Select the item node in the list, drag it to the empty repeating section, and select Section With Controls to add three text boxes surrounded by a lot of unneeded white space, as shown here:**

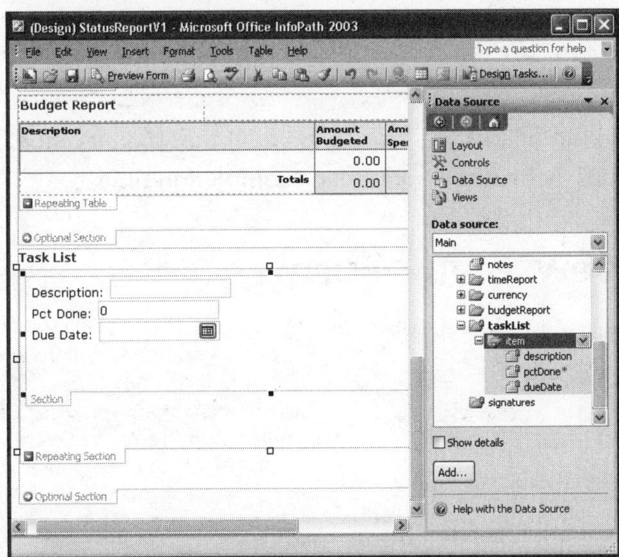

3. **Press Ctrl+Z twice to return the section to a repeating table, and save your changes.**

As a general rule, repeating elements that have only a few short fields and, especially, numeric values–such as the Status Report's three examples–should be added as repeating tables. The Rss2v1 form you create later in this chapter has a repeating section because some of the elements are text boxes that require long, descriptive text.

Testing Your Modified Form for Usability

Now that you've completed the modifications to the Status Report form, it's time to give the design a test drive with the procedure on the next page.

▶ Test the Status Report form

1. **Choose the Fill Out A Form task pane from the task pane menu.**
2. **Click the Custom Status Report link to open Form1 in data entry mode. Notice that saving the modified template adds it to your most recently used (MRU) list in the File menu.**
3. **Complete a sample form, and save it in the same folder as the template, and then close the form and design windows.**
4. **Ask one of your colleagues to fill out the form, and verify that the placeholder prompts and default values make sense and reduce completion time.**

Using the sample files

The completed StatusReportV1.xsn template and a sample XML data document (SR9876-1.xml) are located in your C:\Microsoft Press\Introducing InfoPath 2003\Chapter04\StatusReportV1 folder. Compare your template modifications and data documents with the samples.

Starting with a New, Blank Form

It's a better practice to base a form on an existing XML document than to design a form from scratch. Creating a form template and XML schema from a sample XML document ensures that your form design can produce usable data documents. If you don't have a well-formed .xml file to use and don't want to write one in Notepad, you can design the XML data document's schema in the Data Source task pane. Before you embark on designing the data document and form simultaneously, create the document design on paper and review it with the form's users or your organization's developers to make sure that it contains elements or attributes for all required data values.

Avoiding ad hoc template and document designs

It's a very uncommon practice to create a form from scratch. The information in this section is provided for completeness only. If you plan to use existing XML documents or schemas or intend to write an XML test document on which to base your form design, skip to the section "Creating a Template from an XML Document."

When you start a design with a new, blank form, InfoPath automatically adds to the data source a default root element named *myFields*, which can contain group and field elements. A *group* contains one or more child elements, which can be either groups or fields. Groups bind to required or optional form sections; repeating groups bind to repeating sections or repeating tables. *Fields* bind to HTML controls. Fields represent either elements or attributes; most simple XML documents don't include attributes.

You can use either or a combination of the following two design approaches when starting from an empty form:

- Add and define groups and fields in the Data Source task pane, and then bind sections to the groups and controls to the fields using the drag-and-drop method described earlier in this chapter. When you drag a field to the form, InfoPath adds a friendly name label to the left of the control.
- Add sections and controls from the Controls task pane in from the top to the bottom of the form. Adding a section adds a consecutively numbered group, starting with group1 to the form's data source. Adding a control adds a consecutively numbered field of the controls data type to the data source. This method doesn't add a label for the control.

Avoiding ad-hoc data document structure

The most important aspect of InfoPath form design is the structure and content of the form's XML data document. The goal of form design is to make entering or editing content an easy and foolproof task for users, not to define the document's structure. Although dragging sections and controls from the Controls task pane to the form work area might appear to be the simplest way to create a new form, you must assign meaningful element names to the sections and fields in the Data Source task pane. You'll probably need to alter the sequence of sections and fields in the data document with the Move, Move Up, or Move shortcut menu options. Thus, you'll find that designing the data source first and then adding sections and controls to the form is the more efficient form design process.

This section's example is based on a modified version of the Contacts-WellFormed.xml document from Chapter 3, with two added date attributes. (Contacts-WellFormed.xml is located in your C:\Microsoft Press\Introducing InfoPath 2003\Chapter03\XMLDocs folder.) The root element name is *contacts*, which contains a repeating child group, *contact*, which in turn has *dateAdded* and *dateUpdated* attributes. The *contact* group has two text fields, *firstName* and *lastName*, and a *personal* child group. The *personal* group contains *address*, *city*, *state*, *zipCode*, *phone*, and *eMail* fields.

Defining Groups and Fields in the Data Source Task Pane

To begin creating your XML data source by defining its groups and fields, follow these steps.

▶ **Start a new Contacts form**

1. **With InfoPath open and the Fill Out A Form task pane active, click the Design A Form link.**
2. **In the Design A Form task pane, click the New Blank Form link to activate the Design Tasks task pane.**
3. **Click the Data Source link to activate the Data Source task pane, which contains a single myFields node.**

4. Right click the myFields node, and choose Properties from the shortcut menu to open the Field Or Group Properties dialog box.
5. Change the group name to a more descriptive root element name, **contacts**, as shown here:

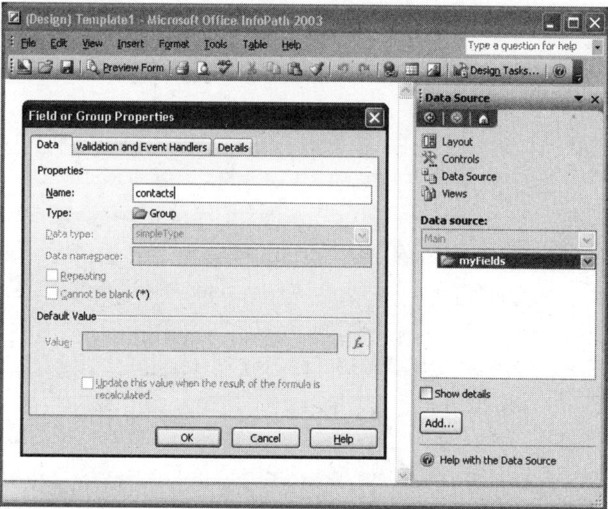

6. Click OK to close the dialog box, and click the task pane's Add button to open the Add Field Or Group dialog box to add the *contact* repeating group.
7. Type **contact** in the Name text box, select Group from the Type drop-down list, and select the Repeating check box, as shown here. Click OK to close the dialog box.

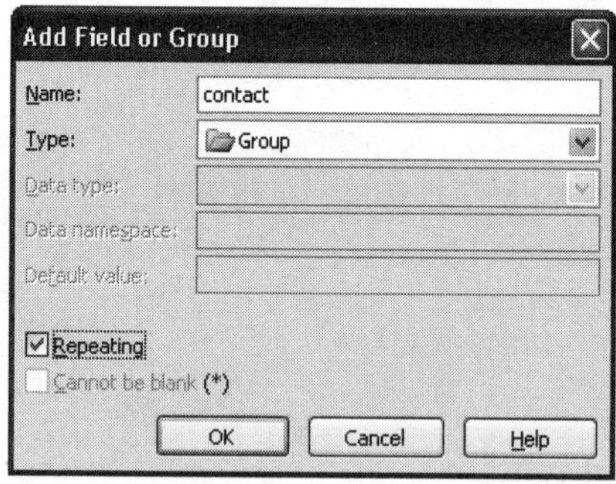

Avoiding element and attribute sequence problems

Be careful to add attributes and elements in the exact sequence you want them to appear in the XML data document. InfoPath lets you move an element to another group or an attribute to another element or group, but you can't move elements or attributes within a group.

▶ Add attribute fields to the group

1. With the contact repeating group node selected, click Add to add the first of the two date attributes to the contact group.
2. In the Add Field Or Group dialog box, type **dateAdded** as the attribute name, select Field (Attribute) from the Type drop-down list, and select Date (Date) from the Data Type drop-down list, as shown here, and click OK.

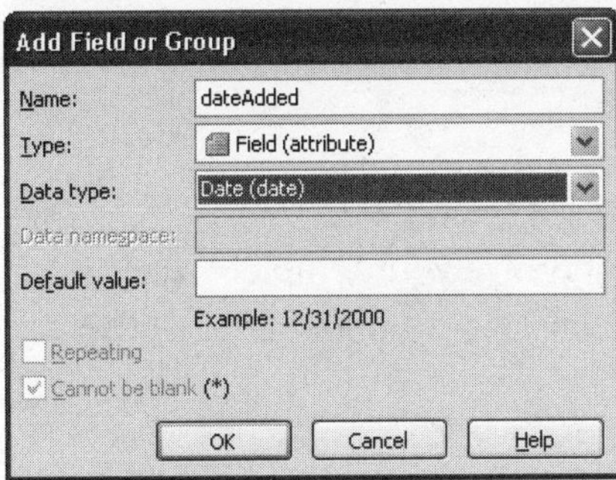

A red asterisk (*) following the name in the Data Source list indicates elements or attributes that have required values. Elements can have blank date or numeric field values, but attributes can't.

3. Click Add, and repeat step 2, but type **dateUpdated** as the name.

▶ Add element fields and a subgroup to the contact group

1. With the contact node selected, click Add to add the group's *firstName* element.
2. In the Add Field Or Group dialog box, type **firstName** as the element name, accept the default Field (Element) as the Type and Text (String) data type, and select the Cannot Be Blank check box, as shown here:

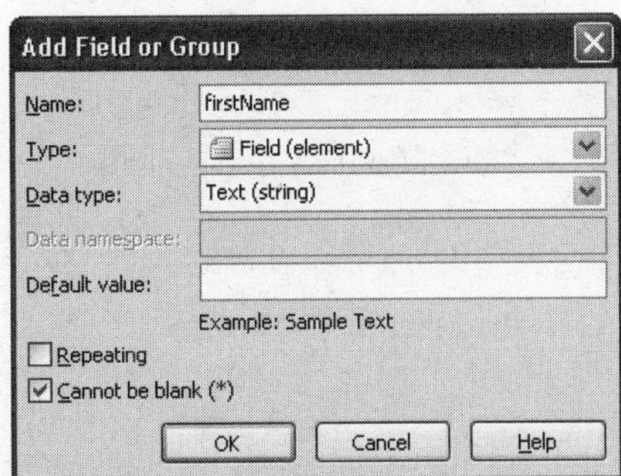

3. Click OK, repeat step 2 for the *lastName* element, and click OK to add the element. Notice that element node icons have a lighter gray background than attribute icons.

4. **With the contact node still selected, click Add to add the *personal* element as a nonrepeating group, as shown here:**

5. **Press Ctrl+S, click Save in the dialog box, and save your template as ContactsCh4.xsn or the like in a new ContactsCh4 subfolder of your My Documents\Infopath folder.**

If you select the Show Details check box in the Data Source task pane, your Data Source list appears as shown in Figure 4-3. The data type names listed under the node names are XML schema datatypes, such as *string* for text fields. When you add default values, the value appears after the data type name.

Figure 4-3 This Data Source list for the contacts form has initial groups, attributes, and elements added.

Using Drag-and-Drop to Add Sections and Controls

The drag-and-drop method of adding sections and controls from the data source is the easier of the two approaches described in the section "Starting with a New, Blank Form," earlier in this chapter. The contacts root element binds to the form automatically, so the first child element of the root and its element and attributes contribute sections and controls to the form.

To add the sections and controls you've specified so far, drag the contact node onto the form. Choose Repeating Section With Controls from the shortcut menu that opens when you release the left mouse button. InfoPath automatically adds the controls and labels and an optional section for the empty personal group to the repeating section. Your form appears as shown in Figure 4-4.

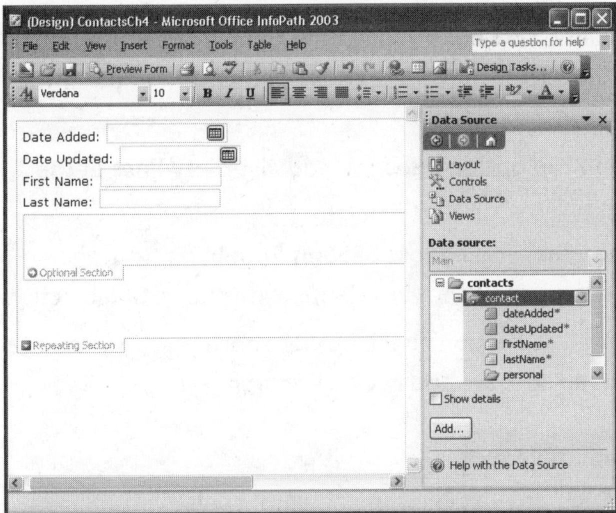

Figure 4-4 Dragging the contact node to the form generates a repeating section with controls for attributes and elements and an empty optional section for the personal group.

The default control arrangement wastes space on the form by stacking controls vertically and adding empty lines to the sections. InfoPath adds nested sections as optional sections; for this example, the *personal* element isn't optional. To rearrange the controls, conserve form area, and change the optional section to a required section, do the following.

▶ Customize the default sections and controls

1. **Hold down the Shift key, select the four text boxes, and then right-click the Last Name text box and select Properties from the shortcut menu to open the Properties (Multiple Selection) dialog box. Click the Align button to align the text box contents with the label text, and click OK to close the dialog box.**
2. **Position the insertion point to the right of the Date Added date picker, press Delete, and add 10 spaces to separate the Date Added and Date Updated controls. Move the insertion point to the right of the Date Updated date picker and press Enter to add an empty line.**
3. **Position the insertion point after the First Name text box, press Delete, and add 4 spaces.**

4. Select the First Name text box, and drag the right-middle sizing handle to the right to increase the available text width. (As you increase the text box's width, the Last Name label and text box move to the right.)
5. Repeat step 4 for the Last Name text box, making its width approximately equal to the First Name text box. (If you increase the width beyond the right margin, the text box moves to the next line.)
6. Click to the right of the Last Name text box to select the repeating section, and drag the right margin of the form to within a few pixels of the right edge of the text box.
7. Delete all but one empty line in the optional section and all empty lines in the repeating section.
8. Right-click the Optional Section tab, and choose Section Properties from the shortcut menu to open the dialog box of the same name with the Data tab active.
9. Clear the Allow Users To Delete This Section check box, as shown here, to change the optional section to a required section, and click OK to apply your change:

10. Press Ctrl+S to save your changes.
11. Click Preview Form. The form at this point, shown in Figure 4-5, won't win any graphic design awards, but it is operable. You will notice the red asterisks in the Date Added, Date Updated, First Name, and Last Name text boxes indicating that entries are required for these fields.
12. Click Close Preview.

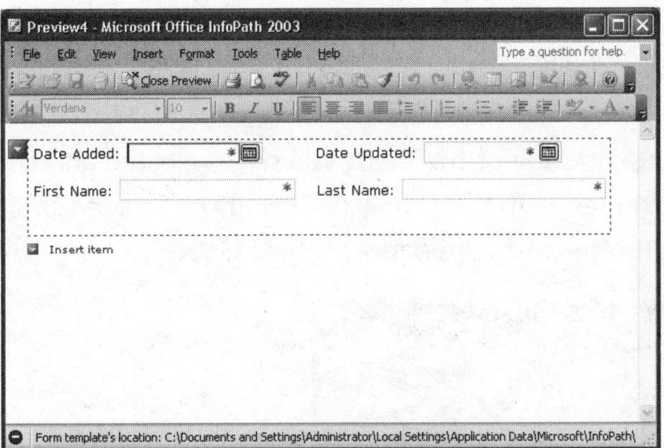

Figure 4-5 The contacts form has attribute and element controls rearranged and the optional personal section changed to a required section.

Adding Elements and Controls Simultaneously

The alternative to dragging and dropping a section with its controls is adding a text box or other control to the main form or a section. In this example, you'll add text box controls and elements to the personal section. The process is cumbersome, so here you'll add only fields for the *address* and *city* elements.

To add the two controls and elements and then perform the required fix-up, follow these steps.

▶ Add *address* and *city* elements to the form

1. **Press Ctrl+F1 to reopen the Data Source task pane, if it isn't open.**
2. **Click the Controls link to make the Controls task pane active.**
3. **With the Automatically Create Data Source check box selected, drag the Text Box control to the section to add a text box bound to the new field1 field.**
4. **Press Enter, and repeat step 3 to add a second text box bound to the field2 field.**
5. **Open the Data Source task pane, and right-click the field1 node and select Properties from the shortcut menu to open its Field Or Group Properties dialog box.**
6. **Replace field1 in the Field Name box with address, select the Cannot Be Blank check box, and click OK to apply your changes.**
7. **Repeat steps 6 and 7 for field2, renaming it city.**

8. **Add Address: and City: labels to the left of the two text boxes. Remove the blank line between the text boxes, and align the labels with the text boxes in the contact section.**
9. **Select both text boxes, right-click one of the items you have selected and choose properties from the shortcut menu. In the Properties (Multiple Selection) dialog box that appears, click Align. Your form appears as shown here:**

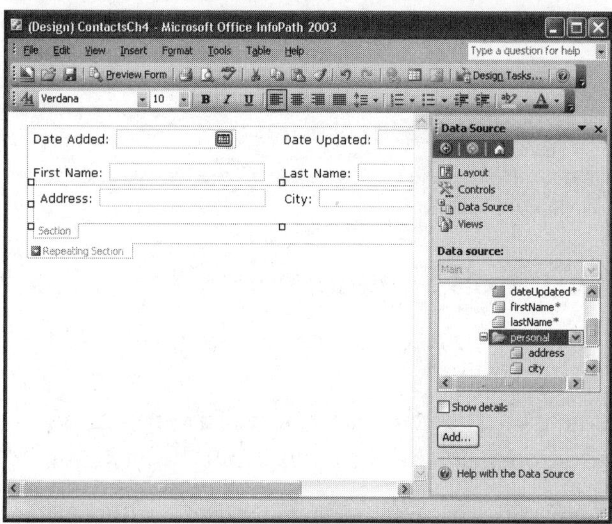

Completing and Testing the ContactsCh4 Template

You still have four elements to add to the template: *state*, *zipCode*, *phone*, and *eMail*. It's faster to add these elements by adding the fields to the Data Source list, as you did in the section "Defining Groups and Fields in the Data Source Task Pane," earlier in this chapter. Make *state* and *zipCode* required (select the Cannot Be Blank check box), and specify the *phone* and *eMail* fields as optional. Drag the four fields to the personal section, align the text boxes and labels, adjust the label and text box sizes and locations to conform approximately to those shown in Figure 4-6, and save your changes.

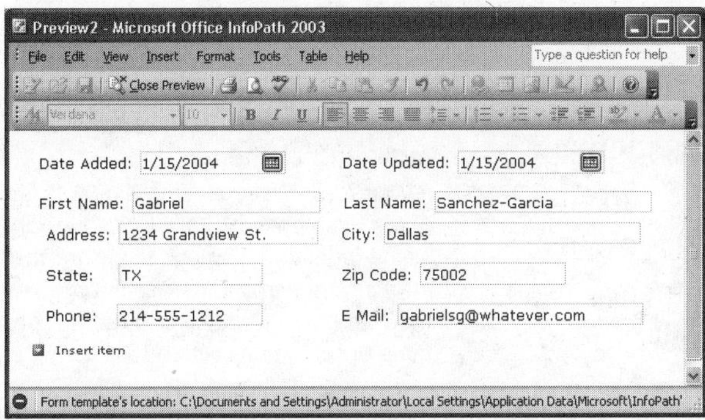

Figure 4-6 Preview mode displays the final version of the Contacts form.

> **Removing or changing "my" namespace**
>
> InfoPath's default possessive namespace won't be acceptable to most XML developers or IT management. You'll undoubtedly need to substitute a default namespace, which eliminates the prefixes, or an alternative namespace declaration and prefix. The section "Getting Rid of the *my:* Namespace," later in this chapter, shows you how to make either of these changes.

Your work isn't complete until you verify the XML data document produced by the form. Make the Fill Out A Form task pane active, click the link for the name you gave the form (ContactsCh4 for this example), and fill in a couple of records. Save the data document, and then open it in Notepad. Figure 4-7 shows the sample data document–less the XML declaration and InfoPath processing instructions (PIs)–after reformatting it for readability. The ubiquitous *xmlns:my* namespace declaration appears at the top of Figure 4-7, and *my:* prefixes each element and attribute name.

ContactsCh4.xml - Notepad

```
<my:contacts
xmlns:my="http://schemas.microsoft.com/office/infopath/2003/myXSD/2003-11-01T2
1:43:32" xml:lang="en-us">
        <my:contact my:dateAdded="2004-01-15" my:dateUpdated="2004-01-15">
                <my:firstName>Gabriel</my:firstName>
                <my:lastName>Sanchez-Garcia</my:lastName>
                <my:personal>
                        <my:address>1234 Grandview St.</my:address>
                        <my:city>Dallas</my:city>
                        <my:state>TX</my:state>
                        <my:zipCode>75002</my:zipCode>
                        <my:phone>214-555-1212</my:phone>
                        <my:eMail>gabrielsg@whatever.com</my:eMail>
                </my:personal>
        </my:contact>
        <my:contact my:dateAdded="2004-01-15" my:dateUpdated="2004-01-15">
                <my:firstName>Robert</my:firstName>
                <my:lastName>Johnson</my:lastName>
                <my:personal>
                        <my:address>550 Petroleum Blvd.</my:address>
                        <my:city>Houston</my:city>
                        <my:state>TX</my:state>
                        <my:zipCode>72001</my:zipCode>
                        <my:phone>713-555-1212</my:phone>
                        <my:eMail>rjohnson@somewhere.com</my:eMail>
                </my:personal>
        </my:contact>
</my:contacts>
```

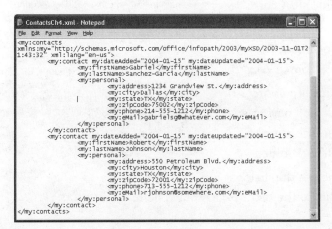

Figure 4-7 This sample XML data document was produced by the contacts template with the default InfoPath namespace declaration and element/attribute prefixes.

Creating a Template from an XML Document

If you found the preceding exercise a bit too complex, you'll appreciate InfoPath's automatic form generation capability. The Data Source Wizard delivers an almost-completed form in a minute or less, if the XML data document you specify to create the data source is well-formed, not overly complex, and representative of the final production version.

Making sure InfoPath recognizes repeating elements

If your form has repeating elements, use a data document with at least two instances of the repeating element to ensure that InfoPath's schema inference engine interprets the element correctly and binds a repeating table or repeating section to the element. You can change a nonrepeating group to a repeating group by using the Field Or Group Properties dialog box's Data tab, but it's better to get the section or table type right initially.

The example in this section is based on a simplified version of a publicly available Really Simple Syndication version 2.0 (RSS 2.0) document at *www.oakleaf.ws/rss.xml*. Your organization can use the form you create in this section to establish its own RSS 2.0 feed–an XML document usually named rss.xml–to notify employees and customers of new content available from a Web site. The orange XML buttons you see on Web pages open rss.xml or a similarly named file, which usually is in RSS 2.0 format.

To create the initial version of the RSS 2.0 form, Rss2v1.xsn, follow these steps.

Getting a Grip on RSS 2.0?

RSS 2.0 is a de facto industry standard for syndicating weblog content. Several earlier RSS versions—including 0.91, 0.92, and 0.93—remain in limited use. Most weblogging tools generate RSS 2.0 XML files automatically as the author adds content. Desktop applications or Microsoft Outlook add-ins called *aggregators* or *readers* simplify checking for new content and viewing the designated pages. RSS 2.0 is equally useful for advertising new Web site content. You can learn more about RSS 2.0 and its specification at *blogs.law.harvard.edu/tech/rss*. Visit *www.oakleaf.ws/infopath/* for additional details about this chapter's sample RSS 2.0 file and its schema.

▶ **Create a form from an existing XML document**

1. **Close and reopen InfoPath, and click the Design A Form link in the Fill Out A Form dialog box.**

2. **Click the New From XML Document Or Schema link to start the Data Source Wizard.**
3. **In the first wizard screen, click Browse to display the Open dialog box, and navigate to your C:\Microsoft Press\Introducing InfoPath 2003\Chapter04\Rss2v1 folder.**
4. **Double-click Rss2v1.xml to close the dialog box and add the path and file to the text box, as shown here:**

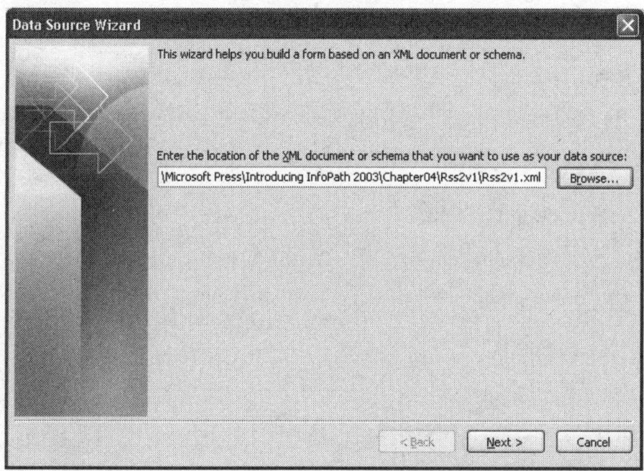

5. Click Next, accept the No option (the default) in the second wizard screen, and click Finish, which opens a message box asking whether you'd like to use data from the sample document to provide default values for the form, as shown here:

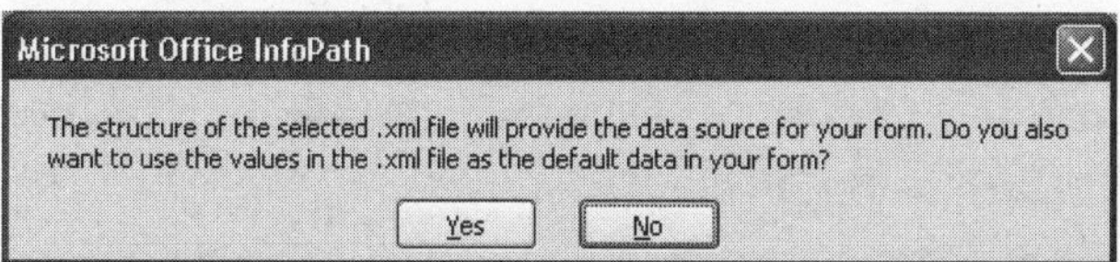

6. For this example, click Yes to close the message box and add the document's single attribute and all elements to the Data Source list.
7. Drag the channel node to the form, and select Sections With Controls from the shortcut menu that opens when you release the left mouse button to add all controls except the text box for the *version* attribute to the form, as shown here:

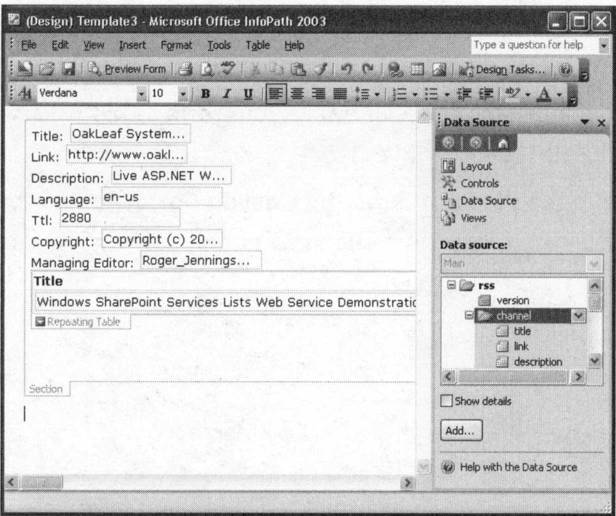

Adding a Missing Attribute and Fixing the Initial Form Layout

A control for the *version* attribute isn't important, because the default value (2.0) applies to all instances of RSS 2.0 data documents you create. It's a good practice, however, to provide controls for all attributes and elements in the initial design. InfoPath adds repeating tables for repeating sections–in this example, *item*. RSS 2.0 items contain too much text to display in a repeating table of reasonable length, so you should change the repeating table to a repeating section to accommodate wide single-line and multiline text boxes.

Adding extra fields to the data source
Fields you add to the data source that aren't in the XML document on which you base the form gain the inevitable *my:* namespace prefix. The RSS 2.0 specification doesn't permit namespace prefixes, although local namespace declarations are allowed to indicate added fields that aren't covered by the specification. If the sample XML document doesn't contain all the elements you need, it's easier to add all extra elements to the data source document than to fix the namespace problem later.

To add the missing attribute, change the repeating table to a repeating section, and remove most empty lines from the design, follow these steps.

▶ Modify the default section with controls

1. **Add the missing *version* attribute's text box to the form by dragging the version node to the left of the Title label and pressing Enter.**
2. **Right-click the Repeating Table tab, and choose Change To, Repeating Section from the shortcut menu. All *item* fields disappear from the repeating section.**
3. **Drag the item node to the repeating section, and choose Controls from the menu that appears when you release the mouse button. (You already have a section, so don't choose Section With Controls.)**
4. **Use the mouse pointer to select the three empty lines below the repeating section, and press Delete.**
5. **Do the same for the empty lines below the Link text box of the repeating section.**
6. **Press Ctrl+S, click Save in the message box, and save your form as Rss2v1.xsn in a new \My Documents\InfoPath\Rss2v1 folder.**
7. **Choose File, Properties to open the Form Properties dialog box, type RSS 2.0 Version 1 in the Form, and click OK to close the dialog box.**

Figure 4-8 shows the result of the changes you made in the preceding steps.

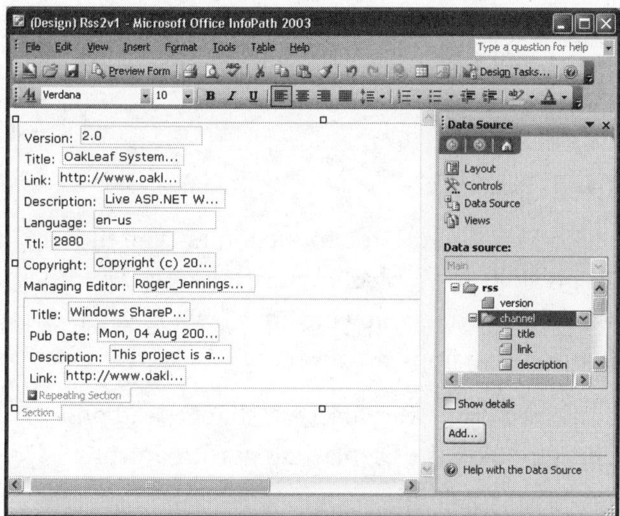

Figure 4-8 This is the Rss2v1.xsn template after adding a missing attribute, changing a repeating table to a repeating section, and removing empty lines.

Performing a Quick Check of the Template's Data Document

Before you expend time and energy optimizing the form design for data entry, it's a good policy to inspect the XML data document produced by the form. Adding default values when you generate the design simplifies the test process; you can change or delete the default values when you tweak the form's design.

To create a test data document to compare against the document you specified as the data source, using Rss2v1.xml as an example, follow these steps.

▶ Create a test document from the template

1. **Open the Fill Out A Form task pane, and click the RSS 2.0 Version 1 link to open an instance of Form1 with default values provided for all fields.**

2. **Scroll to the end of the items, click the Insert Item button or click an empty region of the repeating section to select the entire section, and press Ctrl+Enter to add a duplicate item to the document.**
3. **Press Ctrl+S and save the document as RssTest1.xml or the like in the template's folder.**
4. **Open the data document in Notepad, and compare its contents with the original version. Disregard the InfoPath PIs and formatting (white space) differences, which have no effect on most readers/aggregators.**

If you followed the steps in the two preceding procedures carefully, you'll find no significant differences between Rss2v1.xml and RssTest1.xml other than the group and fields of *item* element you added.

Optimizing the Form for Data Entry

If you're interested in using the RSS 2.0 form to create production rss.xml files or you want to show off your new design skills to your colleagues, take a few minutes to modify the form's layout for easier data entry. Following are a few redesign suggestions that take less than 10 minutes to implement:

- Make fields whose default values you don't want users to change read-only fields. Select the Read-Only check box on the Display tab of the control's Properties dialog box.
- Move seldom-changed or read-only fields above the data entry fields, and separate them from the primary fields with a horizontal line. Select the label and text box, and then cut and paste the combination where you want it. Choose Insert, Horizontal Line to add a line below the insertion point.
- Adjust the width of text boxes to suit their expected content.
- Use the Text Box Properties dialog box's Display tab to enable multiline text boxes for text box controls that contain lengthy text, such as descriptions. Select the Wrap Text check box for these controls, and choose the appropriate Scrolling action: Expand To Show All Text or Show Scrollbar When Necessary.
- Align all text boxes with their labels. To increase the space between text boxes on successive lines, select all text boxes, right-click a text box, and select Properties to open the Properties (Multiple Selection) dialog box., Click the Align and Apply buttons, replace the default 1 px Top Margin value with **3** px, and click OK to close the dialog box.
- Add horizontal lines between sections to make the transition between sections evident to users. Chapters 5 and 7 show you how to add layout tables with borders and background colors that make individual sections evident.

Figure 4-9 shows a preview of the final version of the template with the preceding layout enhancements. The entire channel section is read-only for this example, because the example is for an entire Web site.

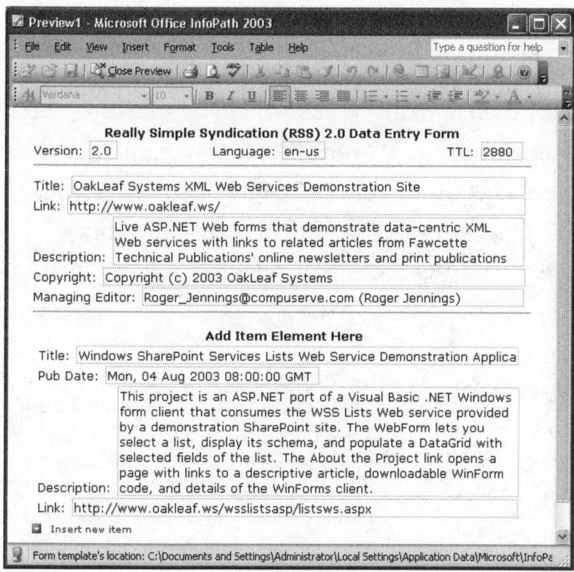

Figure 4-9 A few quick formatting fixes improve the Rss2v1.xsn template's usability.

> **Using the sample files**
> You'll find the final version of Rss2v1.xsn in your C:\Microsoft Press\Introducing InfoPath 2003\Chapter04\Rss2v1 folder, along with the Rss2v1.xml source file and the RssTest1.xml comparison document.

Adapting the RSS 2.0 Form for Production Use

The only modifications you need to make to the Rss2v1.xsn schema to create rss.xml files for your organization's internal or external Web site is to replace the default values of *channel* elements with the appropriate text and remove the default values from *item* elements. Chapter 12 will show you how to make the Rss2v1.xsn template available to users from a server share or an intranet Web site.

You can merge new *item* elements in other forms using the technique you learned in the section "Merging Forms," in Chapter 2. RSS files require a last-in, first-out (LIFO) format with the most recent addition at the top of the list. For RSS files, open the form with the new content, and merge the existing production file.

Basing a Template on an XML Schema

If you have an existing schema that conforms to the W3C XML Schema recommendation, InfoPath can generate a form design from it in most cases. The same recommendation for document-based forms applies to schema-based forms: start simple. As an example, you can create a data source from a very complex schema, such as the schema for business documents that conform to Universal

Business Language (UBL) requirements. But you probably won't be able to create a usable form automatically from a schema of this complexity.

One of the disadvantages of using an XML schema to create the data source is that sections are *locked* unless explicitly declared *open* (for modification) by an added *xsd:any* element. You can't add new elements or attributes to a locked data source. InfoPath's sample forms' schemas are open, but most schemas aren't, for good reason: altering an existing schema when creating an InfoPath form probably would make the XML data document invalid in a workflow process.

Creating and Refining a Schema for a Data Document

If you don't have a schema on which to base a form, it's a more straightforward process to create a form from an XML data document than to design your own schema. But you might encounter a situation in which the form design must handle different versions of a document with optional sections to support the differences. One approach to this problem is to fabricate a sample source document that contains elements and attributes for all document versions. In this case, you must change sections that don't appear in all documents to optional sections.

Exploring UBL schemas and data documents

Your C:\Microsoft Press\Introducing InfoPath 2003\Chapter04\UBL-Op70 folder contains a schema for a complete UBL Invoice document—UBL_Library_0p70_Invoice.xsd—that imports the other three schemas in the folder. InfoPath can create a data source from the schema, and you can drag the top-level *invoice* element to the form to add sections and cotrols to the form automatically.

The folder also contains a sample instance (XML data document) of an office supply invoice—OfficeSupplyInvoiceInstance.xml—on which you can base a form design, but the form contains a myriad of nested optional sctions, which make it extremely difficult to complete. (The invoice instance's *xsi:schemaLocation* value has been modified to prevent use of its schema and allow InfoPath to infer the schema.)

Another approach is to let InfoPath merge multiple XML documents when you create the form's data source in the Data Source Wizard. If you start with the simplest document, InfoPath designates sections added by other document versions as optional sections.

An alternative to creating the schema with InfoPath is to use the Microsoft XSD (XML Schema Definition) Inference 1.0 tool to generate an initial schema from one XML data document instance and then refine the schema by adding elements and attributes from other related document instances. This tool generates basic XML schemas that typify those in common use for simple business documents.

> **Avoiding multiple schemas**
> The Microsoft XSD Inference 1.0 tool creates an individual schema for each namespace declared in the source .xml file. You must import the additional schema(s) to the primary schema in this case. The UBL_Library_0p70_Invoice.xsd schema mentioned in the preceding section uses schema import operations. Importing schemas is beyond the scope of this chapter.

This section's examples use an abbreviated version of Rss2v1.xml and a second document–Rss2v2.xml–for refining the schema. Rss2v2.xml doesn't include the optional *language*, *ttl*, and, *copyright* elements, but it does have an added *docs* element, an *image* element with subelements to add an image file that displays the site's logo, and a *guid* element with an *IsPermaLink* attribute.

To infer a schema for Rss2v1.xml and refine it with Rss2v2.xml and then save the resulting schema file, follow these steps.

> **Using the sample files**
> Your C:\Microsoft Press\Introducing InfoPath 2003\Chapter04\Rss2v2 folder contains the two sample data documents, schemas created from each of the two documents, and other files you create in the procedures in later sections in this chapter.

▶ Use the Microsoft XSD Inference 1.0 tool to generate a schema

1. **Start Internet Explorer, and open the Microsoft XSD Inference 1.0 tool at *apps.gotdotnet.com/xmltools/xsdinference/*.**
2. **Click Browse to open the Choose File dialog box, and navigate to your C:\Microsoft Press\Introducing InfoPath 2003\Chapter04\Rss2v2 folder.**
3. **Double-click Rss2v1.xml to select the file, and click Infer Schema to generate the initial schema, as shown here:**

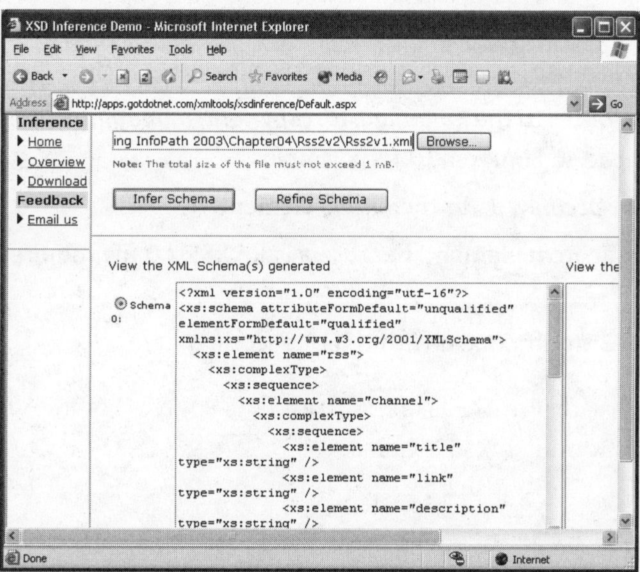

4. **Click Browse, double-click Rss2v2.xml in the Choose File dialog box, and click Refine Schema to add the missing elements and attribute to the schema.**
5. **Click in the schema text box, press Ctrl+A to select all its contents, and press Ctrl+C.**
6. **Start Notepad, and press Ctrl+V to paste the contents to the file.**
7. **Replace *utf-16* with UTF-8 as the encoding method, and save the file as Rss2v1+2.xsd with UTF-8 encoding in a new \My Documents\InfoPath\Rss2v2 folder. InfoPath requires UTF-8 encoding for all XML document types.**

See Also You can learn more about the Microsoft XSD Inference 1.0 tool by clicking the Overview link on the tool's Web page, scrolling to the bottom of the page, and following the links to articles about XSD schemas and use of the tool.

Modifying an Inferred Schema for InfoPath

You need to make minor modifications to the inferred schema to create a usable form from the schema. The XSD Inference 1.0 tool assumes that a single instance of each element is required The tool also detects multiple occurrences of elements, such as *item*, and adds a *maxOccurs="unbounded"* attribute for these elements. Many RSS 2.0 elements aren't mandatory, and it's a good practice to add a *minOccurs="0"* attribute to these elements. A *minOccurs="0"* attribute accommodates document versions that don't contain the element, which is one of the purposes of this exercise.

To modify the Rss2v1+2.xsd schema to accommodate both document versions, follow these steps.

▶ **Edit the inferred schema**

1. **Open Rss2v1+2.xsd in Notepad.**
2. **Add *minOccurs="0"* attributes to the *language*, *ttl*, *copyright*, *managingEditor*, and *docs* elements. Look ahead to Figure 4-10 for examples.**
3. **Add *minOccurs="0" maxOccurs="1"* to the *image* element.**
4. **Add *minOccurs="1"* to the *item* element, because a valid RSS 2.0 file requires at east one item.**
5. **Save the file as Rss2v1+2Modified.xsd with UTF-8 encoding.**

At this point, the schema is ready for use as an InfoPath data source. Figure 4-10 shows most of the Rss2v1+2Modified.xsd schema.

Rss2v1+2Modified.xsd - Notepad

File Edit Format View Help

```
<?xml version="1.0" encoding="UTF-8"?>
<xs:schema attributeFormDefault="unqualified" elementFormDefault="qualified"
xmlns:xs="http://www.w3.org/2001/XMLSchema">
  <xs:element name="rss">
    <xs:complexType>
      <xs:sequence>
        <xs:element name="channel">
          <xs:complexType>
            <xs:sequence>
              <xs:element name="title" type="xs:string" />
              <xs:element name="link" type="xs:string" />
              <xs:element name="description" type="xs:string" />
              <xs:element name="language" type="xs:string" minOccurs="0"/>
              <xs:element name="ttl" type="xs:unsignedShort" minOccurs="0"/>
              <xs:element name="copyright" type="xs:string" minOccurs="0"/>
              <xs:element name="managingEditor" type="xs:string"
minOccurs="0"/>
              <xs:element name="docs" type="xs:string" minOccurs="0"/>
              <xs:element name="image" minOccurs="0" maxOccurs="1">
                <xs:complexType>
                  <xs:sequence>
                    <xs:element name="url" type="xs:string" />
                    <xs:element name="title" type="xs:string" />
                    <xs:element name="link" type="xs:string" />
                    <xs:element name="width" type="xs:unsignedByte" />
                    <xs:element name="height" type="xs:unsignedByte" />
                  </xs:sequence>
                </xs:complexType>
              </xs:element>
              <xs:element minOccurs="1" maxOccurs="unbounded" name="item">
                <xs:complexType>
                  <xs:sequence>
                    <xs:element name="title" type="xs:string" />
                    <xs:element name="pubDate" type="xs:string" />
                    <xs:element name="description" type="xs:string" />
                    <xs:element name="link" type="xs:string" />
                    <xs:element name="guid" minOccurs="0">
                      <xs:complexType>
                        <xs:simpleContent>
                          <xs:extension base="xs:string">
```

Figure 4-10 These modifications to the Rss2v1+2.xsd schema accommodate multiple document versions with an optional section.

Deciding on data types

It's a common practice to assign data types other than the default *xs:string* for business documents and to add *xs:minInclusive* and *xs:maxInclusive* attributes to limit the range of numeric values. Specifying datatypes other than *xs:dateTime*, *xs:date*, and *xs:boolean* isn't as critical for InfoPath schemas, because you can use data validation rules to test for appropriate numeric values in text boxes. If you control the schema for a form, however, it's a good practice to assign appropriate datatypes to all non-string elements.

One of the advantages of using the XSD Inference 1.0 tool is that it infers XML Schema datatypes from values in the XML source document. For example, the tool detects that the version element's value is 2.0, so it's assigned the *xs:decimal* data type. Numeric data types without decimal values receive the smallest numeric datatype that will accommodate the element's value, such as *xs:unsignedByte* for values less than 255 and *xs:unsignedShort* (highlighted in Figure 4-10) for values between 256 and 65,535. Elements and attributes with a *"true"* or *"false"* value become *xs:boolean*. If the *pubDate* value had used XML Schema's ISO 8601 date and time formatting standard (*CCYY-MM-DDThh:mm:ss±zz:00*), its data type would be *xs:dateTime*. Scroll through Rss2V1+2Modified.xsd to inspect all non-string data types.

Creating a Form from the Modified Schema

The process of creating a form from an XML schema is almost identical to that for creating a form from an XML data document, as described in the section "Creating a Template from an XML Document," earlier in this chapter. You substitute the schema's .xsd file for an .xml file in the second page of the Data Source Setup Wizard.

When you create the template from the Rss2V1+2Modified.xsd schema, save it as **Rss2v2.xsn** in the folder containing the schemas. The primary difference you see in the Data Source task pane's list is a small lock symbol overlaid on field and group icons, which indicates the node is locked for most modifications.

The change you made to the *image* element in the preceding section lets you change the default image section to an optional section by opening the Section Properties dialog box and selecting the Allow Users To Delete This Section check box. Figure 4-11 shows the initial form design generated from the Rss2v1+2Modified.xsd schema. Create a test data document from the new template, save it as **Rss2v1+2Modified.xml**, and check its contents by opening it in Notepad.

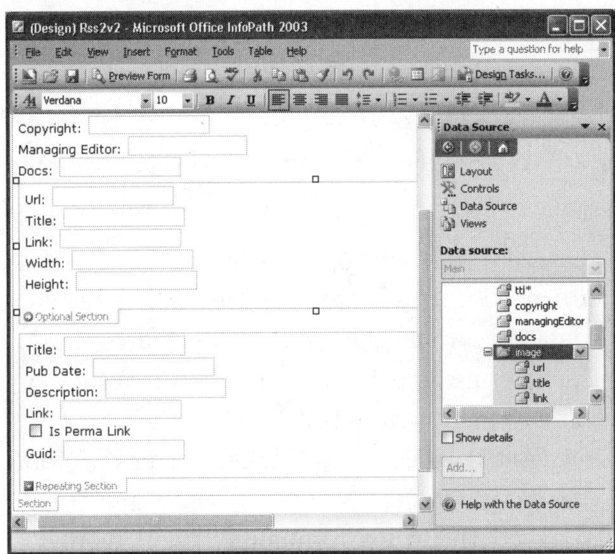

Figure 4-11 This initial form design is based on the Rss2v1+2Modified.xsd schema.

Copying a Form Design and Adding New Elements

Reworking the new form layout to correspond with that in the section "Optimizing the Form for Data Entry," earlier in this chapter, takes only a few minutes, but laying out and formatting a more complex form can take several hours. You can take advantage of your prior design by using copy-and-paste methods to copy the design to your new form. When you paste the sections and fields to the new form, you must rebind them to the appropriate node in the Data Source list.

▶ **Replace the template's sections and controls**

1. **With Rss2v2.xsn open, click in the work area, press Ctrl+A to select the entire design, and then press Delete to delete all sections and controls.**

2. Open another InfoPath instance, and open the C:\Microsoft Press\Introducing InfoPath 2003\Chapter04\Rss2v1\Rss2v1.xsn file in design mode.
3. Click in Rss2v1.xsn's work area, press Ctrl+A, and press Ctrl+C to copy the sections and their controls to the Clipboard.
4. Switch back to the Rss2v2.xsn instance, click in its work area, and press Ctrl+V to paste the copied elements, as shown here. Red exclamation marks indicate sections and controls that aren't bound to Data Source nodes.

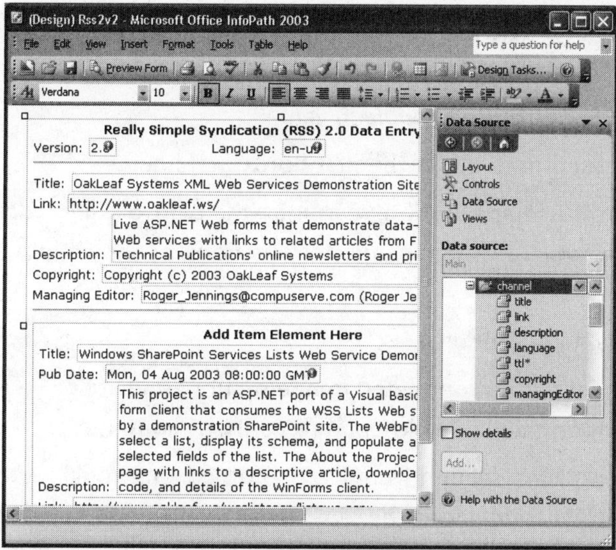

5. Close the Rss2v1.xsn instance.
6. Scroll to the Section tab at the bottom of the form, right-click the tab, and choose Change Binding from the shortcut menu to open the Section Binding dialog box, expand the nodes, and select the channel section node, as shown here:

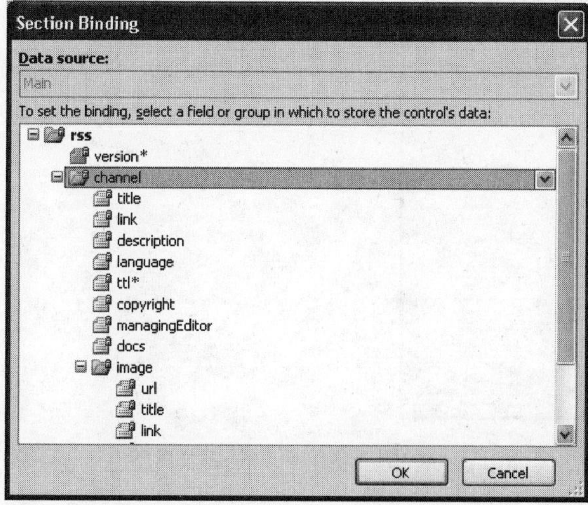

7. Click OK to close the dialog box and change the binding.
8. Repeat steps 6 and 7 for each channel field, the item section, and its fields. (Skip the image section node, which you add later.) Default text box values disappear when you change bindings to a node without a default value specified.

▶ Add the missing controls and optional section

1. Drag the docs node to a position under the Managing Editor text box. (Look ahead to Figure 4-12 for new control locations.)
2. Drag the guid node below the item section's Link text box.
3. Drag the IsPermaLink attribute node to the right of the Guid text box. InfoPath adds a check box to set IsPermaLink's *xs:boolean* value.
4. Drag the optional image section to under the first horizontal line.
5. Remove empty lines from the image section, rearrange the controls, and add another horizontal line between the image and item sections, as shown in Figure 4-12.
6. Save your template as **Rss2v2Copied.xsn**.
7. Create a test data document with a completed image section, save it as **Rss2v2Copied.xml**, and open the file in Notepad to verify its contents.
8. Attempt to remove the only item section from Rss2v2Copied.xml. You'll receive the error message *The item cannot be removed*. This message indicates that InfoPath adheres to the schema's requirement of at least one item element in a form.

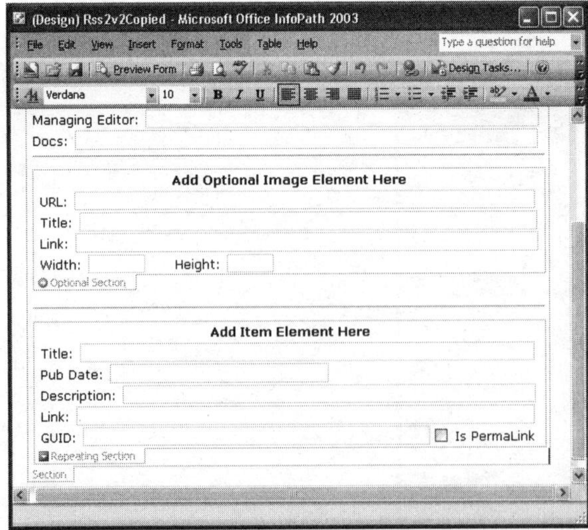

Figure 4-12 This final version of the modified Rss2v2.xsn form has design tweaks to add optional sections and controls.

Using Existing XML Data Documents with a New Template

When you alter the structure of the data source for a form, InfoPath automatically updates data documents you open with the modified template. If you change the template's name, location, or both, you must manually edit existing data documents' PIs to point to the renamed or relocated template.

The RssTest1.xml data document you created in the section "Performing a Quick Check of the Template's Data Document," earlier in this chapter, is a good candidate for verifying that the final Rss2v2Copied.xsn schema works with earlier data documents. RssTest1.xml's PIs point to the Rss2v1.xsn template in your My Documents\InfoPath\Rss2v1 folder.

To make a copy of RssTest1.xml that opens in Rss2v2Copied.xsn, follow these steps.

▶ Change RssTest1

1. **Copy RssTest1.xml from your My Documents\InfoPath\Rss2v1 folder to your My Documents\InfoPath\Rss2v2 folder, and rename the copy RssTest1Copied.xml.**
2. **Open RssTest1Copied.xml in Notepad, and change the value of the URL-encoded href attribute from href="file:///C:\Path\Rss2v1\Rss2v1.xsn" to href="file:///C:\Path\Rss2v2\Rss2v2Copied.xsn".**
3. **Save the file with UTF-8 encoding.**
4. **Double-click Rss2v2Copied.xml to open it in Rss2v2Copied.xsn. The optional image section is missing from the data document, as indicated by the two closely spaced horizontal lines between the channel and item sections. The expected menu button for the image section doesn't appear when you position the mouse pointer in that region.**
5. **Right-click in the active form area to open a shortcut menu with Insert Item and Insert Image choices, as shown on the next page.**

Encoding URLs

Internet URLs don't permit spaces and certain punctuation marks. URL-encoding replaces restricted characters with a percent sign (%) followed by the hexadecimal code for the ASCII character. As an example, *%20* is the code for a space. You won't need to change the partial *Path* prefix in the preceding example if you stored the files in the recommended subfolders of My Documents\InfoPath.

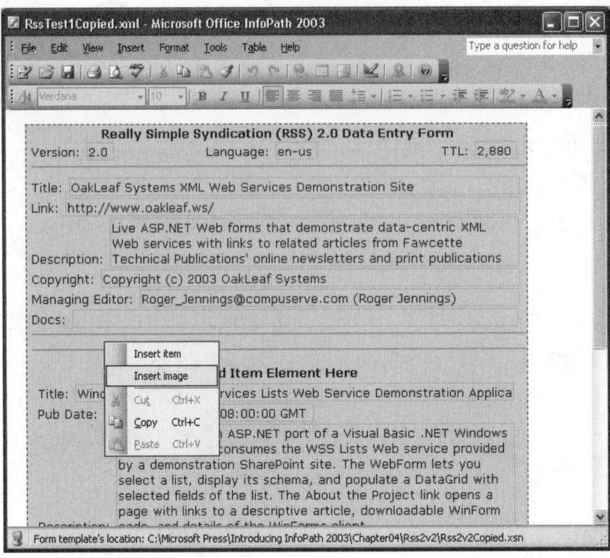

6. If you want to add an optional image section to the form, choose Insert Image, and complete the section data.

Getting Rid of the *my:* Namespace

It would be reasonable to expect that you could extract the template files and simply remove or replace the *my:* namespace prefix, and if replacing *my:* with another namespace name, change *xmlns:my* to *xmlns:tns* (or whatever) in every file. This technique works when you replace the *my:* namespace prefix with another prefix, but it usually doesn't work when you remove the namespace prefix. In the latter case, attempting to open manifest.xsf displays schema error messages. It's possible to manually alter the schema, but doing this is impractical for even moderately complex documents.

Using the sample files

Completed sample files for the next two sections are located in your C:\Microsoft Press\Introducing InfoPath 2003\Chapter04\ ContactsTns and ContactsNoNS folders.

Replacing the *my:* Namespace with a Different Name

The ContactsCh4.xsn template you created in the section "Starting with a New, Blank Form," earlier in this chapter, is an especially egregious example of "my mania." Even the standard schema.xsd file turns into myschema.xsd when you create a data source from scratch. To remove all vestiges of *my* from the project (except from myschema.xsd) and replace them with *tns* (short for for *this namespace*), follow these steps

▶ **Replacing all instances of my: in a project**

1. Make backup copies of ContactsCh4.xsn and ContactsCh4.xml.
2. Open ContactsCh4.xml in Notepad.
3. Choose Edit, Replace. In the Find And Replace dialog box, type **my:** in the Find What text box, type **tns:** (or another namespace prefix you want to use) in the Replace With text box, and click Replace All.
4. Replace *my* in the *xmlns:my* declaration of the contacts element with **tns**, as shown here:

```
<?xml version="1.0" encoding="UTF-8"?><?mso-infoPathSolution
solutionVersion="1.0.0.3" productVersion="11.0.5779" PIVersion="1.0.0.0"
href="file:///C:\Microsoft%20Press\Introducing%20InfoPath%202003\Chapter04\Con
tactsCh4\ContactsCh4.xsn"
name="urn:schemas-microsoft-com:office:infopath:Contacts-from-Scratch:-myXSD-2
003-11-01T21-43-32" ?><?mso-application progid="InfoPath.Document"?>
<tns:contacts
xmlns:tns="http://schemas.microsoft.com/office/infopath/2003/myXSD/2003-11-01T
21:43:32" xml:lang="en-us">
        <tns:contact tns:dateAdded="2004-01-15" tns:dateUpdated="2004-01-15">
                <tns:firstName>Gabriel</tns:firstName>
                <tns:lastName>Sanchez-Garcia</tns:lastName>
                <tns:personal>
                        <tns:address>1234 Grandview St.</tns:address>
                        <tns:city>Dallas</tns:city>
                        <tns:state>TX</tns:state>
                        <tns:zipCode>75002</tns:zipCode>
                        <tns:phone>214-555-1212</tns:phone>
                        <tns:eMail>gabrielsg@whatever.com</tns:eMail>
                </tns:personal>
        </tns:contact>
        <tns:contact tns:dateAdded="2004-01-15" tns:dateUpdated="2004-01-15">
                <tns:firstName>Robert</tns:firstName>
                <tns:lastName>Johnson</tns:lastName>
                <tns:personal>
                        <tns:address>550 Petroleum Blvd.</tns:address>
                        <tns:city>Houston</tns:city>
                        <tns:state>TX</tns:state>
                        <tns:zipCode>72001</tns:zipCode>
                        <tns:phone>713-555-1212</tns:phone>
                        <tns:eMail>rjohnson@somewhere.com</tns:eMail>
                </tns:personal>
        </tns:contact>
</tns:contacts>
```

5. Press Ctrl+S to save the modified file, and close it.
6. Open ContactsCh4.xsn in design mode. Choose File, Extract Files, and extract the template files to the current folder.
7. Open each extracted file, and repeat steps 3, 4, and 5. Be especially careful not to omit step 4.
8. Right-click manifest.xsf, and choose Design from the shortcut menu to open the manifest file in design mode.
9. Choose File, Save As, and save your file as **ContactsCh4.xsn**.
10. Open ContactsCh4.xml to verify that your namespace changes work correctly.

Removing the *my:* Namespace

The easiest method of removing a namespace is to create a sample XML data document, remove the namespace prefixes from it, and create a new, blank form from the document. Use the techniques from the sections "Creating a Template from an XML Document" and "Copying a Form Design and Adding New Elements," earlier in this chapter, to create the new template and schema. The "On Your Own" section at the end of this chapter provides abbreviated instructions for removing namespace prefixes.

Chapter Summary

InfoPath's Data Source Wizard makes creating data sources for new form templates a quick and easy process. You can base the data source for a form on a sample XML data document or an XML schema. If you don't have a schema for your document, you can let InfoPath infer the schema or use the Microsoft XSD Inference 1.0 tool to create one. Alternatively, you can design your data source and form interactively, but starting from scratch is a more tedious and error-prone process. Designing an XML data document and its schema in the Data Source task pane adds an undesirable *my:* namespace prefix to the resulting document.

Dragging a data source node–often the first child of the root node–to InfoPath's work area adds sections and their controls to the form automatically. If the data source is based on a data document or schema, InfoPath adds labels to the controls automatically. Depending on the form's data source, repeating groups generate repeating tables or repeating sections with controls. You can modify data sources you create from scratch or from data documents; data sources created from XML schemas are locked. You can't add, remove, or alter elements or attributes of a locked schema.

InfoPath's capability to copy and paste sections and controls from one template to another simplifies form cloning, but you must reestablish binding between form objects and their data sources.

InfoPath lets you change the namespace declaration and prefix of a form by extracting the template files and replacing the current namespace name in all documents, including any data documents you created previously. Removing a namespace usually requires creating a new template from a data document that has the namespace prefixes removed.

Q&A

Q. I have an XML schema and a sample data document for my form. What's the better choice for use as the data source generated by the Data Source Setup Wizard?

A. The easiest way to decide on the better approach is to try both. Schemas often include many attributes and elements that production documents don't use. A form generated from such a schema will require substantial reworking, if you don't selectively add sections and controls for the elements that you know are required. On the other hand, if the XML data document contains a wide variety of data types, using a schema eliminates the need to specify a data type for non-string elements and ensures that values entered in a form conform to the data types without the need for adding declarative validation rules or Visual Basic .NET validation code.

Q. Do my XML data documents require a namespace declaration?

A. There's no hard and fast rule regarding use of namespace declarations and namespace qualifiers for elements and attributes. As an example, RSS 2.0 documents don't use namespaces for RSS content, although namespaces are permitted to extend the document. Unless your document must be assigned a default namespace or use namespace prefixes to conform to an external requirement, stick to "not in a namespace" documents.

Q. How do I remove the *my:* namespace prefix that results from adding fields to an existing form without namespace prefixes?

A. Depending on the type of fields you add, you might be able to use the approach described in the section "Replacing the *my:* Namespace with a Different Name," earlier in this chapter, with an empty Replace With text box. If that doesn't work, you're probably stuck with the more tedious process described in the section "Removing the *my:* Namespace."

Q. Does InfoPath impose a limit on the size or complexity of a schema or form design?

A. There are no published limitations, but caching large, complex forms consumes a substantial amount of RAM. If InfoPath uses up your PC's RAM and uses the Microsoft Windows XP or Windows 2000 or later paging file to store cached data, you'll notice dramatically reduced performance. The UBL samples mentioned in this chapter can bring InfoPath to its knees on a Windows XP computer with 500 MB RAM.

On Your Own

Here's an abbreviated step-by-step exercise for removing a namespace (in this case, *my:*) from a form:

1. Copy the ContactsCh4.xml file you created in the section "Replacing the *my:* Namespace with a Different Name" to a new folder–in this example, My Documents\InfoPath\ContactsNoNS.
2. Replace all instances of *my:* with nothing (by leaving the Replace With text box empty).
3. Remove the InfoPath PIs and the namespace and language attributes from the root *contacts* element so that it appears as *<contacts>*.
4. Save the file as **ContactsNoNs.xml** with UTF-8 encoding.
5. Use the Data Source Wizard to create a data source for the new template.
6. Copy the form sections and controls from ContactsCh4.xsn.
7. Bind the sections and controls to the appropriate groups and fields of the data source.
8. Change the optional personal section to a required section.
9. Create a test document to verify that the namespace prefix is gone.

CHAPTER 5

Laying Out Forms

In this chapter, you will learn how to:

- **Establish a strategy to maintain consistency in overall form layout and design**
- **Set default view widths and specify the default font family and size for each control type**
- **Add a layout table with a standard title and empty row to contain other form design elements**
- **Add a layout table and insert controls in its cells**
- **Decorate layout tables with borders of varying widths**
- **Add a repeating table to a form, calculate default values, and format numeric cells for currency and percentage values**
- **Embed existing layout and repeating tables in a new layout table with a title**
- **Draw tables using a freehand pencil and eraser cursors**

For more information:

- **See Chapter 7, "Formatting Forms," for additional table and control design options.**
- **Review "Navigating Documents with XPath" in Chapter 3, "Understanding Form Technologies," for an overview of XPath expressions.**
- **Refer to "Calculating Values with the Expression Box" in Chapter 6 for additional examples of XPath expressions.**

To work through this chapter:

- You need experience in creating data sources from XML data documents, which is explained in Chapter 4, "Creating a Template from an XML Document."
- You should be familiar with manipulating Microsoft Office InfoPath 2003 tables, as described in Chapter 2, "Adding Tables to Rich Text Boxes."
- You should have installed in your C:\Microsoft Press\Introducing InfoPath 2003\Chapter05 folder the sample files from the CD that accompanies this book. You will use the XML data documents in the subfolders as the data source for the forms you create in this chapter.

The Contacts and RSS 2.0 data entry forms you designed in Chapter 4, "Creating Forms," didn't take advantage of the versatile layout features available in InfoPath. The labels and text box controls you added to form sections by choosing Section with Controls appear on individual lines. You can place label and text-box pairs in the same line by deleting line-feed equivalents and then align text boxes horizontally within a section by adding spaces and trimming widths. It's not easy to get the horizontal alignment right without changing the font size of the spaces you add, and inline labels for multi-line text boxes align at the bottom of the text box.

InfoPath's layout tables solve text alignment problems and enable you to establish a consistent form design strategy for your organization. Placing sections and controls within layout tables gives you the tools you need to tweak your design for better readability and improved data entry efficiency. Layout tables let you add outside borders to your form and its sections and, if you choose, controls contained in table cells. You can add individual layout tables for a form header and each section of the form. Alternatively, you can nest multiple layout tables within a single table that contains a heading.

This chapter deals with layout and repeating tables, along with the text box controls they contain; Chapter 7 delves into the details of table, section, and control formatting, including conditional formatting.

Adhering to Design Standards

Most organizations observe a set of graphic design standards for stationery, business forms, brochures, product specification sheets, Web pages, and other publicly accessible and internal media. These standards usually include logos and specific font families for the organization name and document text, and they often include layout guidelines for print publications and Web pages. The goal is to present a consistent, memorable "corporate" image to employees and the public at large, regardless of the organization's business, charitable, or governmental purpose. InfoPath's sample forms adhere to a standard design pattern that uses layout tables to maintain a consistent graphic "flavor."

The forms you create probably will be for "internal use only," and your employer might not have graphics standards for internal printed or electronic documents. In this case, work with your colleagues to establish standards for form design, such as form headings, font families and sizes, and section layout.

Adding Layout Tables from the Task Pane

Chapter 2 introduced you to working with InfoPath tables in data entry mode in the "Adding Tables to Rich Text Boxes" section. InfoPath provides a similar design mode capability for adding layout tables with cells to contain sections and controls, but extends the standard Table menu choices with a Layout task pane. Choosing the Layout task pane displays a set of standard layout tables. The Insert Layout Tables list's first selection, Table With Title, adds a default two-row, single-column table with placeholders for the title text and other form content. Figure 5-1 shows the master layout table for this chapter's first example.

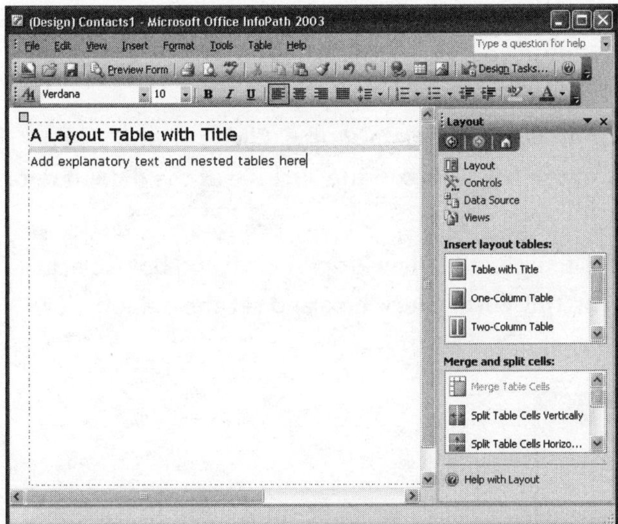

Figure 5-1 You add this single-column, two-row layout table by double-clicking the Table With Title item and replacing the placeholder for the title and optional text.

The remaining standard layout tables have one, two, and three columns and one row. You can specify a custom table with the number of rows and columns you set in the Insert Table dialog box that opens when you click the Custom Table. The Merge And Split Cells list offers selections that correspond approximately to the Table menu's choices. You use the Merge And Split Cells selections when you modify parent and nested tables in later sections.

The following sections show you how to add a master table with a title to a form, add a repeating section to the master table, and add a layout table with text box controls in the repeating section.

Creating the Initial Contacts1 Template

In this section, you create a simple form to understand the capabilities of basic layout tables. A modified version of the Contacts-WellFormed.xml data document from Chapter 4 is a good choice for the data source for the form. The Contracts1Source.xml sample file has two contact entries with required personal and optional business address sections.

To create the data source for the Contacts1 template and add the master (title) table to the form, follow these steps.

▶ Add a data source and master layout table

1. **Start InfoPath, click the Design A Form link on the Fill Out A Form dialog box, and click New From XML Document Or Schema link to start the Data Source Wizard.**

2. Click the Browse button to open the Open dialog box, navigate to your C:\Microsoft Press\Introducing InfoPath 2003\Chapter05\Contacts folder, and double-click Contacts1Source.xml.
3. Click Next and then click Finish to create the data source. Click Yes when the message box asks if you want to use the values in the .xml file as the default data for your form.
4. Choose Format, View Properties to open the View Properties dialog box, select the Use A Custom Layout Width For This Form check box, and set the default view width to **600** pixels, as shown here:

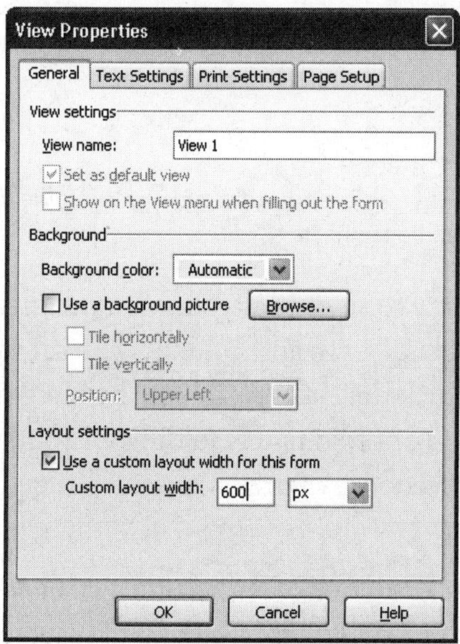

5. Click the Layout link in the Data Source task pane, and click Table With Title to add the default two-row table.
6. Replace the Click To Add Title placeholder with **Contacts Form 1**, and click the Click To Add Form Content placeholder to delete it.
7. Delete the default empty line above the master table to minimize the form's top margin.
8. You'll nest all other controls in this master table, so drag the table's lower dashed line to the bottom of the work area. (Refer to Figure 5-3 for sizing.)
9. Save your template as Contacts1.xsn in a new subfolder of My Documents\InfoPath.
10. Choose File, Properties to open the Form Properties dialog box, type **Contacts with Master Table Test** as the Form Name, and click OK to close the dialog box.

Adding a Repeating Section, Layout Table, and Controls

Contacts1.xsn's data source has three basic form components: name, personal address (required), and business address (optional). For this example, you add the contacts group section to the empty cell of the master table, insert and size a three-column layout table, and then add First Name and Last Name labels and text boxes to the leftmost and rightmost table cells. Follow these steps to add the form elements.

▶ Add a data source and master layout table

1. **Open the Data Source task pane, drag the contact repeating group from the Data Source list to the layout table's empty row below the title, and select Repeating Section from the shortcut menu that opens when you release the left mouse button.**
2. **Click to select the section, drag its bottom sizing handle to the bottom of the table, and click inside the section to select it.**
3. **Open the Layout task pane, scroll to the Three-Column Table item, and click it to add the table to the top of the repeating section. Click each of the three "Click to add form content" placeholders to remove them, as shown here.**

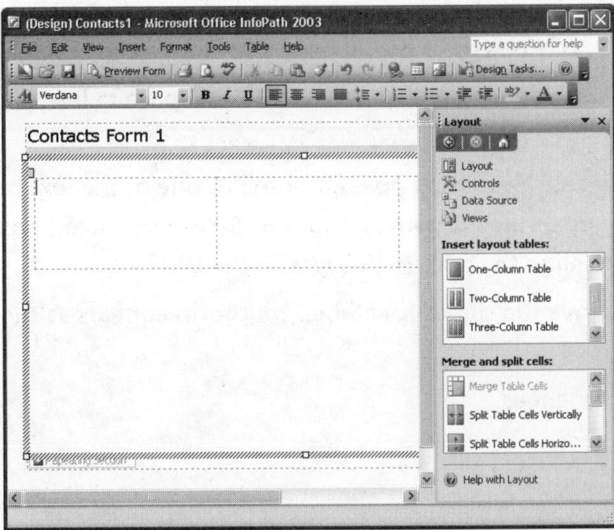

4. **Right-click the left column (A) of the table, choose Table Properties to open the dialog box of the same name, and click the Column tab.**
5. **Each column is 195 pixels wide, for a total of 585 pixels, because section and table margins occupy about 15 pixels of the master form's 600-pixel width. Set the width of column A to 285 pixels, as shown on the next page.**

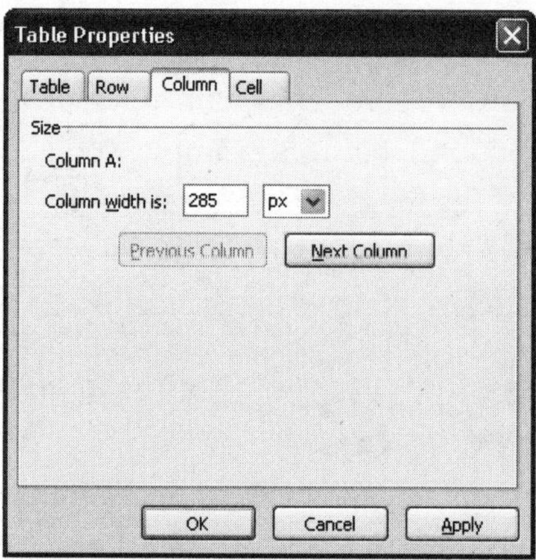

6. Click Next Column, and set the width of column B to **15** pixels. The middle column acts as a separator for the two columns that will contain First Name and Last Name controls.
7. Click Next Column again, set the width of column C to **285** pixels, and click OK to close the dialog box.
8. Click the Data Source link, expand the contact node, drag the firstName node to column A, and drag the lastName node to column C to add labels and text boxes to the cells.
9. Reduce the width of the text boxes to fit the labels and text boxes on a single line.
10. Drag the bottom of the layout table up to remove the extra space below the text boxes.
11. Select the First Name and Last Name text boxes, right-click one of the text boxes, and choose Properties to open the Properties (Multiple Selection) dialog box. On the Size tab, click Align to align the text vertically with the label.
12. Delete any empty lines above the single-row table. Your form appears as shown below.
13. Press Ctrl+S to save your changes.

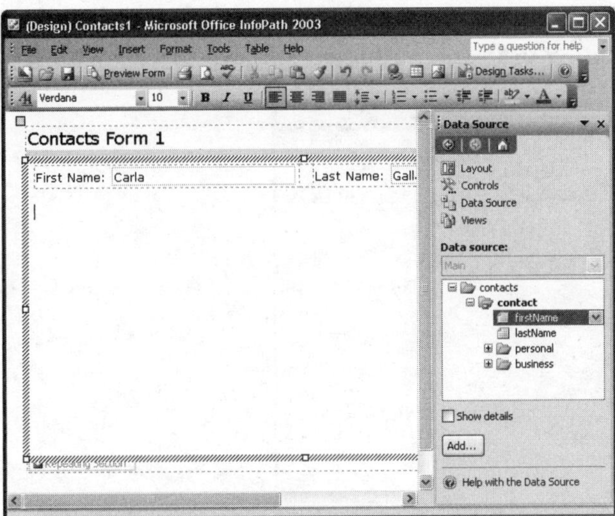

Adding Controls in a Layout Table

One approach to adding sections to a master table is to add a section without controls, insert an empty layout table in the section, and then drag the section's fields from the Data Source list to the table's cells. This method becomes tedious if the section contains many fields.

InfoPath offers a shortcut for adding a layout table with labels and controls to an entire section automatically. The only issue with this approach is that the controls insert a two-column table with a row for each field in the section. Most fields don't require the default text box width to display their data. Changing the table from two to four columns to halve the number of rows requires splitting cells, cutting and pasting cell content, and then removing the empty table rows.

Adding a Layout Table with Controls

To add the personal group as a nested layout table, with labels and text boxes in individual table columns, and prepare to split the table cells, follow these steps.

▶ Add a layout table for the personal group

1. **Open the Data Source task pane, and drag the personal group from the Data Source list to a position to the right of the Last Name text box to insert it under the First Name and Last Name table.**
2. **Choose Controls In Layout Table from the shortcut menu that opens when you release the left mouse button.**

3. **Close the task pane, and drag the right border of the newly inserted table so that it aligns with the right border of the upper table, as shown here.**

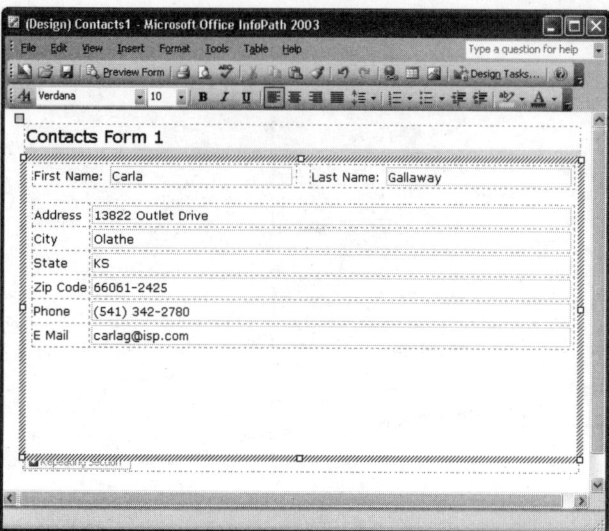

Splitting Table Cells and Moving Cell Contents

InfoPath's table-editing features ease the drudgery of redesigning layout tables with controls. The split cells feature lets you add as many new columns to a layout table as you need to move fields to the same row. If you're familiar with modifying Microsoft Office Word 2003 tables, you'll find that InfoPath's table-reconfiguration process is similar.

To split the personal section's table so that it resembles the design of the first layout table you added and move content from columns to rows, follow these steps.

▶ Rearrange the personal section layout table

1. **Click the Address label to select the table, move the mouse pointer slightly above the second column (where it turns into a downward-pointing arrow), and click to select all cells in the second column.**
2. **Choose Table, Split Cells to open the Split Cells dialog box.**
3. **Set the Number Of Columns to 4, and clear the Merge Cells Before Split check box, as shown here.**

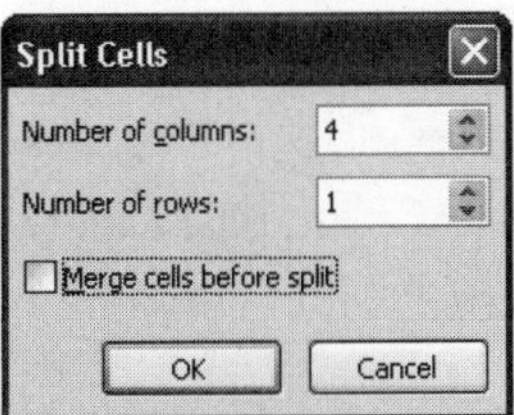

4. Click OK to split the cells, and adjust the width of the columns to match approximately the width of the labels, text boxes, and empty column of the upper table.
5. Select the City label and its text box, press Ctrl+X to cut the selection to the Windows Clipboard, click in row 1 of the fourth column (D), and press Ctrl+V to paste the two controls.
6. Repeat step 5 for the Zip Code label and text box, but paste them below the City row.
7. Repeat step 5 for the E Mail label and text box, but paste them below the Zip Code row.
8. Cut and paste the State and Phone labels and text boxes into rows 2 and 3 of the left columns.
9. Select the three empty table rows, and press Delete to remove them. Your table appears as shown here.

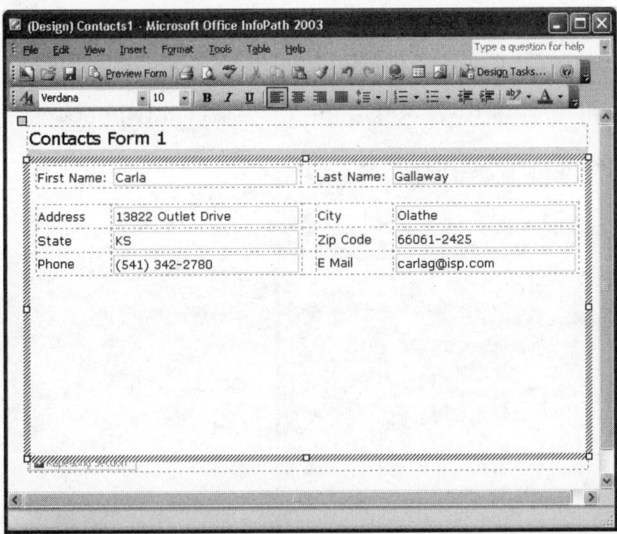

Adding a Row and Merging Content from Another Table

The firstName, lastName, and personal fields are required, so it makes sense to merge the contents of the first two tables. Moving the labels and controls of the first table to the second table also eliminates differences in text alignment between the tables.

To add a new top row to the second table, move the contents of the first table to the newly added row, and delete the first row, follow these steps.

▶ Merge the names and personal tables

1. **Click the Address label, and choose Table, Insert, Rows Above to add a new row to the table.**
2. **Cut the First Name label (without the colon) from the first table, and paste it into column A of the second table.**
3. **Repeat step 2 for the Last Name label, and paste it into column D.**
4. **Cut and paste the First Name and Last Name text boxes into columns B and E.**
5. **Click in the first table, and choose Table, Delete, Table to remove it.**
6. **Select the two text boxes that you just moved, open the Properties (Multiple Selection) dialog box, on the Size tab, set the Bottom Padding and Bottom Margin value to 1 pixel, set the Width value to 100 %, and click OK to apply the settings. (Using the Align feature in a table with multiple rows reduces the row height, and text boxes and labels in separate columns align automatically.)**
7. **Adjust the width of the State, Zip Code, and Phone text boxes to accommodate their content. The U.S. Postal Service probably will appreciate your observance of their trademark by changing Zip Code to ZIP Code.**
8. **Add a caption in one of the empty rows above the table, as shown here.**

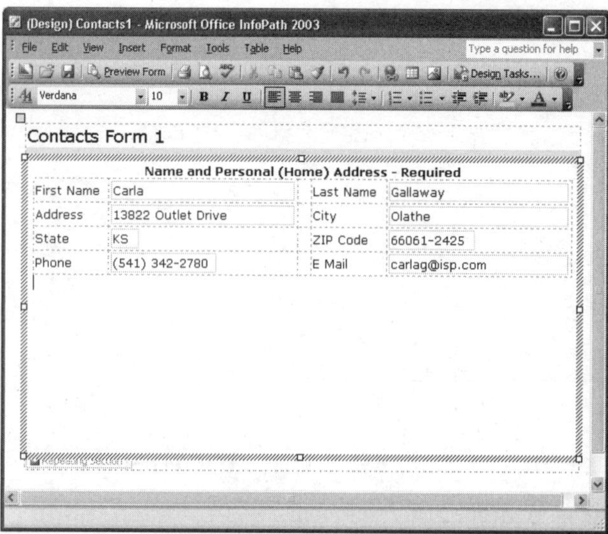

9. **Delete any remaining empty lines above the table, and save your changes.**

Using an Optional Section with a Layout Table

Adding the optional business group to the form shows you how to add an optional section without controls to the repeating section and then add a layout table with controls to the optional section.

To add an optional section with a layout table for the business group, follow these steps.

▶ **Add the optional section and controls**

1. **Open the Data Source task pane, drag the business group node below the personal group table, and choose Section.**
2. **Right-click the Section tab, and choose Section Properties to open the Section Properties dialog box.**
3. **Select the Do Not Include The Section In The Form By Default option, and select the Allow Users To Insert The Section check box to make the section optional.**
4. **Select the Show Insert Button And Hint Text check box, and type Click Here to Insert Business (Work) Address or something similar in the text box, as shown here. If you don't mark the check box, the optional section placeholder isn't visible. Click OK.**

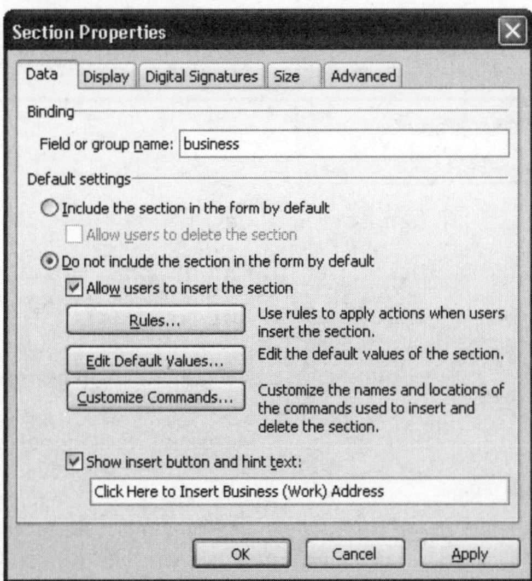

5. **Drag the business group node to the optional section, and choose Controls In Layout Table to add a two-column, nine-row table. Expand the width of the table to the full width of the optional section.**

6. **Select column B, split the column into four columns (remembering to deselect the merge columns option), adjust the column widths, and relocate label/text-box pairs as you did earlier in the section "Splitting Table Cells and Moving Cell Contents." Look ahead to Figure 5-4 for layout guidance.**
7. **State and ZIP Code labels and resized text boxes fit within a single right column, so split row 3, column E into three columns, and move these two label/text-box pairs to the split cells.**
8. **Delete the four empty rows, add a caption, reduce the height of the optional section and repeating section, and drag the bottom of the master table to the bottom of the repeating section.**
9. **Save your changes, and click Preview Form to check your work so far. Figure 5-2 shows the preview with the optional section added.**

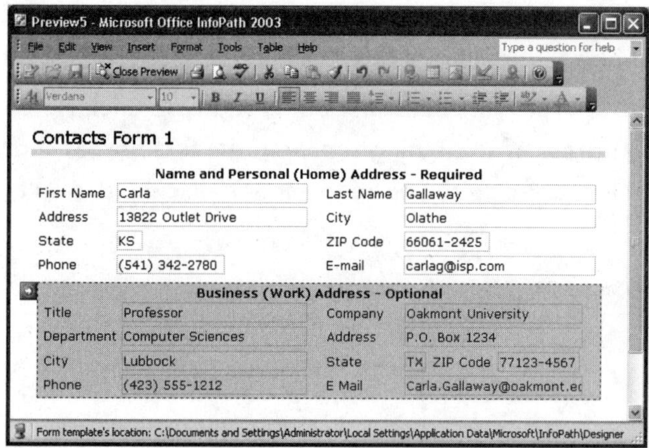

Figure 5-2 This preview shows the Contact1.xsn template's final design.

The examples in this chapter illustrate layout and formatting techniques but don't duplicate topic coverage in previous chapters, such as specifying required fields and testing templates. However, it's a good practice to verify that the forms you create with a new design methodology generate the data document you're expecting and that repeating sections merge correctly. To perform the test, create two forms using the default data, and then merge them to verify that all fields of repeating sections appear in the merged document.

Using the sample source and merged files

Your C:\Microsoft Press\Introducing InfoPath 2003\Chapter05\Contacts folder contains the completed Contacts1.xsn template and two sample data documents, Contacts1Test.xml and Contacts1Merge.xml, which have been merged into Contacts1Test+Merge.xml to verify that the repeating sections merge correctly

Adding Table Borders

At this point, the form you've produced is short on graphic accouterments. You can spiff up the form a bit by adding borders to your tables. Adding borders, like adding dividing lines, aids users in identifying specific form sections. You also can add cell divider lines.

Following are methods for adding specific types of borders to the tables you added to the Contacts1.xsn template:

- ✦ To add a border around the master form, click the master table's selection handle at the upper left of the table, and choose Table, Borders and Shading. Then click the Outline button, and select a border width, such as 2 1/4 points. For each border that you want make different, click it and make the changes. (If you don't click the four outside border buttons, the width remains the default 1 point.) Borders around the entire table don't contribute to usability; add them only if they're needed to conform to graphic standards.
- ✦ Use the same technique to add an outside border to an individual table, but reduce the width to 1 1/2 points or fewer. To improve readability, set label cell Left Padding to 3 pixels.
- ✦ When you add the border around a master form with a title, the light gray border under the title disappears. To restore it, add a horizontal, 6-point, light gray inside border to the master form. It's also a good design practice to add a space in front of the title text.
- ✦ If you decide to add inside (cell) borders, accept the default 1-point width.

Figure 5-3, on the next page, illustrates that adding borders around all table elements leads to a harsh appearance and contributes little or nothing to the form's usability. (This version is Contacts1Borders.xsn.)

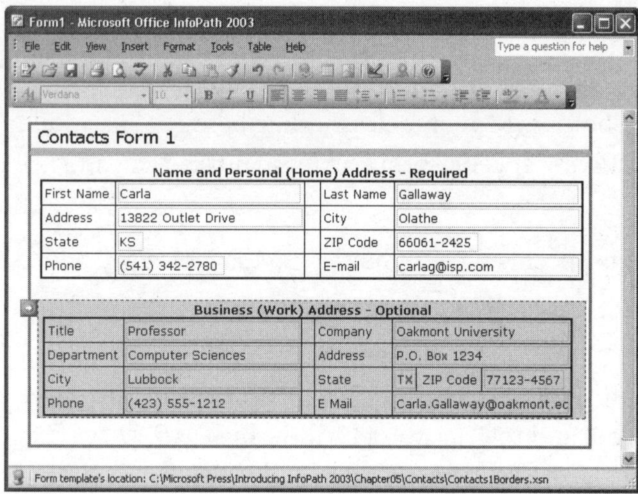

Figure 5-3 This version of the Contacts1 form has every possible border added.

Working with Repeating Tables

The Status Report form and most other sample InfoPath forms include repeating tables. The form examples you've worked with so far in this book don't have sections that suit repeating tables well because most text boxes contain lengthy content. Sales orders, invoices, and similar business documents include line items that lend themselves to display in repeating tables. As an example, a sales order created from a query against the Access Northwind database's Orders and Order Details tables includes order-specific information and multiple line items. The line items include several numeric data types, which give you the opportunity to explore InfoPath's numeric formatting features and receive a preview of calculating sums with expression boxes.

Creating a Data Source from an Attribute-Centric Data Document

The source document for the repeating table exercise is a modified data document generated by the Northwind Traders Order Entry and Editing Form that you saw in Figure 1-6 of Chapter 1, "Presenting InfoPath 2003." InfoPath generates complex attribute-centric XML data documents from Microsoft Access and SQL data sources, as you'll discover in Chapter 13, "Connecting Forms to Databases."

All data documents you've seen so far are *element-centric* XML, which uses element values to hold the data and attribute values for metadata. (The common definition of *metadata* is "data about data," such as the *dateAdded* and *dateUpdated* attribute values of the Chapter 4 ContactsCh4.xml data document.) *Attribute-centric* XML delivers the data as attribute name/value pairs. For this example and those in Chapter 13, the attribute name is the field name of the table specified by the element name. Figure 5-4 shows the 11072.xml data source document in Microsoft Internet Explorer 6.

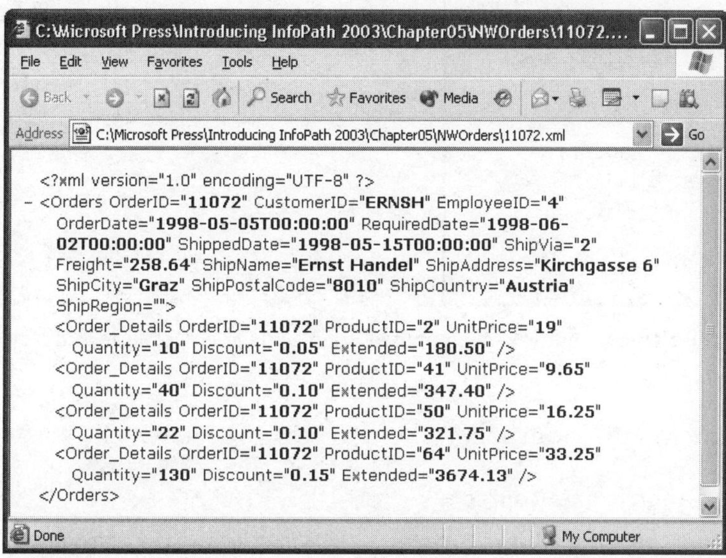

Figure 5-4 This attribute-centric data document was generated from the Northwind Orders and Order Details tables. An underscore substitutes for the space in the Order Details table name.

Avoiding attribute-centric documents

Don't create attribute-centric data documents unless you're forced to for compatibility with existing XML applications. ActiveX Data Objects (ADO) and the early XML features of Microsoft SQL Server 2000 generate attribute-centric XML documents, but element-centric XML is the norm for almost all current XML-based applications, such as XML Web services and custom projects you create with ADO.NET in the .NET Framework.

Compare the attribute-centric structure of 11072.xml with the element-centric version of the same Northwind database records in Figure 5-5. Access 2003 exported the records for order 11072 to the 10072EC.xml file. The *_x0020_* element of the *Order_x0020_Details* repeating group substitutes for the space in the Order Details table name, and the field that's equivalent to the Extended attribute is missing. Both files are in the C:\Microsoft Press\Introducing InfoPath 2003\Chapter05\NWOrders folder. The following example uses an attribute-centric source document to show you how to create a repeating table from an attribute-centric source document's repeating elements.

Figure 5-5 This is part of the element-centric version of the Orders and Order Details records for Northwind order 11072.

To create a data source from 11072.xml, follow these steps.

▶ Create the attribute-centric data source

1. **Close and reopen InfoPath, click Design A Form in the Fill Out A Form dialog box, and in the Design A Form task pane, click New From XML Document Or Schema.**
2. **Select C:\Microsoft Press\Introducing InfoPath 2003\Chapter05\NWOrders\11072.xml as the source document for the form, and use default values for the form.**
3. **From the Data Source list in the Data Source task pane, drag the Orders node, which represents an individual document, to the work area, and choose Controls In Layout Table. InfoPath adds controls from the Orders table fields in a sequence unrelated to their order in the source document and the Order_Details line items as an empty, unlabeled bulleted list.**
4. **Delete the unusable Bulleted List in the bottom right table cell.**
5. **In the Data Source list, right-click the Order_Details repeating field (element) node, and choose Repeating Table to add the repeating table below the Orders table. Friendly field names appear as bold labels in the repeating table's header row. Again, InfoPath adds the attributes in an apparently random sequence to the table.**
6. **Delete the Order Details label and text box in the rightmost table cell. Removing the Order Details element in the table allows new line items to be added.**

7. **Select and cut the Extended label, paste it into the header of the rightmost empty cell, and then cut and paste the text box under the label. You must cut and paste labels and text boxes of repeating tables in separate operations.**
8. **Repeat steps 6 and 7 for the Order ID label and text box, but place them in the leftmost empty cells.**
9. **Move the Unit Price label and text box one column to the right, and then do the same for the Product ID pair.**
10. **Finally, move the Quantity pair to column B and delete the empty column.**
11. **Readjust the column widths, as shown here.**

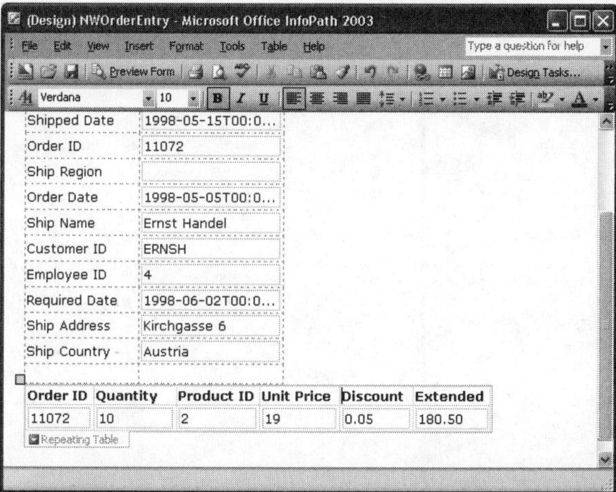

12. **Choose File, Properties, to open the Form Properties dialog box, type Northwind Order Entry Test in the Form Name text box, and click OK.**
13. **Press Ctrl+S or click Save, and save your form as NWOrderEntry.xsn in a new \My Documents\InfoPath\NWOrders folder.**

Changing Data Types and Rearranging the Orders Table

You read in Chapter 4 that, unlike the Microsoft XSD Inference 1.0 tool, InfoPath doesn't attempt to infer data types from the data in source documents. This means you must change the data type of each date and numeric field manually. When you change the data type, you lose default values, if present. You also have the option of applying the techniques you learned earlier in the chapter to coalesce the Orders table into fewer rows.

To change the field data types and add new default values, do the following.

▶ Change the field data types

1. In the Data Source list, right-click the Freight node and choose Properties to open the Field or Group Properties dialog box.
2. Choose Decimal (double) from the Data Type list, type **258.64** as the Default Value (as shown here), and click OK. (You lose the original default values when you change the data type, and adding temporary default values makes designing and testing the form easier.)

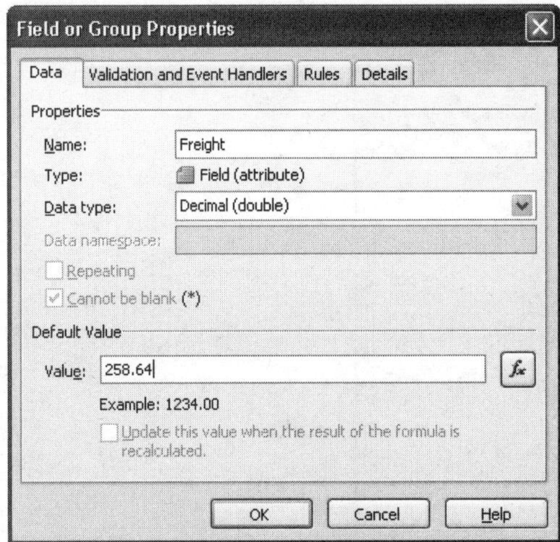

3. Repeat steps 1 and 2 for the Ship Via (Data Type = Whole Number (integer); Default Value = **2**), OrderID (Data Type = Whole Number (integer); Default Value = **11072**), and Employee ID (Data Type = Whole Number (integer); Default Value = **4**) fields.
4. Repeat steps 1 and 2 for the three date fields, selecting Date (date) as the Data Type, and typing **5/5/1998**, **6/2/1998**, and **5/15/1998** as the default values for the OrderDate, RequiredDate, and ShippedDate, respectively.
5. Change Quantity and ProductID to Whole Number (integer) with defaults of **10** and **2**, respectively. (InfoPath changed the data type of the OrderID field to integer when you completed step 3; don't add a default value to this field.)
6. Change Unit Price, Discount, and Extended to Decimal (double) with defaults of **19.00**, **0.05**, and **180.50**, respectively.
7. Press Ctrl+S to save your changes.

If you have the patience, rearrange the Orders table to two sets of columns with labels and text boxes that match the sequence of the attributes in Figure 5-4, and change the three date text boxes to date picker controls. After about 10 minutes of heavy-duty cutting and pasting, your table appears as shown in Figure 5-6.

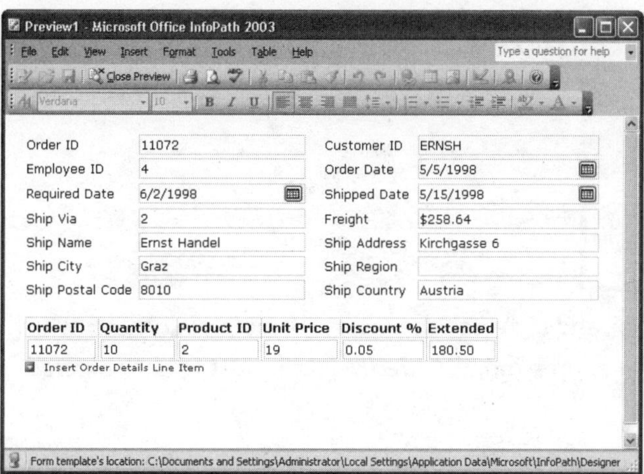

Figure 5-6 The Orders and Order Details tables appear as shown here after considerable time and energy spent moving cells.

Specifying a Default Value from Another Field Value

The InfoPath Insert Formula feature lets you assign a value from one control (the source) as the default value of other controls for fields of the same data type (targets). When you update the source control's value, target controls update in unison. As an example, the Order ID values in the repeating table must correspond to the Order ID value of the Orders group. If you change the Order ID in the layout table, existing and added Order Details rows must receive the new Order ID value. The value you set in the source control overrides default text box and data source values. To give the Insert Formula feature a test, follow these steps.

▶ **Assign the master Order ID value to Order Details elements**

1. **Right-click the empty Order ID text box in the Order Details repeating table, and choose Text Box Properties to open the Text Box Properties dialog box.**
2. **Click the function (fx) button under the Default Values heading to open the Insert Formula dialog box.**
3. **Click the Insert Field or Group button to open the Select A Field Or Group dialog box.**
4. **Scroll to and select the OrderID attribute field of the Orders group, as shown on the next page.**

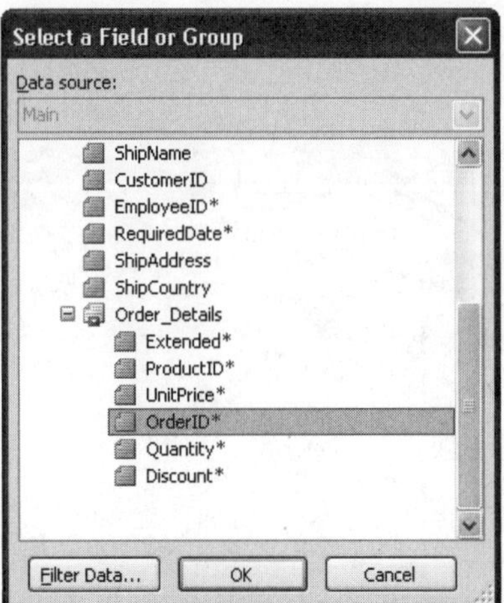

5. **Click OK to close the dialog box and return to the Insert Formula dialog box, which displays an abbreviated XPath expression, *@OrderID* that points to the selected attribute field, as shown here.**

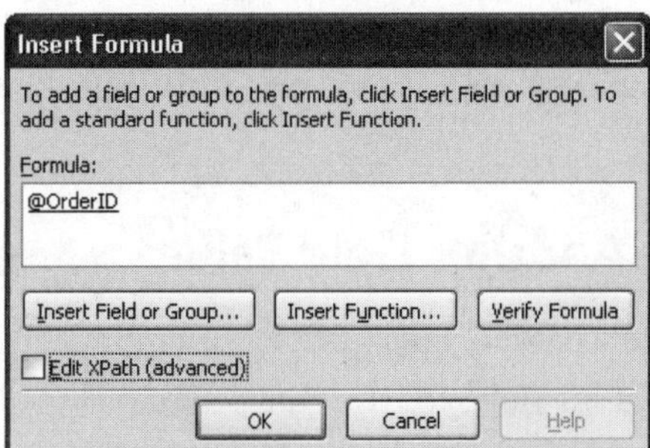

6. **Select the Edit XPath check box to display the full XPath expression for the attribute value, */../..@OrderID*, click OK to close the dialog box and copy the abbreviated expression to the Default Value text box, and click OK again to close the Text Box Properties dialog box.**
7. **Click Preview Form, and change the Order ID value in the layout table to another number to update the Order ID values in the repeating table.**
8. **Click the Insert Item button or link to add a new Order Details item, and verify that the new row uses the same default value.**
9. **Close the preview, and save your changes.**

Using the Insert Formula Feature to Calculate Default Values

The Insert Formula feature makes it easy to write XPath expressions for computing numeric field values, such as the extended amounts for order or invoice line items.

The Extended field in the Order Details section is a good candidate for demonstrating this capability.

To add a calculated default value–Quantity * Unit Price * (1 - Discount)–for the Extended field, follow these steps.

▶ Calculate the extended value of Order Details items

1. **Right-click the Extended text box in the Order Details repeating table, and choose Text Box Properties to open the Text Box Properties dialog box.**
2. **Click the function button to open the Insert Formula dialog box, click the Insert Field or Group button to open the dialog box, and double-click the Quantity field to add it to the Formula text box.**
3. **Type * after the *@Quantity* expression, and repeat step 2, but double-click the UnitPrice field.**
4. **Type *(1- after the *@UnitPrice* expression, and repeat step 2, but double-click the Discount field, and type) after the *@Discount* expression. Your Formula text box appears as shown here.**

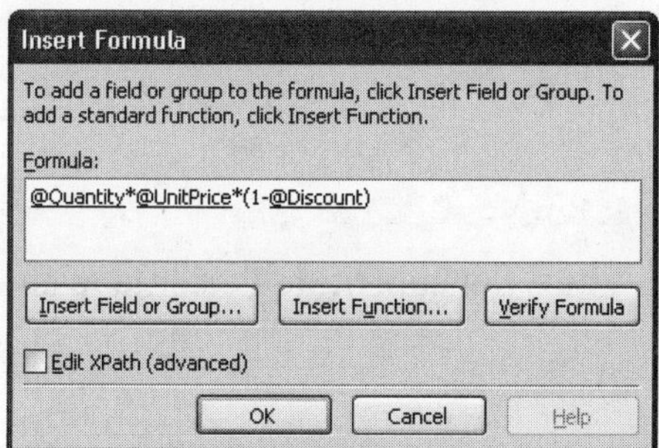

5. **Click Verify Formula to check your entry, click OK to insert the abbreviated XPath expression in the Default Value text box, and click OK to close the dialog box.**
6. **Open a preview; alter Quantity, Unit Price, and Discount values to verify the calculated default value; and save your form design changes.**

Additional decimal values that sometimes appear are the result of rounding errors, which you will learn to disguise in the next section.

Formatting the Repeating Table's Numeric Text Boxes

The XML Schema specification doesn't provide a currency or percentage data type, but InfoPath lets you format the text boxes for entering currency and percentage values. Special numeric formatting is available for the Decimal (double) data type only. Formatting doesn't affect the element or attribute values of the XML data document.

To format the Unit Price and Extended text box for currency (US$ for this example) and the Discount text box as percentage, follow these steps.

▶ **Format text boxes bound to decimal fields**

1. **Right-click the Unit Price text box, choose Text Box Properties to open the Text Box Properties dialog box, and click Format to open the Decimal Format dialog box.**
2. **Select the Currency option, and select 2 from the Decimal Places list, as shown here. (The Auto Decimal Places option doesn't add trailing zeros to integer values.) Click OK twice to close the dialog boxes.**

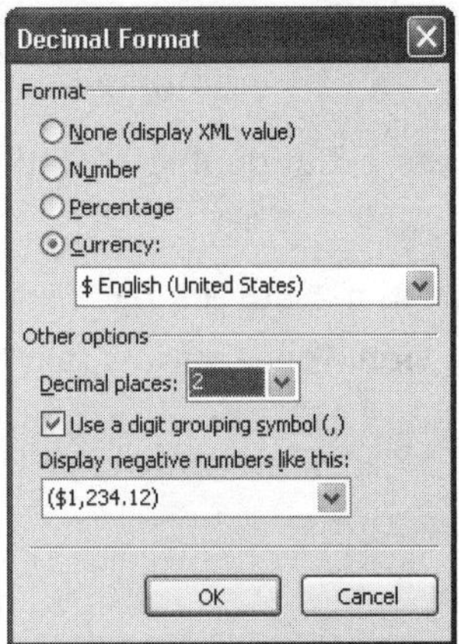

3. **Repeat steps 1 and 2 for the Extended text box.**
4. **Repeat steps 1 and 2 for the Discount text box, but substitute Percentage and 0 Decimal Places in step 2.**
5. **Save your form.**

Figure 5-7 shows the repeating table with numeric formatting added. InfoPath doesn't add a % symbol for percentage values; adding **%** before or after the Discount label lets users know the value is a percentage.

Summing Numeric Values in a Table Footer

Repeating tables have an optional footer that's useful for displaying summarized numeric data. You add a footer by selecting the Include Footer check box on the Display tab of the Repeating Table Properties dialog box. As you learned in Chapter 3, expression boxes use XPath *sum( )* expressions to calculate the totals and aren't bound to fields. Chapter 6, "Adding Basic Controls and Lists," covers expression box controls in detail.

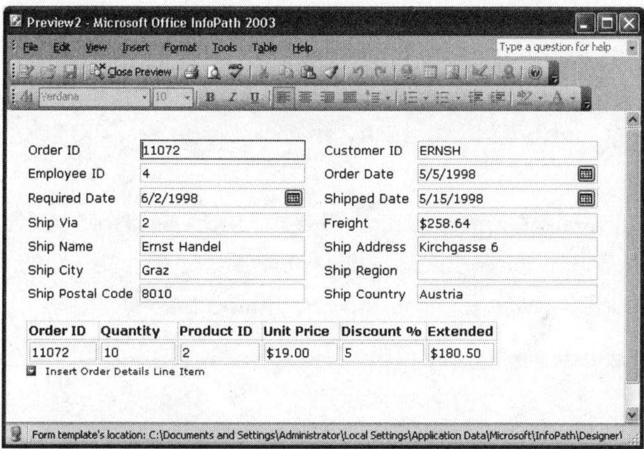

Figure 5-7 This preview shows text box values formatted for U.S. currency and percentage.

To add a table footer and total the Quantity and Extended fields, follow these steps.

▶ **Add a table footer with total values expression boxes**

1. **Right-click the Repeating Table tab, choose Repeating Table Properties to open the Repeating Table Properties dialog box, and click the Display tab.**
2. **Select the Include Footer check box, as shown here, and click OK to add the footer row.**

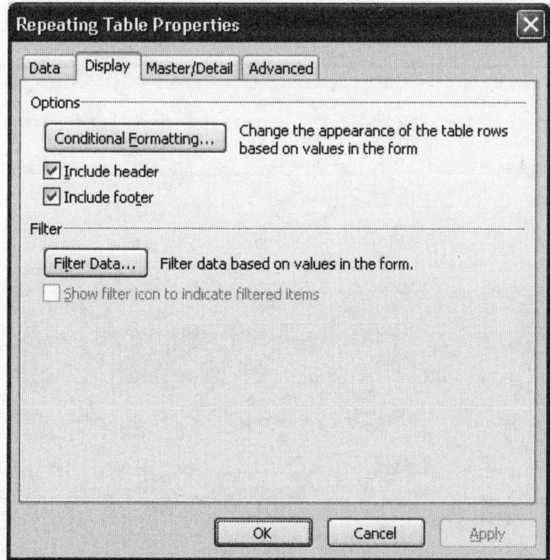

3. **Press Ctrl+F1 to display the task pane, if it's not open, and click the Controls link.**
4. **Scroll to the Expression Box item in the Insert Control list, and drag the control to the Quantity footer cell. Field name identifiers appear for all form fields, and the Insert Expression Box dialog box opens.**

5. **Click the function button to the right of the text box to open the Insert Formula dialog box, click Insert Field or Group to open the Select A Field Or Group dialog box, select Quantity under the Order_Details node, and click OK to add the XPath expression that points to the Quantity field to the Insert Expression Box's XPath text box.**
6. **Prefix the XPath expression with sum(, and add a closing parenthesis after *@Quantity*, as shown here. (XPath expressions are case sensitive; typing Sum(, for example, causes an error.) Click OK twice to close the two dialog boxes.**

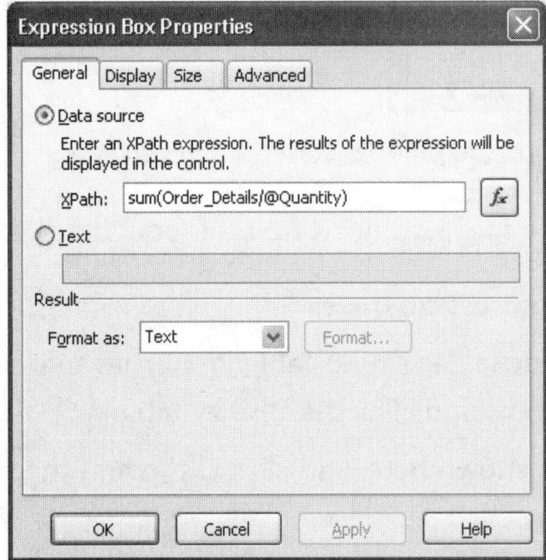

7. **Repeat steps 4 through 6 for the Extended field.**
8. **Right-click the Extended expression box, choose Expression Box Properties to open the Expression Box Properties dialog box, select Decimal from the Format As list, click Format, select Currency, 2 Decimal Places, and click OK twice to format the Extended total.**
9. **Save your form.**

The generalized XPath expression *sum(groupName/@attributeName)*, which appears in the Insert Expression Box's text box, totals attribute values in repeating sections or tables. Omitting the @ symbol totals element values. Figure 5-8 shows your form with the two added expression boxes. The Extended total is 1.#QNAN, which is InfoPath's code for not a number, in design mode, because the individual values aren't calculated until you open a preview or a form.

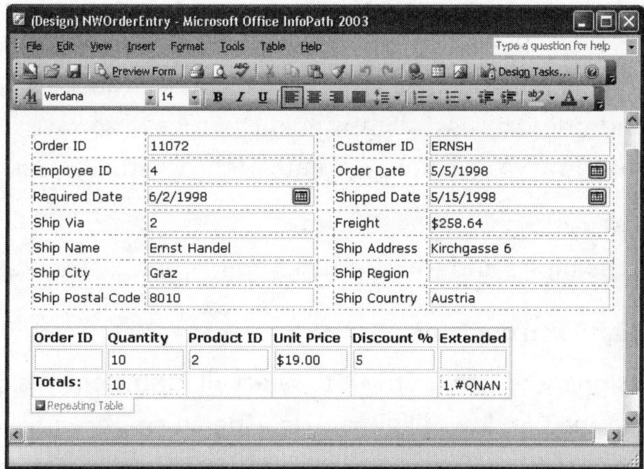

Figure 5-8 This repeating table footer contains expression boxes for summing the Quantity and Extended fields.

Test the expression boxes you added by clicking Preview Form, selecting the repeating table, and pressing Ctrl+Enter to add a few Order Details entries, as illustrated in Figure 5-9.

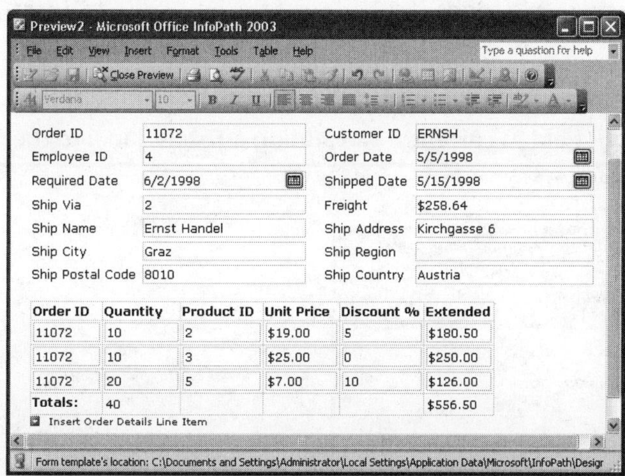

Figure 5-9 This form preview shows totals for the four default and one added Order Details entries.

Create, save, and use Notepad to compare a test form with the original data document to ensure that the two documents have identical structures. The test form opens with a single default Order Details item, so the number of *OrderDetails* elements will differ from the original. The only structural difference between the original and the InfoPath form (other than the PIs) is the substitution of element closing tags for the shortcut element closing syntax of the original document.

Adding a Master Table Ex Post Facto

The design of the NWOrderEntry form is decidedly bland, so you might want to spruce it up with a master table and title. This is a slightly chancy process, so save and make a backup copy of NWOrderEntry.xsn before you embed the existing tables and controls in a master table.

To add a master table and embed the tables and their controls, follow these steps.

▶ Insert a table with a title and all form controls

1. Open NWOrderEntry.xsn in design mode, press Ctrl+A to select all form elements, and press Ctrl+X to cut them to the Windows Clipboard, leaving an empty work area.
2. Press Ctrl+F1 to open the task pane, if it's not open, click the Layout link, click Table With Title to add a single-column table to the form, and close the task pane.
3. Type **Northwind Order Entry Form** as the title.
4. Click the bottom cell of the table to remove the prompt, and press Ctrl+V to paste the Windows Clipboard contents into the cell.
5. Drag the right edge of the master table to the right edge of the embedded Orders table.
6. Add finishing touches to your form, such as removing the empty line at the top of the form, formatting the Freight field as currency, and adding a **Totals:** label to the repeating table's footer, as shown here.

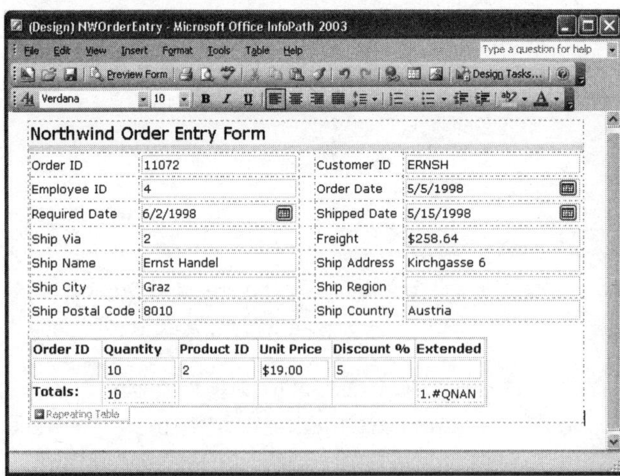

7. Save your form.

Drawing a Table

The InfoPath Tables toolbar contains a Draw Tables button that enables you to design specialized tables by drawing freehand. This feature is similar to the Draw Tables feature of Microsoft Word but the behavior of the pencil differs from the pencil in the Word version. As mentioned in the "Adding Tables to Rich Text Boxes" section in Chapter 2, drawing tables–especially layout tables–isn't an easy process for anyone other than professional Web page designers. One potential application for drawing freehand tables is to trace data entry locations from a temporary form background image that you create by scanning a paper form.

Following are basic instructions for drawing InfoPath tables:

- To add a table to the working area, click the Draw Table button to enable the pencil cursor, and drag the pencil diagonally to create a table in the overall size you want.
- To add a vertical cell divider, drag the pencil vertically. Once you've added a table, dragging the pencil diagonally does nothing.
- To add a horizontal cell divider, drag the pencil horizontally.
- To disable the pencil cursor and return to the insertion point cursor, double-click the table twice or click the Draw Table button.
- To add borders as you draw the table, open the toolbar's Border Style list, select the type of border to add, and open the Border Width list to specify the thickness.
- To remove a cell divider, click the Eraser button, hold the left mouse button down and drag the mouse over the divider until you highlight it, and then release the mouse button.
- To delete a table, click its selection button with the selection (arrow) cursor, and press Delete.

Other table-editing features, such as changing the size or position of cell dividers, are similar to those for layout tables. You also can apply split, merge, and other table-menu operations to freehand tables. Figure 5-10 shows a freehand table with a few sample RSS 2.0 labels and text boxes and the pencil cursor selected.

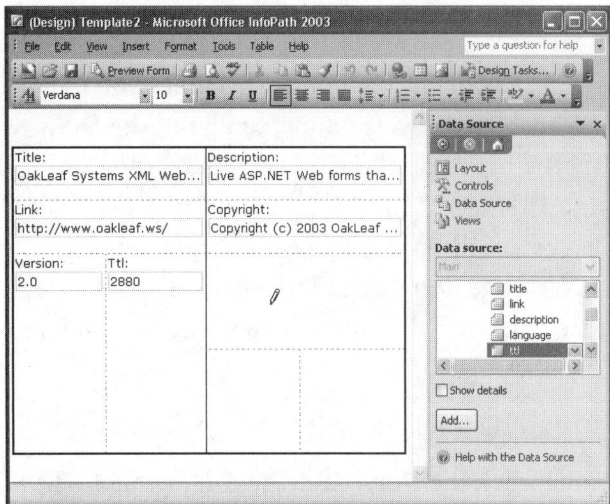

Figure 5-10 Use the Draw Tables' pencil cursor to draw a table and add cell dividers.

Chapter Summary

Layout tables are one of InfoPath's most powerful form-design features. A single-column layout table with a heading row and a second row to contain all other form elements is the most common starting point in producing InfoPath forms.

Conventional sections with controls add labels and text boxes automatically but require manual formatting operations to place label/text-box pairs on a single line and align text box edges to achieve an attractive form layout. InfoPath's layout tables for data source groups automatically place labels and text boxes in adjacent cells, which eliminates vertical and horizontal text-alignment problems. Automatic label and text box insertion creates a row for each field's label and text box. Placing more than one label/text-box pair in a row requires splitting table cells followed by cut-and-paste operations to reduce the number of rows.

Repeating tables are preferable to repeating sections for entering numerical data stored in fields of repeating groups because they conserve valuable "real estate" in the form. Repeating table footers can hold expression boxes to display the sums of numeric columns. The Insert Formula dialog box simplifies calculating expression box and default field values using XPath expressions.

InfoPath lets you use a pencil tool to draw custom tables that aren't easy to create by specifying the number of rows and columns of a custom layout table. In most cases, you'll find that using standard or custom layout table selections from the Layout task pane are a better starting point for conventional InfoPath forms.

Q&A

Q. Is it better to use a separate one-row title table with individual layout tables or to embed layout tables in the second row of a title table?

A. The only advantages of a two-row title table with nested sections, layout, and repeating tables are the option to add a border around the entire form and apply a background color to only the active area of the form. An independent title table lets you copy it to the other forms you create and modify it as necessary. An independent title table probably is a better approach when you've added a logo graphic or applied other special formatting to titles that are common to all or most forms.

Q. Is there any limit to the depth of nesting layout tables?

A. The only limitation on nesting depth is space on the form to accommodate controls at the lowest level in the nesting hierarchy. Assuming that group layout tables are embedded in a master layout table for the form, the practical limit is likely to be three or possibly four nesting levels.

Q. Why is element-centric XML preferred over attribute-centric XML?

A. A basic purpose of XML is to create structured or semi-structured documents with human-readable content. Attributes, because they're contained *within* element tags, are considered part of the structure of documents, not their content. Human-readable content belongs between opening and closing element tags. The relatively minor reduction in size of an attribute-centric versus an element-centric document doesn't justify intermingling structural and content information.

Q. Can I add controls other than text boxes to the data rows of a repeating table?

A. Yes, if the fields have appropriate XML schema data types, such as *date*, *dateTime*, or *boolean*, which bind to date picker or check box controls. Multiple numeric fields bound to a set of option buttons is another suitable choice. InfoPath's sample Applicant Rating form illustrates the use of option buttons in a layout table, but they're sometimes also useful in repeating tables to display and calculate total scores in footer expression boxes.

On Your Own

Here's an additional exercise to test your layout skills:

1. Create a new RSS 2.0 form based on the Rss2v3.xml source document in your C:\Microsoft Press\Introducing InfoPath 2003\Chapter05\Rss2v3 folder that duplicates this form.

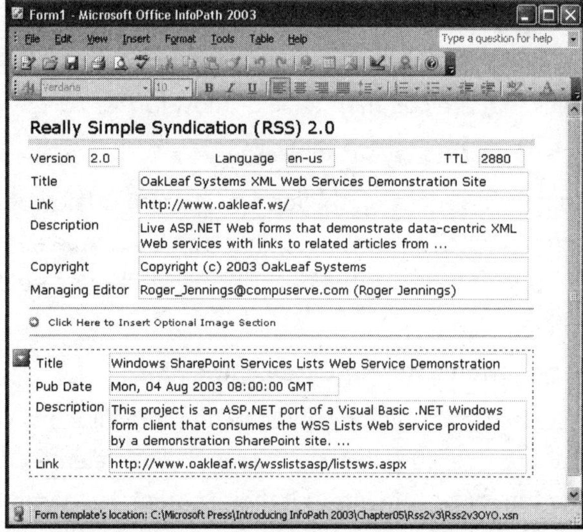

2. Start by adding a single table with a title, and then add a layout table with controls for the channel group in the empty row of the master table.
3. Add a horizontal line, an optional section for the image group, and a layout table with controls for the group.
4. Add a horizontal line, a repeating section for the item group, and a layout table with controls for the group.
5. Split cells, move the controls to positions shown in the step 1 screen capture, and delete empty rows and lines. Change the two Description text boxes from single-line to multi-line.
6. Optionally, add borders to tables.
7. Save and test your form.

CHAPTER 6

Adding Basic Controls and Lists

In this chapter, you will learn how to:

- **Classify controls by type, associate controls with field data types, and set property values that are common to most controls**
- **Add conventional and rich text boxes, hyperlinks, and three types of lists to your form**
- **Describe the format of XML Schema's *date* and *dateTime* datatypes**
- **Create drop-down lists and list boxes with items populated from data you type or add from secondary data sources**
- **Add option buttons to option groups and insert check boxes bound to True/False (*boolean*) fields**
- **Use XPath expressions to display calculated numeric values in expression boxes, and add Base64-encoded images and ink drawings to forms**

For more information:

- **Refer to the section "Navigating Documents with XPath," in Chapter 3, for XPath terminology.**
- **See the section "Summing Numeric Values in a Table Footer," in Chapter 5, for help completing the "On Your Own" exercise at the end of this chapter.**
- **See Chapter 9, "Working with Advanced Form Elements," for descriptions and examples of the new control and section types added to the original version of Microsoft InfoPath 2003 in Service Pack 1 (SP-1).**
- **Refer to Chapter 13, "Connecting Forms to Databases," and Chapter 14, "Designing InfoPath Web Service Clients," for creating secondary data sources from database tables and queries or XML Web services.**
- **Review the World Wide Web Consortium (W3C) XML Schema Part 2: Datatypes recommendation at *www.w3.org/TR/xmlschema-2/*.**

To work through this chapter:

- You need experience working with layout and repeating tables, which you gained in Chapter 5, "Laying Out Tables."
- You should be familiar with formatting text and adding other elements to rich text boxes from working through the section "Formatting Rich Text Data," in Chapter 2, "Filling Out Forms."
- You need an understanding of the XML Schema terminology outlined in the section "Validating Documents with XML Schemas," in Chapter 3, "Understanding Form Technologies."
- You should be familiar with XPath expressions from reading the section "Navigating Documents with XPath," in Chapter 3, and completing the procedures in the sections "Using the Insert Formula Feature to Calculate Default Values" and "Summing Numeric Values in a Table Footer," in Chapter 5.
- You need the sample files from the CD that accompanies this book installed in your C:\Microsoft Press\Introducing InfoPath 2003\Chapter06 folder. As in previous chapters, you use the XML data documents in the subfolders as the data source for the forms you create in this chapter.

The preceding chapters have concentrated on standard text boxes bound to fields as the primary controls for entering data, with a few examples of the date picker control and one instance of a check box to set True/False (*boolean*) values. It's a good bet that most of your production forms will consist primarily of text boxes, date pickers, drop-down lists, and expression boxes.

Runners-up in the control popularity contest include check boxes, option buttons and groups, list boxes, lists (plain, bulleted, and numbered), pictures, rich text boxes, and ink pictures. Rich text boxes trail the HTML-based control ratings, because rich text Extensible Hypertext Markup Language (XHTML) content is uncommon in structured XML documents, because its structure isn't governed by a schema. At the time this book was written, ink picture controls weren't yet heavily in use, because Tablet PCs were still a relatively new technology and therefore not very common.

This chapter explains how to add, format, and customize behavior of basic InfoPath controls that are bound to text, numeric, logical, or Base64-encoded fields in the form's XML data document. The emphasis is on basic controls and lists that you haven't worked with in earlier chapters. Most procedures use a sample form that's similar to the NWOrderEntry.xsn template that you created in Chapter 5, but this version has an element-centric XML data document as its data source. You'll modify this template and then use the final version in Chapter 7, "Formatting Forms," and Chapter 8, "Validating Form Data," and in Part IV, "Programming InfoPath Forms."

Adding advanced controls and sections

This chapter describes the set of controls and related objects included with the initial InfoPath 2003 version, which Microsoft released in October 2003 with the other Microsoft Office System 2003 applications. InfoPath 2003 SP-1 adds three new controls—file attachment, vertical expression box, and scrolling region—and several new section types, and it lets you add custom (ActiveX) controls to forms. Chapter 9 covers the elements added by SP-1.

InfoPath 2003 SP-1 classifies controls as Standard, Repeating and Optional, File and Picture, Advanced, and Custom controls. This chapter covers all of the Standard and File and Picture controls, except file attachment, and includes expression box and ink picture controls, and hyperlink text box controls, which the SP-1 version categorizes as Advanced.

Relating Controls to Data Types

This chapter categorizes controls by their most commonly assigned field data types: text or rich text (*xsd:string*); date, time, or date and time (*xsd:date*, *xsd:time*, or *xsd:dateTime*); numeric (*xsd:integer* or *xsd:double*); logical (*xsd:boolean*); and image (*xsd:base64binary*). (InfoPath's and most other XML-aware applications' schemas use the *xsd:* or *xs:* namespace prefix to designate XML Schema datatypes.)

Differentiating between *data type* and *datatype*

You've probably noticed that this book distinguishes the words *data type* and datatype. *Data type* refers to InfoPath's "friendly" name for the data type, such as Whole Number. The corresponding XML Schema *datatype*—in this case, *integer*—appears in parentheses in the Properties dialog box's Data Type list.

Figure 6-1 shows the design of a template (IPControls.xsn) with working examples of the 13 controls that this chapter discusses.

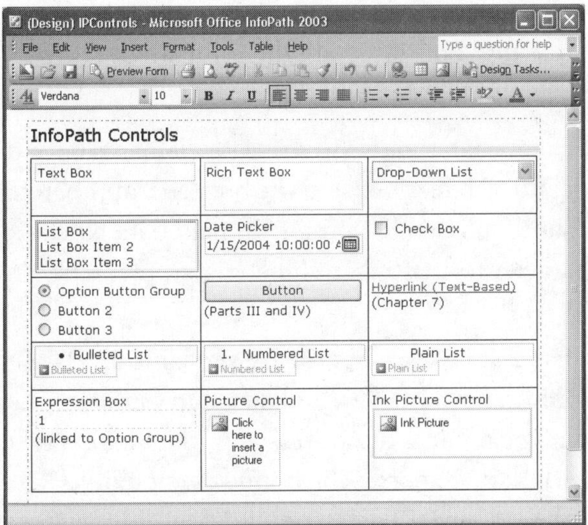

Figure 6-1 This template has examples of the 8 standard InfoPath controls, a text-based hyperlink control, the three types of repeating lists, an expression box, and graphical picture and ink picture controls.

See Also Part III, "Working with Databases and Web Services," and Part IV, "Programming InfoPath Forms," cover the use of buttons in your forms. Chapter 7 describes the text-based version of a hyperlink control; you add a hyperlink that obtains its values from the data source's fields in the section "Bound Hyperlink Controls" later in the chapter.

Figure 6-2 illustrates each of the components of Figure 6-1 in data entry mode with a GIF bitmap and simulated ink drawing added by the user to the two graphical controls.

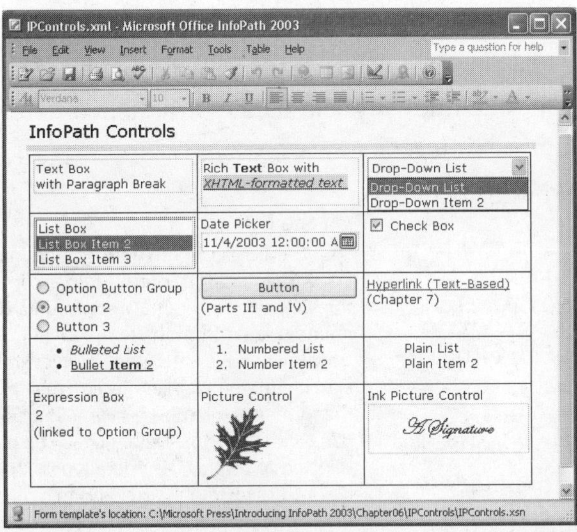

Figure 6-2 This is the form generated by the design of Figure 6-1 with user-added character formatting, list items, and graphics.

Many controls can be bound to one of several different InfoPath field data types and their corresponding XML Schema datatypes. Following are the InfoPath data type categories assigned to the controls shown in Figures 6-1 and 6-2:

- **Text and rich text** The XML Schema datatype is *xsd:string* for elements bound to the IPControls form's text box and rich text box and the bulleted, numbered, and plain lists. The rich text box and bulleted list's InfoPath field data type is rich text (XHTML) to permit character formatting; numbered and plain list examples bind to text fields.
- **Hyperlink** A *hyperlink* control has display and link values, similar to an HTML hyperlink (anchor), and is read-only in form preview and data-entry modes. The sample form has static values you type in Link To Address and Display Text text boxes on the control's Edit Hyperlink dialog box. The bound version links either or both values to a field of the *xsd:anyURI* datatype. *URI* is an abbreviation for Uniform Resource Identifier. The most common type of URI in InfoPath forms is an Internet URL, but the XML Schema recommendation doesn't specify the format of *xsd:anyURI* values.
- **Date and time** Date picker controls support *xsd:date* or *xsd:dateTime* XML Schema datatypes. The date picker example is bound to an *xsd:dateTime* element. You can't bind a date picker control to a field of the *xsd:time* data type.
- **Numeric** The preferred datatype for elements bound to the drop-down list and list box controls is *xsd:integer,* but *xsd:string* is permissable. By default, these controls return the position of the selection as a numeric value; 1 denotes the first value, which usually is the default. Text that appears in the list is called the *display name.* The numeric value and display name are called value/display name pairs. Option button groups also return numeric values assigned by default to each button of the group. The InfoPath field data type assigned to these three controls is Whole Number (integer).
- **Logical** The check box control binds to a True/False field of the *xsd:boolean* datatype. Check boxes can return *true* and *false* or *1* and *0* for the checked and unchecked states, respectively. You can specify blank for either state, but doing so isn't common.
- **Image** The picture and ink picture controls bind to fields of the *xsd:base64Binary* datatype, which corresponds to InfoPath's picture data type.

On the CD

Your C:\Microsoft Press\Introducing InfoPath 2003\Chapter06\IPControls folder contains the IPControls.xsn template, two data documents created from the template (IPControls.xml and IPControlsNoGraphics.xml), and extracted template files. Review the fields for the form in the template's Data Source task pane with the Show Details check box selected to display their data types. Open IPControlsNoGraphics.xml and myschema.xsd to explore the default control values and their corresponding XML Schema datatypes.

Setting Common Control Properties

Before you get into the detailed descriptions of individual controls and how to use them, the Size and Advanced tabs of the *ControlType* Properties dialog box deserve explanation. You used a few of the Size tab's features in earlier chapters, but this will be your first introduction to the Advanced tab.

Changing the Size of Controls

The Size tab's layout is identical for all controls, but some elements are disabled for specific control types. Figure 6-3 shows the Text Box Properties dialog box Size tab with InfoPath's default settings.

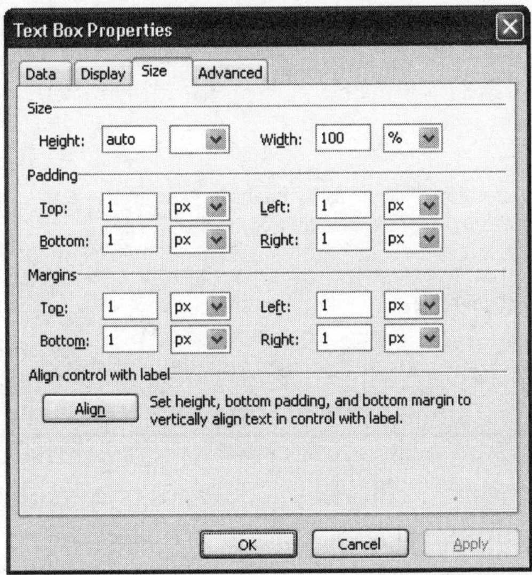

Figure 6-3 The Size tab of the Text Box Properties dialog box displays default values for the IPControls form's text box control.

The following list describes the purpose of the settings in the Size tab's three sections:

- **Size** Sets the height and width of the control. The default value of Height is Auto, which adjusts the vertical dimension to suit the font size of controls that contain text, or the original size of a graphics image. The Height setting isn't available for drop-down list boxes, so it's disabled. The Width setting defaults to 100% of the available width of the control's layout table cell or 130 px (pixels) for most controls that aren't contained in layout tables. Use the Width setting to adjust the size of controls to maintain vertical alignment of their right borders.

The Width setting doesn't change the appearance of check boxes and option buttons; it only affects the space the control occupies.

- **Padding** Sets the space between the contents of the control and its border. The default Padding value is 1 px for most controls. Padding is disabled for drop-down lists, list boxes, check boxes, option buttons, picture controls, and ink picture controls.
- **Margins** Set the space between the border of the control and adjacent controls; the default value is 1 px for most controls. Picture and ink picture controls disable Margin settings. If a layout table contains these controls, set the table's cell Padding values rather than its Margin values. You can change the margins of all controls at once by selecting the entire table and applying new cell Padding values.

The drop-down lists adjacent to each setting text box offer a choice of eight units of measurement. Pixels (px) is the default and most common setting for all InfoPath control size adjustments.

See Also **You can customize the border and background color of controls by changing settings in the Borders And Shading dialog box. Chapter 7 covers formatting layout tables and controls.**

Specifying Advanced Control Properties

On the Advanced tab, you can add a Screen Tip or an accessible name, assign a specific position for the control in the tab order sequence, and specify a shortcut key (Alt+*Key*) for setting the focus to a control. The view's stylesheet (view1.xsl for this example) stores the advanced setting values. Each control of the IPControls example has advanced settings applicable to the control type. Figure 6-4 shows the Advanced tab for the IPControls example form's text box control.

Here are the Advanced tab control settings options:

- **ScreenTip** Useful for explaining the purpose, required formatting, or other special characteristics of the control, such as its shortcut key assignment. Some controls, such as ink picture controls, substitute accessible names for ScreenTips.
- **Tab Index** Lets you customize the tab order. A 0 Tab Index value specifies the default tab order–left-to-right, top-to-bottom. Only controls that can receive the focus appear in the tab order. Expression boxes, empty ink pictures, and unselected option buttons can't receive the focus. Assign Tab Index numbers starting with **1** to set a custom tab order. The IPControls example form has a custom top-to-bottom, left-to-right tab sequence.

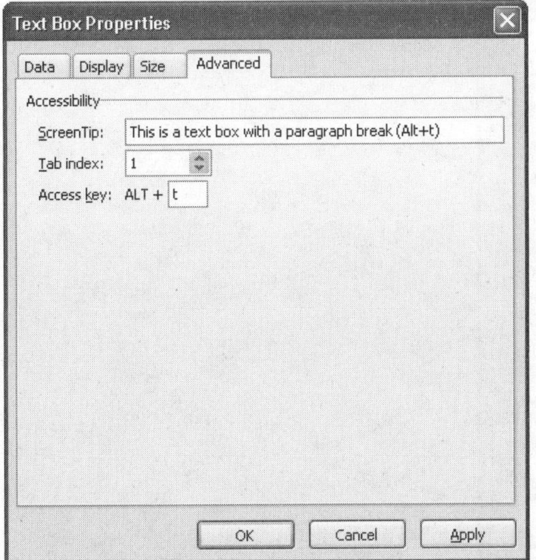

✦ **Figure 6-4** The Advanced tab of the Text Box Properties dialog box lets you set Screen Tips and shortcut keys, and change the control's tab order.

✦ **Shortcut keys** Provide quick navigation to controls that can receive focus. Shortcut keys work for most controls except bulleted, numbered, and plain lists. All controls on the IPControls form have shortcut key combinations, which are noted in the Screen Tip for the control.

Avoiding shortcut key conflicts

Don't assign shortcut key combinations, such as Alt+T or Alt+O, that conflict with InfoPath's menu bar shortcuts—in this case, Tools and Format. Shortcut keys assigned to controls override the menu shortcuts and make them inoperable, as demonstrated by the use of Alt+T for the IPControls form's text box control.

Working with Controls for Text Data

Chapters 4 and 5 described most text box design-mode details in the context of form design and layout. Chapter 2 provided a detailed explanation of the rich text box's capabilities in data entry mode. For the sake of brevity (and tree conservation), this chapter doesn't repeat the previous content. This following sections concentrate on the InfoPath and XML Schema data types that are compatible with text-based controls.

Text Boxes

Text boxes are InfoPath's most versatile control type. You can bind text boxes to fields of almost all of the InfoPath field data types–picture is the only excluded data type–as shown in Figure 6-5. (XHTML, which also is excluded, is an InfoPath format, not an XML Schema datatype.)

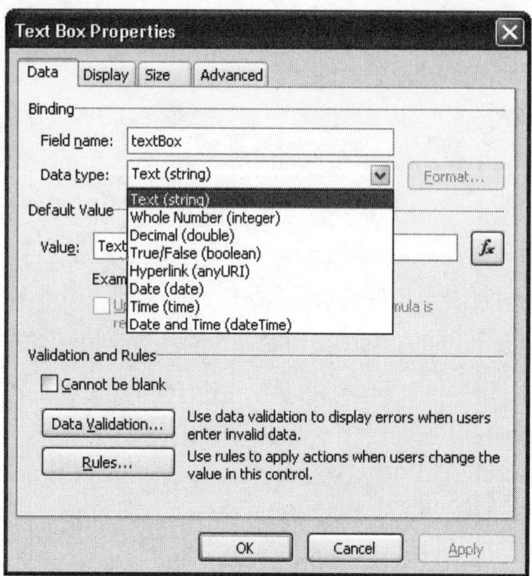

Figure 6-5 These InfoPath data types and their corresponding XML Schema datatypes are compatible with the text box control.

The default XML Schema datatype for fields you add to the form's data source is *xsd:string*. When you select an InfoPath data type on the Text Box Properties dialog box's Data tab, InfoPath changes the XML Schema datatype to correspond to your selection, if your schema isn't locked. (Basing a form on a custom schema, rather than an XML document locks the schema.) XML content, with the exception of *xsd:base64Binary* (encoded) data, is readable text; thus, it's possible to assign any text box content–including numbers and dates–to elements of the *xsd:string* datatype. Using the *xsd:string* datatype for numbers and dates defeats the datatype checking provided by the associated schema and doesn't let you specify formatting of decimal places, currency, or date values.

Text boxes support linefeeds if you select the Paragraph Break check box on the Display tab of the Text Box Properties dialog box. InfoPath doesn't add an HTML *
* tag for a paragraph break; instead, a carriage return/linefeed pair is embedded within the XML document. (To see this, you can open IPContacts.xml in Notepad, and scan for *Paragraph Break*, which has a trailing carriage return/linefeed pair.) The price of mixing content and presentation in an XML data document, which is a questionable practice at best, is loss of formatting of InfoPath data documents that you open in Notepad or other basic text editors. Raw XML code that's missing white space (indents before and line-breaks after element tags) is very difficult to read.

A more useful addition, which has appeared in SP-1, is the ability to limit the length of the text by selecting the Limit Text Box To check box and specifying the maximum number of characters in the Characters spin box, as shown in Figure 6-6.

Limiting the number of characters prevents errors when submitting forms that update limited-width fields in database tables.

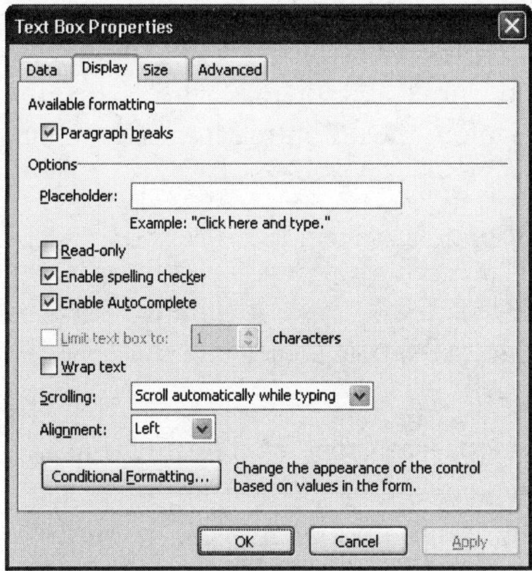

Figure 6-6 The Text Box Properties dialog box's Display tab has controls to permit recognition of paragraph breaks and limit the maximum number of characters users enter in text boxes.

Rich Text Boxes

InfoPath denotes rich text boxes' XHTML content by a local namespace declaration–*xmlns="http://www.w3.org/1999/xhtml"*–following the tag name. As an example, here's the XML code for the sample form's rich text box:

```
<my:richTextBox>
Rich <strong xmlns="http://www.w3.org/1999/xhtml">Text</strong>
Box with <em xmlns="http://www.w3.org/1999/xhtml">
<font style="BACKGROUND-COLOR: #ffff00">
<u>XHTML-formatted text </u></font></em>
</my:richTextBox>
```

The section "Formatting Rich Text Data," in Chapter 2, explains how to enter rich text in data-entry mode, and the section "Restricting the Contents of Rich Text Boxes," in Chapter 4, describes how to limit users' choices of inserted objects and text formatting.

Bound Hyperlink Controls

You haven't yet seen an example of InfoPath's Hyperlink field, which corresponds to XML Schema's *xsd:anyURI* (any Uniform Resource Identifier) datatype. The primary purpose of the Hyperlink field is to provide URLs that link to Web pages in XML data documents. Note that you also can add Universal Resource Names (URNs) as URIs. The bound hyperlink's display is the same as the IPControls form's Hyperlink (Text-Based) example.

To test a bound hyperlink format with the IPControls.xsn template, follow these steps.

▶ **Add a text box bound to a hyperlink field**

1. **Open IPControls.xsn in design mode, activate the Data Source task pane, and select the Show Details check box.**
2. **Right-click the textBox field, and choose Properties from the shortcut menu to open the Field Or Group Properties dialog box.**
3. **In the Data Type drop-down list, select Hyperlink (anyURI), and add the URL *http://www.oakleaf.ws/infopath* as the Default Value, as shown here:**

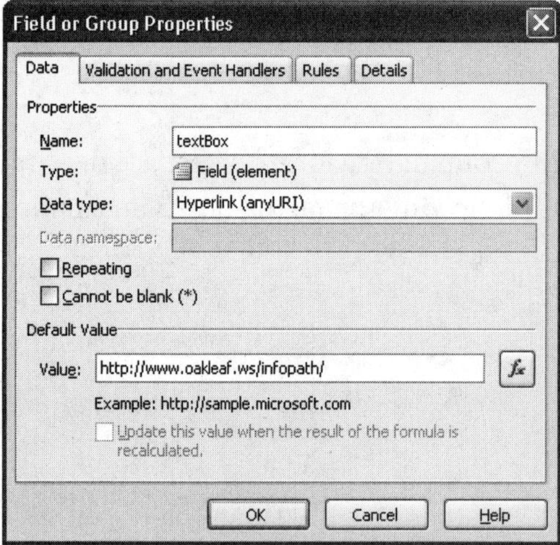

4. **Close the dialog box, and drag the textBox field under the original text box to format the text as a hyperlink. (You must add a new text box control to gain hyperlink formatting; changing the data type of an existing text box doesn't work.)**
5. **Right-click the hyperlink control, and choose Edit Hyperlink from the shortcut menu to open the dialog box of the same name. Select the Text option in the Display section, and type OakLeaf InfoPath Web Site in the adjacent text box, as shown here. (If you select the Address option in the Link To section and type an address in the adjacent text box, the control no longer binds to an *anyURI* field and becomes a text-based hyperlink.)**

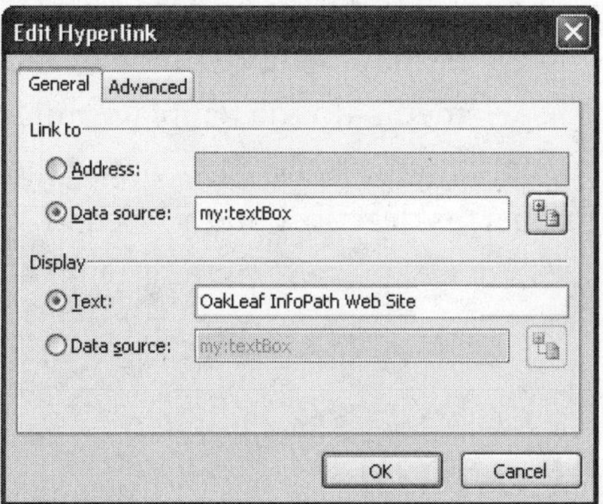

6. **Click OK, and click Preview Form to display the name you typed as Display Text, and if you specified a valid URL, click the text to follow the link.**
7. **Right-click the hyperlink, and observe that all shortcut menu items are disabled. However, you can edit the Link To value of the text box.**
8. **Click Close Preview, and close IPControls.xsn without saving your changes.**

Bulleted, Numbered, and Plain Lists

A group with a repeating field accommodates the three types of InfoPath's XML lists, which default to the Text (*string*) data type. You can add a small button and an adjacent link to prompt users to add a new list item by selecting the Data tab's Show Insert Button And Hint Text check box and typing a prompt in the associated text box, as shown in Figure 6-7.

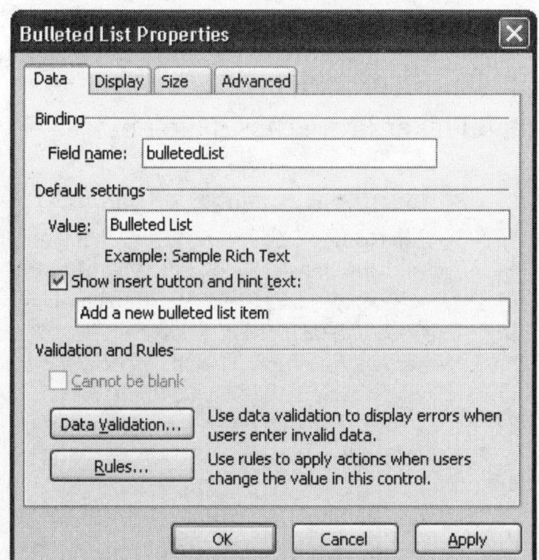

Figure 6-7 Prompt the user to add list items by selecting the Show Insert Button And Hint Text check box and replacing the default *Insert item* text with a more descriptive phrase.

The three empty bulleted list items that the sample Status Report form displays when creating a new data document appear as a result of template modifications–the addition of two empty *<sr:item></sr:item>* elements–to the template.xml file. If you want to encourage users to fill out more than one bulleted item, use the Edit Default Values dialog box to specify the number, as described in the section "Customizing Templates by Editing Default Values," in Chapter 11, "Setting Template and Digital Signing Options."

Binding the Date Picker Control

The date picker control is self-explanatory, but XML Schema's representation of the *xsd:date*, *xsd:dateTime*, and *xsd:time* datatypes deserves a bit more detail. As mentioned in Chapter 4, the XML Schema Part 2: Datatypes recommendation uses International Standards Organization (ISO) 8601 format to specify date, time, or date and time instances. (The *xsd:duration* datatype specifies date and time intervals.)

The ISO 8601 format for date and time is *CCYY-MM-DDThh:mm:ss*, where *CC* is the century, *YY* is the year, *MM* is the month, and *DD* is the day of the month. *T* is the time separator, and *hh:mm:ss* represent hours, minutes, and seconds, which can include a decimal value. A minus sign (-) preceding *CCYY* indicates years before the Common Era. As an example, *2004-04-01T10:00:00* represents 10:00 A.M. on September 1, 2003. A *0000* value for the century and year is prohibited.

InfoPath translates an empty text box to an element similar to *<my:datePicker xmlns:xsi="http://www.w3.org/2001/XMLSchema-instance" xsi:nil="true"></my:datePicker>*. To accept a *nil* value, the schema definition for the field must contain a *nillable="true"* attribute, as in *<xsd:element name="datePicker" nillable="true" type="xsd:dateTime"/>*. Clearing the DatePicker Properties dialog box's Cannot Be Blank check box on the Data tab makes date values nillable.

An optional *Z* time-zone separator followed by a plus sign (+) or minus sign (-) enables specifying the difference in *hh:mm* format between local time and Universal Coordinated Time (UTC), also known as Zulu (Z) or Greenwich Mean Time (GMT). Unlike many other Microsoft XML-based applications and programming tools, InfoPath doesn't append the time zone information.

Dealing with Null date values

Microsoft SQL Server's SQLXML 3.0 and later add-ins translate Null date values to *0001-01-01T00:00:00Z{+|-}HH:00*. The actual value is *0001-01-01T00:00:00.0000000Z-08:00* for servers running on Pacific Standard Time (PST). If you type **1/1/0001 00:00:00 AM** as the default value in design mode or the actual value in data entry, InfoPath converts the value to 1/1/2001 12:00:00 A.M. InfoPath also can't handle negative century/year values. The only permissible value for a Null (empty) date value is a blank value in the date picker control's text box, which translates to *nil* for *nillable* date values.

Using Drop-Down Lists and List Boxes

Chapter 2 introduced the use of a drop-down Currency list in data entry mode, but none of the sample forms that you've worked with so far in design mode include drop-down lists. The NWOrdersEC.xsn template and its element-centric data source have fields–such as ShipVia and EmployeeID–that lend themselves to selection by drop-down lists. Figure 6-8 shows a preview of NWOrdersEC.xsn with default data supplied by the 11066.xml source document. Each section of the form represents a data source group: CustomerInfo, OrderInfo, and LineItems.

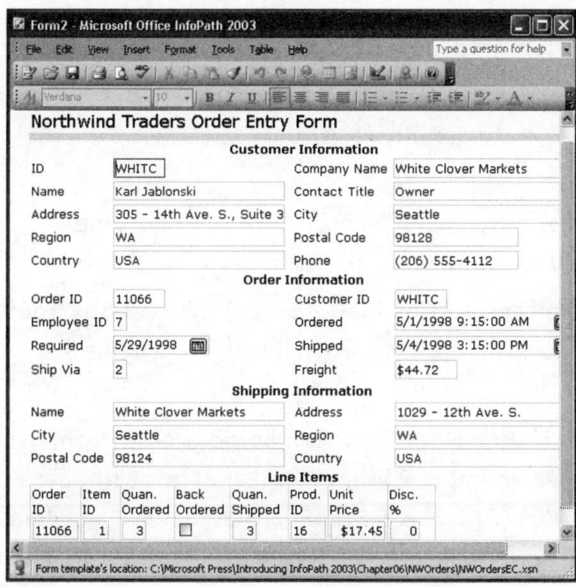

Figure 6-8 This is the initial version of the NWOrdersEC form in preview mode.

> **Using the sample files**
> Your C:\Microsoft Press\Introducing InfoPath 2003\Chapter06\NWOrders folder contains the NWOrdersEC.xsn template, which is the starting point for adding drop-down lists for the following three sections and for adding option button groups in the section "Option Buttons and Groups," later in this chapter. The completed version of the template is ...\NWOrdersFinal\NWOrders.xsn.

Drop-down lists and plain list boxes share common design mode features. Drop-down lists consume much less form real estate than plain list boxes, which makes drop-down lists the more popular type. The following sections deal with drop-down lists only; list boxes differ only in appearance.

As mentioned near the beginning of this chapter, items in drop-down lists consist of value/display name pairs. InfoPath offers five alternatives for populating drop-down lists: manually entered values you type on the Data tab of the Drop-Down List Properties dialog box, an XML data document, a database table, a Web service, or a Microsoft Windows SharePoint Services library or list. The following section covers the first option—manually entered values, which are similar to Microsoft Access's value lists for combo and list boxes. The section "Using Secondary Data Sources with Lists," later in this chapter, covers XML documents as a secondary data source. Chapters 13 and 14 show you how to use database tables or queries and XML Web services as secondary data sources.

Populating Lists with Manually Entered Values

To add list items, values, and display names manually and embed them in your form, follow these steps.

▶ **Replace the Ship Via text box with a drop-down list**

1. **Navigate to your C:\Microsoft Press\Introducing InfoPath 2003\Chapter06\NWOrders folder, and open the NWOrdersEC.xsn template in design mode.**
2. **Activate the Data Source task pane, and expand all group nodes to become familiar with the structure of the data source.**
3. **Right-click the Ship Via text box, and choose Change To, Drop-Down List Box from the shortcut menu to morph the control to a drop-down list that occupies the entire layout table cell.**
4. **Right-click the drop-down list, and choose Drop-Down List Box Properties from the shortcut menu to open the Drop-Down List Box Properties dialog box with the Data tab active. The Data tab's List Box Entries section contains a default Select item with no value and a 2 item added from the text box's default value, as shown here:**

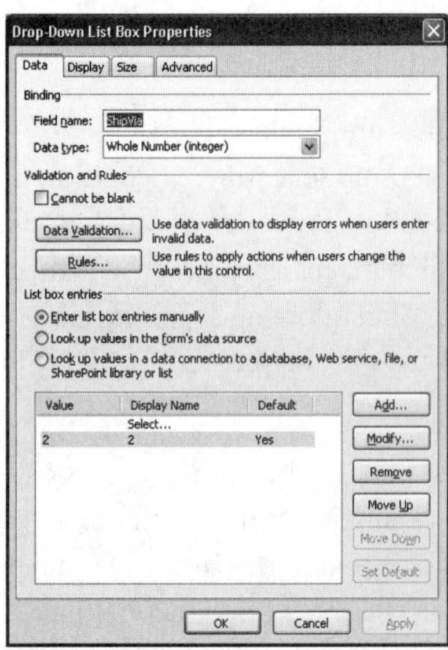

5. Select the first entry in the List Box Entries list, and click Modify to open the Modify Choice dialog box. Leave the default empty Value because the ShipVia field isn't required and needs a blank value, change *Select...* to **Select Shipper**, and click OK.
6. Click Set Default to make Select Shipper the default item.
7. Select the 2 item, and click Remove to delete it.
8. Click Add to open the Add Choice dialog box, type **1** as the Value and **Speedy Express** as the Display Name. Click OK to add the item.
9. Click Add again, but specify **2** and **United Package** in the Add Choice dialog box. Repeat the step again and add **3** and **Federal Shipping**. Your ShipVia list now appears as shown here:

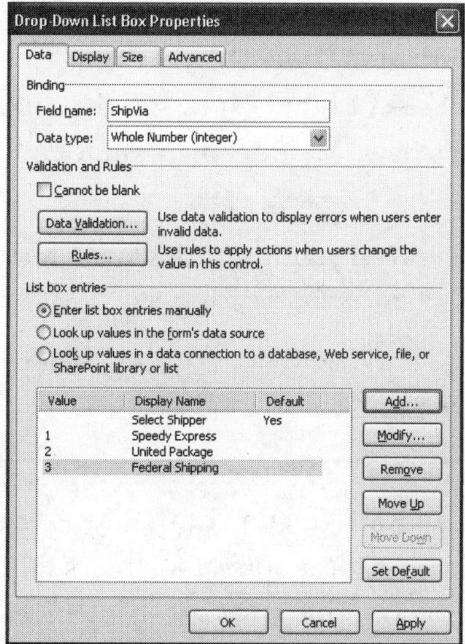

10. Click OK to apply your changes. Reduce the width of the control, click Preview Form, and open the list to verify the items, as shown here:

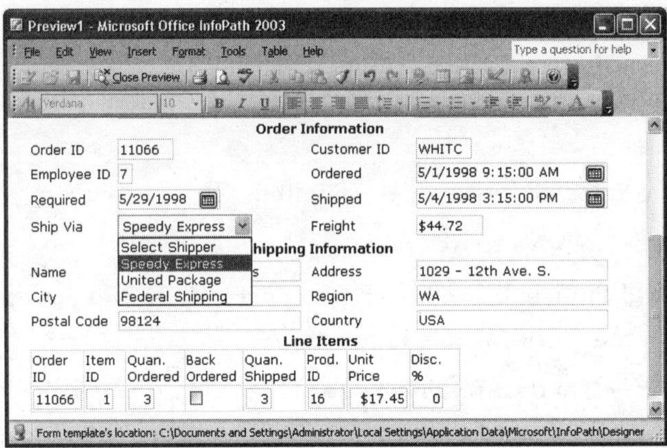

11. **Close the preview, and press Ctrl+S to save your changes, and choose File, Close to close the form**
12. **Choose File, Fill Out a Form, and click the Northwind Order Entry (EC) link to open the form with the template's default values. Select United Express in the drop-down list, save the form as NW11066.xml in a new \My Documents\InfoPath\Controls folder, and close it.**
13. **Reopen NW11066.xml to verify that InfoPath saved your drop-down list setting, and then close the form.**

Using Secondary Data Sources with Lists

Typing even a moderately short list in the Drop-Down List Properties dialog box can become tedious. In many cases, you can export an XML document that can serve as a secondary data source to populate the list. The ...\Chapter06\NWOrders folder contains four element-centric XML documents exported from Microsoft Office Access 2003 queries: CustLookup.xml, EmplLookup.xml, ProdLookup.xml, and ShipLookup.xml. In this section, you'll take advantage of the Data Connection Wizard to use an XML document as a secondary data source for a drop-down list. The source document is EmplLookup.xml. To replace the Employee ID text box with a drop-down list based on an XML document, follow these steps.

▶ Create a drop-down list populated by a secondary data source

1. **With the NWOrdersEC form open in design mode, convert the Employee ID text box to a drop-down list using the method described in step 3 of the previous procedure.**
2. **Open the Drop-Down List Box Properties dialog box, select the Look Up Values In A Data Connection To A Database, Web Service, File Or SharePoint Library Or List option, and click Add to open the Data Connection Wizard.**

3. Accept the default XML Data File option in the first page of the Wizard, and then click Next.
4. Browse to the C:\Microsoft Press\Introducing InfoPath 2003\Chapter06\NWOrders folder.
5. Double-click EmplLookup.xml to select it and close the dialog box, and click Next.
6. In the next screen of the wizard, accept the default data source name, leave the Automatically Retrieve Data When This Form Is Opened check box selected, and click Finish. You'll see the message box shown here:

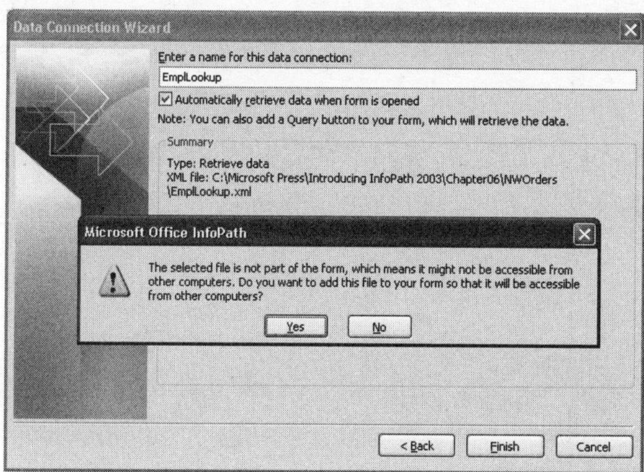

7. Click Yes to include the secondary data source document in the NWOrdersEC.xsn template, and return to the Drop Down List Box Properties dialog box.
8. Click the Select XPath button to the right of the empty Entries text box to open the Select A Field Or Group dialog box, and select the EmplLookup group node, as shown here. (The dataroot group and generated attribute nodes are artifacts of Access's Export As XML feature.)

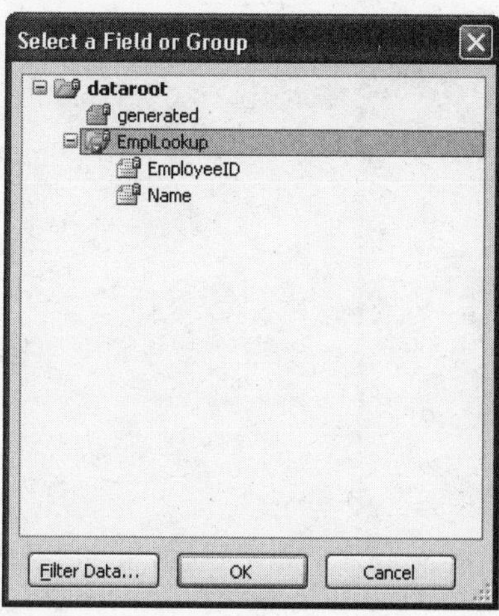

9. Click OK to return to the Properties dialog box, which automatically populates the Value and Display Name text boxes with EmployeeID.
10. The Name field, which concatenates the Employees table's FirstName and LastName fields, should serve as the Display Name value, so click the Select XPath button to the right of the Display Name text box to open the Select Field Or Group dialog box again.
11. Double-click the Name node to specify it as the Display Name value and return to the Properties dialog box, which now appears as shown here:

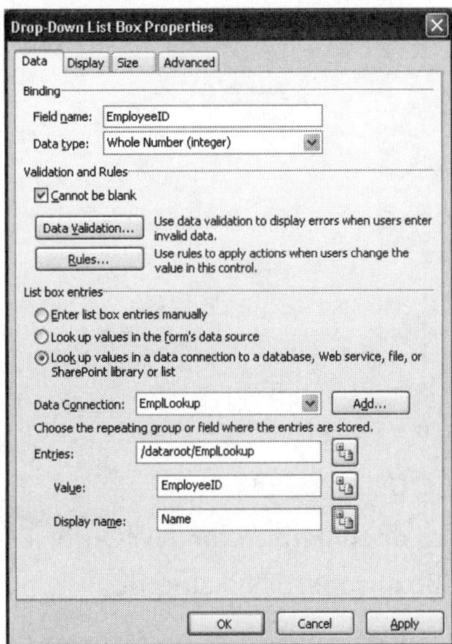

12. Click OK, click Preview Form, and open the Employee ID drop-down list. The original default value (7) for the EmployeeID field applies to the morphed drop-down list, so Robert King, the seventh name in the list, is selected by default, as shown here:

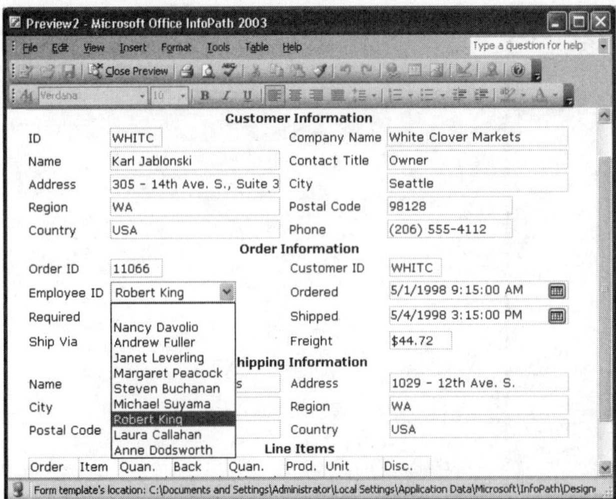

13. Save your template design, and repeat steps 12 and 13 of the previous procedure to verify that the form preserves changes you make to the EmployeeID list selection.

You might have noticed that the Cannot Be Blank check box was selected by default on the Drop-Down List Properties dialog box's Data tab, but the drop-down list contains a blank item at the top. Selecting the empty item displays a schema validation warning (a red asterisk).

Linking Lists to Text Boxes

In many cases, you probably want to display the value of a drop-down list selection, which often corresponds to the primary key field of a table, in an adjacent text box. Binding two controls to the same field synchronizes their values but adds a spurious Information icon to the controls that states the obvious–*Control stores duplicate data.* You can safely disregard this icon.

To display a list's selected value in a text box and synchronize the list selection with a value typed in a text box, follow these steps.

► **Bind a text box to the Ship Via drop-down list's value**

1. **Add a couple of spaces in front of the Ship Via drop-down list, move the insertion point to the left margin of the cell, and choose Insert, Text Box to open the Text Box Binding dialog box.**
2. **Expand the OrderInfo node, and double-click the ShipVia node, as shown here, to add a label and text box bound to the ShipVia field:**

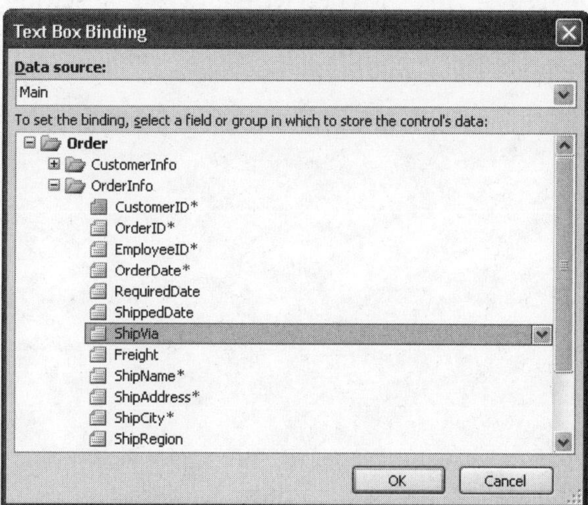

3. **Delete the added label, and reduce the width of the text box so that both controls are on a single line.**
4. **Repeat steps 1 through 3 for the Employee ID drop-down list, binding the text box to the EmployeeID field.**
5. **Save your template design, preview the form, and verify that the text box values synchronize with drop-down list selections and vice versa.**

Adding Check Boxes and Option Buttons

Check boxes and option buttons share a common property–they have two states: *on* (selected) or *off* (cleared.) Check boxes bind to a single field; multiple option buttons automatically form an InfoPath *option (button) group*, which also binds to a single field. If you've designed Access forms, you'll find the default behavior of InfoPath's check boxes and option groups to be almost identical to their Access counterparts.

Adding Check Boxes

The NWOrdersEC.xsn template includes a check box to indicate whether an order line item was backordered. Check boxes most commonly bind to fields of the XML Schema's *boolean* datatype, which is specified for the backordered field, but it's possible to specify any of the eight InfoPath data types that are valid for text boxes. Figure 6-9 shows the default settings for check boxes bound to fields of InfoPath's True/False (*boolean*) data type. Value When Cleared and Value When Checked settings are limited to (Blank), TRUE, FALSE, 0, or 1. The TRUE and FALSE settings set element values to *true* and *false*. The XML Schema specification allows *0* or *1* values, but *true* or *false* are preferred.

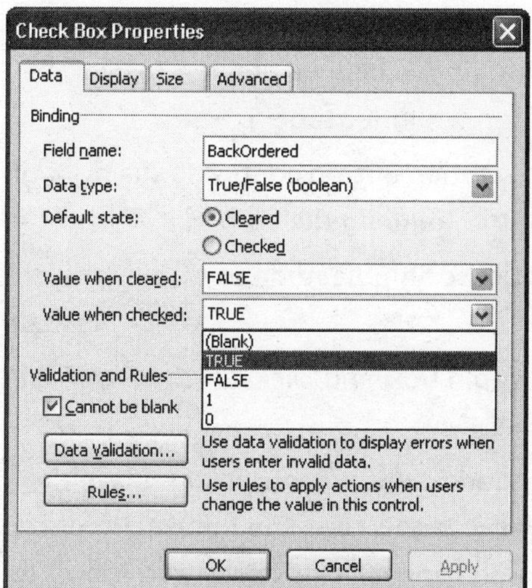

Figure 6-9 This Data tab for a check box control displays the value options for the control's checked state.

If you select an InfoPath data type other than True/False (*boolean*), you can type appropriate text in the Value When Cleared and Value When Checked text boxes–even dates and times. You could reverse the True/False logic by selecting FALSE or 0 for checked and TRUE or 1 for cleared, but doing so is definitely not recommended.

Option Buttons and Groups

When you add an option button to a form, InfoPath displays the dialog box shown in Figure 6-10. Although you can select a single option button, doing so violates the ground rules of UI design: an option group must contain two or more buttons, and only one button of the group can be selected at a time. By default, InfoPath assigns option buttons sequential numeric values, starting with 1.

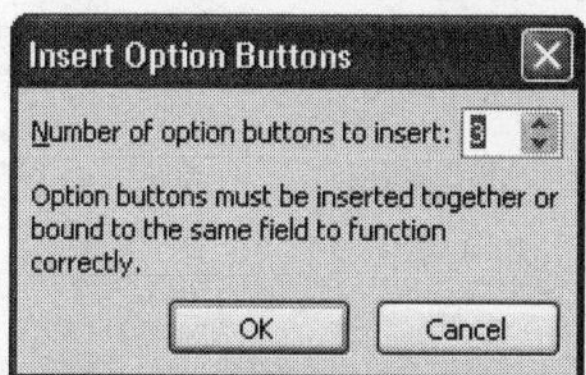

Figure 6-10 The Insert Option Button dialog box, showing the default number of buttons selected.

To replace the NWOrdersEC.xsn template's Ship Via drop-down list with a three-button option group, follow these steps.

▶ **Add an option group with four option buttons**

1. Select and delete the Ship Via drop-down list. (If you choose Change To, Option Button, InfoPath inserts a single option button without a label.)
2. Activate the Controls task pane, and drag the Option Button control to the right of the Ship Via text box to open the Option Button Binding dialog box.
3. Expand the OrderInfo node, and double-click the ShipVia node to display the Insert Option Button dialog box.
4. Select 4 in the Number Of Options To Insert spin box, and click OK to insert four option buttons with Ship Via labels in the cell.
5. Delete the linefeed equivalents after the first and third buttons, and replace the labels with **None**, **Speedy**, **United**, and **Federal**. In this case, the Information icon that warns about double-bound controls doesn't appear. Optionally, add spaces to the left of the Speedy label to align it vertically with the None button, as shown here:

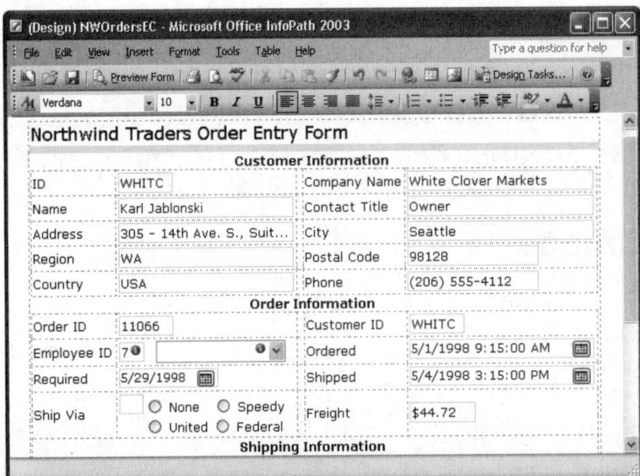

6. Right-click the None option button, choose Option Button Properties from the shortcut menu, remove the 1 value, and select the This Button Is Selected By Default check box, as shown here:

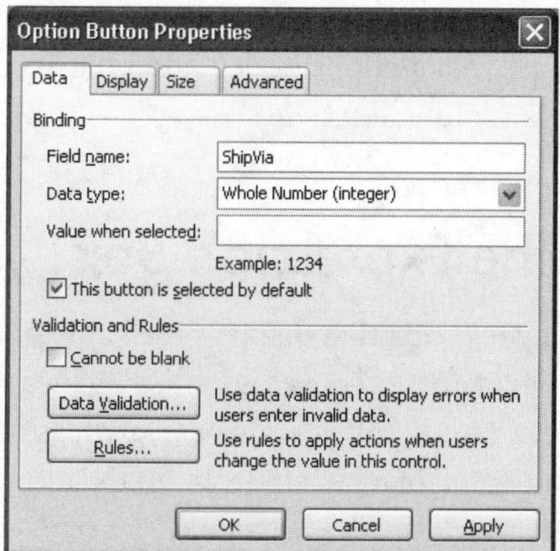

7. **Click OK to close the dialog box, right-click each of the remaining three buttons, choose Option Button Properties from the shortcut menu, and substitute 1, 2, and 3 for their values.**
8. **Click Preview Form, and click the three option buttons to verify that the buttons and the adjacent text box are bound to the ShipVia field, as shown here:**

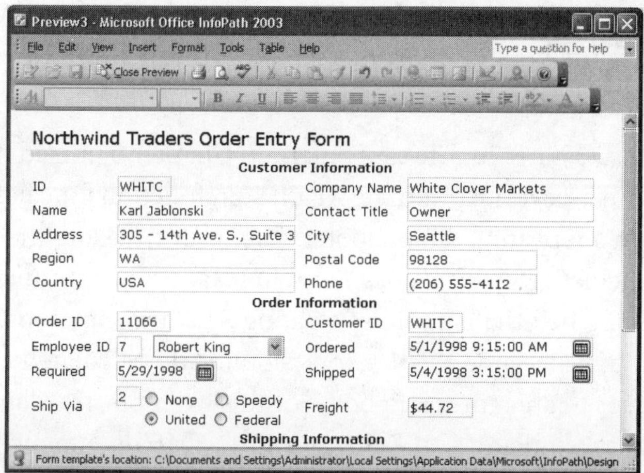

9. **Option buttons aren't an efficient use of form real estate, so press Ctrl+Z repeatedly to undo the changes, or close the template and do *not* save your changes.**

Here's a general InfoPath form design recommendation: Use drop-down lists or conventional list boxes, not option groups, for situations in which more than two or three buttons are required. Drop-down lists usually are the best choice, unless you want the user to see all or most options without taking any action. In the latter case, consider using a conventional list box instead. The sample Applicant Rating form that you can open from the Fill Out A Form dialog box's Sample Forms list is an exception to the recommendation because of its clever use of option buttons to calculate average rating values for several optional sections. Calculating the average ratings requires code to execute multiple XPath functions.

Calculating Values with the Expression Box

An expression box is an unbound, read-only text box that displays the value of an XPath expression. The most common use of expression boxes is to display the result of mathematical operations on numeric field values, but you also use expression boxes to display text values, such as the full name of a person from firstName and lastName field values. As you learned in Chapter 3, XPath is a language for navigating the in-memory representation of XML documents–called the *XML Document Object Model*, or XML DOM–to select specific nodes and subnodes by name. If you specify a leaf node or an attribute name as the expression, XPath returns the value of the node or attribute to the expression box. XPath also offers aggregate functions, such as *sum* and *count*, and common mathematical operators for addition, subtraction, multiplication, and division of numerical field values. XPath also has string functions, such as *concat* for concatenating (combining) strings and *substring* for extracting partial string values. The JScript behind InfoPath's sample forms makes extensive use of XPath expressions and operators.

The section "Summing Numeric Values in a Table Footer," in Chapter 5, introduced you to the read-only expression box control and the XPath sum function for calculating totals of numeric values in a repeating table's footer. The section "Using the Insert Formula Feature to Calculate Default Values," also in Chapter 5, introduced you to the Insert Formula dialog box that simplifies creating XPath expressions. In this section's procedure, you use the same XPath expression to add calculated extended order line item values to an expression box. For this example, the data source for the NWOrderEC.xsn template is an element-centric XML document, so the XPath expression you create doesn't include the @ symbols that designate attribute values. Instead of using the Insert Field Or Group dialog box to add fields to the XPath expression, you type the XPath expression into the Insert Formula dialog box's Formula text box, because typing the expression is faster than selecting individual fields and then editing the expression.

To add an Extended Amount expression box to the LineItem repeating table, follow these steps.

▶ Add an expression box and an XPath expression

1. Open the NWOrdersEC.xsn template in design mode, and scroll to the LineItem repeating table.
2. Select the Disc. % column, and choose Table, Insert, Columns To The Right to add a column for the expression box. Increase the width of the column by about half its default width.
3. Position the insertion point in the added column's bottom cell, choose Insert, More Controls to activate the Controls task pane. In the Insert Controls list, scroll to and click the Expression Box item to open the Insert Expression Box dialog box.
4. Click the Edit Formula (*fx*) button to the right of the XPath text box to open the Insert Formula dialog box.
5. Type **QuanOrdered * UnitPrice * (1 - Discount)** in the Formula text box, and click the Verify Formula button to test your expression, which adds underlines to the field names, as shown here:

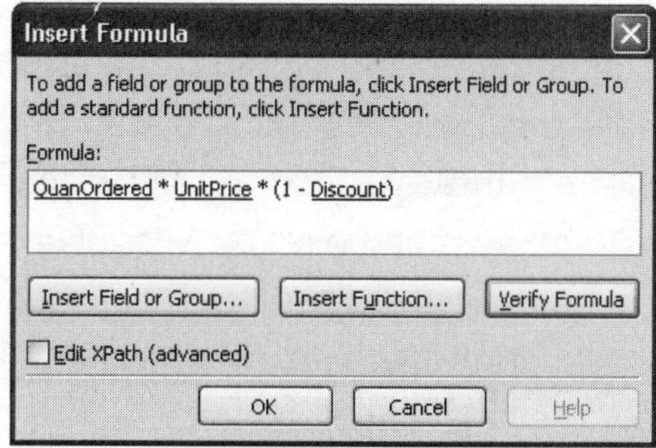

6. Click OK twice to close the two dialog boxes, right-click the newly inserted expression box, choose Expression Box Properties from the shortcut menu to open its Properties dialog box, and select Decimal in the Format As list on the General tab. Click the Format button to open the Decimal Format dialog box, select Currency as the format and 2 for Decimal Places, and click OK twice to apply the formatting. The expression box displays *$52.35* as the calculated value from the default values for QuanShipped, UnitPrice, and Discount.
7. Type **Extended Amount** as the expression box's label, select the expression box, and click the Align Right button.

8. **Click Preview Form to test the calculation by adding two or more line items with different quantity and discount values, as shown here:**

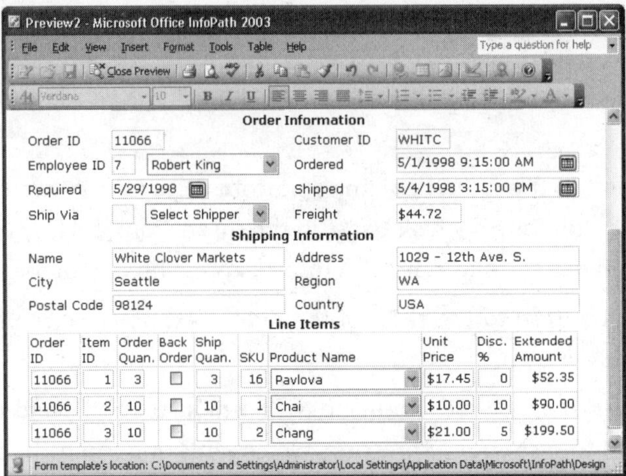

9. **Close the preview, and save your template changes.**

Calculations of this type are the most common use for expression boxes added to the data row of repeating tables. You use XPath functions to add counts, sums, and averages–calculated by dividing the sum by the count–to expression boxes in table footers. Unfortunately, you can't total values of expression boxes by XPath expressions you type in the XPath text box of the Expression Box Properties dialog box's General tab. You must add code to perform calculations with expression box values, because expression boxes aren't bound to data source fields. Chapter 17, "Writing Advanced Event Handlers," illustrates summing expression box values with Visual Basic .NET code.

Incorporating Pictures

Adding pictures to a form is a straightforward process, although the methods differ from those you used in Chapter 2 to add pictures to rich text box controls. Conventional picture and ink picture controls store the binary values of Graphics Interchange Format (GIF) files in elements of XML Schema's *base64Binary* datatype. (Conventional picture controls can use most common graphics file types; ink picture controls are limited to GIF images.) Conventional picture controls also support linked images; ink picture controls don't.

The Gory Details of Base64 Encoding

IETF RFC 2045, "Multipurpose Internet Mail Extensions (MIME) Part One: Format of Internet Message Bodies" (at *www.ietf.org/rfc/rfc2045.txt*) defines Base64 Content-Transfer-Encoding in section 6.8. The objective of Base64 encoding is to permit binary data to be expressed by groups of 6-bit representations of printable ASCII characters. The allowable 65-character ASCII subset includes A through Z, a through z, 0 through 9, + and /, and the equal sign (=), which is a padding character. The subset doesn't include characters—such as <, >, ', " and &—that are illegal within XML element and attribute values. Encoding binary data occurs in 3-byte (24-bit) chunks, which the encoding processor converts to four 6-bit character codes ranging from 0 through 63. The output chunk for four printable characters represented in conventional 8-bit ASCII is 4 bytes, which causes a 33 percent increase in the size of Base64-encoded data.

See Also Base64 encoding supports both ASCII and EBCDIC as input and output, but Base64 is used more commonly for encoding binary data. For more information about ASCII and EBCDIC standards, see the sidebar "Encoding Text," in Chapter 3. Open the IPControls.xml file—mentioned in the section "Relating Controls to Data Types," earlier in this chapter—and scroll to the <my:pictureControl ...> element to see an example of a Base64-encoded GIF image.

The word *what* encoded as Base64 is *d2hhdA==*. The four input characters become six encoded characters plus two characters of padding represented by the two equal signs. The padding characters, which occur at the end of the encoded stream, compensate for two missing characters in the second 3-byte chunk; *wha* is the first 3-byte chunk. Base64 decoders interpret the first padding character encountered as a shortcut to the end of the data stream.

Adding Picture Controls

Adding a picture control to a template automatically adds a field of the Picture (base64Binary) InfoPath data type to the data source. When you drag a picture control to a template, the Insert Picture Control dialog box opens, as shown in Figure 6-11. In this dialog box, you can choose between incorporating the Base64-encoded image data in the data document (as a *base64Binary* element or attribute value) or adding a link to a valid URI for the image (as an *anyURI* element or attribute value). The URI must point to a file that's accessible to all potential users from a server share or a valid Internet or intranet URL for an image file.

Figure 6-11 The Insert Picture Control dialog box lets you choose whether to embed the Base64-encoded graphic in the data document or add a link to the file.

The picture control adds by default a placeholder for images to be inserted by the user, as shown in Figure 6-1. You can substitute a default picture for the placeholder in design mode by clicking the Browse button on the Data tab of the Picture Properties dialog box, shown in Figure 6-12, and specifying a file or an Internet URL in the Insert Picture dialog box's File Name text box. Your C:\Microsoft Press\Introducing InfoPath 2003\Chapter06\IPControls folder includes the OakLeaf.gif file for the leaf logo shown earlier in Figure 6-2. You can insert the same image using a link to *http://www.oakleaf.ws/OakLeaf.gif.*

Keeping XML data documents self-contained

It's tempting to specify URLs for linked images rather than embedding large amounts of image data in the data document. If your data document is a message in a workflow process, such as an insurance claim, the linked image file might not be accessible to all workflow intermediaries. Despite the added message overhead, it's a safer—and thus a better—practice to include the Base64-encoded information in the XML data document. Doing this is especially important if you digitally sign the document. Chapter 11 describes how to add digital signatures to a form.

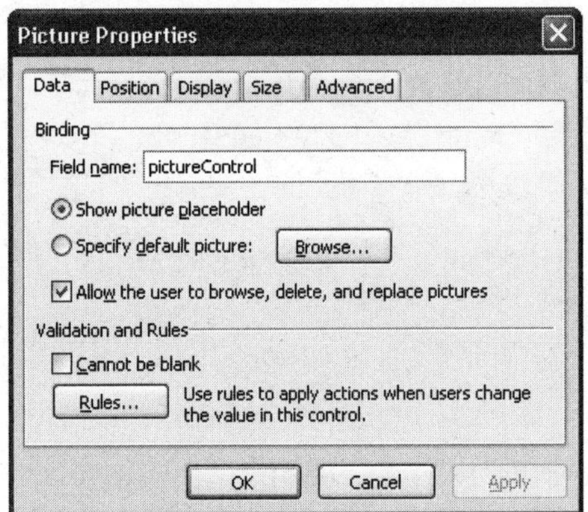

Figure 6-12 The Picture Properties dialog box's Data tab has controls for adding a default image and restricting users' ability to browse for images.

You can prevent users from changing the default image by clearing the Allow The User To Browse For New Pictures check box, but doing this is counterproductive–the default image becomes embedded in every data document users produce. If you want to add a static graphic to a form, it's much more efficient to choose Insert, Picture and embed an image in the form's template.

The Position tab in the Picture Properties dialog box controls text wrapping; you can choose In Line With Text, Left, or Right wrapping styles. Only the Height and Width text boxes are enabled on the Size tab.

Using Ink Picture Controls

Ink picture controls add an empty region to the form in which Tablet PC–equipped users can ink their signatures or draw sketches. InfoPath saves the strokes as a Base64-encoded GIF file for compatibility with conventional PCs, Web sites, and databases. The only property values you can change using the Ink Picture Properties dialog box are the field name, the height and width, and the settings on the Advanced tab.

Converting strokes to text

The Tablet Input Panel (TIP) appears when Tablet PC users give the focus to an editable control, such as a text box or a bulleted list. As users enter strokes in the TIP, the operating system converts the strokes to characters in the text box. Other controls, such as date pickers, drop-down lists, list boxes, and option buttons, respond to the stylus directly.

Chapter Summary

InfoPath's set of 13 basic controls and lists contribute to form design versatility. Some general-purpose input controls, such as text boxes, can bind to fields of all but one of the nine XML Schema datatypes that InfoPath supports. Special-purpose input controls bind to specific data types–date picker controls bind only to *date*, *time*, or *dateTime* elements or attributes, and picture controls store image data as *base64Binary* element values. Rich text boxes bind to *string* elements; InfoPath's XHTML data type is an identifier for formatted text, not an XML Schema data type. Bulleted, numbered, and plain lists bind to *string* elements and support optional XHTML character formatting. General-purpose input controls, including bound hyperlinks, also bind to *anyURI* elements, which usually contain URNs or URLs, but aren't limited to these constructs.

Drop-down lists, list boxes, and option button groups are selection controls, which limit users' choices to two or more values. Selection controls have value/display name pairs; the value of the selected item or option binds to an element or attribute. (Option button display names are labels.) The *integer* datatype is most common for selection control values, but you can bind the value to other common XML Schema datatypes. Check boxes, which are limited to selected or cleared states and don't have display names, usually bind to *boolean* fields but offer the same datatype choices as other selection controls.

You create value/display name pairs for drop-down lists or list boxes by adding item entries on the Data tab of the Properties dialog box. Alternatively, you can use the Data Connection Wizard to create a secondary data source that provides the value/display name pairs. The wizard can generate secondary data sources from XML documents, database tables or queries, or XML Web services. XPath expressions specify the secondary data source fields for values and display names.

Expression boxes are unbound, read-only text boxes that display the result of XPath expressions. XPath expressions perform calculations on numeric fields or manipulate text values. The most common use of expression boxes is counting rows and computing totals or averages of numeric values in repeating tables or sections.

Q&A

Q. Why should I be concerned with control data types, taking into account that XML data documents store all values as text?

A. The need for data type checking of XML data documents (infosets) was one of the primary incentives for the development of the XML Schema recommendation. One of InfoPath's strong points is schema-based validation of all form data entry values, which is called *strong (data) typing* by many XML-aware applications. If you type alphabetic characters in a text box bound to an *integer* or a *double* element, InfoPath flags the data type error with a dashed red outline and displays a *This form includes errors. Do you still want to save it?* message when you attempt to save the form. You can save a form with errors, but you can't submit it to a database or an XML Web service. Declarative data validation can detect some data type entry errors but isn't an adequate substitute for strong data type checking by the form's schema.

Q. Why is InfoPath's Whole Number (*integer*) the most common data type for list box values?

A. The original source or ultimate destination for information contained in XML data documents often is a database. Primary key values relate a display name to a particular row of a database table or query. As an example, an EmployeeID value uniquely identifies a record in the Northwind database's Employees table. The most common primary key data type is a 32-bit integer partly because most databases support automatic generation of sequential-integer primary key values. Some tables use character values, such as the five-letter CustomerID field of Northwind's Customers table, as the primary key, but this practice is less common.

Q. How do I update an XML file that serves as the secondary data source for a list box?

A. The answer depends on whether you incorporated the XML source file in the template file. If you don't specify inclusion in the template file, you can replace the XML file with an updated version or edit it with an XML-aware application. In this case, all users must have access to the file from a server share when they open a new form or edit an existing form. If you incorporate the XML file in the template, you must rebuild the template's .xsn file each time you change the XML file's contents.

Q. Are links to image files on a public Web site safe enough for a picture control?

A. Not for forms of moderate or higher importance. When you link a file, even to a well-known and professionally maintained site, you add uncertainty to the validity of the form. If the form's recipient can't connect to the site and download the image, the workflow process is interrupted. In many cases, form intermediaries are server-based processes that might be blocked from direct Internet access by a firewall.

On Your Own

This additional exercise tests your understanding of secondary data sources and XPath expressions that populate expression box controls. You add a Product Name drop-down list and three expression boxes to the NWOrdersEC.xsn form. Figure 6-13 shows a preview of the Line Items section's final appearance.

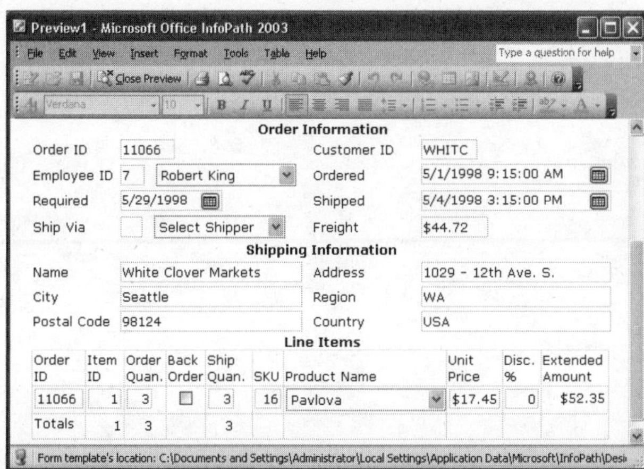

Figure 6-13 A preview of the Northwind Traders Order Entry form after adding the controls in this exercise.

1. Open the NWOrdersEC.xsn form in design mode, change the Prod. ID column name to **SKU**, and reduce the width of the Quan. Ordered, Quan. Shipped, and SKU columns, as shown in Figure 6-13, to make more space for adding the Product Name drop-down list.
2. Expand the width of the Line Item table to the border of the master table. Add a table column to the right of the SKU column, and adjust the column widths to leave as much room as possible for the added list.

3. Add a drop-down list that uses the ProdLookup.xml file as its secondary data source.
4. Add a footer to the repeating table with **Totals** as the label in its first column.
5. Add an expression box in column B to count the number of line items in the order. The XPath expression is *count(OrderInfo/LineItems/LineItem)* to display the number of items in a group. For this example, the XPath expression requires the full path to the group or field.6. Add expression boxes in columns C and E to total the quantities ordered and shipped. The XPath expressions are *sum(OrderInfo/LineItems/LineItem/QuanOrdered)* and *sum(OrderInfo/LineItems/LineItem/QuanShipped)*, respectively.
6. Format all expression boxes as Whole Number, and right-align their contents.
7. Test your form in preview mode, save the template, and save a data document with several line item entries to verify that the form works as expected.

CHAPTER 7

Formatting Forms

In this chapter, you will learn how to:

- **Establish a standard format for the InfoPath forms you create**
- **Apply color schemes to master tables and background colors to forms**
- **Embed a logo or other image in a form**
- **Add preformatted headings in table cells**
- **Add hyperlinks to graphics and text**
- **Format table cells and controls with borders and background colors**
- **Apply conditional formatting to text box controls**
- **Use the Format Painter to apply a selected special text format to labels and controls**

For more information:

- **See the World Wide Web Consortium's (W3C) Cascading Style Sheets level 1 recommendation at *www.w3.org/TR/REC-CSS1*.**
- **Go to msdn.microsoft.com, expand the Web Development node of the table of contents, and click the Cascading Style Sheets node to learn more about how Microsoft implements the CSS specification in Microsoft Internet Explorer.**
- **Preview the section "Validating Numerical Values" in Chapter 8 for additional expressions that you can use for conditional formatting.**

The preceding three chapters of Part II in this book, "Designing InfoPath Forms," concentrate on the technicalities of creating, laying out, and adding sections and controls of various types to forms. This chapter takes a different tack; it deals primarily with form presentation issues, such as the use of graphics and colors to embellish your form designs, and using conditional formatting to alter the appearance of text box controls. Working through this chapter's exercises won't turn you into a full-fledged graphic artist, but you'll learn some techniques to give your forms a more professional appearance and, hopefully, make them easier on users' eyes. You'll also learn how to minimize data entry errors using conditional

To work through this chapter:

- You need experience working with Microsoft InfoPath layout tables, which are described in Chapter 5, "Laying Out Forms."
- You should be familiar with picture, date picker, drop-down list box, and check box control characteristics in data entry and design modes. Chapter 2, "Filling Out Forms," and Chapter 6, "Adding Basic Controls and Lists," cover these subjects.
- You should have the sample forms for this chapter from the CD that accompanies this book installed in your C:\Microsoft Press\Introducing InfoPath 2003\Chapter07 folder. The sample forms are required to complete the exercises in this chapter.

formatting. Conditional formatting lets you change the appearance of, hide, or disable controls in response to field value changes.

The black and white screen captures in this book will make it difficult for you to see the effect of altering colors. You'll find that performing the exercises in this chapter will be much more illustrative.

Adopting an Organization-Wide Format

The section "Adhering to Design Standards" in Chapter 5, "Laying Out Forms" describes the benefits of establishing a uniform approach for designing master layout tables and their embedded contents. Most example forms in Chapter 5 and successive chapters use a standard, two-row master table in which the form title appears in the first row and all other form components appear in the second row. This base design lets you add a standard background color to the master table for all forms you create.

The figures in this book and the examples in this chapter use the standard Microsoft Windows XP theme. If your organization has adopted a custom Windows XP color scheme or theme, you'll undoubtedly want to adopt background, control, and, possibly, border colors for tables, controls, or both that complement the scheme. Bear in mind that you're not designing a Web page or advertising your organization wares or services with InfoPath forms. The best policy for adding color and graphic images to forms is conservatism—regardless of your political persuasion.

Applying Color Schemes and Background Colors

InfoPath comes with 17 predefined color combinations, which you select in design mode from the Color Schemes task list, as shown in Figure 7-1. Each combination has six color squares, but most schemes have duplicate colors in positions 4 and 6 (numbered from left to right). You apply a color scheme to your form's master layout table by clicking the name of the scheme in the Color Schemes task pane. Layout tables, repeating tables, and sections are transparent by default, so they receive the color scheme's background color if you haven't previously applied shading to a table or section. (The 25 sample InfoPath forms use the Blue color scheme, but they don't embed sections and repeating tables in a master layout table.)

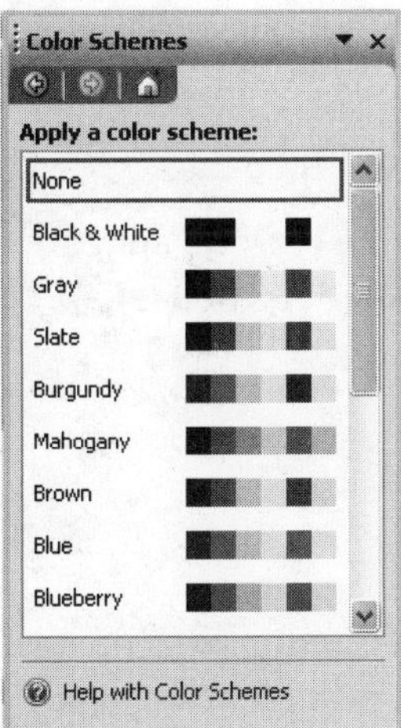

Figure 7-1 The Color Schemes task list lets you select one of 17 predefined sets of colors for form, table, and control backgrounds and text.

Here's how InfoPath applies the colors of the scheme you select to a form's master layout table:

- The title background receives the color of position 1, and the title text changes from black to the color in position 4.
- The title underline changes to the color of position 2.
- The background of row 2 in the master table becomes the color of position 4.
- Default repeating table borders, which are the same color as the default title underline, also receive position 4's color. Table borders you add aren't affected, unless you accidentally made them the same color as the default repeating table borders (which isn't likely).
- The background of controls, such as text boxes, color pickers, and drop-down lists, remains white.

This chapter's exercises use the NWOrderCh6.xsn template in your C:\Microsoft Press\Introducing InfoPath 2003\Chapter07\NWOrdersCh6 folder. This template is a copy of the NWOrdersFinal.xsn example form from Chapter 6.

The Bright Blue color scheme is well suited to Windows XP's default theme. The position 1 color almost matches the title bar color in the InfoPath window, and the position 3 color is similar to the toolbar background. To add the Bright Blue color scheme to the NWOrdersCh6.xsn template, follow the steps on the next page.

▶ Apply a color scheme

1. **Open NWOrdersCh6.xsn in design mode.**
2. **Choose Format, Color Schemes to activate the Color Schemes task pane.**
3. **In the task pane, click Bright Blue in the Apply A Color Scheme list. The appearance of the title and content rows in your master table changes, as shown here.**

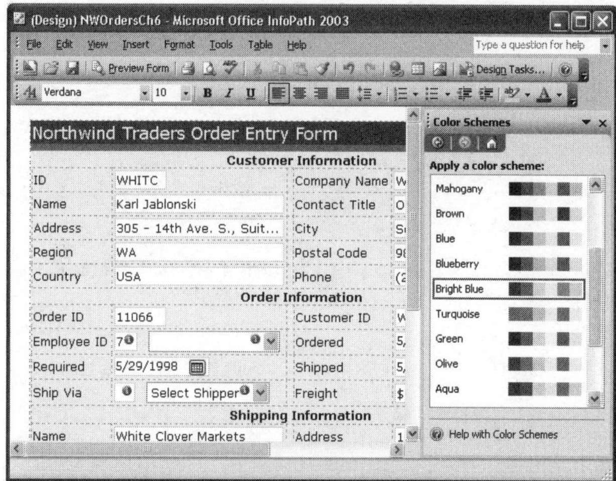

4. **Click Preview Form to check the changes. If necessary, scroll to the bottom of the form to verify that adding the color scheme changed the repeating tables default border to the position 2 color.**
5. **Close the preview, and save the template as NWBrightBlue.xsn in a new \My Documents\InfoPath\Formatting subfolder.**

If you want to remove the color scheme and revert to the original design, click None in the Apply A Color Scheme list.

To establish a uniform brightness level within the form's window, which users might find easier on their eyes, you can surround the master table with a background color. You add a background color by choosing Format, Background Color to display the View Properties dialog box. The default Background Color selection is Automatic, which translates to no applied color (the window's background color). Opening the list displays a color picker control. After you apply a color scheme to a form, the scheme's six colors appear as selections in square buttons at the top of the color picker, as shown in Figure 7-2. (Before you apply a color scheme, these buttons aren't present.)

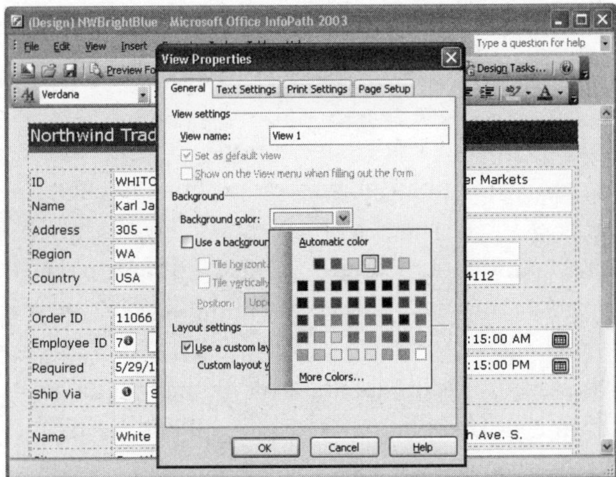

Figure 7-2 This template has the color of position 4 (*primaryLight*) applied as the view's background color.

To add a background color to the NWBrightBlue.xsn template, follow these steps.

▶ **Apply a background color**

1. **With NWBrightBlue.xsn open in design mode, choose Format, Background Color or Format, View Properties to open the View Properties dialog box with the General tab active.**
2. **Open the Background Color list, and choose one of the six scheme colors—position 4 for this example.**
3. **Click OK to add the background color to the outside of the master table.**
4. **Open a maximized preview to check the form's appearance.**
5. **Save your changes.**

To remove a background color, open the View Properties dialog box and choose Automatic in the Background Color list box. As an alternative to a background color, you can add a picture (a bitmap image) to serve as the form's background.

Embedding Logos and Static Graphics

The section "Picture Controls" in Chapter 6 explains how to add picture controls whose binary data is embedded in Picture (*base64Binary*) fields of the form's XML data document. You also can embed logos or other static graphics in templates. If you've worked with Microsoft Access forms, an InfoPath embedded picture corresponds to an Access image control with an embedded bitmap, such as that of the

Switchboard form in the Northwind sample database. You can insert a picture from a file or from a clip art image. For clip art images, use the process described in the Chapter 2 section "Inserting Pictures into Rich Text Boxes."

The examples in this section use the Northwind Traders logo captured as a Graphics Interchange Format (GIF) file from the Switchboard form and modified to change the background color from dark gray to the *primaryLight* background color. You don't need to change the background color of transparent GIF files. Adding an image to a form adds a FileName.ext copy of the original graphics file to the .xsn file, where FileName is eight random hexadecimal characters (0 to 8 and A to F), and ext is the source file's extension. You might see a thumbs.db database file in the template's folder after you add a logo or other image. This file holds thumbnail images for graphics files in the folder; it isn't required, and you can safely erase it.

Adding the logo to a vacant or added table cell makes it easier to control the spacing between a logo or graphic and its surrounding text, as well as the alignment of the image. To add, resize, and pad a logo included with the sample files for this chapter, follow these steps.

▶ Insert a logo from a file

1. **With the NWBrightBlue.xsn template open in design mode, position the cursor at the start of the Customer Information label.**
2. **Choose Table, Insert, Rows Above to add another row to the master table. (The added row includes an underline.)**
3. **Press Ctrl+L, or click the toolbar's Align Left button to remove the inherited centered alignment.**
4. **With the cursor in the added row, choose Table, Split Cells, specify 2 columns and leave the default 1 row in the Split Cells dialog box, and click OK to create two columns.**
5. **Click in the left column of the added row, and choose Insert, Picture, From File to open the Open dialog box, which defaults to your My Pictures folder.**
6. **Navigate to your C:\Microsoft Press\Introducing InfoPath 2003\Chapter07\ NWBrightBlue folder, double-click the NWLogoBrightBlue.gif image, which has a background color that matches the *primaryLight* color in the Bright Blue color scheme, and drag the bottom of the row to the bottom of the picture, as shown here.**

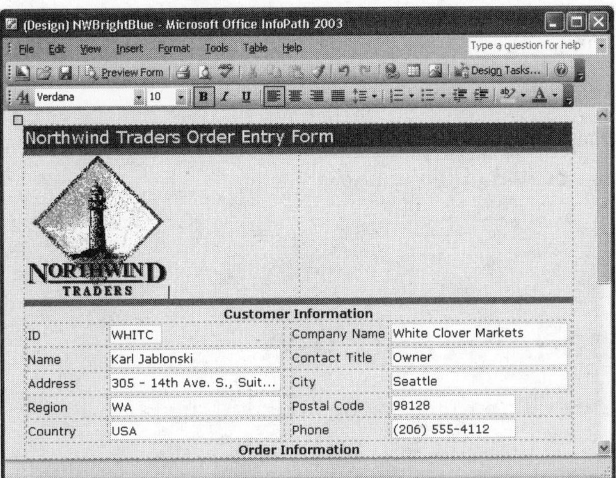

▶ Resize and reposition the logo

1. The logo is rather large, so click the image and press Alt+Enter or right click the image, and choose Format Picture to open the dialog box of the same name.
2. Click the Size tab, type a smaller value, such as **85**, in the Height text box, and click Apply to test the new size, as shown here.

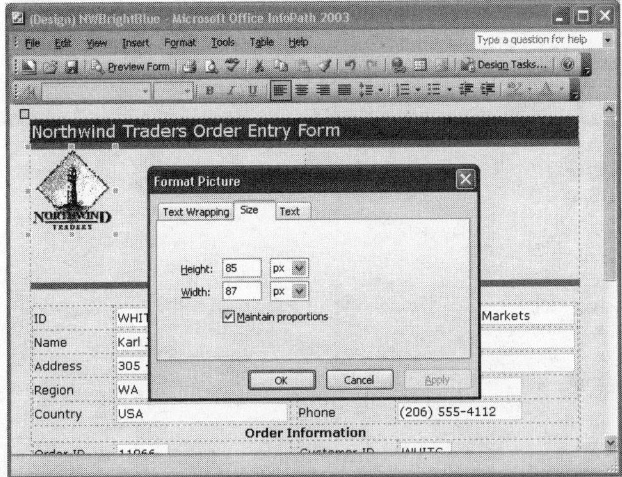

3. Click the Text tab and type alternate text for the logo, such as **Northwind Traders Logo**, and click OK to close the dialog box. The alternate text appears when users select the Always Expand ALT Text For Images check box under the Accessibility heading of Internet Explorer's Advanced tab of the Internet Options dialog box.
4. Right-click the left cell outside the image region, choose Table Properties, and click the Cell tab.

5. **Add a top and bottom margin to the logo by specifying 5 pixels of padding to the top and bottom of the cell, leave the default 1 pixel left and right padding, and click OK to close the dialog box.**
6. **Drag the bottom of the row up to the bottom of the image, and drag the cell divider to the right of the newly padded image.**
7. **Save your changes.**

Working with Headings and Text

A lot of empty space lies to the right of the logo you added in the preceding section, so a natural inclination is to fill the hole with a slogan, organization propaganda, or user instructions. Giving in to this temptation lets you try adding InfoPath's preformatted headings to a table cell.

The Pick Formatting To Apply list in the Font task pane has HTML heading styles 1 through 5, Normal (10-point Verdana is the default), and Clear Formatting choices. Applying a color scheme assigns the *primaryVeryDark* color to headings. The larger headings enable you to add outlandishly formatted text, as shown in Figure 7-3. ("Before" has the orange *accentDark* color applied.)

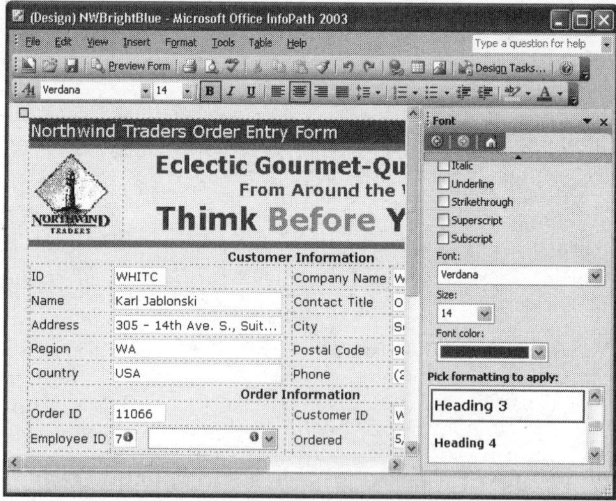

Figure 7-3 This is an example of overdoing the addition of headings and applying a garish font color to a form with the Bright Blue color scheme.

To add and format headings in the cell to the right of the logo that you added to the NWBrightBlue.xsn template, follow these steps:

▶ **Add, center, and format headings**

1. **In the NWBrightBlue.xsn template, position the cursor in the cell to the right of the picture.**
2. **Press Ctrl+D or choose Format, Font to open the Fonts task pane and select Heading 2 (18-point Verdana bold.)**
3. **Type a few words, such as Eclectic Gourmet-Quality Foods.**
4. **Press Enter to create a new line, select Heading 3 (14 point), and type From Around the World.**
5. **Press Enter again, select Heading 1 (24 point), and type a user warning, such as Think Before You Type.**
6. **Center the text that you just typed.**
7. **Use the mouse to select a word, such as "Before," to emphasize, open the Font Color list in the task pane, and select the position 5 color (*accentDark*), which applies the selected color's complement to the currently selected text.**
8. **Click the emphasized word to deselect it and display the selected color, orange for this example.**
9. **Save the changes, if you like them.**

If you want to remove the formatting, select the text and click the Clear Formatting item in the Pick Formatting To Apply list.

You also can apply the color scheme to the labels on your form, although doing this might reduce their contrast if you haven't applied a bold attribute. The three bold form section headings are good candidates for the *primaryVeryDark* color.

Adding Hyperlinks to Forms and Images

Hyperlinks (HTML anchors) that you embed in forms aren't InfoPath controls because they don't bind to an XML Data document field. In this respect, hyperlinks are similar to embedded images. You can place a text-based (label) hyperlink at any location in the form or add a hyperlink to a graphic. To give both techniques a try with links to Microsoft sample Web pages for hyperlinks in the Northwind sample database's Suppliers table, follow these steps.

▶ **Add a hyperlink to a table cell**

1. **With the NWBrightBlue.xsn template open in design mode, delete the third heading line you added in the preceding exercise, press Enter to add a new line, and click the Normal formatting item in the Font task pane.**

2. Click Ctrl+K or choose Insert, Hyperlink to open the Insert Hyperlink dialog box.
3. For this example, type this URL in the Address text box: **http://www.microsoft.com/accessdev/sampleapps/mayumi.htm**.
4. In the Text text box in the Display section, replace the automatically added URL with the text to appear in the cell, **Mayumi's (on the World Wide Web)**, as shown here.

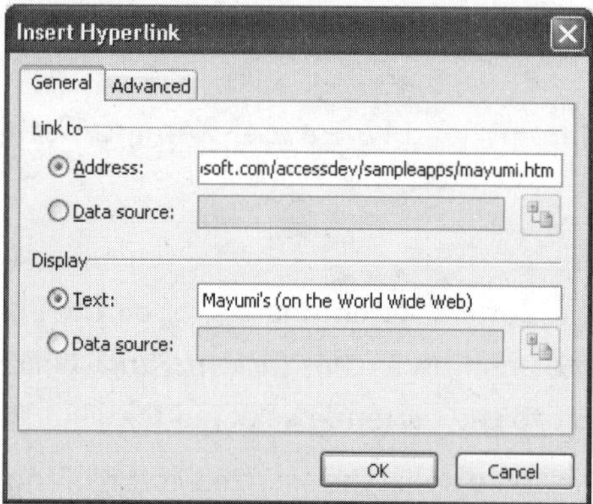

5. Click OK to add the Hyperlink.
6. If you want to change the font color of the hyperlink, select the text, open the Font task pane, and select a color from the Font Color list. Optionally, apply bold formatting to the link.
7. Choose Preview Form, and click the hyperlink to test it.

▶ **Add a hyperlink to an embedded image**

1. Right click the image, the Northwind logo for this example, and choose Hyperlink to open the Insert Hyperlink dialog box. Adding a hyperlink to an image disables the Display option buttons and text boxes.
2. In the Address text box, type the URL for the link, **www.microsoft.com/accessdev/sampleapps/PlutzerE.htm**, for this example.
3. Click OK to add a hyperlink and a blue border to the image.
4. Choose Preview Form, and click the image to test its hyperlink.
5. Close the preview, and save your changes.

Figure 7-4 shows the result of adding the text and image hyperlinks to the form. You can't change the style or color of the border that the hyperlink adds to an image in InfoPath's user interface. You can remove the border by selecting the logo, choosing Tools, Borders and Shading, and clicking the None button on the Borders tab. Your C:\Microsoft Press\Introducing InfoPath 2003\Chapter07\NWBrightBlue\ folder contains NWBrightBlueLogo.xsn, which includes all modifications you made in the preceding exercises.

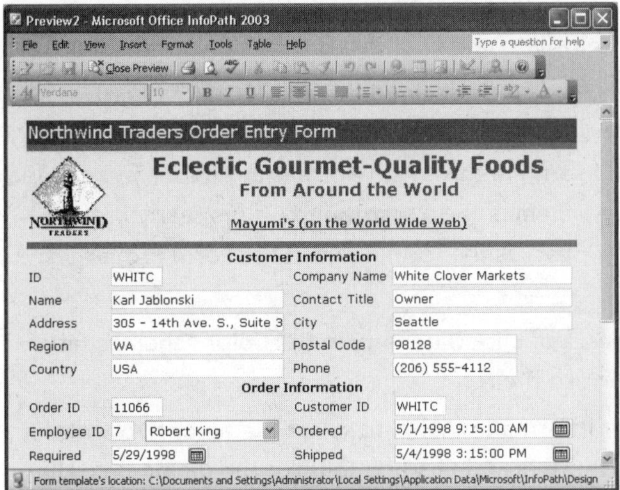

Figure 7-4 This preview of the NWBrightBlue.xsn template shows the added text and image hyperlinks.

Formatting Tables, Cells, and Controls

The Chapter 5 section "Adding Table Borders" briefly describes the process for adding outside and inside borders to layout tables and applying padding to cell contents. The sections that follow explain the formatting process in greater detail and describe how to add colors from a selected color scheme to individual tables and controls and their borders. Like the preceding examples, these exercises start with a copy of the NWOrdersCh6.xsn template but use a different color scheme–Blueberry.

Formatting and Adding Borders to Tables

It's often useful to distinguish individual layout tables from one another, such as Customer Information from Order Information, or relate specific table elements to one another using background colors. For this example, you assign one background color to the Customer Information table and the Shipping Information rows of the Orders table, and another background color to all other Order Information elements, including the Line Items repeating table header. Adding outside and inside borders to tables is optional, but borders make the Customer, Order, and Shipping Information sections consistent with the default design of the Line Items repeating table. Adding a small left margin to the labels by cell padding improves the overall appearance of the form.

To change the background colors of the NWBlueberry.xsn template, apply table borders, and add left cell padding with InfoPath's multiselect feature for table cells, follow these steps.

▶ **Create a copy of the source template and change table background colors**

1. Navigate to your C:\Microsoft Press\Introducing InfoPath 2003\Chapter07\NWOrdersCh6 folder, open NWOrdersCh6.xsn in design mode, and save it as NWBlueberry.xsn in the \My Documents\InfoPath\Formatting folder you created in the section "Applying Color Schemes and Background Colors" early in the chapter. Assign **NWBlueberry (Test)** as the form name in the Form Properties dialog box, and click OK.
2. Choose Format, Color Schemes, and click Blueberry in the Color Schemes task pane to apply the color scheme to the form.
3. Click in front of the Customer Information label to select the second row of the master form, choose Format, Borders and Shading to open the dialog box, click the Shading tab, select the No Color option, and click OK to remove the shading from the master table.
4. Click in the Customer Information table ID cell or any other cell, choose Table, Select, Table to select all cells in the subtable.
5. Choose Format, Borders And Shading, click the Shading tab in the dialog box, select the Color option, open the color picker, select the background color in position 3 (*primaryMedium*), and click OK to apply the background color to the first table.
6. Repeat steps 4 and 5, but select the Order Information table, and apply the color in position 4 (*primaryLight*) to the table.
7. Select the row containing the Shipping Information label. On the Shading tab in the Borders and Shading dialog box, select No Color to remove its background color.
8. Use the mouse to select the three Shipping Information rows. On the Shading tab in the Borders and Shading dialog box, select the same color as you did for the Customer Information table in step 5 (*primaryMedium*) to visually relate the entries to the Customer Information table.

▶ **Add table and row borders**

1. Select all cells of the Customer Information table, and choose Format, Borders and Shading.

2. On the Borders tab in the Borders and Shading dialog box, open the color picker, select the position 5 color (*accentDark*), click the Outline and Inside buttons, and then click OK to add a border to all selected cells.
3. Select column C (the narrow separator column), and open the Borders tab in the Borders and Shading dialog box.
4. Select the same color as you did in step 2, click the None button to clear all borders, and then click the two buttons at the bottom of the diagram to preserve the vertical borders, as shown here.

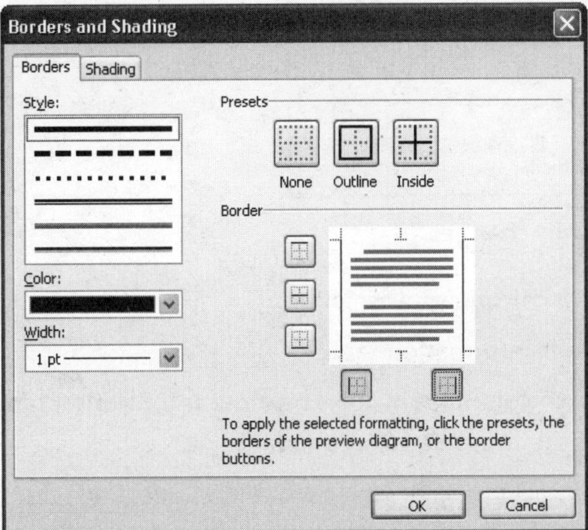

5. Click the Shading tab, select the No color option, and click OK.
6. Repeat steps 1 and 2 for the Order Information and Shipping Information table.
7. Repeat steps 3, 4, and 5 for the Order Information section, but select the four cells in column C.
8. Repeat step 6 for the three Shipping Information rows, and open the form in preview mode. The form appears as shown here.

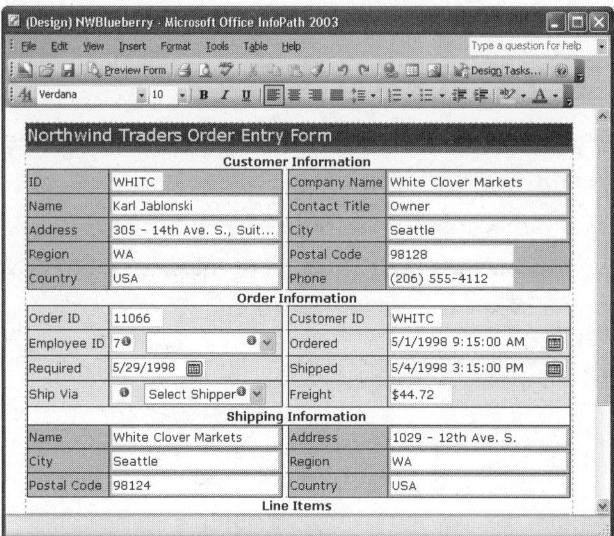

9. Close the preview, and save your changes.

▶ Pad all label cells at once with column multiselection

1. Click the ID cell of the Customer Information table.
2. Press Ctrl, drag the mouse down column A of the Customer Information table to select the four cells, and drag the mouse down Column D.
3. Repeat step 2 for columns A and D in the Order Information table, and your form in design mode with the six label columns selected appears as shown here.

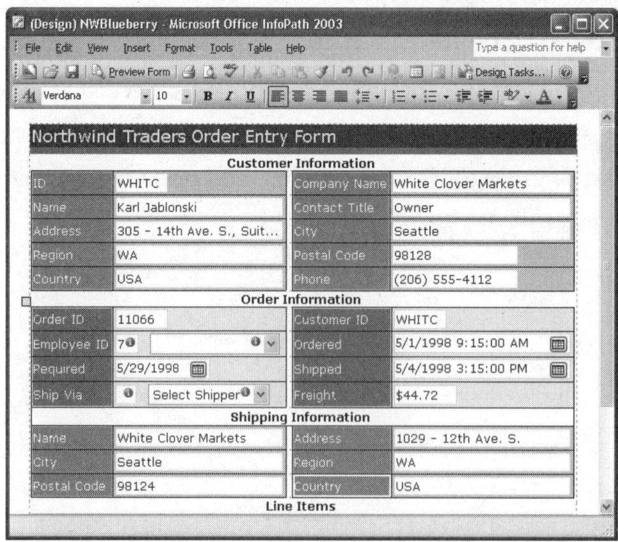

4. **Choose Table, Table Properties to open the Table Properties dialog box, click the Cells tab, type 3 as the Left Padding value, and click OK to apply the 3-pixel padding to all selected cells.**
5. **Adding the padding causes the Company Name label to occupy two lines, so remove Name, and change the Name label of the Shipping Information section to Company.**

Adding Borders to Text Boxes

The default borders for text boxes often appear to vanish when you add table background colors. You can make the borders reappear by applying a darker color to them. The following steps also show you how to use InfoPath's multiselect feature for controls.

▶ **Add visible borders to all applicable controls at once**

1. **Click the Order ID text box, press Ctrl, and then click each text box and date picker in the first three sections to select them. (You can't change the border style of controls that have built-in borders, such as drop-down list boxes, so don't select them.) Your form in design mode appears as shown here.**

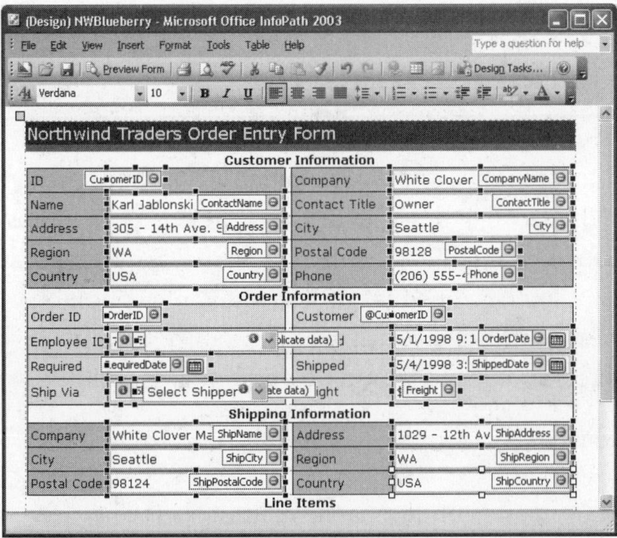

2. **Choose Format, Borders And Shading, open the color picker, select the position 1 color, which is dark enough to be visible, and click the Outline button.**
3. **Click OK to apply borders to all controls in the first three form sections. Preview the form, which appears as shown here.**

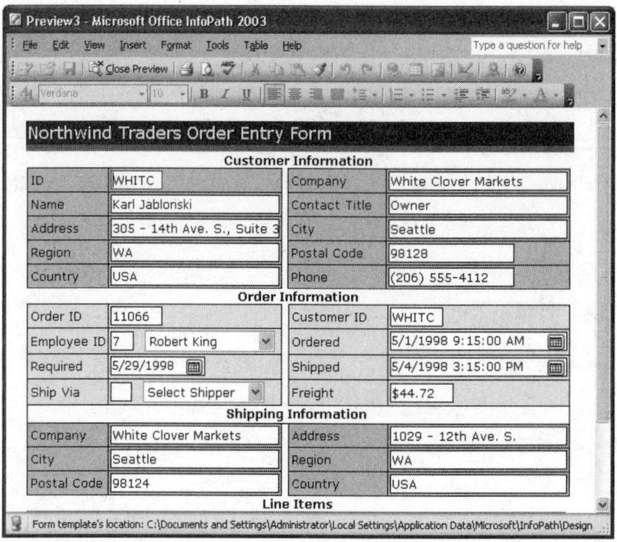

A drawback to adding darker borders to controls is that the blue border surrounding an empty control with the focus is difficult to discern from unselected controls, although the presence of the cursor in the selected text box mitigates the problem. You probably won't notice this potential issue with forms that have default values.

Applying Conditional Formatting

Conditional formatting is one of the most important features you can use in InfoPath to alert users of out-of-range, undesirable, or suspect values when they're entering data. Conditional formatting doesn't flag those values as errors; usually, it provides users a visual clue that the data is or might be incorrect. Chapter 8 describes declarative data validation rules that define erroneous entries. You apply conditional formatting primarily to text boxes; conditional formatting is disabled for date pickers, both list box types, check boxes, and option groups. Conditional formatting can apply any or all font attributes, change the font and background colors, or hide or disable the control.

These are some typical applications for conditional formatting alerts:

- Highlighting costs that are close to or exceed budget limits. As an example, if a cost item is within 90 percent of the budgeted amount, color the value orange and apply a bold attribute. If the cost is more than 100 percent of budget, color the value red and apply bold underline attributes, which is an undesirable or–in some governmental agencies–an out-of-range condition.

- ✦ Detecting differences in text values, such as a shipping address that differs from the billing address. In many cases, these addresses differ, but the data entry operator should be made aware of the suspect entry in case of a typographical error.
- ✦ Hiding controls in response to the setting of another control, such as hiding shipping address text boxes if a Same As Bill To check box is selected.

To apply conditional formatting to a control, choose Format, Conditional Formatting to open the Conditional Formatting dialog box, which initially displays an empty Conditions With Formatting list. Alternatively, open the control's Properties dialog box, click the Display tab, and click the Conditional Formatting button to open the dialog box. Click Add to open the Conditional Format dialog box, and specify the field name, a comparison expression, and a constant or field value in the three text boxes, as illustrated in Figure 7-5. The two open lists hide the Font Color (bright orange) and Background Color (dark blue) selections in the figure; although this figure shows both lists open, only one list can open at a time.

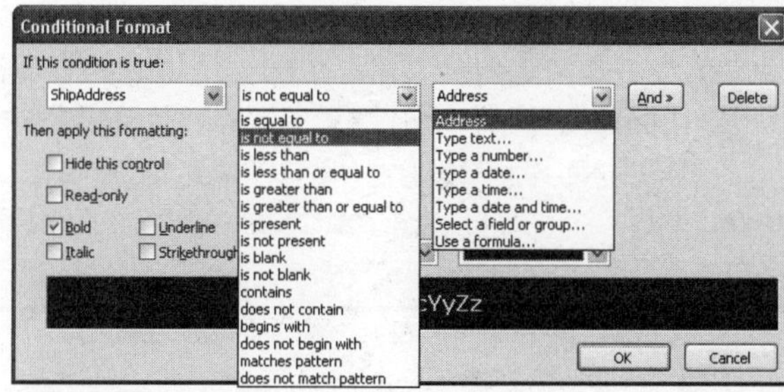

Figure 7-5 This image shows selections available in the comparison expression and compare-to values of the Conditional Format dialog box.

As an example of conditional formatting, the NWBlueberry.xsn template's default ShipAddress and PostalCode field values aren't the same as the Address and PostalCode field values. When you open a preview of the form, the expression shown in Figure 7-5 applies the conditional formatting to the text box bound to the ShipAddress field, as shown in Figure 7-6.

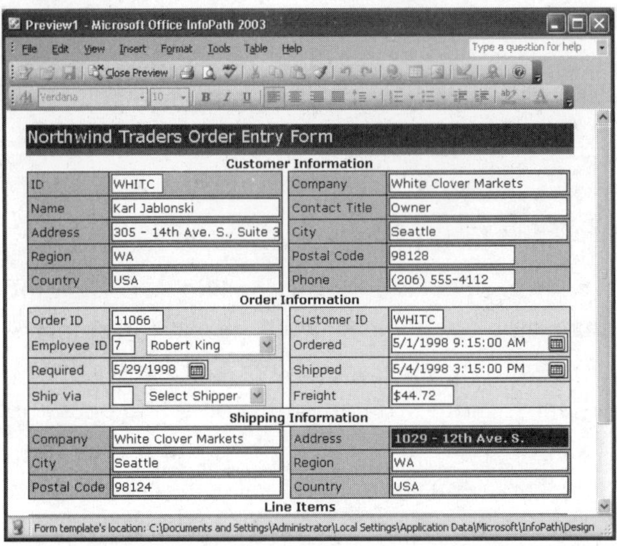

Figure 7-6 Grab the data entry operator's attention with orange and blue conditional formatting applied to the Shipping Information Address text box that's bound to the ShipAddress field.

Understanding Conditional Formatting Logic

The most common type of programming logic is *positive*; if the condition is satisfied, the expression evaluates as *true*. Multiple expressions can use *and* logic to draw a final conclusion–if *Expression1* is true and *Expression2* is true, and so on, the final result evaluates as *true*. An alternative is *or* logic– if *Expression1* is true or *Expression2* is true, the final result evaluates as *true*. InfoPath conditional expressions also provide a *not* version for most conditions, so you can specify a condition that evaluates as *false*.

As an *and* logic example, you might not want to highlight empty Shipping Information text boxes when adding a new order for a customer. In this case, you add another condition with *and* logic–*ShipAddress is not blank*–as shown in Figure 7-7.

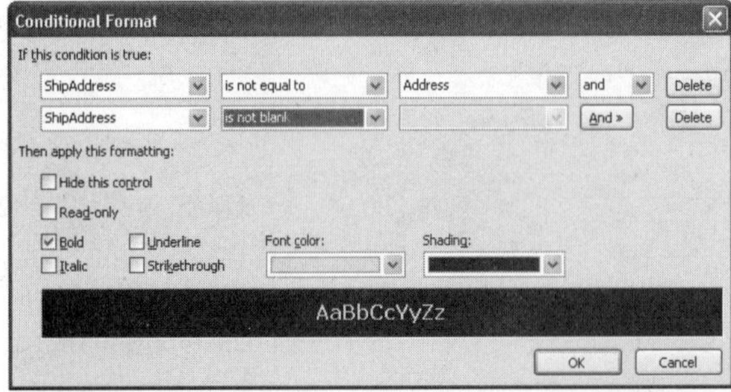

Figure 7-7 A second expression that uses the *not* operator demonstrates multiple conditional formatting criteria.

If you need another condition, such as testing whether an asterisk (*) in a shipping address field represents "same as customer's corresponding billing address field," add another *and* condition– *ShipAddress is not **.

In the Conditional Formatting dialog box, you can add multiple sets of conditions, which is the equivalent of adding parentheses around multiple logical expressions to cause them to be evaluated as a group. Multiple condition sets are limited to the *or* operator–if any condition group evaluates as true, conditional formatting is applied to the control. The following sections show you how to establish single and multiple condition sets.

Testing Text Values

The preceding section defined potential criteria for acceptable values of the text box bound to the ShipAddress field. In this exercise, you add those criteria and extend their application to text boxes bound to the ShipCity, ShipRegion, ShipPostalCode, and ShipCountry fields. Instead of an asterisk, the ShipAddress text box accepts "Same as Bill To Address (*)" as an acceptable entry, in preparation for exercises in later sections.

To set up conditional formatting for the NWBlueberry form's Shipping Information section, follow these steps.

▶ **Add the initial criterion**

1. **With the NWBlueberry.xsn template open in design mode, select the Address text box of the Shipping Information section, and choose Format, Conditional Formatting to open the dialog of the same name, as shown here.**

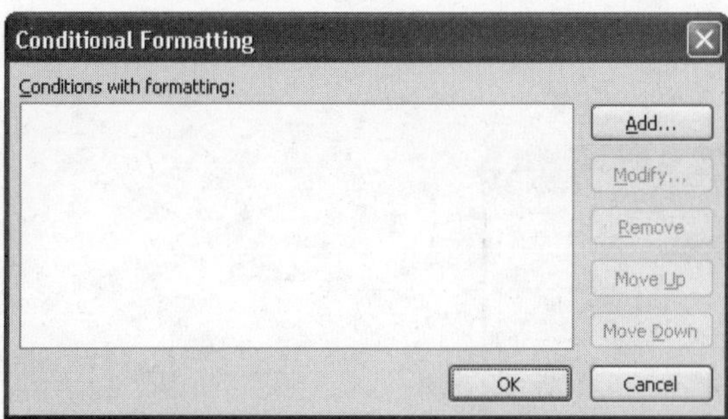

2. **Click Add to open the Conditional Format dialog box, with the ShipAddress field specified in the first drop-down list. (You can select any field in the selected group from this list, or click the Select A Field Or Group item to open a dialog box in which you select a field from another group.)**

3. Select the comparison operator Is Not Equal To in the second text box, and choose Select A Field or Group in the third list to open the Select a Field or Group dialog box.
4. Expand the CustomerInfo node, and double-click Address to close the dialog box and substitute Address in the third list. (Refer to Figure 7-5.)
5. Select the Bold check box, open the Font Color picker, choose light orange, open the Shading picker, and select medium blue. (The six color scheme color buttons don't appear in this version of the color picker.)

▶ Add the second and third criteria and test the result

1. Click the And button to expose a second criterion row, and select Is Not Blank in the comparison operator text box.
2. Click And again, select Is Not Equal To in the second list and Type Text in the third list, and type * in the text box. InfoPath adds double-quotes around the text when you press Tab to leave the field, as shown here.

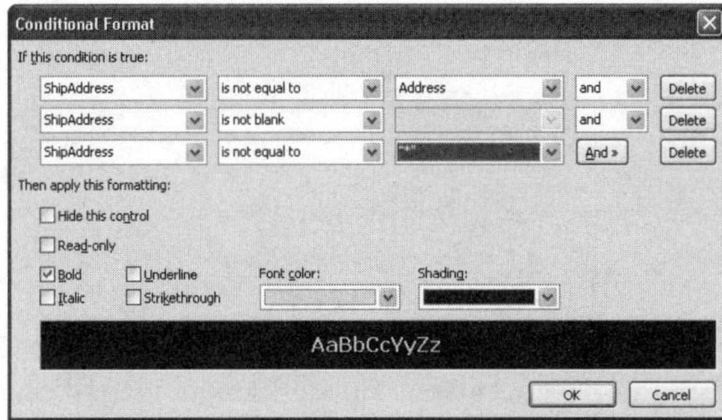

3. Click OK to return to the Conditional Formatting dialog box, which displays part of the complete expression you added and has Modify and Remove buttons enabled, as shown here.

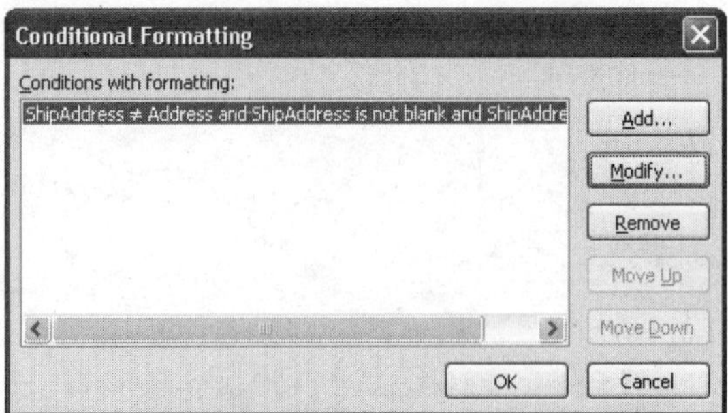

4. Click OK to apply the conditional formatting expressions to the text box, and click Preview Form, which opens with the text box bound to the ShipAddress field highlighted. (Refer to Figure 7-6.)

5. Test the first condition by copying and pasting the contents of the Address text box in the Customer Information section to the Address text box in the Order Information section and pressing Tab. The highlighting disappears because the two field values are equal.
6. Test the second condition by deleting the text you pasted to leave a blank text box and pressing Tab. The text box contains a red asterisk, which denotes that an empty text box violates the form's XML schema, but the text isn't highlighted.
7. Type * in the text box, and press Tab to verify the last criterion.

▶ **Add the remaining four * criterion fields**

1. Repeat steps 1 through 5 and 1 through 4 of the preceding two exercises, respectively, for the City and Country text boxes, comparing the values to the City and Country values of the CustomerInfo section.
2. The ShipRegion and ShipPostalCode aren't required fields; the schema allows an empty value and won't flag an omission. For the text boxes bound to these two fields, don't add the second Is Not Blank criterion.
3. Optionally, emulate a software quality assurance (QA) specialist and perform the tests in steps 5 through 7 of the preceding section.

▶ **Add the "Same as Bill To Address (*)" criterion**

1. Select the Shipping Information's Company text box, and repeat steps 1 through 4 of the "Add the initial criterion" exercise.
2. Repeat steps 1 though 5 of the "Add the second and third criteria and test the result" exercise, but in step 2 type **Same as Bill To Address (*)** in the text box.

Conditional Formatting Based on a Non-Blank Value

Optional ShipVia and Freight field values are required if the order has been shipped, which is indicated by a non-blank value in the nillable ShippedDate field. You can apply conditional formatting to the ShipVia text box, the associated drop-down list box, or both. The example in this section formats the text box. Testing the Freight field value requires two expression groups that use the *Or* operator to disallow a blank value or a value less than $5.00. Northwind Traders' minimum shipping and handling charge is assumed to be $5.00.

To add conditional formatting to the ShipVia and Freight fields, follow these steps.

▶ Add criteria to the Ship Via text box

1. **Select the Ship Via text box, choose Format, Conditional Formatting, and click Add to open the Conditional Format dialog box.**
2. **With ShipVia in the first list, select Is Blank from the comparison operator list, and click the And button.**
3. **Select ShippedDate from the first list and Is Not Blank from the comparison operator list, choose the Bold text box, and assign the light orange font and medium blue background colors, as before.**
4. **Click OK twice to add the criteria.**

▶ Add criteria groups to the Freight text box

1. **Select the Freight text box, and open the Conditional Format dialog box.**
2. **With Freight in the first list, select Is Less Than from the comparison operator list, select Type a Number in the third list, type 5, and click the And button.**
3. **Select ShippedDate from the first list and Is Not Blank from the comparison operator list, select the Bold check box, and assign the light orange font and medium blue background colors, as shown here.**

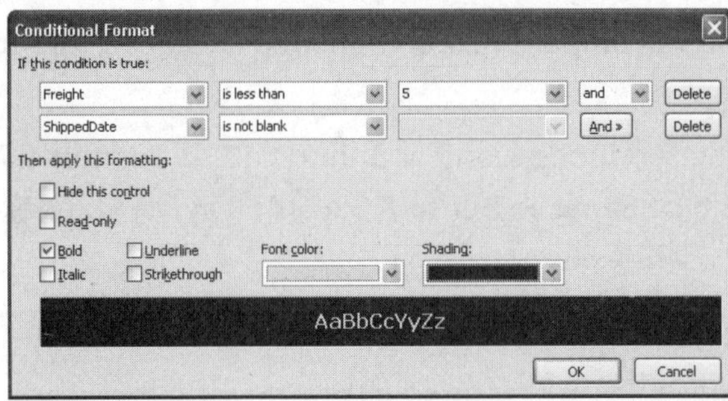

4. **Click OK to return to the Conditional Formatting dialog box, and click Add to open a second, empty Conditional Format dialog box.**
5. **With Freight in the first list, select Is Blank from the comparison operator list, and click the And button.**
6. **Select ShippedDate from the first list and Is Not Blank from the comparison operator list, select the Bold check box, and assign the font and background colors.**
7. **Click OK to return to the Conditional Formatting dialog box, which displays both expressions in its Conditions With Formatting list, as shown here.**

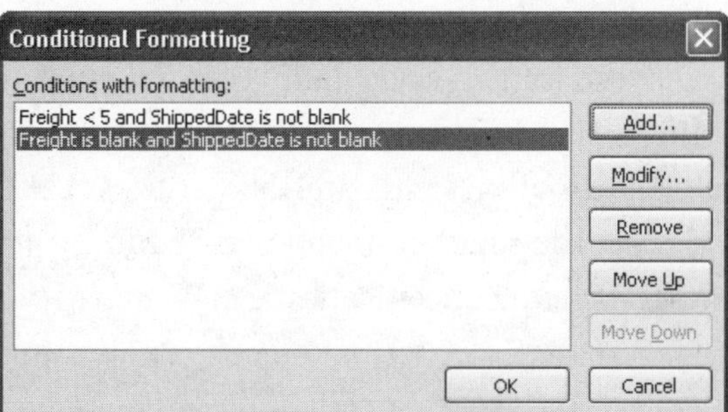

8. **Click OK to apply the conditional formatting expressions to the Freight text box.**
9. **Save your changes, click Preview Form, and test the expressions with and without a Shipped date value. Your form in Preview mode with the default Shipped value, and missing Ship Via and invalid Freight values, appears as shown in Figure 7-8.**

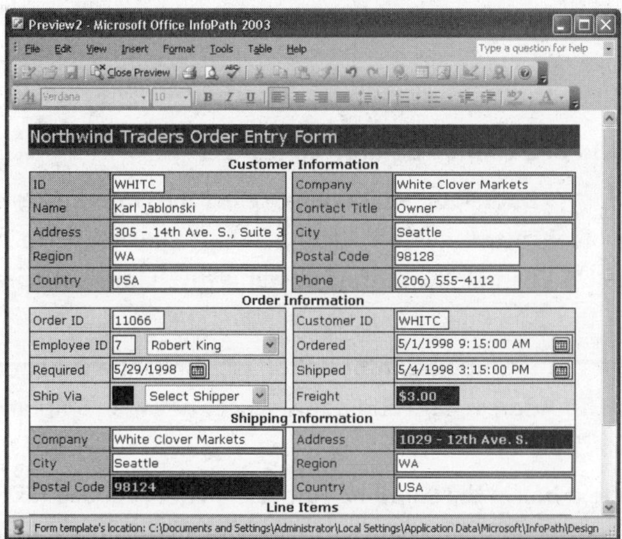

Figure 7-8 This preview of the NWBlueberry.xsn template shows conditional formatting applied to Ship Via, Freight, and Shipping Information fields.

Hiding Controls Conditionally

One of the most useful features of conditional formatting is its capability to hide controls that don't require values under a specified condition. For example, all but a few of Northwind Traders' orders have the same billing and shipping addresses. In this case, it makes sense to default shipping addresses to billing addresses when an element or attribute value specifies the same address. One approach is to use the Insert Formula dialog box to add default Shipping Address values from the Customer table's address field values, as described in the section "Adding Workflow-Dependent Rules" in Chapter 10, "Adding Views to a Template."

Alternatively, you can establish generic default values for a shipping address that's identical to the billing address. You prepared for this eventuality with the conditional formatting expressions in the preceding section–Same as Bill To Address (*) for Company and * for all other Shipping Information fields are valid entries. Valid entries are required in hidden controls that the schema specifies as requiring at least one character (*minLength="1"*). The XML Schema specification calls *minLength* a *constraining facet*.

The next exercise adds a check box with a default *true* value bound to a *Boolean* attribute value specifies that the Shipping Information controls are hidden by default. The check box's value is metadata, so an attribute–rather than an element–is the appropriate field type.

Hiding controls also demonstrates the use of multiple conditional formatting expressions for a control. To add a bound check box to a new True/False (boolean) field and apply an additional conditional formatting expression group to control visibility of the Shipping Information controls, follow these steps.

▶ Add a new True/False field and change default values

1. **Open the NWBlueberry form's Data Source task pane, select the OrderInfo group, add a new True/False (Boolean) attribute field named IsShipToSameAsBillTo, and set the default value to TRUE. The field (with the inevitable *my:* namespace prefix) appears at the bottom of the Data Source list.**
2. **Drag the field to the right of the Shipping Information label, change the check box's label to Same as Bill To Address, and add a few spaces between Shipping Information and the check box.**
3. **Right click the Company text box in the Shipping Address section, choose Text Box Properties, and replace the Default Value with Same as Bill To Address (*). Be sure to capitalize the default value correctly, because comparisons are case sensitive.**
4. **Replace the Default Value of the remaining five Shipping Information text boxes with *.**
5. **Save your changes, and click Yes when asked if you want to overwrite the form with the new version that has an altered data source.**

▶ Selectively hide Shipping Information controls

1. **Select the Company text box in the Shipping Information section, choose Format, Conditional Formatting, and click the Conditional Formatting text box's Add button to add another expression group.**
2. **In the Conditional Format text box, select the IsShipToSameAsBillTo field.**

3. **Select Is Equal To from the comparison operator list, and select TRUE in the third list.**
4. **Select the Hide This Control check box. Your expression appears as shown here.**

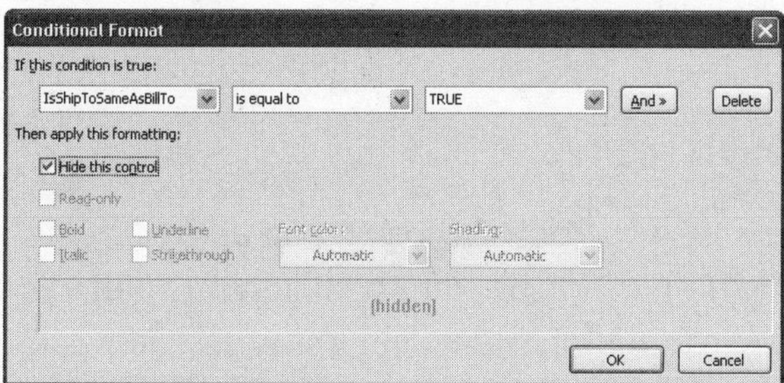

5. **Click OK to return to the Conditional Formatting dialog box with the added second criterion group (a single-statement expression) in its Conditions With Formatting list, and click OK to add the conditional formatting expressions.**
6. **Repeat steps 1 though 5 for the remaining five text boxes.**
7. **Save your changes, and preview the form to verify the controls are hidden when the check box is selected and visible when it's cleared.**
8. **Create and test a new form from the template, as illustrated in Figure 7-9.**

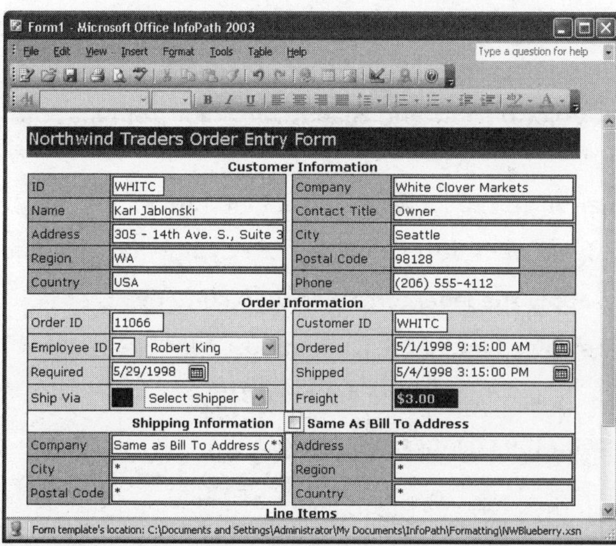

Figure 7-9 This test form created from the final version of the NWBlueberry.xsn template has two text boxes that contain inappropriate values.

The final version of the NWBlueberry.xsn form that incorporates the conditional formatting expressions added to this point is in your C:\Microsoft Press\Introducing InfoPath 2003\Chapter07\NWOrdersFinal folder.

The conditional formatting exercises you worked through in the preceding few sections only scratch the surface of what you can accomplish with conditional formatting. The next chapter, which covers data validation, uses similar expressions for validating text data.

Using the Format Painter

The Format Painter toolbar button lets you copy the formatting of a control or text and apply it to other controls or text on the form. InfoPath's Format Painter feature is similar to that of all Office 2002 or later applications, such as Access. You select the control or text with the format you want to copy, click or double-click the Format Painter button, and then click the text or control to apply the formatting. Double-clicking the Format Painter button locks the button in the enabled state to let you apply formatting to multiple text or control instances. You click the button again to disable the locked button. Unlike the Format Painter in Access, the InfoPath version doesn't apply the source control's conditional formatting rules to the target control.

To give the Format Painter a test, follow these steps.

▶ Apply a label format to other labels and controls

1. **Open your NWBlueberry.xsn template in design mode, if it isn't open.**
2. **Select both characters of the ID label in the Customer Information table, click the Bold button, click the Font Color button, and change the color from black to dark red.**
3. **Double-click the Format Painter button to lock it in the enabled state.**
4. **Click a few other labels in the Customer Information table to change their format.**
5. **Click a couple of text boxes to apply the label format to their contents.**
6. **Click one of the date picker controls to apply the formatting.**
7. **Click the Format Painter button to return it to the disabled date.**
8. **Close the template without saving the changes you made.**

The Format Painter is especially handy if you decide to change the formatting of many text items, controls, or both in a form.

Chapter Summary

InfoPath's panoply of custom formatting features make it easy to design attractive forms. You can apply one of InfoPath's 17 color schemes to the title and second row of a master table, and then use any of the scheme's lighter colors to apply a background color to the entire form, individual embedded layout tables, individual table cells, or controls. You also can use the selected scheme's colors for table and control borders.

You can embed images from graphics files or clip art in pictures that InfoPath saves as part of the form template. You also can apply unbound hyperlinks to embedded images or descriptive text for the link. Views contain the data for embedded hyperlinks. InfoPath has a set of five predefined HTML headings that range in font size from 24 to 8 points.

You minimize the probability of data entry errors or omissions by taking advantage of InfoPath's declarative conditional formatting of text box controls. The Conditional Format dialog box makes it easy to generate simple or complex logical expressions that alter the appearance of or hide individual controls. If you can't create a single expression to implement the conditional formatting rules you need, the Conditional Formatting dialog box lets you add additional sets of rules, which are evaluated by a built-in *Or* operator.

Q&A

Q. Can I create my own custom color schemes?

A. No. InfoPath color schemes are hard-coded. However, you can create your own set of custom colors by clicking the More Colors item in a color picker to open the Color dialog box, and typing decimal values (0 to 255) in the Red, Green, and Blue text boxes. InfoPath doesn't save custom colors between sessions; a session ends when you close InfoPath.

Q. How do I embed a clip art picture in a form?

A. Choose Insert, Picture, From Clip Art to open the Clip Art task pane, and follow the same procedure as you did when inserting a clip art picture in a rich text box. (See the Chapter 2 exercise, "Inserting an Image from the Clip Art Task Pane.")

Q. Can I apply conditional formatting to values in repeating table rows?

A. You bet. The next chapter shows you how with data validation and conditional formatting examples.

Q. Can I use different conditional formatting colors to indicate the severity of a data entry problem?

A. Yes. Add multiple conditional formatting expression groups with different settings for the Font Color and Shading properties.

On Your Own

Here are additional exercises to test your understanding of conditional formatting expressions:

1. Apply an additional conditional formatting expression for the Freight text box that's true if the order hasn't been shipped and the Freight text box contains a value greater than 0.

2. Add a conditional formatting expression to the Required Date control that's true if the Required date isn't blank and is less than or equal to the Ordered date.

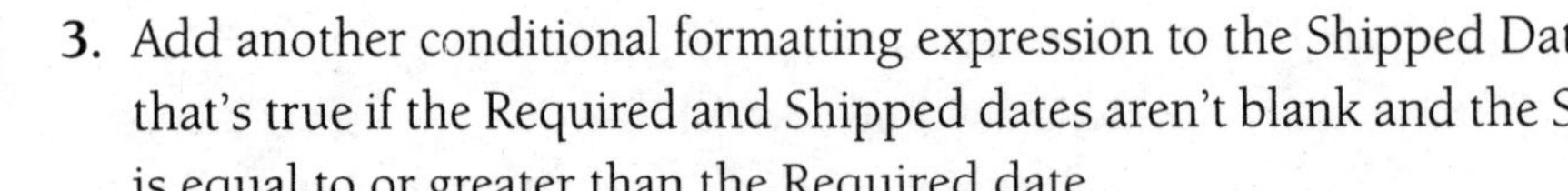

3. Add another conditional formatting expression to the Shipped Date control that's true if the Required and Shipped dates aren't blank and the Shipped date is equal to or greater than the Required date.

CHAPTER 8

Validating Form Data

In this chapter, you will learn how to:

- **Describe how data validation differs from conditional formatting and apply data validation rules to text boxes, list boxes, and date picker controls**
- **Use multiple comparison operators to validate numeric data, and use regular expressions to validate the formatting of text boxes**

For more information:

- **Browse the XPath Developer's Guide at the Microsoft Developer Network (MSDN) site. Go to *msdn.microsoft.com*, and search for "XPath Developer." (Include the double quotation marks.)**
- **See the World Wide Web Consortium (W3C) XML Path Language (XPath) Version 1.0 specification at *www.w3.org/TR/xpath*, especially section 2.5, "Abbreviated Syntax," and section 3.4, "Booleans."**

Garbage in, garbage out (GIGO) is an axiom of the information technology industry. Organizations spend billions of dollars per year cleansing databases of erroneous and inconsistent information. In many cases, the errors remain undetected until database users discover them–usually inadvertently–or data analysis software (called *online analytical processing*, or OLAP) returns obviously unreasonable results. Most mistakes are typographical, but many errors result from missing, incomplete, or duplicate entries.

Validation during data entry has proven to be the best and easiest method of minimizing data errors and inconsistencies. Limiting users' data entry choices with selections from drop-down lists is another way to minimize bad data collection. If you've designed Microsoft Access tables, you've probably applied at least some data validation tests for data entry errors, such as missing field values, incorrect or improbable date entries, and invalid or unreasonable numeric values. InfoPath's approach to declarative (design mode) validation methodology differs from Access's, but InfoPath can accomplish similar results. However, you must add programming code to handle some data entry tests, such as numeric date differences, that are easy to express as Access validation rules but not with InfoPath's declarative approach.

To work through this chapter:

- You should be familiar with the application of conditional formatting to text boxes as described in the section "Applying Conditional Formatting," in Chapter 7, "Formatting Forms." Completing that section's conditional formatting exercises is helpful, but not required, for this chapter's procedures.
- You should have a basic understanding of Boolean logic and know how *And* and *Or* operators act on True/False operand pairs. You don't need to be a programmer to understand this chapter; experience with the Microsoft Visual Basic for Application (VBA) *Not*, *And*, and *Or* operators is useful but not essential.
- You should have installed in your C:\Microsoft Press\Introducing InfoPath 2003\Chapter08 folder the sample files from the CD that accompanies this book. If you didn't complete Chapter 7's data validation examples, you'll find the completed Northwind Traders Order Entry Form's template, NWOrdersCh07.xsn, in the C:\Microsoft Press\Introducing InfoPath 2003\Chapter08\NWOrdersCh07 folder. This template is required to get the most out of this chapter's exercises.

Comparing Data Validation and Conditional Formatting

The section "Applying Conditional Formatting," in Chapter 7, introduced you to logical expressions that warn users of missing or mismatched text data. That chapter's "On Your Own" section included exercises for flagging some erroneous date values. You use similar expressions as data validation rules, but data validation doesn't just highlight text box controls with bad or suspect data. Data validation errors display a red asterisk or apply a dashed red border to controls containing entries that violate the rules. All standard controls–except buttons–have data validation features enabled.

An error message appears when you try to save or submit a data document that contains validation errors, as shown in Figure 8-1. You can't submit a data document with data entry errors to an Access or a SQL Server database, an XML Web service, a Microsoft SharePoint forms library, or a Web site. You can save the offending form as an XML data document–presumably for subsequent correction–by clicking Yes in the message box.

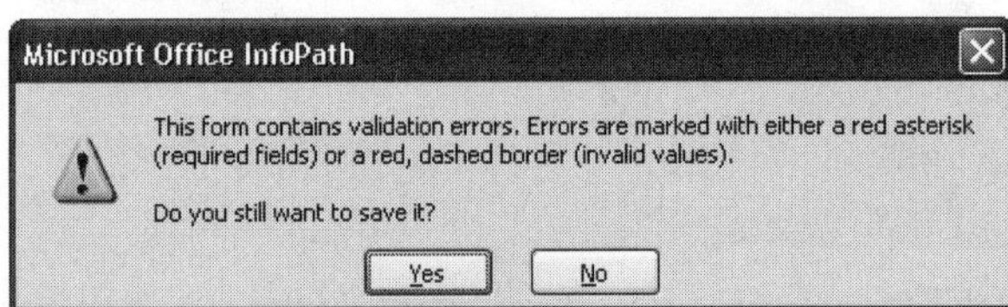

Figure 8-1 This error message appears when you attempt to save a form with a validation error or a missing required field value.

You apply validation to data in a selected control by choosing Format, Data Validation or by opening the *ControlType* Properties dialog box and clicking Data Validation to open the Data Validation (*ControlName*) dialog box. Clicking the Data Validation (*ControlName*) dialog box's Add button for a new rule or clicking the Modify button for an existing rule opens a second Data Validation (*ControlName*) dialog box, shown in Figure 8-2. This dialog box is quite similar to the Conditional Format dialog box. Instead of text formatting controls, the Data Validation dialog box has a drop-down list that lets you specify whether to display a ScreenTip and delay error messages until requested, or display the error message when the offending control loses the focus. You add the ScreenTip and error message, which usually are identical, in the two text boxes. If you delay error messages, users can find multiple errors on complex forms by choosing Tools, Go To Next Error (Ctrl+Shift+E). They can display the error message by choosing Tools, Show Error Message (Ctrl+Shift+S).

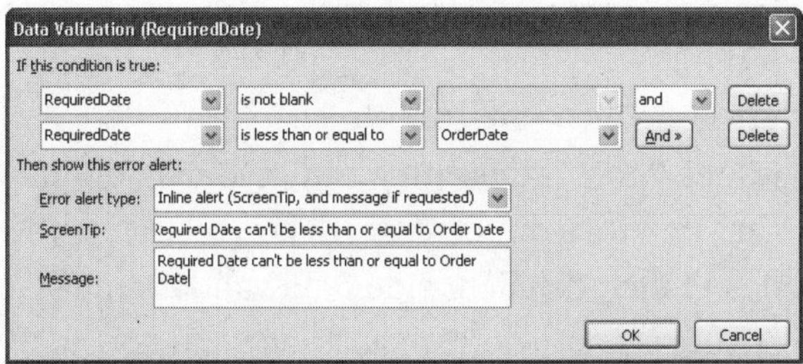

Figure 8-2 The Data Validation dialog box is similar to the Conditional Formatting dialog box.

An important difference between data validation and conditional formatting is where InfoPath stores the rules in the template's .xsn file. The manifest.xsf file contains data validation expressions and message definitions, which apply to the data document and, thus, to all views. View transform files (view1.xsl for the default view) store conditional formatting expressions, which apply only to the view to which you add the expressions. This design preserves the separation of content-related actions (data validation) and presentation-related changes (conditional formatting).

Data vs. Schema Validation

The XML Schema recommendation incorporates data validation capabilities, which are enforced by *constraining facets*, such as the *minLength="1"* example in the section "Hiding Controls Conditionally," in Chapter 7 or the *maxLength="##"* value you specify by the Limit Text Box To ## Characters spin box on the Text Box Properties dialog box's Display tab. Almost all XML Schema datatypes support *enumeration facets*, which restrict values to members of a list of valid values, and *pattern facets*, which require values to adhere to a format specified by a *regular expression*. (InfoPath SP-1 data validation can test conformance to a regular expression with the Matches Pattern or Does Not Match Pattern condition. The section "Validating Text Box Patterns" near the end of the chapter describes how to validate a text box with a regular expression.)

If you base your form on an existing schema that includes constraining, enumeration, or pattern facets, InfoPath's schema validation feature identifies erroneous field values with a dashed red border around the offending control. You don't need to duplicate schema-based constraints with data validation expressions.

A few software analysts have complained that InfoPath doesn't add facets to the form's schema for declarative data validation, which would conform to the open XML Schema standard; they denigrate InfoPath's template-based validation rules as "proprietary," meaning "not standards-based." It's exceedingly difficult to design XML schemas that include constraints on a field value based on the value of another field, and (perhaps) impossible if the constraints depend on values of more than one other field. InfoPath uses XPath 1.0—a W3C recommendation—to define data validation rules. Thus, the "not standards-based" argument is tenuous, at best.

Validating Text Boxes with Custom Expressions

Order entry forms and invoice forms are good examples of InfoPath forms that require validation of several text box values. Most order entry and invoicing operations use *online transaction processing* (OLTP) with a direct network connection to the database. If the data entry program doesn't include client-side data validation tests and relies on database constraints to ensure server-side data accuracy and consistency, users receive an error message from the server. Sending data that produces a server-side error and returns a message is called a *round-trip*. One of the goals of client-side data validation is to minimize round-trips to the database server.

When order entry or invoicing operations take place through an intermediary over a wide area network, such as an XML Web service accessed via the Internet, round-trips caused by bad input data consume substantially more computing resources and usually are much slower than round-trips in a traditional OLTP environment.

The rules you specified in Chapter 7 for the Northwind Traders form's shipping address text boxes also apply to data validation, except the rules that alert users to differences between billing and shipping addresses–these rules are advisory, not mandatory. There are a few additional rules you might want to apply by data validation, such as requiring Postal Code values for all Country values except Ireland. (In Ireland, only Dublin City has postal codes.) Another important data validation rule is based on the fact that most addresses in the Northwind sample database don't have Region entries, but U.S., Canadian, and Brazilian addresses require Region values for states and provinces. The first validation test is simple, so it serves as an easy introduction to the data validation process.

Applying and Testing a Simple Validation Rule

To add the Postal Code data validation rule to a copy of the final version of the Northwind Traders form from Chapter 7 and test the result, follow these steps.

▶ **Add the required PostalCode rule**

1. **Open the NWOrdersCh07.xsn template, located in your C:\Microsoft Press\Introducing InfoPath 2003\Chapter 08 folder, in design mode and save it in a new folder, such as My Documents\InfoPath\Validation. Change the Form Name to NWOrdersCh07 Test.**
2. **Right-click the Postal Code text box in the Customer Information section of the form, and choose Text Box Properties from the shortcut menu.**

3. In the Text Box Properties dialog box, click the Data Validation button to open the Data Validation (PostalCode) dialog box. Click Add to open the second dialog box of the same name.
4. Leave the default PostalCode field in the first list, select Is Blank in the operator list, and click the And button.
5. In the added row, select Country in the first list, select Is Not Equal To in the operator list, select Type Text in the third list, and type **Ireland** in the text box.
6. Leave the default Error Alert Type setting of Inline Alert, and, in the Screen Tip box type **All countries except Ireland require postal codes**. Copy and paste the entry to the Message box. Your entries appear as shown here:

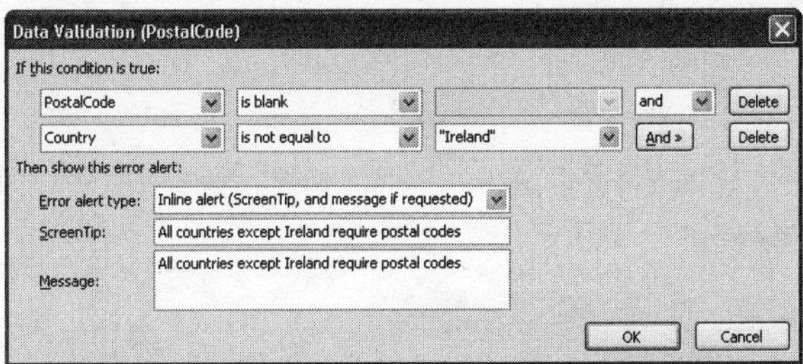

7. Click OK to close the dialog box. Note that the contents of the Message box and the XPath expression appear in the Conditions With Data Validation box of the first Data Validation dialog box. Click OK twice to close the two remaining dialog boxes and save your rule.
8. Optionally, apply the same rule to Postal Code box in the Shipping Information section of the form, and save your changes.

▶ **Test the PostalCode validation rule**

1. Press Ctrl+F1 to open the task pane, switch to the Fill Out A Form task pane, and click the NWOrdersCh07 Test link in the task pane to open a temporary form.
2. Delete the Postal Code, press Tab, and observe the Postal Code text box's red asterisk, which indicates that a required field value is missing. Rest the mouse pointer on the text box to display the ScreenTip, as shown here:

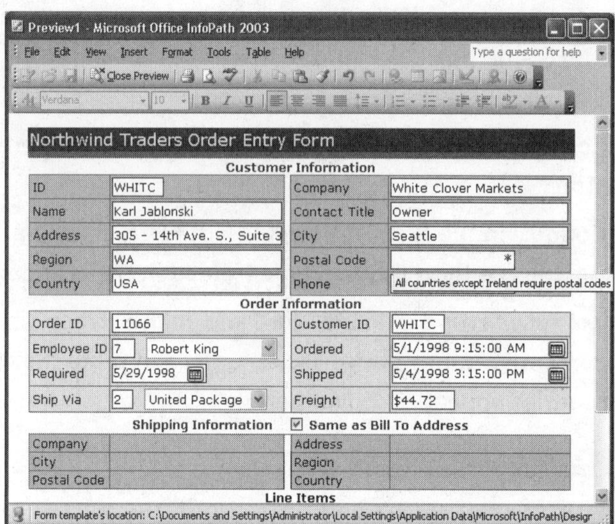

3. Select the Postal Code text box, and choose Tools, Show Error Message to display a strangely wide message box with the error message shown here:

4. Click OK, and then choose File, Save As, which displays an ordinary error message:

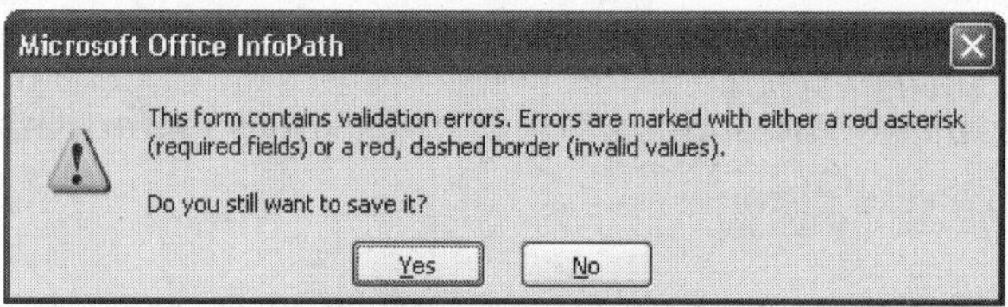

5. Click No to abandon the save operation, replace USA with **Ireland**, and press Tab. The red asterisk disappears.
6. If you added the validation rule to the Postal Code box in the Shipping Information section in step 8 of the preceding procedure, give that rule a quick test. Clear the Same As Bill To Address check box, clear the Postal Code box, and type **USA** in the Country box to display the effect of the combination of data validation and conditional formatting.
7. Close the form without saving your changes.

Working around data validation's case-sensitivity problem

If you replace Ireland with **IReland** and press Tab, the red asterisk reappears, which shows that InfoPath's declarative text-based data validation is case-sensitive and, therefore, susceptible to minor typographic errors. One solution to the problem of case sensitivity is to replace the Country box with a drop-down list containing the names of all countries in which the organization does business, which assures that the Country values are correct. Another—but less trustworthy—solution is to write data validation code that compares the uppercase Country value with an uppercase constant—IRELAND for this example. The latter approach ensures proper spelling but not capitalization of Country values.

Applying the Region Validation Rule

The conditional formatting expressions you added in Chapter 7's procedures and the Postal Code validation rule you added in the previous section use the XPath *and* operator. This section introduces you to using the XPath *or* operator in conjunction with an *and* operator. If you're familiar with logical expressions in VBA, you would expect to be able to use parentheses to specify logical operator precedence, as in the statement *Region = "" And (Country = "USA" Or Country = "Canada" Or Country = "Brazil")*, which would deliver the rule you need. InfoPath translates your selections and entries in the Data Validation and Conditional Format dialog boxes to XPath expressions. The problem is that XPath 1.0 doesn't recognize parentheses for operator precedence. XPath's operator precedence is fixed, and *or* is at the bottom of the precedence pecking order. Thus, the data validation expression shown in Figure 8-3 works for USA, but it doesn't work for Canada or Brazil. If a Region value is present, typing Canada or Brazil in the Country text box adds a red border to the Region textbox, because the second *or* operator disregards the *and* operator

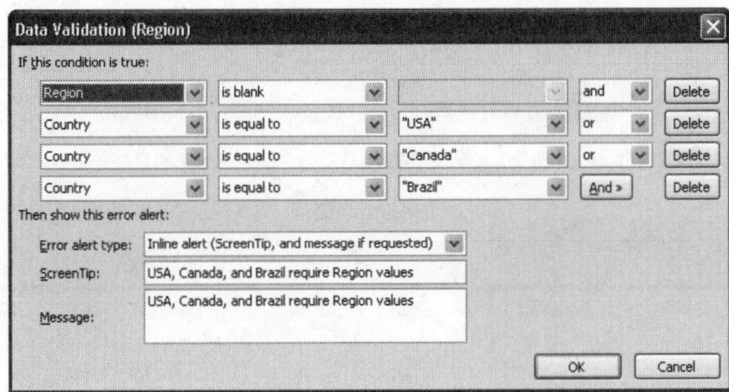

Figure 8-3 The XPath expression represented by the conditions shown here doesn't work correctly because of operator precedence issues.

See Also To learn more than you might want to know about XPath's operator precedence rules, see the section 3.4, "Booleans" in the XML Path Language (XPath) Version 1.0 recommendation at *www.w3.org/TR/xpath*.

Reversing the order by deleting the first *And* condition and adding it after the last *Or* condition doesn't solve the precedence problem. In this case, the expression works for Brazil only. This means that you must duplicate the Region Is Not Blank expression for each Country value. InfoPath limits you to a maximum of five conditions in an XPath expression, so you need multiple expression groups to handle the Region validation rule. One alternative is to add three Region Is Blank And Country = "*CountryName*" expression groups. You can save a bit of work by adding one expression group for USA and Canada, and a second expression group for Brazil.

Follow these steps to add the first validation expression set for USA and Canada to the Region field of the NWOrdersCh07 Test form's Customer Information section.

▶ **Add the Region validation rule for USA and Canada**

1. With the form open in design mode, right-click the Region text box in the Customer Information section, and choose Text Box Properties from the shortcut menu.
2. In the Text Box Properties dialog box, click the Data Validation button to open the Data Validation (Region) dialog box. Click Add to open the second dialog box of the same name.
3. With Region selected in the first list, select Is Blank from the operator list, and click And to add another condition row.
4. Select Country in the first list and Is Equal To in the operator list. Select Type Text in the third list, type **USA** in the text box, and click And.
5. Open the And/Or list in the preceding row, and select Or in preparation for the next condition entry.
6. Repeat steps 4 and 5, but type **Canada** in step 4.
7. Type **USA, Canada, and Brazil require Region values** in the ScreenTip and Message text boxes. The Data Validation dialog box appears as shown here.

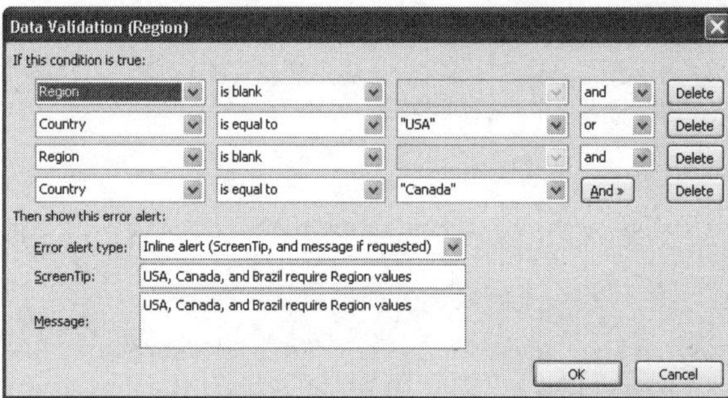

8. Click OK three times to close the text boxes and add the validation rule.
9. Click Preview Form, leave the default USA Country value, clear the Region field, and press Tab to verify that the field now shows a validation error.
10. Change USA to **Canada**, press Tab, and verify that validation works for the second condition pair.
11. Change Canada to **UK** (or any other country name except USA or Canada), press Tab, and verify that an empty Region value doesn't have a red asterisk
12. Close the preview, and save your template changes.

As mentioned in Chapter 7, InfoPath applies the equivalent of a VBA *Or* operator to multiple expression groups. To add the second expression group for Brazil, follow these steps.

▶ Add the Region validation rule for Brazil

1. **Repeat steps 1 through 3 of the preceding procedure.**
2. **Select Country in the first list, Is Equal To in the operator list, select Type Text in the third list, and type USA in the text box.**
3. **Type USA, Canada, and Brazil require Region values in the ScreenTip and Message text boxes.**
4. **Click OK three times to to add the second expression group and close the dialog boxes.**
5. **Repeat steps 9 through 12 of the preceding procedure, but type Brazil in step 10.**

Using Other Text Comparison Operators

InfoPath's declarative logical operators include several choices that you haven't encountered in previous conditional formatting or data validation exercises: Contains, Does Not Contain, Begins With, and Does Not Begin With. Contains tests a field value for an occurrence anywhere in the value of one or more consecutive characters you specify in the Type Text box. Begins With tests a field value for the occurrence of characters at the start of the value.

The next exercise uses the Contains and Begins With operators to test if values in the Shipping Information field contain the defaults when you clear the Same As Bill To Address check box. Adding Contains and Begins With validation rules demonstrates the effect of adding a validation rule to a field with conditional formatting.

To apply Contains and Begins With validation rules, follow these procedures.

▶ Apply a Contains condition to the Company (ShipName) field

1. **With the Northwind Traders form open in design mode, right-click the Shipping Information's Company text box, choose Text Box Properties, click Data Validation, and click Add to open the second Data Validation (ShipName) dialog box.**
2. **With ShipName selected in the first list, select Contains from the operator list, choose Type Text in the third list, and type (*) in the text box. (An asterisk might be present in a company name, but an asterisk enclosed in parentheses is very unlikely.)**
3. **Click And, and select IsShipToSameAsBillTo in the first list, Is Equal To in the second list, and FALSE in the third list.**

4. Type **A company name is required** or the like in the ScreenTip text box, and copy the entry to the Message text box, as shown here:

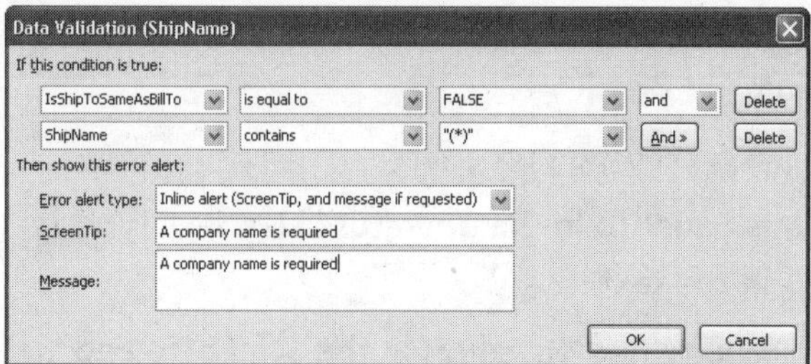

5. Click OK three times to apply the rule and close the dialog boxes. Save the changes that you made to the form.
6. Click Preview Form, and clear the Same As Bill To Address check box. In this case, a dashed red border indicates an invalid field value.

▶ **Apply a Begins With expression to other Shipping Information fields**

1. Repeat steps 1 through 5 of the preceding procedure, but in step 2 choose ShipAddress in the first list, Begins With in the operator list, and type * in the text box. In step 4, replace *A company name* with **An address**. (You use Begins With instead of Is Equal To to prevent users from accidentally leaving the asterisk in the first character position.)
2. Repeat the same steps for the remaining four text boxes, changing the ScreenTip and Message box text to correspond to the field names. Optionally, change the ScreenTip and Message box text for the ShipRegion and ShipPostalCode fields to correspond with the conditional formatting values you applied in Chapter 7.
3. Save your changes, click Preview Form, and clear the Same As Bill To Address check box to verify that you've applied a data validation rule to each text box, as shown here by the dashed red borders around each of the six Shipping Information text boxes:

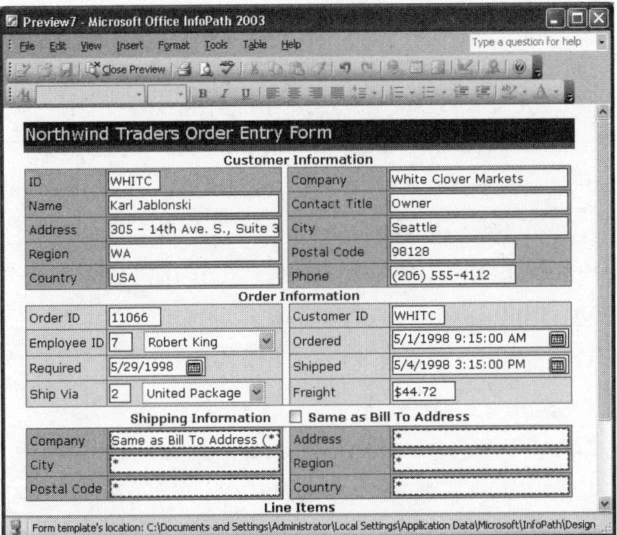

4. **Type entries in the text boxes that don't correspond with the Customer Information field values to test the combination of data validation and conditional formatting.**
5. **Close the preview to return to design mode.**

Whether conditional formatting of Shipping Information values is applicable at this point is a judgment call. If most shipping address fields are likely to be the same as billing address fields, the conditional formatting tests are useful. Otherwise, conditional formatting might distract data entry operators.

Testing Numeric Values

XPath automatically detects whether a node value is a string or number. Comparison values, such as [Not] Less Than, [Not] Less Than Or Equal To, [Not] Equal To, [Not] Greater Than or Equal To, and [Not] Greater Than, apply to numeric values, as you'd expect, and also to string values. When testing string values, these operators test the numeric Unicode value of the first character. If the string has more than one character, the test continues until a mismatch occurs with a successive character. If no character mismatch occurs, the values are equal; otherwise, the result is greater or less than the comparison value. If the comparison value you type in the text box is "BB", a "BC" field value returns true for the Is Greater Than comparison, and "BA" returns true for Is Less Than.

The Line Items repeating list in the Northwind Traders Order Entry Form contains several numeric values that require validation to ensure data consistency. Here are the validation rules for LineItem field values, expressed in positive-logic terms, that you apply in this section's exercise:

- The OrderID attribute value must match the Order Information section's OrderID element value. You can use the Insert Formula feature to apply the OrderID element value as the default value of the attribute, but users can change the value if you don't make the OrderID attribute's text box read-only.
- QuanOrdered must be greater than 0 and not greater than 100, which is Northwind's maximum order limit for a single item.
- QuanShipped must be less than or equal to QuanOrdered.
- The BackOrdered field value must be true if QuanShipped is less than QuanOrdered and must be false if QuanShipped equals QuanOrdered. You can use the Insert Formula feature to set the value of the BackOrdered field, but users can change the value if the control isn't read-only.
- The Discount value must be 0 for QuanOrdered values less than 5 units and less than or equal to 25 percent.

Follow these steps to add and test the preceding data validation rules for the Line Items list.

▶ Validate the OrderID attribute and the QuanOrdered and QuanShipped fields

1. **With the Northwind Traders form open in design mode, right-click the Order ID box in the Line Items section, choose Text Box Properties, click Data Validation, and click Add to open the second Data Validation (OrderID) dialog box.**
2. **With OrderID selected in the first list, select Is Not Equal To in the comparison operator list, and Select A Field Or Group in the third list.**
3. **In the Select A Group Or Field dialog box, and double-click OrderID under the OrderInfo node.**
4. **Add text, such as Line item Order ID value must match Order ID, to the ScreenTip and Message text boxes, and click OK three times to apply the rule and close the dialog boxes.**
5. **Open the Order Quan. box's Data Validation (QuanOrdered) dialog box, leave the default QuanOrdered in the first list, select Is Less Than in the second list, select Type A Number in the third list. Type 1 in the text box, and click And to add the second row.**
6. **Select Or from the And/Or list in the preceding row, leave the default QuanOrdered in the first list, select Is Greater Than in the second list, select Type A Number in the third list. Type 100 in the text box, add Order quantity must**

be 1 or more and less than 100 as the ScreenTip and message text, and click OK three times to add the rule and close the dialog boxes.

7. Open the Ship Quan. box's Data Validation (QuanShipped) dialog box, leave the default QuanShipped in the first list, select Is Greater Than in the second list, and select Select A Field Or Group.
8. In the Select A Group Or Field dialog box, expand the LineItem node, and double-click QuanOrdered. Add **Quantity shipped can't be greater than quantity ordered** as the ScreenTip and Message text, and click OK three times to apply the rule and close the dialog boxes.
9. Save your changes, preview the form, test the rules you've added so far, and return to design mode.

If the QuanOrdered rule doesn't work correctly, you probably forgot to change And to Or in step 6.

The following exercise shows you how to combine two sets of And and Or operators in a single data validation rule for the BackOrdered field, and validate a field of the Decimal (*double*) data type.

▶ Validate the BackOrdered and Discount fields

1. Open the Back Order check box's DataValidation (BackOrdered) dialog box, leave the default BackOrdered in the first list, select Is Equal To in the second list and FALSE in the third list, and click And to add a new row.
2. Accept And in the preceding row; select QuanShipped in the first list, Is Less Than in the second list, and Select A Field Or Group in the third list; and specify the QuanOrdered field for comparison
3. Click the And button to add a new row, and change And to Or in the preceding row.
4. Leave the default BackOrdered, select Is Equal To and TRUE, and click And.
5. Accept And in the preceding row; select QuanShipped, Is Equal To, Select A Field Or Group; specify the QuanOrdered field for comparison: and add ScreenTip and Message text, as shown on the next page.

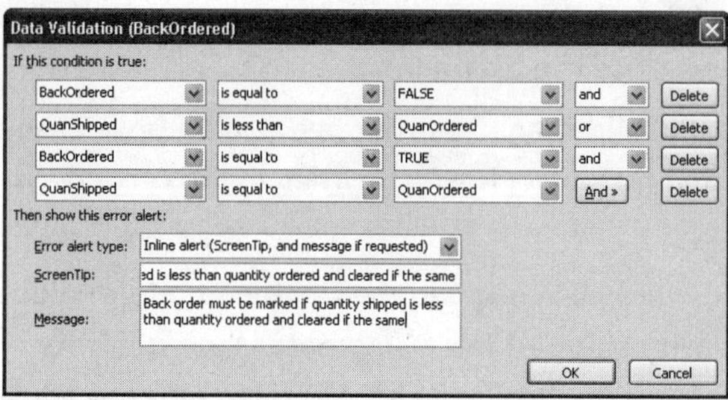

6. Click OK three times to add your rule for the BackOrdered field.
7. Open the Discount text box's Data Validation (Discount) dialog box, leave the default Discount, select Is Greater Than and Type A Number, type **0** as the comparison value, and click And.
8. Accept And in the preceding row; select QuanOrdered, Is Less Than, and Type A Number; type **5** as the comparison value, and click the And button to add a new row.
9. Change And to Or in the preceding row, leave the default Discount, select Is Greater Than, select Type A Number, and type **0.25** as the comparison value.
10. Add ScreenTip and Message text, as shown here:

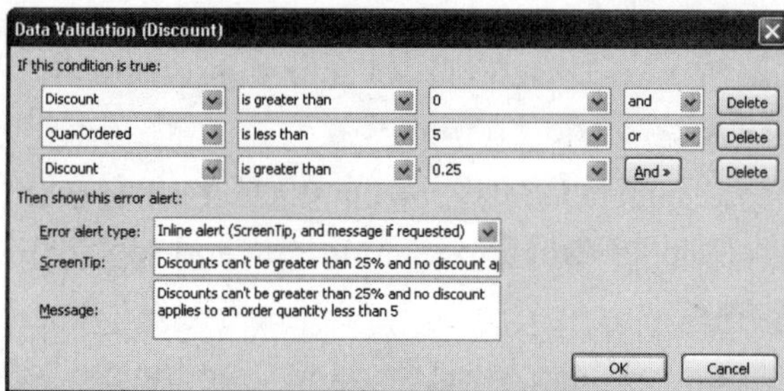

11. Click OK three times to add the validation rule, save your changes, and open a preview to test the two rules you added with values such as those shown here:

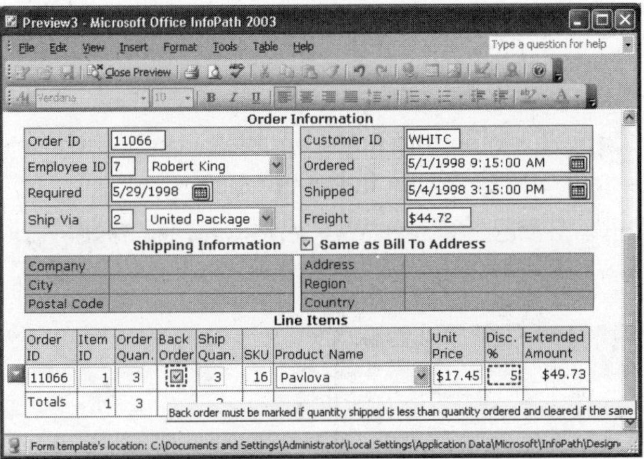

Validating List Box Values

List boxes return text or numeric values; data validation expressions for list boxes are the same as those for text boxes of equivalent data types. Alternatively, if you have a text box bound to the same field as the list box, you can apply the data validation rule to the text box.

The following example assumes that Speedy Express (list box value = 1) makes deliveries to U.S. destinations only. The Same As Bill To Address option complicates the validation expression. If you select the Same As Bill To address check box, the expression must test the Customer Information section's Country field instead of the ShipCountry field. The data validation expression in VBA syntax is shown here:

(ShipVia = 1 And IsShipToSameAsBillTo = True And Country <> "USA") Or (ShipVia = 1 And IsShipToSameAsBillTo = False And ShipCountry <> "USA")

The Data Validation dialog box has a maximum of five conditions and the preceding requires six conditions. Thus, you must add a second expression group for the expression to the right of the *Or* operator in the VBA example above.

To add the Speedy Express constraint to the Ship Via drop-down list and test the result, follow these steps.

▶ Validate the Ship Via drop-down list

1. **Open the Ship Via drop-down list's Data Validation (ShipVia) dialog box.**
2. **Leave the default ShipVia in the first list, select Is Equal To, select Type Number, type 1 in the text box, and click And to add a new row.**

3. Select the IsShipToSameAsBillTo attribute in the first list, select Is Equal To, select TRUE, and click And to add a new row.
4. In the first list, select the Select A Field Or Group item to open the Select A Field Or Group dialog box. Expand the CustomerInfo node, double-click Country, select Is Not Equal To, select Type Text, and type **USA** in the text box.
5. Add appropriate ScreenTip and Message text. Your entries for the first expression group appear as shown here:

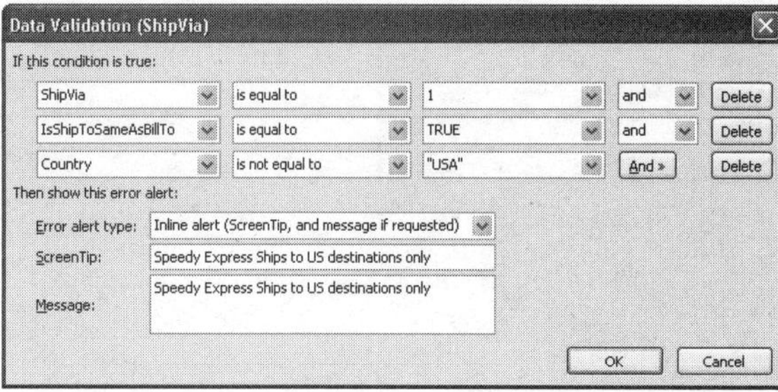

6. Click OK to add the first validation expression group, and click Add to add another expression group.
7. Repeat steps 2 and 3, but select FALSE as the value in step 3.
8. Select ShipCountry, Is Not Equal To, Type Text, and type **USA** in the text box.
9. Add the same ScreenTip and Message text you added in step 5, click OK three times to close the dialog boxes, apply the second expression group, and save your changes.

▶ **Test your validation rule**

1. Click Preview form, and select Speedy Express in the Ship Via list. The form's default values don't violate the validation rule.
2. Change the Shipping Information section's Country value to **UK** or any country name other than USA to test the first (declarative) expression group. The expression flags the Ship Via box and the drop-down list as containing a bad entry because both controls are bound to the ShipVia field, as shown here:

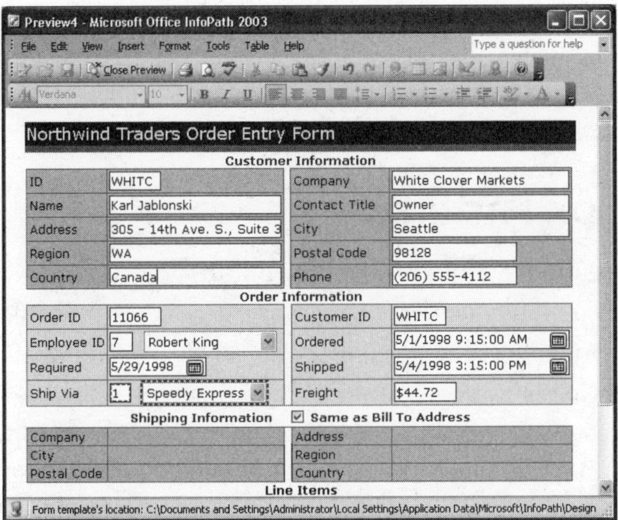

3. **Clear the Same As Bill To Address check box. The text and list remain flagged, because data in the Shipping Information section's Country box is invalid at this point.**
4. **Type USA in the Shipping Information section's Country box, and press Tab to apply the value and remove the data validation flag from the Ship Via controls.**
5. **Type UK in the same Country box, and press Tab to apply the value and verify that a value that is valid for the ShipCountry field but not for Speedy Express in the ShipVia field flags the two controls.**

Testing Date Picker Values

The section "Conditional Formatting Based on a Non-Blank Value," in Chapter 7, showed you how to test for the presence of values in date picker controls, and that chapter's "On Your Own" section suggested an additional exercise for conditionally formatting the Order ID text box if the Required date value is present and less than or equal to the Ordered date. Conditional formatting and data validation logical expressions are identical.

You can compare date picker values with a fixed date value you type in a text box, which is seldom useful, or with other Date (*date*) and DateAndTime (*dateTime*) InfoPath field data types. (The Time (*time*) field data type is a special case and isn't applicable to date picker control values.) InfoPath treats dates as numeric values in declarative expressions, but uses a special string-comparison function (*msxsl:string-compare*) to determine date equality or inequality. The Today function is a useful comparison value for values of the *date* datatype. You can compare a date with your computer's system date by choosing Use A Formula in the third condition list to open the Insert Formula dialog box, clicking Insert Function, and selecting Today from the Functions list.

Validating Text Box Patterns

InfoPath's pattern-matching feature lets you validate or conditionally format special text formatting. The Data Entry Pattern dialog box offers prebuilt regular expressions for U.S. and Canadian telephone numbers, social security numbers, 5-digit ZIP Codes, and ZIP+4 Codes, as shown on the left in Figure 8-4. You can also create your own regular expression by selecting a custom pattern and adding special characters from an Insert Special Character drop-down list. The dialog box on the right in Figure 8-4 shows a pattern for matching the five-letter CustomerID field.

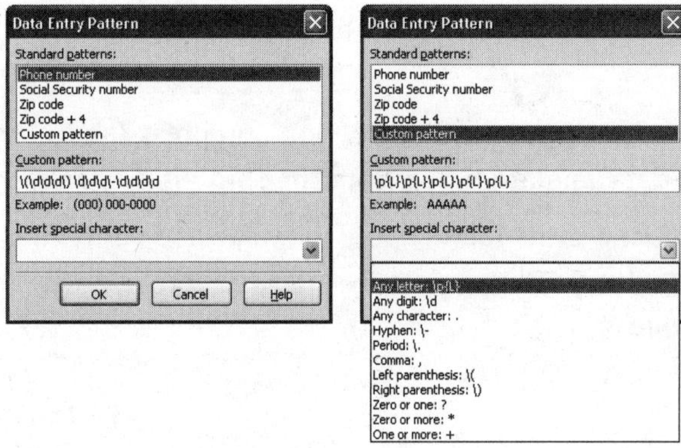

Figure 8-4 The Data Entry Pattern dialog box provides prebuilt regular expressions (left) and lets you create custom regular expressions by adding elements from a drop-down list (right).

See Also For more information about regular expressions, visit *msdn.microsoft.com/library/en-us/cpgenref/html/cpconRegularExpressionsLanguageElements.asp*. This page has links to a wide range of regular expression topics.

To validate the format of U.S. and Canadian telephone numbers, follow these steps.

▶ **Use a regular expression to test phone number formatting**

1. Open the Phone text box's Data Validation (Phone) dialog box, and click Add.
2. Leave the default Phone in the first list, select Does Not Match Pattern, and select Select A Pattern to open the Pattern Matching dialog box.
3. Accept the default Phone Number pattern, and click OK.
4. Click And; select Country, Is Equal To, Type Text; and type **USA**.

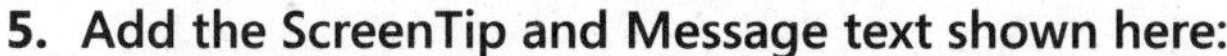

5. **Add the ScreenTip and Message text shown here:**

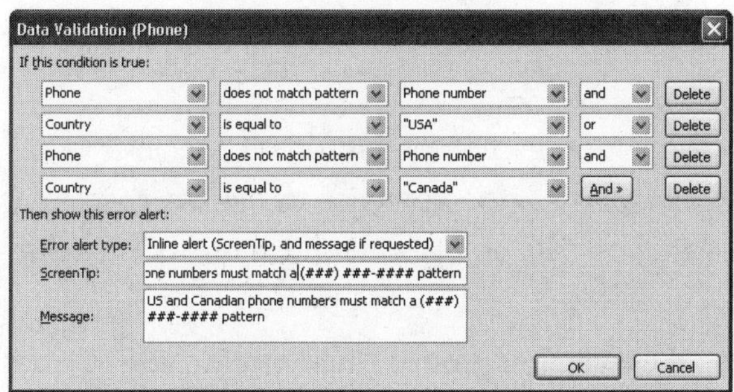

6. **Click OK to add the expression group, click Add, and repeat steps 2 through 5, but type Canada in step 4.**
7. **Click OK three times to apply the data validation rule, and save your changes.**
8. **Open a preview, and change the Phone box contents with USA and Canada as text box values to verify the validation rule.**

Chapter Summary

Data validation by data entry applications such as InfoPath is critical to maintaining organization-wide data accuracy and consistency, especially if the data isn't submitted immediately to a database that has built-in data validation rules. InfoPath's data validation features closely resemble those for applying conditional formatting. Both features use standards-based XPath expressions. View .xsl files store expressions for conditional formatting; the manifest.xsf file holds data validation expressions, which apply to all views of a form. The primary difference in the data validation UI is substitution of a ScreenTip and message box for conditional formatting property values and the inability to add multiple expression groups.

If a validation rule requires more than five expressions or contains both *And* and *Or* operators, you must add expression groups to complete the rule. XPath includes common comparison operators for numeric and text values; InfoPath treats date values as numeric for comparison purposes. You use less than, less than or equal to, greater than or equal to, and greater than operators primarily with numeric and date values. Pattern matching with regular expressions lets you validate the format of text box values; you also can use pattern matching with conditional formatting.

Q&A

Q. Can I validate rich text boxes and other basic control types that weren't covered in this chapter?

A. Yes. Data validation applies to all controls except the button picture, ink, file attachment, and expression box types. It's a good practice to validate check box and option button group values where possible, but validating rich text box and list (bulleted, numbered, or plain) content isn't a common practice.

Q. Is there a limit to the number of expression groups that I can include in a data validation rule?

A. There's no published limitation on the number of expression groups for data validation or conditional formatting. The practical limit is your ability to avoid conflicting conditions in multiple expression groups.

Q. Can I compare a Date (*date*) field value with a DateAndTime (*dateTime*) value?

A. Yes. You can verify that the comparison behaves as expected in the first "On Your Own" exercise.

On Your Own

Here are some additional exercises to test your expertise with data validation rules:

1. Add a data validation expression to the Required date picker that's true if the Required date isn't blank and is less than or equal to the Ordered date.
2. Add a validation rule to the Ship Via drop-down list that restricts use of Federal Shipping to orders destined for locations outside the United States.
3. Add a validation rule to the Ship Via drop-down list that restricts Speedy Express to destinations within the contiguous United States. Alaska, Hawaii, Puerto Rico, and the U.S. Virgin Islands (AK, HI, PR, and VI) aren't allowed as Region values.

CHAPTER 9

Working with Advanced Form Elements

In this chapter, you will learn how to:

- **Add a master/detail repeating table and section to a form**
- **Apply filters to repeating tables and sections**
- **Use data in the form to populate drop-down list boxes**
- **Add a drop-down list that's populated by a filtered drop-down list**
- **Work with event-based rules**
- **Establish user roles for workflow applications and assign users to the roles**
- **Add File Attachment controls to a form**
- **Insert ActiveX controls in a form and connect the control values to field values**
- **Change main data sources and use data documents with embedded schemas**

For more information:

- **See the "Using Drop-Down Lists and List Boxes" section of Chapter 6, "Adding Basic Controls and Lists," for more details about secondary data sources for drop-down lists.**
- **Refer to "The Gory Details of Base64 Encoding" sidebar of Chapter 6 for the details of Base64 encoding of file attachments.**

Microsoft InfoPath 2003 Service Pack 1 (SP-1) is much more than a traditional Microsoft Office service pack update, which usually delivers bug fixes and security patches. As discussed in the Introduction and Chapter 1, "Presenting InfoPath 2003 SP-1," SP-1 adds a multitude of new features to the original version of InfoPath 2003. An extended Office System 2003 beta cycle gave the InfoPath development team the time required to overcome a few limitations in the original product and add functionality requested by beta testers and early InfoPath adopters. The upgrade performed by SP-1 easily qualifies as a new "point" release, such as InfoPath 1.1 or even InfoPath 2004, but the product name remains InfoPath 2003.

To work through this chapter:

- You should be familiar with adding standard controls, such as list boxes, and repeating tables and sections to a form.
- Your test computer should be connected to a Microsoft Windows 2000 or later Active Directory domain for testing user roles, but a network connection isn't essential.
- You must have installed the sample files from the CD that accompanies this book in your C:\Microsoft Press\Introducing InfoPath 2003\Chapter09 folder. The DataSources subfolder contains the XML files you need to complete exercises in this chapter.

You've already encountered many SP-1 improvements in the preceding chapters. This chapter concentrates primarily on SP-1's advanced enhancements that apply to InfoPath elements with which you're already familiar–sections, controls, and data sources. Later chapters discuss more SP-1 changes and additions as you encounter them in sections and exercises.

Designing Master/Detail Forms

Master/detail forms are one of the most useful features added by SP-1. The purpose of master/detail forms is to improve the efficiency of forms that work with large amounts of data, such as lists of products, orders, employees, and the like. InfoPath's master/detail feature automatically adds a repeating table and repeating section to a form. The repeating table (master) displays a few important fields of a repeating group and, by default, the repeating section (detail) shows all group fields. The following two sections describe how to create a master/detail form from a single repeating group and from two related repeating groups linked by a key field value.

Creating a Master/Detail Form Bound to a Single Repeating Group

Default master/detail forms rely on a data source with a single repeating group. In this case, the InfoPath master/detail form displays two views of a single repeating group's fields. A repeating table at the top of the form displays a row for each group instance, and a repeating section below the table displays in text boxes the field values of the table row you select.

The basic objective of the default master/detail design is to permit users to easily view and edit a large number of items, such as a list of products or customers, whose field text boxes won't fit in a repeating table of reasonable width. You remove repeating table columns that users won't need to identify the group instance they want to view or edit. Clicking a table row synchronizes the form's details section with the selection, as shown in Figure 9-1.

Filtering long lists

The master repeating table's number of rows becomes a problem when users edit long lists. Fortunately, InfoPath provides a filter feature to display subsets of lists, such as products by category. The section "Filtering Repeating Tables and Sections" later in this chapter describes how to add a drop-down list to filter a master/detail form based on a field value, such as CategoryID, for a Products list form.

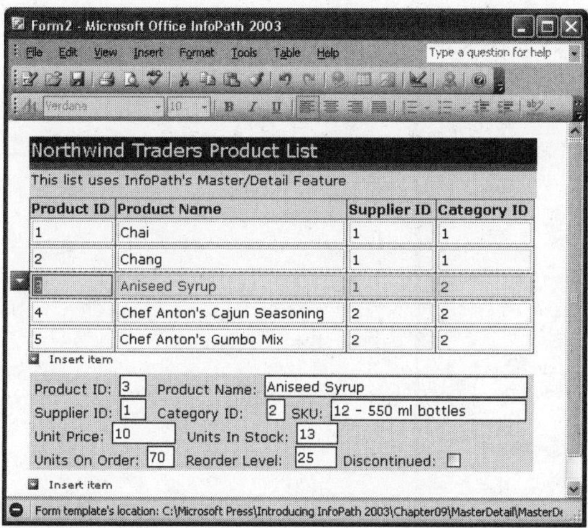

Figure 9-1 This master/detail form displays an XML document with five Product elements. Selecting a row of the repeating table displays the selected Product node's child elements.

To create and test a default master/detail form from a modified XML data document generated from the Products table of the Microsoft Access 2003 Northwind database, do the following.

▶ Add a default master/detail table and section to a new form

1. **In InfoPath, click the Design A Form link in Fill Out A Form dialog box to display an empty form with the Design A Form task pane active.**
2. **Click the New From XML Document Or Schema link to start the Data Source Wizard.**
3. **Click Browse and navigate to the C:\Microsoft Press\Introducing InfoPath 2003\Chapter09\DataSources folder, double-click Products.xml, and click Next and Finish to create the form's data source. Click Yes to use default values in the form.**
4. **Click the Controls link in the Data Source task pane, scroll to the Sections category of the Insert Controls list, and click the Master/Detail item to open the Master/Detail Binding dialog box.**
5. **Select and expand the Product group, as shown here, to bind the master repeating table and detail section to the group.**

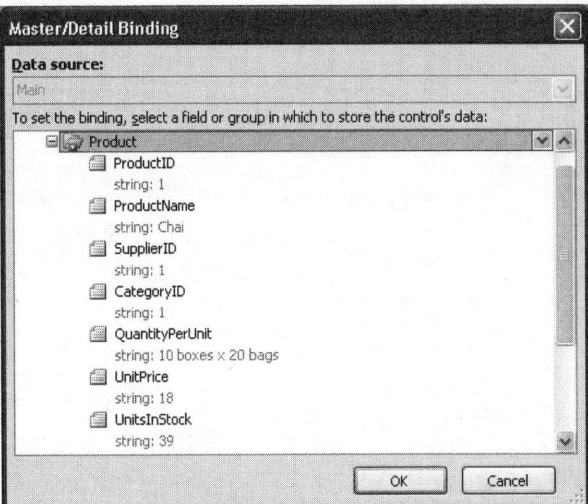

6. Click OK to add the default repeating table and its repeating detail section to the form, as shown here with empty lines at the bottom of the detail section removed.

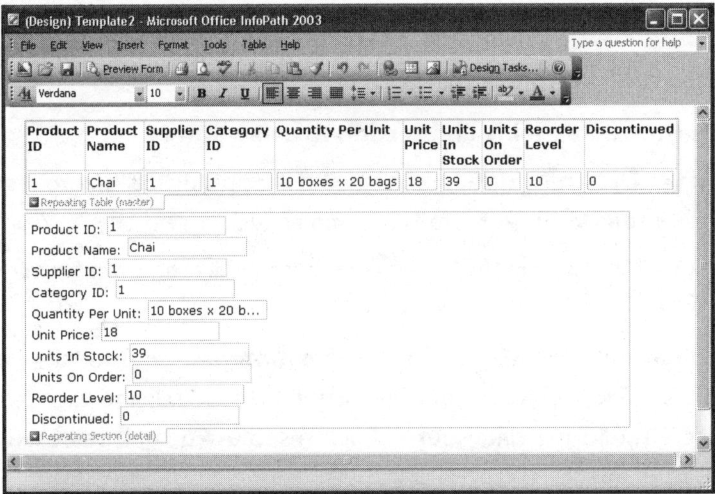

7. The master repeating table duplicates all data in the detail section, so select the Quantity Per Unit column and all columns to the right of it, and choose Table, Delete, Columns to remove them.

8. Resize the remaining four columns, and reduce the width of the detail section, as shown here.

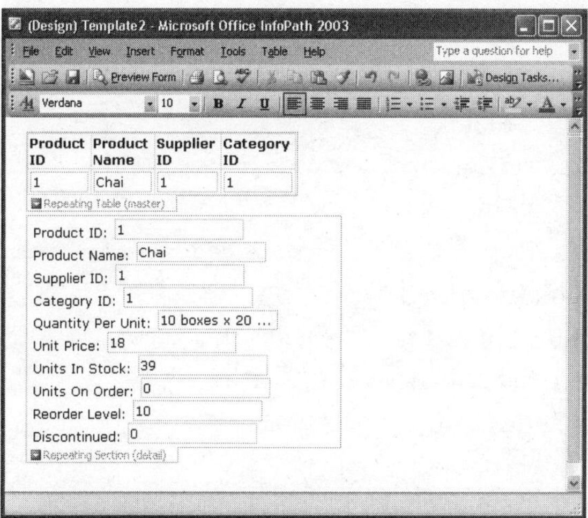

9. Save the template as **ProductsMD.xsn** in a new My Documents\InfoPath\MasterDetail folder, choose File, Properties, and name the form **ProductsMD Test 1**.

10. Press Ctrl+F1 to activate the task pane, choose Fill Out A Form, and click the ProductsMD Test 1 link to open a new Form1, whose repeating table contains 77 rows.

11. Scroll to the end of the list, select a row in the master table, and verify that the data in the details section reflects the selection, as shown here.

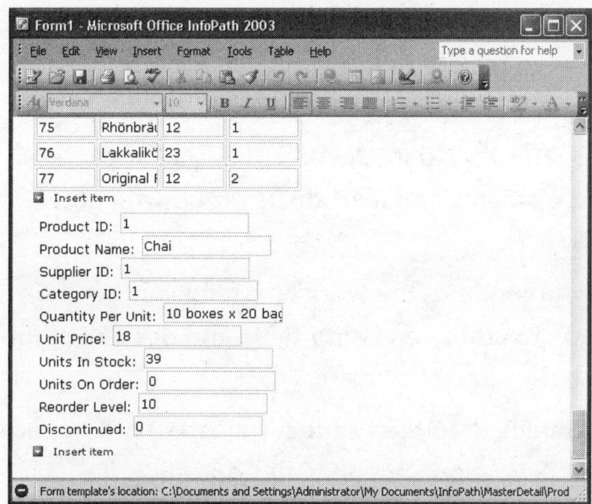

12. Save the form as **ProductsMD1** for use in the next section's exercise, and close it.

Linking Master/Detail Elements by a Key Field

You can modify master/detail relationships on the Master/Detail tab of the Properties dialog box for the Repeating Table (master) section or the Repeating Section (detail) section. This feature lets you add a repeating section from a related repeating group, and then link the added section by a common (key) field value. For example, if your form is based on an XML data document with Suppliers and Products nodes, you can link a detail section bound to the Product group to the Supplier table by the SupplierID value. This approach approximates the design of an Access master/child form that has a continuous subform for the child records. In this case, the repeating section can have multiple instances.

To create a master/child form based on the Supplier and Product repeating groups of the ProductsSuppliers.xml sample data document, follow these steps.

Fixing XML data documents exported by Access 2002 and later

When you use the Export to XML feature in Access to create an XML data document that serves as the data source for an InfoPath form *and* use the default values for testing the form and creating an initial XML data document, you must verify that the document's data structure is consistent for all elements. Access omits elements that have null values, instead of including a self-closing tag, such as *<Region />*.

If you want to use the exported document to provide temporary default values for testing or creating an initial XML data document, you must manually insert self-closing tags for all missing elements. Alternatively, you can create a copy of the table to export and use an update query to change null text values to empty strings (""), null numeric values to 0 or an improbable value, and null date/time values to 1/1/1900 or the like. You don't need to make these changes if you don't add the data as default values, but you'll find that the default sequence of fields in repeating tables and sections isn't the same as that of the data source.

▶ Create a master/detail form linked by key field values

1. **Repeat steps 1 through 3 of the preceding exercise, but open SuppliersProducts.xml in step 3. This XML data document has a Suppliers group with three Supplier child elements and a Products group with 10 Product child elements.**
2. **Drag the Supplier repeating group node to the work area, and choose Master/Detail as the section type to add a repeating table and details section to the form.**
3. **Delete the Repeating Section (detail), drag the Product repeating group under the repeating table, and choose Repeating Section with Controls.**
4. **Right-click the Repeating Section tab, choose Repeating Section Properties to open the Properties dialog box, and click the Master/Detail tab.**
5. **Select the Set As Detail option button to enable the controls related to master/detail relationships.**

6. Open the Link To Master ID drop-down list, and select the ID of the master repeating table, which is the only available, non-blank list item.
7. Select the By Key Field option for linking the master and detail elements, click the Select XPath button to the right of the Key Field (master) text box to open the Select Field or Group Dialog box, and double-click Supplier ID.
8. Select the XPath button to the right of the Key Field (detail) text box to open the Select Field or Group Dialog box, and double-click Supplier ID. The Master/Detail tab appears, as shown here. (Your Link To Master ID value might differ).

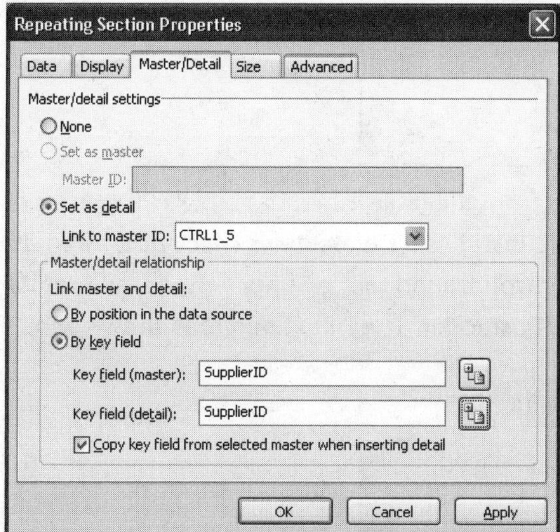

9. Click OK to close the dialog box and add the master/detail relationship. Click Preview Form.
10. Verify that three repeating section items appear for the default selection, Supplier ID 1.
11. Click the second row of the Supplier table, and verify that the four repeating sections show 2 as the Supplier ID.
12. Optionally, remove non-essential Supplier fields, reformat the detail section, and preview the form. The modified form preview appears, as shown here.

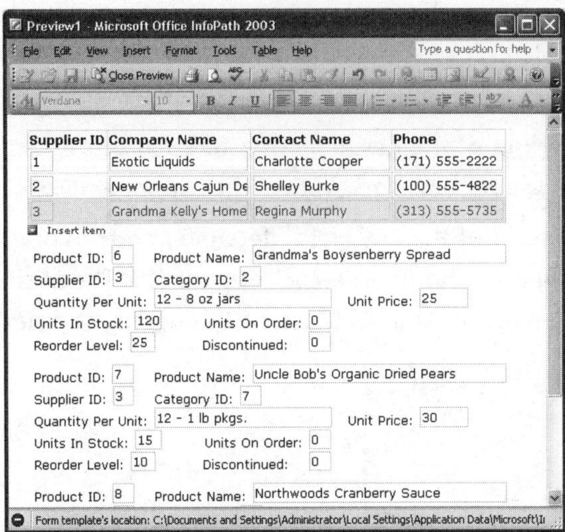

13. **If you remove Supplier columns from the table, open the table's Properties dialog box, and clear the Allow Users To Insert And Delete Rows check box. Alternatively, add a repeating section with controls bound to the Supplier node, and set its Link Master And Detail option to By Position In The Data Source, as shown here.**

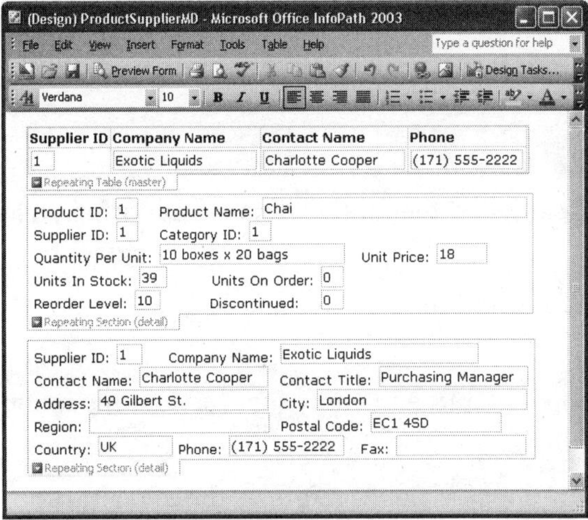

14. **Save your template as ProductSupplierMD.xsn in the My Documents\InfoPath\MasterDetail folder, and name the form ProductSupplierMD Test 1.**

You can change a repeating detail section to and from a repeating table, but you can't change a master repeating table to a repeating section with controls. The Select A Control dialog box in the Change To, More menu item doesn't contain a Repeating Section With Controls item.

Filtering Repeating Tables and Sections

As mentioned in the preceding section, viewing and editing long lists isn't practical without a method for limiting the number of rows of the repeating table. To solve this problem, InfoPath's filter feature lets you apply a filter to repeating tables and sections. You apply the filter to the master table of master/detail forms. The most common way to apply a filter criterion is to make a selection from a drop-down list box. Drop-down list boxes must be bound to a field of the data source, so you must add to the data source an element or attribute to store the filter criterion value. A filter criterion is metadata, not document content, so an attribute is the better field type choice. You add the attribute to the repeating group's parent node–Products, for this example.

The Specify Filter Conditions dialog box, which is similar to the Conditional Formatting and Data Validation dialog boxes, lets you determine how the filter behaves based on the drop-down list box selection. For example, a Show All or empty selection displays all records, and the drop-down list box's value field specifies the filter criterion value. If you add an alphabetic filter, for example, your list box would display Show All and 26 capital letter A through Z items. InfoPath stores filter conditions–such as conditional formatting criteria–in views, so you can specify a different dynamic (list box) or static (text value) filter criterion for a particular view.

The master/detail filter example in this section is based on the Northwind database's Categories list, which lets you select products in one of eight categories. To add the drop-down list box to the form, to set the list box's value field as the filter criterion value, and to learn how filters work in a form, follow these steps.

▶ Add a drop-down list of categories

1. **Open the ProductsMD1.xsn template you created in the section "Creating a Master/Detail Form Bound to a Single Repeating Group", activate the Data Source task pane, select the Products root node (not the Product child node), and click Add to open the New Field or Group Properties dialog box. Type productsFilter as the Name, select Field (attribute) as the Type, and leave the default Text (string) as the Data Type Value, as shown here.**

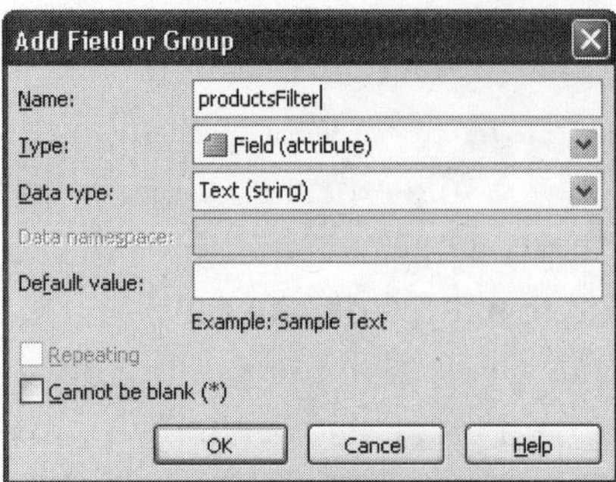

2. Click OK to add the new my:productsFilter attribute, add an empty line above the repeating table, type **Select a Product Category:** as the label, and choose Insert, Drop-Down List Box to open the Drop-Down List Box Binding dialog box.
3. Select the productsFilter attribute, and click OK.
4. Open the drop-down list's Properties dialog box, select the Look Up Values In A Data Connection option, and click the Add button to start the Data Connection Wizard.
5. Accept the default XML Document option, click Next, click Browse, navigate to the C:\Microsoft Press\Introducing InfoPath 2003\Chapter09\DataSources folder, and double-click Categories.xml. Then click Next, and click Finish to add the secondary data source, and click Yes to add the data document as a template resource file.
6. On the Data tab of the Drop-Down List Box Properties dialog box, click the Select XPath button to the right of the Repeating Group text box to open the Select A Field Or Group dialog box. Select the Category group, and click OK.
7. Click the Select XPath button to the right of the Display Name text box, select CategoryName in the Select Field or Group dialog box, and click OK. The Drop-Down List Box Properties dialog box appears, as shown on the next page.

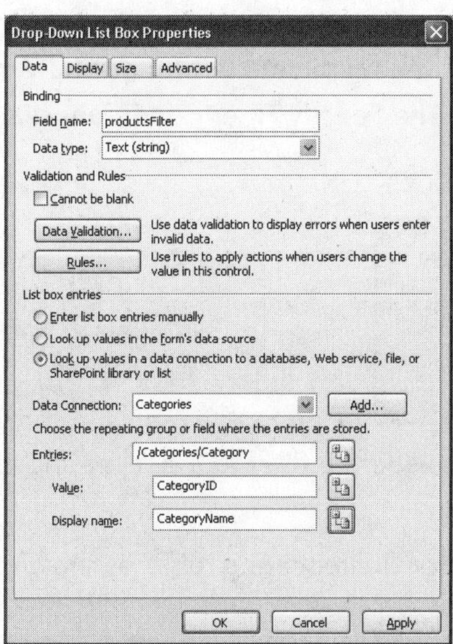

8. Click OK to close the Properties dialog box, remove the added Products Filter label from the first line of the form, and add **(blank to select all products)** to the right of the list.
9. Open the Properties dialog box for the Repeating Section (detail), and clear the Allow Users To Insert And Delete The Sections check box. You can't add a new product to a repeating section that's bound to a filtered master repeating table.
10. Click OK, choose Preview Form, and verify that the list contains an empty display name. Close the preview, and save your template changes.

▶ Apply the filter to the CategoryID field

1. Right-click the master repeating table, and open its Properties dialog box, leaving the Data tab active.
2. Change Insert Item in the text box to **Insert New Product**, and click the Display tab.
3. Click the Filter Data button to open the dialog box of the same name, and click Add to open the Specify Filter Conditions dialog box.
4. Select CategoryID in the first list, accept Is Equal To in the condition list, open the third list, choose Select A Field Or Group to open the dialog box of the same name, select the my:productsFilter attribute, and click OK.

5. Click And to add a new condition row, change the preceding row's And operator to Or, choose Select A Field Or Group, select the my:productsFilter attribute, click OK, and select Is Blank in the condition list. The Specify Filter Conditions dialog box appears, as shown here:

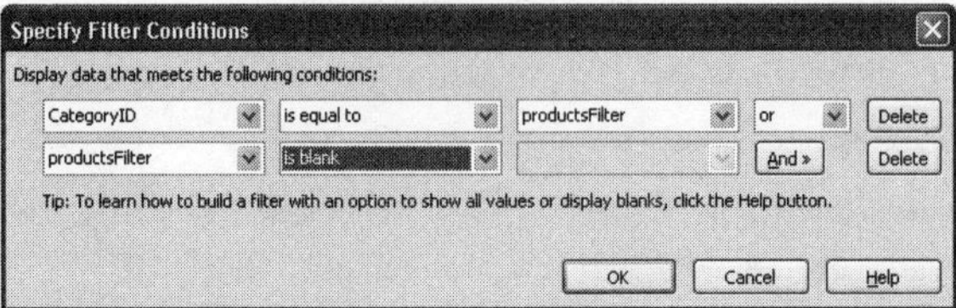

6. Click OK three times to close the dialog boxes add the filter to the repeating table. Open a form preview.
7. Select a category in the drop-down list to filter the repeating table, as shown here.

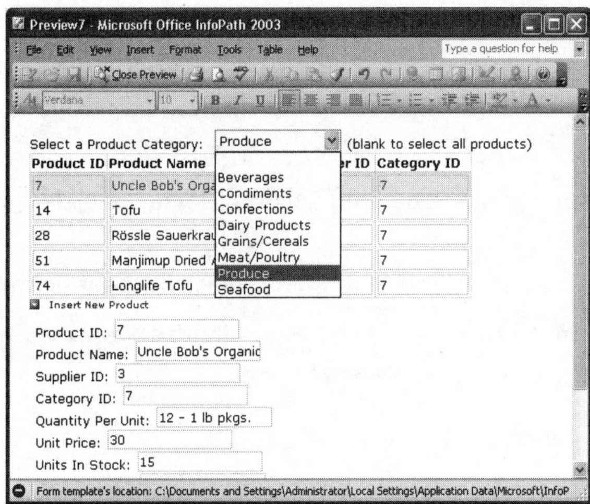

8. Select a few other categories, and then select the empty item in the list and verify that all repeating table items reappear.
9. Create an XML data document named **ProductsMD2.xml** from the template, and save it with a category selected.

▶ Test new product addition and filter behavior

1. Open ProductsMD2.xml, and select a category other than Beverages.
2. Click the repeating table's Insert New Order button, or link to insert a new product with the default values for the first Product element, Chai. Notice that filtered items have a small yellow filter symbol (a funnel) at the upper left of their selection buttons, but the selection button for the added item with a CategoryID value of 1 doesn't display the filter symbol, as shown here.

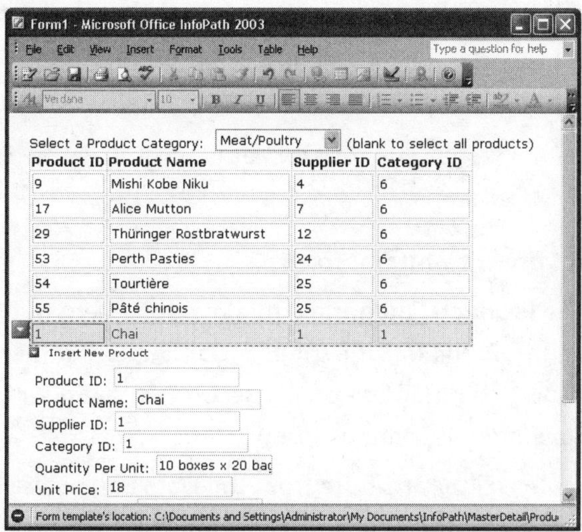

3. **Select the Beverages category, scroll to the bottom of the repeating table, and verify that the added product appears at the bottom of the list with a funnel symbol.**
4. **Select the category value in effect during the addition, and verify that the added item no longer appears in the list.**
5. **Close ProductsMD2.xml without saving your changes.**

You also can apply filters to independent repeating sections that aren't linked to repeating tables and to independent repeating tables.

Displaying secondary data sources in the Data Sources task pane

Another new SP-1 feature is the ability to display the main data source and all secondary data sources for a form in a list in the Data Sources task pane. Open the drop-down list, select the Categories (secondary) item, and expand the Category node to display its fields.

Populating Lists with Form Data

A major deterrent to populating lists from secondary data sources whose values are stored in template resource files is having to update the resource file to accommodate periodic changes. The alternative is linking to a data source on a server share, but this prevents disconnected users from accessing the network data source. One solution to this problem is to include the secondary data source as a separate repeating group in the XML data document, and to use the new capability in SP-1 to populate list boxes from the repeating group. This lets you add or delete items from list boxes bound to the group by adding a repeating section for the group to another view that's dedicated to list box maintenance.

ProductsCategories.xml is a sample data source document that's similar to the SuppliersProducts.xml source document that you used earlier in the section

"Emulating an Access Master/Child Form." The Product repeating group acts as the main data source for the form, and the Category repeating group provides the data source for the drop-down category list.

To design a master/detail form that uses the Category repeating group as the data source for the filter list box, follow these steps.

▶ Create the drop-down list and use it to filter a form

1. **Create a new template from the ProductsCategories.xml data document in the C:\Microsoft Press\Introducing InfoPath 2003\Chapter09\DataSources folder, and add master/detail sections as you did in the earlier section, "Creating a Master/Detail Form Bound to a Single Repeating Group."**
2. **Drag the Products group's productsFilter attribute from the Data Source list to above the repeating table, and change the text box to a drop-down list box.**
3. **Open the list box's Properties dialog box, select the Look Up Values In A Form option on the Data tab, click the Select XPath button to the right of the Repeating Group text box, and double-click Category in the Select A Field Or Group dialog box.**
4. **Click the Select XPath button to the right of the Display Name text box, and double-click CategoryName. Your Data tab appears, as shown here.**

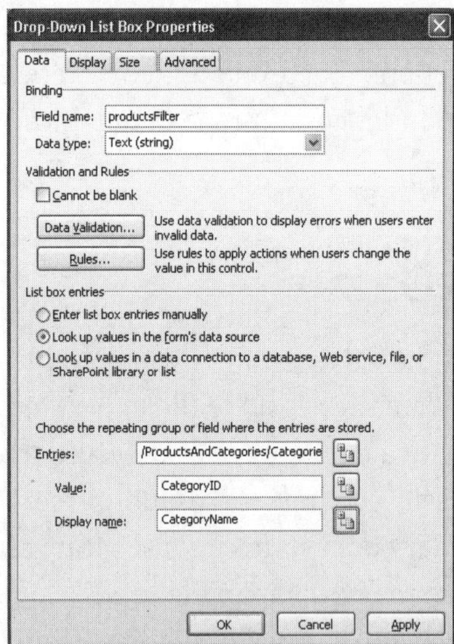

5. **Preview the form, and open the drop-down list box to verify that it contains a blank item and the eight category names.**

6. **Repeat steps 1 through 9 from the "Apply the filter to the CategoryID field" exercise in the earlier section, "Creating a Master/Detail Form Bound to a Single Repeating Group."**
7. **Optionally, you can save your form as ProductsMDListDS.xsn in the My Documents\InfoPath\MasterDetail folder and name the form ProductsMDListDS Test 1.**

Cascading Drop-Down List Box Selections

InfoPath lets you filter a secondary data source or the repeating section of a form that serves as the data source of a list box. This capability lets you use a primary (parent) list box to determine the list items of a secondary (child) list box. As an example, a Country list box can limit choices in a City list box to those cities in the selected country. In this case, the repeating section must contain elements with Country and City child elements for each city. CountryCity.xml in the C:\Microsoft Press\Introducing InfoPath 2003\Chapter09\DataSources folder is an example of the required repeating section structure. Cascading list boxes aren't limited to a two-level hierarchy; as an example, you can add a Continent list box and replace the Country data source with a ContinentCountry repeating section in the form.

You can use cascading list boxes to filter the form's contents at any level in the hierarchy. The following example filters customer data generated from the Northwind sample database's Customers table by country or city.

Staying in touch with list-management reality

Incorporating the metadata for cascading drop-down lists as repeating sections in the XML data document complicates InfoPath's role as a list-management tool. The user or programming code must update the metadata when the values of corresponding fields of repeating section(s), which serve as the form's data source, change. Thus, the example in this section uses repeating sections of the data document to store the list boxes' data. Unlike lists based on relational tables, maintaining synchronization between document content and metadata isn't a trivial task. The example is intended to demonstrate the use of cascading list boxes, and isn't a recommendation to use this technique in a real-world list-management application. For the sake of simplicity, the example uses elements, rather than attributes, to store metadata values.

▶ **Create the test form and add the drop-down list boxes**

1. **Create a new template from the CustomersLists.xml data document in the C:\Microsoft Press\Introducing InfoPath 2003\Chapter09\DataSources folder, expand the Customers node, drag the Customer repeating group to the work area, and choose Master/Detail to add a repeating table and section to the form.**
2. **Remove all but the Customer ID, Company Name, City, and Country columns from the master repeating table, adjust the widths of the columns to suit their content,**

and save your form as **CustomersMDCity.xsn** in the \My Documents\InfoPath\ MasterDetail folder, and add **CustomersMDCity Test 1** as the form name.

3. Open the Data Source task pane, drag the CustomersList node's listCountry attribute above the master table, change the text box to a drop-down list box, and delete List from the label.
4. Open the list's Properties dialog box, select the Look Up Values In A Form option on the Data tab, click the Repeating Group's Select XPath button to open the Select A Field Or Group dialog box, expand the Countries node, and double-click the Country node.
5. Leave the default periods in the Value and Display Name fields, which are references to Country, in the Value and Display Name text boxes, and click OK. Preview the form to verify that the Country list contains the correct values, and then close the preview.
6. Drag the listCountryCity attribute to the right of the Country list, change the label to City, and change the text box to a drop-down list box.
7. Repeat step 4, but expand the CountriesAndCities node, double-click the CountryCity repeating group, and specify City as the Value and Display Name. The Drop-Down List Box Properties dialog box appears, as shown here:

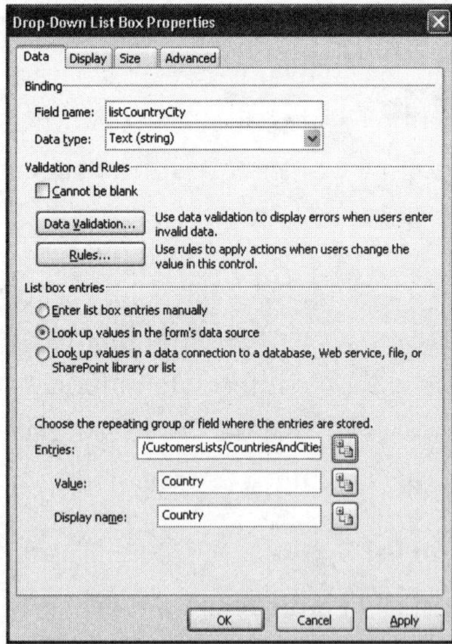

8. Preview the form, verify that the City list begins with Buenos Aires and ends with San Cristobal, and then save your changes.

▶ Filter the CountryCity group

1. Reopen the Cities list's Properties dialog box, click the Repeating Group's Select XPath button to open the Select A Field Or Group dialog box with the CityCountry node selected, and click the Filter Data button to open the Filter Data dialog box.
2. Click Add to open the Specify Filter Conditions dialog box, accept Country and Is Equal To in the first two lists, choose Select A Field Or Group in the third list, and double-click the listCountry node.
3. Click the And button to add another condition, and change And to Or.
4. Choose Select A Field Or Group in the first list, double-click the listCountry node, and select Is Blank in the condition list. The Specify Filter Conditions appears, as shown here.

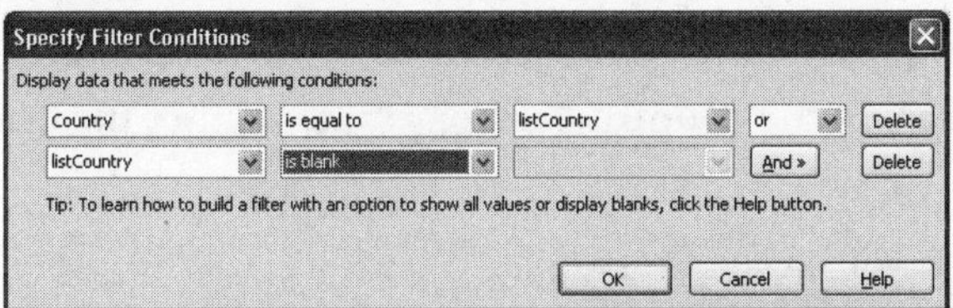

5. After you apply the filter the Value and Display Name field names change from City to Country, so change them back to City. Click OK four times to close the dialog boxes and return to the work area. Preview the form.
6. Select an item in the Country list, such as USA, open the City list to verify that the cities correspond to the country, and the select another country or no country. Notice that the City list retains an entry for the last city you selected. This artifact is related to the filter behavior mentioned in step 2 of the "Test new product addition and filter behavior" exercise in the "Filtering Repeating Tables and Sections" section.

▶ Filter the master table by the Country or City drop-down value

1. Open the Properties dialog box for the Customer repeating table, click the display tab, click the Filter Data button, and click Add to open the Specify Filter Conditions dialog box.
2. Select City in the first list, accept Is Equal To, choose Select A Field Or Group, and double-click listCountryCity.
3. Click And to add another condition, change And to Or, choose Select A Field Or Group in the first list, double-click listCountryCity, select Is Blank, and click OK to add the condition group.
4. Click Add to add another condition group, select Country in the first list, accept Is Equal To, choose Select A Field Or Group, and double-click listCountry.

5. **Click And to add another condition, change And to Or, choose Select A Field Or Group in the first list, double-click listCountry, select Is Blank, and click OK to add the condition group. Your Filter Data dialog box appears, as shown here.**

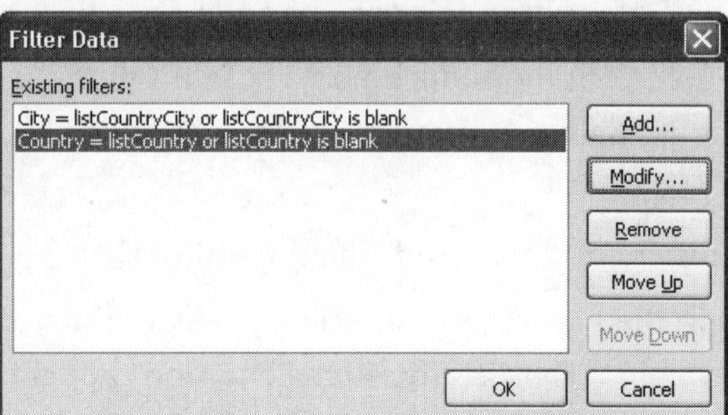

6. **Save your changes, and open a preview. Rows for all customer elements appear with both drop-down lists empty. Select a country, such as UK, with an empty City list box to display all customers in the country. Select a city to restrict the list to customers in the city, as shown here.**

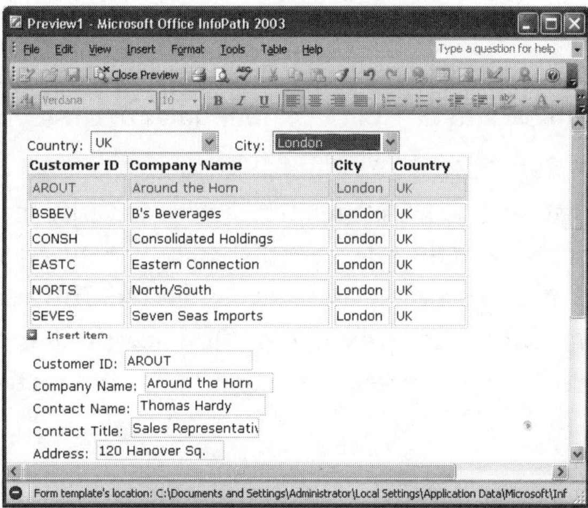

Applying Event-Based Rules

InfoPath SP-1 adds a new rules feature that lets you intercept events created by user actions and specify a course of actions, which is subject to a set of conditions you designate for each action. Applying declarative event-based rules minimizes the need to write InfoPath event handlers with programming code.

You can establish rules to handle the following events:

- **Form open.** Choose Tools, Form Options, to open the Form Options dialog box, click the Open and Save tab, and click the Rules button to open the Rules For Opening Forms dialog box.
- **Form submit from the toolbar button or File menu.** Choose Tools, Submitting Forms to open the Submit Options dialog box, select the Enable Submit option, choose Custom Submit Using Rules from the Submit list, and click the Rules button to open the Rules For Submitting Forms dialog box.
- **Button click.** Add a button control to a form, double-click it to open the Button Properties dialog box, and click the Rules button to open the Rules dialog box.
- **Control value change.** Open the control's Properties dialog box, click the Rules tab to display the Rules list, and click Add to open the Rule dialog box, as shown in Figure 9-2.

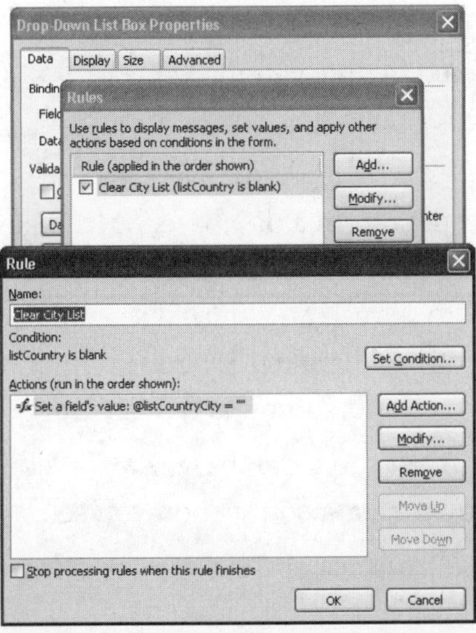

Figure 9-2 This rule sets the CustomersMDCity form's City list box value to blank when you select a blank Country value.

Invoking a rule is subject to conditions for the rule that you specify in a Condition dialog box, shown in Figure 9-3, which is identical to the Specify Filter Conditions dialog box. You can add multiple condition sets, which apply to actions in the same way that multiple expression sets apply to conditional formatting or data validation operations.

Figure 9-3 This condition specifies that the rule of Figure 9-2 is invoked only when you select a blank Country list box.

Following is a list of the actions you can initiate from an event:

- **Show A Dialog Message.** Displays a message box with the text message you specify and an OK button.
- **Show A Dialog Expression.** Displays a message box containing the result of a formula as the message and an OK button.
- **Switch Views.** Displays the view of a name you select from a list. You can specify a view based on the user's role or a button click. (Roles are the subject of the following section, "Creating and Assigning Roles.") This option isn't available for control value change events. Using the Switch Views action is one of the topics of Chapter 10, "Adding Views to a Template."
- **Set a Field's Value.** Sets the value of a selected field to a static value or the result of a formula you specify in the Insert Formula dialog box. You can't change the field value of the control that initiates a control value change event.
- **Query Using a Data Connection.** Requests data from a database, XML Web service, or Microsoft SharePoint list specified by the data connection you select. You can invoke this action from a button click to refresh an external secondary data source supplied by a database or Web service. Chapter 13, "Connecting Forms to Databases," and Chapter 14 cover query and submit actions.
- **Submit Using a Data Connection.** Sends updates to a database, XML Web service, SharePoint list, or Web site specified by the data connection you select.
- **Open a New Form to Fill Out.** Opens a new instance of the template's data document.
- **Close the Form.** Closes the active data document with the opportunity to save changes, if any.

Figure 9-4 shows the actions available in the Action dialog box's Action list for the control value change event. You can add multiple actions for an event, which execute in sequence or after processing an action with the Stop Processing Rules When This Rule Finishes check box selected. (See Figure 9-2.)

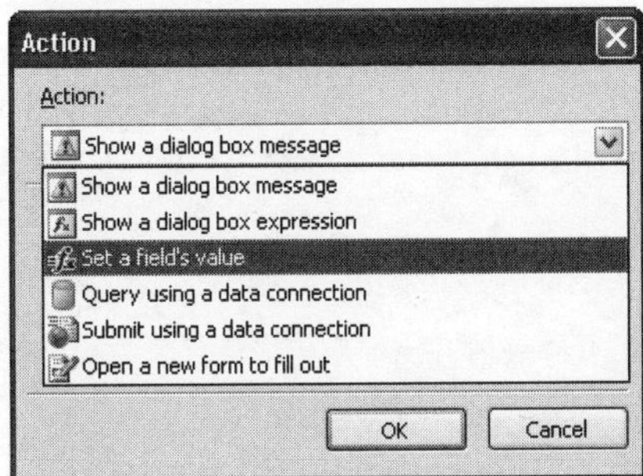

Figure 9-4 This subset of actions is available to handle a control value change event.

The CustomersMDCity.xsn form you created in the preceding section has a minor defect: when you select the empty item in the Country list with a non-blank City selection, the master/child elements don't change. The form should display all customers when you select the empty Country item. Fixing this defect provides a good example of adding a simple rule to a form.

To add a rule that sets the City text box value to an empty string (blank) when you select the empty item in the Country text box, follow these steps.

▶ Add a control value changed event rule

1. **Open the CustomersMDCity.xsn template in design mode, if you closed it.**
2. **Right-click the Country drop-down list box, open its Properties dialog box, and click the Rules tab.**
3. **Click the Add button to open the Rule dialog box. In the Name text box, replace Rule 1 with Clear City List.**
4. **Click the Set Condition button to open the Condition dialog box, leave the default listCountry in the first list, select Is Blank in the second list, and click OK to add the condition.**
5. **Click Add Action to open the Action dialog box, select Set A Field's Value in the Action list, click the Field's Select XPath button to open the Select Field or Group dialog box, and double-click the listCountryCity attribute.**
6. **Leave the Value text box empty to specify an empty string (""), as shown here.**

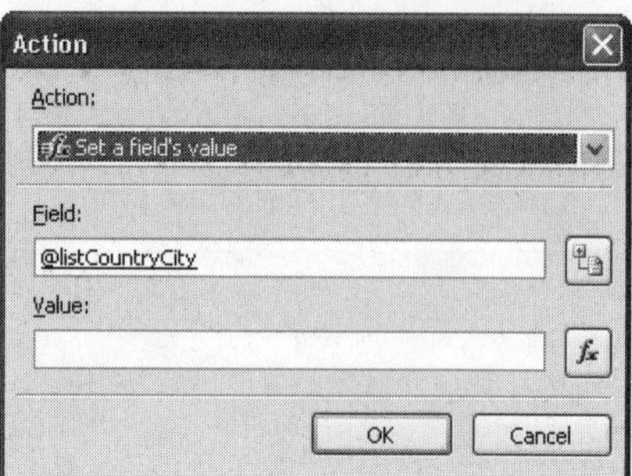

7. **Click OK three times to close the dialog boxes and apply the rule.**
8. **Open a preview, select a country and city, and then select the blank value in the Country list to verify that the City list clears and all customer rows appear in the repeating table.**
9. **Save your template changes.**

Rules are a very powerful addition to the InfoPath 2003 feature set. The remaining chapters in Part III of this book contain several more examples of applying rules to views and forms that connect to databases or consume Web services.

Creating and Assigning User Roles

User roles are an essential element of workflow processing. As an example, any employee can initiate an expense report form, but only a supervisor can approve it, and, if the requested reimbursement is more than $1,000 or the initiating employee is a supervisor, a manager's approval might be needed. The roles in this workflow scenario are Employee (called the form's initiator), Supervisor, and Manager. You can specify rules with actions that depend on the role membership of the person who opens the form. For this scenario, the expense report might have different views for Employees, Supervisors, and Managers. The rule displays the appropriate view when the user opens the form.

Establishing roles is a two-step process: you add a role for the template and then add Windows user accounts or security groups; or you add the name of a field that contains a value of user, supervisor, or manager logon (DOMAIN/Username) to the new role. Figure 9-5 shows the UI for adding a Supervisor role and a domain user to the role. The process is similar to adding a new security group to an Active Directory domain or organization unit, or a local group to your computer, and then adding members to the group.

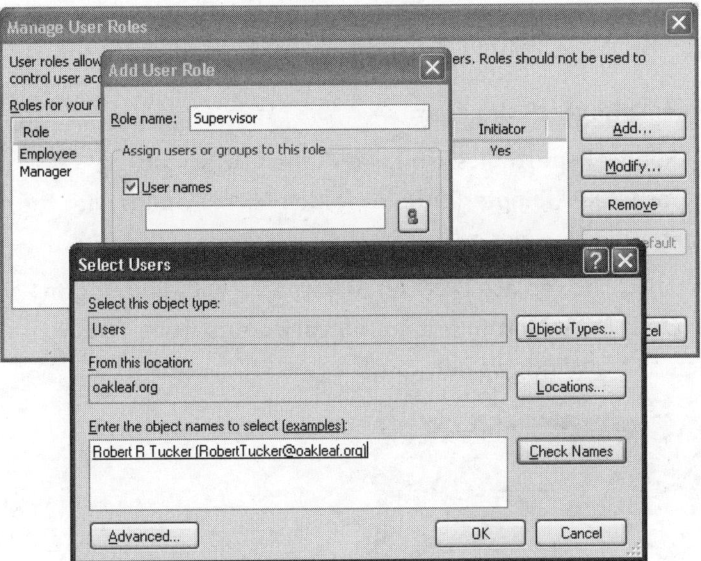

Figure 9-5 You can add a new role and add users, groups, or both in a single operation with InfoPath's Manage User Roles, Add User Role, and Select Users or Select Groups dialog boxes.

The security group analogy doesn't mean that roles provide data security. Even if you restrict members of a role to a read-only view of the data, determined users can edit the XML data document using Notepad. Form users without role membership are assigned to the designated default role, which must be present if you add roles to the form.

User roles are most effective when you and the users of your forms have accounts in a Windows 2000 or later Active Directory domain. If you assign a security group to a role, the form's user must be connected to the network to resolve the username's group membership when opening the form. In addition, the form must be published in a Microsoft Internet Explorer 6.0 local intranet zone or on a trusted site. By default, forms opened from server shares and Web sites in the user's domain are in the local intranet zone. The Automatic Logon With Current Username And Password (the default) or Automatic Logon Only In Intranet Zone option must be selected in the User Authentication, Logon section at the end of the Settings list of Internet Explorer's Security Options dialog box.

The ExpenseReportRoles.xsn template example–derived from InfoPath's Expense Report (Domestic) sample form–demonstrates the use of user logon names that are stored in form fields to determine which of two views a user sees when opening the form. The form has two roles: Employee and Manager. Typing your logon name in the Employee Logon Name text box opens the default Employee/Initiator view;

doing the same in the Manager Logon Name text box opens the Manager/Approver view. To test the ExpenseReportRoles form and explore its design, follow these steps.

▶ Open and test the ExpenseReportRoles form

1. **In InfoPath, open the ExpenseReportRoles.xsn form in the C:\Microsoft Press\Introducing InfoPath 2003\Chapter09\Roles folder. Form1 opens with the default Employee/Initiator view active.**
2. **Scroll to the Manager table, and replace DOMAIN\Username with your logon name, as shown here. (Omit DOMAIN\ to use your local user account if your computer isn't connected to a Windows network.)**

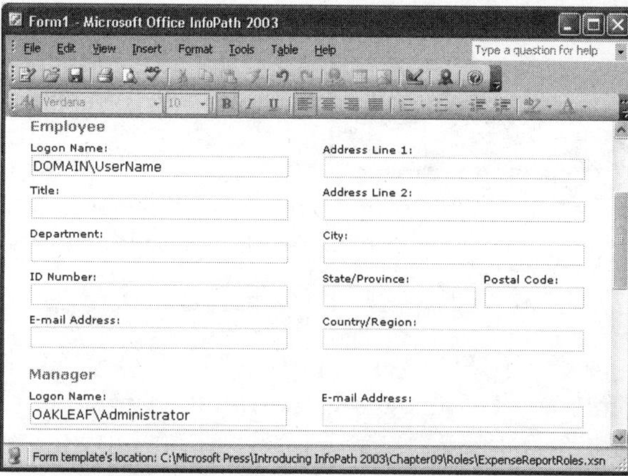

3. **Save the data document as UserAsManager.xml in a new My Documents\ InfoPath\Roles folder, and close it.**
4. **Reopen UserAsManager.xml, which now displays the Manager/Approver view.**
5. **Replace DOMAIN\Username in the Employee table with your logon name, as shown here.**

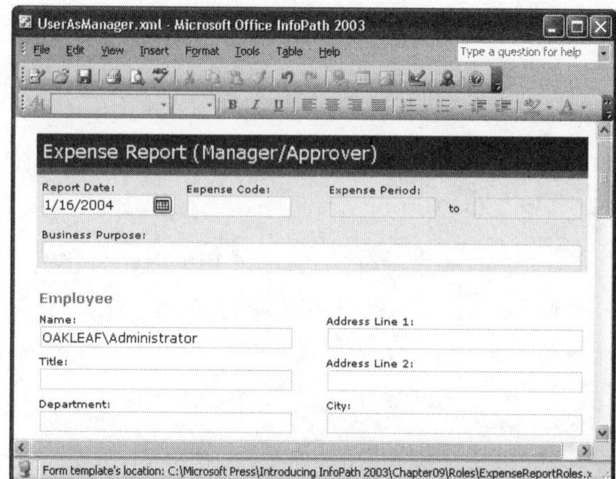

6. Replace your logon name in the Manager table with **DOMAIN\Username** or some other invalid account, and repeat step 3, but save the document as **UserAsEmployee.xml**.
7. Reopen UserAsEmployee.xml to display the Employee/Initiator view.

▶ Explore the User Roles and Form Opening Rules

1. Click the Design This Form button, and choose Tools, User Roles to open the Manage User Roles dialog box, as shown here.

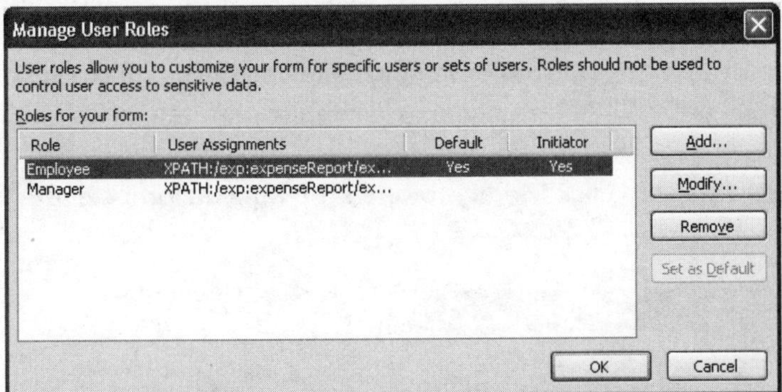

2. Select one of the roles (Manager, for this example), click Modify to open the Modify User Role dialog box, and then click the User Names From The Form text box's Select XPath button to open the Select A Field Or Group dialog box, as shown here.

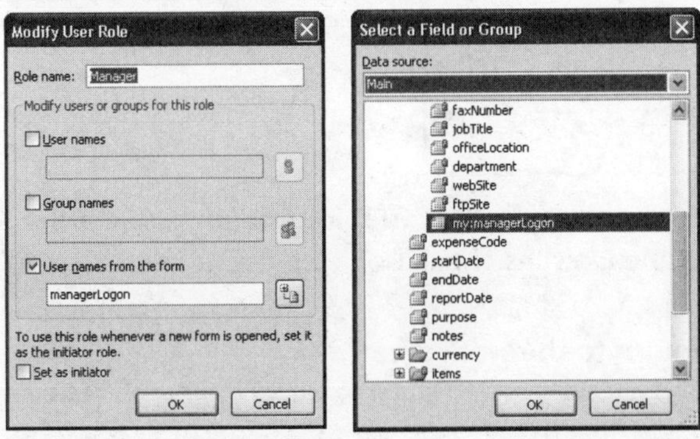

When a my:managerLogon field is added to the Manager node, it stores the Manager Logon Name value. A similar my:employeeLogon field stores the Employee Logon Name value.

3. Click Cancel three times to return to the form, and choose Tools, Form Options to open the Form Options dialog box, click the Open and Save tab, and click Rules to open the Rules For Opening Forms dialog box.

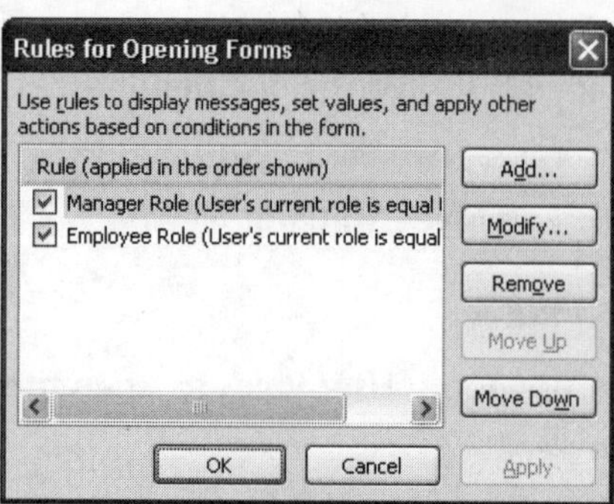

For this example, the rule application sequence isn't important because the manager and employee logons always differ and only one of the rules is invoked. If you specify groups or multiple user names, rule application sequence might be important.

4. **Select the Manager role, and click Modify to open the Rule dialog box, as shown here.**

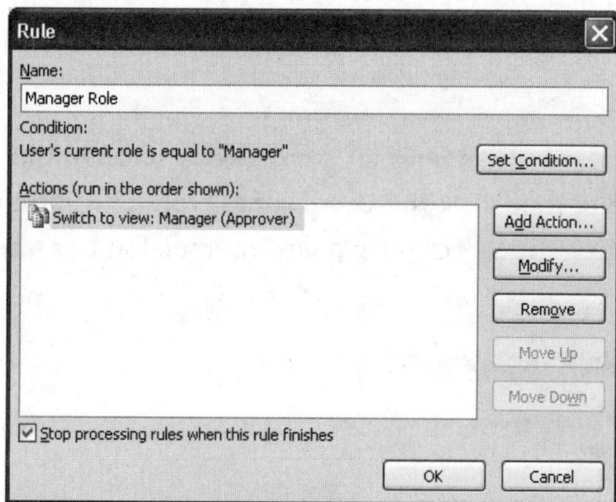

When rule application sequence is important, you might need to select the Stop Processing Rules When This Rule Finishes check box to prevent executing rules with lower priorities.

5. **Click Cancel three times to return to the work area.**

You also can take advantage of user roles using conditional formatting. For example, you can make specific employee-entered fields read-only for managers, as shown in Figure 9-6, or designate manager-entered approval fields as read-only for employees.

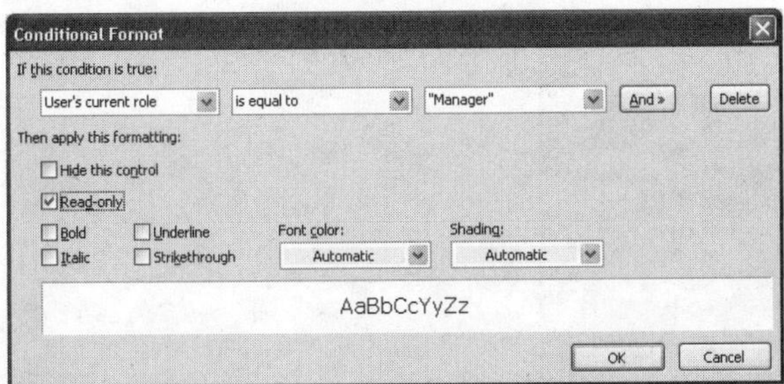

Figure 9-6 Conditional formatting with user role criteria enables specifying controls of a view as read-only for users in a specific role. You also can hide the view's optional sections or controls in optional sections.

Adding File Attachments

The File Attachment control lets you incorporate files of supported types as Base64-encoded data. Supported file types include ASCII or UTF-8 text, most Office System application documents, Web pages, and files of other types that aren't on InfoPath's list of verboten extensions in the note at the end of this section.

▶ Add an attachment to the Expense Report sample form

1. In InfoPath, click the Sample Forms link, select the Expense Report (Domestic) form, and click the Design This Form link.
2. Scroll to the optional Notes section, change Notes to **Trip Report Attachment**, and delete the notes rich text box.
3. Select the expenseReport root node in the Data Source task pane's list, and click add to open the Add Field or Group dialog box. Type **tripReport** as the name, select Picture Or File Attachment (base64) as the Data Type, leave the remaining default values, and click OK.
4. Drag the my:tripReport field to the table cell formerly occupied by the rich text box, and select File Attachment from the menu to add a default Click Here To Attach A File placeholder, as shown here.

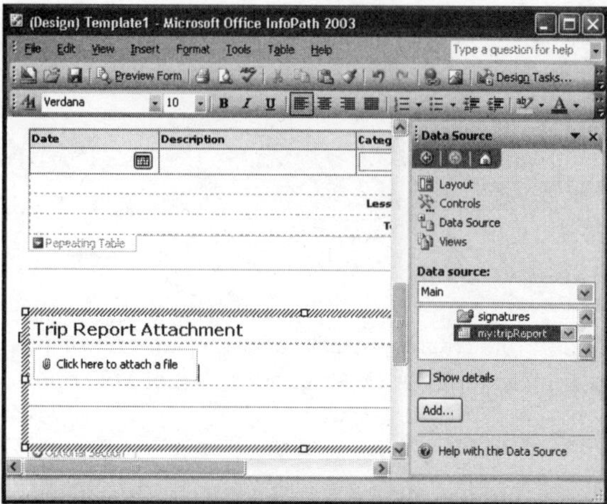

5. Right-click the placeholder, and choose File Attachment Properties to open the dialog box. If you have a Microsoft Word or text document to provide a preformatted file for a trip report, select the Specify Default File, click the Browse button, navigate to the file, and double-click it. If you want to limit the file types that users can attach, select the Allow The User To Attach Only The Following File Types check box, and type their extensions, separated by semicolons, as shown here.

6. Click OK to return to the work area, choose File, Save As, save your template as **ExpenseReportAttachment.xsn** or the like in a new My Documents\InfoPath\Attachments folder, and name your form **ExpenseReportAttachment Test 1**.

7. Select the Fill Out A Form task pane, click the link for the template you saved to open Form1, scroll to the Trip Report table, and click the placeholder to open the File Attachment dialog box. Navigate to a .doc or .txt file, double-click it to add its Base64-encoded content to the form, and replace the placeholder with the document's name, type, and size.

8. **Right-click the document to display the menu options for file attachments, as shown here.**

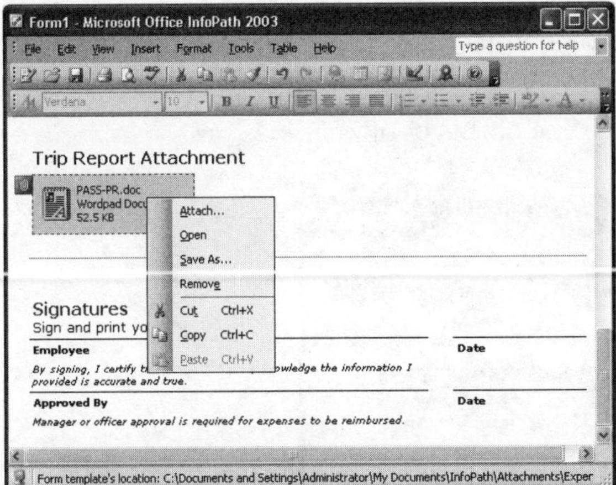

9. **Save Form1 as ReportWithWordAttachment.xml or the like, and then check the data document's file size, which is 74K for the 52K Word document used for this example.**

10. **Double-click to open the file. It opens in Word with a randomly generated file name.**

The document size without an attachment is 4K, which results in a net increase of 70K for the 52K attachment. The increase in size is the result of Base64 encoding of the binary file, as described in Chapter 4's "The Gory Details of Base64 Encoding" sidebar.

Practicing safe file attachment

Microsoft designates the following file extensions as unsafe for file attachments to InfoPath forms: .ade, .adp, .app, .asp, .bas, .bat, .cer, .chm, .cmd, .com, .cpl, .crt, .csh, .exe, .fxp, .hlp, .hta, .inf, .ins, .isp, .its, .js, .jse, .ksh, .lnk, .mad, .maf, .mag, .mam, .maq, .mar, .mas, .mat, .mau, .mav, .maw, .mda, .mdb, .mde, .mdt, .mdw, .mdz, .msc, .msi, .msp, .mst, .ops, .pcd, .pif, .prf, .prg, .pst, .reg, .scf, .scr, .sct, .shb, .shs, .tmp, .url, .vb, .vbe, .vbs, .vsd, .vsmacros, .vss, .vst, .vsw, .ws, .wsc, .wsf, and .wsh. Notice that Access documents (.ade, .adp, .mda, .mdb, .mdt, .mdw, .mdz) and Visio (.vsd) files can't be attached to InfoPath forms.

Using ActiveX Controls in Forms

SP-1 delivers the capability to add simple, single-value ActiveX controls–such as scroll bar sliders, spin buttons, and progress bars–to forms and bind their value to a field of the appropriate data type. You also can bind the value of ActiveX controls written specifically for InfoPath to the entire XML text content of a group, or directly to the InfoPath Document Object Model (DOM) node. Custom-written ActiveX controls are beyond the scope of this book.

The exercise in this section adds three types of ActiveX controls that install as part of the Windows XP or later operating system, or as part of Office 2000 or later. You use SpinButton and ScrollBar controls to set the values of text boxes and control the display of ProgressBar controls, as shown in Figure 9-7. InfoPath supports installation of controls that aren't installed on users' computers by adding .cab files to the project, which also is beyond the scope of this book.

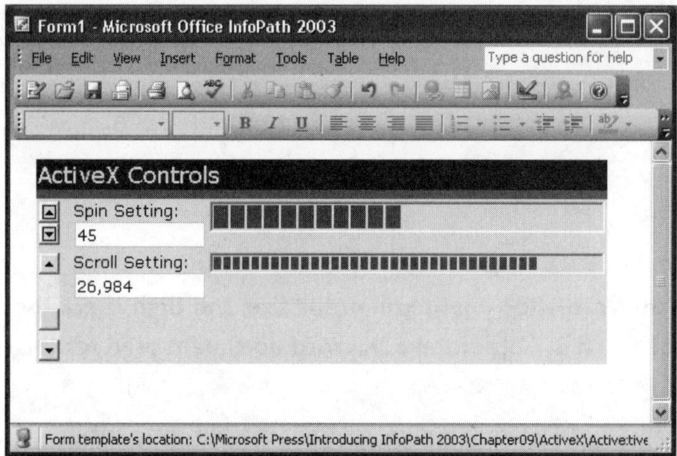

Figure 9-7 This form demonstrates the use of ActiveX SpinButton and ScrollBar controls to set the default values of fields that control the display of ProgressBar controls.

To add the four controls to the Insert Control list's Custom Controls section and then to a demonstration form, and use the SpinButton and ScrollBar controls to set the default value for the ProgressBar controls, do the following.

▶ Add SpinButton, ScrollBar, and ProgressBar controls to a form

1. **In InfoPath, design a new form using the ActiveXControls.xml data document in the C:\Microsoft Press\Introducing InfoPath 2003\Chapter09\ActiveX folder as its data source. Add a Table With Title to the form, split the second row into three columns, and add a row below the second row. Optionally, add a color scheme to the form.**
2. **In the Data Source task pane, change the data type of each element to Whole Number (integer), and replace the missing default value with the original default value: 50 for spinValue and spinSetting, and 16000 for scrollValue and scrollSetting.**
3. **Open the Controls task pane, and click Add or Remove Custom Controls to open the dialog box of the same name.**

4. Click Add to open the Add Custom Control Wizard's first dialog box, and scroll to and select the Microsoft Forms 2.0 SpinButton control, as shown here.

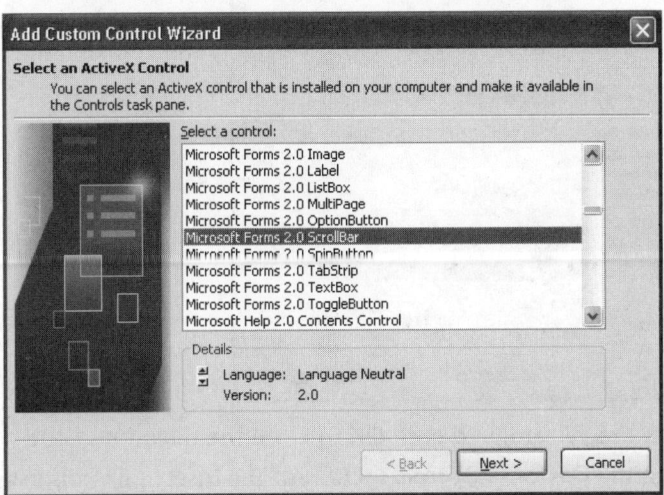

5. Click Next to accept the default Don't Include A .cab File option, and click Next to display the Specify A Binding Property dialog box. Leave the default Value as the binding property, as shown here.

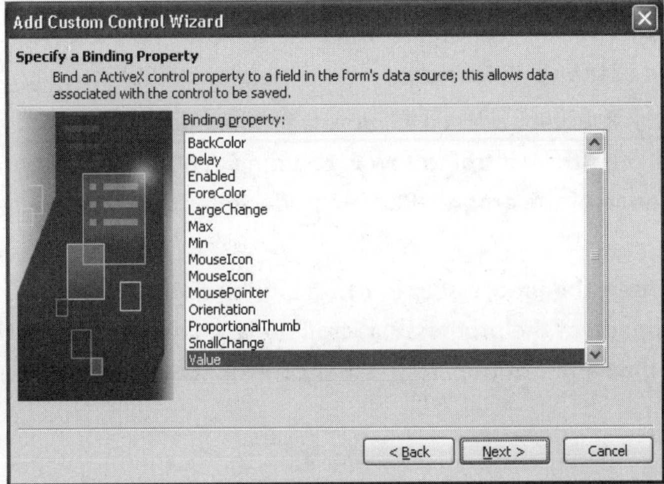

6. Click Next, leave the default Enabled as the Enable or Disable Property and True in the list box, and click Next to open the Specify Data Type Options dialog box.
7. Leave the default Field (element or attribute) selection. All ActiveX controls you add in this section have numeric Value properties, so clear the default Text (string) check box, select the Whole Number (integer) text box, and select the same data type in the Default Data Type list, as shown here.

8. Click Finish to dismiss the Wizard, and click OK to close the dialog and add the custom control to the Custom Controls section of the Insert Controls list.
9. Drag the added control to row 2, column A of the table to add a vertically oriented spin button. Bind the button to the spinSetting subnode of the spinButton node.
10. Repeat steps 3 through 8, except insert a Microsoft Forms 2.0 ScrollBar control in step 4, drag the control to row 3, column A, and bind the control to the scrollSetting subnode of the scrollBar node.
11. Repeat steps 3 through 8, except insert a Microsoft ProgressBar Control, Version 6.0, in step 4, drag the control to row 2, column C, and bind the control to the spinValue subnode of the progressBarSpin node. Refer to Figure 9-7 for sizing.
12. Repeat step 11, but insert the ProgressBar in row 3 and bind the control to the scrollValue subnode of the progressBarScroll node, and size it appropriately. As you reduce the height of the ProgressBar control, the number of its elements increases.

13. Right-click the second ProgressBar, open its Properties dialog box, click the General tab to display the control's properties sheet values, and change the Max value to **32767**, as shown here.

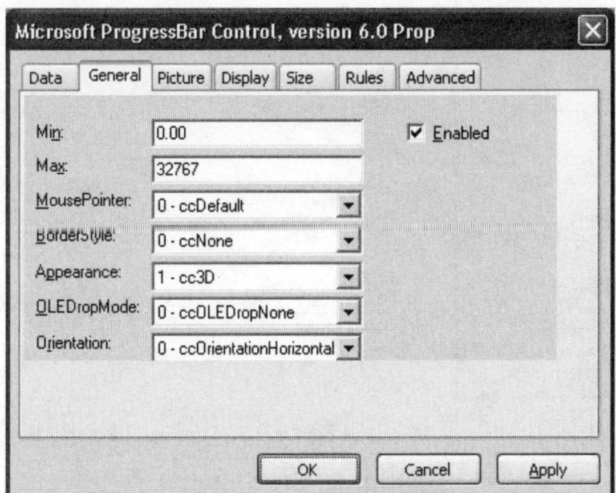

The default maximum value of a ScrollBar control is 32,767; the default maximum value of SpinButton and ProgressBar controls is 100. Microsoft Forms 2.0 controls don't have a properties sheet, so their Properties dialog boxes don't have a General page.

14. Save your template as **ActiveXDemo.xsn** or the like in a new My Documents\InfoPath\ActiveX folder, and assign **ActiveXDemo - Test1** as the form name.

▶ **Add text boxes, hook up the ProgressBars, and test the form**

1. In the Data Source task pane, drag the spinSetting field to row 2, column B, and the scrollSetting field to row 3, column B.
2. Open the spinValue field's Properties dialog box, click the Insert Formula button, click Insert Field or Group, expand the spinButton node, double-click spinSetting, and click OK.
3. Verify that the Update This Value When The Result Of The Formula Is Recalculated check box is selected, as shown on the next page.

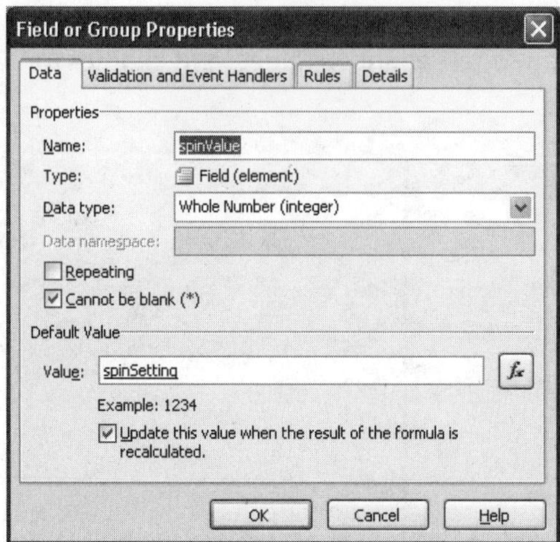

4. **Click OK to connect the ProgressBar to the specified field, and repeat steps 2 and 3 for the scrollValue field, except select scrollSetting in the Select A Field Or Group dialog box in step 2.**
5. **Preview the form, and verify that the SpinButton and ScrollBar controls change the values in the text boxes and the ProgressBars' display.**
6. **Save your changes.**

Using Advanced Main Data Source Features

InfoPath SP-1 adds the ability to convert the main data source of a form to a modified version of the original data source without having to manually modify the template files. SP-1 also supports creating data sources from XML documents that have embedded schemas. The following two sections describe this added InfoPath functionality.

Converting the Main Data Source of a Form

The primary data source in the release version of InfoPath was cast in concrete. Once you created a form from an XML document, schema, database table or query, or Web service, even a minor change to a primary data source required you to create a new form template. InfoPath SP-1 lets you change the main (formerly primary) data source to a modified version that has a similar structure. You also can change the data source from an XML data document to a related XML schema, but you can't change from an XML data document or schema source to a Web service or other data connection (or vice versa). InfoPath maps dependent data to the new data source, where possible. Controls bound to fields or sections that are missing in the converted data source display a warning icon.

Follow these steps to convert the data source for the ProductsMD.xsn template that you created earlier in the chapter to a data source with added fields.

▶ Change the ProductsMD.xsn template's main data source

1. **Open the ProductsMD.xsn template, if it isn't open.**
2. **Choose Tools, Convert Main Data Source to start the Data Source Wizard.**
3. **Click Browse, navigate to the C:\Microsoft Press\Introducing InfoPath 2003\Chapter09\DataSources folder, double-click ProductsExt.xml, and click Next, Finish, and Yes to replace the main data source and its default values.**
4. **Choose Save As, and save your file as ProductsMDExt.xsn in a new My Documents\InfoPath\AdvancedDS folder, and add ProductsMDExt Test 1 as the form name.**
5. **Open a preview, and verify that the category filter works properly.**
6. **Close the preview, rearrange the existing controls and their labels, drag the added CategoryName and CompanyName fields from the data source list, and, optionally, modify the layout, as shown here.**

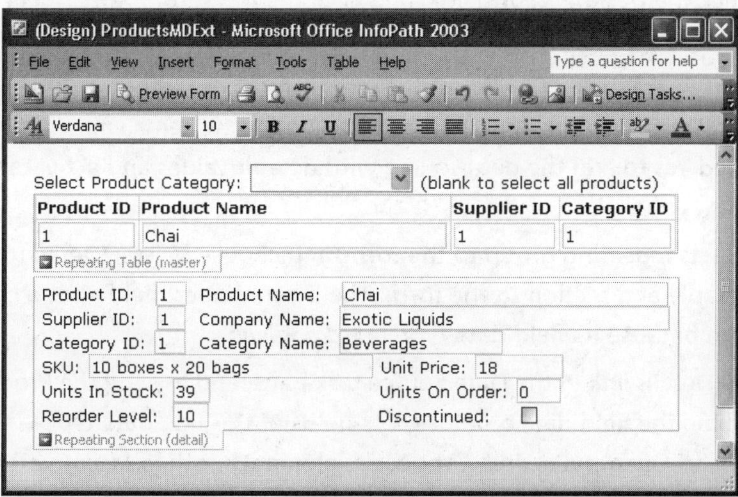

7. **Open a final preview, save your template changes, and exit InfoPath.**

Creating a Data Source from an Embedded Schema

Data documents with embedded XML schemas are relatively uncommon; in most cases, documents that require schema validation include attributes that specify the namespace and location of the associated schema. Access 2002 and later let you export XML documents that include an embedded XML Schema, such as the ProductsSchema.xml file used in this section's exercise. The .NET Framework represents ADO.NET *DataSet* objects in DiffGram format, which includes a complete schema for the XML document returned as the payload from an XML Web service.

The advantage of using an embedded or associated schema to define the main data source is that the schema establishes the data types and other constraints when creating XML data documents from the template. The downside of this approach is that the schema is locked, unless the schema contains elements of the *xsd:any* datatype, which enables InfoPath schema modifications. Schemas containing the *xsd:any* datatype are as uncommon as embedded schemas.

To create a master/detail form from the Northwind database's Products table that includes an embedded schema, do the following.

▶ Create a simple form based on an embedded schema

1. **In InfoPath, click the Design A Form link, and click the New From XML Document or Schema link to start the Data Source Wizard.**
2. **Click Browse, navigate to the C:\Microsoft Press\Introducing InfoPath 2003\Chapter09\DataSources folder, and double-click ProductsSchema.xml. Then click Next, Finish, and Yes to add the data source with default values and activate the Data Source task pane.**
3. **Drag the Products repeating group to the form, and choose Master/Detail to add the repeating table and section to the form. The Discontinued field adds a check box to the form because its field data type is *xsd:boolean*.**
4. **Click the Show Details link in the Data Source task pane, and expand the Products group to examine the field data types. Access fields of the Text data type—ProductName and QuantityPerUnit—appear as elements of the *xsd:simpleType* datatype, and only the Discontinued field has a default value.**
5. **Optionally, save the form as ProductsEmbedXSD.xsn in the ...\Chapter09\AdvancedDS folder, with ProductsEmbedXSD Test 1 as the form name.**

Chapter Summary

InfoPath SP-1 adds a remarkably useful set of advanced features to the first release of InfoPath 2003. The most important of the added elements is the master/child with its repeating table and linked repeating section. Master/child tables make it practical to manage long lists that incorporate detail fields. InfoPath's new filtering feature is especially applicable to master/child lists, but you also can filter independent repeating tables and sections.

Drop-down lists get a major facelift. You can populate a drop-down list from a form's repeating section, which simplifies list updates, and you can cascade parent/child lists to provide multiple drop-down lists to filter repeating tables, sections, or both. Declarative event-based rules replace complex programming code for intercepting form-based events and taking action based on conditions that you specify. User roles for workflow applications, combined with rules, let you specify what view members of a role see when they open a form or which controls are visible or read-only.

SP-1 extends the ability of *base64Encoded* fields to storing attachments of common, e-mail–safe file types. Other helpful SP-1 features include the capability to change the main (formerly primary) data source for a form without starting a new form design from scratch. XML documents with embedded schemas aren't common–except in ADO.NET DataSets–but you can create new forms from such documents and establish strong field typing without manual schema modifications.

Q&A

Q. Can I incorporate a repeating table in the repeating section of a master/child form?

A. Yes, if your detail data source has the correct hierarchical structure. An example of a form of this type would be a list of customers, their orders, and the orders' line items. In this case, the repeating line item field must be a child of the order field, because you can't cascade master/detail forms. (A repeating section can't be a master *and* a detail section.) The following "On Your Own" section suggests creating an example of a repeating detail section that contains a repeating table.

Q. Is it necessary to enclose repeating elements, such as <*Order*> or <*Item*> within parent <*Orders*> or <*Items*> tags?

A. No, but it's a generally accepted XML document design practice. Full-featured text editors make it easy to add the parent tags to XML files formatted with white space (linefeeds or carriage-return/linefeed pairs and indent spaces or tabs). Notepad can't easily handle the required search and replace operations with white space–formatted .xml files.

Q. Can I assign users to roles if their Windows XP or Windows 2000 workstations are members of a Windows NT 4.0 domain?

A. Yes, but you can't use the Select Users or Select Groups dialog boxes to assign users or groups to roles. These dialog boxes depend on Active Directory to validate your entries. You can type user logins manually in the User Names text box of the Add User Role or Modify User Role dialog boxes. You also can assign Windows NT 4.0 domain users to roles by storing their logon names in the form.

On Your Own

Here's an additional exercise that demonstrates the use of repeating tables within repeating sections:

1. Create a new form from the CustomersOrdersItems.xml data document in the C:\Microsoft Press\Introducing InfoPath 2003\Chapter09\DataSources folder.
2. Add a master/detail repeating table from the Customer repeating group.
3. Remove unimportant columns from the master table, and reformat the detail section text boxes to conserve vertical space.
4. Add another detail section from the Order repeating group, and link it to the master table by CustomerID key fields. The Item repeating group within the Order group adds a repeating table to the repeating section.
5. Reformat the Order section's text boxes to conserve vertical space.
6. Preview your template and save it.
7. Save an XML data document from the template.

CHAPTER 10

Adding Views to a Template

In this chapter, you will learn how to:

- **Create an alternative, simplified view of a form**
- **Modify views of a form to selectively display sections and controls**
- **Design views for distribution by e-mail or as e-mail attachments**
- **Add default and multiple print views to a form**
- **Create a Microsoft Word print view from an XSLT file**

For more information:

- **See the sections "Adding Controls in a Layout Table" and "Working with Repeating Tables," in Chapter 5, "Laying Out Forms," for altering layout and repeating tables.**
- **See the section "Applying Conditional Formatting," in Chapter 7, "Formatting Forms" for help with conditional formatting expressions.**

To work through this chapter:

- You need experience adding sections to a form and manipulating layout and repeating tables.
- You must understand conditional formatting and data validation techniques.
- You must know how to establish event-based rules to set default values.
- You should have installed in your C:\Microsoft Press\Introducing InfoPath 2003\Chapter10 folder the sample files from the CD that accompanies this book.

Up to this point on your Microsoft InfoPath 2003 learning curve, you've worked only with default views of forms. This chapter introduces you to forms with multiple views that users choose from the View menu. Hiding data entry sections and controls when they're not required for a particular activity is a typical use for multiple views. You can also add a rule that determines the role of the user and switches to the appropriate view.

Multiple views also let you repurpose a form to serve several functions. A typical use for multiple views is adapting an order entry form to deliver an order acknowledgment, print acknowledgments, and generate invoices with e-mail and printing views added. Each view is based on the same XML data document. The document's status in the order workflow process determines the content of fields and the conditional formatting rules that apply at each step.

Adding a Simplified Form View

Removing unneeded elements from a form's default view is the quickest and easiest way to add a new view to a form. The example in this section assumes that unneeded elements have default values for new forms or obtain their values from an existing XML data document that users edit. Here's the basic process:

1. Create and name a new, empty view.
2. Copy the original form's contents to the new view.
3. Remove the unneeded objects from the new view.
4. Rename the original default view.
5. Assign the added view as the default view.

The following procedure removes the required Channel and optional Image sections from the default view of the RSS 2.0 form. Your C:\Microsoft Press\Introducing InfoPath 2003\Chapter10\Rss2v4 folder contains a formatted version of Chapter 4's Rss2v4.xsn template. To add the simplified view to this template, follow these steps.

▶ **Add a new view by pasting a copy of the default view**

1. **Navigate to C:\Microsoft Press\Introducing InfoPath 2003\Chapter10\Rss2v4, and open the Rss2v4.xsn template in design mode.**
2. **Press Ctrl+A to select all form elements, and press Ctrl+C to copy the elements to the Clipboard.**
3. **Choose View, Manage Views to activate the Views task pane.**
4. **Click the Add A New View link to open the Add View input box, and type Items Only as the New View Name, as shown here:**

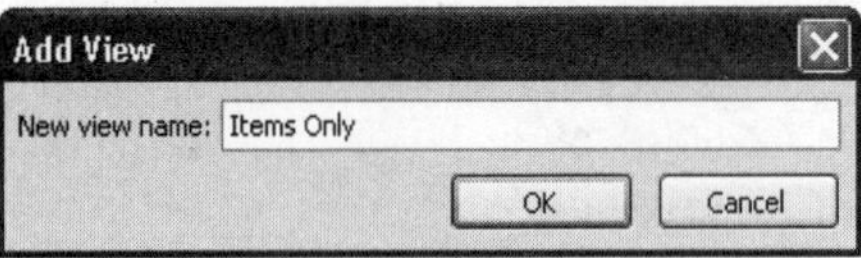

5. **Click OK to add the new, empty view.**
6. **Press Ctrl+V to paste the copied form elements to the view.**
7. **Click the Version label to select the first embedded layout table, click the table's selection handle to select all elements, and press Delete to remove the table.**
8. **Click the Section tab to select the Image section, and press Delete to remove it.**
9. **Remove the horizontal line and the spaces above and below it.**
10. **Drag the bottom of the master table up to the bottom of the Repeating section tab. Your form now appears as show here:**

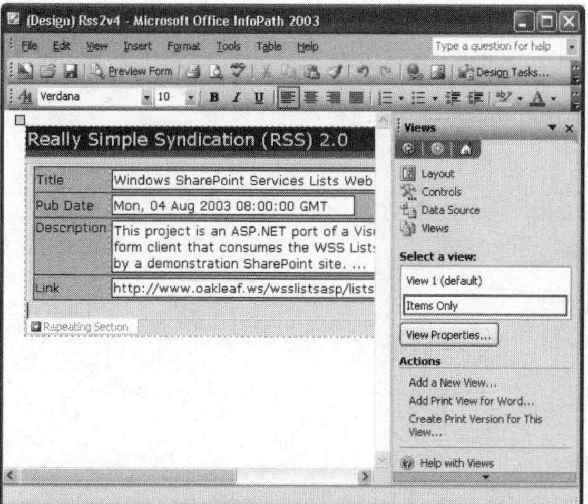

11. In the Views task pane, double-click the View 1 (Default) item in the Select A View drop-down list to open the View Properties dialog box.
12. In the View Name text box on the General tab, replace View 1 with **All Sections** or the like, as shown here:

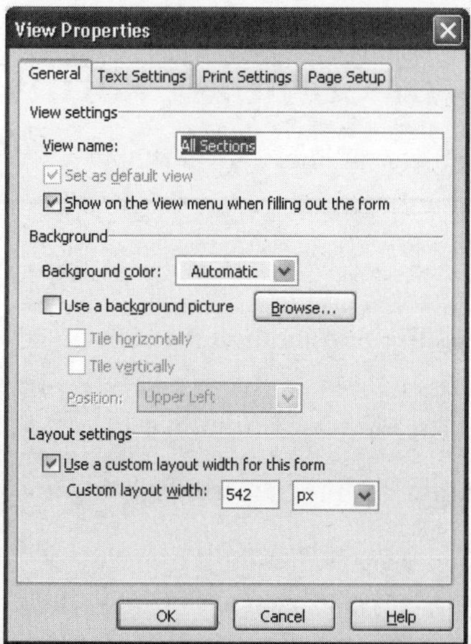

13. Click OK to close the properties window and save your changes.
14. Open the Items Only drop-down list, and select Set As Default to make Items Only the default view.
15. Click Preview Form to display the default view.
16. Choose View, All Sections to display the original form version.
17. Save your changes, open the Rss2v4.xml sample data document in the same folder as Rss2v4.xsn, and check both form views.

Figure 10-1 shows the default Items Only view of the Rss2v4.xml test data document, which has multiple items.

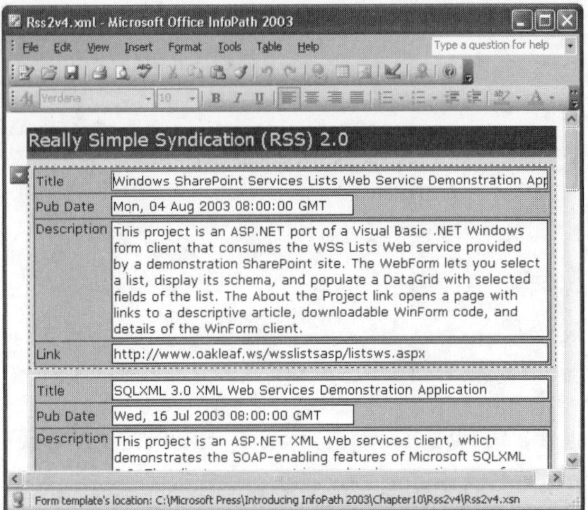

Figure 10-1 Select the simplified Items Only view, shown here, or the All Sections view of a sample RSS 2.0 data document by choosing a View menu option.

Presenting Multiple Views of Complex Forms

The Northwind Traders Order Entry form is an example of a form that can serve at least two purposes: order entry and editing, and invoice generation and editing. These processes represent the order processing workflow's starting and ending points, unless someone cancels the order or invoice. You can add other views for e-mailing order acknowledgments and invoices to the purchaser and specify a view as the default printing view. The section "Designing a Default Print View," later in this chapter, describes modifications to adapt the view for printing.

Following are basic design guidelines for creating multiple views of a complex form:

- Plan to copy and paste elements of the initial default view to new views. Copying and pasting sections and controls between views maintains their binding to primary data sources and, for list boxes, secondary data sources.
- Add an *integer* field to specify the workflow status. You can use this value to determine the view that appears when users open a data document.
- Place groups of controls that shouldn't appear in all views in their own sections. You can remove sections from a view, but you can't selectively hide or show individual layout table rows. Conditional formatting enables hiding individual controls on a per-view basis.

- Design the most complex view first, when possible, and apply all conditional formatting rules to that view. Doing this lets you base other views on a single view for consistency.
- Modify conditional formatting rules as necessary for the specific view. Data validation rules apply to all views.

Creating an Invoice Entry View from the Northwind Order Entry Form

The NWOrdersCh10.xsn template in your C:\Microsoft Press\Introducing InfoPath 2003\Chapter10\NWOrdersCh10 folder is a modified version of the ...\Chapter08\NWOrdersFinal\NWOrdersFinal.xsn template. New fields, secondary data sources, and controls have been added to better represent a real-world order entry form and provide for issuing an invoice.

Table 10-1 describes the fields added to the NWOrdersCh10.xsn data source's OrderInfo and Invoice Info groups.

Table 10-1 Fields Added to the OrderInfo and InvoiceInfo Group in NWOrdersCh10.xsn

Field Name	Type	Purpose	Datatype	Required
my:CustOrderID	Element	Customer order number. (In use, substitute buyer name if no order number is provided.)	string	Yes
my:PaymentTerms	Element	Code for payment terms defined by the PaymentTerms secondary data source (PaymentTerms.xml).	*integer*	Yes
my:WorkflowStatus	Attribute	Code for the current link in the workflow chain as defined by the WorkflowStatus secondary data source (WorkflowStatus.xml).	*integer*	Yes
my:LastUpdated	Attribute	Date and time of last update by workflow process or manual entry. (Should default to system time, which requires code.)	*dateTime*	Yes
my:UpdatedBy	Attribute	Initials of data entry operator. (Defaults to *WF*, for workflow process.)	*string*	Yes
my:InvoiceInfo	Section	Has the OrderID attribute (described next in this table) and contains the InvoiceID and InvoiceDate elements.	*N/A*	Yes
OrderID	Attribute	Primary key value of the order for this invoice.	*integer*	Yes
InvoiceID	Element	Sequential invoice number (primary key) assigned by the workflow process or a database lookup.	*integer*	No
InvoiceDate	Element	Defaults to shipping date (rule-based).	date	No
my:CustOrderID	Element	Customer order number. (In use, substitute buyer name if no order number is provided.)	string	Yes

Figure 10-2 shows a test form created from the NWOrdersCh10.xsn template that you modify in this and later sections. The Order Information section has the added Cust. Order and Terms controls. The added Status section has the (workflow) Status and Last Updated controls. The Status section is for internal use only and doesn't appear in views of the form you create that are sent to the customer.

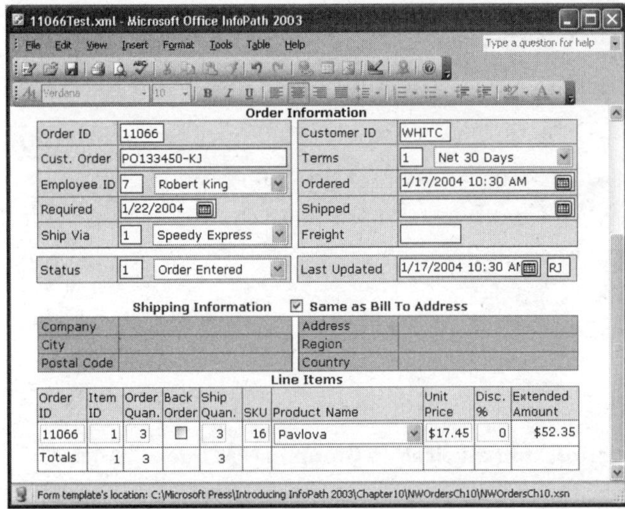

Figure 10-2 This template and its test data document are the starting point for adding invoice generation and other views.

To create a new InvoiceEntry view, as illustrated in Figure 10-3, and save a sample XML data document for use in subsequent exercises, follow these steps.

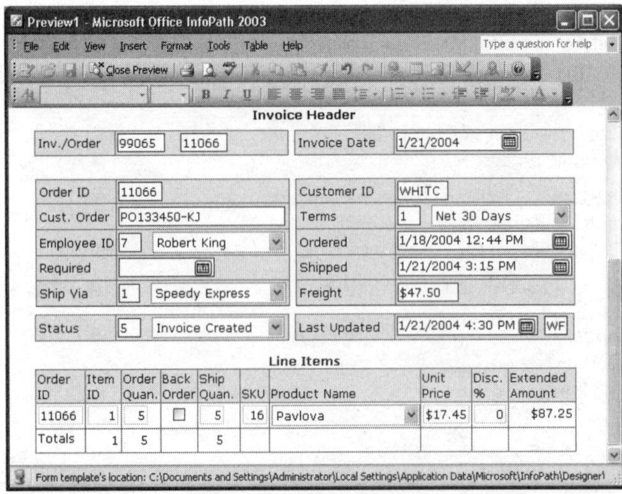

Figure 10-3 The InvoiceEntry view of a test XML data document illustrates most changes you make in this section to a copy of the original OrderEntry view.

▶ **Start an invoice entry view**

1. Navigate to the C:\Microsoft Press\Introducing InfoPath 2003\Chapter10\NWOrdersCh10 folder, and open the NWOrdersCh10.xsn template in design mode.
2. Press Ctrl+A, and then press Ctrl+C to copy the view to the Clipboard.
3. Choose View, Manage Views to activate the Views task pane, which displays OrderEntry (Default) in the Select A View list.
4. Click the Add A New View link to open the Add View input box, and type **InvoiceEntry** as the View Name.
5. Click OK to close the dialog box and open the new, blank view, and press Ctrl+V to paste the Order Entry view.
6. Change Order Entry in the title cell to **Invoice Generation**. Choose File, Save As, change the file name to **NWOrdersViews.xsn**, save your changes in a new \My Documents\InfoPath\Views folder, and change the form name to **NWOrdersViews - Test1**.

Invoices often have a different layout than order entry forms. As an example, bill to and ship to information is adjacent in most paper invoice forms. Invoices also require an invoice number and invoice date; invoice date usually is the same as the shipped date. Invoices commonly use different terms than order entry forms to describe their sections. Do the following to make these changes to the InvoiceEntry view.

▶ **Rearrange the form and add the Invoice Header section**

1. With the Invoice Entry view active, select the Shipping Information layout table, press Ctrl+X, position the insertion point at the beginning of the Order Information label, and press Ctrl+V to move the layout table to its new location below the Customer Information layout table.
2. Delete the empty line above the Line Items repeating table, preview your changes, and return to design mode.
3. Position the insertion point at the end of the Order Information label, choose Insert, More Controls to activate the Controls task pane, and click the Section item in the list to open the Section Binding dialog box.
4. Double-click the my:InvoiceInfo node to bind the new section to the node.
5. To shortcut the layout table generation process, select the first row of the Order Information layout table, and copy it to the Clipboard. Click inside the new, empty section, paste the table row, and remove the two empty lines.

6. Change Order ID to Inv./Order, and add a few spaces in front of the Order ID text box. Move the insertion point to the left border of column B, click Text Box in the Insert Controls list, and bind the new text box to the my:InvoiceInfo group's InvoiceID field. (The OrderID text box doesn't have a label, because it's hidden in the invoice sent to customers.)
7. Remove the added label, shorten the text box, remove the digit-grouping symbol, and apply an outline border to the text box with the first color of the Blueberry color scheme.
8. Right-click the OrderID text box, choose Change Binding from the shortcut menu, and double-click the InvoiceInfo's OrderID attribute in the Text Box Binding dialog box. If the default value appears with a digit-grouping symbol, remove it.
9. Change the Customer ID label to Invoice Date, delete the Customer ID text box, and drag a date picker control bound to my:InvoiceInfo's InvoiceDate field to the cell.
10. Remove the added label, shorten and add a border to the date picker control, and change the date format to short date (M/D/YYYY).
11. Change the Customer Information label at the top of the form to Bill To, the Shipping Information label to Ship To, and the Order Information label to Invoice Header.
12. Optionally, reverse the positions of ID and Company in the first table row, and change the labels to more invoice-like terminology, as shown here in preview mode:

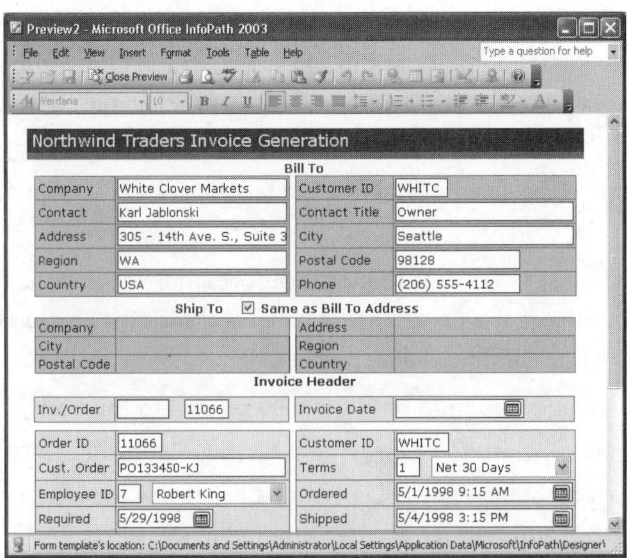

13. **Preview the form and examine both views by selecting each view from the View menu.**
14. **Return to design mode, and save your changes.**

For views that represent steps in a workflow, each document might have a numeric code to represent its current status. The sample form's Status drop-down list has nine choices, ranging from Order Canceled (0) to Invoice Canceled (9). The two views you've created so far represent the Order Entered (1) and Invoice Created (5) steps in the workflow process. In the following example, the data document file name is the Order ID value, a hyphen, and the workflow status code. To create the two data documents, follow these steps.

▶ Create test data documents

1. **Activate the task pane, choose Fill Out A Form, and click the form name link to open the default OrderEntry view as Form1.**
2. **Change the Ordered and Required dates to more recent values, clear the Shipped date picker control, clear the Freight text box, and match the Last Updated date to the Ordered date.**
3. **Add an item to the Line Items table, set Ship Quan. values to 0, and select the Back Order check box to eliminate the data validation errors. (You'll fix this problem in the next section.)**
4. **Save the test form as 11066-1.xml in the template's folder. *11066-1* corresponds to the Order Entered status. (Open the Status drop-down list to see all the steps in the workflow.)**
5. **Choose View, InvoiceEntry; add an arbitrary Invoice number; and add identical Invoice Date, Shipped, and Last Updated dates. Select a shipper, add a freight amount, select Invoice Created as the Status of the workflow, and specify Ship Quan. values for both line items, as shown here:**

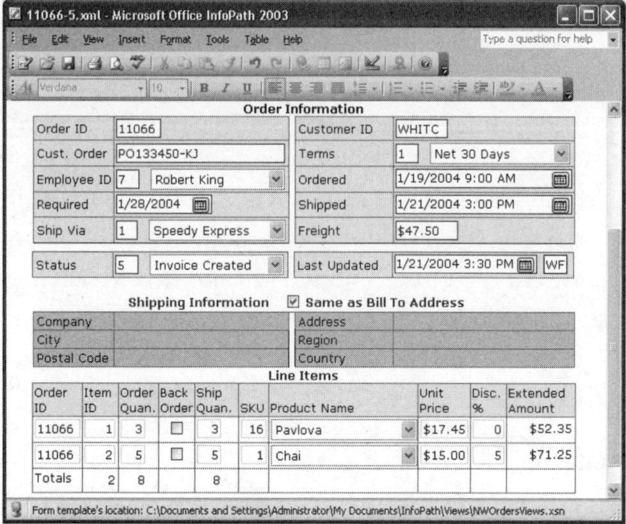

6. **Choose Save As, save the form as 11066-5.xml for Invoice Created status tests, and return to design mode.**

Making Workflow-Dependent Changes

A workflow status code is important as a criterion for handling view-dependent changes to conditional formatting and data validation expressions. For this example, the Line Items table's Back Order and Ship Quan. fields aren't applicable to order entry operations, and 3 as the default Order Quan. and Ship Quan. values isn't appropriate for a real order entry form. You must also change the Extended expression box to display extended amounts based on Order Quan. rather than Ship Quan. for the OrderEntry view.

To make the required changes to the OrderEntry view, follow these steps.

▶ Change default values and data validation expressions for order entry

1. **Select the OrderEntry view, and in the Line Items table, change the default Order Quan. value to 1 and the default Ship Quan. value to 0.**
2. **Right-click the Back Order check box, choose Check Box Properties to open the Properties dialog box, and click Data Validation. With the first Conditions With Data Validation entry selected, click Modify to open the Data Validation (BackOrdered) dialog box.**

3. **Click the And button, and select Select A Field Or Group. Double-click my:WorkflowStatus under the OrderInfo node in the Select A Field Or Group dialog box, select Is Greater Than Or Equal To and Type A Number, and type 5 in the text box, as shown here:**

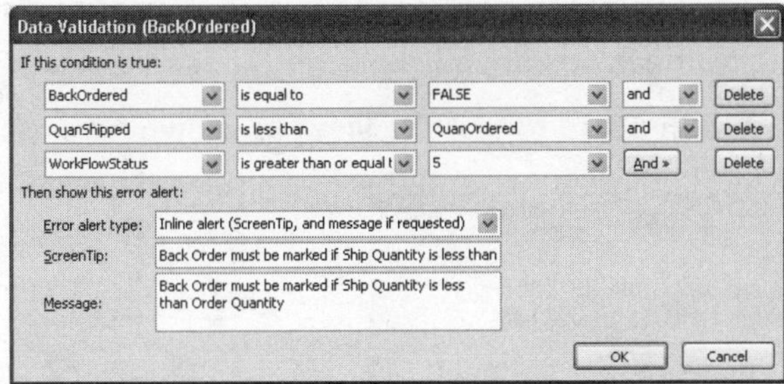

4. **Click OK three times to close the dialog boxes and save changes to the data validation rule.**
5. **Open the Data Source task pane, double-click OrderDate, delete its Default Value and click OK to save your changes. Do the same for RequiredDate, ShippedDate, and Freight.**
6. **Close the template, save your changes, and double-click 11066-1.xml.**
7. **Clear the two Back Order check boxes to verify that the validation rule works for this view.**
8. **Close and save 11066-1.xml, and open 11066-5.xml.**
9. **Verify that the Back Order check boxes show data validation flags based on the ordered and shipped quantities, and then close 11066-5.xml.**

Multiple views created from an initial default view often include controls that aren't applicable to all views. In the OrderEntry view, the Line Items repeating table shouldn't contain controls that are related to shipping, which occurs later in the order processing workflow. Thus, you delete the Back Order check box and Ship Quan. text box. The Extended expression box value is based on the QuanShipped field, so you must change the XPath expression to use the QuanOrdered field.

▶ Remove unneeded Line Items controls and update the Extended expression box

1. **Reopen the NWOrdersViews.xsn template in design mode, and switch to OrderEntry view, if necessary. (In design mode, InfoPath opens the last active view by default.)**
2. **Select the Back Order and Ship Quan. columns, and press Delete to remove them.**

3. Open the Extended expression box's Properties dialog box, change QuanShipped to **QuanOrdered** in the XPath box, and click OK to save your changes. The default Extended value is equal to the Unit Price amount.
4. Increase the width of the table to match that of the Shipping Information section, and adjust the widths of the three rightmost columns to permit increasing the available width of the Product Name drop-down list.
5. Save your changes, and open 11066-1.xml to test the view, as shown here:

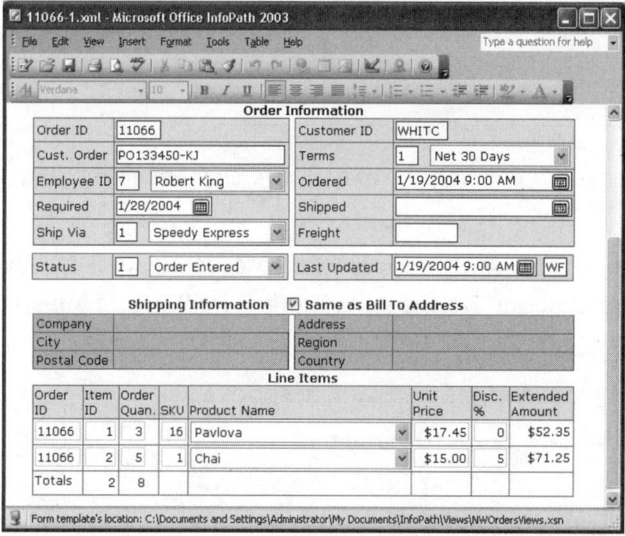

6. Close 11066-1.xml and open 11066-5.xml, switch to InvoiceEntry view, and verify that this view's Extended expression box responds as expected to changes in Ship Quan.

Adding Workflow-Dependent Rules

Rules that supply default date and time values and automatically open the view for the current workflow status speed form completion and minimize data entry errors. In this section, you'll add rules to set the value of the Last Updated date picker control to the current date and time when the user opens a form at any stage in the workflow process, to set the OrderDate value when entering a new order, and to open the InvoiceEntry view if the Workflow ID value is 5 (Invoice Created).

To add these three rules, follow these steps.

▶ Add rules to set dates and change the default view

1. With the NWOrdersViews template open in design mode, choose Tools, Form Options, to open the dialog box, and click the Open and Save tab. Click the Rules button to open the Rules for Opening Forms dialog box, click Add to open the Rule dialog box, and change the Name of the rule to **Set Last Updated**.
2. Click Add Action to open the Action dialog box, and select Set A Field's Value in the drop-down list. Click the Field box's Set XPath button at the right of the Field text box to open the Select A Group Or Field dialog box, and double-click the LastUpdated attribute under the OrderInfo node.
3. Click the Value box's Formula (*fx*) button to open the Insert Formula dialog box, and click Insert Function to open the dialog box of the same name. Select Date And Time in the Categories list and Now in the Functions list, as shown here:

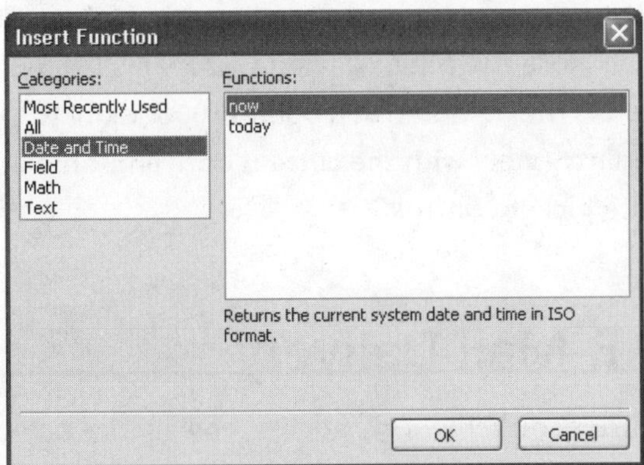

4. Click OK to close the dialog box and verify your Action settings, as shown here:

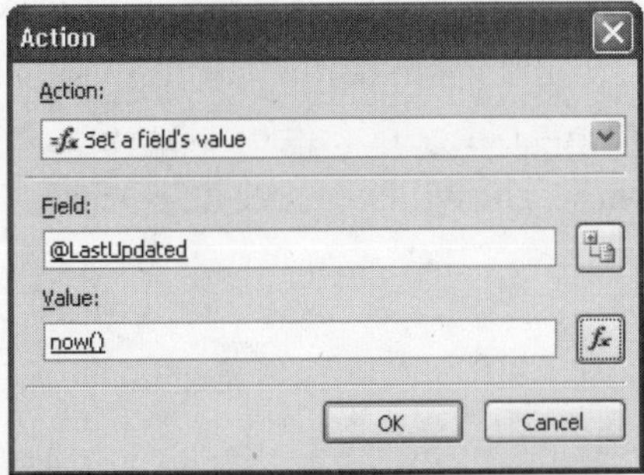

5. Click OK twice to return to the Rules For Opening Forms dialog box, and click Apply to save your rule.
6. Click Add to add another rule, name the rule **Set Order Date**, and click Set Condition to open the Condition dialog box.

7. Click Select A Field Or Group in the first list, double-click the WorkFlowStatus attribute in the dialog box, accept Is Equal To, select Type A Number, and type **1**, as shown here:

8. Click OK, and repeat steps 2 through 5, but select the OrderDate attribute in step 2.
9. Click Add again, name this rule **Show InvoiceEntry View**, and specify a WorkFlowStatus Is Equal To 5 condition.
10. Click Add Action, select Switch Views as from the drop-down list, select InvoiceEntry in the Views list, and click OK four times to close the dialog boxes apply the last condition.
11. Save your changes, preview the OrderEntry view to verify the default Order Date and Last Updated values, and then close the preview window. Open 11066-5.xml to verify that the InvoiceEntry view is the default. Then open 11066-1.xml to verify that it opens in the default OrderEntry view with the current date and time in the Order Date and Last Updated date picker controls.

Modifying Views for E-Mail Delivery

Sending messages to customers for order confirmation and perhaps invoice payment requires modifying views that are optimized for data entry. The OrderEntry and InvoiceEntry views contain information that isn't germane to the purchaser, and you'll need to add a section for address information below the title bar. The following procedure shows you how to hide information from the e-mail recipient based on the Order Acknowledged workflow status and how to change conditional formatting rules that don't apply to the view. The e-mail view, shown in Figure 10-4, serves as the source for the default print view of the form.

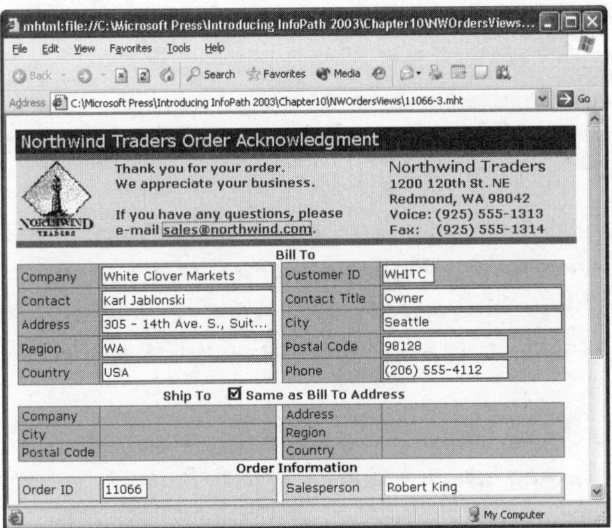

Figure 10-4 The OrderAcknowledgment view of the 11066-3.xml data document shows the changes needed to generate a fully formatted e-mail order acknowledgment. The e-mail link is active in the static .mht attachment.

To create an e-mail OrderAcknowledgment view that you can send with an XML file or export as an .mht file for an e-mail attachment, follow these steps.

▶ Create and modify an OrderAcknowledgment view

1. With the NWOrdersViews template open in design mode, copy the OrderEntry view to the Clipboard, add a new view named **OrderAcknowledgment**, and paste the OrderEntry elements into it.
2. Change Entry in the title to **Acknowledgment**, position the insertion point in front of the Customer Information label, and choose Tables, Insert, Rows Above.
3. Decrease the height of the added row to less than 1 inch, add a the fourth scheme color as the row's shading color, click the Align Left button, and split the cell into three columns.
4. With the insertion point in column A, choose Insert, Picture, From File, navigate to the C:\Microsoft Press\Introducing InfoPath 2003\Chapter10\NWOrdersCh10 folder, and double-click NWLogoBlueberry.gif to insert the image. Change the height to **80** px.
5. Adjust the column widths, and add the text shown in Figure 10-4 to columns B and C. When you add the e-mail address, InfoPath automatically creates a Mailto link.
6. Optionally, rearrange the form and change the section labels to better resemble the InvoiceEntry view.

7. Select the Status section, delete it from the view, and remove the space between Order Information and Line Items.
8. The values in the three value text boxes adjacent to the drop-down lists in the Order Information section aren't meaningful to customers, so delete them and set the width of the drop-down lists to 100%.
9. Delete the duplicate Customer ID label and text box, and delete the Shipped label and date picker control, which isn't applicable to an order acknowledgment. Rearrange the remaining controls so that you can delete an empty table row. (Refer to Figure 10-4 for layout guidelines.) Finally, add the prefix **Est.** to the Freight label.
10. Select the Est. Freight box, and choose Format, Conditional Formatting. Remove the three Conditions With Formatting list items, and click OK to remove the text box's conditional formatting for this view.
11. Preview the form to verify the design, save your changes, and open 11066-1.xml for a final test.
12. In the default data entry view, select Order Acknowledgment in the Status list, and save the form as **11066-3.xml**.
13. Switch to the OrderAcknowledgment view, and add an estimated freight amount to verify the conditional formatting change you made in step 10.
14. Choose File, Export To, Web. Save the file as **11066-3.mht**, and double-click the file in Windows Explorer to open the exported file in Internet Explorer.

Designing a Default Print View

The default print view prints automatically when you choose File, Print or File, Print Preview. You designate the default view for printing on the Print Settings tab of the View Properties dialog box. You can design other views for printing, but (obviously) only one view can be the default.

Views you design for e-mail distribution are logical candidates for conversion to print views. To create a default print view from the OrderAcknowledgment view, which you designed in the preceding section, follow these steps.

▶ **Create a default print view from the OrderAcknowledgment view**

1. Open the OrderAcknowledgment view in design mode, copy its contents to the Clipboard, add a new view named **PrintOrderAck**, and paste the elements to the new view.

2. Double-click the PrintOrderAck item in the Select A View list to open the View Properties dialog box, and select the Print Settings tab.

3. Click the Header or Footer buttons to add a header, footer, or both to your form. You can type text and select AutoText codes to customize headers and footers, as shown here:

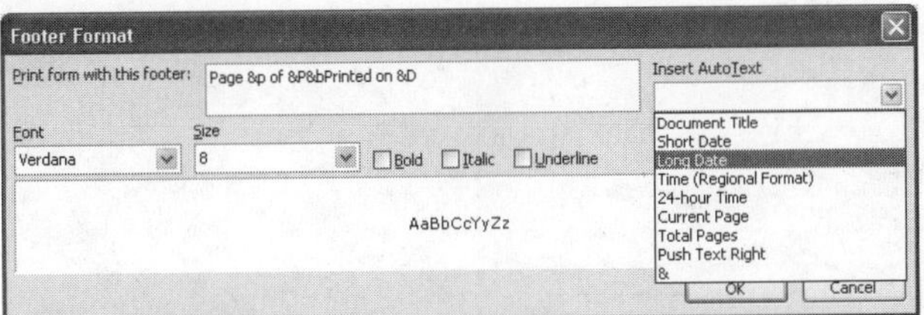

4. Select the Page Setup tab to specify a particular printer, paper size, or paper source or to change margins. Click OK to close the dialog box.
5. Switch to the OrderAcknowledgment view, click View Properties, and click the Print Settings tab. Select PrintOrderAck in the Select An Existing View To Use When Printing This View list, and click OK.
6. Preview the form, and choose File, Print Preview to verify the default printing view assignment for the OrderAcknowledgment view.
7. Borders around text boxes detract from the design. Close both preview windows, use Ctrl+click to select every text box and date picker control in the view, and choose Format, Borders And Shading, to open the Borders And Shading dialog box. Click the None button to remove the borders, and then click OK.
8. The Customer Code label and some Line Items labels wrap to two lines, so adjust the width of table columns to prevent incorrect wrapping.
9. The logo bitmap has a background color that is printed, so replace it with the NWLogoPrint.gif file from the same location as the logo you added in the preceding section. (NWLogoPrint.gif has a white background.)
10. To make it evident to users that the form is intended for printing, remove the shading color from row 2 of the master form and all other layout tables. (InfoPath doesn't print table or form shading colors by default, so this step is optional.)
11. If you want to print background colors or images, choose Tools, Options, and select the Print Background Colors And Print Background Pictures check box on the General tab. (This setting applies to all views.)
12. Save your changes, open 11066-3.xml, choose File, Print Preview for a final test, and print the form.

Figure 10-5 shows the 11066-3.xml data document open in print preview mode.

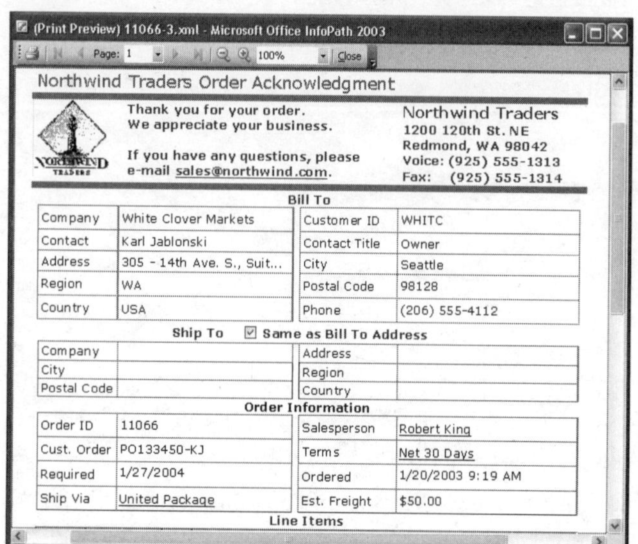

Figure 10-5 Print preview confirms that the default OrderAcknowledgment print view is ready for use.

Adding a Microsoft Word Print View

A Microsoft Word print view applies a custom .xsl file that transforms an InfoPath form into an HTML document that contains Word formatting tags, and then uses the Microsoft Office System 2003's Microsoft Office Image Writer print driver to create a Microsoft Document Imaging (.mdi) or TIFF (.tif) bitmap file from the document. You can print the .mdi or .tif file or apply Office's optical character recognition (OCR) feature to the image to generate a formatted Word .htm, .doc, or .rtf file. The tricky part of the process is authoring the .xsl file, which requires XSLT expertise and a working knowledge of the Word XML document schema.

Word print views are best suited to simple forms with few controls and a large quantity of plain text content, such as paragraphs contained in a text box of a repeating section. This section's example consists of excerpts from the text of a Microsoft press release.

To create a sample Word print view, generate a printable .mdi file, and create Word .htm and .doc files with Office's OCR feature, follow these steps.

▶ Create, test, and save a Word print view

1. Open the sample PDC2003PR.xml document in your C:\Microsoft Press\Introducing InfoPath 2003\Chapter10\WordPrintView folder. If you're interested in viewing the transform file, open WordView.xsl in Internet Explorer.
2. Click the Design This Form button to switch to design mode, and click the Views link to activate the Views task pane.
3. Click the Add Print View For Word link to start the Add Print View For Word Wizard, and click Next.
4. Click Browse, double-click the transform file for the form (WordView.xsl in the template's folder for this example), and click Next.
5. Type **Print Word View** as the name of the view, and click Next and Finish to complete the wizard.
6. Double-click the View1 (Default) entry in the Views task pane to open the View Properties dialog box, click the Print Settings tab, select Print Word View as the default print view, click OK, and save your changes.
7. Choose Windows Start, Settings (if necessary), Printers And Faxes to open the Printers And Faxes dialog box, right-click Microsoft Office Document Image Writer, and choose Set As Default Printer on the shortcut menu.
8. Close and reopen PDC2003PR.xml, and choose File, Print to open the Save As dialog box. (The File, Print Preview menu item is disabled for Word print views.)
9. Navigate to the template folder, change the file name from Document1.mdi to **PDC2003PR1** or the like, and click Save. A fully formatted version of your InfoPath data document opens in a Microsoft Office Document Imaging window, as shown here:

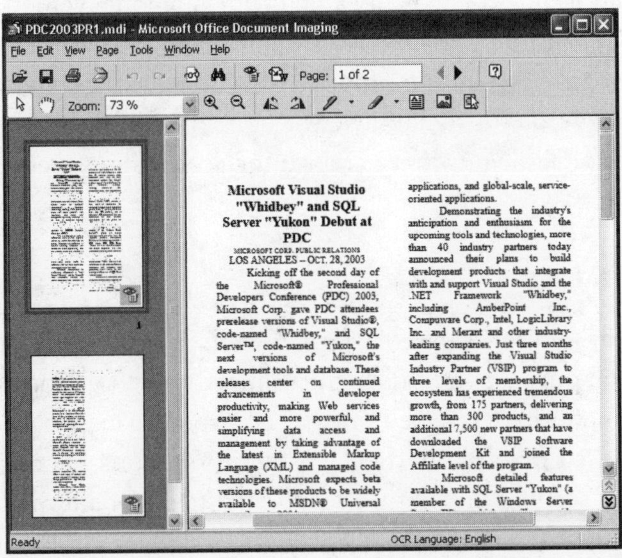

Microsoft Visual Studio "Whidbey" and SQL Server "Yukon" Debut at PDC

MICROSOFT CORP. PUBLIC RELATIONS
LOS ANGELES – OCT. 28, 2003

Kicking off the second day of the Microsoft® Professional Developers Conference (PDC) 2003, Microsoft Corp. gave PDC attendees prerelease versions of Visual Studio®, code-named "Whidbey," and SQL Server™, code-named "Yukon," the next versions of Microsoft's development tools and database. These releases center on continued advancements in developer productivity, making Web services easier and more powerful, and simplifying data access and management by taking advantage of the latest in Extensible Markup Language (XML) and managed code technologies. Microsoft expects beta versions of these products to be widely available to MSDN® Universal

applications, and global-scale, service-oriented applications.

Demonstrating the industry's anticipation and enthusiasm for the upcoming tools and technologies, more than 40 industry partners today announced their plans to build development products that integrate with and support Visual Studio and the .NET Framework "Whidbey," including AmberPoint Inc., Compuware Corp., Intel, LogicLibrary Inc. and Merant and other industry-leading companies. Just three months after expanding the Visual Studio Industry Partner (VSIP) program to three levels of membership, the ecosystem has experienced tremendous growth, from 175 partners, delivering more than 300 products, and an additional 7,500 new partners that have downloaded the VSIP Software Development Kit and joined the Affiliate level of the program.

Microsoft detailed features available with SQL Server "Yukon" (a member of the Windows Server

10. **Click the Send Text To Word toolbar button to open the eponymous dialog box, click Browse, navigate to the template folder, and click OK twice. If you haven't installed Word's OCR feature, you're asked to install it from the Office 2003 CD-ROM or a network share. Word performs an OCR operation on the document and then opens a PDC2003PR.htm file.**
11. **Save a copy of the file as a Word Document (*.doc), as shown here:**

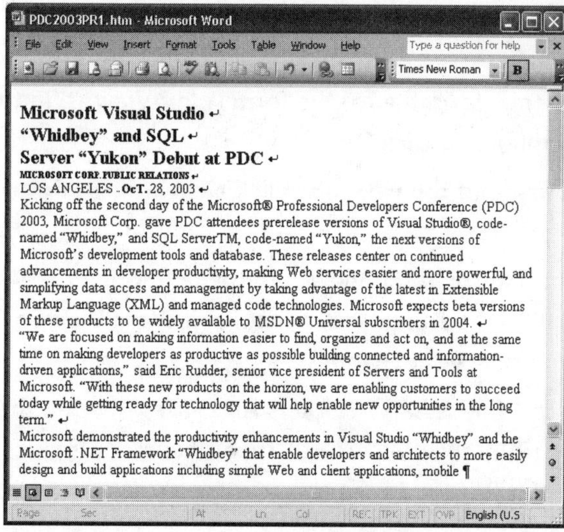

12. **Close Word and the Document Imaging window, save your changes, and reset your default printer to its original setting.**

You can substitute a rich text box for a plain text box, but only basic text formatting, such as bold or italic font attributes, appears correctly in a final .doc file. Files named PDC2003PR-RT contain basic rich-text formatting. Font colors are lost in the OCR process, and tables with multiple lines of text appear in the default font (Verdana) in an .htm document but don't covert properly to tables in .doc files. Files named PDC2003PR-RT2 demonstrate the formatting problem with tables in .doc files. You can't remove a Word print view from the default view; restore the Backup Copy of PrintView.xsn in the current folder if you want to repeat the preceding exercise.

Chapter Summary

InfoPath's capability to display multiple views of a form is an important incentive for adopting InfoPath as a general-purpose XML data entry and editing tool. Copying and pasting form design elements between views makes repurposing existing views easy. Pasted elements retain their bindings to the data source's sections, elements, and attributes. You can delete sections and controls you don't need for alternative views, add new sections and controls to the view, and alter conditional formatting to suit the view's purpose. Data validation rules apply to all form views.

Multiple views enable a single form to accommodate changes in data entry operations and document content at each step in an automated workflow environment. You can customize views for e-mail distribution as .xml or .mht files and define a default printing view. Choosing File, Print Preview or File, Print in data entry mode automatically opens the select view's default print view. Printing to Microsoft Office Document Imaging files and applying OCR to create formatted Word .htm and .doc files is an alternative if you have the requisite XSLT authoring skills.

Q&A

Q. Is there a limit to the number of views I can add to a template?

A. There's no published or theoretical limit to the number of views, but the size of your template file for a complex form increases with each view you add. For example, the original NWOrdersCh10.xsn file's size is 14,636 bytes and contains 128 KB of compressed files. Adding the three additional views increases the file's size to 37,866 bytes and the size of the extracted files to 354 KB. You'll probably encounter noticeable performance impairment with template files larger than 200 KB or so, which corresponds to about 2 MB of compressed files.

Q. Recipients need Internet Explorer to open forms e-mailed as .mht files. Is there an alternative for recipients who use other browsers?

A. Yes. The InfoPath 2003 Software Development Kit (SDK) includes a Downlevel command-line tool (XDown.cmd) to transform form views to formatted HTML with an XDown.xsl transform. The process isn't simple, and some InfoPath features might not display correctly. If you've installed the InfoPath 2003 SDK, open the InfoPath 2003 SDK documentation, expand the Tools node, and read the "Using the Downlevel Tool" topic.

Q. Can I change the data document's file name automatically based on a workflow status or the current view?

A. Yes. The form must be fully trusted and you must write programming code to accomplish this feat. Fully trusted forms are one of the subjects of Chapter 12, "Publishing Form Templates." Chapter 16,

On Your Own

Here are a few additional exercises that you can use to test your view and rule design prowess:

1. Create an e-mail version of the InvoiceEntry view.
2. Create a print version of the InvoiceEntry e-mail view.
3. Modify the print version to more closely resemble a printed form by increasing the form's width to about 7.5 inches, decreasing the font size to 8 pt, and rearranging the Ship To and Bill To tables as side-by-side address blocks without labels. (You can use the Text tab of the View Properties dialog box to change the size of all the view's controls at once.)
4. Add a rule to set the Customer ID value in the Order Information or Invoice section equal to the Customer ID value in the Customer Information or Bill To section.
5. Add a rule that applies only to the InvoiceEntry view to set the value of the my:InvoiceInfo group's OrderID attribute to the OrderID value of the OrderInfo group.

CHAPTER 11

Setting Form Template and Digital Signing Options

In this chapter, you will learn how to:

- ✦ **Enable form protection**
- ✦ **Disable InfoPath design mode during installation of InfoPath 2003 on users' computers**
- ✦ **Restrict users from merging or submitting forms**
- ✦ **Prevent users from saving, exporting, printing, or e-mailing data documents**
- ✦ **Remove unneeded fields from new forms**
- ✦ **Add digital signatures to entire data documents or parts of documents with a Client Authentication certificate**
- ✦ **Add custom HTML task panes to forms, specify how InfoPath handles form upgrades, specify the script programming language, and export a version of the form for users who do not have Microsoft InfoPath 2003 SP-1 installed**

For more information:

- ✦ **See "Windows 2000 Certificate Services and PKI," Chapter 16 of the *Microsoft Windows 2000 Server Resource Kit*. Search for *Web enrollment* on *www.microsoft.com*, and click the link under the Technical Resources heading.**
- ✦ **See the topic "Certification Authority Web Enrollment Services" in the Windows 2000 Server documentation. Click the More Technical Resources Results link to display the link to this topic. Both articles apply to Microsoft Windows Server 2003.**

To work through this chapter:

- ✧ You should have installed in your C:\Microsoft Press\Introducing InfoPath 2003\Chapter11 folder the sample files from the CD that accompanies this book.
- ✧ You need an Internet connection to submit forms by the HTTP *POST* protocol to the OakLeaf Web site.
- ✧ You should have some experience with the use of digital certificates for authenticating documents, such as e-mail messages.
- ✧ You must have a commercial Client Authentication certificate that supports digital document signing or access to a Microsoft Windows 2000 or later certificate server from which you can obtain a Client Authentication certificate and, if the certificate server isn't in your Trusted Certificate Authorities list, access to the certificate server's certificate (.crt) file.

The Form Options dialog box is a catchall for setting form design properties that aren't accessible through menu options or task panes. This chapter shows you how to use features on the dialog box's General, Open and Save, Digital Signature, and Advanced tabs. Chapter 12, "Publishing Form Templates," will show you how to configure settings on the Form Options dialog box's Security and Form Library Columns tabs.

Enabling Form Protection

After spending a few hours designing and testing a new or modified form for production, you certainly don't want users to be able to alter the template at will by clicking the Design This Form button or choosing Tools, Design This Form and opening the form's template in design mode. When you publish your template to a server share, to an Internet Information Services virtual directory on your company's intranet, or to a Windows SharePoint Services site, unauthorized template changes affect all users of the production form.

See Also The sections "Sharing Templates from a Network Folder" and "Publishing Templates to an Intranet Site" in Chapter 12 will cover deployment of URL-based, untrusted (*sandboxed*) or fully trusted, digitally signed templates to server shares and intranet Web servers. These two sections will also show you how to secure shared templates against user modification.

To rein in users who are tempted to modify a form's template, choose Tools, Form Options to open the Form Options dialog box with the General tab displayed. Select the Enable Protection check box, as shown in Figure 11-1, and click OK to save your changes. Form protection disables the Design This Form toolbar button and the Tools, Design This Form menu option.

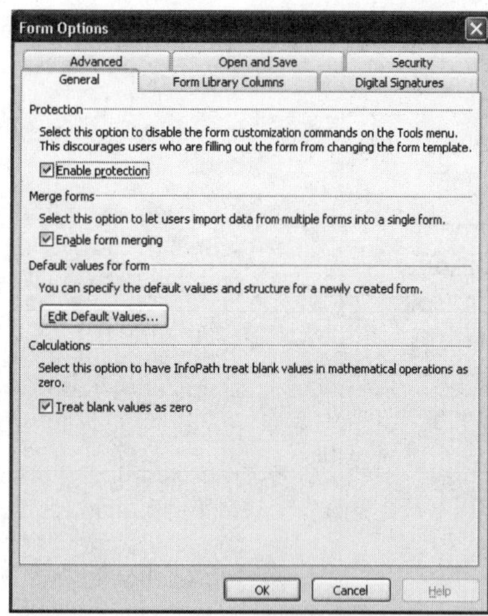

Figure 11-1 Selecting the Enable Protection check box on the General tab of the Form Options dialog box is the first step in protecting templates against modification by users.

Form protection doesn't prevent users from attempting to modify the template. Users must have Read access to the shared template file, which requires at least Read permission for the server share, shared folder, and .xsn file. This means that users can open the .xsn file,

Testing the Enable Protection feature

The Rss2v4Prot.xsn template in your C:\Microsoft Press\Introducing InfoPath 2003\Chapter 11\Rss2V4 folder has protection enabled. Double-click the template file to display the warning message shown in Figure 11-2.

regardless of whether they have permission to save changes to the file. Anyone opening a protected .xsn file receives the warning shown in Figure 11-2.

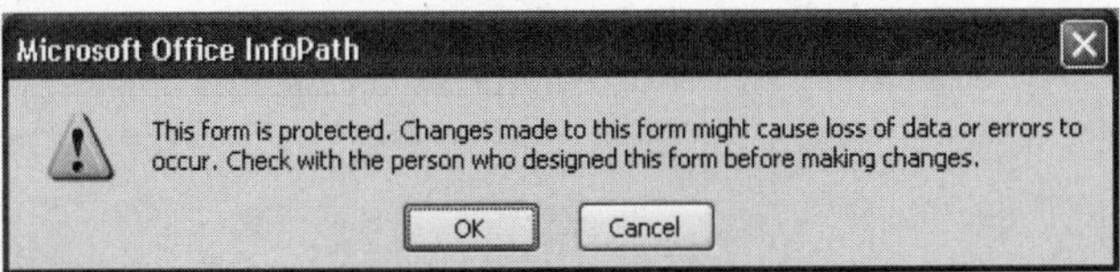

Figure 11-2 This warning message appears when anyone (including you) opens a protected template on the local computer or from a server.

Disabling InfoPath Design Mode

If your organization has acquired InfoPath as part of Microsoft Office Professional Enterprise Edition 2003, you can request that InfoPath be installed on users' computers with design mode disabled. Step 10 of the Microsoft Office 2003 Custom Installation Wizard's process displays a dialog box for setting individual installation options for all Office System 2003 applications. Figure 11-3 shows the expanded Microsoft InfoPath 2003 node with a Miscellaneous subnode. This subnode has a single setting–Disable InfoPath Designer Mode.

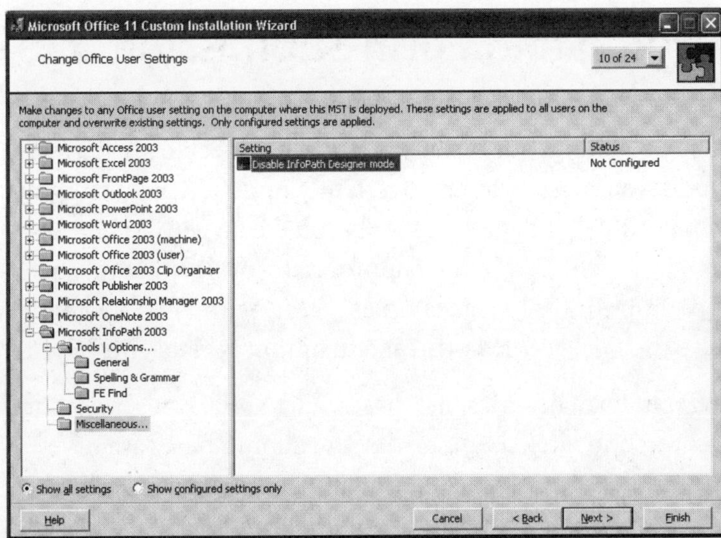

Figure 11-3 The Disable InfoPath Designer Mode setting is accessible in step 10 of the Office System 2003 installation configuration process.

Double-clicking the setting item opens the Disable InfoPath Designer Mode Properties dialog box. Selecting the single check box and selecting the Apply

Changes option, as shown in Figure 11-4, and then clicking OK disables design mode for all users who have InfoPath installed with this configuration.

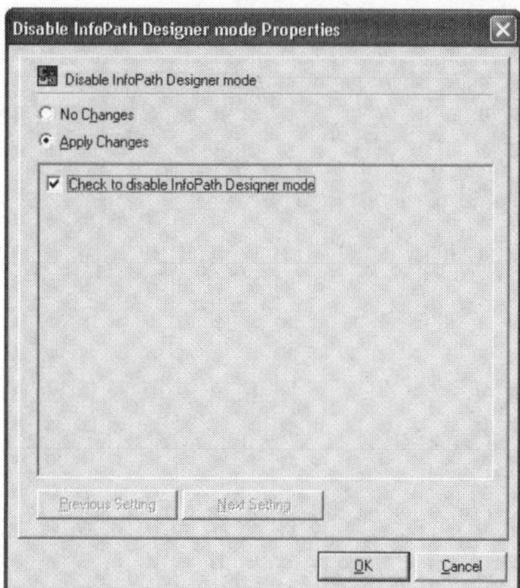

Figure 11-4 These settings disable design mode for Office System 2003 installations that use this wizard configuration.

See Also To learn how to emulate the registry change that the Custom Installation Wizard makes to disable design mode, see the section "Disabling Design Mode for Deployed Fully Trusted Forms," in Chapter 12.

Controlling Merging and Form Submission

The General tab of the Form Options dialog box has an Enable Forms Merging check box that's selected by default. If your form isn't designed specifically for merging, clear the check box to prevent users from inadvertently or deliberately merging data documents. As examples, RSS 2.0 data documents you create with Rss2v4.xsn are designed for merging, but merging is totally inappropriate for documents you create with the Northwind Order Entry form examples. Clearing the Enable Forms Merging check box disables the File, Merge Forms menu option in data entry mode.

Submitting forms to SharePoint form libraries, databases, and XML Web services are advanced topics that are covered in later chapters, but you should be aware of another restriction that you can apply to forms–specifying how users can submit a form. You specify submission options by choosing Tools, Submitting Forms to open a dialog box of the same name, which offers the following selections in the Submit To list:

- **E-Mail** Opens the Message dialog box specified by the selected data connection and sends the data document as an e-mail attachment to the named recipients

- **Web Service** Sends updated form content to an XML Web service method that's designed for receiving data

- **SharePoint Form Library** Sends the data document to an existing form library of a Windows SharePoint Services site to which the form's template has been published
- **Web Server (HTTP)** Sends the form to a Web page that accepts HTTP *POST* operations
- **Custom Submit Using Form Code** Specifies a Microsoft JScript, Visual Basic Scripting Edition (VBScript), or Visual Basic .NET event handler for the *OnSubmitRequest* event that's triggered when users click the Submit button or choose File, Submit
- **Custom Submit Using Rules** Lets you specify rules that select one or more data connections to use for form submission, depending on conditions you apply to the rules.

The Do Not Enable Submit option, which disables the File, Submit menu option in data entry mode, is the default selection.

See Also Chapter 12, "Publishing Form Templates," covers submitting forms to SharePoint form libraries, because you must publish the template to create the library before you can submit a form to it. Chapter 13, "Connecting Forms to Databases," and Chapter 14, "Designing InfoPath Web Service Clients" cover submitting forms to databases and XML Web services. These operations require enabling submissions.

Submitting a Form Through HTTP

You can submit a form to a Web page that processes HTTP *POST* operations. The protected version of the RSS 2.0 form (Rss2v4Prot.xsn) has HTTP *POST* submission enabled. A simple ASP.NET Web page at *www.oakleaf.ws/ipsubmit/ipsubmit.aspx* accepts the *POST* submission. A production version of this page might automatically update your intranet or Internet Web server's rss.xml file.

To explore form submission options and test the submission process, follow these steps.

▶ **View submission options and submit the RSS 2.0 form**

1. **Navigate to your C:\Microsoft Press\Introducing InfoPath 2003\Chapter 11\Rss2V4 folder, and open the Rss2v4Prot.xsn template in design mode. Click OK to dismiss the protection warning message.**
2. **Choose Tools, Submitting Forms to open the Submitting Forms dialog box. As you can see, the Enable Submit and Submit Through HTTP options are selected, the URL for the OakLeaf submission page is provided, the Enable The Submit Menu**

Item On The File Menu check box is selected, and a modified menu caption is provided:

3. Click the Submit Options button to open the eponymous dialog box with the default options selected, as shown here. (If you substitute a custom message, the Details button shown in step 6 doesn't appear in the Success Message box.)

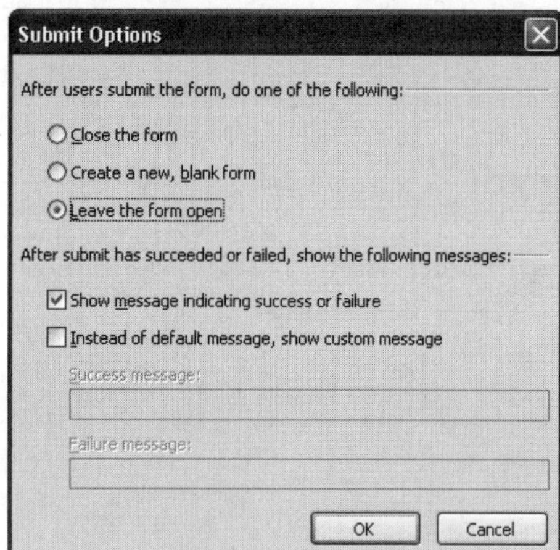

4. Click OK twice to close the two dialog boxes, and then click Preview Form.
5. Click the Submit To OakLeaf Site button or choose File, Submit To OakLeaf Site to post the data document to the Web server. The following message box will appear, indicating that the *POST* operation succeeded:

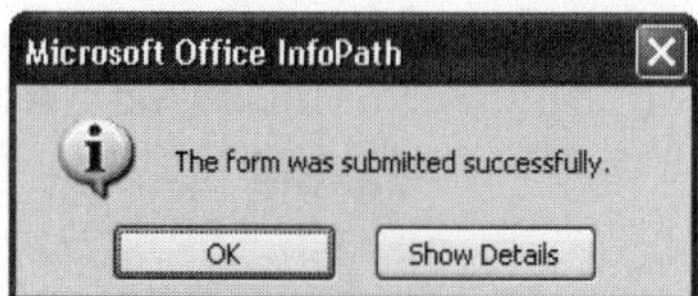

6. **Click the Show Details button to display the posted data in a browser window, as shown here:**

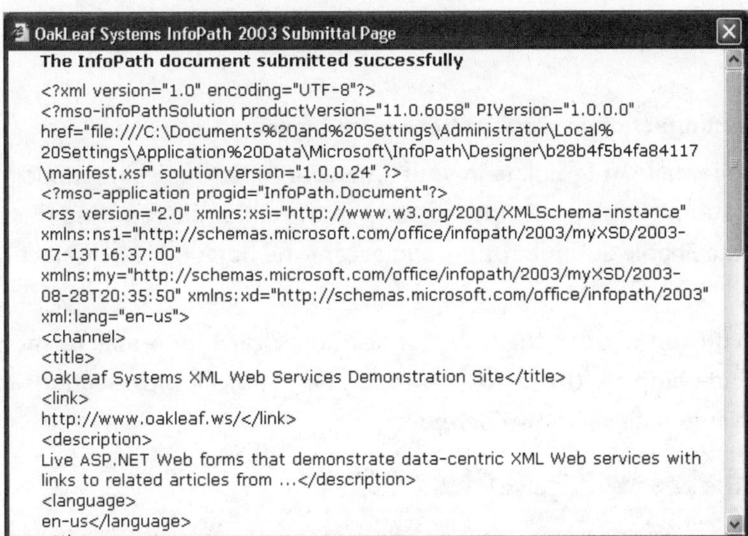

The processing instructions reflect the location of a temporary copy of the manifest.xsf file—not the .xsn file—in a subfolder of your Documents and Settings folder. (This is your only opportunity to see the modification to the processing instructions for previews.)

7. **Close the browser window and the preview.**
8. **Choose Tools, Submitting Forms, and select the Do Not Enable Submit option to disable the remaining dialog box controls.**
9. **Open a second preview window, and verify that the Submit menu option is disabled.**
10. **Close the preview window and InfoPath without saving your changes.**

> **Creating your own ASP.NET page for *POST* operations**
> If you have Microsoft Visual Studio .NET 2003 or Visual Basic .NET Standard Edition 2003 installed and you have experience with ASP.NET, you can add your own version of the OakLeaf IPSubmit Web page to a local Web server. Microsoft Visual C# .NET and Visual Basic .NET code files (IPSubmit.cs and IPSubmit.vb) are located in your C:\Microsoft Press\Introducing InfoPath 2003\Chapter 11\ASPNetCode folder. Open a new Web Application project, and replace all of the code behind an empty designer page with the text from the appropriate file.

Submitting a Form Through E-Mail

Submitting a form through e-mail is similar to sending a form as an e-mail attachment but requires defining a data connection for the transmission. One advantage of submission over sending is that the template stores the recipient, subject, and comment information so that users don't need to type the information each time they submit the form. Another benefit of e-mail submission is the option to use the Insert Formula dialog box to insert e-mail addresses and add other transmission-related data from form field values. You must have Microsoft Office Outlook 2003 installed on your computer to submit a form through e-mail.

To give the Data Connection Wizard's e-mail submission feature a try, follow these steps.

▶ Create a data connection and submit the form by e-mail

1. **Open the Rss2v4Mail.xsn template in your ...\Rss2v4 folder in design mode, choose Tools, Submitting Forms Options to open the dialog box bearing the same name, select the Enable Submit option, and accept the default E-Mail selection of the Submit list.**
2. **Click the Add button to open the Data Connection Wizard for e-mail form submission, and complete the form with To, Cc, Bcc, Subject, Introduction, and Attachment Name data, as shown here:**

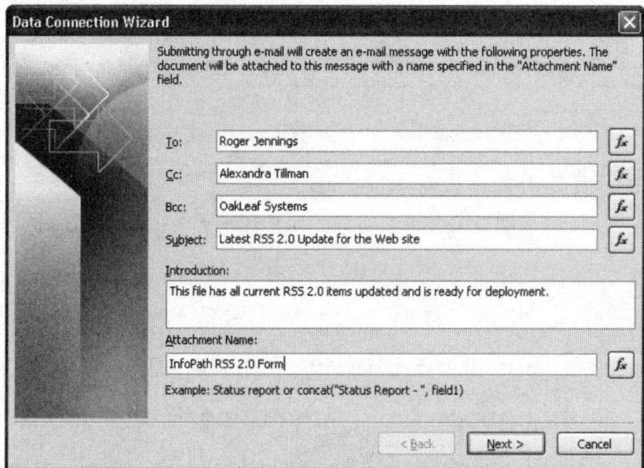

   If your form has fields containing e-mail addresses or other information for the connection fields, click the Insert Formula (*fx*) button to the right of the corresponding text box, and specify the field name with the appropriate value.

3. **Click Next, type a Name for the data connection, such as Rss2v4 E-Mail Submit, and click Finish to complete the wizard. In the Submitting Forms dialog box, add by E-Mail to the caption, as shown here:**

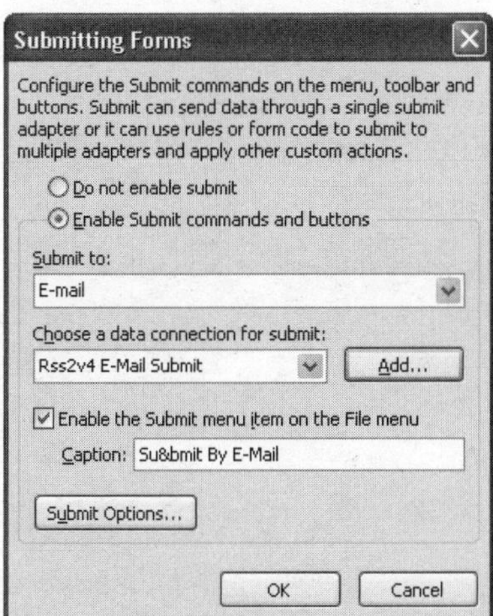

4. Click OK to close the dialog box and create the data connection, open a form preview window, and click the Submit By E-Mail button to open the *Subject*-Message dialog box. Place the insertion point in the Attachment description to enable the View Attachment button, as shown here:

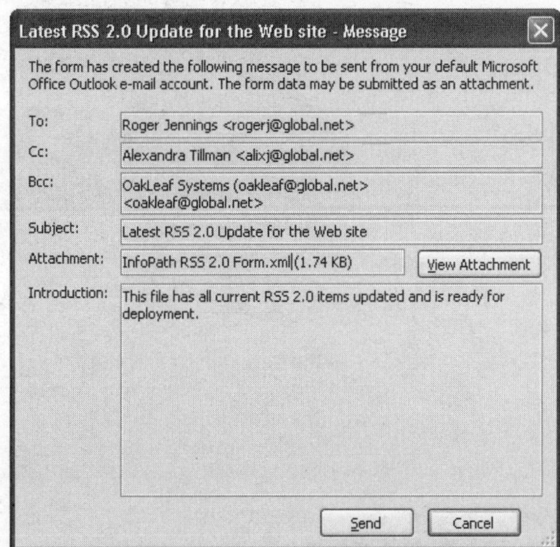

(E-mail addresses in this section's figures are fictitious.)

5. Click OK to acknowledge the successful transmission. Outlook 2003 recipients open the *Subject*-Message (HTML) dialog box with the text of the introduction and the XML file attachment, as shown on the next page.

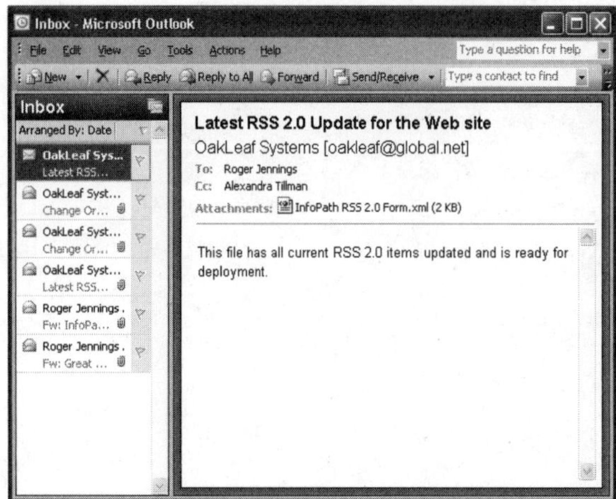

Recipients of forms sent or submitted by e-mail must have InfoPath installed and network, Web server, or SharePoint access to a published copy of the form's template. If you submit the Rss2v4Mail form as a message to your e-mail address and receive the message on the computer running InfoPath, you can double-click the Rss2v4Mail.xml attachment and edit it with the local template. Submitting a preview causes the e-mailed form to be read-only.

Setting empty numeric elements to 0 and assigning templates to a custom category

InfoPath 2003 SP-1 adds two new features to the General tab of the Form Options dialog box: Calculations and Form Category. Selecting the Treat Blank Values As 0 check box (the default) converts empty (*nil*) numeric element values to 0 when used in formulas. If you clear this check box, any calculation that encounters a *nil* value returns *nil* (*null*), which is unlikely to be what you want to happen.

Selecting the Enable Custom Category check box and specifying a category name lets you categorize templates. Each category you add appears after Sample Forms under the Fill Out A Form dialog box's Form Categories heading. Clicking a category link displays the forms you've added to the category. Removing all forms in a category removes the category name.

Limiting a Form's Feature Set

The Form Option dialog box's Open and Save tab, shown in Figure 11-5, Enable Features section has check boxes that let you prevent users from saving and autosaving the data document, exporting a form as an .mht file or to a Microsoft Excel worksheet, printing the form, or sending the document by e-mail. Clearing all check boxes has the effect of preventing users from preserving or distributing copies of confidential forms. In this case, the only means of saving confidential form data is to submit the form by the method specified in the Submitting Forms dialog box. Obviously, you must prevent users from modifying the template to make this confidentiality scenario effective. Chapter 12 shows you how to prevent users from modifying templates that you publish to server shares, Web servers, and SharePoint form libraries.

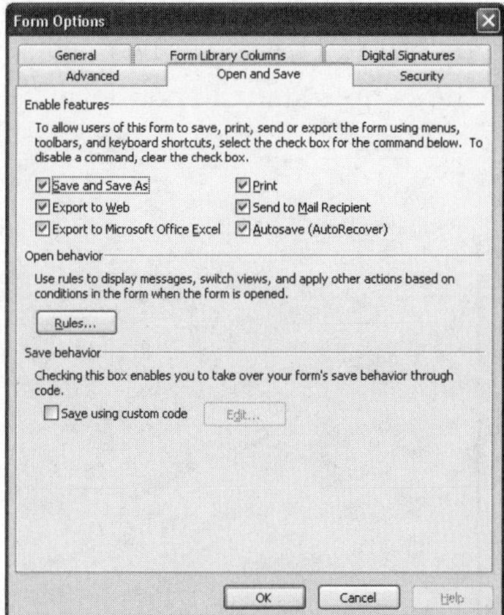

Figure 11-5 The Open and Save tab has check boxes that control users' ability to save, export, print, and send the template's data documents.

Clicking the Rules button in the Open and Save tab's Open Behavior section displays the Rules For Opening Forms dialog box. The section "Adding Workflow-Dependent Rules" in Chapter 10, "Adding Views to a Template," describes the use of this dialog box for setting field values and specifying the default view when opening a form.

Selecting the Save Using Custom Code check box in the Open and Save tab's Save Behavior section enables the Edit button. Clicking Edit opens the Microsoft Script Editor (MSE) with a JScript or VBScript handler for the *OnSaveRequest* event. Chapter 17, "Writing Advanced Event Handlers," shown you how to program the *OnSaveRequest* event with Visual Basic .NET code.

Removing Unused Fields from New Forms

Forms based on schemas that have many optional sections, fields, or both create data documents with empty element values for these fields. The sample InfoPath forms provide examples of schemas that generate data documents with mostly empty elements. If your form doesn't have sections or controls bound to optional elements, you can use InfoPath's Edit Default Values dialog box to reduce the size of the XML data document substantially. Modifications you make in this dialog box don't affect the schema; changes affect only the template's template.xml file, which InfoPath uses as the starting point for new forms. The sample.xml file doesn't reflect the modifications.

You open the Edit Default Values dialog box by clicking the Edit Default Values button on the Form Option dialog box's General tab. Figure 11-6 shows two instances of the Edit Default Values dialog box for the sample StatusReport form.

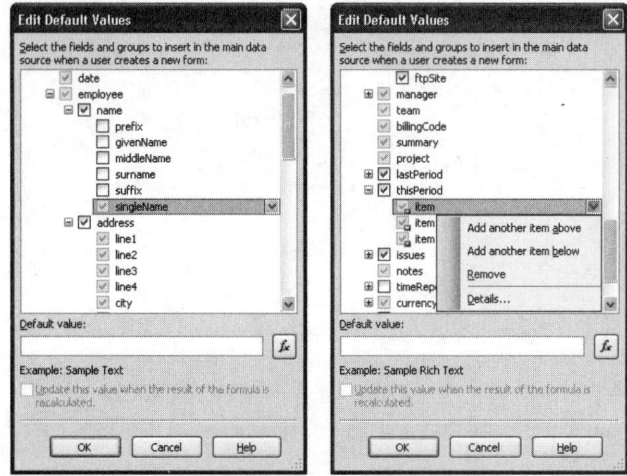

Figure 11-6 Clearing enabled check boxes in the Edit Default Values dialog box removes the sections or fields from new data documents (left). You add or remove default repeating sections with menu items (right).

Here's a brief explanation of how the InfoPath's Edit Default Values feature works:

- Disabled check boxes represent sections and fields that are bound to the form's required sections and controls.
- Enabled check boxes with green check marks represent unbound or not-required sections or fields. (A not-required section or field has a *minOccurs="0"* attribute value.) Clearing the check box removes the section or field from the data document.
- Enabled section check boxes can contain disabled check boxes. Clearing a section check box clears the check boxes for all child sections and elements, so don't remove sections that contain disabled check boxes, such as the *employee/name* section shown on the left in Figure 11-6, which has a required *singleName* element. Instead, remove individual child elements or sections.

- Cleared section check boxes represent optional sections. Selecting these check boxes changes an optional section to a required section or a repeating section. You can specify the default number of occurrences of required repeating sections or rows of repeating tables by right-clicking the node and choosing Add Another ItemName Above, Add Another ItemName Below, Remove, or Details as shown on the right in Figure 11-6.

- The Default Value check box is enabled for most enabled fields. When it's enabled, you can specify a default value for the field as an alternative to specifying a default value on the Data tab of a control's Properties dialog box or the .
- You can specify a default value based another field value or XPath function by clicking the Insert Formula (*fx*) button to open the Insert Formula dialog box and clicking the Insert Field Or Group or Insert Function button.

Saving a StatusReport form with only the Date field populated generates a 3539-byte data document that contains only 10 data bytes. Eliminating unneeded sections and fields reduces the size to about 17 bytes.

To take the Edit Default Values dialog box for a test drive with the StatusReport template, follow these steps.

▶ Reduce the size of new status report documents

1. **Start InfoPath, and click the Design A Form link on the Fill Out A Form task pane to activate the Design task pane.**
2. **Click the Customize A Sample link, and double-click Status Report on the Sample Forms tab.**
3. **Save the template as SREditDefaults.xsn or the like in a new \My Documents\InfoPath\SREditDefaults folder.**
4. **Open the Fill Out A Form task pane, click the link to the newly saved template, and save the form as SRDefault.xml to provide a baseline for the data document size reduction process of the remaining steps. Close the form to return to design mode.**
5. **Choose Tools, Form Options to open the Form Options dialog box, and click the Edit Default Values button.**
6. **Clear the five enabled check boxes under the *employee/name* section. The *name* section isn't designated as required, but one of its elements—*singleName*—is bound to a control.**
7. **Scroll to the *employee/address* section, and clear its check box.**
8. **Clear all remaining *employee* check boxes except the *emailAddressPrimary* and the *department* check boxes; these two elements are bound to text box controls.**

9. **Repeat steps 6 through 8 for the *manager* section and its children. (The manager's *emailPrimaryAddress* element isn't bound to a control, but it might be useful in future form versions.)**
10. **Click OK twice to close the dialog boxes and apply the changes. Verify in design mode that you haven't removed any fields bound to controls, and then save your changes. You must save the template to create a new data document with the edited defaults.**
11. **Repeat step 4, but save the data document as SREdited.xml to check its size—about 1526 bytes. (The actual size varies with the length of the template's path and file name.)**
12. **Optionally, open the two data documents in Notepad to compare their contents.**

The sample Status Report form has bulleted lists that have three bullets by default and three optional repeating tables. You can change the default number of bullets or other list items and require repeating sections or tables in the Edit Default Values dialog box.

Adding Digital Signatures to Forms

InfoPath supports the use of X.509 digital certificates to enable applying digital signatures to an entire form or to individual groups or fields of a form. InfoPath stores the digital signature data for an entire form in the data document's signatures group. Assigning signatures to individual form groups or fields adds signatures subgroups to the document's signatures group.

Applying a digital signature ensures recipients that a data document or its specific groups or fields originated from a specific person or computer and hasn't been modified by anyone else. If anyone alters the document's content subsequent to signing, the digital signature won't match a value (called a *hash*) that's calculated from the file's text. If the entire form is signed, the data document is read only. In this case, you must remove the digital signature to modify the data document with InfoPath. InfoPath SP-1 forms also support multiple digital signatures; this feature enables auditable, multistep approval processes. Saving a copy of the data document with all required signatures prevents any signing party from repudiating an action, such as initiation or approval of a document.

See Also To gain a better understanding of XML digital signatures, read "An Introduction to XML Digital Signatures," at *www.xml.com/pub/a/2001/08/08/xmldsig.html*, and "Enabling XML Security," at *www-106.ibm.com/developerworks/xml/library/s-xmlsec.html/index.html*.

Trusting the Certificate Authority

All users who need to digitally sign forms or verify the digital signatures of signed forms must trust the certificate authority (CA) that issues digital signing certificates to users. The CA for the examples in this section and in the following digital signature–related sections is a Windows Server 2003 member server (OakLeaf-MS2K3) in a Windows 2000 ActiveDirectory domain running stand-alone Certificate Services with Web enrollment support installed. This configuration is common for intranets and extranets; *extranets* permit designated business partners to access specific parts of an organization's intranet. Extranet users must have access to the CA's certificate (.crt) file to add your organization's CA to their trusted CA lists, and they must be able to request and obtain certificates from the CA's certificate server.

If you already have a personal digital certificate that supports digital signing, skip to the section "Signing and Cosigning a Form," later in this chapter. Otherwise, follow these steps to determine whether your computer trusts the CA.

▶ Verify that the local computer trusts the CA

1. **Start Internet Explorer, choose Tools, Internet Options to open the Internet Options dialog box, and select the Content tab.**
2. **Click the Certificates button to open the Certificates dialog box, and select the Trusted Root Certification Authorities tab.**
3. **Scroll to the name of your CA (OakLeafRootCA is the sample CA in this and the following exercises), and verify that the Intended Purpose list displays <All>, as shown here: if not, the list must include <Non-Repudiation Signing>, which is required for digitally signing InfoPath forms. (Free or low-cost commercial e-mail signing certificates won't work.)**

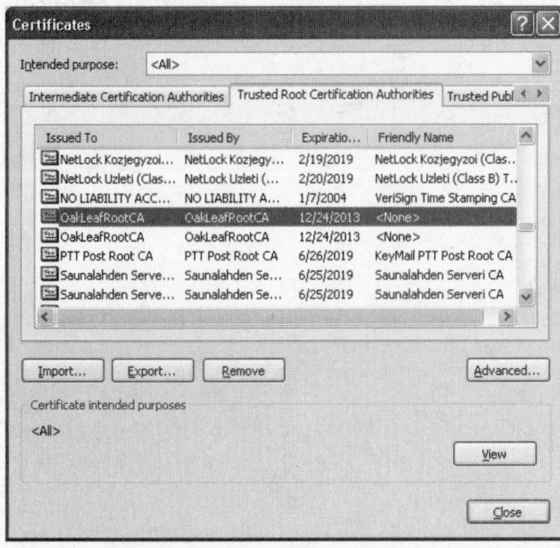

4. **If the name of your CA isn't listed, ask your network administrator for the location of the CA's certificate file, click Import to start the Certificate Import Wizard, and follow the wizard's instructions to add the CA to the Trusted Root Certification Authorities list.**
5. **Click Close, and then click OK.**

Obtaining a Digital Signing Certificate

The most common method of obtaining a certificate from a Windows 2000 and later certificate server is the Web enrollment process. The procedures aren't significantly different for a Windows 2000 or Windows 2003 enterprise CA, but they vary slightly depending on whether the CA issues certificates automatically or requires an administrator to approve certificate issuance. If your organization has established an enterprise CA, you probably have the required Client Authentication certificate. If so, skip to the next section.

Enabling Web enrollment on a Windows Server 2003 computer running SharePoint

Installing Windows SharePoint Services as the default Web site on a certificate server disables Web enrollment's Active Server Pages (ASP). To reenable Web enrollment, you must remove the certsrv virtual directory from SharePoint management. Run the SharePoint Central Administration tool, and click the Configure Virtual Server Settings, Default Web Site, and Define Managed Paths links to open the Define Managed Paths page. Type **certsrv** in the Path box, select the Excluded Path option, and click OK to add certsrv to the Excluded Paths list.

Follow these steps to obtain a digital signing certificate from a Windows 2000 or 2003 server CA.

▶ Obtain an advanced certificate from the CA

1. **In Internet Explorer, type the URL or server name of the certificate server followed by /certsrv/ to open the Welcome page of the Microsoft Certificate Services Web site, as shown here:**

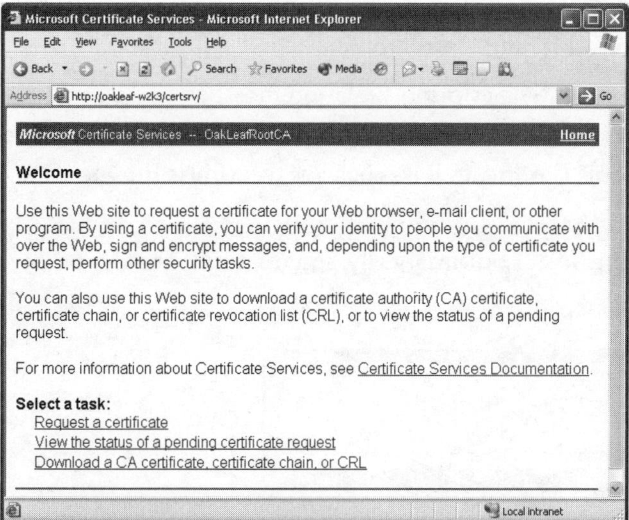

2. Click the Request A Certificate link to open the Request A Certificate page.
3. Click the Advanced Certificate Request link to open the next page.
4. Click the Create And Submit A Request To This CA link to open another Advanced Certificate Request page.
5. Fill out the Identifying Information section, and leave the default Client Authentication Certificate in the Type Of Certificate Needed list.
6. Leave the default key options, unless you have a reason for doing otherwise. For this example, the Key Size is increased to 2048 bytes for additional security:

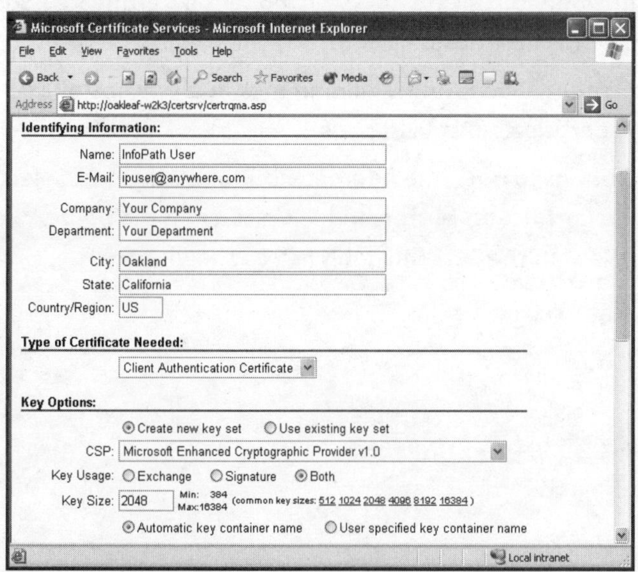

7. Scroll to the Additional Options section, type a Friendly Name for the certificate, such as **InfoPath Signing Cert**, and click Submit.
8. Click Yes to dismiss the Potential Scripting Violation message and submit the request. If your CA issues certificates automatically, a Certificate Issued page opens. Click the Install This Certificate link, click Yes to dismiss the message, and skip to step 13.
9. Most CA's don't issue certificates automatically, so you might see the following Certificate Pending page:

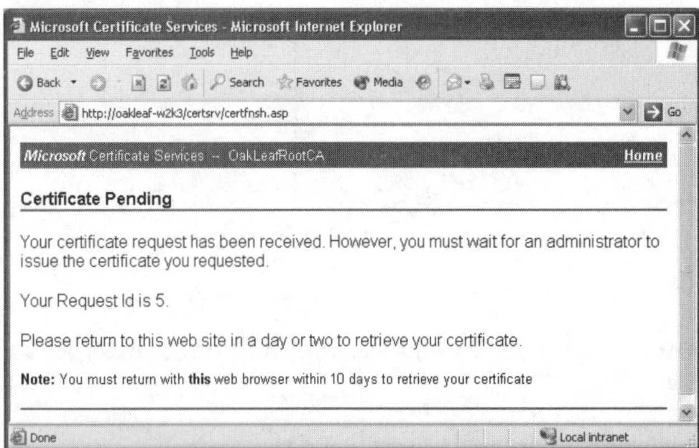

10. After the CA administrator issues your certificate, return to the page you specified in step 1, and click the View The Status Of A Pending Certificate Request link to open a page of the same name.
11. Click the Client Authentication Certificate link, which opens a Certificate Issued page, and click the Install This Certificate link.
12. Click Yes to dismiss the Potential Scripting Violation message box, install the certificate, and display a Certificate Installed page.
13. Choose Tools, Internet Options to open the Internet Options dialog box. Select the Content tab, and click the Certificates button. In the Certificates dialog box, verify that the certificate is present in the Personal tab's list, as shown here:

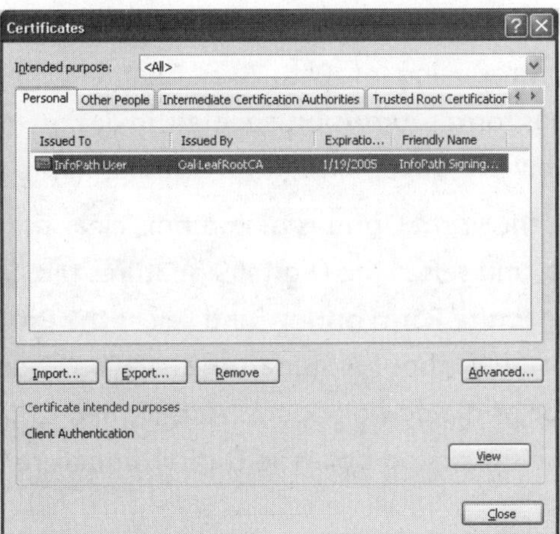

14. **With your signature item selected, click View to open the Certificate dialog box, click the Details tab, scroll to and select Key Usage in the list. The usages shown here should appear in the text box:**

15. **Click OK, click Close, and click OK to close the dialog boxes, and then close Internet Explorer.**

Signing and Cosigning an Entire Form

InfoPath's developers made signing entire forms a simple, point-and-click operation. To sign a form, you must enable digital signatures in design mode on the Form Options dialog box's Digital Signatures tab.

The following four procedures show you how to enable signing an entire document, add your signature to a document, test for modified documents, and emulate an approval cosignature.

▶ Specify digital signing in design mode

1. Navigate to your C:\Microsoft Press\Introducing InfoPath 2003\Chapter11\Rss2v4 folder. Open Rss2v4Prot.xsn, which has form submission enabled, in design mode, and save it as **Rss2v4Sign.xsn** to a new My Documents\InfoPath\Signing folder.
2. Choose Tools, Form Options to open the Form Options dialog box, clear the Enable Protection on the General tab, and select the Digital Signatures tab. Select the Enable Digital Signatures For The Entire Form option, and select the Prompt Users To Sign The Form If It Is Submitted Without A Signature check box. Submission is enabled, so the Submitting Forms dialog box opens. Add **Signed** to the caption, and click OK to close to close the dialog box. The Digital Signature tab appears as shown here:

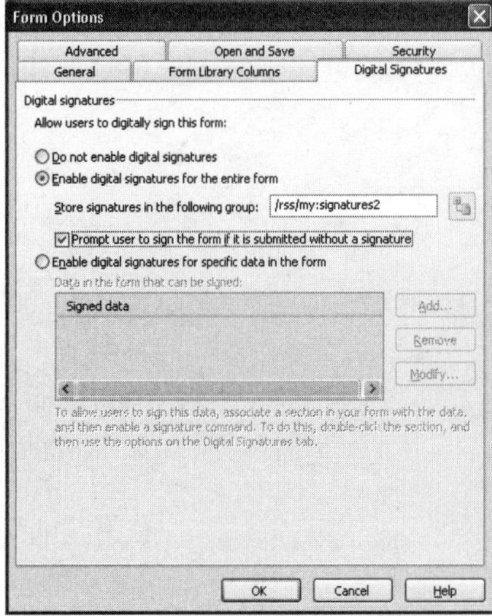

3. Click OK to close the Form Options dialog box and save the changes. Save the template, and click Overwrite to close the warning message box.
4. Save an unsigned data document as **Rss2v4NoSign.xml**. You will notice that you don't receive a prompt when you save an unsigned form that has submission enabled. The warning appears only if you submit the form.

▶ Sign the entire data document

1. Open a new Form1. Enabling digital signatures in step 2 of the preceding procedure enables the Digital Signatures toolbar button and the Tools, Digital Signatures menu option.

2. Click the Digital Signatures button to open the Digital Signatures dialog box, and click the Add button to start the Digital Signature Wizard. Click Next to accept

Entire Form as the signature scope and open a certificate list in the second wizard screen, as shown here:

3. Select the certificate you want to use, and click Next to display the third wizard screen, which displays key information about the certificate. Type a comment to accompany your signature, if you want, as shown here:

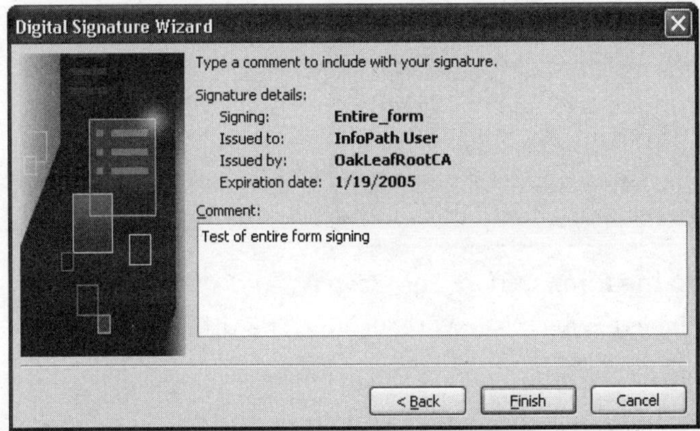

4. Click Finish to display the Digital Signature Wizard's confirmation screen. Select the I Have Verified This Content Before Signing check box to enable the Sign button, as shown on the next page.

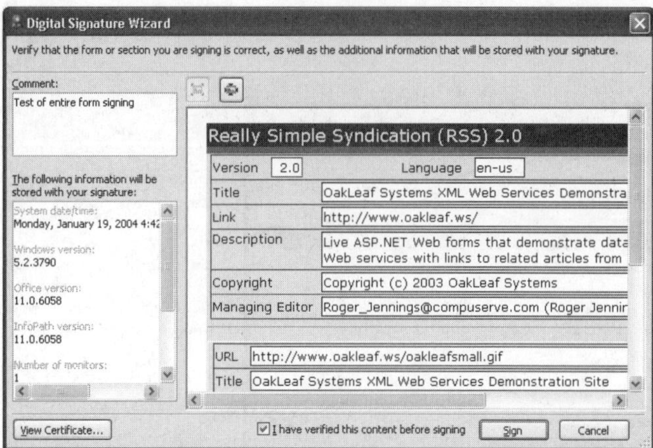

5. Click Sign to display the Digital Signatures dialog box, shown here:

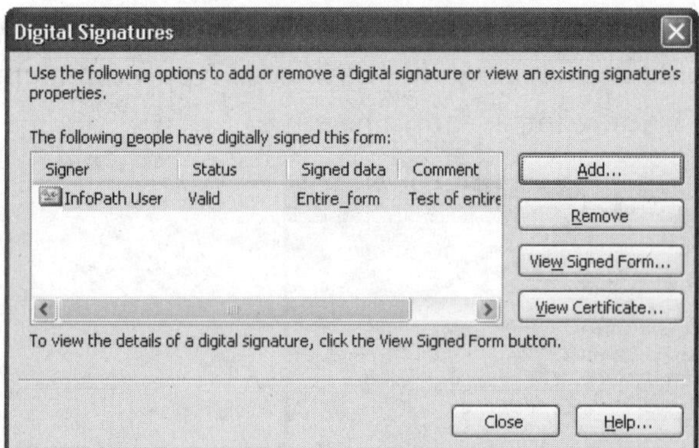

6. Click Close to return to the form. Choose File, Save As, and save the form as **Rss2v4Sign1.xml** or the like, which is now read-only. The title bar adds the [Signed] to the file name.
7. If you want to edit the form, click the Digital Signatures button, click the Remove or Remove All button, click OK, and click Yes to confirm your action. Selecting the Prompt Users To Sign The Form If It Is Submitted Without A Signature check box in step 2 of the preceding exercise and submitting the form to the OakLeaf Web site without adding a signature displays the following prompt:

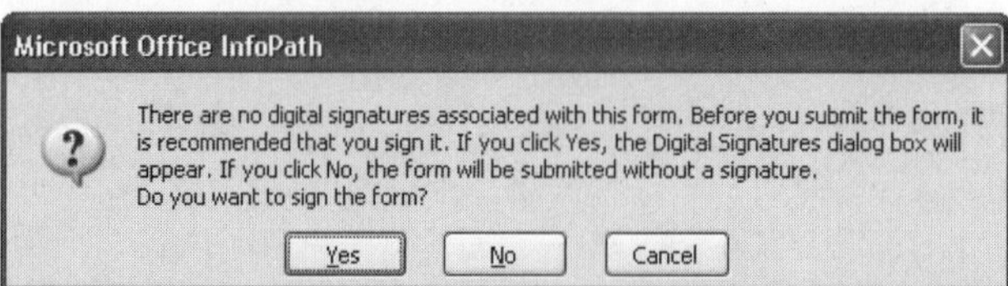

8. With the form re-signed if you removed the signature, choose File, Submit To OakLeaf Web Site, and click Show Details to open the browser window with the

data document's content. Scroll until you reach the <*my:signatures#*> element, as shown here:

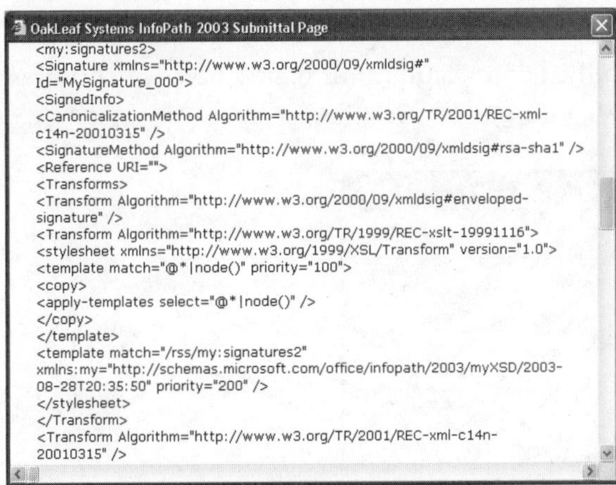

```
OakLeaf Systems InfoPath 2003 Submittal Page
<my:signatures2>
<Signature xmlns="http://www.w3.org/2000/09/xmldsig#"
Id="MySignature_000">
<SignedInfo>
<CanonicalizationMethod Algorithm="http://www.w3.org/TR/2001/REC-xml-
c14n-20010315" />
<SignatureMethod Algorithm="http://www.w3.org/2000/09/xmldsig#rsa-sha1" />
<Reference URI="">
<Transforms>
<Transform Algorithm="http://www.w3.org/2000/09/xmldsig#enveloped-
signature" />
<Transform Algorithm="http://www.w3.org/TR/1999/REC-xslt-19991116">
<stylesheet xmlns="http://www.w3.org/1999/XSL/Transform" version="1.0">
<template match="@*|node()" priority="100">
<copy>
<apply-templates select="@*|node()" />
</copy>
</template>
<template match="/rss/my:signatures2"
xmlns:my="http://schemas.microsoft.com/office/infopath/2003/myXSD/2003-
08-28T20:35:50" priority="200" />
</stylesheet>
</Transform>
<Transform Algorithm="http://www.w3.org/TR/2001/REC-xml-c14n-
20010315" />
```

9. **Continue to scroll through the content added to the data document by the digital signature, which includes the Base64 encoded signature and certificate.**
10. **Close the browser window, and save two copies of the signed form as Rss2v4Sign2.xml and Rss2v4Sign3.xml for use in the following procedures.**

Adding a digital signature increases the XML data document's size from about 1640 bytes to 19 KB. Base64-encoded copies of the digital signature, user's certificate, and a PNG bitmap of the form add most of the bulk.

Enabling digital signatures doesn't affect the document's original schema, which you can confirm by extracting the template files and opening schema.xsd in Notepad. Instead, InfoPath adds a myschema.xsd file to the template, which adds the *signatures* section and imports schema.xsd. The myschema.xsd schema doesn't validate the structure of the *signatures#* section; the *xsd:any* data type and *processContents="lax"* attribute permit unstructured content in the section. The W3C XML-DSig schema for digital signatures is close to 10 KB in size, so its omission from the InfoPath-generated schema is understandable.

▶ Test a forged signed document

1. **Open Rss2v4Sign2.xml in Notepad, make a change to the content to simulate a forgery, such as adding (Modified) to the *channel/title* element, and save the file.**
2. **Open Rss2v4Sign2.xml in InfoPath. The form displays the following invalid digital signature message:**

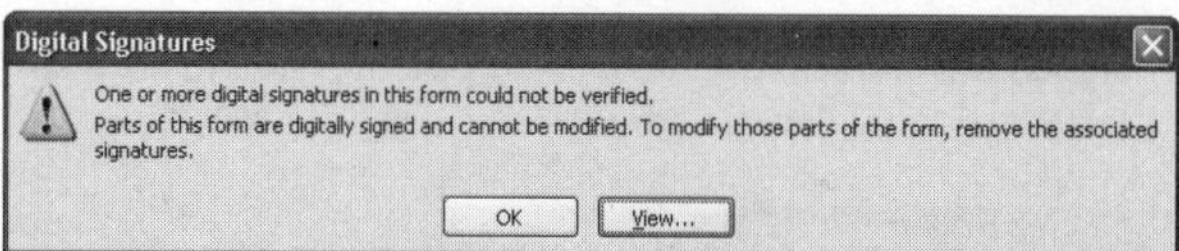

3. Click the View button to open the Digital Signatures dialog box, which states that the signature is invalid, as shown here:

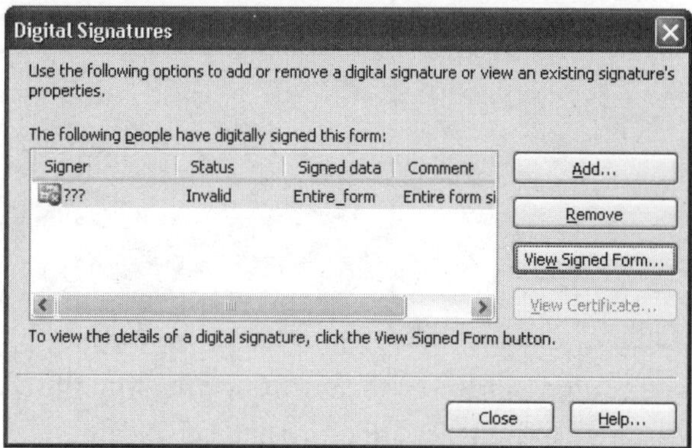

4. Remove the digital signature, click Close to permit editing of the document, and save the unsigned form.

▶ Simulate a cosignature

1. Create a simulated digital signing certificate for another person. (This would appear to defeat nonrepudiation, but it doesn't. The forgery can be detected by comparing the person's real and simulated Base64-encoded certificates.)
2. Open Rss2v4Sign3.xml in InfoPath, click OK to dismiss the digital signature message box, and click the Digital Signatures button. Click Add in the Digital Signatures dialog box, and click Next to display the second screen of the Digital Signature Wizard.
3. Select the certificate you added in step 1, add an approval comment, and return to the Digital Signatures dialog box. The added signature appears as shown here:

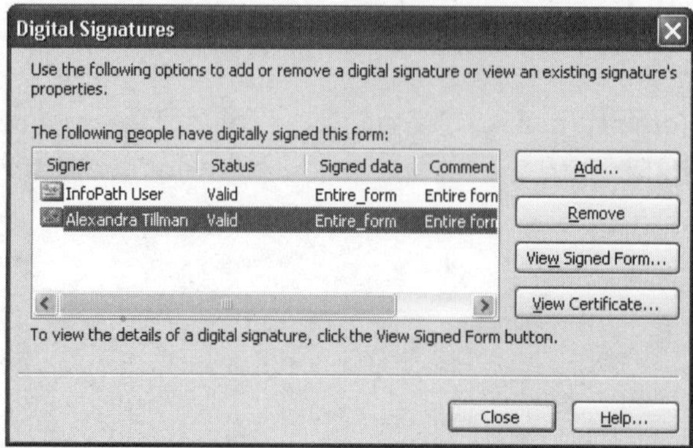

4. **Save the cosigned document, which has grown to 36 KB.**

Signing Individual Form Groups or Fields

An alternative to signing the entire form is to sign, cosign, or countersign individual groups or fields of a form. When you sign individual fields or groups, you have the option to specify a single signature, cosigning (all signatures are independent), or countersigning (each signature signs the preceding signatures). To countersign one group and cosign another group of the Rss2v4Sign.xsn template you created in the preceding section, "Signing and Cosigning an Entire Form," follow these steps.

▶ Enable digital signatures for individual groups

1. **Open Rss2v4Sign.xsn in design mode and save a copy as Rss2v4DS.xsn in the same folder.**
2. **Choose Tools, Form Options, select the Digital Signatures tab, and select the Enable Digital Signatures For Specific Data In The Form option to enable the Data In The Form That Can Be Signed list and its Add button.**
3. **Click the Add button to open the Signed Data dialog box, and click the Select XPath button to open the Select A Field Or Group dialog box. Expand the *channel* node, select the *image* node, and click OK.**
4. **Type a name for the signed data, such as ImageData, select the Each Signature Signs The Preceding Signatures (Counter-Sign) option, and modify the Signature Confirmation Message, as shown here:**

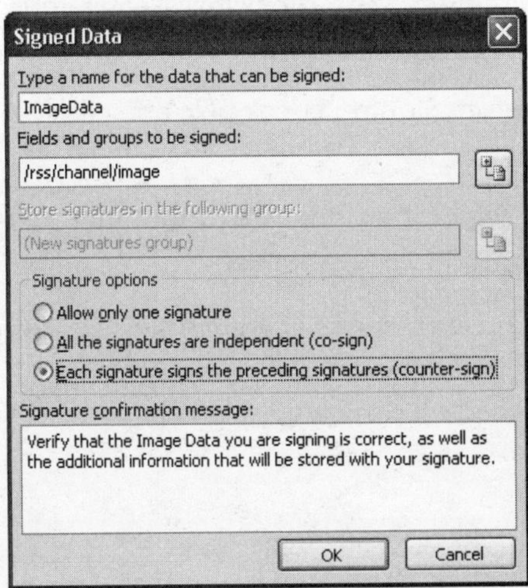

5. **Click OK to add the signed data item to the list.**
6. **Repeat steps 3 through 5, but select the *item* node in step 3. In step 4, change the name from ImageData to ItemData, and select the All The Signatures Are**

Independent (Co-Sign) option instead of Each Signature Signs The Preceding Signatures (Counter-Sign). The Digital Signatures tab of the Form Options dialog box now appears as follows:

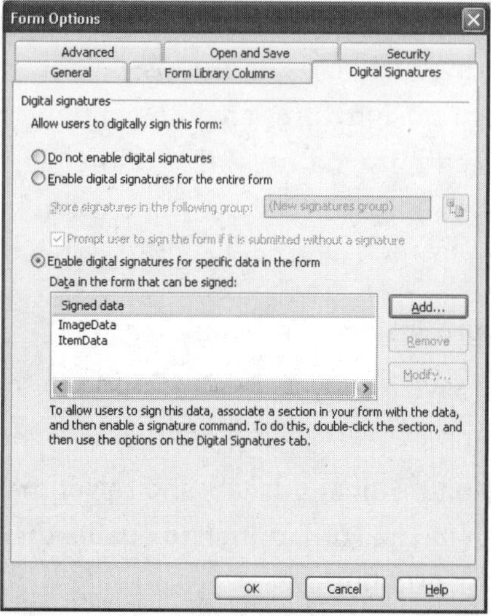

7. Click OK to enable countersigning and cosigning the two groups, and save your template changes, overwriting the original Rss2v4DS.xsn version.

▶ Sign, countersign, and cosign the groups

1. Open a new Form1 from the Rss2v4DS template, and click the Digital Signatures button to start the Digital Signature Wizard.
2. Accept the default ImageData signed data block, and click Next. Select your certificate, and click Next. Add a comment, and click Finish.
3. Select the I Have Verified This Content Before Signing check box, and click Sign to return to the Digital Signatures dialog box.
4. Click Add, and repeat steps 2 and 3, but select the signature of the other person that you added in the preceding procedure.
5. Click Add, and repeat steps 2 through 4 for the ItemData signed data block. The Digital Signatures dialog box appears as shown here:

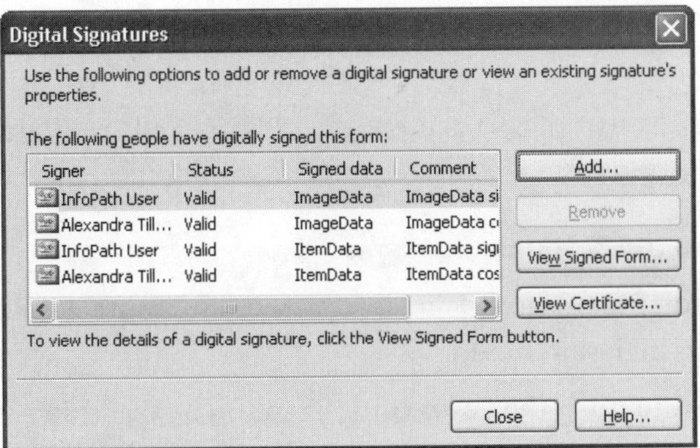

6. **Click Close to apply the signatures, and save your form as Rss2v4DS1.xml, which now weighs in at 71 KB.**
7. **Submit the form, and inspect the Web server's return message.**

Setting Advanced Form Options

The Advanced tab of the Form Options dialog box has controls for specifying the following options:

- Enabling and adding custom task panes. You create custom task panes as HTML files, which often include links to script functions that program InfoPath operations or display data.
- Changing the form version number and specifying how InfoPath upgrades forms to the latest version.
- Changing the default scripting language from JScript to VBScript. Adding custom script in script.js or script.vbs disables the Form Script Language list. Adding Visual Basic .NET code behind InfoPath forms is discussed in of Part IV of this book, "Programming InfoPath Forms."
- Exporting pre-SP-1 versions of the template for use by users without InfoPath 2003 SP-1 installed. Pre-SP-1 versions don't implement SP-1 features; if your form depends on SP-1 features–such as rules, formulas, digitally signed form groups or fields, or .NET managed code–don't expect the exported template to behave correctly.

Adding a Custom Help Task Pane

Custom task panes are HTML documents that users can open in data entry mode. The most common use for custom task panes is providing users with help for filling out forms, especially complex forms. Your C:\Microsoft Press\Introducing InfoPath

2003\Chapter11\Rss2v4 folder contains a very simple HTML file (Rss2v4TaskPane.htm).

To add Rss2v4TaskPane.htm as a custom task pane to the Rss2v4.xsn template, which has two views, follow these steps.

▶ Add a custom task pane to the Resource Manager

1. Navigate to your C:\Microsoft Press\Introducing InfoPath 2003\Chapter11\Rss2v4 folder, and open Rss2v4.xsn in design mode.
2. Choose Tools, Form Options to open the Form Options dialog box, and select the Advanced tab.
3. Select the Enable Custom Task Pane check box, and click Resource Manager to open the Resource Manager dialog box.
4. Click Add to open the Add File dialog box, navigate to the template's folder, double-click Rss2v4TaskPane.htm to add it to the Resource Manager dialog box's Resource Files In This Form list, and click OK.
5. Open the Task Pane Location list, and double-click the Rss2v4TaskPane.htm item, and click OK to close the dialog.
6. Open the Task Pane Location list, select the Rss2v4TaskPane.htm item, and add a title for the new task pane, as shown here:

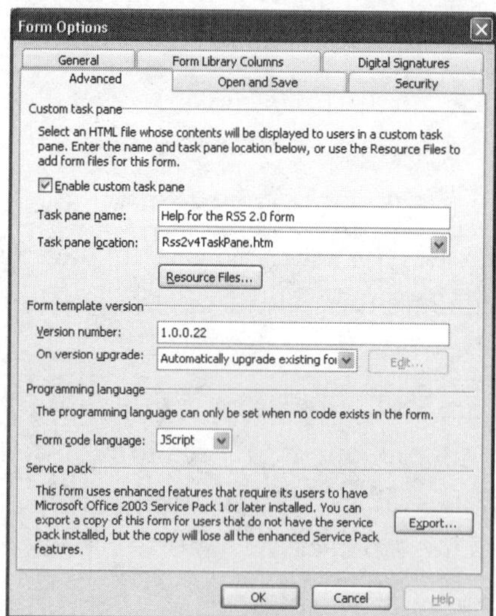

7. Click OK to close the dialog box, and then click Preview This Form. The custom task pane opens by default, as shown here:

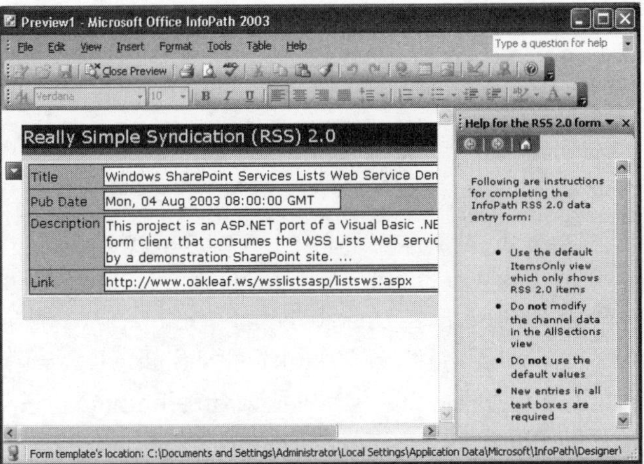

Understanding Form Versioning

InfoPath's template version number consists of four groups of up to four digits separated by periods. InfoPath documentation doesn't describe the usage of the groups, which you can interpret as *InfoPathVersion.FormMainVersion.FormSubVersion.FormBuildNumber*. The default value for a new template is 1.0.0.1. Each time you save a change to a template, InfoPath increments the value of the rightmost group by 1.

The On Version Upgrade list offers the following three selections:

- **Automatically Upgrade Existing Forms** The default.
- **Do Nothing (Existing Forms Might Not Work Properly)** Avoid this selection, because upgrades might cause previously-saved forms to fail to open or display errors when users open them.
- **Use Script Event** Enables the Edit button so that you can add custom programming code to handle the form's *onVersionUpgrade* event.

InfoPath automatically upgrades earlier data documents to the new form version by default. Unless you receive a warning message that previous forms won't be compatible with the new design, InfoPath lets users open forms created with an earlier template version.

InfoPath stores (caches) a copy of an untrusted or a digitally signed (fully trusted) template on the local drive when users first open the template. Each time the user opens a form, InfoPath attempts to check the current template version. If the user's computer can't connect to the networked template location, InfoPath continues to use the cached copy, even if it's out of date. Otherwise, InfoPath updates the user's cached version. You must upgrade custom-installed (unsigned) fully trusted forms manually by reinstalling them on users' computers.

Chapter Summary

InfoPath's Form Options dialog box delivers a potpourri of design mode form property settings. The General tab lets you enable form protection, which disables the Design This Form toolbar button and File, Design This Form menu option. You also can disable form merging and open the Edit Default Value dialog box with the General tab selected. The Edit Default Value dialog box lets you eliminate unneeded sections and fields from new data documents you create from schema-based forms, such as InfoPath's sample forms. The Edit Default Value dialog box also enables you to change optional sections to required sections and specify the default number of list items, repeating sections, and rows of repeating tables. The Tools, Submitting Forms menu option lets you specify whether users can submit forms and, if they can, write custom messages for submission success or failure.

The Form Option Dialog box's Digital Signatures tab is devoted to digital signatures, which deliver nonrepudiation features to entire InfoPath documents or individual groups or fields of documents. You can enable or disable digital signatures and specify a warning prompt if a user submits a form that's not signed. Adding digital signatures to a form requires a personal Client Authentication certificate, which you obtain from a commercial CA or your organization's certificate server.

The Form Option dialog box's Advanced tab lets you add a custom task pane to a form, specify a new template version number, control how InfoPath handles form upgrades, and change the default scripting language from JScript to VBScript, if you're writing script instead of Visual Basic .NET code and haven't added script to your form already. You also can export a copy of the template with SP-1 features removed.

Q&A

Q. Can I disable design mode for users by any means other than the Office 2003 Custom Installation Wizard's Disable InfoPath Designer Mode setting?

A. Yes. You can add an entry to users' registries, as described in the section "Disabling Design Mode for Deployed Fully Trusted Forms," in Chapter 12.

Q. Is it common to encounter XML data documents that contain what appear to be unneeded, empty fields?

A. Yes. In many cases, the schema for business documents requires elements to be present but permits empty text fields and nillable fields of other data types in required elements. Later steps in the workflow process add values to empty or nillable fields

Q. Is there a limit on the number of digital signatures I can add to a form?

A. There's no published limit, but the data document grows by about 17 KB with each added signature. Decrypting digital signatures is a resource-intensive process, so you can expect opening a form to slow a bit with each signature you add.

Q. How can I take advantage of single-signature, cosign, and countersign options for an entire form?

Select the Enable Digital Signatures For Specific Data In The Form check box on the Form Options dialog box's Digital Signatures tab, click Add, open the Select A Field Or Group dialog box, and select the root node of the form–*rss* for the examples in this chapter. Signing the root node is as effective as signing the entire form.

Q. How can I ensure the security of an InfoPath data document that I send over the Internet?

A. Use Secure HTTP (HTTPS) for all data document transmissions over the Internet. HTTPS encrypts the data on the Web server, and Internet Explorer decrypts it on the client. You need a commercial Web server certificate if the recipient doesn't trust your organization's CA.

Q. Can I add more than one custom task pane to a form?

A. No. InfoPath supports only one custom task pane.

On Your Own

Here are two additional exercises to test your digital signing and custom task pane skills:

1. Add digital signatures to the NWOrders data documents you created in the procedures in Chapter 10, "Adding Views to a Template." (If you didn't complete Chapter 10's procedures, the final version of the template and data documents are in your C:\Microsoft Press\Introducing InfoPath 2003\Chapter10\NWOrdersFinal folder.)
2. Write the HTML code for a detailed custom task pane for the final version of Chapter 10's NWOrders template that has multiple views, and add the task pane to the form.

CHAPTER 12

Publishing Form Templates

In this chapter, you will learn how to:

- **Describe InfoPath's built-in form security models**
- **Create security groups and user accounts for accessing shared templates**
- **Publish templates to a shared network folder**
- **Secure shared templates to prevent modification by users**
- **Publish secure production templates to a Web server**
- **Publish templates to a Windows SharePoint forms library and secure them from unauthorized modification**
- **Submit XML data documents to a Windows SharePoint Services forms library**
- **Create fully trusted forms by signing the template with a code signing certificate**
- **Create and deploy unsigned fully trusted templates with JScript or Windows Installer (.msi) installation files**

For more information:

- **See the topic "Understanding Fully Trusted Forms" in the "Technical Articles" chapter of the documentation for the InfoPath 2003 SDK.**
- **See the topic "Using the Forms Registration Tool" in the "Tools" chapter of the documentation for the InfoPath 2003 SDK.**

To work through this chapter:

- You need to know how to add user accounts and security groups to a Microsoft Windows 2000 or later Active Directory domain or to a stand-alone computer that emulates a file server. You also need a basic understanding of Windows 2000 and later file server share, folder, and file security features.
- You should have installed in your C:\Microsoft Press\Introducing InfoPath 2003\Chapter12 folder the sample files from the CD that accompanies this book for creating custom-installed forms.
- You must have Microsoft Internet Information Services (IIS) version 5 or later installed for Web deployment of InfoPath templates, or a network administrator must create a remote IIS virtual directory for sharing templates from your intranet Web site.
- You must have Microsoft Windows SharePoint Services installed on a computer running Windows Server 2003, and you must be a member of a site's Web Designer or Administrator group.
- You need a code signing certificate from a commercial certificate authority (CA) or a Windows 2000 Server or later certificate server to publish digitally signed fully trusted forms.
- You must install the Microsoft Office InfoPath 2003 Software Development Kit (SDK) from the CD that accompanies this book to create unsigned fully trusted forms.
- You need Microsoft Visual Basic .NET 2003 Standard or Microsoft Visual Studio .NET 2003 Professional (or later) installed on your computer to create Microsoft Installer (.msi) packages for deploying unsigned fully trusted forms to users' computers.

Publishing templates to shared folders, Web sites, or SharePoint form libraries requires a basic understanding of InfoPath's built-in form security features and file-system permissions that you assign to Active Directory security groups. Form security, which is based on Internet Explorer security zones, determines whether your form can access resources–databases and Web services in another domain, for example–that aren't part of the form template. If design mode wasn't disabled when InfoPath was installed on users' computers or their registries haven't been modified to disable design mode, you must restrict users' ability to save changes to template designs by restricting their file-system permissions to read-only template access.

Understanding this chapter's network architecture

This chapter's procedures use two Windows Server 2003 member servers (OakLeaf-MS15 and OakLeaf-W2K3) in a Windows 2000 Active Directory domain (*oakleaf.org*). OakLeaf-W2K3 runs Windows SharePoint Services. The procedures assume that you log on to the computers as a member of the local Administrators group. You'll encounter minor differences in the appearance of security-related dialog boxes if you're running Windows XP Professional or Windows 2000 Workstation or Server as a member of an Active Directory domain or in stand-alone mode. However, these differences don't affect the basic approach to securing your InfoPath templates and XML data documents.

Understanding InfoPath Form Security Models

InfoPath's three form security models correspond to Internet Explorer's *content zones*, which appear on the Security tab of Internet Explorer's Internet Options dialog box You specify the security model for your form on the Security tab of the Form Options dialog box, as shown in Figure 12-1.

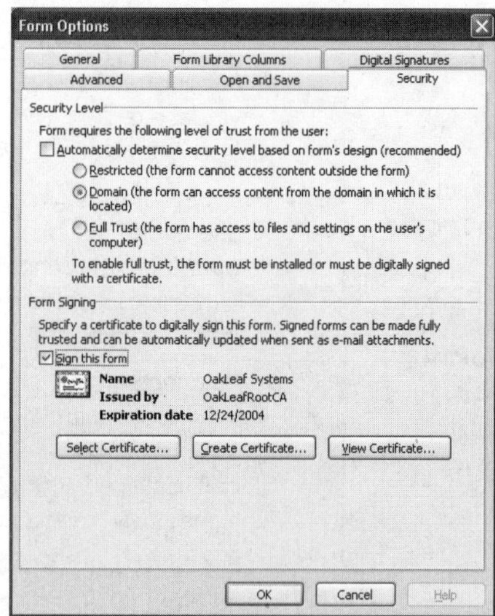

Figure 12-1 The Form Options dialog box's Security tab lets you specify the security level of the form and add a digital signature to create a fully trusted form.

Following are InfoPath's three form security level options and their corresponding Internet Explorer 6.0 content zones:

- **Restricted** Corresponds to Internet Explorer's Restricted Sites zone (high security). The form cannot access resources that are external to the form, such as ActiveX controls. Users can open and save forms, but script code can't access the file system or other computer resources. The Restricted model prevents use of custom task panes, data connections (except submission by e-mail), managed code (Visual Basic .NET or C#), and roles.

- **Domain** Corresponds to Internet Explorer's Local Intranet zone (medium-low security) or forms running on the local computer during development. Forms can access resources–such as databases and Web services–within a single domain. For example, a form running in the local oakleaf.org domain cannot access Web services provided by a server in the public oakleaf.ws domain. Templates deployed to server shares on a local area network (LAN) are considered to be in the same domain. ActiveX controls, custom task panes, roles, and managed code are enabled. The Domain model (also called *sandboxed forms*) is the most common security scenario for published InfoPath forms.
- **Full Trust** Corresponds to Internet Explorer's Trusted Sites zone (low security). Fully trusted forms permit cross-domain data access, permit running ActiveX controls that aren't marked safe for scripting, provide added managed code flexibility, and eliminate some security-based prompts you receive at the Domain security level. You must sign the form with a code signing certificate, as described in the section "Creating Fully Trusted Forms by Code Signing," later in this chapter, or deploy the fully trusted form to users' computers using the techniques described in the section "Distributing Custom-Installed Templates."

By default, InfoPath analyzes your form and its programming code to automatically assign the most restrictive security model. You can override automatic security model assignment by clearing the Automatically Determine Security Level (Recommended) check box and selecting one of the three security model options. None of the forms you've created so far or this chapter's examples requires the Full Trust option.

Identifying the security mode of a form
An icon in the lower left corner of the form identifies the form's security level. A red circle with a horizontal white bar indicates Restricted level. A picture of a computer monitor indicates Domain level, and a green circle with a check mark indicates Full Trust level. These icons are small versions of Internet Explorer's content zone icons.

Creating Test User Accounts and Security Groups

This chapter's template sharing examples require setting up three user accounts and two security groups for testing template security settings. Basing template access on security group membership makes it easy to add new InfoPath users and developers with common security privileges. The test user accounts play an important role in InfoPath form deployment to shared folders, intranet Web sites, and Windows

SharePoint Services sites. Here are descriptions of the test accounts and their security group membership:

- **IPUser** An ordinary user of InfoPath forms who's a member of the InfoPathUsers security group and, by default, the file server's local Users group by virtue of membership in the Active Directory Domain Users group.
- **IPDesigner** A user who's permitted to add and modify template designs. IPDesigner is a member of the InfoPathDesigners, InfoPathUsers, and Users security groups. If you want IPDesigner to be able to create new file shares, the account must be a member of the file server's local Power Users group.
- **AnyUser** An account that's a member of the default Users group only. You use this account to verify that a user without InfoPathUsers or InfoPathDesigners group membership can't gain read access to the template or XML data documents.

If you're a member of the Domain Admins or higher security group for your Active Directory network, create these users and groups, and assign the IPUser and IPDesigner accounts to their security groups with the Active Directory Users And Computers tool. Otherwise, ask your network administrator to add the temporary accounts and groups for you. If you're not connected to a Windows 2000 or later domain, create local security groups and user accounts on your computer.

Disabling design mode doesn't protect shared templates

Disabling design mode on users' computers during InfoPath installation or by changing the user's *DisableDesigner* registry value doesn't provide adequate security for shared templates. Changing the *DisableDesigner* registry value is the subject of the section "Disabling Design Mode for Deployed Fully Trusted Forms," later in this chapter. If users know the registry key value to enable design mode or install their own copy of InfoPath, they can modify unsecured templates.

Sharing Templates from a Network Folder

Publishing templates to a shared file server folder is the simplest and most common scenario for sharing InfoPath template files. As mentioned in the section "Enabling Form Protection," in Chapter 11, you must configure share, folder, and file security settings to allow members of designated security groups to open the template. You prevent ordinary network users from saving changes to InfoPath templates by granting them read-only permissions for the server share and its folders. If you want members of InfoPathUsers to store XML data documents in the shared template folder, they must have read-write permissions for the share and the folder.

In this case, you must apply file-level security and omit write permission for the template file to prevent InfoPathUsers members from changing the template.

By default, members of Windows 2003 Server's Users group have read permissions for all folders, the ability to create files and folders, and the ability to write and append data. Users inherit these permissions from the root folder of the logical drive. You can remove these permissions from the root, but doing so might disrupt routine operations of a file server or your computer. (Network administrators usually remove default permissions for the Users group from production file servers.) All user accounts you add become members of the local Users group, either directly or by membership in Active Directory's default Domain Users security group. If your computer or the file server has default Users group permissions, you must remove the Users group permissions from the shared template folder.

Creating the Server Share and Setting Permissions

The first step in the file-share deployment process is to add the shared folder and set its share permissions. For this example, you store individual templates in subfolders of the shared folder. The subfolders inherit their permissions from the shared folder, which simplifies adding new shared templates. You can modify subfolder permissions to grant particular groups or users access to the template. To create the share and set its permissions, follow these steps.

▶ Create and share the \Shared\InfoPath Templates folder

1. **In Windows Explorer, create a \Shared folder on any logical drive, and add an InfoPath Templates subfolder.**
2. **Right-click the InfoPath Templates subfolder, choose Sharing And Security from the shortcut menu to open the InfoPath Templates Properties dialog box, and select the Share This Folder option.**
3. **Type the share name—IPTemplates for this example—and a brief description of the share, as shown here:**

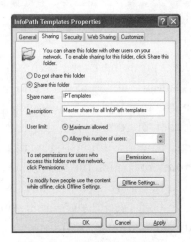

4. Click the Permissions button to open the Permissions For IPTemplates dialog box. If the Everyone group is present, select it, and click the Remove button.
5. Click Add to open the Select Users, Computers, Or Groups dialog box, which displays the default location for entries—your Active Directory domain or local computer name. Click Locations if you need to change the location of the user and group accounts you created in the preceding section.
6. Type ***ServerName*\Administrators; InfoPathDesigners; InfoPathUsers** in the text box, and click Check Names to verify that the groups exist, which is indicated by an underline, as shown here:

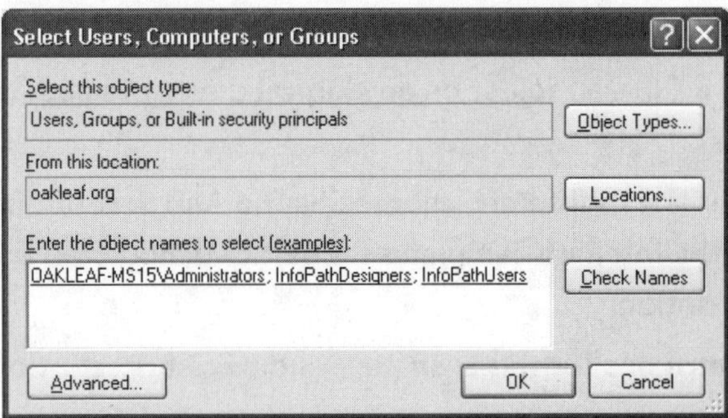

7. Click OK to close the dialog box and return to the Permissions For IPTemplates dialog box.
8. With the InfoPathDesigners group selected, leave the default Read permission, and select the Allow Change check box, as shown here:

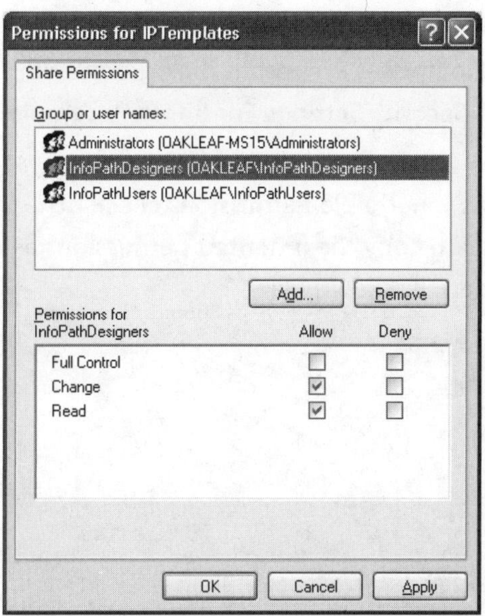

9. **Click Apply, and click the InfoPathUsers group to verify its Read permission. Grant the InfoPathUsers group Change permissions *only* if members must store XML data document in subfolders of the share.**
10. **Finally, give the local Administrators group Full Control privileges.**
11. **Click OK to close the dialog box and return to the InfoPath Templates Properties dialog box, click Offline Settings, select the Files Or Programs From The Share Will Not Be Available Offline option, and click OK. (Making files available offline reduces their security level.)**
12. **Click Apply to apply the share permissions.**

Setting Folder Permissions

The local Users (*ComputerName*\Users) group inherits default Read & Execute and special Create Files/Write Data and Create Folders/Append Data folder permissions from the root folder of the drive. You can't remove local members of the local Users group from the permissions list without removing the group's inherited permissions. Denying permissions doesn't work, because members of the InfoPathDesigners group are members of the local Users group, so they are locked out also.

Replace all inherited permissions with local permissions, remove the local Users group permissions, and add folder permissions for the InfoPathUsers and InfoPathDesigners groups by following these steps.

▶ **Set folder permissions and add a subfolder**

1. Click the Security tab of the InfoPath Templates Properties dialog box, and click Advanced to open the Advanced Security Settings For InfoPath Templates dialog box.
2. On the Permissions tab, clear the Allow Inheritable Permissions check box, and click Copy in the Security message box to copy the inherited permissions as not-inherited to the folder and its subfolders, as shown here:

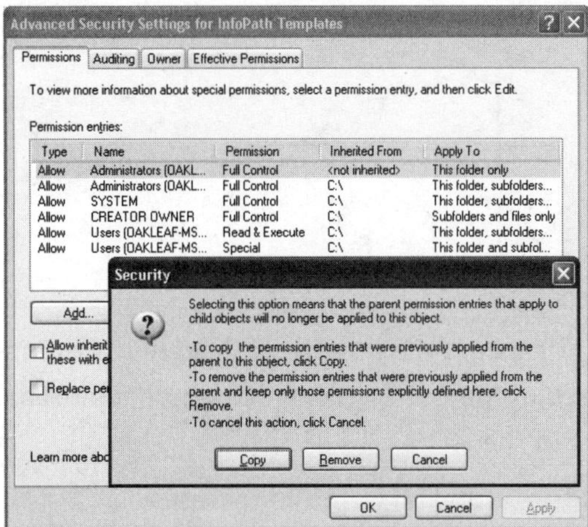

3. Select the Users group's Special permission item, and click Remove.
4. Repeat step 3 for the Users group's Read & Execute permissions, and click OK.
5. Repeat steps 5 and 6 of the preceding procedure, without adding the *ServerName*\Administrators group, to add the InfoPathDesigners and InfoPathUsers groups to the Group Or User Names list.
6. Select the InfoPathDesigners group, and select the Allow column's Modify check box, as shown here:

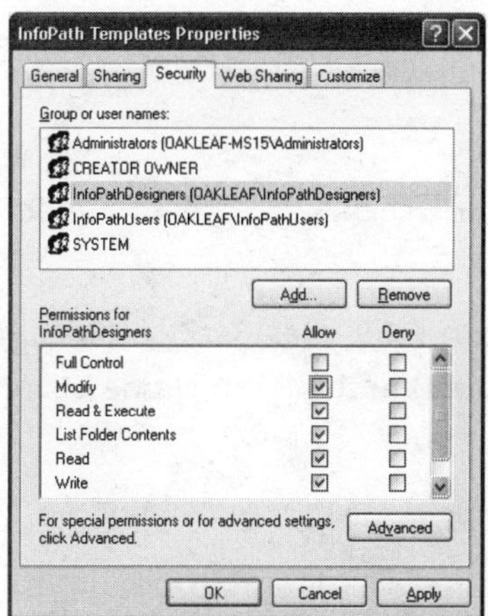

7. **Verify that the InfoPathUsers group has Read & Execute permissions, select the CREATOR OWNER account, select the Allow column's Full Control check box, and click OK to apply the folder security settings and close the dialog box.**
8. **In Windows Explorer, add a subfolder to \Shared\InfoPath Templates—Rss2v4 for this example—to contain the published template. Right-click the subfolder, choose Sharing and Security from the shortcut menu, click the Security tab, and verify inherited permissions for the InfoPathDesigners and InfoPathUsers groups.**
9. **Select the CREATOR OWNER account, select the Allow column's Full Control check box, and click OK to apply the changes. Adding these privileges assures that you have full control of the files and folders you add, regardless of your security group membership.**

Publishing and Testing the Shared Template

The final step in the shared-file deployment process is to use InfoPath's Publishing Wizard to copy the template to the file share with its Uniform Naming Convention (UNC) path embedded in the manifest.xsf file. All data documents that users create from the template include the UNC path in their processing instructions. After you publish the template, you must verify that the security settings you applied in the preceding two sections work as expected. This example uses the Rss2v4.xsn template, so you can test design mode restrictions easily, and assumes that you are emulating a file server on your local computer. A production installation would use a protected template, such as Rss2v4Prot.xsn.

Follow these steps to publish the sample template to the shared folder and test its security settings.

▶ Publish the template

1. Navigate to your C:\Microsoft Press\Introducing InfoPath 2003\Chapter11\Rss2v4 folder, and open Rss2v4.xsn in design mode.
2. Choose File, Publish to start the Publishing Wizard, click Next, accept the default To A Shared Folder option, and click Next.
3. Click Browse, navigate to your C:\Shared\InfoPath Templates\Rss2v4 folder, and click OK, and changeRss2v4 to **Rss2v4 (Shared)** in the Form Name box, as shown here:

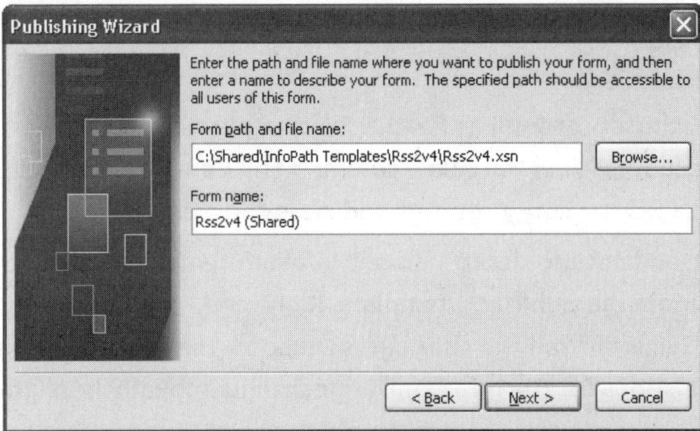

If you're publishing to a remote file server rather than your computer, type the UNC path to the share, which appears as the default location in the next step.

4. Click Next, and replace the local path with the UNC path to the file—***ServerName*\IPTemplates\Rss2v4\Rss2v4.xsn** for this example—as shown here:

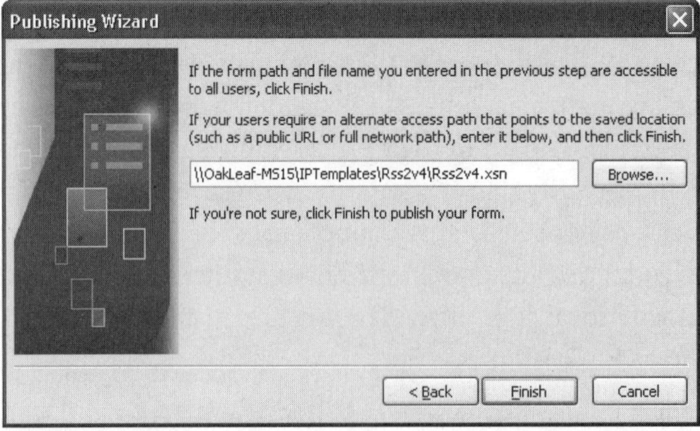

5. Click Finish to display the final wizard screen, which lets you send e-mail messages to users and open the file from its new location:

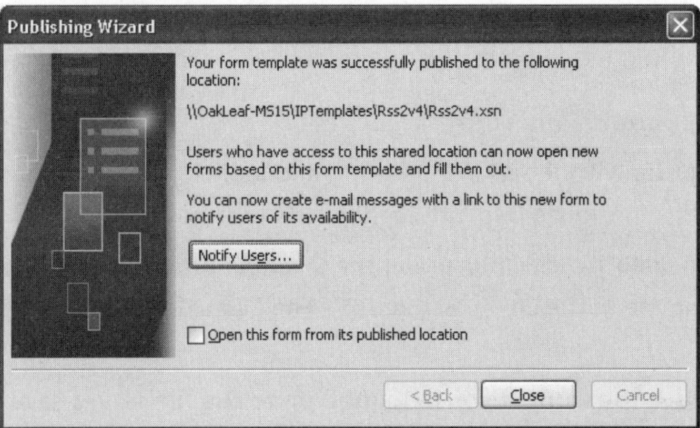

The Notify Users button is present if you have Microsoft Outlook 2003 installed on your computer.

6. **Click Notify Users to open a default Microsoft Outlook e-mail message that you can send to members of the authorized security groups, as shown here:**

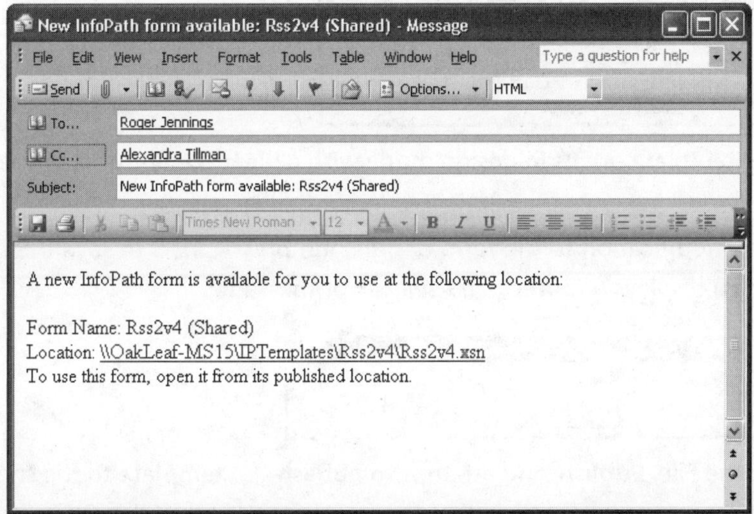

7. **Close Outlook, select the Open This Form From Its Published Location check box, and click Close to open a new Form1 and close the Publishing Wizard.**
8. **Save the form with default values as Rss2v4.xml in the shared folder.**

Making it easy for users to open templates

In your e-mail notification message, suggest that users create a named Network Place with the UNC path to the template's shared folder. Alternatively, enclose a desktop shortcut to the .xsn file. Unfortunately, right-clicking the .xsn item in the Network Places list or the enclosed shortcut exposes a Design menu option.

Deploying the template to a shared folder isn't complete until you've verified that the security settings you applied in the preceding section work as expected. To test the shared template with logon accounts in the InfoPathUsers and InfoPathDesigners security groups, follow the steps on the next page:

▶ **Test group and user permissions**

1. **Log on to your computer with the IPUser account, and launch InfoPath. Windows Installer runs briefly to configure InfoPath for the new user account.**
2. **In the Fill Out A Form dialog, click Open under the Open A Form heading. Type the UNC path to the template in the Open dialog box's File Name box, and click Open to open Form1.**
3. **Verify that you can save the form. If you're logged on to the file server, save the form in My Documents, which is the only server folder that permits the IPUser account write access.**
4. **Click the Design This Form button. You receive the slightly misleading message shown here, stating that the file is currently in use:**

5. **Click Yes. The template opens in design mode with a [Read-Only] suffix in the title bar.**
6. **Make a minor modification to the form design, and press Ctrl+S to save the template, which displays a *form is read-only* error message:**

7. **Click OK, choose File, Publish, and attempt to publish the template to the share. You'll see the same message stating that the form is read-only. Click OK.**
8. **Log off as IPUser, log on as IPDesigner, save the form and its template to the shared folder, and republish the template, overwriting the original version.**
9. **Log off as IPDesigner, log on as AnyUser, and repeat step 2. You receive the following message that verifies that AnyUser can't open the Rss2v4.xsn template or the Rss2v4.xml data document:**

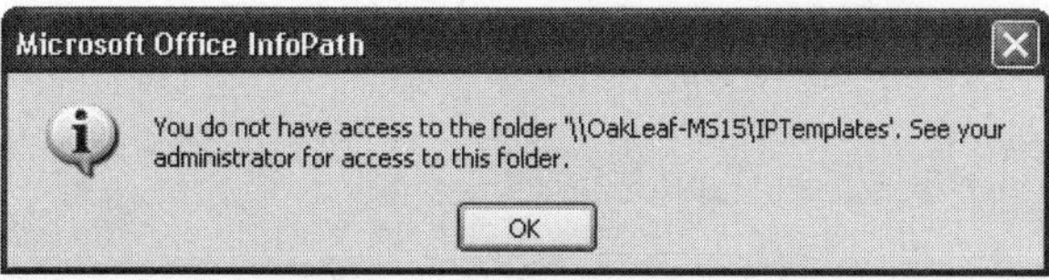

10. Click OK and log off as AnyUser, and log on with your administrative account for the file server.

At this point, you've verified that no one but members of the local Administrators group, which includes Domain Admins, and the InfoPathDesigners group can modify the template. The form is ready for production use after you've enabled protection, as described in the section "Enabling Form Protection," in Chapter 11.

Publishing Templates to an Intranet Site

Access to InfoPath forms via HTTP is an alternative to using shared folders. From the user's perspective, there's little difference between the two methods: the URL to the template or file replaces the UNC path. Many large organizations provide off-site workers with virtual private network (VPN) remote access connections to the internal network, which permits secure access to templates in shared folders. Connecting via the Internet with secure HTTP (HTTPS, also called Secure Sockets Layer, or SSL) to a Web server that requires client authentication certificates provides somewhat less security at considerably lower overall cost than dedicated VPN remote access.

Publishing InfoPath templates to a Web server using the Publishing Wizard is almost identical to the procedure for shared folders, but requires more up-front work. This section's procedures use your test computer as the Web server and require that you log on as a member of the local Administrators group. Here are the basic requirements for publishing InfoPath templates to a Web server:

- The virtual directory (VDir) must not permit anonymous access, which is disabled by default in IIS 6. Integrated Windows authentication (the default) is required to support folder and file security for InfoPath templates.
- Write access must be enabled to permit publishing and modifying the template and saving forms to the VDir's folder.
- Web Distributed Authoring and Versioning (WebDAV) must be enabled. WebDAV is disabled in IIS 6 and enabled in IIS 5 by default. To enable WebDAV with IIS 6's Internet Information Services (IIS) Manager, expand the *ServerName* node, click Web Service Extensions, select the WebDAV item in the Web Service Extension list, and click the Allow button, as shown in Figure 12-2.

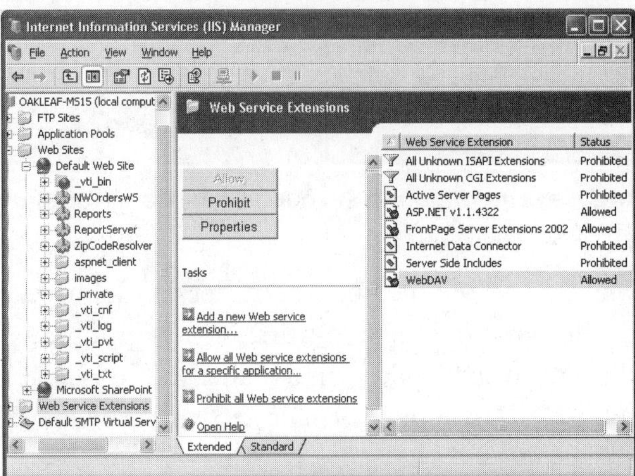

Figure 12-2 You must enable the WebDAV Web service extension to publish InfoPath templates to a Windows Server 2003 intranet site.

- If Windows SharePoint Services are running on the Default Web Site, you must exclude the template's VDir from paths managed by SharePoint using the method described in the section "Obtaining a Digital Signing Certificate," in Chapter 11.
- You can't publish a template to a Web server that's protected by Microsoft's Urlscan Internet Server Application Programming Interface (ISAPI) filter without explicitly permitting use of the HTTP *OPTIONS*, *PUT*, *DELETE*, *LOCK*, and *UNLOCK* verbs and inclusion of .exe extensions in the requested URL. It's not a common practice to install a Urlscan.dll filter on well-protected intranet Web sites, but permitting the extra HTTP verbs and .exe extensions in requesting URLs defeats much of the added site security provided by Urlscan.
- IIS 6 requires assigning a registered Multipurpose Internet Mail Extensions (MIME) type for each extension of files it serves, including .xsn for InfoPath templates. To verify that the .xsn extension is registered, right-click the *ComputerName* node in Internet Information Services (IIS) Manager, and choose Properties from the shortcut menu. Click the MIME Types button to open the MIME Types dialog box, scroll to the bottom of the list of registered MIME types, and verify that the MIME type for .xsn files is present, as shown in Figure 12-3. If not, click the New button to open the MIME Type input box, type **.xsn** in the Extension box, type **application/octet-stream** in the MIME Type box, and click OK three times.

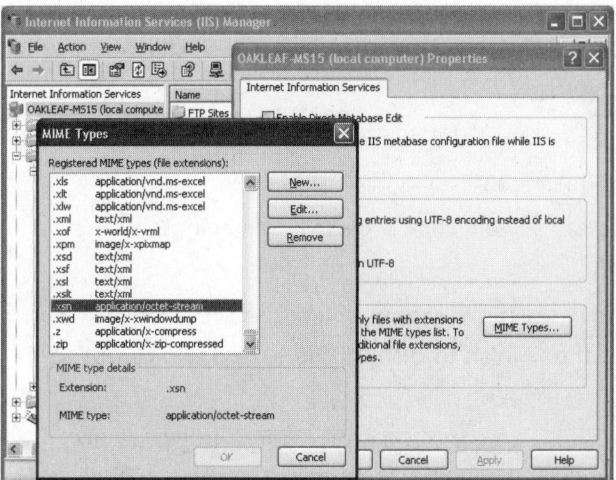

Figure 12-3 IIS 6 requires an application/octet-stream MIME type entry for .xsn files to permit sending template files to clients' caches.

If any of the preceding requirements aren't met, you'll receive the message shown in Figure 12-4 when you attempt to publish your template.

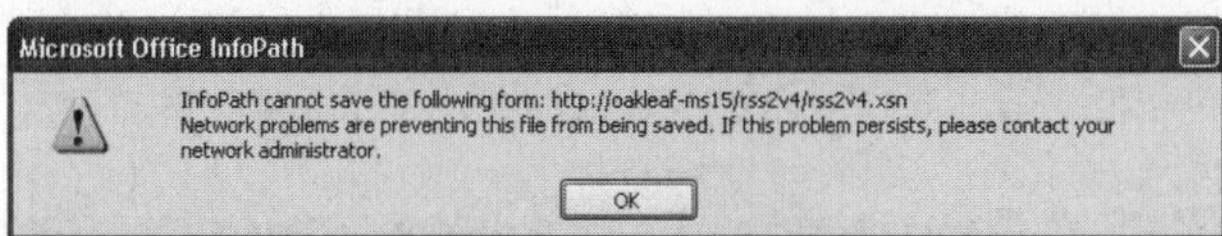

Figure 12-4 This vague error message indicates a virtual directory configuration problem.

Creating an IIS Virtual Directory

After you've taken care of the prerequisites, the next step is to create or specify a local folder to store the published template and an IIS VDir that specifies the local folder as its content source. For initial testing of Web site deployment, you create a new subfolder of the default Web site content folder–\Inetpub\wwwroot. Creating a test VDir for an unsecured content folder minimizes the probability of errors when publishing your first form to a Web site. You'll apply share and folder security for the template in the section "Publishing a Secured Template to the Web Site," later in this chapter.

To create a VDir to which you publish an InfoPath template, follow these steps.

▶ **Add a virtual directory and set its properties**

1. **Add to your \Inetpub\wwwroot folder a subfolder for your template—Rss2v4 for this example.**

2. Launch IIS Manager, expand the *ServerName* and Web Sites nodes, right-click the Default Web Site node, and choose New, Virtual Directory to start the Virtual Directory Creation Wizard. Click Next.
3. In the Virtual Directory Alias screen type the name of the virtual directory in the Alias box—**Rss2v4** for this example—and click Next.
4. In the Web Site Content Directory screen, click Browse, and navigate to the subfolder you added in step 1.
5. In the Virtual Directory Access Permissions screen, select the Write Permissions check box, and click Next and then Finish to dismiss the wizard and return to IIS Manager.
6. Right-click the virtual directory you added, and choose Properties from the shortcut menu to open the *VDirName* Properties dialog box.
7. On the Virtual Directory tab, verify that the Write check box is selected, as shown here, and then select the Directory Security tab. If you have Windows SharePoint Services installed, select DefaultAppPool from the Application Pool drop-down list. (IIS 5 doesn't support multiple application pools.)

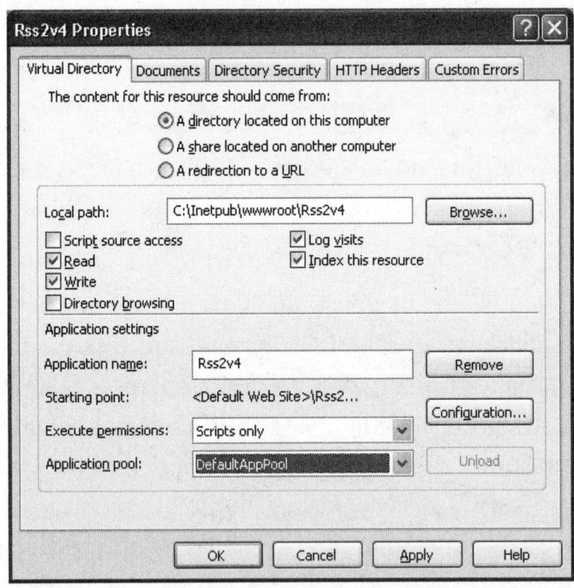

8. Select the Directory Security tab, and click the Authentication And Access Control section's Edit button to open the Authentication Methods dialog box. Clear the Enable Anonymous Access check box, verify that the Integrated Windows Authentication check box is selected, as shown here, and then click OK:

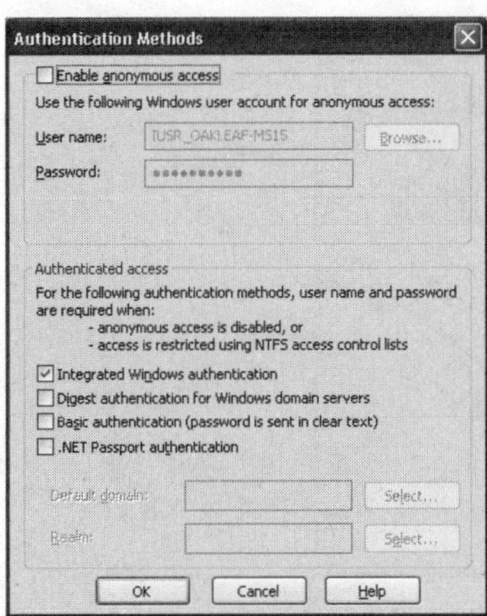

9. **If your site has a server certificate to enable HTTPS, click the Secure Communications section's Edit button to open the Secure Communications dialog box, select the Require Secure Channel (SSL) check box, and specify options for 128-bit encryption and client certificates.**
10. **Click OK to apply your changes, close the Properties dialog box, and return to IIS Manager.**

Testing Web Publication of Unsecured Templates

As mentioned earlier, publishing a template to a Web site is very similar to publishing to a shared folder. One difference is that each template must have its own VDir. Follow these steps to publish Chapter 11's Rss2v4.xsn template to the Rss2v4 VDir.

▶ **Publish and open a test template**

1. **Navigate to your C:\Microsoft Press\Introducing InfoPath 2003\Chapter11\Rss2v4 folder, and open Rss2v4.xsn in design mode.**
2. **Choose File, Publish to start the Publishing Wizard, and click Next.**
3. **In the second wizard screen, select the To A Web Server option, and click Next.**
4. **Type the URL for the VDir as http://*servername*/*vdirname*/*template*.xsn, and change (For Protection) to (Web Server), as shown here:**

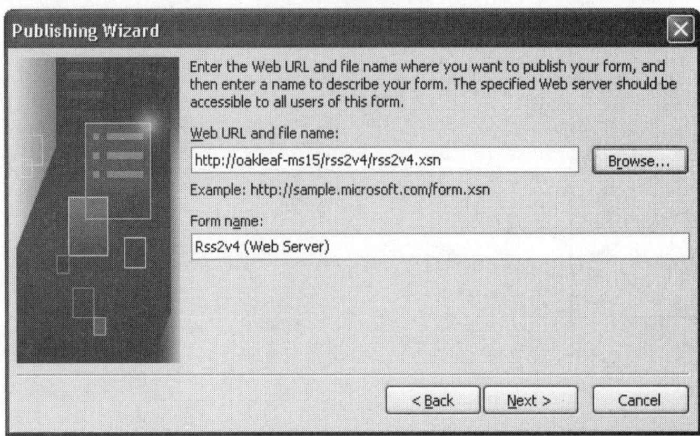

5. Click Next, confirm the location, and click Finish and Close to publish the template. If you receive the error message shown earlier in Figure 12-4, double-check that your Web server and VDir meet the requirements listed earlier, in the section "Publishing Templates to an Intranet Site." Otherwise, this File Download dialog box opens:

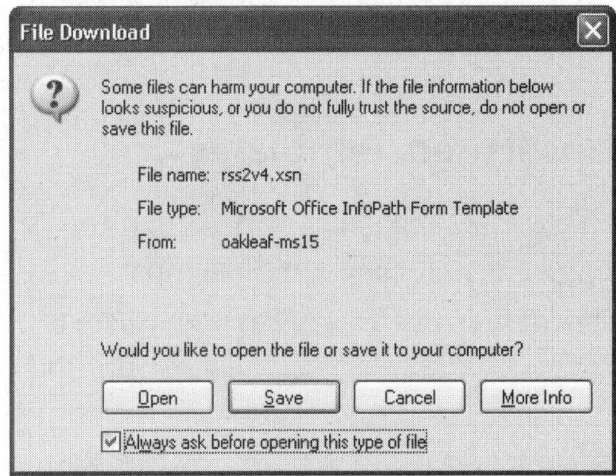

6. Clear the Always Ask Before Opening This Type Of File check box to prevent the message from reappearing, and click Open to launch your local copy of InfoPath with Form1 active.
7. Press Ctrl+S to open the Save As dialog box, type **http://*servername*/ rss2v4/ rss2v4.xsn** in File Name box, and click Save to verify that you can save data documents to the VDir's folder. (Existing files of the same name are overwritten without warning.)
8. Click the Design This Form button, make a minor modification to the template, and press Ctrl+S to save the change...

At this point, you've proven that your system configuration and VDir properties comply with InfoPath's requirements for publishing a template to a Web site, but the template is not yet fully secure.

Publishing a Secured Template to the Web Site

Selecting the Write check box on the Virtual Directory tab of the *VDirName* Properties dialog box enables any authenticated Windows user to write to the VDir. Thus, you must rely on file security to restrict ordinary users' ability to make template changes. Fortunately, it's easy to change the VDir's content directory to a previously secured file share; the share can be on any accessible file server, including the computer running IIS for the Web site.

To take advantage of the security settings you applied earlier in this chapter to the *ServerName*\IPTemplates share and its subfolders for Web deployment, follow these steps.

▶ Publish and test the secure Rss2v4 template

1. Navigate to your \Shared\InfoPath Templates\Rss2v4 folder, and make a backup copy of Rss2v4.xsn.
2. Open IIS Manager, and open the Rss2v4 Properties dialog box.
3. Select the Share Located On Another Computer option, type the UNC path to the Rss2v4 folder—***ServerName*\IPTemplates\Rss2v4** for this example—and click OK. If the files in the share don't appear in IIS Manager's file list pane, press F5 to refresh the display.
4. Repeat steps 1 through 4 of the preceding procedure, but change (For Protection) to **(Web Secured)**, and then click Next.
5. Select Overwrite The Existing Form, click Next and Finish, select the Open This Form From Its Published Location check box, and click Close to republish the template and display Form1.
6. Verify that you can save Form1 as Rss2v4.xml, make a minor design change, and save the template.
7. Log off, and then log on as IPUser and open the template in Internet Explorer to verify that you can open Form1.
8. Attempt to save Form1 as **Rss2v4** (or any other name) to display an *InfoPath cannot save the form* message. You might be prompted for your user name and password during this process. Click OK.
9. Click the Design This Form button, and verify that InfoPath displays a *Do you want to open a read-only copy instead?* message.
10. Log off, and then log on as IPDesigner. Verify that you can save Form1 as **Rss2v4.xml**, change to design mode, and save a design change.
11. Log off and log on with your administrative account.

You've now proven that file-share and folder security that you apply to a shared folder also works for Web site deployment with Windows integrated authentication. To reconfigure the Rss2v4.xsn template to file-share access, rename the Web-based template, and restore the copy you saved in step 1 of the preceding procedure.

Publishing Templates to SharePoint Form Libraries

Windows SharePoint Services is a Web-based portal application that enables collaboration among members of teams, workgroups, or small departments. Windows SharePoint Service's out-of-the-box features include document and form sharing libraries, announcements, image galleries, links, contact and task lists, discussion groups, and surveys. Windows SharePoint Services is a no-charge add-on to Windows Server 2003 and doesn't require client access licenses (CALs). Another Windows SharePoint Services selling point is management simplicity, which enables users to set up and administer their own sites.

Windows SharePoint Services has a site-based security system based on the following four groups:

- **Administrator** Members of this group have full control of the site and can add users to any group. Installing Windows SharePoint Services adds the server's Administrator account to this group.
- **Web Designer** Members can create, edit, and delete Windows SharePoint Services pages, such as document and form libraries. Members of the InfoPathDesigners test group belong here. You must be a member of the Web Designer or Administrator group to publish an InfoPath template to a Windows SharePoint Services forms library.
- **Contributor** Members can add content to libraries and lists. Windows SharePoint Services stores the XML data documents that users create, so this is where you add members of the InfoPathUsers test group.
- **Reader** Members have read-only access to the site. You can add the AnyUser test account to this group if you want to verify that ordinary users can't add data documents to the forms library.

You must add individual user accounts to Windows SharePoint Services sites; attempting to add a group, such as *DOMAIN*\InfoPathDesigners, causes an error. You can add members to multiple site security groups, but there's no apparent advantage to doing this. Windows SharePoint Services stores the published template, so you can't apply file-share or folder security to templates in forms libraries. Fortunately, only members of the site's Administrator and Web Designer groups can save template changes.

Publishing a Template and Specifying Column Names

The Rss2v4Prot.xsn template that you modified in Chapter 11 is a good candidate for testing deployment to a SharePoint site because the template is protected. The Form Option dialog box's Form Library tab lets you specify the fields that appear in the columns of the form library list (also known as *promoting columns*). You also can change the column name for any field. It's simpler, however, to specify and rename the columns to include during the publication process.

To publish the Rss2v4Prot.xsn template to a Windows SharePoint Services site, follow these steps.

▶ **Publish Rss2v4Prot with promoted columns**

1. **Navigate to your C:\Microsoft Press\Introducing InfoPath 2003\Chapter11\Rss2v4 folder, and open Rss2v4Prot.xsn in design mode.**
2. **Choose File, Publish to start the Publishing Wizard, and click Next.**
3. **Select the To A SharePoint Form Library option, and click Next.**
4. **Accept the default Create A New Form Library option, and click Next.**
5. **Type the URL for the default site as http://*servername*/ for intranet access, and click Next.**
6. **Type the name of the form library—RSS 2.0 for this example— in the Name text box and a brief description in the Description text box. Click Next.**
7. **Click the Add button to open the Select A Field Or Group dialog box.**
8. **Expand the item node, if necessary, and select the *item* section's title field. When you select a repeating field, the dialog box enables the Choose A Function To Use On Repeating Data list.**
9. **Change title to Title in the Column Name box, and leave the default first item, as shown here, because you add RSS 2 items in last-in-first-out (LIFO) sequence. Click OK to add the column.**

10. Repeat steps 7, 8 and 9 for the pubDate and link fields, and change their names to **Pub Date** and **Link**.
11. Repeat step 10 for the item group, and rename it **Items**. The only function applicable to groups is *count*. Your list appears as shown here:

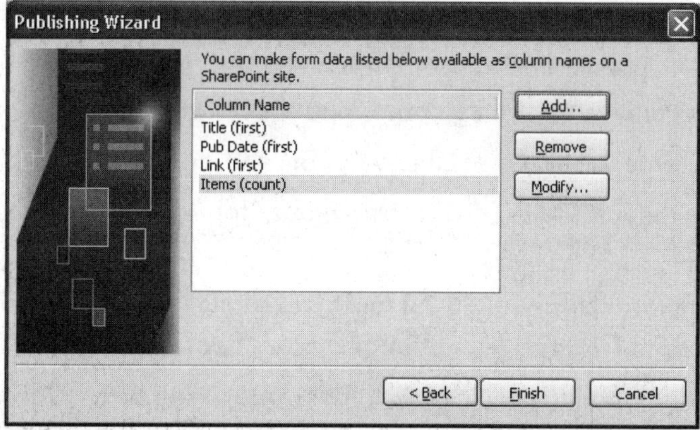

12. Click Finish to open the last wizard screen, select the Open This Form From Its Published Location check box, write down the URL for the form library, and click Close to open this new form library page, shown here:

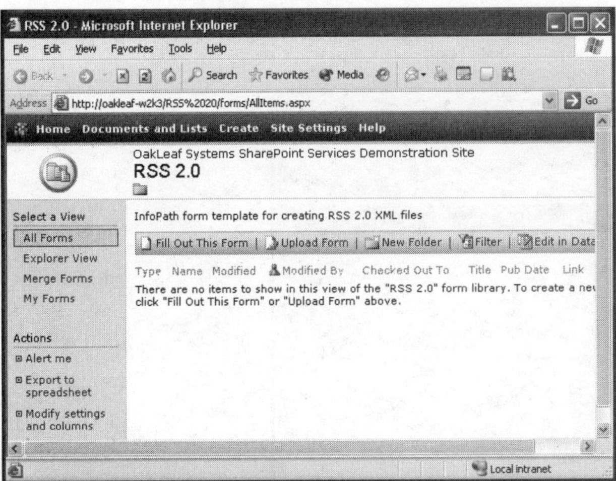

After you publish the form template to the SharePoint site, you should become familiar with the process of adding new data documents to the form library and modifying the form template. To add a new data document to the library and confirm that you can modify the library's template, follow these steps.

▶ Test the template with an Administrator account

1. **On the form library page, click Fill Out This Form to open Form1 in your local copy of InfoPath.**
2. **Press Ctr+S to save the form, which opens a Windows SharePoint Services Save As dialog box. Save the form as Rss2v4 (Administrator) or the like, as shown here:**

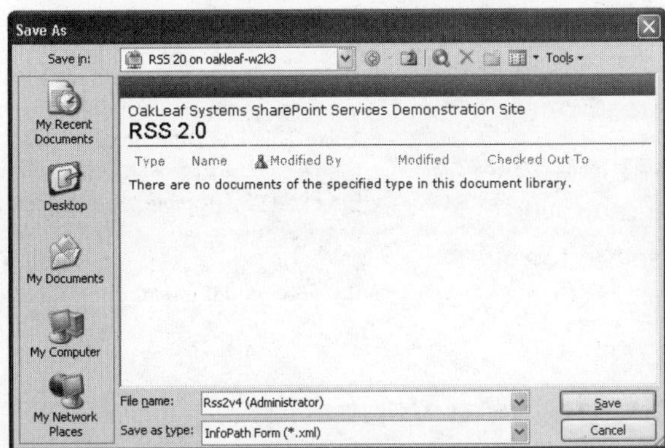

3. **Close the form, and click the library page's Edit In Datasheet View button to open an Office Web Components 11.0 Datasheet control to display the list in a grid. (The Edit In Datasheet View button displays an error message if you haven't installed Office System 2003 on the client computer.)**

4. **Click the Task Pane button to display icons and links for actions that apply to the list only, as shown here:**

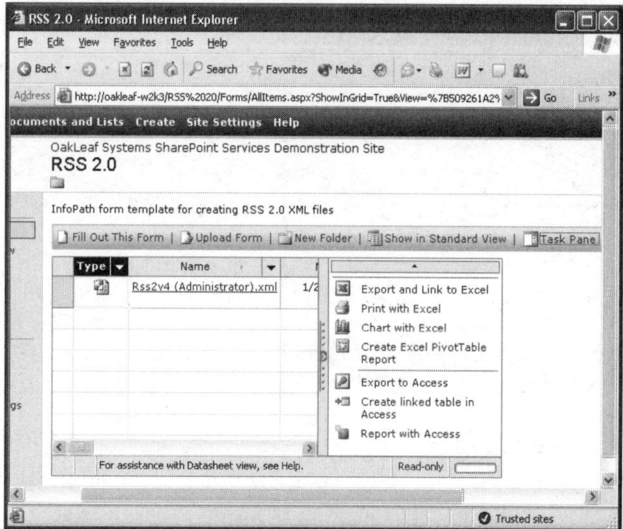

5. **Click the form's Type icon or Name link to open it, choose File, Design A Form to activate the Design A Form task pane, and click the On A SharePoint site link to display the Open From SharePoint Site dialog box.**
6. **Type the site URL drop-down list's text box, and click Next to open a list of form libraries on the site. Select the RSS 2.0 item, and click Open. Click OK in response to the *This form is protected* message. (If another user has the form open, you receive a This form is in use message, and design mode is read-only.)**
7. **Make a minor design change to the template, press Ctrl+S to verify that you can save design changes, and then close the form.**

> **Removing unnecessary columns in a new default list view**
>
> SharePoint's default columns aren't likely to be very interesting to users, but you can't remove any columns from the default (All Forms) view. To add a new view, click the Modify Settings and Columns link, scroll to the Views section, and click Create A New View. Click Datasheet View, give the view a name, and select the Make This The Default View check box. Clear the Name, Modified, Modified By, and Checked Out To check boxes, scroll to the bottom of the page, and click OK to create the view. Click the Go Back To RSS 2.0 link to see the new default view.

Assigning Test Users to Groups and Verifying Template Security

Your SharePoint template publishing project isn't complete until you've verified that InfoPathUsers group members can save data documents but not template changes and InfoPathDesigners members can do both. To add the IPUser, IPDesigner, and the AnyUser accounts as site users, assign them to site security groups, and test their write privileges, follow these steps.

▶ **Add site users and assign them to groups**

1. Click the Site Settings menu button near the top of the page to open the page of the same name, click the Administration section's Manage Users link to open that page, and click the Add Users button to open the Add Users: *SiteName* page.
2. In the Users box, type the user names to add in ***Domain\UserName*** or ***ComputerName\UserName*** format, separated by semicolons, and select the Reader site group check box. For this example add, **IPDesigner**, **IPUser**, and **AnyUser**, as shown here:

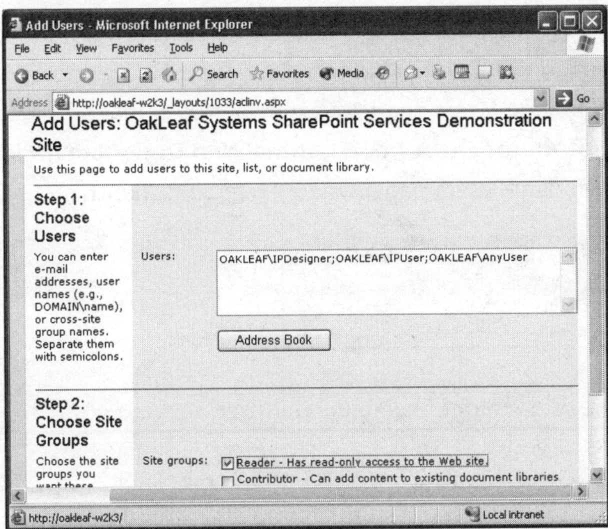

3. Scroll to the bottom of the page, and click Next. Assign fictitious e-mail addresses to the added users.
4. Clear the Send The Following E-Mail check box, if it's selected, and click Finish to return to the Manage Users page.
5. Select the IPDesigner check box, click the Edit Site Groups Of Selected Users button to open the Edit Site Group Membership page, clear the Reader check box, and select the Web Designer check box, as shown on the next page.

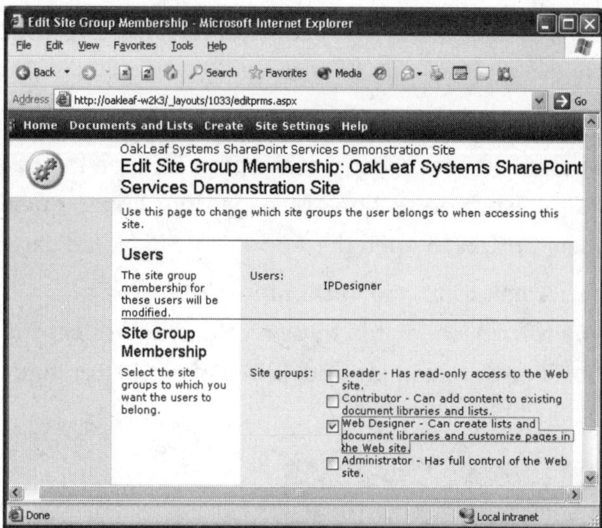

6. Click OK to return to the Manage Users page, and repeat step 5 for the IPUser account, but select the Contributor check box—not the Web Designer check box. Click OK to return to the Manage Users page, which now looks like this:

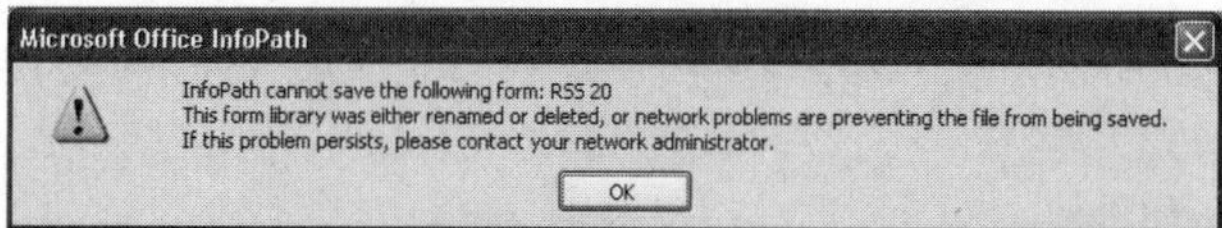

Templates published to shared folders and Web sites required tests to confirm security settings, and you should verify SharePoint form library security. To confirm security settings for RSS 2.0 forms and the template, follow these steps.

▶ Test users' ability to save forms and template design changes

1. Log off as an Administrator, log in as **IPDesigner**, click the Documents And Lists menu button, and click the RSS 2.0 link to activate the RSS 2.0 form library page.
2. Repeat steps 1 through 3 and 6 through 8 from the procedure "Test the Template with an Administrator Account," earlier in this chapter, to verify that Web Designer group members can save forms and template design changes. In this case, save Form1 as **Rss2v4 (IPDesigner)**.
3. Repeat steps 1 and 2, but log in as **IPUser**, and verify that you can save Form1 as **Rss2v4 (IPUser)**. When you attempt to save a template modification, you receive this message:

4. **Repeat steps 1 and 2, but log in as AnyUser, and verify that you receive the following or a similar message when you attempt to save Form1 and that you receive the error message in step 4 when you attempt to open a template in design mode from the SharePoint site.**

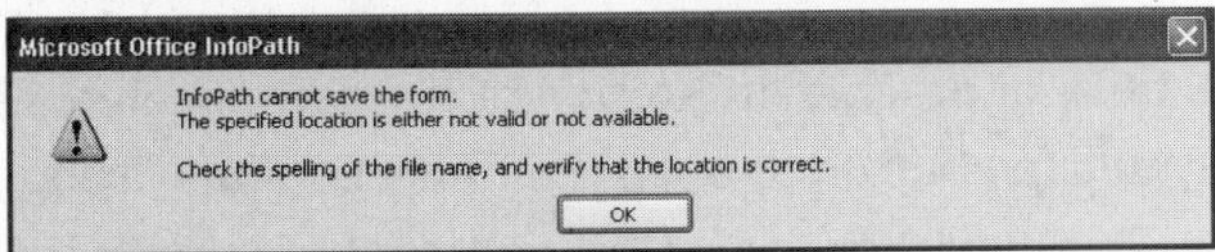

5. **If you're very concerned about form security, add AnyUser to the local Power Users group, and repeat step 4.**
6. **Log off as AnyUser and log on with your administrative account.**

The preceding procedure should be sufficient to demonstrate to the most security-conscious InfoPath designers that SharePoint's security groups are capable of protecting shared templates from unauthorized modification.

Submitting Documents to a SharePoint Forms Library

Save As is the simplest method for adding a form to or updating a form in a SharePoint forms library. If you want to prevent users from saving copies of a data document to their local computer or elsewhere or sending forms by e-mail, you must disable features on the Form Options dialog box's Open and Save tab and change the design to submit the form to the SharePoint library. For this example, you replace the OakLeaf Web Site data connection with a data connection to the SharePoint site. You must be logged on with an Administrator account for the SharePoint site to be able to save the template design change.

To restrict the form to submission only and specify the SharePoint site as the data connection, follow these steps.

▶ Change Open and Save features and the data connection

1. **In the form library, click Fill Out This Form to open a new Form1, and change to design mode as you did in the preceding examples.**

2. Choose Tools, Form Options to open the Form Options dialog box, click the Open and Save tab, clear all check boxes, and click OK to apply the restrictions.
3. Choose Tools, Submitting Forms to open the Submitting Forms dialog box, select Submit To A SharePoint site, and click Add to start the Data Connection Wizard.
4. Type **http://*servername/libraryname*** in the SharePoint Form Library box. For this example, the URL is *http://oakleaf-ms2k3/RSS%2020*. (The URL is the first three elements of the URL you wrote down in step 11 of the "Publish Rss2v4Prot with promoted columns" procedure in the section "Publish the Template and Specify Column Names.")
5. If you want to add a date, time, or other identification to the data document's file name, click the Insert Formula (*fx*) button to open the Insert Formula dialog box, type **concat("*FormName* - ", today())** or **concat("*FormName* - ", now())** in the Formula box, and optionally, select the Allow Overwrite If File Exists check box, as shown here:

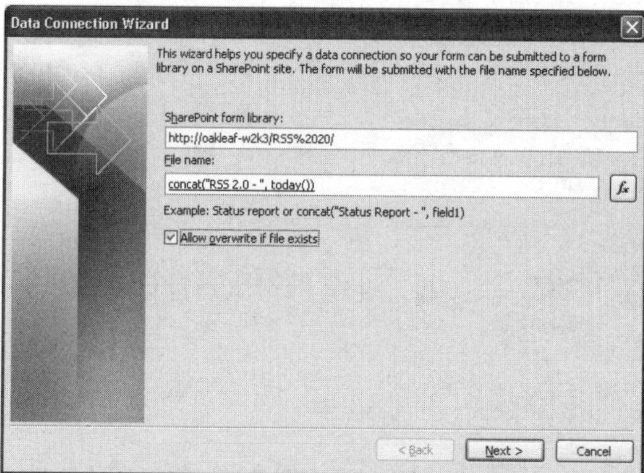

6. Click Next, and type a name for the data connection. Click Finish to return to the Data Connections dialog box, and click Close to return to the Submitting Forms dialog box. Change the caption to **Su&bmit to SharePoint Site,** and click OK.
7. Close the template, save your changes, and close the form.

▶ Test form submission to the site

1. Click the Submit To SharePoint site button, and click OK to acknowledge the *Form was submitted successfully* message.
2. Verify that the form name you specified in step 5 of the preceding exercise appears in the Name column, as shown here:

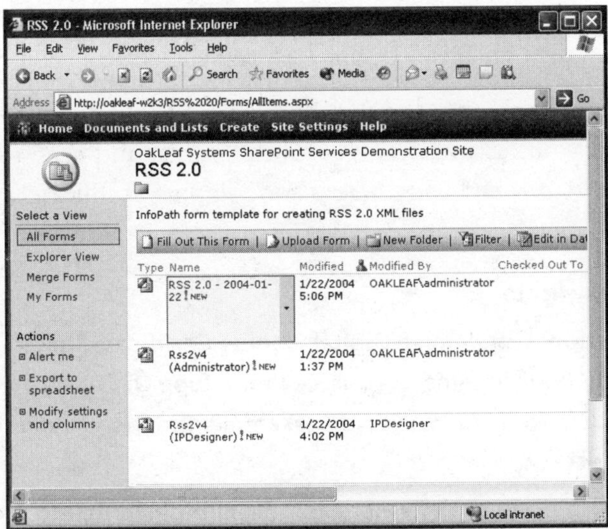

3. Open the form to verify that the submission truly succeeded.

If you receive an error message when attempting to submit the form, you probably mistyped the URL in step 4 of the preceding exercise. Open the form in design mode, choose Tools, Data Connections to open the Data Connections dialog box, and click Modify to open the first Data Connection Wizard dialog box. Verify that the URL matches the URL in the Internet Explorer Address bar, up to but *not including* /Forms/AllItems.aspx … . Make any necessary changes, complete the wizard steps, save the changes, and try submitting again.

Creating Fully Trusted Forms by Code Signing

If you need to take advantage of any features that aren't permitted by InfoPath's Domain security model, such as cross-domain data access, you must specify the Full Trust security model. When you specify Full Trust, you have two choices: adding a digital signature from a code signing certificate to the form or creating and deploying a custom-installed template. A code signing certificate differs from a client authentication certificate. Most commercial CAs provide code signing certificates. If you install a code signing certificate obtained from your organization's certificate server, users of your forms must trust the CA. If you've implemented digital signatures for data documents, users already trust the organization-wide CA.

It's far simpler to obtain a code signing certificate, if you don't have one, and apply a digital signature to the form than it is to deploy custom-installed templates. Another advantage of signed templates is that users automatically receive updates to cached templates. Custom-installed templates require reinstallation for each template change. Thus, you should use digitally signed templates unless you or your IT staff absolutely refuse to implement an X.509 public key infrastructure.

The following procedure makes the assumption that you've already obtained a client authentication certificate from your organization's certificate server and need to obtain a code signing certificate. If you already have a code signing certificate, skip this exercise.

▶ Obtain a code signing certificate

1. Follow the steps in the section "Obtaining a Digital Signing Certificate," in Chapter 11, except in step 5, specify Code Signing Certificate in the Type Of Certificate list, and specify an appropriate friendly name. For this example, the friendly name is **InfoPath Code Signing Cert**.
2. After you install the certificate, launch Internet Explorer, choose Tools, Internet Options, select the Content tab, and click the Certificates button.
3. Verify in the Certificates dialog box that the certificate is present and that its intended purpose is Code Signing, as shown here:

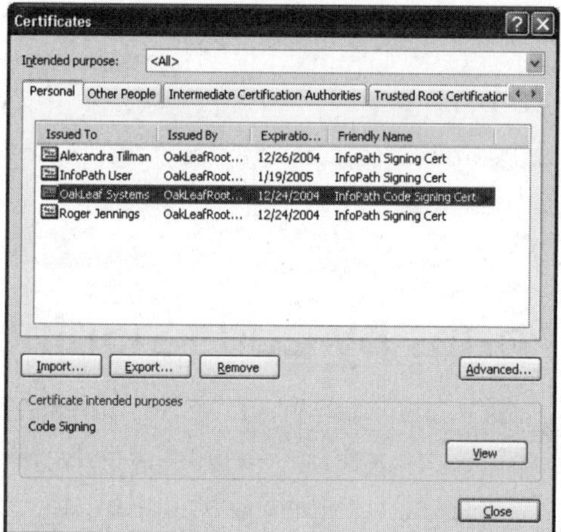

4. Optionally, click View to view a detailed description of a typical code signing certificate.
5. Close the dialog boxes and Internet Explorer.

▶ Sign a form

1. Open one of the forms you published to a shared folder or Web server in design mode. This procedure uses the Rss2v4.xsn form published to the \\OakLeaf-MS15\Shared\IPTemplates\Rss2v4 folder. When opening the form, type the UNC path or URL for the form.

2. Choose Tools, Form Options to open the Form Options dialog box, select the Security tab, and select the Sign With A Specific Certificate option, which enables the Select Certificate button.
3. If your code-signing certificate doesn't appear as the default, click Select Certificate to open the Select Certificate dialog box, and with your code signing certificate selected in the list, click OK.
4. Clear the Automatically Determine Security Level check box, and select the Full Trust option, as shown here:

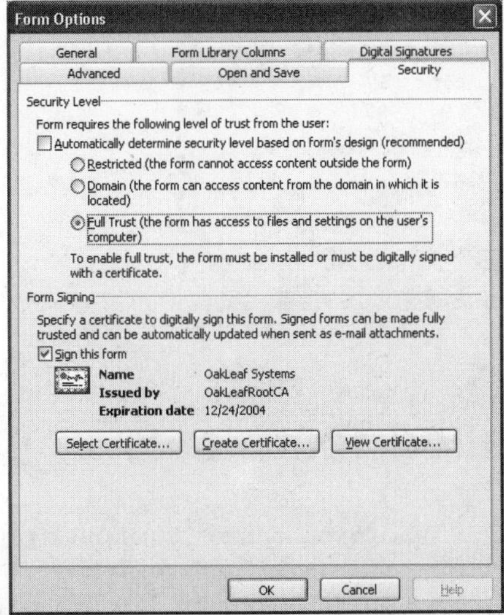

5. Click OK to apply the new security model, and save your template changes.
6. Reopen the template, which displays a Security Warning dialog box if the certificate publisher isn't included in Internet Explorer's Trusted Publisher's list.
7. Select the Always Trust Files From This Publisher And Open Them Automatically check box to enable the Open button, as shown here:

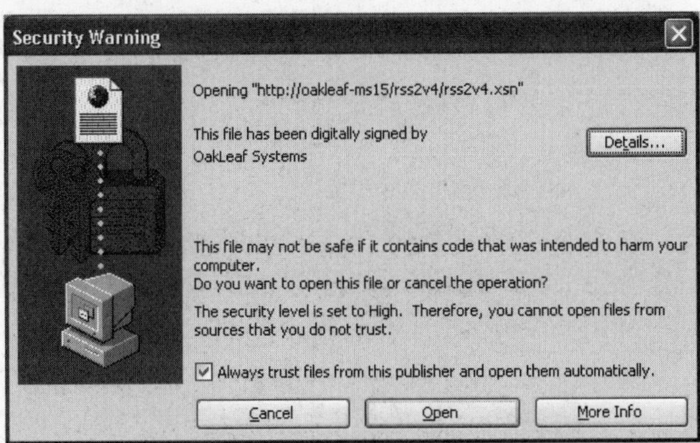

8. **Click Open to add the certificate to Internet Explorer's Trusted Publishers list and open the form. The green check box in the form's lower left corner confirms the form is fully trusted, as shown here:**

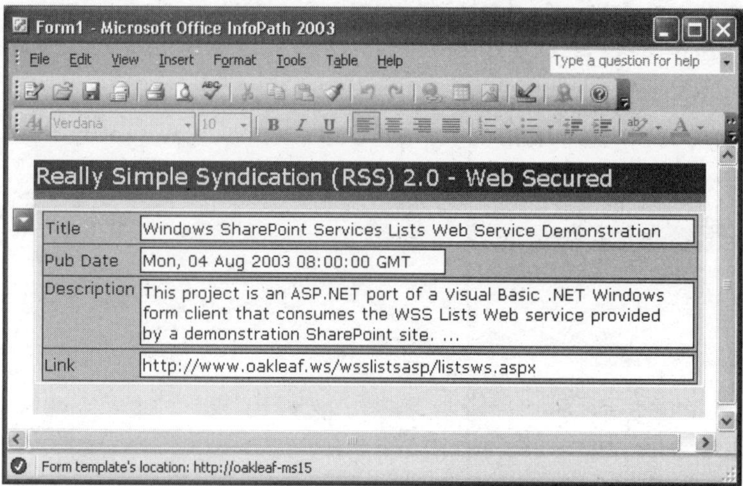

Distributing Custom-Installed Templates

Custom-installed templates–formerly called *URN-based* templates–let you create fully trusted InfoPath templates that users install on their Windows 2000 or later workstations, which must have InfoPath 2003 installed to be useful. Custom-installing a template adds a registry entry, which includes the well-formed path to the template. The purpose of custom-installed forms is to create fully trusted forms that don't require the code to be signed.

The downside of custom-installed forms is the need for users to obtain and install templates with a JScript (*TemplateName*.js) installation or Windows Installer (*TemplateName*.msi) file. You need Visual Basic .NET Standard Edition 2003 or Visual Studio .NET Professional Edition 2003 installed on your computer to create a Windows Installer file.

Simplifying installation of custom-installed forms for users

If you *must* distribute production templates for custom-installed forms and you don't have Visual Studio .NET 2003 installed, purchase a copy of Visual Basic .NET Standard 2003 so that you can create Windows Installer files. You'll recover the initial cost quickly by eliminating help desk calls from users attempting to install the templates with the JScript file. Making it easier for users to choose the directory in which to install the template is another benefit of a Windows Installer file. You'll also need Visual Basic .NET Standard 2003 or Visual Studio .NET 2003 to create InfoPath Projects, the subject of Part IV of this book, "Programming InfoPath Forms."

Making Regform.exe easier to use
Use Windows Explorer to add a copy of Regform.exe to your \WINDOWS\system32 (Windows XP and Server 2003) or \WINNT\system32 folder (Windows 2000). The copy lets you access Regform.exe from any folder without typing the path.

You create the fully trusted template and the JScript or Windows Installer file with a command-line form registration tool named *Regform.exe*. Regform.exe is a part of the Microsoft InfoPath 2003 SDK, which you can download from *http://msdn.microsoft.com/office/understanding/infopath/devdocs/*. If you install the SDK with InfoPathSDK.msi to the default location, you'll find Regform.exe in your \Program Files\Microsoft Office 2003 Developer Resources\Microsoft Office InfoPath 2003\Tools folder.

Using Regform for JScript Installation

If you don't have Visual Basic .NET Standard or Visual Studio Professional 2003 installed, you're stuck with the JScript installation process. The standard command-line syntax for a JScript installation, assuming that you have a copy of Regform.exe in your ...\system32 folder, is shown here:

regform.exe /U urn:Template:Company /T Yes "d:\full path\source template.xsn"

The */U* switch specifies the template's URN, which must begin with *urn:* and contain no spaces. */T Yes* specifies a fully trusted form, and the final argument is the well-formed path to the template you're converting. The URN must be unique to each template. (If the full path or template name contain spaces, you must surround the argument with double quotation marks.)

Here's a sample command-line instruction to create a fully trusted version of the Rss2v4FtJs.xsn template in your C:\Microsoft Press\Introducing InfoPath 2003\Chapter12\Rss2v4Js folder:

regform.exe /U urn:Rss2v4FtJs:OakLeaf /T Yes "C:\Microsoft Press\Introducing InfoPath 2003\Chapter12\Rss2v4js\Rss2v4FtJs.xsn"

Regform.txt, in your C:\Microsoft Press\Introducing InfoPath 2003\Chapter12 folder, contains the full syntax for Regform.exe instructions.

When you execute the preceding instruction from the Command Prompt window, either by typing it or running a .cmd (batch) file containing the instruction, Regform.exe performs the following operations:

- Creates a backup copy of the source template–Rss2v4FtJs.bak for the preceding instruction example.

- Extracts the template files, modifies the manifest.xsf file to specify a fully trusted template, and uses Makecab.exe to re-create the .xsn file. (Makecab.exe is a utility for creating compressed cabinet files.)
- Generates a 4300-byte *TemplateName*.js file–Rss2v4FtJs.js for this example–to run on the client.

You'll probably find that fewer errors result if you create in Notepad a .cmd batch file to execute the preceding instruction. Your C:\Microsoft Press\Introducing InfoPath 2003\Chapter12\Rss2v4Js folder contains a sample template source file and FtJs.cmd batch file, which you execute from the Command Prompt window, as shown in Figure 12-5.

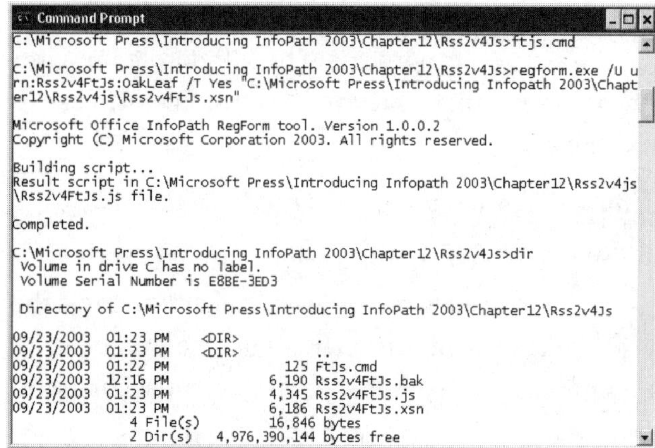

Figure 12-5 Executing the sample FtJs.cmd batch file creates these form backup, JScript installation, and modified .xsn files.

Installing the sample modified template creates the following registry key: *HKEY_LOCAL_MACHINE\SOFTWARE\Microsoft\Office\11.0\InfoPath\SolutionsCatalog\urn:Rss2v4FtJs:OakLeaf*.

To emulate installing the .js and modified .xsn files on a client computer, follow these steps.

Making sure users can run fully trusted forms

The Options dialog box's Allow Forms That I Install With A Custom Setup Program To Have Access To Files And Settings On My Computer check box is selected by default, but it's possible that InfoPath users might have altered this setting. This check box must be selected to open a fully trusted custom-deployed form.

▶ Use the JScript file to install the fully trusted template on a client

1. In Windows Explorer, create a new folder for the template, **\Program Files\InfoPath Form Templates\Rss2v4FtJs** for this example, on the same machine.

2. **Navigate to your C:\Microsoft Press\Introducing InfoPath 2003\Chapter12\ Rss2v4Js folder, and double-click the FtJs.cmd file to create the fully trusted version of Rss2v4FtJs.xsn and generate the Rss2v4FtJs.js script.**
3. **Copy *TemplateName*.xsn and *TemplateName*.js to the new folder. For this example, copy Rss2v4FtJs.xsn and Rss2v4FtJs.js from your C:\Microsoft Press\Introducing InfoPath 2003\Chapter 12\ Rss2v4Js folder.**
4. **Double-click the Rss2v4FtJs.js file, and click Yes and OK to acknowledge the two messages shown here:**

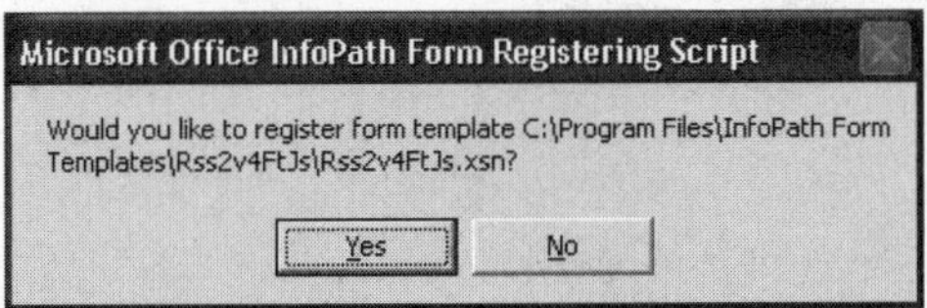

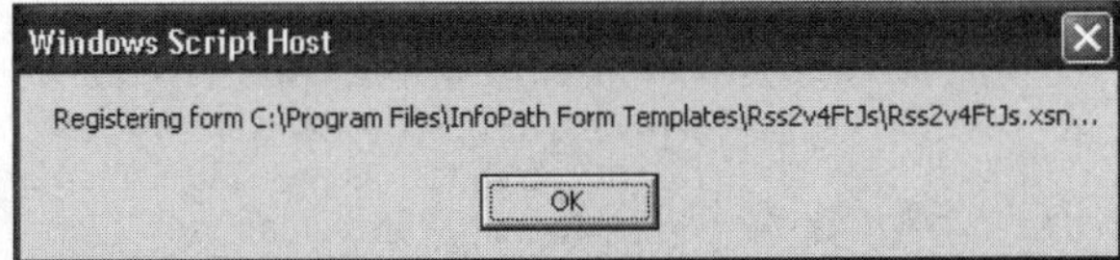

5. **After registration is complete, this confirmation message appears:**

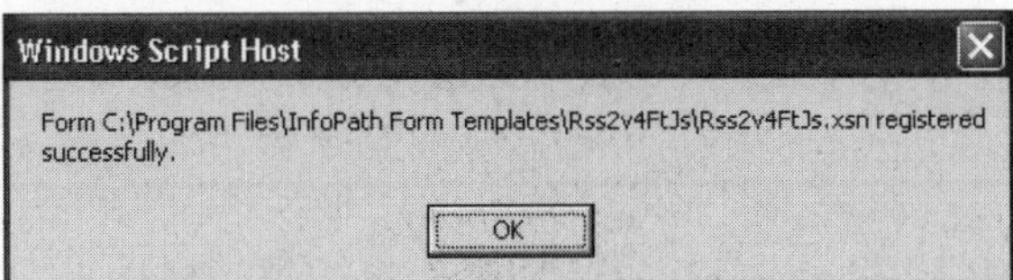

6. **Click OK, and double-click Rss2v4FtJs.xsn to open the fully trusted form and verify the registration, which is indicated by a trusted sites icon (green circle with a check mark) and the form's URN at the bottom left of the form.**

To uninstall the Rss2v4FtJs.xsn file on your computer, follow these steps.

▶ **Uninstall the template from a client with the JScript file**

1. **Choose Start, Run, and type the following path in the Open box: "C:\Program Files\InfoPath Templates\Rss2v4FtJs\Rss2v4FtJs.js" /uninstall. The double quotation marks are required for paths or file names with spaces. Click OK, and acknowledge the three messages shown here:**

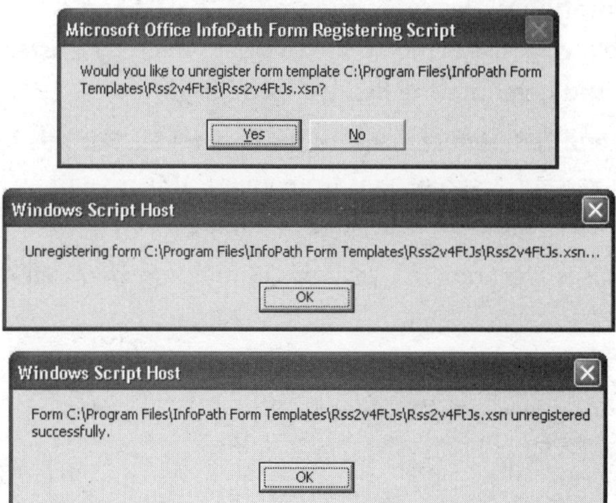

2. **Double-click Rss2v4FtJs.xsn. You'll receive an error message, which verifies that the form has been uninstalled.**
3. **Repeat step 1 to verify that the JScript code reports an error if you attempt to uninstall a form more than once.**

Specifying silent installation or a different folder

The JScript installation file accepts a */silent* switch to eliminate installation prompts and close the empty InfoPath instance during registration. Users can specify a different installation folder with a */d "d:\path\file-name.xsn"* switch.

Creating a Windows Installer File with Regform

Creating a Windows Installer file is as easy as generating a JScript installation file; you don't even need to know how to launch Visual Basic .NET or Visual Studio .NET to create the .msi file. You add a */MSI* command-line switch to the Regform.exe instruction (after the */T Yes* switch) and execute the instruction from the folder containing the source template file. The Regform.exe instruction with */MSI* does the following:

- Generates a temporary Visual Studio .NET Setup project, Setup.vdproj, in your \Documents and Settings*UserName*\Local Settings\Temp\1\Regform folder.
- Creates a modified copy of the *TemplateName*.xsn file, and adds the copy and a helper file named Caction.exe to the project.
- Compiles the project to Setup.exe and Setup.msi in the ...\Regform\Release folder.
- Copies Setup.msi as TemplateName.msi to the current folder.

Your C:\Microsoft Press\Introducing InfoPath 2003\Chapter12\Rss2v4Msi folder contains a sample template source file (Rss2v4FtMsi.xsn) and FtMsi.cmd batch file with the */MSI* switch, which you execute from the Command Prompt window, as shown in Figure 12-6. The folder includes Rss2v4FtMsi.msi installer file, which you can use if you don't have Visual Basic .NET 2003 Standard Edition or Visual Studio .NET installed.

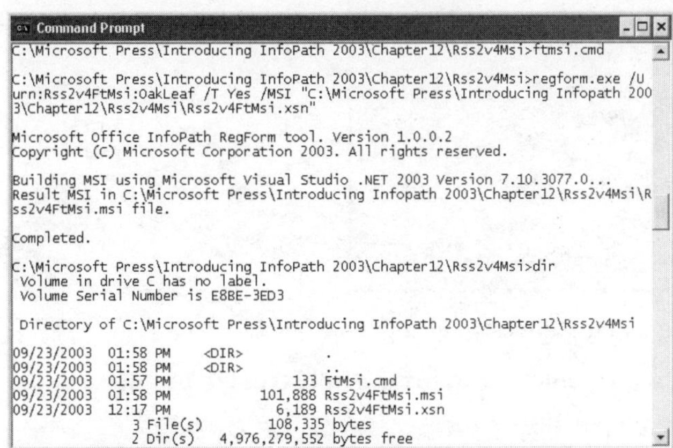

Figure 12-6 Adding the /MSI command-line switch generates the TemplateName.msi Windows Installer file.

To install the Rss2v4FtMsi.xsn template to a folder on your test computer by using the Rss2v4FtMsi.msi installer file in your C:\Microsoft Press\Introducing InfoPath 2003\Chapter12\Rss2v4Msi folder, follow these steps.

▶ Emulate client installation with a Windows Installer file

1. **Copy *TemplateName*.msi to any location on the client machine. For this exercise, copy Rss2v4FtMsi.msi.**
2. **Double-click the Rss2v4FtMsi.msi file to start Windows Installer, and click Next.**
3. **Add the template name (without the extension) to the default destination folder, C:\Program Files\InfoPath Form Templates\, and accept the default Just Me option to install the template for the current user only, as shown on the next page.**

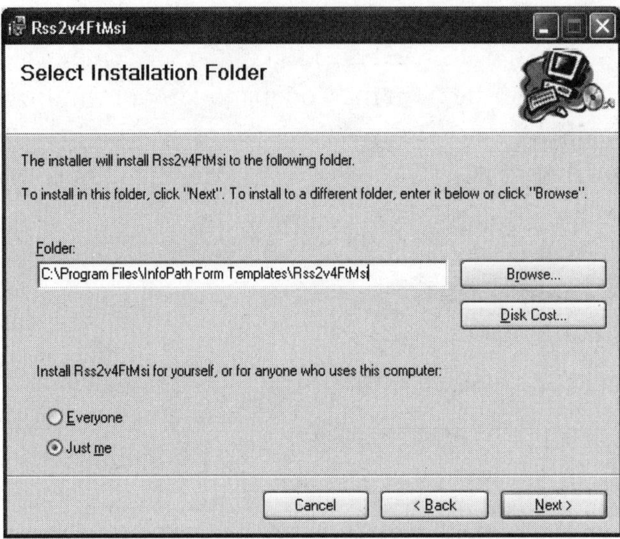

4. **Click Next twice to complete the installation, and then click Close.**
5. **Navigate to the destination folder, which contains the fully trusted template and a hidden ca*TemplateName*.exe helper file.**
6. **Verify that the trusted sites icon appears at the bottom of the form, and that you can save forms and modify the template design.**
7. **Run the installer again to uninstall the template by selecting the Remove *TemplateName* option and clicking Finish. Alternatively, users can uninstall the template by using Control Panel's Add Or Remove Programs tool.**

Disabling Design Mode for Deployed Fully Trusted Forms

The only practical method for preventing users from modifying of custom-installed templates is to prevent users from entering design mode. The section "Disabling InfoPath Design Mode," in Chapter 11, describes how to use the Custom Installation Wizard to disable design mode during InfoPath setup. If users already have InfoPath installed with design mode enabled, you can disable it by adding the following registry DWORD (32-bit) value name and data: *HKEY_CURRENT_USER\Software\Microsoft\Office\11.0\InfoPath\Designer\DisableDesigner* = *0x00000001*. You must have local Administrator privileges to change registry values. Disabling design mode removes InfoPath's Design This Form button, Design A Form task pane, and the File, Design A Form menu option.

Warning
Making changes to the Windows registry might cause serious problems that could require you to reinstall the operating system. Before making any change to the registry, use the Backup Utility to create a backup of the System State and your boot folder and be sure to have the system recovery disk available. On computers running Windows XP or Windows Server 2003, use the Automated System Recovery Wizard to create a recovery disk and a backup of your local system partition the hard drive.

To disable design mode on a user's computer, follow these steps:

▶ **Add the DisableDesign DWORD value**

1. **Close InfoPath, if it's open. Choose Start, Run, type regedit in the Open box, and click OK to open the Registry Editor.**
2. **Expand the *HKEY_CURRENT_USER* node, and navigate to and select the *HKEY_CURRENT_USER\Software\Microsoft\Office\11.0\InfoPath\Designer* key.**
3. **Choose Edit, New, DWORD Value to add a New Value #1 entry to the key with a default value of 0x00000000 (0).**
4. **Change the entry's name to DisableDesigner, right-click the entry, and choose Modify from the shortcut menu to open the Edit DWORD Value dialog box.**
5. **Type 1 in the Value Data box, as shown here:**

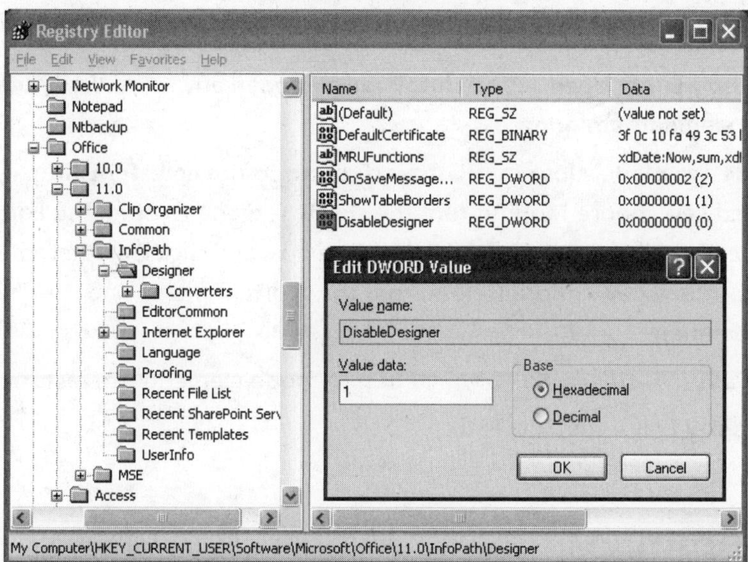

6. **Click OK to set the value and close the dialog box. Your added value looks like the figure on the next page.**

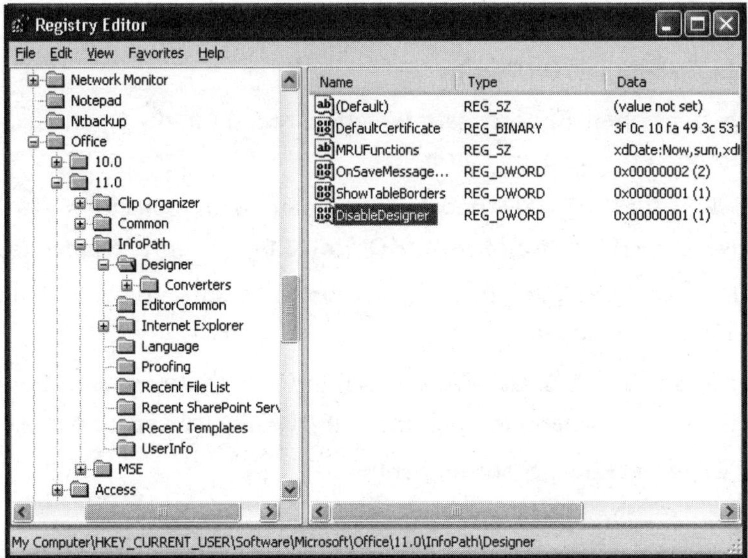

7. **Keep the Registry Editor open, launch InfoPath, and open any form. Verify that all design mode elements are gone.**
8. **To reinstate design mode, close InfoPath, and return to the Registry Editor. Right-click the added key, choose Modify from the shortcut menu to open the Edit DWORD Value dialog box, type 0 in the Value Data box, and click OK. Alternatively, right-click the added key, choose Delete from the shortcut menu, and click Yes to confirm the deletion.**
9. **Reopen InfoPath to verify that all original design mode elements are restored.**
10. **Close the Registry Editor and InfoPath.**

Chapter Summary

InfoPath lets you publish templates to shared folders, intranet Web sites, or Windows SharePoint Services sites. Publishing templates to shared folders and Web sites exposes your templates to accidental or malicious modification by ordinary users. Securing templates from unauthorized changes requires applying group-level or user-level security to server shares and folders. If authorized template users must store data documents to the folder containing the template, you must add file-level security to protect the template. The folder-level and, optionally, share-level security provisions are the same for templates shared by file and Web servers. Securing templates that you publish to a SharePoint site is simpler, because only members of the Web Designer and Administrator groups for the site can save template modifications.

Copies of conventional InfoPath templates cached on users' machines are sandboxed, which means that code behind the forms can't access local system resources, create instances of Component Object Model (COM) objects, or run ActiveX controls that aren't marked safe for scripting. Templates that require these capabilities must be installed and registered on users' computers as fully trusted. The InfoPath 2003 SDK offers the Regform.exe command-line tool to create fully trusted templates, which users install with a JScript installation script or a Windows Installer file. You must have a license for Visual Basic .NET Standard 2003 or Visual Studio .NET Professional 2003 to create Windows Installer files.

Q&A

Q. How do I apply file-level security to further protect my shared templates?

A. Applying file-level security is identical to the process for applying folder-level security, with a few minor exceptions. You must remove permissions inherited from the folder security settings, copy them as not-inherited settings for the template file, and clear the Allow Modify and Allow Write check boxes.

Q. Can users of a template opened from a Windows SharePoint Services site's forms library save InfoPath data documents to a location other than the SharePoint library?

A. Yes. Choosing File, Save As defaults to the SharePoint forms library, but users can save the .xml file to any folder or Web site for which they have write permissions.

Q. Can users submit InfoPath data documents to a Web site from a SharePoint forms library?

A. Yes, but they receive a warning message that states: *This page is accessing information that is not under its control. This poses a security risk. Do you want to continue?"* Clicking OK submits the form successfully.

Q. Why would I need to create a fully trusted form?

A. If your form doesn't include programming code that requires a fully trusted form, you might want to use a fully trusted form to avoid cross-domain warning messages for forms that access databases or Web services, which are the subject of Part III of this book, "Working with Databases and Web Services."

Q. Can a developer with Visual Studio .NET Professional 2003 create a Windows Installer file for me?

A. Yes, but the developer must have a licensed copy of InfoPath to run Regform.exe and test the installation files.

On Your Own

Here are a few additional exercises that will increase your competence for sharing secure InfoPath templates:

1. Create a shared folder named NWOrders that contains the NWOrdersFinal.xsn template from Chapter 10, "Adding Views to a Template," and apply share and file permissions for the InfoPathDesigners and InfoPathUsers groups.
2. Verify template security with the IPUser and IPDesigner accounts.
3. Change the share and folder permissions to permit members of the InfoPathUsers group to save data documents to the folder but not modify the NWOrdersFinal.xsn template.
4. Verify template security.
5. Create a new IIS VDir that uses the NWOrders folder (not the share) as its content location.
6. Verify template security.
7. Add digital signatures to the other forms that are shared, including forms shared from a SharePoint forms library.

PART III

Working with Databases and Web Services

Part III shows you how to use Microsoft Access or SQL Server database tables as the main data source for forms and then submit additions or updates to table records. You also learn how to use database queries to populate drop-down list and list box controls. Examples of forms that interact with simple and complex XML Web services demonstrate InfoPath 2003 SP-1's prowess as a Web service client.

CHAPTER 13

Connecting Forms to Databases

In this chapter, you will learn how to:

- **Use the Data Connection Wizard to create a main data source for a form bound to Jet or SQL Server tables**
- **Create a default query and data entry view of a data-bound form**
- **Add data entry controls to the default view**
- **Edit and delete parent and child table records with a Submit Changes button**
- **Apply conditional formatting rules to buttons to prevent data entry errors**
- **Add and delete parent and child table records**
- **Create secondary data sources for list boxes from Jet or SQL Server tables**
- **Change the primary data source for a data-bound form**

For more information:

- **See the section "Using Secondary Data Sources with Lists," in Chapter 6, "Adding Basic Controls and Lists," for more detailed information about adding secondary data sources for list boxes.**

To work through this chapter:

- You need to know how to add layout tables with controls and how to rearrange layout tables, as described in Chapter 5, "Laying Out Forms."
- You need Microsoft Access 2000 or later with the sample databases installed on your computer or network read/write access to the Northwind.mdb sample database. (The Microsoft Office System 2003 Setup program with default options doesn't install Northwind.mdb.)
- You need read/write access (at least *db_datareader* and *db_datawriter* roles) to the Northwind sample database of Microsoft SQL Server 2000 Service Pack 3 (SP-3) or later or to NorthwindCS, the sample database for Microsoft SQL Server Desktop Engine (MSDE) 2000 SP-3 or later, for the client/server examples.
- You should be familiar with relational database terminology. Some experience using Access 2000 or later is helpful, and familiarity with Access data project's SQL Server designer is useful but not essential for the client/server samples.
- You'll find it useful, but not essential, to be familiar with adding secondary data sources based on static XML documents.

The Data Connection Wizard in Microsoft InfoPath 2003 lets you connect forms to Jet (Access) .mdb database files and Microsoft SQL Server 2000 SP3 and later databases, including the Microsoft SQL Server Desktop Engine (MSDE). You can issue queries to retrieve records, edit records, add new records, submit your changes, and delete records, if you have the required database permissions. You also can specify tables or queries to populate secondary data sources for drop-down and conventional list boxes. This chapter's examples require create (insert), retrieve (query), update, and delete permissions for the Jet or SQL Server sample databases. You can execute stored procedures to retrieve data, but supplying variable argument values to a stored procedure requires adding code behind your form, which is one of the subjects of Part IV of this book, "Programming InfoPath Forms."

InfoPath 2003 won't replace Microsoft Access as a rapid application development (RAD) tool for retrieving and editing relational data, nor can it compete with the versatility offered by data-bound Microsoft Visual Basic 6 or Microsoft Visual Studio .NET Windows forms. However, InfoPath enables Office System 2003 power users and developers to create basic Jet-based and SQL Server–based online and offline data query and editing forms quickly and easily. If you're familiar with ActiveX Data Objects (ADO) disconnected recordsets, InfoPath's ADOAdapter provides similar retrieve, disconnect, edit, reconnect, and update capability.

Downloading MSDE Release A

If you purchased the stand-alone version of Microsoft InfoPath 2003 and don't have Microsoft Office 2002 or later installed on your machine or didn't install MSDE when you installed Office, you can download and install MSDE Release A from *www.microsoft.com/sql/msde*. Release A is the desktop version of SQL Server 2000 with Service Pack 3a.

The default format for saved InfoPath data documents is an ADO *Recordset* object transformed to an XML document, which has an unconventional, attribute-centric structure. The structure corresponds to an ADO Rowset schema, which is written in Microsoft's Annotated XML-Data Reduced (XDR) language. The XML Schema recommendation has caused XDR to become obsolete, but many production Visual Basic 6 and C++ applications continue to use ADO recordsets. Complex document structure and a nonstandard schema severely limit the utility of saved ADO-style XML data documents in workflow processes.

Using the Data Connection Wizard

The InfoPath Data Connection Wizard calls the Office Data Connection Wizard to create an .odc file for Jet and SQL Server data sources. The wizard embeds required data from the .odc file in the manifest.xml file and creates a default query and data-entry form when you complete the multistep data source definition process. To use the Data Connection Wizard with Jet or SQL Server databases, you'll need to know these basic guidelines for defining main data sources that generate updatable data entry and editing forms:

- Codeless data entry forms are best suited for creating and editing forms for a single record of one table, which can have one child table. An example is a query view that accepts an order number and returns order information to a data entry view. You add a section or layout table with controls for order header data and a repeating table for line items to the data entry view.

- As a rule, master/detail sections aren't well suited to displaying multiple master records and their dependent child records, because the master record usually contains detailed information that isn't easily viewed in a repeating table.
- Adding a second child table makes the data entry form read-only. As an example, adding a related customer record as a child of an order record with line items prevents submitting changes to the database.
- InfoPath queries don't support wildcard searches–for example, *LIKE 'A%'* to return all records whose specified field value begins with the letter *A*. Query values must match corresponding field values exactly; the database determines case-sensitivity of string values. (You can write code to enable wildcard searches, but the code is very complex.)
- Deleting a parent record with child records requires enabling cascading deletions for the related table. Cascading deletions are a property of the database's relationship object.

The following two sections show you how to use the Data Connection Wizard to establish a connection to Jet and SQL Server databases and generate the default view from the tables you specify. The resulting forms will be used in procedures later in this chapter.

Creating a Query and a Data Entry Form with a Jet Connection

Connections to Access (Jet) databases use the Microsoft Jet 4.0 OLE DB Provider to generate ADO *Recordset* objects. To create a connection to the Northwind.mdb sample database, follow these steps.

▶ Create a connection to a local copy of Northwind.mdb

1. **Start InfoPath, click the Fill Out A Form dialog box's Design A Form link, and click the Design A Form task pane's New From Data Connection link to start the Data Connection Wizard.**
2. **Select the Database (Microsoft SQL Server Or Microsoft Office Access Only) option, and click Next.**
3. **Click Select Database to open the Select Data Source dialog box, shown here:**

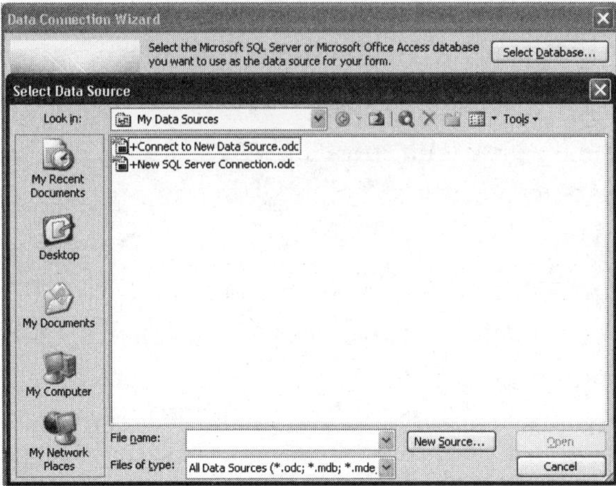

4. Double-click the +Connect To New Datasource.odc item to open the Welcome To The Data Connection Wizard screen.
5. Select Other/Advanced in the list, and click Next to open the Data Link Properties dialog box.
6. Select Microsoft Jet 4.0 OLE DB Provider in the OLE DB Provider(s) list, as shown here:

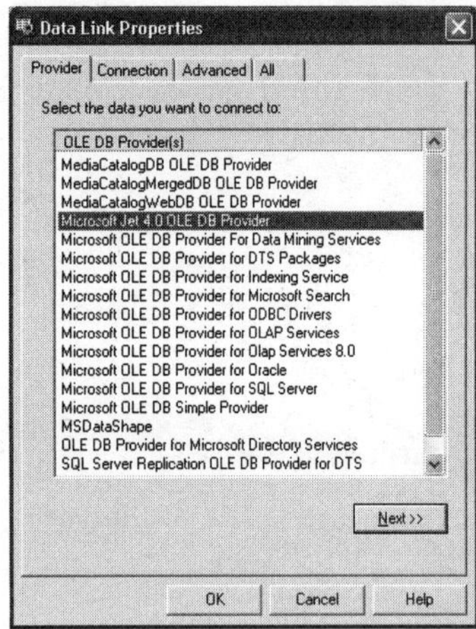

7. Click Next. On the Connection tab, click the browse (...) button to the right of the Database Name box to open the Select Access Database dialog box. Navigate to your copy of Northwind.mdb, which is in your \Program Files\Microsoft Office\Office11\Samples folder by default, and double-click Northwind.mdb to close the dialog box and add its well-formed path to the Database Name box. Leave the default Admin user with a blank password.

Connecting to a secure Jet database

If you're connecting to a secure Jet database, you must provide User Name and Password values and then click the All tab of the DataLink Properties dialog box. Select the Jet OLEDB: System Database property in the Name list, click Edit Value, type the well-formed path to the System.mdw workgroup file, and click OK. If you want to maintain database security, don't select the Save Password In File check box in step 10.

8. **Click the Test Connection button to verify the connection, as shown here:**

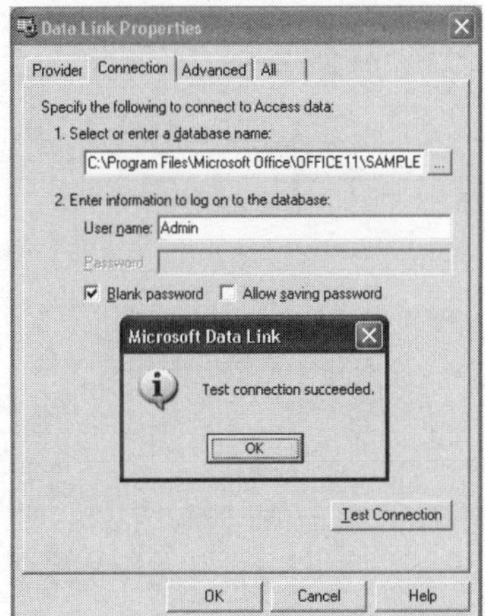

9. **Click OK twice to close the dialog boxes and go to the Data Connection Wizard's Select Database And Table screen, which displays all tables and queries in the database. The following procedures use the Orders table as the parent table, so scroll to and select Orders, as shown here:**

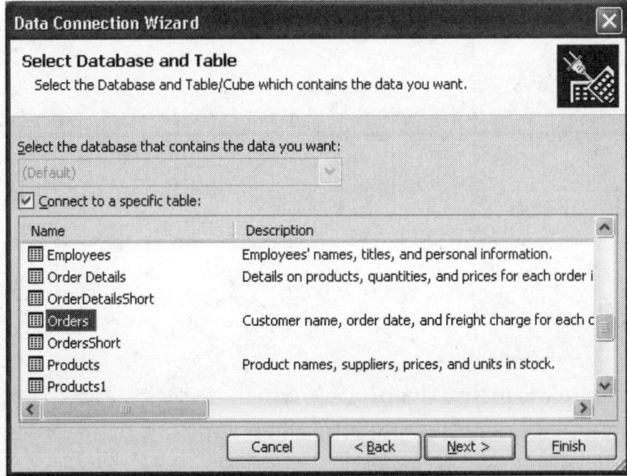

10. **Click Next, and replace (Default) Orders.odc with a more descriptive name for the data connection—NWOrdersJet.odc for this example. Leave all the remaining default values, as shown here:**

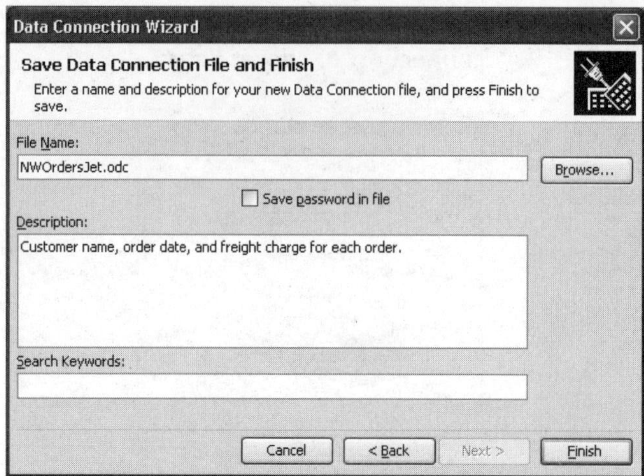

11. Click Finish to complete the wizard and open a dialog box that displays the Orders table's fields.
12. You need order line items for the form, so click Add Table to open the Add Table Or Query dialog box, and select the Order Details table, as shown here:

13. Click Next to open the Edit Relationship dialog box, which displays OrderID as the primary and foreign key fields for the relationship. Click Finish to display the Orders and Order Details tables in the Data Source Structure tree view list.
14. Click the Edit SQL button to open the Edit SQL dialog box, and click Test SQL Statement to verify the query, which is written in the SHAPE command syntax of the MSDataShape Provider, as shown here:

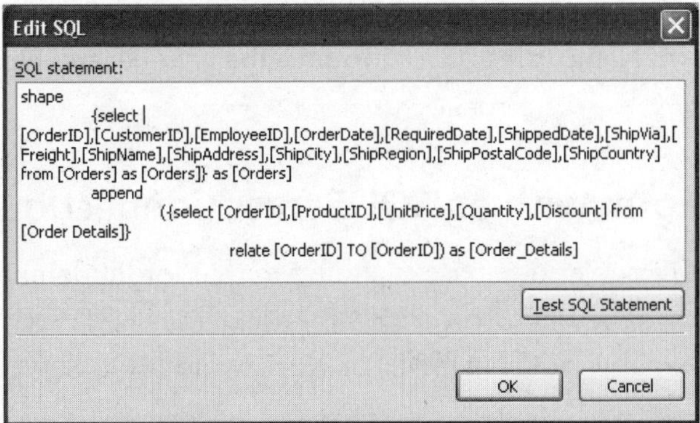

See Also To learn more about SHAPE command syntax, which enables InfoPath to handle hierarchical recordsets, go to *msdn.microsoft.com*, search for the term *Q189657* in the Microsoft Knowledge Base, and open the "HOWTO: Use the ADO SHAPE Command" article.

15. **Click OK twice, and with the Orders table selected, click the Modify Table button to open the Sort Order dialog box. You need a single Orders record and its related Order Details records for this example, so clear the Allow Multiple Records From This Table To Be Displayed In The Form check box, as shown here:**

Caution: If you don't clear this check box, your Order/Order Details form won't work.

16. **Click Finish, and click Next to display a summary of your selections. Name the data connection NWOrdersJet, verify that the Submit Status value is Enabled in the Summary section, and click Finish to generate the default form with New Record and Run Query buttons.**

17. **Type Northwind Order Form - Jet in the title table's first row, delete the second row, save the template to a new NWOrdersJet subfolder of My Documents\ Infopath as NWOrdersJet.xsn.**

18. Choose File, Properties to open the Form Properties dialog box, assign Northwind Order Form - Jet as the Form Name, press Ctrl+S to save the change, and close InfoPath.

Generating a Default Form with an SQL Server Connection

Creating a connection to an SQL Server database is similar to that for Jet database connections, but SQL Server uses the Microsoft OLE DB Provider for SQL Server. To create a connection to the NorthwindCS (MSDE) or Northwind (SQL Server) sample database, follow these steps.

▶ **Create a connection to an SQL Server instance**

1. Repeat steps 1 through 3 of the preceding procedure.
2. Double-click the +New SQL Server Connection.odc item to open the Data Connection Wizard's Connect To Database Server screen.
3. Type **localhost** if SQL Server or MSDE is running on your computer. Otherwise, type the network (NetBIOS) name of the remote server running SQL Server or MSDE. Leave the default Use Windows Authentication option if your logon account has read/write access to the Northwind or NorthwindCS database, as shown here. Otherwise, select the Use The Following User Name And Password option and type your user name and password if the server is set up for SQL Server security.

4. Click Next to open the Select Database And Table screen. Click the drop-down arrow to display the Select The Database That Contains The Data You Want list, select Northwind or NorthwindCS, and select the Orders table, as shown here:

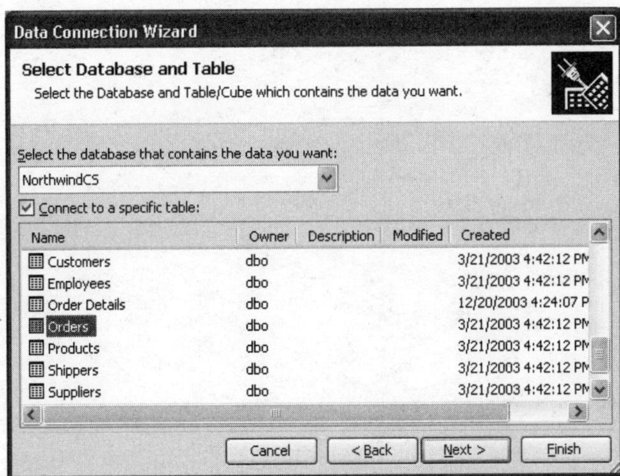

5. **Repeat steps 10 through 16 of the preceding procedure, but change the name of the file to NWOrdersSQL.odc in step 10 and the name of the data connection to NWOrdersSQL in step 16.**
6. **Add Northwind Order Form - SQL Server as the title, delete the second title table row, and save the template to a new NWOrdersSQL subfolder of My Documents\Infopath. For the SQL Server version, the template file name is NWOrdersSQL.xsn in the NWOrdersSQL subfolder, and the Form Name is Northwind Order Form - SQL Server.**

Adding Controls to a Default Form

The Data Connection Wizard generates a data source with queryFields and dataFields groups; the data source fields are identical for Jet and SQL Server sample databases. The wizard generates the default form shown in Figure 13-1 for either connection type. The two empty layout tables are intended to contain query and data entry controls. This chapter's procedures use a simple query that returns a specified Orders record and its related Order Details records. The first step is to add an Order ID text box to the query layout table to specify the Orders record. You then replace the empty data entry layout table with a layout table with controls.

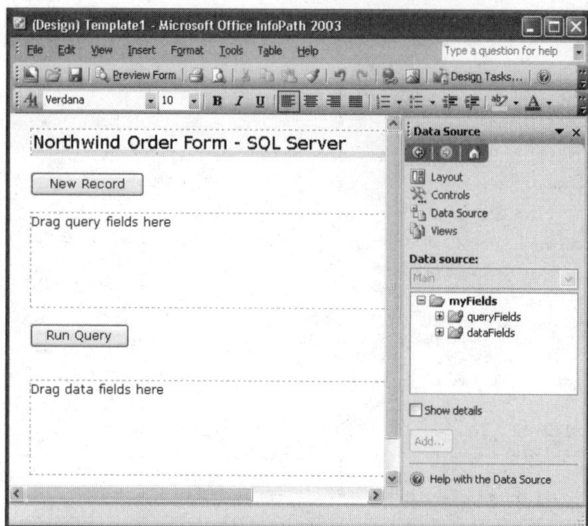

Figure 13-1 The Data Connection Wizard creates this default form for all connections to Jet or SQL Server databases.

To add the initial set of controls to a form based on either Jet or SQL Server tables, follow these steps.

▶ Add controls and test the initial form design

1. **With the NWOrdersJet.xsn or NWOrdersSQL.xsn template open in design mode and the Data Source task pane active, expand the queryFields and q:Orders nodes, and drag the OrderID field to the upper (query) layout table.**
2. **Decrease the width of the Order ID box, and drag the bottom of the query table up to the bottom of the text box.**
3. **Select the query table, and split it into four columns. Drag the Run Query button to column B and the New Record button to column C, insert a horizontal line below the table, and remove the empty lines above and below the table.**
4. **Delete the lower layout table, drag the dataFields node below the horizontal line, and select Section from the shortcut menu. You bind the empty section to the dataFields node, so you can add a layout table with controls for the Orders field and a repeating table for the Order_Details field.**
5. **Expand the dataFields node, drag the d:Orders group to the added section, and select Controls In Layout Table from the shortcut menu to add the controls for the Orders fields.**
6. **Expand the d:Orders node, drag the Order_Details node inside the section below the Orders layout table, and select Repeating Table from the menu.**

7. **Reduce the widths of the repeating table's fields and the section, and save your changes.**
8. **Optionally, increase the width of the table, split column B into three cells, and rearrange the fields to conserve vertical space. The form with the table coalesced appears as shown here:**

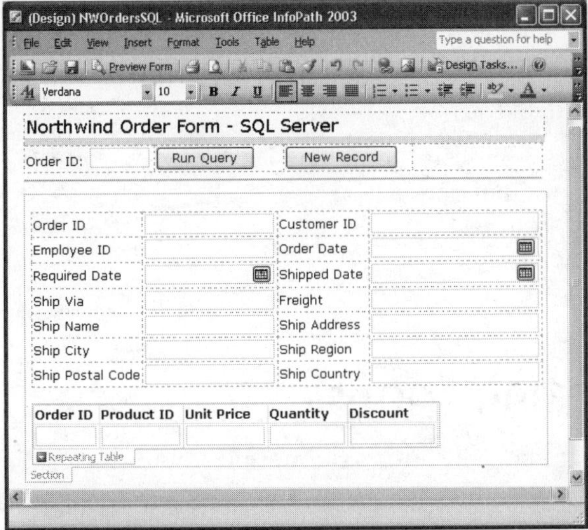

9. **Save your changes, activate the task pane, select Fill Out A Form, and click the form's friendly name link to open a new Form1.**
10. **Type a valid OrderID value, such as 11066, in the text box, and click Run Query to display data from the selected Orders record and related Order Details records:**

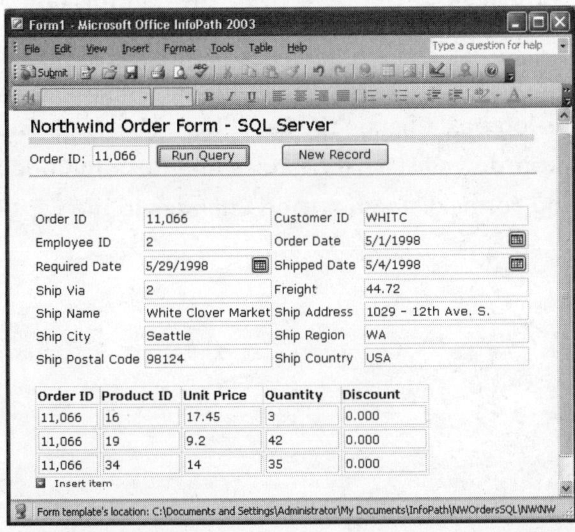

11. **Save the data document in the template's folder as NW11066.xml or the like.**

If you're interested in the data document's structure, open the 9 KB NW11066.xml file with Notepad. The *<dfs:queryFields>* and *<dfs:dataFields>* elements contain the data for the query and data entry sections of the form, which totals about 1870 bytes. The remaining 7 KB consists of an embedded schema and the original data before editing in the data entry tables. InfoPath uses the original data to prevent concurrency errors; if the data in the tables doesn't correspond to the original data, InfoPath displays an error message when you submit your changes.

Fixing fractional value rounding errors

The Discount field values for some Order Details records display rounding errors, such as 0.050000001 instead of 0.05. The errors result from using Jet's Single data type instead of Double or Decimal for the Discount field. SQL Server's NorthwindCS database inherited the errors by importing the Single value as the SQL Server real data type. InfoPath interprets Single or real values with rounding errors as Not A Number (NaN) when performing XPath calculations on these values. To fix the problem, change the Discount field's data type to Decimal (4,2) or Decimal (5,3) to permit values up to 99.99 or 99.999.

Editing and Submitting Forms

The Data Connection Wizard automatically adds a Submit button to the form's toolbar, which lets you submit edited values for the selected order to the database tables. This button isn't likely to be easily identified by users, and its location is inconsistent with other buttons on the form. To add and configure a more evident Submit Changes button, follow these steps.

▶ Add a Submit Changes button

1. With the Northwind Orders Form in design mode, activate the Controls task pane, and drag a button control to the right of the New Record button.
2. Right-click the button, and choose Button Properties from the shortcut menu to open the Button Properties dialog box. Change the Label from Button to **Submit Changes**, and in the Action drop-down list, change Rules And Custom Code to Submit to open the Submitting Forms dialog box. Add **Changes** to the Caption box, as shown here:

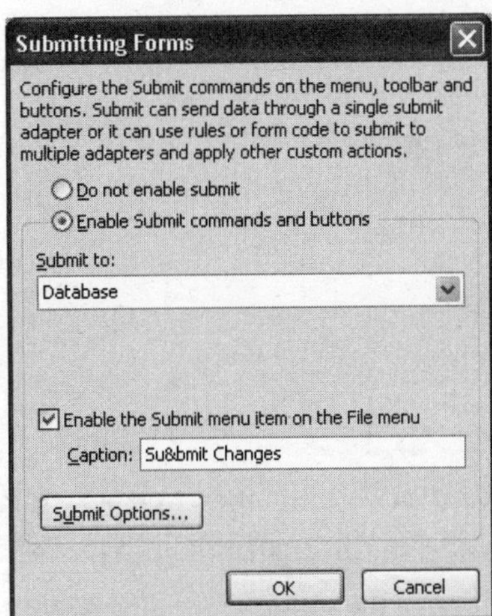

3. **Click Submit Options to open the Submit Options dialog box, and accept the default Leave The Form Open option. Select the Instead of Default Message, Show Custom Message check box, and add appropriate Success and Failure messages, such as these:**

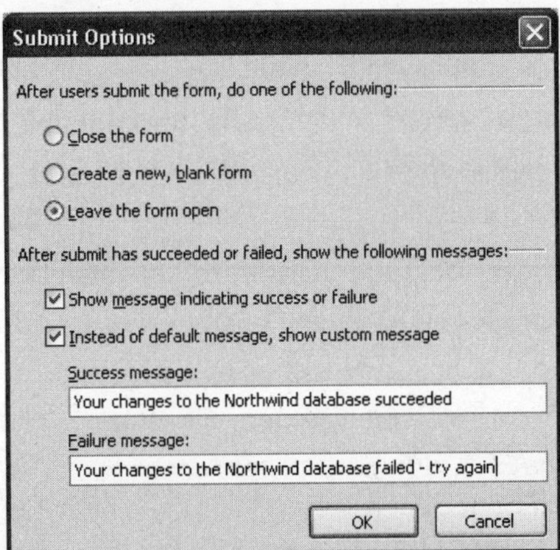

4. **Click OK twice to close dialog boxes and save your changes, and then save your template changes.**

The data in the cached recordset returned from a query and the template's schema combine to enforce data concurrency rules and constraints on data values when you submit the form to the database. To test the submit process, follow these steps:

▶ **Test data submission, concurrency issues, and constraint violations**

1. **Give the new button a try by opening a preview, running a query for Order ID 11066, making no changes, and clicking the Submit Changes button or choosing**

File, Submit Changes. In the custom Failed message that appears, click Details to display this explanation:

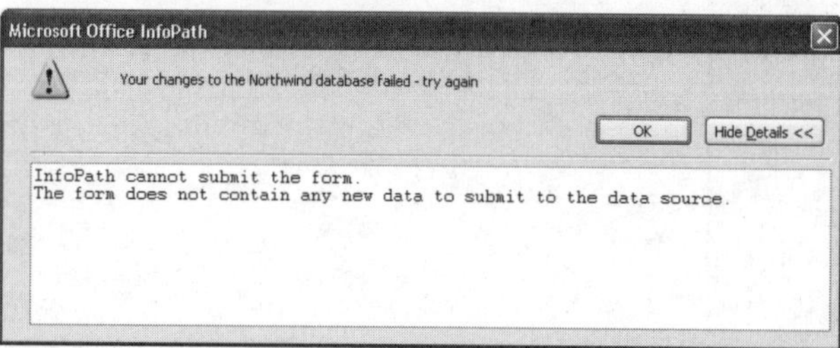

2. **Click OK, and make a minor change to the record, such as changing the Employee ID value to 5. Then click Submit Changes. You receive the custom Success message. (If your update fails, you probably don't have write permission for the tables.)**
3. **To verify that InfoPath performs concurrency tests, keep the preview open, open the NW11066.xml form in another InfoPath instance, and click Query to verify that the Employee ID value changes to the value you typed in step 2.**
4. **Change the Employee ID to a different number, such as 2, click Submit Changes, and close the form without saving changes.**
5. **Return to the preview, enter yet another Employee ID value, such as 8, and click Submit Changes. You'll receive an error message that contains this statement in the Details box: *Row cannot be located for updating. Some values may have been changed since it was last read.***
6. **Click the preview's Query button to refresh the data, click Yes to acknowledge the warning message, type a nonexistent Employee ID value (10 or greater), and click Submit Changes. The error message from SQL Server states: *UPDATE statement conflicted with COLUMN FOREIGN KEY constraint 'FK_Orders_Employees'. The conflict occurred in database 'NorthwindCS', table 'Employees', column 'EmployeeID'.***
7. **Close the preview.**

You've now verified that InfoPath won't submit data that doesn't differ from the original values, performs data concurrency tests, and observes the Order table's foreign key constraints.

Disabling Buttons with Conditional Formatting

If a user clicks the Run Query button with an empty Order ID text box, InfoPath displays the two message boxes shown in Figure 13-2 in succession.

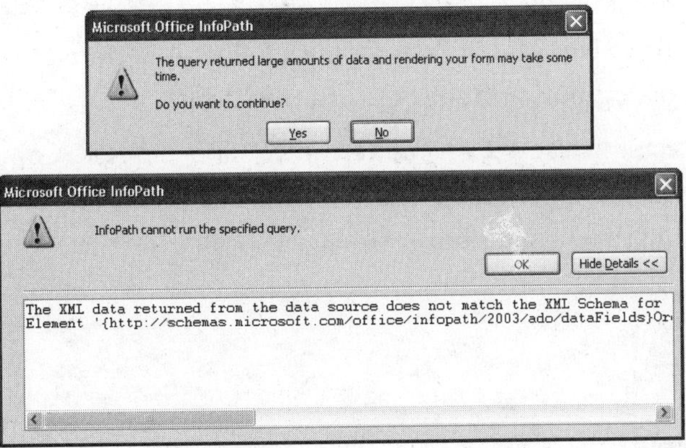

Figure 13-2 These two messages appear when you click the Run Query button without an Order ID value.

Users receive similar error messages if they submit changes without adding foreign key field values. You can use conditional formatting to disable buttons if specific conditions aren't met. In this exercise, you'll disable the Run Query button if a valid Order ID value isn't present and disable the Submit Changes button if required field values aren't provided. You'll also learn how to apply a regular expression pattern-matching test to the Customer ID text box value, which must contain five uppercase letters.

▶ Conditionally disable the Run Query and Submit Changes buttons

1. **Open the Properties dialog box for the Run Query button, click the Display tab, and click the Conditional Formatting button to open the Conditional Formatting dialog box.**
2. **Click Add to open the Conditional Format dialog box. Click Select A Field Or Group, expand the queryFields and q:Orders nodes, and double-click the OrderID field. Select Is Blank as the condition, and select the Disable This Control check box, as shown here:**

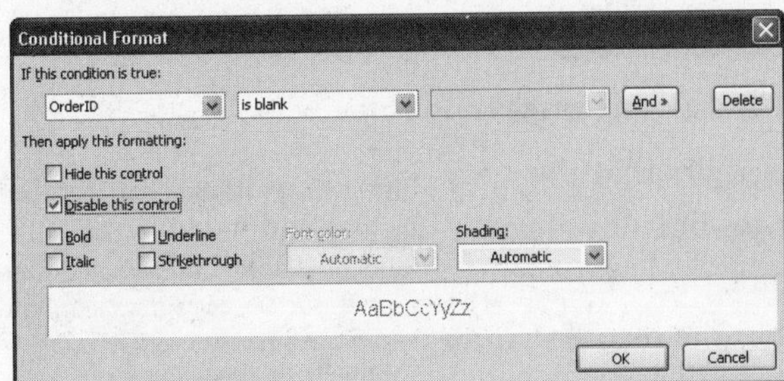

3. **Click OK three times to apply your changes and close the dialog boxes.**
4. **Repeat step 1 for the Submit Changes button.**

5. Repeat step 2, but expand the dataFields and d:Orders nodes, select the CustomerID field, and select Does Not Match Pattern. Click Select A Pattern to open the Data Entry Pattern dialog box, and select Custom Pattern.
6. Open the Insert Special Character list, select Any Letter: \p-{L}, and click OK. Copy and paste the special character five times, as shown here, and click OK twice to return to the Conditional Formatting dialog box.

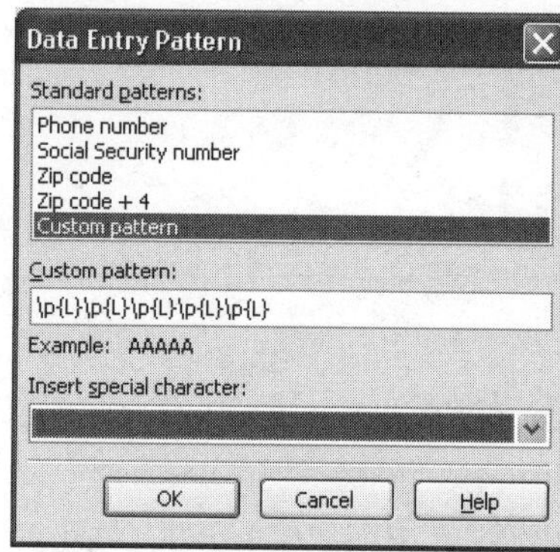

7. Click Add, select Select A Field Or Group, select Employee ID under the d:Orders node, and click OK. Select Is Blank in the condition list, select the Disable This Control Check box, and click OK to return to the Conditional Formatting dialog box.
8. Repeat step 7 for the ShipVia, OrderDate, ShipName, ShipAddress, ShipCity, and ShipCountry fields. Your Conditions With Formatting list for the Submit Changes button appears as shown here:

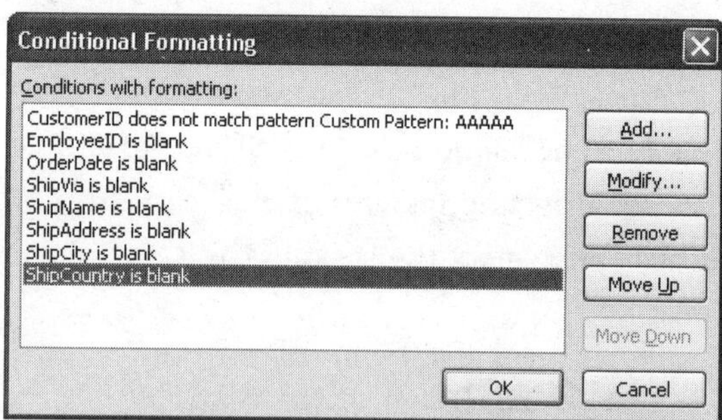

9. Click OK twice to apply the conditional formatting rules.
10. Open a preview window, and verify that the Run Query and Submit Changes buttons are disabled. Add an OrderID value, press Tab, click Run Query, and verify that the resulting data enables the Submit Changes button. Make changes to the Orders values that violate the rules you added to verify the other conditional formatting rules.

Removing the Submit toolbar button and menu item

When you add conditional formatting to a submit button, consider clearing the Submitting Forms dialog box's Enable The Submit Menu Item On The File Menu check box, which also removes the Submit toolbar button. The conditional formatting rules you apply to the button you add to the form don't apply to the Submit menu item or the toolbar button.

Adding and Deleting Records

InfoPath's default New Record button simply clears the form in preparation for adding a new record. Users must type or select required values in the form's controls and click the Submit Changes button to perform an *INSERT* operation on the tables.

InfoPath provides a Delete & Submit button to remove the current record. As mentioned in the section "Using the Data Connection Wizard," earlier in this chapter, deleting a record with dependent child records displays an error message unless the relationship between the parent and child records implements cascading deletions.

Adding New Records

Using a read-only Jet Autonumber or SQL Server identity field to store the OrderID value simplifies adding new records to the Orders and Order Details tables. Autonumber and identity fields automatically add a new 32-bit integer value that's greater by 1 than the largest value that has ever existed in the field. As an example, if you start such a field with 100000, add 100 records, and then delete the 100 records you added, the value for the next record you add will be 100101. It's a common practice to use an Autonumber or identity field as a table's primary key field, which must have a unique value to identify each record.

InfoPath takes full advantage of Autonumber and identity field values by assigning the primary key value to the corresponding foreign key field of related records automatically. In this procedure, InfoPath assigns the Orders table's OrderID value to the OrderID field of Order Details records you add to a new or existing order. Thus, you can remove the OrderID text box and its label from the repeating table to simplify data entry operations. Follow these steps to remove the OrderID column of the repeating table and test the addition of a new Orders record with Order Details records.

▶ Remove the table's OrderID column and test the line item addition

1. **With the Northwind Orders Form template open in design mode, select the Order ID column of the repeating table, and press Delete to remove it.**
2. **Click Preview Form, type a valid OrderID in the text box, and click Run Query.**
3. **Click the Insert Item link or its adjacent button to add an empty Order_Details row.**
4. **Type a valid ProductID value (between 1 and 77) that doesn't duplicate other ProductID values, and type values for Unit Price, Quantity, and Discount. (Discount must be 0 or less than 1).**

5. Click Submit Changes to verify that InfoPath successfully updates the Order Details table without supplying its OrderID value from a bound text box, and click Run Query again to confirm the addition.
6. Click the selector button for the Order Details item you added, select Remove Order_Details, and click Submit Changes to reverse the changes.

▶ Add new Orders and Order Details records

1. With the Northwind Order Form open in design mode, open a new Form1, leave the OrderID box empty, and type a valid CustomerID value, such as **WHITC** or **ALFKI**, and an EmployeeID value between 1 and 9. (InfoPath ignores values in the OrderID box when adding a new record with an Autonumber or identity primary key value.)
2. Add today's date to the Order Date and Required Date fields, specify a ShipVia value between 1 and 3, enter a Freight amount, and type short text values in the required address text boxes.
3. Add a couple of Order Details items, observing the constraints described in step 4 of the preceding procedure. Your data entry form should appear similar to this:

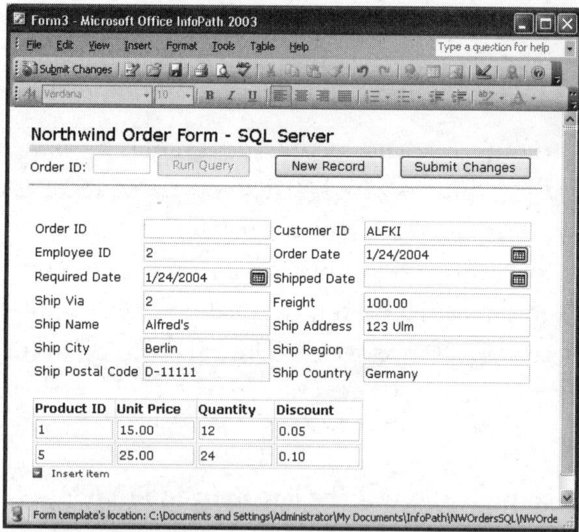

4. Click Submit Changes to add the new record and display the new order number in the Orders section's OrderID box.
5. Verify the added records by typing the new OrderID value in the query's OrderID box and clicking Run Query.
6. Close the form, noting the added Order ID value.

Deleting Records

If you're familiar with the Microsoft Access Relationships window or with SQL Server Database Diagrams, you can alter the relationship between parent and child records to implement cascading deletions. The following procedure is based on unmodified versions of the Northwind and NorthwindCS sample databases, so you must delete the Order Details items manually, submit the changes, and then delete the parent Orders record.

Follow these steps to add a Delete & Submit button and delete the records you added in the preceding procedure.

▶ **Add a Delete & Submit button and delete an Orders record**

1. With the Northwind Order Form template open in design mode, add a new row above the Orders table's first row, and drag the Submit Changes button to column B.
2. Drag a Button control from the Controls task pane to column D.
3. Right-click the button, and choose Button Properties from the shortcut menu to open the Button Properties dialog box. Change the Label to **Delete & Submit**, select Delete & Submit from the Action list, clear the Enable The Submit Menu Item On The File Menu check box, and click OK twice. The button inherits the custom messages you provided when you added the Submit Changes button.
4. Click Preview Form, type the OrderID value for the order you added in the preceding procedure as the query OrderID value, and click Run Query.
5. Click Delete & Submit, click Yes to confirm the deletion, and verify that InfoPath displays a error message containing the explanation *DELETE statement conflicted with COLUMN REFERENCE constraint*. Click OK to dismiss the message.
6. Select and remove the Order Details records you added in the preceding procedure, and click Submit Changes.
7. Click Delete & Submit to delete the Orders record, which erases the Orders section.
8. Verify that the Orders record deletion succeeded by clicking Run Query again, which returns this error message:

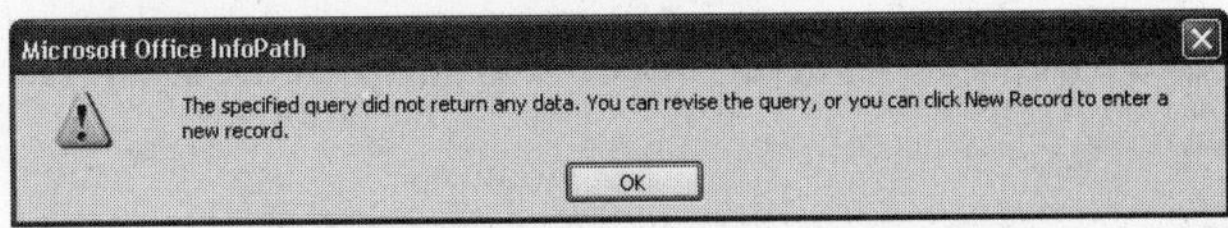

This error message appears when you click Run Query with any invalid OrderID value in the text box.

Creating Secondary Data Sources for List Boxes

The secondary data sources you created to populate drop-down lists in the section "Using Secondary Data Sources with Lists," in Chapter 6, rely on static XML documents. Updating these documents isn't easy, especially if they're embedded in the template's .xsn file. InfoPath's Data Connection Wizard lets you create dynamic secondary data sources that reflect the current values in the underlying table. The only drawback to this approach is that InfoPath must download and cache the secondary data source's rows when you open the form. If your form has several list boxes with many items, opening the form can be delayed by a few seconds or more, depending on the speed of the database connection and the load on the database server.

You must create a new .odc file for each secondary data source you add, because the .odc file specifies the table or query that provides the data. It's a common practice to populate secondary data sources from saved Jet queries or SQL Server views; alternatively, you can write your own SQL SELECT statement to return customized data for drop-down list value names.

Follow these steps to create a secondary data source for a drop-down list that displays the employee names for selections you make in the Northwind form's Order EmployeeID text box and test the added control and its data source.

▶ Create the employee name secondary data source

1. **With the Northwind Orders Form open in design mode, choose Tools, Data Connections to open the Data Connections dialog box, and click the Add button to start the Data Connection Wizard.**
2. **Select the Receive Data option in the first wizard screen, and click Next. Select the Database (Microsoft SQL Server Or Microsoft Office Access Only) option in the next wizard screen, and click Next.**
3. **Repeat the steps you followed for the Jet or SQL Server data source in the section "Using the Data Connection Wizard," earlier in this chapter, but name the ODC file NWEmplLookupJet.odc or NWEmplLookupSQL.odc, as appropriate, and specify Employees as the table name.**
4. **In the wizard's Data Source Structure list, clear all but the EmployeeID, FirstName, and Last Name check boxes.**
5. **Click the Edit SQL button to open the Edit SQL dialog box, and change *select "EmployeeID","LastName","FirstName"* to select "EmployeeID","LastName" + ', ' + "FirstName" as "EmplName", leaving the remainder of the statement the same, as shown here for SQL Server:**

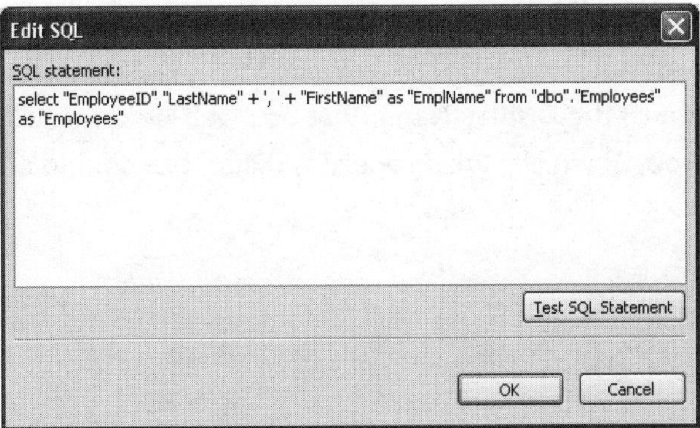
Edit SQL
SQL statement:
select "EmployeeID","LastName" + ', ' + "FirstName" as "EmplName" from "dbo"."Employees" as "Employees"
Test SQL Statement
OK
Cancel

Modifying the SQL statement for a Jet data source

SQL Server queries use identifiers enclosed in quotation marks to accommodate spaces and other punctuation in table and field names; Jet databases use square brackets for this purpose. The full Jet SQL statement for the preceding query is: *select [EmployeeID],[LastName] & ", " & [FirstName] as EmplName from [Employees] as [Employees].*

6. **Click Test SQL Statement to verify your changes, click OK to dismiss the message that warns that you can't represent the statement in a tree view, and click Next. Click Yes to dismiss the warning about unsafe queries.**
7. **Replace Employees with NWEmplLookupJet or NWEmplLookupSQL in the text box, leave the Automatically Retrieve Data When The Form Is Opened check box selected, and click Finish and Close to close the dialog boxes and add the secondary data source.**

To add a drop-down list to the Employee table cell, bind the value of the list box to the secondary data source you added, and display the employee name, follow these steps:

▶ Add an EmplName drop-down list and link it

1. **Reduce the width of the EmployeeID box, and drag a drop-down list from the Controls task pane's list and drop it to the right of the text box, which opens the Drop-Down List Box Binding dialog box.**
2. **Expand the dataFields and d:Orders nodes, and double-click the EmployeeID field to bind the drop-down list to the text box.**
3. **Remove the label, and reduce the width of the control. Right-click the control, choose Properties from the shortcut menu to open its Properties dialog box, and select the Look Up Values In A Data Connection To A Database, Web Service, File, Or SharePoint Library Or List option.**
4. **Select the name you assigned to the secondary data source in step 7 of the preceding procedure in the Data Source list.**

5. Click the Select XPath button to the right of the Entries box to open the Select A Field Or Group dialog box, and double-click the d:Employees node.
6. Click the button to the right of the Display Name text box, and double-click the d:EmplName item. Your Drop-Down List Box Properties dialog box should appear as shown here:

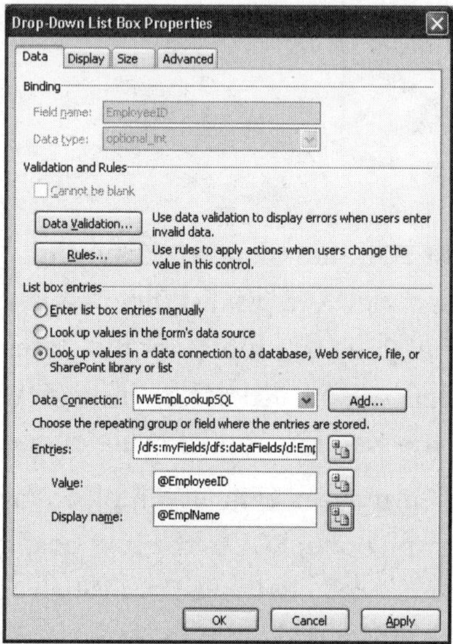

7. Click OK. Optionally, change the Ship Postal Code label to **Ship PostCode**, and decrease the width of column A to leave more width available for the drop-down list.
8. Save your design changes.

▶ Test the linked drop-down list

1. Open a form preview window, type a valid OrderID value, and click Run Query to verify that the drop-down list displays the correct employee name.
2. Change the employee name, and verify that the EmployeeID value changes, as shown here:

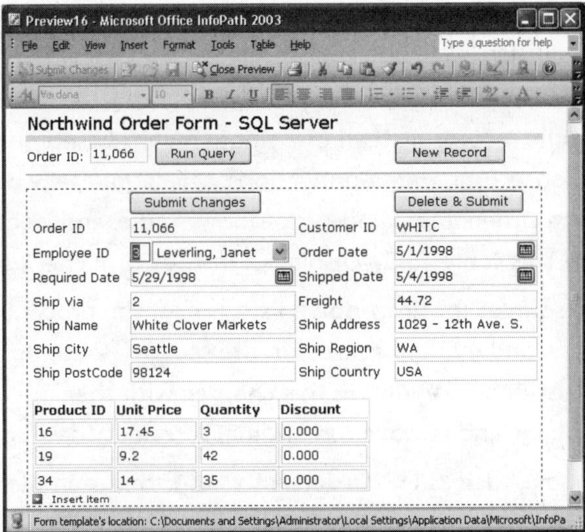

3. **Click Submit Changes, and then click Run Query to verify that the drop-down list is working correctly.**
4. **Close the preview window to return to design mode.**

Changing the Main Data Connection for a Form

You can change the main data connection for the form, if the new data source has the same or a similar structure and field names as the original. This feature is especially useful when you upsize Jet databases to SQL Server or need to change an SQL Server connection's server name from a test to a production server.

To change the data connection for a database from SQL Server to Jet, from Jet to SQL Server, or from one instance of SQL Server to another instance, follow these steps.

▶ Change the main data source from SQL Server to Jet, or vice versa

1. **Choose File, Save As, make a backup copy of your form, close the template, and reopen the original version in design mode.**
2. **Choose Tools, Convert Main Data Source to start the Data Connection Wizard.**
3. **Select the Database (Microsoft SQL Server Or Microsoft Office Access Only) option, and click Next.**
4. **Click Change Database to open the Select Data Source dialog box.**
5. **Repeat the steps of the procedure in the section "Using the Data Connection Wizard," earlier in this chapter, for the new database type. The preceding**

procedures use SQL Server, so this example changes the form to a Jet database by following steps 4 through 16 of the Jet database procedure.

6. If the data entry controls lose their bindings in this process, it's likely that the data connection is returning multiple records instead of a single record based on the query. To fix this problem, choose Tool, Data Connections, select your new data source, click Modify, select the Orders table and click Modify Table, and clear the Allow Multiple Records From This Table To Be Displayed In The Form check box.
7. If you added secondary data sources for drop-down lists, repeat the procedure "Create the employee name secondary data source" in the section "Creating Secondary Data Sources for List Boxes," earlier in this chapter, with the alternative secondary data source, and remove the original secondary data source.
8. Save your form with a new name, such as **NWOrdersJet.xsn** for this example, and name the form **Northwind Orders Form - Jet**

Chapter Summary

InfoPath's capability to create data-bound forms that you can use to edit, add, and delete records from Jet and SQL Server tables is useful for designing basic data entry applications. The Data Connection Wizard automates generation of a default form with Query and New Record buttons. A completed data entry section typically contains a section with controls for the parent table and, for a child table in a one-to-many relationship, a repeating table or section.

Data-bound forms are best suited to editing a single parent table record and, if needed, a single child table's records. Adding a Delete & Submit button lets you delete records, but deleting a record with dependent records requires specifying cascading deletions for the relationship or deleting dependent records before deleting the parent record.

InfoPath lets you create secondary data sources to populate list box controls from queries against tables in Jet and SQL Server databases. If you don't have a saved Jet query or SQL Server view to provide the secondary data source, you can write a custom SQL query to return the data structure you need.

You can change the main data connection for a form from, for example, a Jet to an SQL Server database that you upsize from Jet. You also must change the main data connection if you move an SQL Server database to another server or change from a test database to a production database.

Q&A

Q. Can I bind an InfoPath form to tables of databases other than Access or SQL Server 2000?

A. Yes, but you must write custom code to connect to other databases. An alternative for Oracle and other databases that have .NET native or ODBC data providers is to create a Microsoft ASP.NET XML Web service that connects to the Oracle database and use the Data Connection Wizard to consume the Web service. You'll find a detailed example of this approach at *www.perfectxml.com/InfoPathOracle.asp*.

Q. Is there any limit to the number of secondary data sources for an InfoPath form?

A. No. You can add as many secondary data sources as you need to populate list box controls. To minimize form opening delays and stress on the underlying database, it's a good practice to use static XML files for data that changes infrequently, such as U.S. states and their abbreviations, or countries and their ISO country codes.

Q. Can I populate a list box from an SQL Server 2000 stored procedure?

A. Yes, but you must write an EXEC *ProcName* statement in the Edit SQL Statement dialog box, and users must have *EXECUTE* permission for the procedure. Assigning database users to the *db_datawriter* role doesn't give them blanket *EXECUTE* permissions for the database.

On Your Own

Here are some additional exercises for enhancing your secondary data source and developing general form design skills:

1. Add drop-down lists populated by secondary data sources for selecting CustomerID values by CompanyName, ShipVia by CompanyName, and ProductID by ProductName.
2. Add an Extended expression box to calculate individual Order Details amounts and column totals as described in the section "Calculating Values with the Expression Box," in Chapter 6.
3. Add data validation rules to the form based on the examples in Chapter 8, "Validating Form Data."

CHAPTER 14

Designing InfoPath Web Service Clients

In this chapter, you will learn how to:

- **Describe InfoPath's XML Web service requirements and limitations**
- **Use the Data Connection Wizard and a UDDI registry to add a public XML Web service as a main data source**
- **Design a simple receive-only form based on an XML Web service**
- **Create a Web service main data source for receiving and submitting data**
- **Design a form that retrieves, updates, and inserts records in a Web service–enabled database**
- **Create secondary data sources from Web services to populate drop-down lists**

For more information:

- **Go to the Web Services Development Center at *msdn.microsoft.com/webservices/*, and choose Understanding Web Services, Web Service Basics to read background material on Microsoft's approach to XML Web service technology.**
- **Go to *www.oakleaf.ws/* for live online demonstrations of a wide range of XML Web services created with Visual Studio .NET. Most of these demonstration Web services have links to complete documentation for the ASP.NET Web services and online Web Forms clients.**

Service-oriented architecture (SOA) is a hot topic in the IT industry, and XML-based Web services are one of SOA's primary enablers. Most current applications for XML Web services involve server-to-server communication, but some—especially publicly available utility services—are well suited for server-to-desktop applications. As Web services gain industry-wide acceptance, interaction of desktop productivity applications with Web services will become a common method of communicating with networked servers. One of InfoPath 2003's initial design criteria was to provide an easy-to-use, flexible graphical user interface (GUI) for Web services. Microsoft's *InfoPath 2003 Product Guide* describes InfoPath as the "premier smart client for XML Web services."

To work through this chapter:

- You must be familiar with basic form layout practices and with adding sections and controls to forms.
- You need an Internet connection to consume the publicly available XML Web services for this chapter's procedures. A high-speed connection isn't required because the basic exercises don't send or receive large XML documents.
- You should have experience using the Microsoft InfoPath Data Connection Wizard to create forms from Microsoft Access (Jet) or SQL Server tables, as described in Chapter 13, "Connecting Forms to Databases."

This chapter assumes that you're familiar with basic Web services terminology, such as SOAP (formerly an acronym for Simple Object Access Protocol), Web Services Description Language (WSDL), and Universal Description, Discovery, and Integration (UDDI) services. If these terms are unfamiliar, check out the "For More Information" topics at the beginning of this chapter. You don't need experience with creating or consuming XML Web services applications–or writing script, or Visual Basic .NET code–to complete this chapter's examples.

Understanding InfoPath's Web Service Requirements

InfoPath imposes several restrictions on XML Web services that you can use to create main or secondary data sources without adding Visual Basic .NET code or script to your form. Following are the most important of the Data Connection Wizard's requirements for and restrictions of Web service data connections:

- The Web service must use the SOAP 1.1 *document/literal* (doc/lit) format. Web services have *style* and *use* attributes; the *style* value is either *document* or *rpc*, and the *use* value can be *literal* or *encoded*. (The abbreviation *rpc* is short for *remote procedure call*.) The doc/lit format defines exchanging XML messages with their structures defined by a schema in the WSDL document; doc/lit is the default style for ASP.NET Web services.
- The Web service can't include mandatory *SOAP headers*. SOAP headers are extensions to SOAP messages that, as an example, implement message routing and security features, such as digital signatures and message encryption. InfoPath disregards optional headers.

Using the Data Connection Wizard with XML Web Services

The Data Connection Wizard inspects the Web service's WSDL document to create the XML schema for a main or secondary data source. You can search Microsoft's UDDI 2.0 registry at *http://uddi.microsoft.com* to find Web services that meet your needs or type the URL for the WSDL document in a text box. If the Web service can't derive a schema from the WSDL file and the service requires parameters, you're prompted to provide parameter values. Unlike forms you create from Jet or SQL Server databases, the Data Connection Wizard doesn't add a New Record button.

The Data Connection Wizard supports the following three types of InfoPath forms that consume Web services:

- **Receive-only form** Sends a SOAP 1.1 request message to a Web service, receives SOAP 1.1 response messages, extracts the data from the SOAP 1.1 envelope, and displays the data in sections or layout tables with controls you add to the default form. The request message usually contains one or more parameters to specify the data to be returned. You can save the original or edited data as an InfoPath data document, but you can't submit the data to the Web service.
- **Submit-only form** Sends a SOAP 1.1 message that contains the data from controls bound to the data source to a Web service, but has no provision to display return values. A submit-only form usually performs create (insert) operations on tables in a Web service–enabled database. You add controls to enter new data and configure a submit button to send the data to the Web service.
- **Receive-and-submit form** Combines the features of receive-only and submit-only forms, but requires a common data structure. You specify the group that contains data common to both receive and submit operations in an additional step, and the wizard creates default Query and Data Entry views. As with submit-only forms, you must add and configure a submit button.

Designing a Simple Form to Receive Data

Receive-only forms you create from XML Web services are the simplest of the Data Connection Wizard's three supported form types. Most publicly accessible utility Web services, such as Cdyne Systems' AddressLookup service that's used in this section's procedure, don't permit submitting data. The AddressLookup ASP.NET Web service connects to a database of U.S. Postal Service (USPS) ZIP Code information and has several methods for performing individual operations, such as checking one-line or two addresses. If the address is found, the service returns USPS-standardized address data and related information. AddressLookup is a commercial Web service with monthly service and transaction fees, but Cdyne provides a test license key for evaluation purposes.

See Also You can learn more about the Cdyne AddressLookup Web service at *www.cdyne.com*. The InfoPath Web service client example for the Cdyne service is for test purposes only, and is not intended for commercial or production use.

Previewing the CheckAddress Web Method's SOAP Messages

The SOAP request message to AddressLookup's CheckAddress Web method has five parameters–*AddressLine*, *ZipCode*, *City*, *StateAbbrev*, and *LicenseKey*. *AddressLine* and *LicenseKey* are required; if you provide a *ZipCode* value, you can omit *City* and *StateAbbrev*. The test *LicenseKey* value is *0*. A typical SOAP test request message to the method looks like this:

```
<?xml version="1.0" encoding="utf-8"?>
<soap:Envelope xmlns:soap="http://schemas.xmlsoap.org/soap/envelope/"
    xmlns:xsi="http://www.w3.org/2001/XMLSchema-instance"
    xmlns:xsd="http://www.w3.org/2001/XMLSchema">
  <soap:Body>
   <CheckAddress xmlns="http://ws.cdyne.com/">
     <AddressLine>1300 Broadway</AddressLine>
      <ZipCode />
      <City>Oakland</City>
      <StateAbbrev>CA</StateAbbrev>
      <LicenseKey>0</LicenseKey>
    </CheckAddress>
  </soap:Body>
</soap:Envelope>
```

The method elicits a SOAP response message that contains the USPS's standard address format with ZIP+4 codes and related address information, as shown here:

```
<?xml version="1.0" encoding="utf-8"?>
<soap:Envelope xmlns:soap="http://schemas.xmlsoap.org/soap/envelope/"
    xmlns:xsi="http://www.w3.org/2001/XMLSchema-instance"
    xmlns:xsd="http://www.w3.org/2001/XMLSchema">
  <soap:Body>
    <CheckAddressResponse xmlns="http://ws.cdyne.com/">
      <CheckAddressResult>
        <ServiceError>false</ServiceError>
        <AddressError>false</AddressError>
        <Firm />
        <DeliveryAddress>1300 BROADWAY</DeliveryAddress>
        <PrimaryLow>1300</PrimaryLow>
        <PrimaryHigh>1312</PrimaryHigh>
        <PriEO>E</PriEO>
        <SecEO />
        <SecondaryLow />
        <SecondaryHigh />
        <Secondary />
        <Extra>BROADWAY</Extra>
        <City>OAKLAND</City>
        <StateAbbrev>CA</StateAbbrev>
        <ZipCode>94612-2501</ZipCode>
        <AddressFoundBeMoreSpecific>false</AddressFoundBeMoreSpecific>
        <CarrierRoute>C035</CarrierRoute>
        <County>ALAMEDA</County>
```

```
        <DeliveryPoint>99</DeliveryPoint>
        <CheckDigit>10</CheckDigit>
        <BarCode>f94612250110f</BarCode>
        <NeededCorrection>true</NeededCorrection>
        <CSKey>Z22296</CSKey>
        <RecordTypeCode>S</RecordTypeCode>
        <CongressDistrictNumber>09</CongressDistrictNumber>
        <FIPS>06001</FIPS>
        <FinanceNumber>055508</FinanceNumber>
        <FromLongitude>-122.272080</FromLongitude>
        <FromLatitude>37.804127</FromLatitude>
        <ToLongitude>-122.271780</ToLongitude>
        <ToLatitude>37.804827</ToLatitude>
        <AvgLongitude>-122.271930</AvgLongitude>
        <AvgLatitude>37.804477</AvgLatitude>
        <CMSA>7362</CMSA>
        <PMSA>5775</PMSA>
        <MSA>5775</MSA>
        <MA>084</MA>
        <TimeZone>PST</TimeZone>
        <hasDaylightSavings>true</hasDaylightSavings>
        <AreaCode>510</AreaCode>
        <LLCertainty>90</LLCertainty>
        <CountyNum>1</CountyNum>
        <PreferredCityName>OAKLAND</PreferredCityName>
        <CensusBlockNum>1001</CensusBlockNum>
        <CensusTractNum>4030.00</CensusTractNum>
        <Primary>1300</Primary>
        <PrefixDirection>
        </PrefixDirection>
        <StreetName>BROADWAY</StreetName>
        <Suffix>
        </Suffix>
        <PostDirection>
        </PostDirection>
      </CheckAddressResult>
    </CheckAddressResponse>
  </soap:Body>
</soap:Envelope>
```

Creating a Form Template from an UDDI-Registered Web Service

Follow these steps to create a single-view USPSAddress form based on the CheckAddress method of the AddressLookup Web service.

▶ Create the main data source from a UDDI lookup

1. **Start InfoPath, and click the Fill Out A Form dialog box's Design A Form link. Click the New From Data Connection link to open the Data Connection Wizard, select the Web Service option, and click Next.**
2. **Select the Receive Data option, and click Next.**

3. Click the Search UDDI button to open the Search Web Service dialog box. Leave the defaults in the two drop-down lists, and type **cdyne** in the Search For box. Click Search to display a list of Cdyne Web services registered with Microsoft's UDDI 2.0 site, and select the CDYNE::Address Correction for USA Addresses service entry, as shown here:

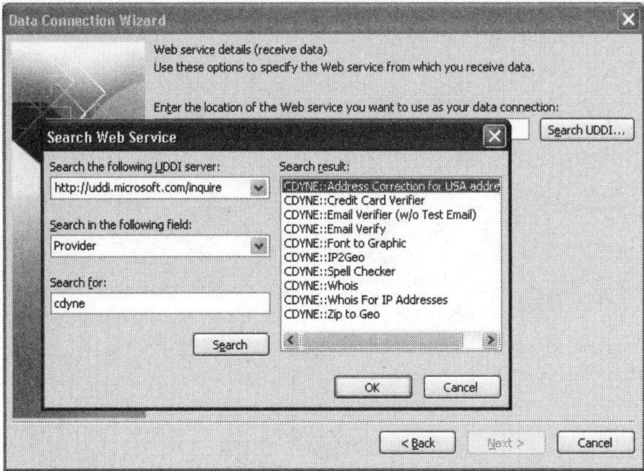

4. Click OK to close the dialog box and add the URL for the WSDL document, *http://ws.cdyne.com/psaddress/addresslookup.asmx?wsdl*, to the location box. (Microsoft ASP.NET Web services generate dynamic WSDL documents, which you access by adding a *?wsdl* suffix to the *ServiceName*.asmx file for the Web service. Most Java-based Web services have a static ServiceName.wsdl file.)

5. Click Next to display a list of Web methods supported by the Web service. Select the CheckAddress method to display its documentation in the Description Of Operation pane, as shown here:

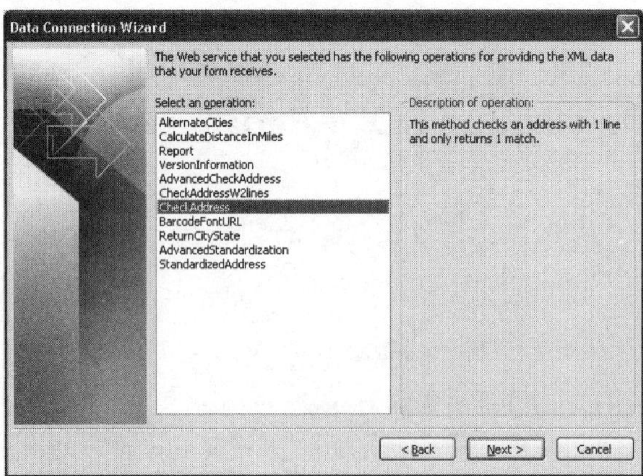

Working around a missing or an inoperable CheckAddress Web method
There is no guarantee that the AddressLocator service or CheckAddress method will continue to offer public access with the *0* test *LicenseKey* value. If you can't connect to the CheckAddress service or AddressLocator returns an error, you can open typical XML data documents in the final version of the USPSAddress.xsn template in the C:\Microsoft Press\Introducing InfoPath 2003\Chapter14\USPSAddress folder.

6. Click Next to display a summary screen. Type **CheckAddressWS** or the like in the name box, and click Finish to close the dialog and create the main data source and a default view for the service.

▶ Add bound controls to the default view

1. Type USPS Address Correction as the form's title, delete the title table's second row, and delete both layout tables.
2. Expand the queryFields node in the Data Source task pane. Drag the s0:CorrectedAddress group, which contains fields for the Web method's five parameters, above the Run Query button, and choose Controls In Layout Table from the menu that appears. Your form should appear as shown here:

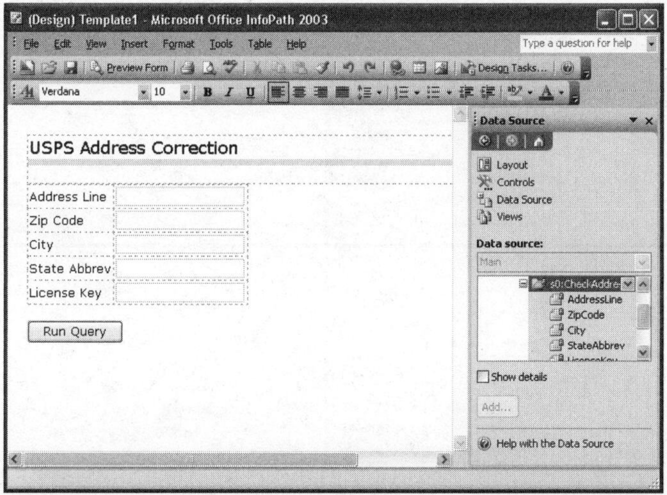

3. Add a column to the table to contain the text boxes for the corresponding SOAP response message values.
4. In the Data Sources task pane, scroll to and expand the dataFields node and its subnodes. Drag the DeliveryAddress field to column C, row 1, and delete its label.
5. Repeat step 4 for the ZipCode, City, and StateAbbrev fields, placing them in rows 2 through 4, and then close the task pane.
6. Delete Line from the Address Line label, change Zip to ZIP, and remove Abbrev and Key from the labels.

7. Increase the width of columns B and C to make room for longer addresses, and adjust the width of the text boxes to suit their content. Your form should now look like this:

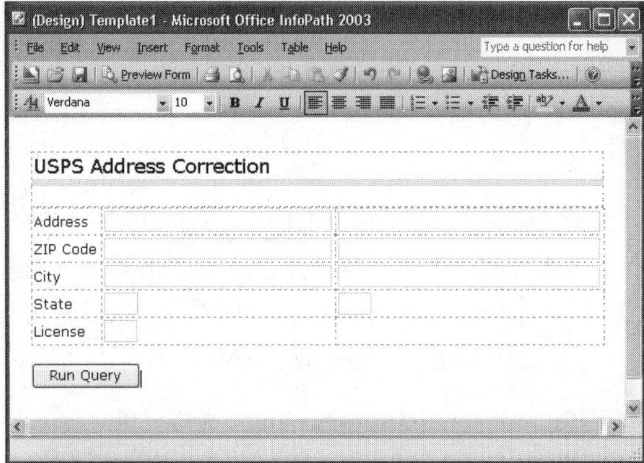

8. Click Preview Form, type a known-good address, with or without a ZIP Code, and 0 as the License in the column A text boxes, and click Run Query to consume the AddressLookup service's CheckAddress Web method. Your preview window should look similar to this:

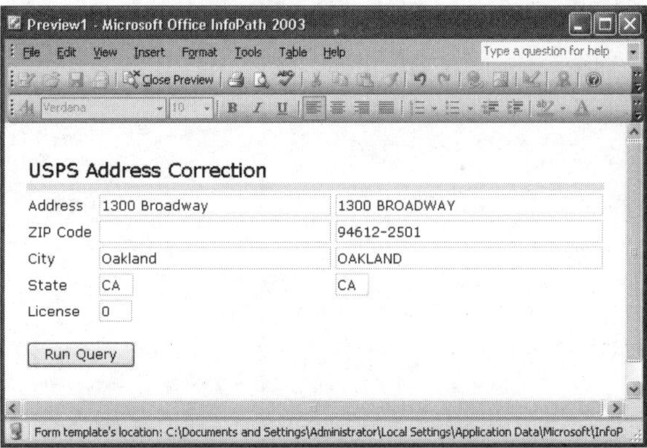

9. Save your template with an appropriate name in a new My Documents\Infopath subfolder named USPSAddress as USPSAddress.xsn or the like, and name the template USPSAddress - Test1.

Detecting addresses with multiple entries

The CheckAddress Web method returns only the Address values you typed and doesn't provide the USPS-standardized address values, if the postal address has multiple entries. If you encounter this situation, try an address for a private residence. The AddressLookup service has another Web method, AdvancedCheckAddress, that returns an array of entries for a single address.

In your C:\Microsoft Press\Introducing InfoPath 2003\Chapter14\USPSAddress folder, you'll find a completed version of the USPSAddress.xsn template and a copy of the WSDL document for the service, AddressLookup.wsdl, which you can open with Internet Explorer. There's also a 1200Broadway.xml file that you can open in Internet Explorer, in case you can't connect to the Cdyne service.

Creating a Form That Receives and Submits Data

Creating a Web service–based InfoPath form that receives and submits persistent data usually requires access to a database service that enables updates. InfoPath data documents generated from Web service–enabled databases have a more conventional structure than those created by the direct database connections that use InfoPath's ADOAdapter. The OakLeaf XML Web services demonstration site provides a NWOrdersWS Web service that permits editing and updating a very large version of the NorthwindCS sample database. The database contains about 200,000 Orders records and 500,000 Order Details records. The Web service uses SQL Server stored procedures to retrieve, update, and create new Orders and Order Details records.

See Also For more information about the database back-end design and data object structures for the NWOrdersWS Web service, see the article "Optimizing SQL Server Data Access," at *www.ftponline.com/vsm/2003_11/magazine/features/jennings/*.

Understanding SOAP Messages from Serialized Objects

Following is the SOAP request message to the GetOrderSP Web method that returns data from a single Orders record and its Order Details records:

```
<?xml version="1.0" encoding="utf-8"?>
<soap:Envelope xmlns:soap="http://schemas.xmlsoap.org/soap/envelope/"
    xmlns:xsi="http://www.w3.org/2001/XMLSchema-instance"
    xmlns:xsd="http://www.w3.org/2001/XMLSchema">
  <soap:Body>
    <GetOrderSP xmlns="http://oakleaf.ws/nworderws">
      <intOrderID>1445151</intOrderID>
    </GetOrderSP>
  </soap:Body>
</soap:Envelope>
```

The SOAP response message contains a serialized Order object within the <GetOrderSPResult> element. The term serialize means to create a hierarchical XML document from an instance of a class or type; deserializing creates a class or type instance from an XML document. Here's an example of the SOAP response message returned from the preceding request message:

```
<?xml version="1.0" encoding="utf-8"?>
<soap:Envelope xmlns:soap="http://schemas.xmlsoap.org/soap/envelope/"
    xmlns:xsi="http://www.w3.org/2001/XMLSchema-instance"
    xmlns:xsd="http://www.w3.org/2001/XMLSchema">
  <soap:Body>
    <GetOrderSPResponse xmlns="http://oakleaf.ws/nworderservice">
      <GetOrderSPResult>
        <OrderID>1445151</OrderID>
        <CustomerID>SPLIR</CustomerID>
        <EmployeeID>5</EmployeeID>
        <OrderDate>1996-08-01T00:00:00.0000000-07:00</OrderDate>
        <RequiredDate>1996-08-29T00:00:00.0000000-07:00</RequiredDate>
        <ShippedDate>1996-08-01T00:00:00.0000000-07:00</ShippedDate>
        <ShipVia>2</ShipVia>
        <Freight>4.54</Freight>
        <ShipName>Split Rail Beer &amp; Ale</ShipName>
        <ShipAddress>P.O. Box 555</ShipAddress>
        <ShipCity>Lander</ShipCity>
        <ShipRegion>WY</ShipRegion>
        <ShipPostalCode>82520</ShipPostalCode>
        <ShipCountry>USA</ShipCountry>
        <OrderDetails>
          <OrderDetail>
            <OrderID>1445151</OrderID>
            <ProductID>22</ProductID>
            <UnitPrice>5</UnitPrice>
            <Quantity>10</Quantity>
            <Discount>0</Discount>
            <Discount>0</Discount>
          </OrderDetail>
        </OrderDetails>
      </GetOrderSPResult>
    </GetOrderSPResponse>
  </soap:Body>
</soap:Envelope>
```

The UpdateOrInsertOrderSP Web method accepts a SOAP request message that's almost identical to the preceding response message. The difference is that a single *<UpdateOrInsertOrderSP ...>* element replaces the *<GetOrderSPResponse ...>* and *<GetOrderSPResult>* elements within the *</soap:Body>* element. Specifying 0 as the *<OrderID>* element's value adds a new order to the database when you click the submit button.

Creating a Data Source and Form Template from a WSDL Document

To create a main data source and a receive-and-submit form from the NWOrdersWS services' GetOrderSP and UpdateOrInsertOrderSP Web methods and then test the form, follow these steps.:

▶ **Create the main data source from a URL**

1. Start InfoPath, and click the Fill Out A Form dialog box's Design A Form link. Click the New From Data Connection link to open the Data Connection Wizard, select the From A Web Service option, and click Next. Leave the default Receive And Submit Data Option, and click Next again.
2. Type the URL for the WSDL document—**http://www.oakleaf.ws/nworderssws/nworderssws.asmx?wsdl** for this example—in the location box, and click Next.
3. Select the Web method for the receive data operation—GetOrderSP for this example—as shown here. (You'll use the other Get methods to populate drop-down lists in the next section, "Using Web Services as Secondary Data Sources.")

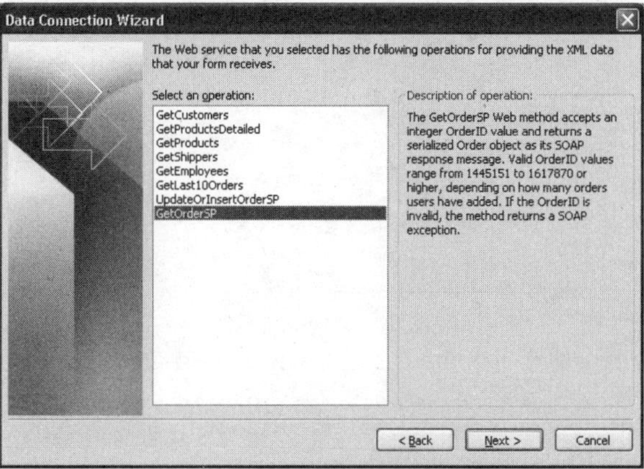

4. Click Next, type **GetOrderSP** as the data connection name, and click Next again to specify the submit data Web method.
5. Leave the URL you typed in step 2, and click Next again.
6. Select the UpdateOrInsertOrderSP Web method, as shown here:

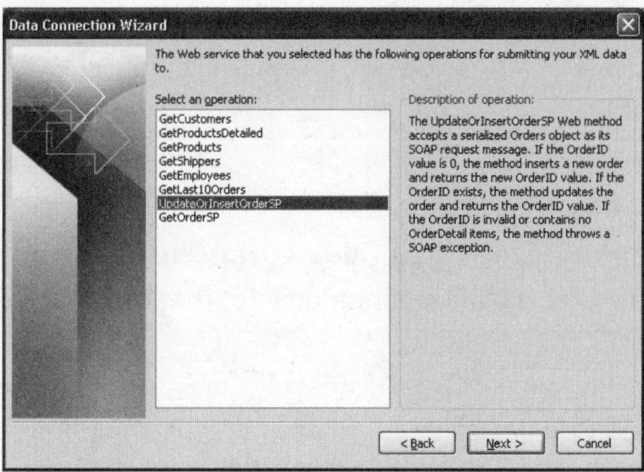

7. Click Next to open the wizard's Parameters screen, and click the Modify button next to the Fields Or Group box to open the Select A Field Or Group dialog box. You specify the group that returns an *Order* object when submitting data to the service.
8. Expand the dataFields node to display the source data for submission—GetOrderSPResult for this example—and select the group, as shown here:

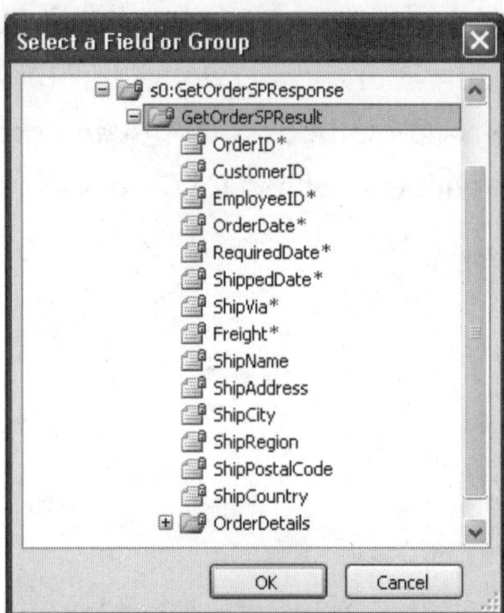

9. Click OK to add the XPath expression for the group to the Field Or Group box, as shown here:

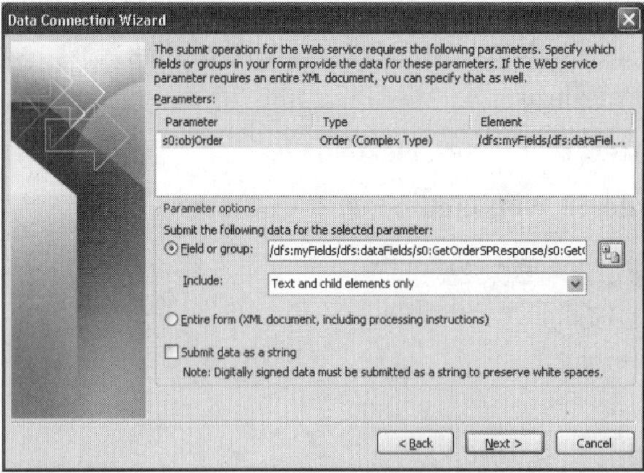

10. Click Next to display the Summary screen, type **UpdateOrInsertOrderSP** in the Name box, and click Finish to create the main data source for the form and display the default view.

▶ Add the query and data entry text boxes

1. Change the title of the form to **Northwind Traders Order Entry and Editing** or the like, remove the second row of the title table, split the upper layout table into

three columns and two rows, and delete the second layout table. Merge the three cells of row 2, and insert a horizontal line.

2. Expand the queryFields node in the Data Source task pane, and drag the intOrderID field to column A, row 1. Remove *Int* from the label, reduce the width of the Order ID text box, and drag the Run Query button to column B, row 1.
3. Expand the dataFields node, drag GetOrderSPResult to below the layout table, and select Section to add a section bound to the *Order* object's data fields.
4. Drag GetOrderSPResult to the added section, and choose Controls in Layout Table from the menu.
5. Expand the OrderDetails node, drag the OrderDetail repeating group to below the layout table, and choose Repeating Table from the menu.
6. Widen the data entry table, split column B into three columns, and rearrange the columns as you did in the section "Adding Controls to a Default Form," in Chapter 13.
7. Reduce the width of the repeating table's columns to suit their contents. Your template should appear as shown here:

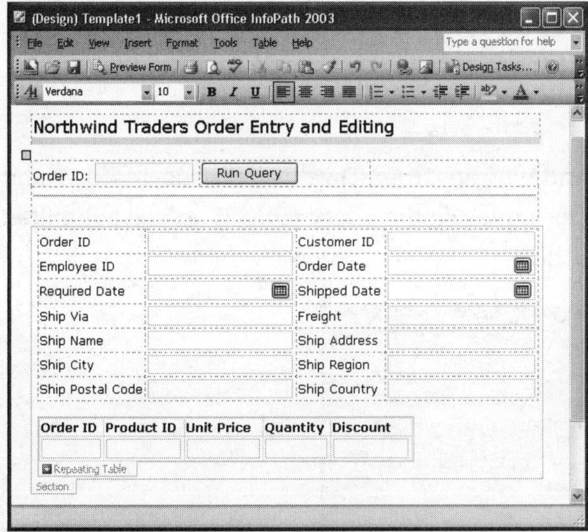

8. Add a button control to column C of the query layout table. Right-click the button, and choose Button Properties from the shortcut menu to open the Button Properties dialog box. Change the Label to **Submit to Web Service**, and select Submit from the Actions list to open the Submitting Forms dialog box.
9. Select Submit To A Web Service, leave UpdateOrInsertOrderSP as the data connection, and clear the Enable The Submit Menu Item On The File Menu check box, as shown on the next page.

(Don't add the custom success and failure messages you specified for the database example in Chapter 13. You need the ability to display message details for the custom SOAP exceptions the service returns when an error occurs.)

10. **Click OK twice to apply the changes, and reduce the width of the Submit To Web Service button.**
11. **Save your template as NWOrdersWS.xsn in a new My Documents\InfoPath\NWOrdersWS subfolder, name the template NWOrdersWS - Test1, and it.**

▶ Test data retrieval, updates, and inserts

1. **Reopen NWOrdersWS.xsn, and type an Order ID value between 1445151 and 1617870—1445152 for this example—in the query table. If no one has edited the record, your form looks like this:**

2. **Make a change to a value, such as Freight, and click Submit To Web Service. Click OK to dismiss the success message.**
3. **Click Run Query again to confirm that your change updated the Orders record.**
4. **Type 0 in the Order ID box below the horizontal line, and click Submit to Web Service to test inserting a new order. (You can't verify the addition, because InfoPath doesn't accept the new order number that the method returns. You'll almost solve this problem in the next section.)**
5. **Test the GetOrderSP method's custom SOAP exception by typing an invalid Order ID query value, such as 100, in the text box and clicking Submit To Web Service. You receive an error message similar to this when you click the Details button:**

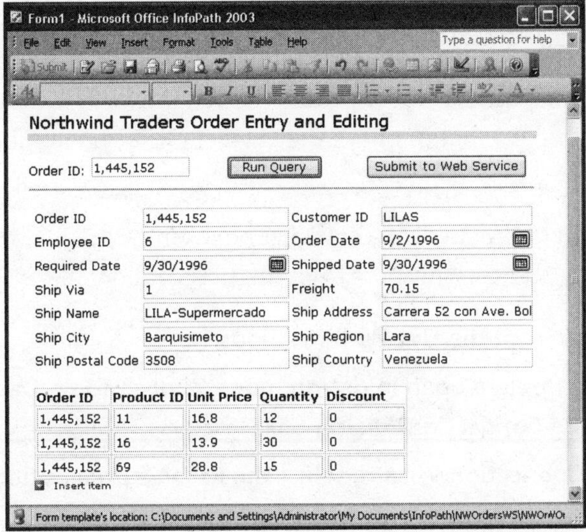

6. **Repeat step 4, but type 100 in the Order ID box to receive an error message similar to that shown in step 5.**
7. **Repeat step 6, but type 0 in the Order ID box, and delete all OrderDetail items. You'll receive this error message *The Order object must have at least one OrderDetail element.***
8. **Add an OrderDetail element with 0 as the Order ID; add an invalid Product ID value, such as 100; and add values for Unit Price, Quantity, and Discount. You'll receive a *SQLClient exception, transaction rolled back* error message. The Web service throws the same exception for invalid Customer ID, Employee ID, and Ship Via codes.**

Unlike forms that connect to database tables, child records require foreign key values, so you can't remove the Order ID column of the repeating table.

Using Web Services as Secondary Data Sources

You can use Web service methods to create a secondary data source that populate drop-down lists. Creating a secondary data source from a Web method with the Data Connection Wizard is similar to the process you used for database tables and queries in the section "Creating Secondary Data Sources for List Boxes," in Chapter 13.

The NWOrdersWS service has five Web methods designed for secondary data source use: GetCustomers, GetProducts, GetProductsDetailed, GetShippers, GetEmployees, and GetLast10Orders. All but the GetLast10Orders method return a serialized object; GetLast10Orders returns an array of integers. A drop-down list of the last 10 orders added to the database is useful to populate a list box that aids in guessing the OrderID value of records you insert in the database. Guesswork is required because the secondary data sources load when you open the form, so newly added orders don't appear in the list unless you close and reopen the form. Updating the form with an added Orders record that displays the correct Order ID text box values requires adding code.

To add secondary data sources to populate drop-down list boxes from the GetLast10Orders, GetEmployees, and GetShippers Web methods, follow these steps.

▶ Add secondary data sources from the Get Web methods

1. **With the NWOrdersWS.xsn template open in design mode, choose Tools, Data Connections to open the Data Connections dialog box.**
2. **Click Add to start the Data Connection Wizard, select the Receive Data option, click Next, select the Web Service option, and click Next again.**
3. **Type http://www.oakleaf.ws/nwordersws/nwordersws.asmx?wsdl in the Location box, copy the URL to the Clipboard for reuse, and click Next.**
4. **Select the GetLast10Orders method, which has no parameters, and click Next.**
5. **Remove Get from the Enter A Name For This Data Connection box, and click Finish to add the secondary data source to the Secondary Data Sources dialog box's list.**
6. **Repeat steps 2 through 5 for the GetEmployees and GetShippers methods. If you have a high-speed Internet connection, add the GetCustomers and GetProducts methods, which have much larger SOAP response messages.**
7. **Click Close to close the Data Connections dialog box.**

▶ Add drop-down list boxes for three secondary data sources

1. **Drag a drop-down list box from the Controls task pane to the right of the upper Order ID text box. The Drop-Down List Box Binding dialog box opens.**
2. **Expand the queryFields node, select intOrderID as the bound field, and click OK.**

3. Remove the list's label, reduce the list's width, and adjust the size of the table cells to accommodate the added control.
4. Right-click the list box, and choose Drop-Down List Box Properties from the shortcut menu to open the dialog box of the same name. Select the Look Up In A Data Connection To A Database, Web Service, File, Or SharePoint Library Or List option.
5. Open the Data Connection list, select Last10Orders, and click the Select XPath button to the right of the Entries box to open the Select A Field Or Group dialog box. Select the int result node, which is a repeating field of integer array values, and click OK. Default self-references (periods or dots) appear in the Value and Display Name text boxes, as shown on the next page.

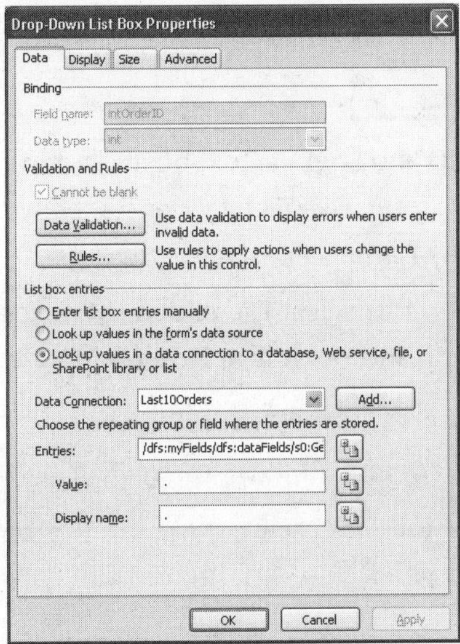

6. Click OK to close the dialog box, right-click the Order ID text box, and choose Properties from the shortcut menu to open its Properties dialog box. Click Format, clear the Use A Digit Grouping Symbol check box, and click OK twice to close the dialog boxes. Also remove the digit grouping symbol from the second Order ID boxes in the data entry section and the repeating table. Optionally, format the Freight and Unit Price text boxes as Currency, and format the Discount text box as Percentage.
7. Click Preview Form, open the added list box, select one of the last orders, and click Run Query to check the Order ID value. Your preview window, with all numeric formatting applied, should look like the figure on the next page.

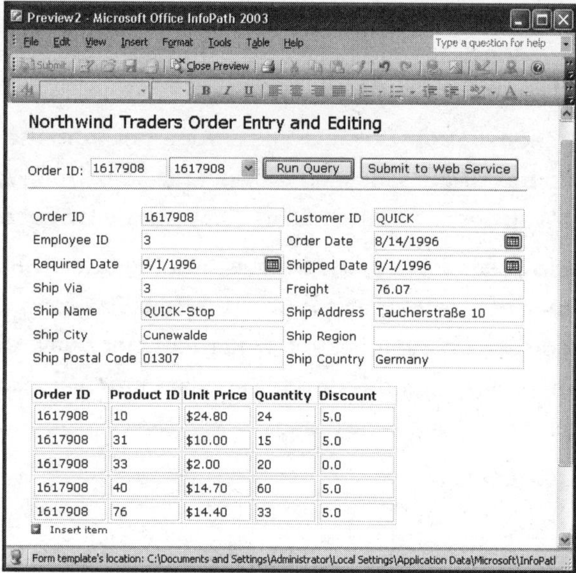

8. **Repeat steps 1 through 5 for the Employee ID and Ship Via text boxes, but in step 5, select the Employee and Shipper repeating groups, respectively, and specify the emplName and shipNamefield as the Display Name values, respectively.**
9. **Save your template changes, and open a new form. Test the added list boxes, save the XML data document as *NWOrderID*.xml, and open it in Notepad to view the data structure.**

Your C:\Microsoft Press\Introducing InfoPath 2003\Chapter14\NWOrdersWS folder contains a copy of the WSDL document for the service, NWOrdersWS.wsdl, and a modified data document, 1445152.xml, which you can open in Internet Explorer for easier reading.

See Also Chapter 17, "Writing Advanced Event Handlers," describes an enhanced version of the NWOrdersWS Web service client that uses managed code behind the form to improve its ease of use. The C:\Microsoft Press\Introducing InfoPath 2003\Chapter24\NWOrdersWS folder includes the Visual Basic .NET source code for the NWOrdersWS ASP.NET XML Web service, which connects to a local instance of SQL Server 2000's Northwind or MSDE's NorthwindCS database. SQL scripts to create the required stored procedures are in the same folder.

Chapter Summary

InfoPath is the first general-purpose GUI for XML Web services that's designed for Windows users rather than developers. The Data Connection Wizard automates the process of designing receive-only, submit-only, and receive-and-submit forms that consume document/literal XML Web services. Creating a single-view, receive-only form from a public XML Web service takes only a few minutes. Receive-and-submit forms take a bit more design effort and don't support New Record or Delete & Submit buttons without adding code to the template. Despite a few other limitations, such as the inability to handle mandatory SOAP headers without writing code, InfoPath can consume most publicly available document/literal Web services. InfoPath also enables creating secondary data sources from document/literal Web services so you can add Web service–populated drop-down lists that are bound to data entry controls.

Q&A

Q. Where can I find more public Web services that work with InfoPath?

A. Try the XMethods Web service registry, at *www.xmethods.com*. Most listed services that specify DOC as the Style value will create receive-only InfoPath forms. The AddressLocator Web service is listed in XMethods's registry. Click the FULL LIST link on the home page, and search for cchenoweth. Click Find Next until you encounter the Postal Address Correction link.

Q. Can I preview a Web service's WSDL document to determine whether it's compatible with InfoPath?

A. Yes. ASP.NET provides a WSDL help document that you can read in Internet Explorer. Type the URL for the .asmx file, but don't include the *?wsdl* suffix. As an example, type http://www.oakleaf.ws/nworderssws/nworderssws.asmx in Internet Explorer to display the help document for the NWOrdersWS service. If the service has a static WSDL file, open it in Internet Explorer, search for *style=* and *use=*, and verify that the attribute values are *document* and *literal*, respectively.

Q. Can InfoPath handle serialized ADO.NET *Dataset* objects as the SOAP message payload for data retrieval and updates?

A. Yes, but *Dataset* objects are related to disconnected ADO recordsets and include a proprietary XML schema for the *Dataset* object that's embedded in the SOAP message. Web services that send or receive *Dataset* objects aren't interoperable with conventional XML Web services running on non-Windows platforms or created with programming frameworks other than .NET. The object structures serialized and deserialized by the NWOrdersWS Web service can be created with Java and any compatible relational database running under UNIX, Linux, or Windows.

Q. How do I handle unknown (Null) date values, such as Shipped Date, with InfoPath?

A. Date picker controls require a date value, unless the data source's WSDL document specifies date values as *nillable*, and the XML Schema specification doesn't define or permit a Null date value. The WSDL document generated by ASP.NET for the NWOrdersWS Web service doesn't add the *nillable=true* attribute to RequiredDate or ShippedDate, so the InfoPath schema that's inferred from the WSDL document doesn't include these attributes.

ASP.NET Web services return *0001-01-01T00:00:00.0000000-08:00* as the *dateTime* value for *NULL* SQL Server *datetime* or Jet DateTime column values. (*-08:00* is the offset from GMT or UCT for Pacific Standard time and varies with your time zone; open the NullDate.xml data document in your ...\Chapter14\NWOrdersWS folder to see an example.) InfoPath's date picker control doesn't recognize this date, and converts a typed 1/1/0001 short date value to 1/1/2001.

The only safe workaround for this problem is to detect January 1 of any year (or 0001 and 2001) in the Web service code and update the table column with a *NULL* value. (The UpdateOrInsertOrderSP Web method implements this workaround. Run a query, type 1/1/0001 in the Required Date or Shipped Date date picker text box, submit an update, and requery the NWOrdersWS Web service.)

Q. Can I add a digital signature to a Web service–based form?

A. Yes, if you submit the data document as text (*string*) to a Web service that's capable of processing a text message and verifying the signature. A string is required because the white space (spaces, tabs, and newline characters) in the message must be preserved. If the Web service requires a complex type, such as a serialized *Orders* object, with digital signatures, data encryption, or both, you must download the Microsoft Web Services Enhancements (WSE) 2.0 add-in from *msdn.microsoft.com/webservices/* and write Visual Basic .NET or C# code to create InfoPath consumer applications that implement the WS-Security specifications. Using WSE 2.0 with InfoPath forms is beyond the scope of this book.

On Your Own

Here are suggestions for additional exercises with forms based on XML Web services:

1. Use conditional formatting to disable the USPSAddress.xsn template's Run Query button unless the Address and ZIP Code text boxes have entries or Address, City and State values are present. Assign tab order 1 through 3 to the query text boxes, and make all returned data text boxes read-only.
2. Modify the design of the USPSAddress.xsn template by adding controls bound to additional data fields, such as County, CarrierRoute, CheckDigit, ServiceError, and AddressError.
3. Add to the NWOrdersWS.xsn template Customer ID and Product ID drop-down lists that you populate from the NWOrdersWS service's GetCustomers and GetProducts methods.
4. Apply the conditional formatting rules from the section "Disabling Buttons with Conditional Formatting," in Chapter 13, to the NWOrdersWS.xsn template.

PART IV

Programming InfoPath Forms

Part IV introduces you to the InfoPath 2003 Toolkit for Visual Studio .NET, which enables substituting managed Visual Basic .NET or Visual C# code for VBScript or JavaScript to implement business logic behind InfoPath forms. You learn how to write and debug simple Visual Basic .NET event-handling procedures, explore the InfoPath Document Object Model (DOM), design procedures that use XPath to retrieve and update DOM data, and create a complete XML Web service client/server solution with a full-featured Web service that runs on your development computer.

CHAPTER 15

Introducing InfoPath Form Template Projects

In this chapter, you will learn how to:

- **Describe the advantages of InfoPath projects that use .NET managed code instead of JScript or VBScript for form event handling.**
- **Create a new InfoPath project, and write a simple Visual Basic .NET event handler for the *OnClick* event of a button control.**
- **Write handlers for the *OnBeforeChange* and *OnAfterChange* events of field values that update the values of other fields with ISO 8601–formatted *date* and *dateTime* values.**
- **Create an InfoPath project from an existing template, write a handler for the *OnAfterChange* event that fires when you add an optional repeating section to a form, and add default RFC1123-formatted *dateTime* values to a *string* field.**
- **Resolve conflicts that occur when opening multiple versions of the same template in data entry mode; copy InfoPath projects from one location to another; create release versions of projects; and publish projects to shared folders, Web servers, and Windows SharePoint Services form libraries.**

For more information:

- **See the index topic "Date and Time Format Strings" in the .NET Framework's help file for more information about the *DateTime* object's formatting options.**
- **Refer to the MSXML 4 Core Services documentation to learn more about the *IXMLDOMNode* and *IXMLDOMNodeList* objects for navigating the XML tree of InfoPath data sources. Search *msdn.microsoft.com* for the term *"MSXML 4.0 SDK"* (include the quotation marks), click the MSXML 4.0 SDK link to open the introduction to the SDK, and scroll to and click the Program With DOM In Visual Basic link for a Visual Basic 6/VBA tutorial.**

To work through this chapter:

- You need Microsoft Visual Basic .NET Standard 2003 or Microsoft Visual Studio .NET Professional 2003 or later installed on your local computer. This chapter refers to both versions as Visual Studio.
- You must download and install the InfoPath 2003 Toolkit for Visual Studio .NET (Toolkit) after installing InfoPath SP-1. The Toolkit is available for download at no charge from a link at *www.microsoft.com/infopath/*.
- You should have experience writing Microsoft Visual Basic 6 code or, preferably, Microsoft Visual Basic for Applications (VBA) code, and familiarity with MSXML Core Services 3 or later and programming the XML Document Object Model (XML DOM). The chapters in Part IV assume that you'll be more comfortable writing Visual Basic .NET code than C# code.
- You should have a working knowledge of elementary Visual Basic .NET programming techniques in the Microsoft Development Environment for .NET and be familiar with .NET Framework 1.1's namespaces and classes. You don't need to be a Visual Basic .NET expert.
- Some experience writing Visual Basic .NET code for Microsoft Excel 2003 or Microsoft Word 2003 projects with the Microsoft Visual Studio Tools for the Microsoft Office System (VSTO) is useful, but not essential.
- You should have installed the sample files from the CD that accompanies this book to provide the data sources for the procedures in this chapter. These folders also contain code snippets that you can paste into the event handler examples.

Several earlier chapters discuss the need to add programming code to Microsoft Office InfoPath 2003 forms to handle tasks that you can't accomplish with InfoPath's declarative programming model. The declarative programming features added by InfoPath 2003 Service Pack 1 (SP-1)–such as the Insert Formula dialog box, event-based rules, and user roles–substantially reduce the need to add programming code to forms. The InfoPath 2003 release version supported only JScript or VBScript programming with the Microsoft Script Editor (MSE). SP-1 lets you create InfoPath 2003 Projects, which substitute managed Visual Basic .NET or C# code for script. You must install the Toolkit to take advantage of SP-1's managed code features.

> **Programming InfoPath forms with JScript or VBScript**
>
> If you're an experienced JScript or VBScript programmer, you might want to apply your scripting skills to form programming. The sample forms installed by InfoPath include JScript event handlers and general-purpose functions that you can use as models for programming your forms. The majority of the InfoPath programming documentation provides JScript—rather than VBScript—examples, which is an odd language choice for an Office application. It's much easier for Office developers to apply their VBA skills to VBScript programming than to JScript programming.
>
> Regardless of your scripting experience, Microsoft Visual C# and Visual Basic .NET are Microsoft's preferred programming languages (in that order, unfortunately), and they represent the future of Microsoft Windows application development. Future versions of InfoPath are likely to be full-fledged .NET implementations; if so, managed code for implementing business logic probably will be a requirement, not an option.

The chapters in Part IV use Visual Basic .NET for all procedures, because most Office developers are accustomed to writing VBA code to automate Office applications. Visual Basic .NET has full parity with C# as a programming language, although each language has a few features that are missing in the other. For example, Visual Basic .NET supports *With ... End With* constructs; C# doesn't. C# offers XML comments, which aren't available in Visual Basic .NET. Building .NET assemblies with either language generates identical Microsoft Intermediate Language (MSIL) code, which the just-in-time (JIT) compiler converts to the same machine-language instructions. Neither language offers a significant performance benefit or penalty.

Comparing Managed .NET Code and Script

The primary distinction between managed .NET code and script is how the code executes: .NET code is compiled, and script is interpreted. A language compiler translates .NET source code into MSIL, and the Common Language Runtime (CLR) JIT-compiles the MSIL to executable (machine) code for a specific processor, such as the 32-bit Intel Pentium or 64-bit AMD Opteron series. The JIT compilation process generates machine code on an as-needed basis; the first time a subprocedure or function executes, the JIT-compiled machine code is cached for reuse. An interpreter reads successive lines of script code and translates each line to machine code every time the script runs. In most cases, compiled code executes faster than interpreted code.

The most important benefits of managed code for InfoPath developers are much easier debugging and early object binding, which enables Microsoft IntelliSense in Visual Studio for statement completion. Building and running managed code opens the form in preview mode. When execution reaches a breakpoint, Visual Studio receives the focus to let you determine the value of variables or object properties at that point. Continuing past the breakpoint returns the focus to the form preview. Another advantage of managed code is that your source code isn't easily accessible to InfoPath users or your competitors. The template stores a reference to an *assembly*, which is a dynamic-link library (DLL) that contains program metadata and MSIL, not source code. Although it's possible to decompile MSIL, you can make it very difficult for others to reverse-engineer your MSIL code with the Dotfuscator obfuscation tool that's included with Visual Studio.

Substituting managed code for script also enables strong typing, which isn't turned on by default for Visual Basic .NET. To enforce strong typing, you must add an *Option Strict On* statement at the beginning of the code or set a language compiler option to enforce strong typing for all Visual Basic .NET projects. When you declare all variables with their data or object types, the language compiler won't let you set the variable's value to a different type. Strong typing prevents declaring variables of the *Object* data type, the .NET equivalent of VBA's *Variant* data type. JScript and VBScript are loosely typed; variables assume the type of the values you assign to them and can change data or object types without notice. Strong typing improves code execution performance and minimizes the potential for run-time errors.

The .NET Framework provides myriad useful classes and methods that aren't present in JScript or VBScript. For example, the InfoPath sample forms require custom *getDateString* and *getTimeString* functions to return date and time in the ISO 8601 pattern that's required by fields of the *xsd:date* and *xsd:dateTime* datatypes. The .NET Framework's *DateTime* class provides standard date/time formatters to return ISO 8601, RFC1123, and many other patterns. RFC1123 is the date format used in the RSS 2.0 examples in this and the preceding chapters. The sections "Responding to *OnAfterChange* Events" and "Taking Action Based on the Value of Another Field," later in this chapter, contain ISO 8601 formatting examples. The section "Adding Managed Code to an Existing Form" demonstrates RFC1123 formatting.

A minor downside of adding managed code to InfoPath templates is the requirement to install the run-time version of the .NET Framework 1.1 on users' computers to provide required classes, and JIT-compile the assembly when the form loads. The 108 MB run-time .NET Framework 1.1 is freely distributable so you can put the Setup.exe file on a server share and instruct users to install it, or users can download .NET Framework 1.1 from the Microsoft Windows Update site, at *windowsupdate.microsoft.com*.

Adding Managed Code Behind a Form

After you install the Toolkit, you can add managed code to an imported copy of an existing form or create a new form in Visual Studio's integrated development environment (IDE). When you open the New Project dialog box, you'll find that the Toolkit has added a new Microsoft Office System Projects icon to the Project Types list, which contains subfolders for Visual Basic and Visual C# projects and an InfoPath Form Template icon, as shown in Figure 15-1. (Installing the VSTO also adds this folder and three template icons for Excel and Word 2003.) If you're using Visual Basic .NET Standard, only Visual Basic Projects appear in the list.

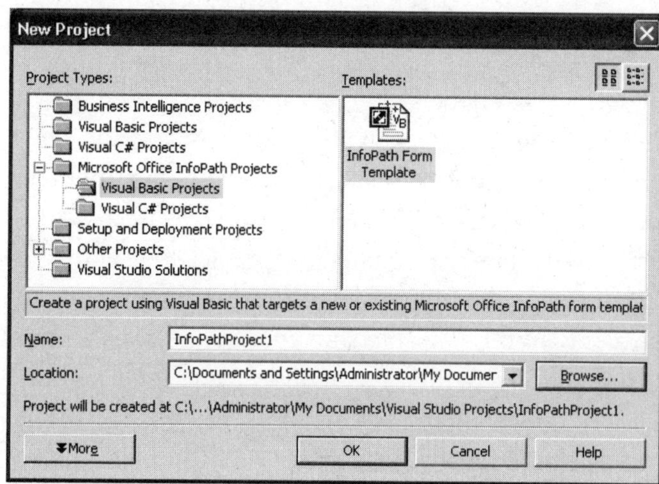

Figure 15-1 The Toolkit adds an InfoPath Form Template icon for Visual Basic and, if installed, Visual C#, and supplies default values for the project name and its folders.

Accepting default settings for the project and clicking OK opens the single screen of the Microsoft Office Project Wizard, which lets you choose between importing a copy of an existing form or creating a new form. Importing a form with JScript or VBScript code disables script operation, but the .js or .vbs files remain in the template file for reference when you replace the script's methods with Visual Basic .NET code. If you select the Create A New Form Template option, the project opens with an empty InfoPathProject1 form in design mode in front of Visual Studio's InfoPathProject1FormCode window, as shown in Figure 15-2. Solution Explorer displays the working file set created by the Toolkit.

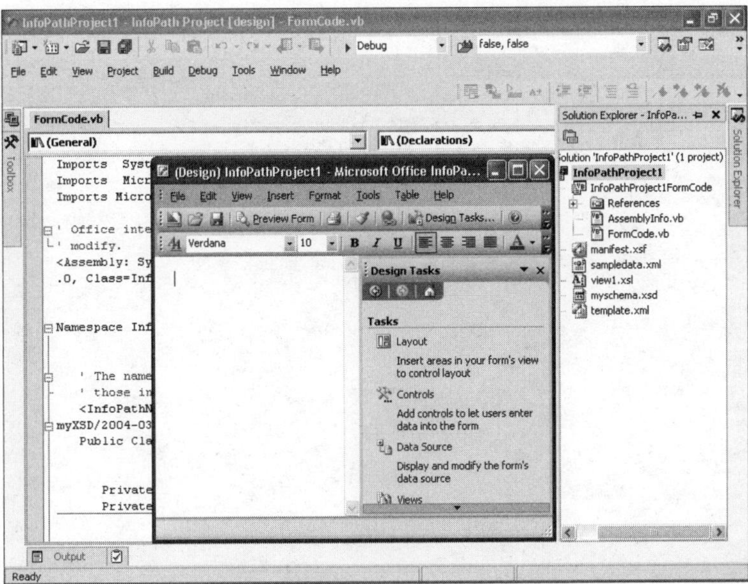

Figure 15-2 Creating a new form template with the default project name opens a new InfoPathProject1 template in design mode and displays the files added to the project by the Toolkit in Solution Explorer.

The Toolkit adds project references to the System namespace and the *Microsoft.Office.Interop.InfoPath.SemiTrust* namespace defined by the primary interop assembly DLL of the same name. Microsoft provides primary interop assemblies (PIAs), which are wrappers for Component Object Model (COM) type libraries, for most Office XP and Office 2003 applications. PIAs install in the global assembly cache (GAC) so they can be shared by all .NET projects. Don't infer from the presence of a PIA that an Office application is .NET-enabled; Microsoft Word 2003, Excel 2003, and InfoPath 2003 SP-1 were the only Visual Studio .NET–enabled Office applications when this book was written.

The Toolkit generates Visual Basic .NET code to create instances of the InfoPath *Application* and *XDocument* objects in a *_Startup* event handler. These two objects are the most important members of the InfoPath object model, which is described in detail in Chapter 16. Figure 15-3 shows the default Visual Basic .NET code added by the Toolkit–commonly called an event-handling stub–with empty lines removed and minor edits for readability. To have Solution Explorer show all files in the project after building and running the default Visual Basic .NET code, choose Project, Show All Files. Notice that the file set includes multiple references to extracted template files.

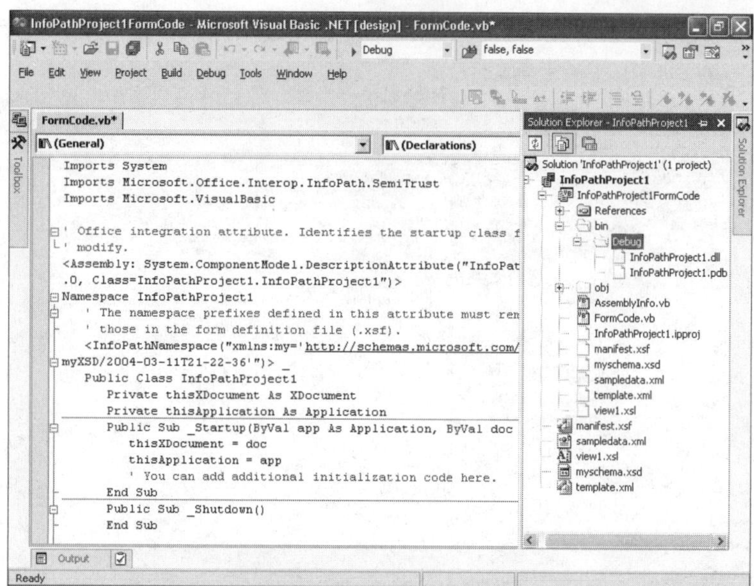

Figure 15-3 Running the default Visual Basic .NET code generated by the Toolkit and choosing Project, Show All Files creates the files and file pointers shown here.

Navigating Project Folders

Visual Studio creates all projects in subfolders of your \My Documents\Visual Studio Projects folder by default. If you accept the default values in the New Project dialog box, click OK, select the Create A New Form Template option in the Microsoft Office Project Wizard's only screen, and click Finish, the template generates a set of files and subfolders in a \My Documents\Visual Studio Projects\InfoPathProject1 folder, which contains only solution (.sln and .suo) files. Your working files, shown in Figure 15-3's Solution Explorer, are in a nested InfoPathProject1 folder and its subfolders. The files that you deploy after building the project in the default debug mode are located in the \My Documents\Visual Studio Projects\InfoPathProject1\InfoPathProject1\bin\Debug folder. InfoPathProject1.xsn is the final template file, InfoPathProject1.dll is the managed code assembly, and InfoPathProject1.pdb contains the debugging symbols. When you compile release versions of your projects, .pdb symbols aren't generated.

Changing file names and locations after creating a project is a chancy process at best, so it's a good practice to decide on a final project name and the initial location for the project files before you start a new InfoPath project. Minimizing the length of the project's path makes it easier to check file locations in the file's Properties dialog box. The examples you create in this chapter run from project subfolders of a C:\IPProjects projects folder and don't create separate subfolders for the solution (.sln and .suo) files.

Adding an Event Handler to a New Form

Your only access to InfoPath's COM objects that the InfoPath PIA exposes is through event handlers and subprocedures or functions invoked by event handlers. The *_Startup* event handler of the code behind the form declares two variables–*thisApplication* and *thisXDocument*. These variables represent the current InfoPath form instance and its data source document. *XDocument* objects contain a *UIObject*, which has an *Alert* method to display InfoPath's standard alert message box. A button with a click event handler that opens an alert box is the simplest example of adding event-handling code behind an InfoPath form.

To add a button and an event handler that displays an alert, follow these steps.

▶ **Create a new project and add a button event handler**

1. **Create a new C:\IPProjects folder to store all InfoPath project examples you create in this chapter and in Chapters 16 and 17.**
2. **Start Visual Studio, and choose Tools, Options to open the Options dialog box. Select the Environment node's Projects And Solutions item, and change the Visual Studio Projects Location to C:\IPProjects. To enforce strong typing with all Visual Basic .NET projects, select the Projects node's VB Defaults item, and set Option Strict to On. Click OK to save your changes.**
3. **Choose File, New, Project to open the New Project dialog box, expand the Microsoft Office InfoPath Projects node, and select the InfoPath Form Templates icon.**
4. **Change the project's Name to IPEvents.Click More and clear the Create Directory For Solution check box to eliminate one subfolder level, as shown here:**

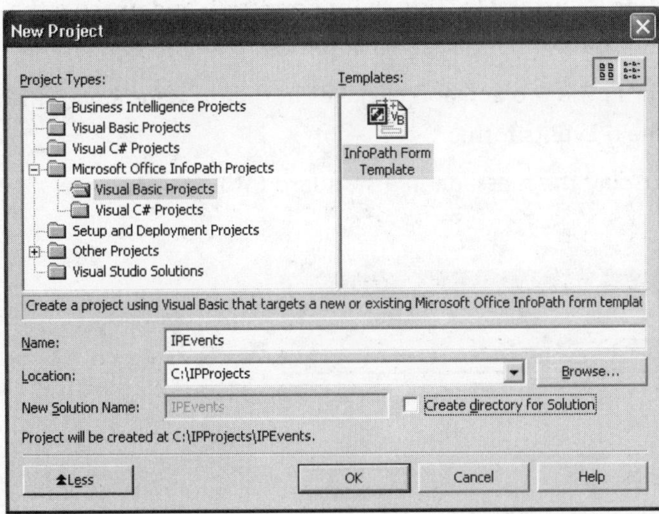

5. Click OK to close the dialog and open the Microsoft Office Project Wizard, leave the default Create New Form Template option, and click Finish to generate the project and open the IPEvents form in design mode.
6. Add *Option Explicit On* and *Option Strict On* statements above the first *Imports* statement. It's a good practice to add *Option Explicit On* and *Option Strict On* because other programmers who work on your form might not have these defaults set.
7. Give the focus to the IPEvents template, add a button control, and open its Properties dialog box. Leave the default Rules And Custom Code item in the Action drop-down list, change the Label value to **Click Event Test**, and set the ID value to **btnClickEvent**, as shown here:

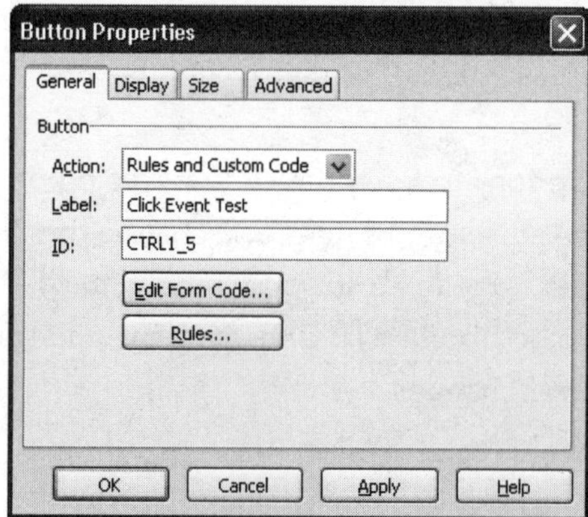

8. Click the Edit Form Code button to add the button's *OnClick* event handler to the *IPEvents* class as a Visual Basic subprocedure and return the focus to Visual Studio.
9. Replace the *'Write your code here* comment in the event handler with **thisXDocument.UI.Alert("Button OnClick event handler")**, and observe the property and method options as you type each period.
10. Press F5 to build and run the project, and click Yes in the message box, which opens a preview of the IPEvents form.
11. Click the button to display the message in a standard InfoPath Alert message box, as shown here:

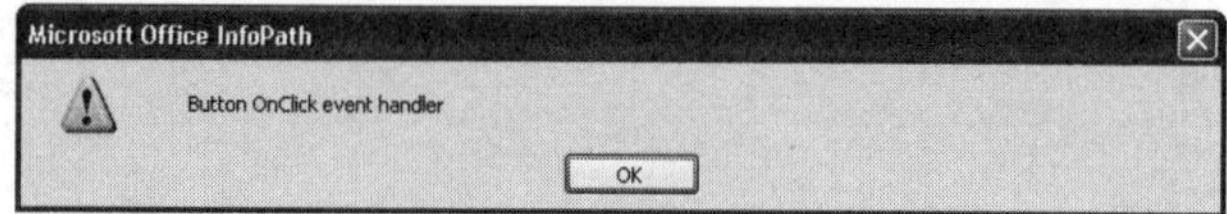

Restoring InfoPath templates that disappear
If you accidentally close the current InfoPath template instance, choose Tools, Open InfoPath or Project, Open InfoPath to restore it.

The event handler's *<InfoPathEventHandler (MatchPath:="btnClickEvent", EventType:= InfoPathEventType.OnClick)>* attribute delegates handling of the InfoPath *OnClick* event to the *btnClickEvent_OnClick* event handler. The *e* parameter's *DocActionEvent* interface has three properties: *ReturnStatus*, *Source*, and *XDocument*. The *ReturnStatus* property is a Boolean value that defaults to *True* and is useful for handing InfoPath events that accept return values and cancel the action if the return value is *False*. The *Source* property returns a read-only *IXMLDOMNode* instance that represents the form's current data source–*my:fields* for the example at this point.

Copying and pasting code snippets
Your C:\Microsoft Press\Introducing InfoPath 2003\Chapter15\IPEvents folder has text files that contain the code snippets you add to the event-handling procedures in the remaining exercises in this chapter. The file name is provided in the step that describes the code to be added.

The *UI* object's *Confirm* method provides the visual equivalent of a Windows forms message box and offers a choice of OK/Cancel, Yes/No, or Yes/No/Cancel buttons. You can use the return value of the message box to control program flow with an *If ... Else ... End If* construct. To change the alert to a confirmation message box, replace the alert statement you added in step 9 of the preceding procedure with the following statements or add them from Confirm.txt:

```
With thisXDocument
  If .UI.Confirm("The source is " + e.Source.baseName + _
        ". Do you want to continue?", XdConfirmButtons.xdYesNo) = _
        XdConfirmChoice.xdYes Then
    e.ReturnStatus = True
   .UI.Confirm("Continuation confirmed.", _
        XdConfirmButtons.xdOKCancel)
  Else
    e.ReturnStatus = False
  End If
End With
```

When you click the button, the upper confirm message box of Figure 15-4 opens. Click Yes to open the message box. Unfortunately, the *Confirm* method doesn't offer a single "OK" button choice to provide a more compact version of an alert.

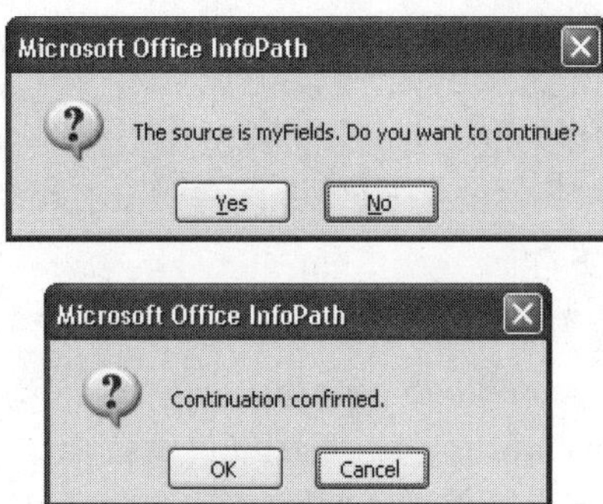

Figure 15-4 Clicking Yes in the first (upper) confirm message box displays the lower one.

Working with Data Source Field Events

Changing data source field values or adding and deleting repeating form sections triggers the following three events:

- ***OnBeforeChange*** Fires after an instruction to change a field value and prior to saving a new value to a field. If the event handler returns a false value to the *ReturnStatus* property of the *DataDOMEvent* argument, InfoPath cancels the field value change. Changing an *XDocument* node value triggers an *OnBeforeChange* event for deletion of the original value and insertion of the new value.
- ***OnValidate*** Fires after *OnBeforeChange* and before *OnAfterChange*, and doesn't recognize return values. The DOM is read-only until execution exits your event handler, so this event is useful primarily for manipulating members of the *Errors* collection.
- ***OnAfterChange*** Fires after changes have been applied to the cached copy of the data source. Like *OnBeforeChange*, the *OnAfterChange* event fires twice when you update a field value.

Adding field event handlers requires a data source and controls to change values. Follow these steps to convert the data source of your form to a simple XML document with fields of multiple data types, and add controls to the form's layout table.

▶ Add a data source and controls to the form

1. **In the form's design view, choose Tools, Convert Main Data Source to start the Data Source Wizard.**

2. **In the first wizard screen, click Browse, and open C:\Microsoft Press\Introducing InfoPath 2003\Chapter15\IPEvents\EventsData.xml. Click Next, and then click Finish to substitute the EventData document structure and its default values for the empty my:fields data source. Click Yes in the message box that asks whether you want to update expressions automatically. Replacing the data source adds several new namespaces to the *Public Class IPEvents*' attribute.**
3. **Open the Data Source task pane, change the data type of the date1 field to Date (date) and the dateTime1 field to Date And Time (dateTime), and change the remaining fields ending in 1 to the data type represented by their name. Leave all fields ending in 2 as the default Text (string) data type.**
4. **Add a two-column, five-row layout table under the button, and drag the element fields to the table cells in left-to-right, top-to-bottom sequence. Drag the eventType attribute to the right of the button to add a label and text box.**
5. **Click Preview This Form, click Yes if the message box asks whether you want to update expressions in the code, and then click Preview This Form again to build and run the project. Your form preview appears as shown here:**

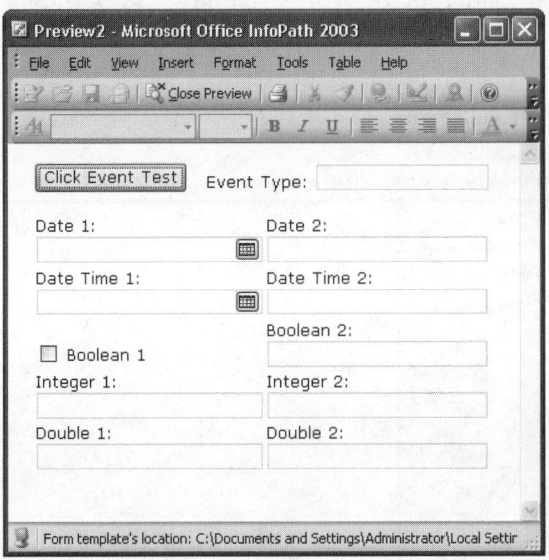

Responding to *OnAfterChange* Events

True/False (Boolean) fields are a good choice for an initial *OnAfterChange* event-handler coding exercise, because the code is very simple. The event handler updates the value of the Boolean 2 text box with a value that corresponds to the state of the

Boolean 1 check box. You specify the target node–an *IXMLDOMNode* object–by applying the *thisXDocument.DOM.selectSingleNode("/eventsData/boolean2")* method and then setting the target node's *text* property value to the *text* property value of the event handler's *e.Source* parameter. The code detects the *e.operation = "Delete"* condition and exits, so only Insert operations are processed.

It's a good programming practice to add structured exception handling to any event handler that might generate a run-time error, because InfoPath projects disregard some run-time exceptions. In this case, your code fails silently, and you might overlook an occasional or even a repetitive exception. Adding a stack trace to the error handler's message supplies the line number on which the error occurred.

Follow these steps to complete the boolean1 event handler with a *Try...Catch...End Try* block for exception handling.

▶ **Add an event handler for the boolean2 field**

1. **Close the preview window to return to design view. Right-click the boolean1 field in the Data Source list, and choose Properties from the shortcut menu to open its Properties dialog box. Click the Validation And Event Handlers tab, and select OnAfterChange in the Events drop-down list, as shown here:**

2. **Click Edit to add the *boolean1_OnAfterChange* event handler to the code and return the focus to Visual Studio, as shown here:**

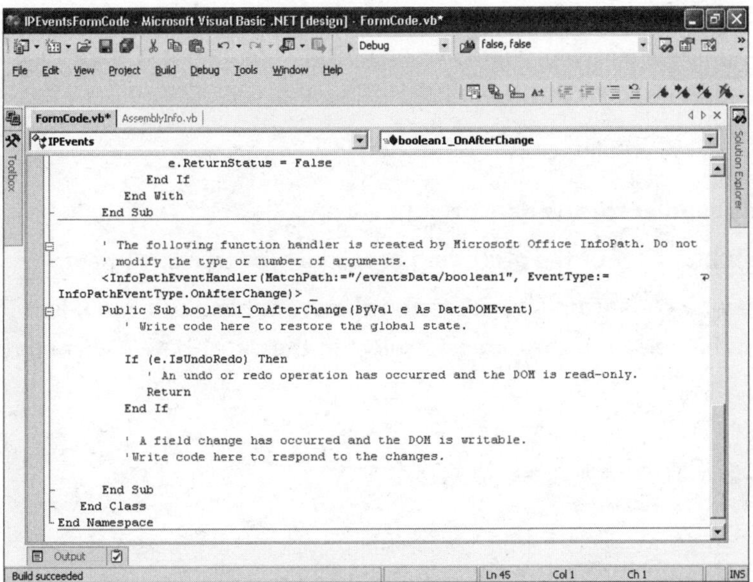

3. **Remove the empty lines and, optionally, the comments, and add the following code from Boolean1.txt after the event handler's *End If* line to update the boolean2 field with the state of the Boolean 1 check box:**

```
If e.Operation = "Delete" Then
   Return
End If
Try
   Dim nodTarget As IXMLDOMNode = _
   thisXDocument.DOM.selectSingleNode("/eventsData/boolean2")
   nodTarget.text = e.Source.text
Catch excBool As Exception
   thisXDocument.UI.Alert(excBool.Message + _
        excBool.StackTrace.ToString)
End Try
```

4. **Press F5 to build and run the project and open a preview window, and test the event handler by clicking the Boolean 1 check box a few times.**
5. **Give Visual Studio the focus, position the insertion point on the first *If* line, and press F9 to set a breakpoint.**
6. **Give the preview window the focus, and then change the Boolean 1 check box's state and halt execution at the breakpoint. Press F11 to step through the procedure, observe that the event fires twice but is processed only once, and then clear the breakpoint by pressing F9 on the highlighted line or by choosing Debug, Clear All Breakpoints.**

Nillable Date (*date*) and Date And Time (*dateTime*) fields present a challenge when you need to convert the Variant data type (Object) of dates returned by the event handler's *e.Source.nodeValue* property to the DateTime data type, which enables easy

ISO 8601 formatting with the *ToString("s")* method and date arithmetic. To avoid run-time errors, you must test for *e.Source.text* values that result from entering empty date values in the date picker's text box.

To create the *date1_OnAfterChange* event handler, follow these steps.

▶ Add an event handler for the date1 field

1. **Repeat steps 1 and 2 for of the preceding procedure for the date1 field.**
2. **Add the following code from Date2.txt after the event handler's *End If* line to update the date2 field with the date you select in the date1 date picker control:**

```
If e.Operation = "Delete" Then
   Return
End If
'Specify date1 as the field to be updated
Dim nodTarget As IXMLDOMNode = _
        thisXDocument.DOM.selectSingleNode("/eventsData/date2")
If e.Source.text = "" Then
   'Date is nil
   nodTarget.text = ""
Try
   'Format the DateTime object as ISO 8601
   Dim strDate As String = _
         CType(e.Source.nodeValue(), DateTime).ToString("s")
   'Remove the time value
   nodTarget.text = Left(strDate, InStr(strDate, "T") - 1)
   'Select the eventsData node
   nodTarget = nodTarget.parentNode
   'Set the attribute value
   nodTarget.attributes(0).text = "date1 Changed"
Catch excDate As Exception
   'Catch runtime errors
   thisXDocument.UI.Alert(excDate.Message + _
         excDate.StackTrace.ToString)
End Try
```

3. **Press F5 to build and run the project and open a preview. Select a date, and verify that the Date 2 text box displays an ISO 8601 date.**
4. **Add a breakpoint at the second *If* statement, and clear the Date 1 text box. Press F11 to step through the procedure, which executes three times, and then clear the breakpoint.**

If you want to see an exception-handling alert, comment the second *Return* statement, add a date value, clear the date value, and press Tab. You'll receive two error messages similar to the one shown in Figure 15-5.

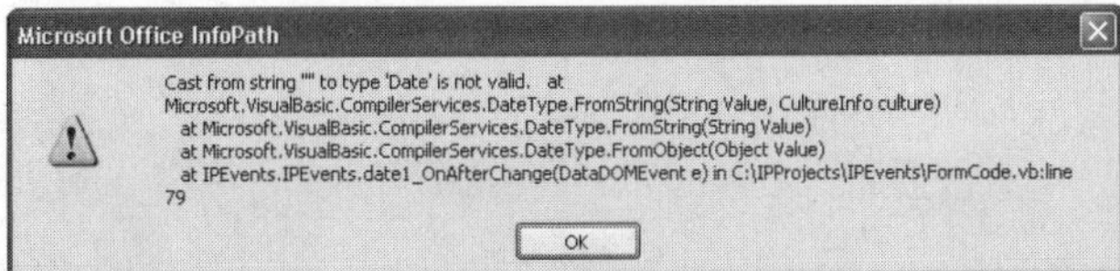

Figure 15-5 A common source of InfoPath event-handler exceptions is attempts to cast a nondate Variant value to the DateTime type, as illustrated by this alert.

Handling *OnBeforeChange* Events

The *OnBeforeChange* event lets you intercept changes, apply business logic to the proposed new value, let users decide whether to make the change with a confirm message box, send a *ReturnMessage* to an alert message box, or any combination of these actions. Your code must handle multiple events correctly to avoid reoccurring confirm message boxes. In this procedure, a *blnHasChanges* flag determines whether the value has been changed by a previous *OnBeforeChange* Insert event. This procedure's event-handler code isn't prone to run-time errors, so exception handling isn't implemented.

Follow these steps to add the *dateTime1_BeforeChange* event handler.

▶ Add an *OnBeforeChange* event handler for the dateTime1 field

1. **In InfoPath design view, right-click the dateTime1 field in the Data Source task pane, and choose Properties from the shortcut menu to open its Properties dialog box. Click the Validation And Event Handlers tab, and select OnBeforeChange in the Events drop-down list.**
2. **Click Edit to add the *dateTime1_OnBeforeChange* event handler to the code and return the focus to Visual Studio.**
3. **Remove the empty lines and, optionally, the comments, and add a *Private blnHasChanged As Boolean* statement immediately after the *Private thisApplication As Application* statement.**
4. **Add the following code from DateTime2OBC.txt after the event handler's *End If* line to display a confirm message box with Yes/No buttons and an alert if the user elects to abandon the changes:**

```
If e.Operation = "Delete" Then
   Return
End If
If blnHasChanged Then
   blnHasChanged = False
   Return
End If
If thisXDocument.UI.Confirm("Do you want to update " + _
   "dateTime2 and dateTime1?", XdConfirmButtons.xdYesNo) = _
```

```
         XdConfirmChoice.xdYes Then
         e.ReturnStatus = True
      True
         blnHasChanged =
         'Cancel the update
         e.ReturnStatus = False
         blnHasChanged = False
         e.ReturnMessage = _
               "DateTime updates were canceled by the user."
      End If
```

5. **Press F5 to open a preview, and change the Date Time 1 date picker value to open a confirm message box. Click No to display the alert with the return message.**
6. **Add a breakpoint at the first *If* statement, change the date, and trace execution to verify that the event fires twice but is processed only once. If you delete the date in the text box and press Tab, the event executes three times, but the flag prevents the confirm message from appearing twice.**

Taking Action Based on the Value of Another Field

The following procedure displays ISO 8601–formatted date and time values for local time or Universal Time Coordinate (UTC) in the Date Time 1 text box, depending on the state of the Boolean 2 check box. The code is similar to that for the *date2_OnAfterChange* event handler, except for addition of the boolean2 field value test and code to change local to UTC time, as shown here:

```
Dim datNodeValue As DateTime = _
   CType(e.Source.nodeValue(), DateTime)
Dim strNodeValue As String
'Get the value of the boolean2 node
Dim nodIsUTC As IXMLDOMNode = _
   thisXDocument.DOM.selectSingleNode("/eventsData/boolean2")
If nodIsUTC.text = "true" Then
   'Use Universal Coordinated Time
   strNodeValue = datNodeValue.ToUniversalTime.ToString("s")
Else
   'Use local time
   strNodeValue = datNodeValue.ToString("s")
End If
```

To add the *dateTime1_OnAfterChange* event handler, follow these steps.

▶ **Add an *OnAfterChange* event handler for the dateTime1 field**

1. **Close the preview window to return to design mode. Right-click the dateTime1 field in the Data Source task pane's list, and choose Properties from the shortcut menu to open its Properties dialog box. Click the Validation And Event Handlers tab, and select OnAfterChange.**

2. **Click Edit to add the *dateTime1_OnAfterChange* event handler to the code and return the focus to Visual Studio.**
3. **Paste the code from DateTime2OAC.txt after the event handler's *End If* line to set the value of the dateTime2 field.**
4. **Test the event handler with Date Time 2 date picker values and empty dates. Clicking the Boolean 1 check box to change the date format. The form, with a UTC date and time, appears as shown here:**

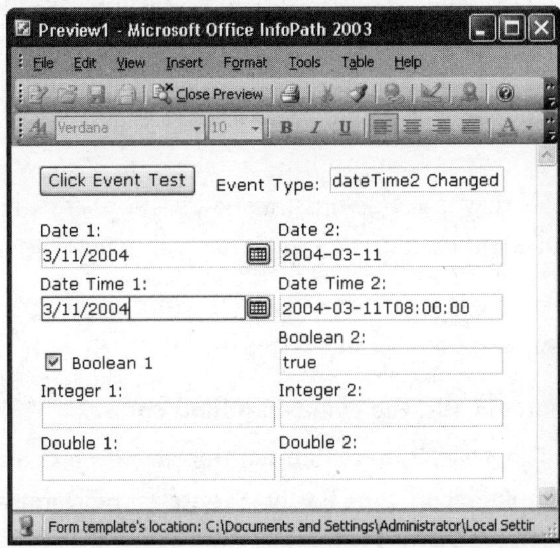

5. **Optionally, set a breakpoint, and trace execution of the code when you change a Date Time 1 value.**

Adding Managed Code to an Existing Form

Creating a new InfoPath project from an existing template is a simple, two-step process if your form doesn't incorporate JScript or VBScript code. Moving to managed code disables the script, and you must rewrite all event handlers in Visual Basic .NET or C#. If your template contains more than 100 lines of script, conversion probably isn't justified unless you need to implement features that the .NET Framework supports and script doesn't. As an example, you need the .NET Framework and the Microsoft Web Services Enhancements (WSE) 2.0- add-on to connect to secure Web services that implement SOAP message encryption and require digital signatures. Digitally signed SOAP messages supplement–but don't replace–digital signatures applied to forms.

RSS 2.0 data documents have a repeating item section with a pubDate field that requires a RFC1123-formatted date string. Repeating sections introduce you to the use of the *IXMLDOMNodeList* object, which contains a collection of repeating *IXMLDOMNode* elements. The object's *length* property returns the number of instances of the repeating section. You can specify the instance you need by an index that's less than the *length* value–for example, *NodeList1(NodeList1.length -1)* points to the last section.

Adding the current time in RFC1123 format when inserting a new section improves data entry efficiency and minimizes typographic errors. The *DateTime.UtcNow* property returns the current UTC time, and the *ToString("R")* method returns the RFC1123 pattern. It's a common practice to add RSS 2.0 items in reverse date/time order (last in, first out) with Insert Above operations, but users can insert new sections in any arbitrary sequence. Thus your code must test all sections for the presence of a pubDate field value and add the current date/time value if it's missing.

To add the RFC1123 date and time to a copy of the Rss2v4.xsn template from Chapter 10, "Adding Views to a Template," follow these steps.

▶ Create the Rss2v4Events project and add the event-handling code

1. Start Visual Studio, and choose File, New, Project to open the New Project dialog box. Click the InfoPath Form Template icon, type **Rss2v4Events** as the Name and, if you didn't set the default folder, type **C:\IPProjects** as the Location.
2. Click OK to open the Microsoft Project Wizard. Select the Open Existing Form Template option, click Browse, navigate to C:\Microsoft Press\Introducing InfoPath 2003\Chapter15\Rss2v4Events, and double-click Rss2v4 (Ch10).xsn.
3. Click Finish. In the message box that appears, assuring you that the original template won't be modified, click OK to open the FormCode.vb window and an InfoPath design mode instance.
4. Add **Option Explicit On** the **Option Strict On** as the first two lines of code.
5. Activate the Data Source task pane, right-click the item section in the Data Source task pane list, and choose Properties from the shortcut menu to open the Properties dialog box. Click the Validation And Event Handlers tab, select the OnAfterChange event, and click Edit to add the *item_OnAfterChange* event handler.
6. Add the following code from Rss2v4Events.txt, which is located in the same folder as the original template, below the *End If* statement:

```
If e.Operation = "Delete" Or e.Site.nodeName <> "item" Then
   Return
End If
```

```
Try
   Dim strXML As String = e.Source.xml
   'Create a list of pubDate node(s)
   Dim lstItems As IXMLDOMNodeList = _
      e.Source.selectNodes("//pubDate")
   'Check all pubDate nodes
   Dim intItem As Integer
   For intItem = 0 To lstItems.length - 1
      Dim nodLastItem As IXMLDOMNode = lstItems(intItem)
      nodLastItem.selectSingleNode("//pubDate")
      If nodLastItem.text = "" Then
            'Get current system time as UTC if pubDate is empty
            Dim datNow As DateTime = DateTime.UtcNow
            'Add the RFC1123 date
            nodLastItem.text = datNow.ToString("R")
      End If
   Next intItem
Catch excInsert As Exception
   thisXDocument.UI.Alert(excInsert.Message + _
      excInsert.StackTrace)
End Try
```

7. **Press F5 and click Yes to build the project and open a preview window. Insert sections above, below, and between other sections to verify that the event handler performs as expected, as shown here:**

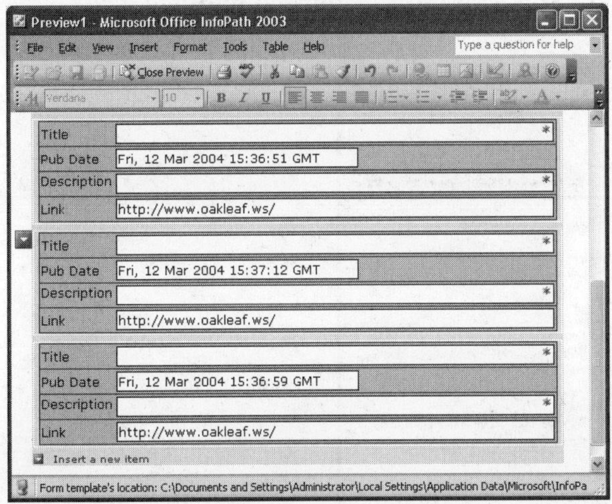

The *e.Site.nodeName* <> *"item"* test in the first statement verifies that the event originated from inserting an item node and not from the change to the pubDate field value. Events lower in the XML document's hierarchy percolate to the root element, a process called *event bubbling*. For more information about the *Site* object and event bubbling, search the InfoPath SDK Documentation for the term *"bubbling"* (include the quotation marks).

Managing Project Relocation and Deployment

The following sections show you how to handle errors that occur when you open a form from a project template in a location other than the *ProjectName* folder, change the location of the InfoPath project files, create a release version of your template, and publish production templates.

Dealing with Template Cache Conflicts

You can create and save a sample data document from the Fill Out A Form task pane in the project's InfoPath design window. In this case, InfoPath use the manifest.xsf file in the project folder as the template and adds it to the local form template cache. Alternatively, you can emulate opening a production Form1 by double-clicking the template file that contains the project's assembly DLL–IPEvents.xsn for this example–in the ...*ProjectName*\bin\Debug folder. Opening Form1 from this folder displays the Form Conflict dialog box shown in Figure 15-6. If you're developing the form template, click the Keep Form On Your Computer button to use the manifest.xsf version. After you complete the form's design, click the Replace Form On Your Computer button to use the FormName.xsn template.

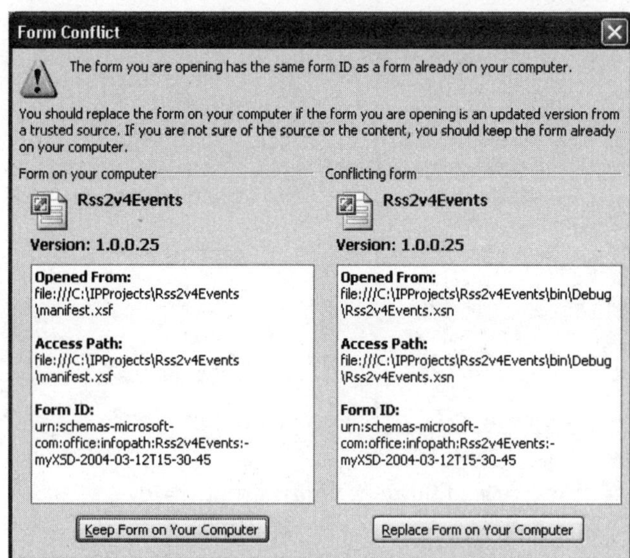

Figure 15-6 This message box appears when you attempt to open a new Form1 from the template's .xsn file in the ...\bin\Debug folder and the manifest.xsf version of the template is in the local cache.

Copying an InfoPath Project to a New Location

Visual Studio users appreciate easy XCopy deployment of their Windows and Web forms projects; moving an entire InfoPath project to a new folder is as easy as using Save As with a conventional template. You can copy the entire project folder to another location and continue development without making any changes to the project. When you open the project, you might receive a warning message that advises you to publish the form from its new location. You can ignore the warning message prior to creating a release version of the project and publishing the template for production use.

Creating a Release Version of the Project

By default, Visual Studio creates and runs InfoPath projects in debug configuration. The debug version of the assembly (*ProjectName*.dll) is slightly larger than the release version, and debug versions of large projects execute more slowly than release versions. The debug symbols (.pdb) file adds unnecessary bulk to the template file. Before you publish a production form, create the release version by choosing Build, Configuration Manager to open the Configuration Manager dialog box. Select Release in the Active Solution Configuration drop-down list, as shown in Figure 15-7, and click OK.

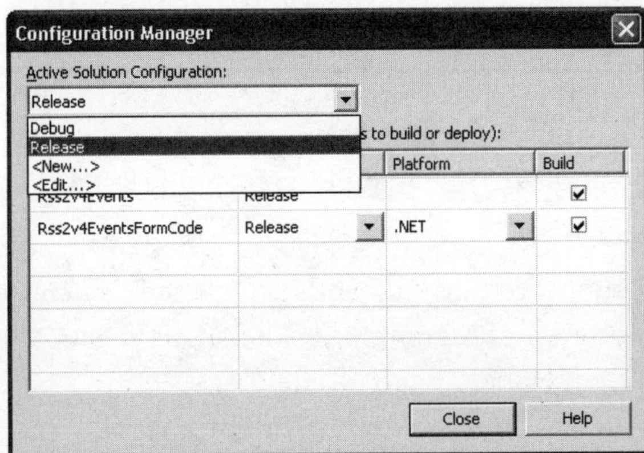

Figure 15-7 Changing the InfoPath project's configuration from Debug to Release generates a production version of the project without a *ProjectName*.pdb file.

Run the project to create a ...*ProjectName*\\bin\\Release folder, which contains release versions of your template and its assembly. The completed projects in your C:\\Microsoft Press\\Introducing InfoPath 2003\\Chapter15\\IPEvents\\IPEvents and ...\\Rss2v4Events\\Rss2v4Events folders have debug and release versions. Debug is the default configuration for these projects.

Publishing Forms with Managed Code

The process of publishing an InfoPath template with managed code to shared folders, Web sites, and SharePoint forms libraries is identical to publishing a template with or without script. Choose Tools, Publish Form to build the form and start the Publishing Wizard. Complete the wizard's steps, as described in Chapter 12, "Publishing Form Templates." The template file contains the assembly DLL. InfoPath publishes your template's release version, if it exists; if not, InfoPath publishes the debug version.

Like forms containing script or ActiveX controls, Domain is the default security mode for forms containing managed code. If your code accesses local computer resources outside of the form, requires cross-domain permissions, or includes references to custom .NET assemblies that aren't signed by Microsoft, you must specify Full Trust as the security mode and specify a code signing certificate to digitally sign the form on the Security tab of the Form Options dialog box. Alternatively, you can deploy a custom-installed template to users' computers.

Chapter Summary

InfoPath projects substitute .NET managed code for script to implement business logic that declarative programming can't handle. You must have Visual Basic .NET 2003 Standard or Visual Studio .NET 2003 Professional or later and the Toolkit for InfoPath 2003 installed to create InfoPath projects with Visual Basic .NET code. This book uses Visual Basic .NET for all programming examples, because Office developers can leverage their VBA skills to write InfoPath event handlers and utility functions or subprocedures.

The Toolkit creates an event-handling subprocedure stub with default code when you specify an event handler by choosing Tools, Programming. Clicking Edit with an event selected on the Validation And Event Handlers tab of a field or section's Properties dialog box also generates a stub. You add code to implement business logic to the stub to complete the event handler. Adding structured exception handling to the code you write ensures that you catch run-time errors that otherwise might not be evident.

Debug is Visual Studio's default configuration for InfoPath projects. To publish a production InfoPath project, you use the Configuration Manager to change to Release configuration, and rebuild your project. You publish the project by choosing Tools, Publish Form in Visual Studio to run InfoPath's Publishing Wizard. The resulting .xsn file includes the .NET assembly that contains the project's MSIL code.

Users must have the .NET Framework 1.1 runtime installed on their computers to JIT-compile the MSIL to executable code.

Q&A

Q. Does InfoPath trigger more than the three events discussed in this chapter?

A. Yes, but *OnBeforeChange*, *OnValidate*, and *OnAfterChange* are the most frequently used event handlers in InfoPath projects. The Programming option on InfoPath's Tools menu provides On Load Event, On Switch View Event, On Context Change Event, and On Sign Event items, which generate the corresponding event handlers. The *OnSubmitRequest* and *OnVersionUpgrade* events let you write code to customize the form submission and upgrade processes. SP-1 adds several more events to InfoPath's repertoire; the next two chapters have code examples for the events not covered in this chapter.

Q. Why do InfoPath projects require programming MSXML objects rather than .NET's more versatile *System.Xml* classes?

A. InfoPath 2003 SP-1 is a conventional Windows application that exposes COM objects to provide access to *Application* and *XDocument* objects. You're limited to manipulating InfoPath COM objects that managed code accesses through the InfoPath PIA. InfoPath, not MSXML, provides the *IXMLDOM*... interfaces that you program with .NET code. SP-1 exposes its classes and interfaces as Automation objects, so Visual Basic 6 or VBA code can manipulate InfoPath objects by adding a reference to the Microsoft InfoPath 1.0 Type Library.

Q. Can I use .NET's *System.Xml* classes to manipulate the data document independent of InfoPath?

A. Yes, you can retrieve the cached XML document's contents as a *String* at any point in the editing process with a *thisXDocument.DOM.xml* instruction. After you add a reference to System.Xml.dll and an *Imports System.Xml* statement to InfoPath's default FormCode.vb, you can populate an in-memory *XmlDocument* instance with a *docXML.LoadXml(thisXDocument.DOM.xml)* statement. You can modify *docXML*, navigate it with an *XPathNavigator* object, import it to a *DataSet* (if the document is relational), and transform it with Extensible Stylesheet Language Transformation (XSLT). Your form must be fully trusted to save the modified document to an .xml file with the *XmlTextReader* class.

Q. Are there any other InfoPath UI objects that I can program with .NET code?

A. Yes. The *XDocument.UI* object provides a *ShowModalDialog* method that displays a dialog box that you define using a conventional HTML file, which can contain script. The form must be fully trusted to open the dialog box. The InfoPath 2003 SDK's documentation offers additional implementation details for the method; type showmodaldialog as the search term and follow the links. You also can display the e-mail message and signature dialog boxes with the *ShowMailItem* and *ShowSignatureDialog* methods.

On Your Own

Here's an additional exercise that uses the Rss2v4Events.xsn template to demonstrate event-handling code reuse:

1. Open the Default Values dialog box, and select the item field check box to make one item instance required.
2. Open a preview window, and observe that the Pub Date text box is empty, because the *OnAfterChange* event doesn't fire in this case.
3. Choose Tools, Programming, On Load Event to add an *OnLoad* event-handling stub.
4. Copy the *Try...Catch...End Try* block only from the *item_OnAfterChange* event handler to the *OnLoad* stub. The *OnLoad* event fires once when you open the form, so you don't need the tests that precede the *Try* statement.
5. The *DocReturnEvent* parameter doesn't provide an *OnLoad* property, but it does have an *XDocument* property that serves a similar purpose. Change the *Dim lstItems As IXMLDOMNodeList = e.Source.selectNodes("//pubDate")* statement to **Dim lstItems As IXMLDOMNodeList = e.XDocument.DOM.selectNodes ("//pubDate")** to substitute *XDocument* for *Source*.
6. Open a preview window, and verify that the Pub Date text box now displays the current date and time.

CHAPTER 16

Navigating the InfoPath Object Model

In this chapter, you will learn how to:

- **Use Visual Studio's Object Browser to explore InfoPath 2003 Service Pack 1 (SP-1) classes, interfaces, enums, and delegates.**
- **Describe InfoPath's *Application* object and its most used members, and write Visual Basic .NET code to return *Application* object property values.**
- **Describe the *XDocument* object, its most important members, and those members' more useful properties and methods.**
- **Use the *SwitchView* method to change views in response to a button click, and add code to the *OnSwitchView* event handler to add the display name to the view's caption.**
- **Write code to determine the number of currently open forms and display their names and the name of the active form in a message box.**
- **Specify a default path and file name for saving a new form, and display the default file name in the each view's title bar.**
- **Test signed sections or fields for the existence and validity of digital signatures.**

For more information:

- **Review the InfoPath 2003 release version's object model by opening the Microsoft Office InfoPath 2003 Software Development Kit (SDK), expanding the InfoPath Developer Reference and InfoPath Object Model Reference nodes, and clicking the InfoPath Object Model Diagram item.**
- **Compare object models for other Microsoft Office applications with the InfoPath 2003 object model in MSDN's "Microsoft Office XP Developer Object Model Guide." Search MSDN for *"XP Developer Object"* (include the quotation marks), and navigate in the TOC pane to an application object model, such as Microsoft Access or Excel.**

To work through this chapter:

- You need the prerequisites for Chapter 15, "Introducing Form Development"—Microsoft Visual Studio .NET or Microsoft Visual Basic .NET and the Microsoft InfoPath 2003 Toolkit for Visual Studio .NET (Toolkit)—installed on your computer. You also need some experience writing Visual Basic .NET code in the Visual Studio environment.
- You need the sample files for this chapter installed from the accompanying CD-ROM to the C:\Microsoft Press\Introducing InfoPath 2003\Chapter16 folder.
- You need a valid digital signing certificate to add digital signatures to individual data source elements, as described in the section "Signing Individual Form Groups or Fields," in Chapter 11, "Setting Template and Digital Signing Options."
- You should be familiar with publishing forms to a Web site and, if you have Microsoft Windows Server 2003 installed, to a Windows SharePoint Services site, as described in the sections "Publishing Templates to an Intranet Site" and "Publishing Templates to SharePoint Form Libraries," in Chapter 12, "Publishing Form Templates."

All Microsoft Office System 2003 applications provide Component Object Model (COM) object or type libraries to expose internal application objects to script, Microsoft Visual Basic for Applications (VBA), Visual Basic 6, and .NET programming languages. *Object models* depict the hierarchy of the application's exposed objects; for Office objects, the top member of the hierarchy is the *Application* object. All other objects are descendants of the *Application* object and represent either individual objects or object collections. Gaining access to an Office application's object or type library from VBA or Visual Basic 6 code requires adding a reference to the library to enable both early binding and the Microsoft IntelliSense feature. Most Office applications export the library from their executable files–for example, Excel.exe exports the Microsoft Excel 11.0 Object Library. As you learned in the section "Adding Managed Code Behind a Form," in Chapter 15, .NET-enabled Office 2003 applications–Microsoft Excel, Word, and InfoPath–use primary interop assembly (PIA) type library wrappers to manipulate the *Application* object and its descendants.

The purpose of an object model diagram is to provide developers with a shortcut to understanding the object hierarchy and to finding objects to fulfill a specific programming requirement. InfoPath's object model is much simpler than that of Access, Excel, or Word. Excel's object model occupies four lengthy Web pages, and Word's takes up seven pages; InfoPath's object model fits on a single page. The InfoPath release version exposed *ExternalApplication* as a COM Automation object; only internal JScript or Microsoft Visual Basic Scripting Edition (VBScript) could access other InfoPath objects. The *ExternalApplication* object's primary purpose was to enable local registration of custom-installed forms. InfoPath SP-1 exposes its entire object hierarchy as Automation objects and through the InfoPath PIA.

Despite the relative simplicity of InfoPath 2003's object model, it's impossible to provide detailed descriptions and examples of all its members in a single chapter of reasonable length. The original InfoPath SDK required more than 200 pages of varying length to document and provide trivial JScript code examples for the object model's collection, object, property, method, event, and enumeration elements. InfoPath SP-1 adds about 100 new elements to the list. Thus, this chapter concentrates on object model elements that are most commonly used in programming InfoPath forms, with emphasis on elements added by SP-1.

Getting Acquainted with Visual Studio's Object Browser

To display the Object Browser, open an InfoPath 2003 project, such as one of those you created in Chapter 15, and choose View, Object Browser or press Ctrl+Alt+J to add a tab to the main window of the integrated development environment (IDE). Figure 16-1 shows the floating version of Object Browser displaying members of the *Application* class. Visual Studio .NET's Object Browser is similar to that of Visual Studio 6, but it displays a different hierarchy in the Objects pane: Project or Assembly, Namespaces, and (if you right-click in the Objects pane and choose Group By Object Type) Classes, Interfaces, Enums, and Delegates. The Members pane lists the selected object's properties and methods with their arguments, data types, and return data types. The bottom pane displays a more detailed version of a selected member's calling syntax.

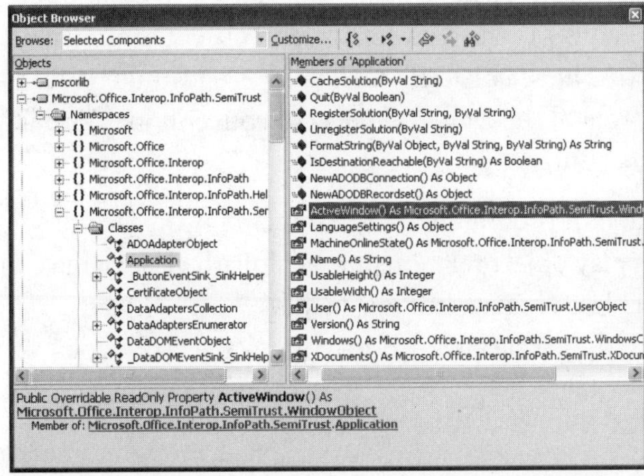

Figure 16-1 The Visual Studio .NET Object Browser's four-level Objects hierarchy doesn't display the hierarchical relationship of classes.

Following are brief descriptions of the four object types provided by the InfoPath PIA:

- **Classes** Represent "blueprints for objects," a term coined in the Visual Basic .NET help files. Classes define the properties, methods, events, and, in some cases, fields of an instance of an object. The *New* keyword creates an instance of a class. InfoPath creates instances of its objects during the startup process, so you need the *New* keyword only to create instances of most .NET Framework classes and custom classes (other than *Shared* classes) that you define.

- **Interfaces** Represent a contract with the class that implements the interface. The class must implement the interface's elements exactly as they are designed. Interfaces are immutable; you can't change an interface after publishing it, because doing so would break the contract with the class. Each InfoPath object has entries under the Classes and Interfaces nodes, but some methods, such as the *IXMLDOM...* interfaces you used in Chapter 15, don't have corresponding classes. MSXML Core Services provides these interfaces to InfoPath, which exposes them to your Visual Basic .NET code. This avoids the need to add a COM reference to Microsoft XML v5.0 or a .NET reference to the *System.Xml* namespace.
- **Enums** Named constants that represent a whole numeric value, which can be of Visual Basic .NET's Byte, Short, Long, or Integer (the default) data type. Unlike Visual Basic 6, you can't substitute a literal number for an enum's value, because enums are strongly typed.
- **Delegates** Define InfoPath events passed to Visual Basic .NET event-handling procedures for button clicks, changes to the data source, and other user-initiated actions, such as changing views. The *<InfoPathEventHandler ...>* attribute preceding *Public Sub...* performs the role of the *Handles* clause of conventional Visual Basic .NET event-handling procedures.

Object Browser's usefulness to InfoPath programmers is hampered by its lack of a hierarchical view of classes to display object relationships. InfoPath class names, except *Application*, have the object class type appended, such as *WindowObject* and *WindowsCollection*. You refer to these objects in code without the class type suffix–*Window* and *Windows*.

Working with the *Application* Object

The *Application* object is the root of the object hierarchy in InfoPath and it provides access to all other objects that the InfoPath PIA exposes. Figure 16-2 shows the top part of the InfoPath SDK's object model diagram. The *XDocuments* collection, which includes an *XDocument* member for each open form, is the most important *Application* object member. *XDocument* objects, which you programmed as *thisXDocument* in Chapter 15, are the subject of this chapter's later sections.

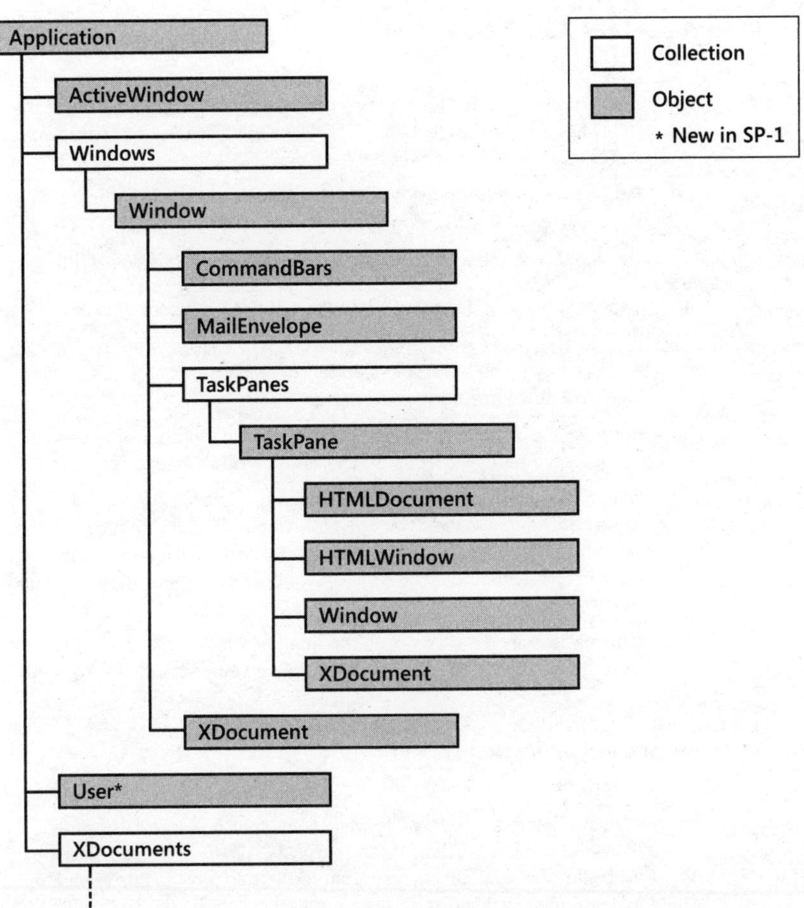

Figure 16-2 The *Application* object's high-level methods and properties are used primarily to determine the current state of the InfoPath project. Event handlers provide the current *XDocument* object as a member of the *e* (*eventArgs*) argument.

Tables 16-1 and 16-2 describe the *Application* object's most commonly used properties–including child objects–and methods; an asterisk identifies items added by InfoPath 2003 SP-1. For information about other properties and methods, click Application in the InfoPath 2003 SDK's object diagram, and then click the Properties or Methods links to open a list of links to applicable help topics.

Table 16-1 Selected Properties of the *Application* Object

Property	Description
*MachineOnlineState**	Returns an *EnumMachineOnlineState* enumeration that has one of the following values: *Online*, *Offline*, or *IEIsInOfflineMode*. The latter two states indicate that the network isn't available.
*UsableHeight**, *UsableWidth**	Returns the maximum value in pixels to which you can set the *Window.Height* and *Window.Width* properties (Integer).
*Window.Height**, *Window.Width**	Gets or sets the specified window's height and width in pixels (Integer).
*Window.Top**, *Windows.Left**	Gets or sets the specified window's top and left margins in pixels (Integer).
*User.IsCurrentUser (strLogin)**	Returns *True* if the login specified by *strLogin* (in DOMAIN\UserName format) is the currently logged in user.
*User.IsUserMemberOf (strGroup)**	Returns *True* if the currently logged in user is a member of the security group specified by *strGroup* (in DOMAIN\GroupName format).
ActiveWindow.WindowType	Gets or sets an *XdWindowType* enumeration that has one the following values: *xdDesignerWindow* or *xdEditorWindow*. During debugging, the value returned by inspecting this property in the *OnOpen* event handler is *xdDesignerWindow*, if the preview window isn't open when you build the project.
ActiveWindow.Caption	Returns the window name from the title bar, such as Preview1 or Form1. During debugging, the value in the *OnOpen* event handler is *Nothing*.

Table 16-2 Selected Methods of the *Application* Object

Method	Description
*IsDestinationReachable (strURL)**	Tests for network connectivity to a server specified by a UNC path to a shared folder, such as \\OakLeaf-W2K3\Shared, or the URL for a Web site or virtual directory,to a shared folder, such as *http://www.oak-leaf.ws/infopath*. The *strURL* argument must contain the share name for UNCs—for example, \\OakLeaf-W2K3 fails with an exception. IP addresses and URLs require a fully trusted form, because the domain can't be predetermined. The method returns *True* if the network resource is accessible.
Quit (blnForce)	Closes the current InfoPath instance. If *blnForce* is *False*, the default, a message prompts users to save changed (dirty) forms. If *blnForce* is *True*, InfoPath closes immediately without saving changes.
*CacheSolution (strURI)**	Checks the currency of a published form's cache and updates the local cache from the published location, if necessary.

The C:\Microsoft Press\Introducing InfoPath 2003\Chapter16\Rss2Events (Ch11) folder contains text files of sample Visual Basic .NET code and a starter Rss2Events project for this chapter's proceduresCh11. Each of the form's two views has a button; you add event handlers for the buttons later in this chapter.

The following code from OnLoadAppCode.txt illustrates the use of several new *Application.User* properties and methods described in Table 16-1:

```
'Application properties and methods examples
With thisApplication
    'Check network connectivity
    Dim blnOnline As Boolean
    If .MachineOnlineState = EnumMachineOnlineState.Online Then
        blnOnline = True
        'Check network resource availability
        Dim blnLAN As Boolean = _
          .IsDestinationReachable("\\OakLeaf-W2K3\Shared")
        Dim blnWeb As Boolean = _
          .IsDestinationReachable("www.oakleaf.ws/infopath/")
    Else
        'Warn user and disable operations that require
        'a network connection
    End If
    'Check user identity and group membership
    'Change OAKLEAF to your domain name
    With .User
        Dim blnIsUserAdmin As Boolean = _
          .IsCurrentUser("OAKLEAF\Administrator")
        Dim blnIsGroupIPDesigners As Boolean = _
          .IsUserMemberOf("OAKLEAF\InfoPathDesigners")
        Dim blnIsGroupIPUsers As Boolean = _
          .IsUserMemberOf("OAKLEAF\InfoPathUsers")
        'Logic to restrict user activities based on user name and/or
        'group membership goes here
    End With
    'Return the InfoPath majorversion.minorversion.build
    Dim strVersion As String = .Version
End With
```

This code tests network connectivity, so code in the first *If* block won't execute if you're not connected to a local area network (LAN) or the Internet. The *Application.User* method supplements the *XDocument* objects's *Role* property, which returns the name of the role assigned to the current user.

To add the code to the *OnOpen* event handler and test the values, follow these steps.

▶ Add and test application properties and methods

1. **Navigate to your C:\Microsoft Press\Introducing InfoPath 2003\Chapter16\Rss2Events (Ch11)Ch11 folder, and double-click Rss2Events.sln to open the project.**
2. **Press F5 to build and run the project, choose View, All Sections to display the alternative view, and then close the preview window.**
3. **In Notepad, open OnLoadAppCode.txt from the project's parent folder with Word Wrap off, and copy and paste the code below the *OnLoad* event handler's *Try* statement.**

4. In the first *If* block, change *\\OakLeaf-W2K3\Shared* to an accessible shared folder.
5. In the *With .User* block, change *OAKLEAF* to your domain name or, if you're not a member of an ActiveDirectory domain, to your computer name. Change login and group names to suit your computer's configuration.
6. Select the *Try* statement, and press F9 to add a breakpoint.
7. Press F5 to execute the code to the breakpoint.
8. Press F11 to step through the code to the *Dim blnLAN...* statement, and pass the mouse pointer over the *blnLAN* variable name, which displays *blnLAN = True.*

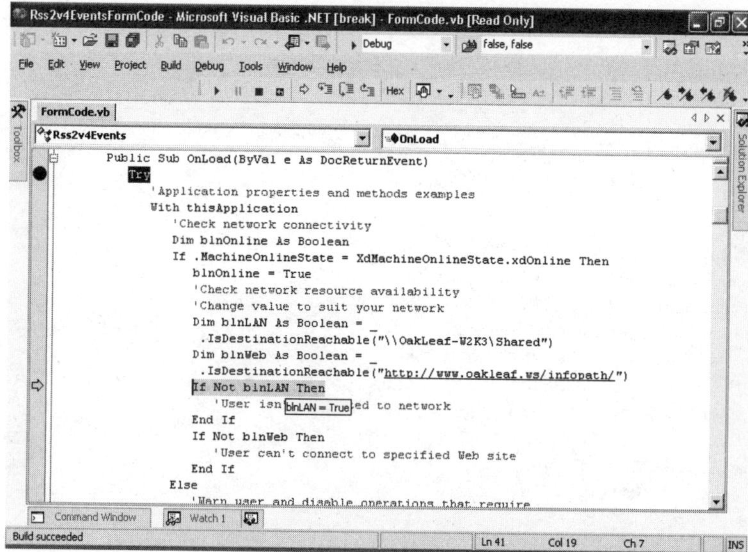

The code you paste from OnLoadAppCode.txt has some additional statements to make inspecting the values easier.

9. Continue stepping through the code, stopping at the *End With* statements and checking the variable values, which are visible only within the code block in which you declare them. The last *With* block doesn't display values.
10. Press F5 to continue execution, verify the size and state of InfoPath's design window, and close the preview window.

You'll add event handlers for the buttons and set the size and state of the InfoPath window later in the chapter.

Exploring the *XDocument* Object

Figure 16-3 shows the InfoPath SP-1 *XDocuments* object model. The *thisXDocument* variable and most event-handling stubs' *e* (*eventArgs*) argument return a reference to the *XDocument* object whose form is being edited and has the focus. The most common use of *XDocuments* is to determine the number of simultaneously open forms and their properties, such as *Caption*.

Table 16-2 describes the *XDocument* object's top-level collections and objects and selected child objects. An asterisk denotes elements added or enhanced in InfoPath SP-1.

Table 16-3 Top-Level Collections and Objects of the *XDocument* Object

Collection or Object	Description
DOM	Returns an *IXMLDOMDocument* instance that represents the complete *XDocument* object as a tree of XML nodes. The *xml* property returns a *String* that you can manipulate with Visual Basic .NET procedural code. Chapter 17 provides *IXMLDOMDocument* programming examples.
Errors	Contains *Error* objects that result from schema or data validation failures. *Error* object properties return detailed information about the source and reason for the failure.
Extension	Returns global script values and provides access to functions in JScript or VBScript files, but not to functions in managed code.
Solution	Has properties that provide information about the Manifest.xsf file; the *DOM* property returns an *IXMLDOMDocument* instance of the file.
DataObjects	Provides access to the release version's *DataAdapter* objects. SP-1's *DataAdapters* collection replaces and makes obsolete the *DataObjects* collection.
*DataAdapters**	Contains members for *DataAdapter* objects, which represent main and secondary data source instances that you create with the Data Connection Wizard. Chapter 17 provides customizing data connection examples.
*SignedDataBlocks**	Contains *SignedDataBlock* objects for each data block that has a digital signature. This object has a *Signatures* collection of *Signature* objects, which contain information about an individual signer of the data block, and a *Certificate* object that provides details about the signer's certificate. The *OnSigned* event returns a *SignEvent* object, which represents a new *SignedDataBlock* object.
Util	Provides *Math* and *Date* child objects and a *Match* method to test field values against a regular expression. Chapter 17 provides examples of complex regular expressions in schemas and for data validation.

Table 16-3 Top-Level Collections and Objects of the *XDocument* Object *(continued)*

Collection or Object	Description
*Util.Math**	Provides access to the aggregate functions of the Insert Formula dialog box—*Avg, Min, Max,* and *Eval*—which take an *IXMLNodeList* object as their argument. *Eval* lets you evaluate an expression, as in *Util.Math.Avg(Util.MathEval(IXMLNodeList, "UnitPrice * Quantity * (1 - Discount)"),* to sum OrderDetails items. *Util.Math* also provides an *Nz* (null-to-zero) function to convert nodes without content to 0 for calculations.
*Util. Date**	Provides *Today* and *Now* functions to return the system date and date/time values as ISO 8610–formatted strings.
*UI**	Provides access to the *Alert* and *Confirm* message boxes you programmed in Chapter 15 and *ShowModalDialog* and *ShowSignatureDialog* methods to display custom and Digital Signatures dialog boxes. The new *SetSaveAsDialogLocation* and *SetSaveAsDialogFileName* methods let you specify the default path and file name for the Save As dialog box.
View	Represents the active form's current view. The *View.Window* property returns a *Window* object for the current view, which has the same collection and object members as Figure 16-2's *Application.Windows.Window* object. The most commonly used members of the *View* object are its *SwitchViews* method and its *View.Window.TaskPanes(0). HTMLDocument* for changing the HTML content of a custom task pane.
ViewInfos	Contains a *ViewInfo* object for each view of the current form, which provides *IsDefault* and *Name* property values.

Tables to fully describe all objects, methods, and properties of the *XDocument* object would require a book of their own. Instead, the procedures in this chapter's remaining sections and Chapter 17's more advanced procedures show you how to program the most commonly used *XDocument* elements.

Working with View Objects and Events

You can make changing views easier for users by adding buttons to execute the *SwitchView("ViewName")* method. The Rss2Events sample form has an All Sections button in the ItemsOnly view and an Items Only button in the AllSections view. If you have several views, it's a good practice to inform users which view is active. Text in a layout table cell can accomplish this objective, but adding the view name to the form window's title bar shows you how to take advantage of the *OnSwitchView* event and the *Caption* property.

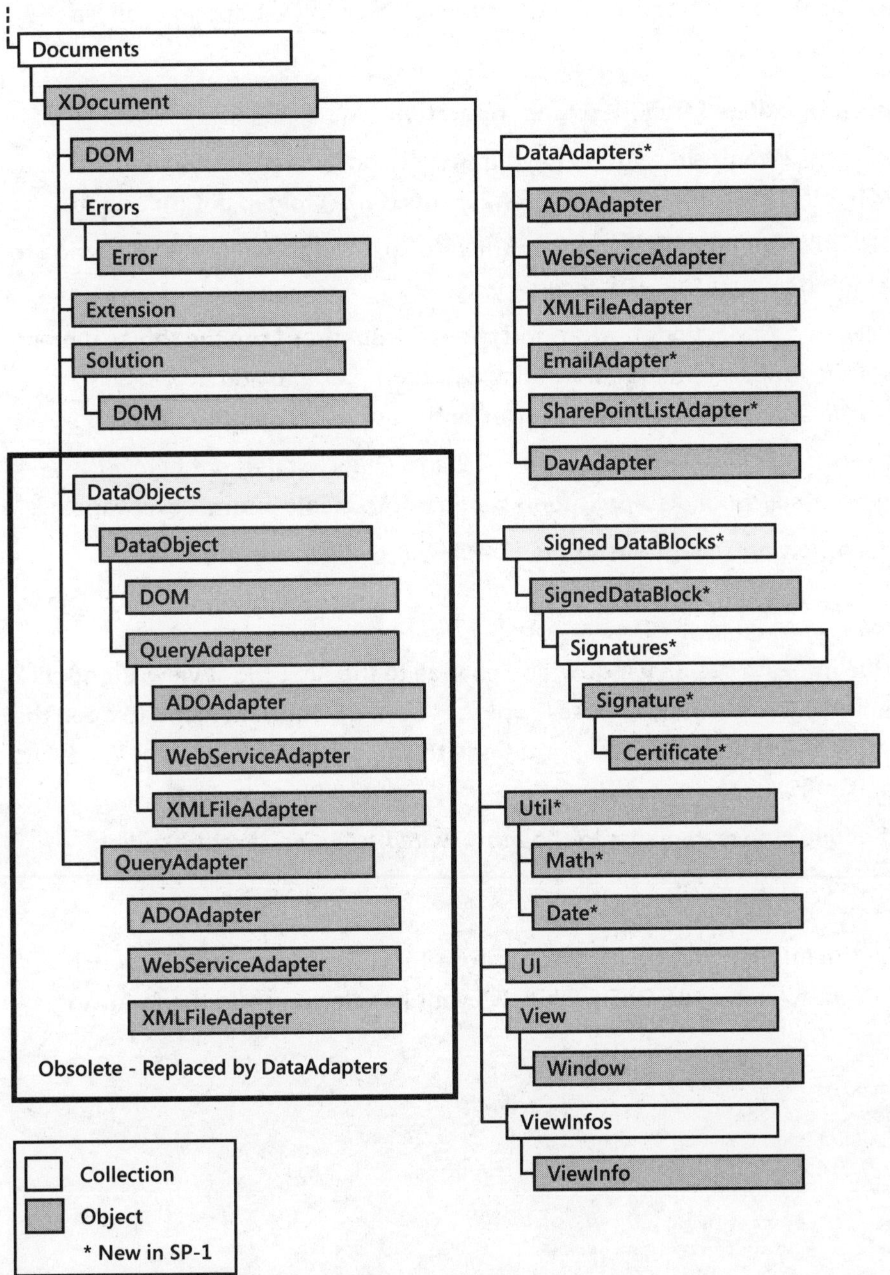

Figure 16-3 InfoPath SP-1 adds three collections and nine objects to the *XDocument* object. The *DataAdapters* collection replaces the InfoPath release version's more complex *DataObjects* collection.

To program the two view buttons and the two view windows' *Caption* properties, follow these steps.

▶ Add event handlers for view-related operations

1. **Open the Rss2Events.sln solution in your C:\Microsoft Press\Introducing InfoPath 2003\Chapter16\Rss2Events (Ch11)\Rss2Events (Ch11) folder, if it isn't open.**
2. **Choose Tools, Open InfoPath, to open the InfoPath design window, and change to the default ItemsOnly view, if necessary.**
3. **Right-click the All Sections button, and choose Properties from the shortcut menu to open the Properties dialog box. Click Edit Form Code to add a *btnViewAll_OnClick* event-handling stub, and close the Properties dialog box.**
4. **Add a *Private strViewName As String = " (Items Only)"* statement below the *Private thisApplication As Application* statement to create a form-level variable.**
5. **Add the following statements to the *btnViewAll_OnClick* event handler:**

```
strViewName = " (All Sections)"
thisXDocument.View.SwitchView("AllSections")
```

6. **Open the InfoPath design window, and change to the AllSections view. Right-click the Items Only button, and choose Properties from the shortcut menu to open the Properties dialog box. Click Edit Form Code to add a *btnViewItems_OnClick* event-handling stub.**
7. **Add the following statements to the *btnViewItems_OnClick* event handler:**

```
strViewName = " (Items Only)"
thisXDocument.View.SwitchView("ItemsOnly")
```

8. **Reopen the InfoPath design window, choose Tools, Programming, On Switch Views Event to create the *OnSwitchView* event handler, and add the following statements:**

```
With thisXDocument.View.Window
   'Remove previous view name
   If InStr(.Caption, " (") > 0 Then
      .Caption = Left(.Caption, InStr(.Caption, " (") - 1)
   End If
   'Add the new view name
   .Caption = .Caption + strViewName
End With
```

9. **Press F5 to build and run the project, click the preview window's view buttons, and verify that Preview1's title bar appears as expected, except when the preview window displays the nondefault AllSections view.**

Testing changes to the UI isn't complete until you verify that the changes behave as expected with multiple forms open, not just a form preview. To verify that *thisXDocument.View.Window* represents the currently active form, follow these steps.

▶ **Test your code with multiple open forms**

1. **Close the preview window, if it's open, and open the design window.**
2. **Select the Fill Out A Form task pane, and click the first entry in the list to open a new form.**
3. **Click both view buttons to add the view name to the form caption.**
4. **Activate the designer, and repeat steps 2 and 3 for at least two more forms.**
5. **Verify that all form captions contain the view name. In this case, the form opens with the default view and view name.**

Programming the *XDocuments* Collection

Testing the *Count* property of the *XDocuments* collection lets you determine how many instances of a template's form are open, as described in Table 16-2. The following code in XDocumentsAlert.txt adds an alert, which displays information about all forms and the active form, to the *btnViewItems_OnClick* event handler:

```
With thisApplication.ActiveWindow
   'Display an informative alert if more than one form is open
   Dim intNumXDocs As Integer = thisApplication.XDocuments.Count
   Dim strXDocNames As String
   Dim strName As String = .Caption
   Dim strType As String = .WindowType.ToString
   Dim strState As String = .WindowState.ToString
   Dim intCtr As Integer
   For intCtr = 0 To intNumXDocs - 1
        'Get the open form's caption in the title bar
        strXDocNames += _
        thisApplication.XDocuments.Item(intCtr).View.Window.Caption + ", "
   Next intCtr
   'Trim the names string
   strXDocNames = Left(strXDocNames, Len(strXDocNames) - 2)
   If intNumXDocs > 1 Then
        'Display details
        thisXDocument.UI.Alert("There are " + intNumXDocs.ToString + _
        " XDocuments in the collection: " + strXDocNames + vbCrLf + _
       "Active Window: " + strName + vbCrLf + "Window Type: " + _
       strType + vbCrLf + "Window State: " + strState)
   End If
End With
```

The preceding code uses the *thisApplication.ActiveWindow* object to point to the currently open form, but *thisXDocument.View.Window* and *e.XDocument.View.Window* work as well. All three objects are pointers to the same *Window* instance.

To add the code from XDocumentsAlert.txt and perform an additional test of the code you wrote in the preceding section, follow these steps.

▶ Add an alert to display information about multiple open forms

1. **Close all open InfoPath windows, and return to Visual Studio's FormCode.vb window.**
2. **Open XDocumentsAlert.txt in Notepad with Word Wrap off, and copy and paste the code above the existing code in the *btnViewItems_OnClick* event handler.**
3. **Press F5 to display a preview window, and repeat the steps in the preceding procedure, but don't close the preview window.**
4. **After you've added three forms and clicked each view button at least once, the alert appears as shown here:**

The alerts you add in this and later sections are intended to display information returned by the managed code you add. If you were programming these objects with JScript or VBScript, you'd be using alerts primarily for debugging purposes. Relying on alerts to return suspect variable values or debugging messages makes trouble-shooting complex script a cumbersome process.

Setting Custom File Paths and Names

Incorrect file locations, names, or both are the probable outcome when users must type or navigate to the path and type file names for InfoPath documents. The *UI* item in Table 16-3 briefly describes the *SetSaveAsDialogLocation* and *SetSaveAsDialogFileName* methods. You can hard-code the path or, for forms that aren't custom-installed, specify the current template file's location by making a minor modification to the *XDocument.Solution.URI* property value, which returns the path and file name of the form's template. Automatically generating unique file names with date/time values or from unique form field values—such as an order or invoice number—minimizes file-naming errors. You invoke the two *SetSaveAsDialog* methods from the *OnLoad*, *OnSaveRequest*, or *OnSwitchViews* event handlers or from any event handler that executes before users choose File, Save for a new form or File, Save As for an existing form.

Setting the Path and File Name in the *OnLoad* Event Handler

The following code from OnLoadSaveAsDefault.txt sets the default path to that of the form's template, which accommodates local forms and those published to a shared folder or Web server. Forms published to SharePoint sites don't require a default path, because SharePoint provides the correct path. The code creates the default file name–Rss*YYYYMMDDThhmm*.xml–from a modified version of the ISO 8601 date and time when the user opens the form.

```
'Set default path (template folder) and file name
'Get the path from the Solution.URI property
Dim strPath As String = e.XDocument.Solution.URI
Dim blnIsWebSite As Boolean'Web and SharePoint sites
Dim blnIsWSS As Boolean 'SharePoint site
Dim blnIsFile As Boolean
Dim strTestFile As String = "file:///"
Dim strTestHTTP As String = "http://"
Dim strTestWSS As String = "/Forms/"
'Set the flags
If InStr(strPath, strTestFile) > 0 Then
   blnIsFile = True
ElseIf InStr(strPath, strTestHTTP) > 0 Then
   blnIsWebSite = True
   If InStr(strPath, strTestWSS) > 0 Then
      blnIsWSS = True
   End If
End If

If blnIsFile Or blnIsWebSite Then
   'Trim the URI for the path to remove the template file
   If blnIsWebSite Then
      strPath = Mid(strPath, InStr(strPath, strTestHTTP))
      strPath = Left(strPath, InStrRev(strPath, "/") - 1)
   Else
      'Remove the prefix
      strPath = Mid(strPath, InStr(strPath, strTestFile) + _
       Len(strTestFile))
      strPath = Left(strPath, InStrRev(strPath, "\") - 1)
      'Replace URL-encoded spaces
      strPath = Replace(strPath, "%20", " ")
   End If
End If
Dim datFile As DateTime = Now
Dim strFile As String = datFile.ToString("s")
'Remove seconds, hyphens and colons
strFile = "Rss" + Left(strFile, InStrRev(strFile, ":") - 1) + ".xml"
strFile = Replace(strFile, ":", "")
strFile = Replace(strFile, "-", "")
'Set the dialog variables
With e.XDocument.UI
   If Not blnIsWSS Then
      'SharePoint determines the path
      .SetSaveAsDialogLocation(strPath)
   End If
   .SetSaveAsDialogFileName(strFile)
   'Temporary alert for testing templates published to
```

```
        'Web and SharePoint sites
        Dim strSaveAs As String = _
         "Solution.URI = '" + e.XDocument.Solution.URI + "'" + vbCrLf
        If blnIsWSS Then
           strSaveAs += "Form file = '" + strFile + "'"
        ElseIf blnIsWebSite Then
           strSaveAs += "Form server, directory, and file = '" + _
              strPath + "/" + strFile + "'"
        Else
           strSaveAs += "Form path and file = '" + strPath + "\" + _
              strFile + "'"
        End If
        .Alert(strSaveAs)
     End With
```

To add the preceding code to the *OnLoad* event handler and test the code with the template on the local file system and deployed to Web and SharePoint sites, follow these steps.

▶ Create default path and file names for a form

1. Close all open InfoPath windows, and return to Visual Studio's FormCode.vb window.
2. Open OnLoadSaveAsDefault.txt in Notepad with Word Wrap off, and copy and paste the code above the *Get All pubDates* comment in the *OnLoad* event handler.
3. Press F5 to build and run the code and display the alert with the original *URI* value and the path and file name for the preview window, similar to that shown here:

   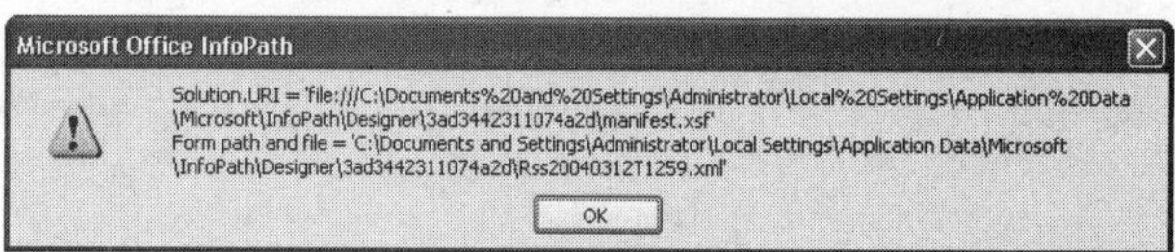

   InfoPath caches preview templates in a randomly named subfolder of My Documents shown in the alert.
4. Close the preview window, and open the designer. Choose File, Fill Out A Form to open the Fill Out A Form dialog box, and click the Recently Used Forms link. Select the Rss2Events form, and then click the Remove This Form link to remove the form from the cache. Close the dialog box.
5. Close the project, navigate to the ...\bin\Debug folder, and double-click Rss2Events.xsn to open a new form, which displays an alert similar to that shown on the next page.

6. **Verify that the path and file names in the alert are correct, close the alert, and type a few characters in the Title and Description boxes. Choose File, Save to verify that the Save dialog box displays the correct path and file name. Save the form for later tests.**
7. **Close the form.**

This chapter's "On Your Own" section provides exercises for publishing the completed form to Web and SharePoint sites and verifying that the form behaves as expected.

Modifying Window Properties in the *OnSwitchViews* Event Handler

The *OnSwitchViews* event fires after the *OnLoad* event when you open a form and each time the user changes the current view. Some *Window* properties–such as *Caption*–aren't accessible in the *OnLoad* event handler, and changing other *Window* properties can result in unpredictable exceptions. Thus, the *OnSwitchViews* event is the better location for initializing custom *Window* properties, such as the title bar text, state (normal or maximized), size, and margins. When you specify a default file name, it's a good practice to replace Form# in a new form's title bar text with the proposed file name. Many forms–especially those that emulate paper forms–should open with a fixed size, regardless of the user's display resolution.

The following code from the OnSwitchViews.txt file replaces Form1 or higher with the default file name, specifies the normal window state, sets a fixed form width and height, and centers the form in the user's display.

```
If (Left(.Caption, 4) = "Form" And Val(Mid(.Caption, 5, 1)) > 0) _
      Or Left(.Caption, 7) = "Preview" Then
   'Replace caption if Form#[#] or Preview
   .Caption = strFileName
End If
'Force normal window state
.WindowState = XdWindowState.xdWindowStateNormal
'Set fixed dimensions
.Height = 380
.Width = 460
If thisApplication.UsableHeight >= .Height And _
      thisApplication.UsableWidth >= .Width Then
   'Center the form
   .Top = (thisApplication.UsableHeight - .Height) \ 2
   .Left = (thisApplication.UsableWidth - .Width) \ 2
End If
```

To add the code from OnSwitchViews.txt and test it, follow these steps.

▶ Add the default file name to the title bar and set the form's size

1. **Close all open InfoPath windows, and return to Visual Studio's FormCode.vb window for the project.**
2. **Add a *Private strFileName As String* declaration after the *Private strViewName* statement near the beginning of the code.**
3. **Add a *strFileName = strFile* statement after the *strFile = Replace(strFile, "-", "")* statement in the *OnLoad* event handler.**
4. **Comment the *.Alert(strSaveAs)* statement in the *OnLoad* event handler.**
5. **Open OnSwitchViews.txt, and copy and paste the code above the *Remove previous view name* comment in the *OnSwitchViews* event handler.**
6. **Press F5 to build and run the program. The preview window, after you click the Items Only button, appears similar to this:**

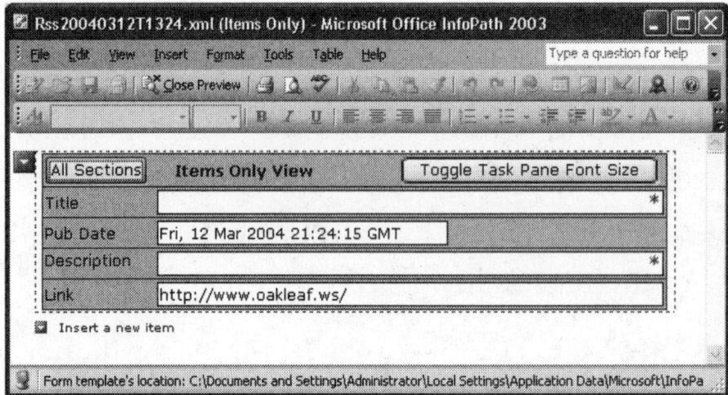

7. **Close the preview window, and open two or more new forms to verify that the form's caption is correct. You must wait up to one minute between successive form additions to verify that the default file name differs because the last two digits of the file name are system-time seconds.**

Testing the *SignedDataBlocks* Collection

When you digitally sign an entire form, you can select the Prompt User To Sign The Form If It Is Submitted Without A Signature check box on the Digital Signatures tab of the Form Options dialog box. There's no corresponding check box for the Enable Digital Signatures For Specific Data In The Form option. Warning the user that the form is missing or has invalid digital signatures requires iterating each member of the *SignedDataBlocks* collection and its *Signatures* collection to detect these conditions.

Listing 16-1 shows the code from the FnTestDigitalSignatures.txt file for the TestDigitalSignatures function, which you can call from the *OnSaveRequest* or *OnSubmitRequest* event handler. If a user receives a warning message box and clicks Yes, the *thisXDocument.UI.ShowSignatureDialog()* statement opens the Digital Signatures dialog box so that the user can correct the problem.

```
Private Function TestDigitalSignatures() As Boolean
   'Iterate SignedDataBlocks members and test for
   'presence and validity of signatures
   Dim strConfirm As String
   With thisXDocument.SignedDataBlocks
      If .Count > 0 Then
         strConfirm = "This document has " + _
          .Count.ToString + " digitally signed data block(s)." + vbCrLf
         Dim intBlock As Integer
         Dim intSig As Integer
         Dim intMissing As Integer
         Dim intBadSigs As Integer
         Dim strSigners As String
         For intBlock = 0 To .Count - 1
            strSigners = ""
            'Iterate the blocks
            With .Item(intBlock)
               'Add the signature name
               strConfirm += "Block " + (intBlock + 1).ToString + _
               " (" + .Name + ") has " + .Signatures.Count.ToString + _
               " signature(s)." + vbCrLf
               'Add the signature relationship
               strConfirm += "The signature relationship is '"
               Select Case .SignatureRelation
                  Case XdSignatureRelation.xdSignatureRelationSingle
                     strConfirm += "Single"
                  Case XdSignatureRelation.xdSignatureRelationCoSign
                     strConfirm += "Co-sign"
                  Case XdSignatureRelation.xdSignatureRelationCounterSign
                     strConfirm += "Counter-sign"
               End Select
               strConfirm += "'." + vbCrLf
               If .Signatures.Count > 0 Then
                  For intSig = 0 To .Signatures.Count - 1
                     'Iterate the signatures and add the signer
                     'and certificate issuer
                     Dim strIssuedTo As String = _
                      .Signatures.Item(intSig).Certificate.IssuedTo
                     strConfirm += "  Signature " + (intSig + 1).ToString + _
                     " is issued to " + strIssuedTo + _
                     " and issued by " + _
                     .Signatures.Item(intSig).Certificate.IssuedBy
                     If .Signatures.Item(intSig).Status = _
                      XdSignatureStatus.xdSignatureStatusValid And _
                      InStr(strSigners, strIssuedTo) = 0 Then
                        strConfirm += " (Valid)"
                     Else
                        strConfirm += " (Invalid)"
                        intBadSigs += 1
                     End If
```

```
                    strSigners += .Signatures.Item(intSig).Certificate.IssuedTo
                    strConfirm += vbCrLf
                 Next intSig
              Else
                 intMissing += 1
              End If
           End With
        Next intBlock
        If intMissing > 0 Or intBadSigs > 0 Then
           'Construct the confirm dialog string
           If intMissing > 0 Then
              strConfirm += intMissing.ToString + _
               " signature(s) are missing"
              If intBadSigs > 0 Then
                 strConfirm += " and " + intMissing.ToString + _
                  " signature(s) are invalid." + vbCrLf
                 strConfirm += "Do you want to sign or fix this document?"
              Else
                 strConfirm += "." + vbCrLf + _
                 "Do you want to sign this document?" + vbCrLf + _
                 "(Disregard co- or counter-signatures that don't apply " + _
                 "at this point)"
              End If
           Else
              If intBadSigs > 0 Then
                 strConfirm += vbCrLf + intBadSigs.ToString + _
                  " signature(s) are invalid." + vbCrLf + _
                  "Do you want to fix this document?"
              End If
           End If

           'Handle response from confirm dialog
           Dim xdConfirm As XdConfirmChoice = _
            thisXDocument.UI.Confirm(strConfirm, _
            XdConfirmButtons.xdYesNoCancel)
           Select Case xdConfirm
              Case XdConfirmChoice.xdYes
                 'Show the signature dialog
                 thisXDocument.UI.ShowSignatureDialog()
                 Return True
              Case XdConfirmChoice.xdCancel
                 'Cancel save if called in OnSaveRequest handler
                 Return False
              Case XdConfirmChoice.xdNo
                 'Not a wise move
                 Return True
           End Select
        End If
     End If
  End With
```

Listing 16-1 The *TestDigitalSignatures* function.

The Rss2Events project in your ...\Rss2Events (Ch11)\Rss2Events (Ch11) subfolder contains two predefined *SignedDataBlocks–ChannelPlusItems* and *Items–*that don't have digital signatures. To add the *TestDigitalSignatures* function to your code and test its execution, follow these steps.

▶ **Add the test function and call it from the *OnSaveRequest* event handler**

1. Close all open InfoPath windows, and return to Visual Studio's FormCode.vb window.
2. Open FnTestDigitalSignatures.txt in Notepad with Word Wrap off, and copy and paste the immediately above the *End Class* statement near the end of the code.
3. Choose Tools, Display InfoPath to open the InfoPath design window. Choose Tools, Form Options in the InfoPath design window to open the Form Options dialog, and click the Open And Save tab. Select the Save Using Custom Code check box, click the Edit button to add an *OnSaveRequest* event-handling stub, close the dialog, and return to the FormCode.vb window.
4. Replace the event handler's stub code with the following:

```
'Test digital signatures before saving form
If TestDigitalSignatures() Then
  e.IsCancelled = e.PerformSaveOperation
Else
  e.IsCancelled = True
End If
e.ReturnStatus = True
```

5. Press F5 to build and run the code, close the preview, and open a new form. Type a few characters in the preview window's Title and Description text boxes, and press Ctrl+S or choose File, Save to display the confirm message box, shown here:

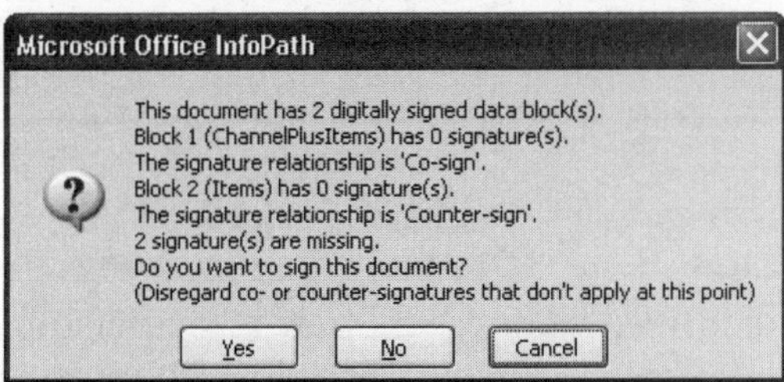

6. Click Yes to open the Digital Signatures dialog box, add one or more signatures to the ChannelPlusItems block, and click Close.
7. Press Ctrl+S again to provide details of the digital signature you added in the message box, which looks similar to this:

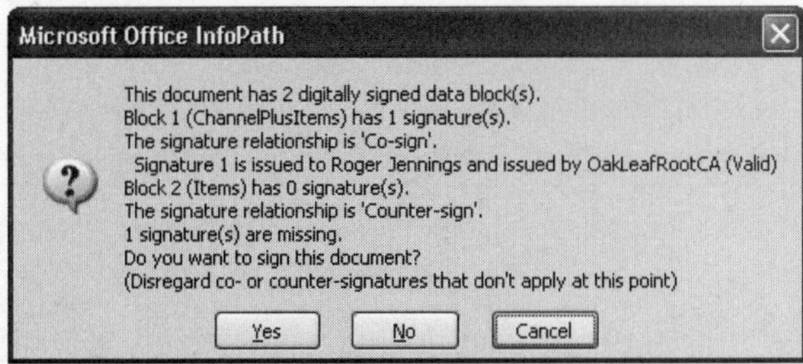

8. **Click Yes, and add a signature to the Items block. Click Close, and press Ctrl+S to verify that the message box no longer appears.**

If you add the same digital signature more than once to a field that requires a co-signature or counter-signature, the confirm message box states that the co-signature or counter-signature is invalid.

Chapter Summary

InfoPath's COM object hierarchy, which you access through the InfoPath PIA, is much simpler than that of other Office applications. Most InfoPath projects involve getting or setting properties and invoking methods of the *Application* and *XDocument* objects and their descendants with event-handling code.

The *Application* object has a set of properties to test for a live network connection and access to file servers and Web sites. The *Application.User* interface has methods to determine whether the form's user name matches a specified logon name and is a member of a particular local or domain-level security group. The *XDocument* objects's *Role* property returns the name of the current user's role.

The *XDocuments* collection's *XDocument* members and their child objects are the primary targets of event-handling code. The *XDocuments.Count* property returns the number of currently open forms; each form has its own *XDocument* instance. The *thisXDocument* variable and *e.XDocument* event argument return the instance of the form with the focus.

This chapter's procedures showed you how to use button controls to change form views; how to add the view name to the form's caption; and how to set default path and file names for saving forms to the local file system, shared folders, Web sites, and Windows SharePoint Services sites. You also learned how to display the default file name in the form's title bar and test individually signed sections or fields for the presence and validity of digital signatures.

Q&A

Q. Can I access InfoPath form controls and their properties with managed code?

A. No. Visual Studio Windows and Web forms projects provide full programmability of controls, but InfoPath doesn't expose controls, which are defined in *ViewName*.xsl files, to .NET or script code.

Q. Can I import VBA or script code to an InfoPath project's FormCode.vb or FormCode.cs window?

A. Yes, with reservations. Most InfoPath VBScript files can be built and run with *Option Strict Off*, and general-purpose Visual Basic 6 and VBA procedures or functions will compile without major modifications. Importing InfoPath JScript files to FormCode.cs requires substantial rewriting, because C# doesn't offer the equivalent of *Option Strict Off*. InfoPath doesn't support Microsoft Visual J# code.

Q. Setting *Option Strict On* generates a large number of errors when building code that runs fine with *Option Strict Off*. Is it worth the effort to fix the type conversion errors?

A. Yes. You should set *Option Strict On* for all Visual Basic .NET projects, except when initially testing Visual Basic 6 projects you convert with the Upgrade Wizard, VBA code you import into the Convert Visual Basic 6 Code dialog box, or VBScript you paste into the FormCode.vb window. *Option Strict Off* enables implicit late binding of *Object* variables. Late binding requires helper objects and reflection to invoke the correct methods when your project runs, and it uses *Variant*-style type coercion to accommodate type conflicts. Early binding eliminates this overhead, enables IntelliSense for strongly typed variables, and disables what many Visual Basic developers call "Evil Type Coercion," or "ETC." Strong typing is especially important for projects that use custom code for database-related operations. To learn more about this subject, search the Visual Studio Help index for *Visual Basic .NET, implicit late binding*.

Q. Why do I get a *Security error* message when I attempt to execute a member of a .NET class that I added to the project?

A. Forms must be fully trusted to execute members of .NET classes that aren't digitally signed by Microsoft or by the European Computer Manufacturers Association (ECMA, the standards body for ECMAScript—formerly JavaScript—and the C# language). Some Microsoft .NET namespaces—such as *Microsoft.mshtml*—require fully trusted forms. You can't sign a form with a code signing certificate while you're debugging it; you must sign the template's .xsn file and test it. An alternative is to specify that all InfoPath managed code runs with full trust on your computer; Chapter 17 shows you how to change the .NET Framework 1.1's security level.

On Your Own

Here are some additional exercises to validate the Visual Basic .NET code you added in this chapter:

1. Publish your form with all procedures completed (or the final version of Rss2Events in your ...\Rss2EventsFinal\Rss2EventsFinal subfolder) to a Web site, using the techniques described in the section "Publishing Templates to an Intranet Site," in Chapter 12. Create multiple forms, and verify that you can save them to the Web server.
2. If you have access to a Windows SharePoint Services site, publish the same form to a library by following the instructions in the section "Publishing Templates to SharePoint Form Libraries," in Chapter 12. Verify that multiple forms, which don't have default path values in this case, behave as expected under SharePoint management.
3. Test submission of the form to the SharePoint site you created in the preceding exercise. See the section "Submitting Documents to a SharePoint Forms Library," in Chapter 12, for instructions.

CHAPTER 17

Writing Advanced Event Handlers

In this chapter, you will learn how to:

- **Use the Microsoft .NET 1.1 Configuration tool to grant full trust to execute managed code**
- **Modify the content of a custom task pane using Microsoft Visual Basic .NET code**
- **Test for missing digital signatures in a form that uses signed code blocks**
- **Generate a customized version of an InfoPath data document and validate it against an external XML schema**
- **Add a form toolbar with standard and custom buttons, write event handlers for toolbar buttons, and test for data validation errors before saving a data document**
- **Copy text data from one field to another, specify a default data document for form previews, and validate formatted data with complex regular expressions**
- **Display running sums in table footer expression boxes**
- **Populate a drop-down list and text box from a single secondary data source**
- **Use managed code to set default values and validate date/time fields**
- **Insert new database records with a Web service client**
- **Create your own NWOrderWS Microsoft ASP.NET Web service, and Migrate InfoPath Web service consumers to a new Web service location**

For more information:

- **See the sections "Creating Fully Trusted Forms by Code Signing" and "Distributing Custom-Installed Templates," in Chapter 12, "Publishing Form Templates" for more information about signing and registering fully trusted forms.**
- **See the section "Adding a Custom Help Task Pane," in Chapter 11, "Setting Template and Digital Signing Options," for more information about adding custom task panes to a form.**
- **Refer to the section "Signing Individual Form Groups or Fields," in Chapter 11, to review adding digital signature blocks to a form.**
- **See the section "Validating Text Box Patterns," in Chapter 8, "Validating Form Data," for more information about using regular expressions to validate field values.**
- **Review the section "Calculating Values with the Expression Box," in Chapter 6, "Adding Basic Controls and Lists," for more information about adding expression boxes to repeating table rows.**

To work through this chapter:

- You should have installed in your C:\Microsoft Press\Introducing InfoPath 2003\Chapter17 folder the sample files from the CD that accompanies this book.
- You must fulfill the prerequisites of Chapter 15, "Introducing InfoPath Form Template Projects," and Chapter 16, "Navigating the InfoPath Object Model."
- You should have some experience with the Microsoft .NET Framework's System.Xml classes. Experience using the Microsoft.mshtml classes is helpful, but not essential.
- You need Microsoft Access 2002 or later with the Microsoft SQL Server Desktop Engine (MSDE) 2000 installed and the NorthwindCS.adp project (or an equivalent) to verify the stored procedures that you add to the NorthwindCS database for a local version of the NWOrdersWS Web service. Alternatively, you can use SQL Server Query Analyzer to run the SQL script and SQL Enterprise Manager to make a required data type change.

The primary purpose of managed event-handling code is to implement business rules that you can't handle with declarative methods–data validation rules, conditional formatting, and roles you establish in InfoPath design mode. Other managed code applications include modifying the content of custom task panes, testing for required digital signatures, displaying calculated values in expression boxes, and saving customized versions of InfoPath XML data documents.

The release version of the Microsoft Office InfoPath 2003 Software Development Kit (SDK) includes 14 Developer Sample Forms to demonstrate Microsoft JScript event-handling code in several scenarios. If you're an accomplished JScript programmer, reviewing the script behind these forms will help you write managed code in Microsoft Visual C# and, to a lesser extent, Visual Basic. NET. This chapter takes an approach that's similar to the Developer Sample Forms by providing examples of forms with complex Visual Basic event handlers. The emphasis is on accomplishing tasks that are required for production versions of the Really Simple Syndication (RSS) 2.0 and Northwind Traders Order Entry and Editing forms that you've progressively developed in the preceding chapters. Another objective of these forms is to demonstrate Visual Basic coding techniques for the new and updated objects, properties, methods, and events in InfoPath 2003 Service Pack 1 (SP-1).

Enabling Full Trust for Managed Code

This chapter's procedures require the Visual Basic .NET event-handling code to run with full trust. You can't digitally sign forms generated from the extracted template files in your project folder. In the .NET Framework's default configuration, you can build–but not run–forms that require full trust for event-handling code. You must specify Full Trust and add a digital signature to the *TemplateName*.xsn file in the project's ...\bin\Debug or ...\bin\Release folder to run the forms. Alternatively, you can register *TemplateName*.xsn by creating a Microsoft Installer (.msi) file with Regform.exe and then executing the .msi file.

Debugging signed or registered forms ordinarily requires a Visual Studio instance connected to the INFOPATH.EXE process. The code in this instance is read-only, so you must open another Visual Studio instance to edit your code and rebuild (but not run) the project. The section "Explore the *SaveRssToFile* Procedure," later in this chapter, shows you how to connect a Visual Studio instance to the INFOPATH.EXE process. Each time you rebuild the project, you must re-sign or reregister *TemplateName*.xsn.

Fortunately, SP-1 provides a workaround for InfoPath developers using managed code. To enable debugging of forms that require full trust, the .NET Framework 1.1 Configuration tool lets you specify full trust for the managed code behind an InfoPath form template. To do so, you add an InfoPath Form Templates code group to the All Code group and assign the new group's project folder and its subfolders Full Trust permissions. Full Trust permissions let you debug and run outside of the InfoPath sandbox managed code that accesses local computer resources without the additional–and inconvenient–INFOPATH.EXE connection. When you're ready to deploy the completed form, add a digital signature to the *TemplateName*.xsn file in the ...\bin\Release folder or create a *TemplateName*.msi file for a registered form.

Working with this chapter's sample forms requires Full Trust permissions for their Visual Basic .NET code. To assign full trust to InfoPath managed code in subfolders of C:\Microsoft Press\Introducing InfoPath 2003\Chapter 17\, as an example, follow these steps.

▶ Run specified InfoPath managed code with full trust

1. **In Control Panel, open the Administrative Tools folder, and double-click the Microsoft .NET Framework 1.1 Configuration shortcut to open the .NET Configuration 1.1 tool's window.**
2. **Expand the Runtime Security Policy, Machine, and Code Groups nodes, as shown here:**

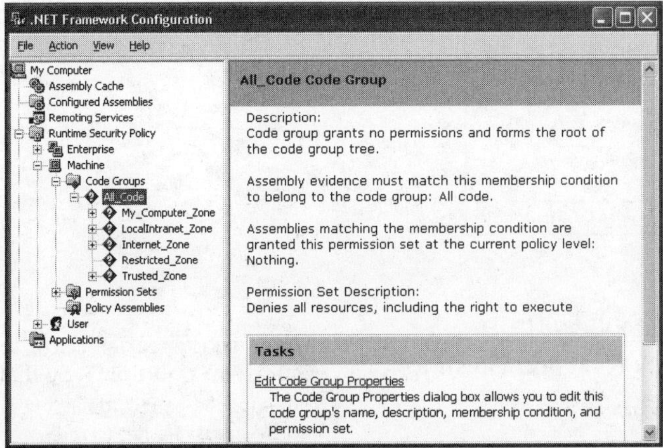

3. **Right click the All_Code node, and choose New from the shortcut menu to open the Create Code Group dialog box. Type InfoPath Form Templates (case sensitive) in the Name box, and optionally add a description, as shown on the next page.**

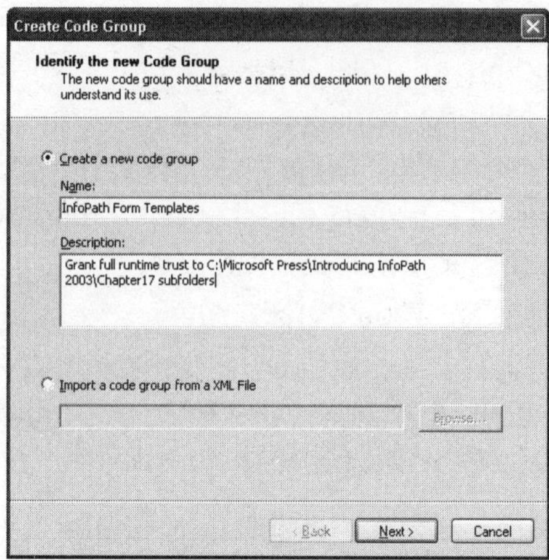

4. Click Next to display the Choose A Condition Type dialog box, and select URL in the drop-down list. Type **file://URLEncodedPathToProjectFolder/* (file://C:/Microsoft Press/Introducing InfoPath 2003/Chapter17/*** for this example) in the URL text box as shown here:

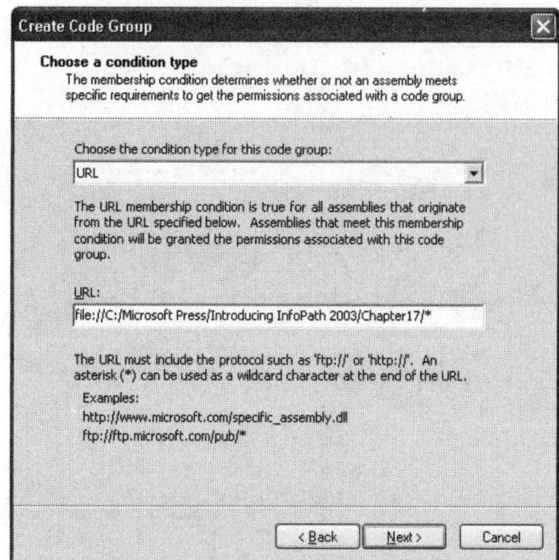

5. Click Next, leave the default FullTrust permission set, and click Next and Finish to complete the full-trust assignment.
6. Close and reopen the .NET Configuration 1.1 window to refresh its data. Your InfoPath Form Templates entry appears under the All_Code node, as shown here:

Typing URL-encoded paths in the Choose A Condition Type dialog box

URL-encoded paths ordinarily require all reverse (black) slashes (\) to be changed to forward slashes (/) and spaces to be replaced with %20. In this case, typing %20 isn't required, and the tool converts reverse slashes after file:// to forward slashes for you. If you substitute %20 for spaces, the tool reverts all instances to spaces. The /* suffix grants full runtime trust to assemblies in the designated folder's subfolders.

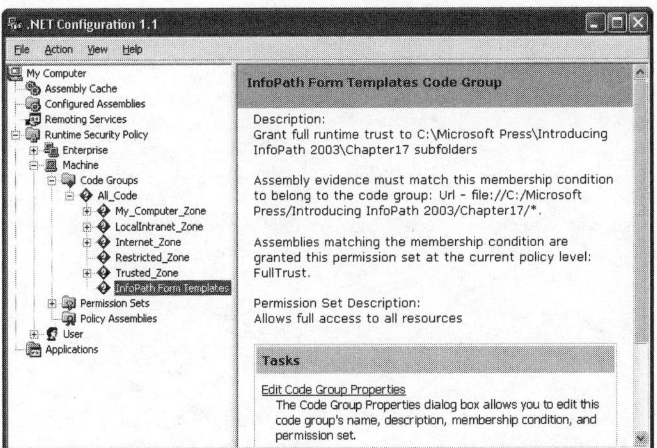

Maintaining runtime security

If you select All Code in preceding step 4, you can't specify a folder and all assemblies on your development machine will run with full trust. In this case, malicious third-party assemblies could access and damage local resources—such as your file system or registry. If you need to assign full runtime permissions to more than one folder simultaneously, see the procedure for adding child nodes to the InfoPath Form Templates node at *www.oakleafe.ws/InfoPath/fulltrust.aspx.*

You can verify and edit the permission set you added in the preceding steps by right-clicking the InfoPath Form Templates node and choosing Properties from the shortcut menu. You *must* complete the preceding procedure to open this chapter's sample forms in preview mode.

Modifying the Text of a Custom Task Pane

InfoPath supports a single custom task pane with HTML and, optionally, JScript or Visual Basic Scripting Edition (VBScript) code that's contained in the HTML resource file you specify on the Advanced tab of the Form Options dialog box. You change the content of a custom task pane by replacing the resource file's code with a *String* variable containing the revised code. Most custom task panes are view-related, so the most common event handler for changing task pane content is *OnChangeView*. Retrieving and setting task pane code requires adding a reference to the .NET-enabled Microsoft.mshtml Component Object Model (COM) component and an *Imports mshtml* statement before or after the *Imports Microsoft.VisualBasic* statement. Creating *mshtml* objects requires a fully trusted form.

The Rss2EventsFinal project, located in the C:\Microsoft Press\Introducing InfoPath 2003\Chapter17\Rss2EventsFinal folder, demonstrates dynamically changing the font size of the *<div id="helptext">* element of the Rss2EventsTaskPane.htm HTML code that's shown on the next page.

```
<html>
  <body bgcolor="#DEEEFF">
    <div id="helptext"><font face="Verdana", size=1>
      Following are instructions for completing the InfoPath
      RSS 2.0 data entry form:
      <ul>
        <li>Use the default ItemsOnly view which only shows RSS 2.0 items</li>
        <li>Do <b>not</b> modify the channel data in the AllSections view</li>
        <li>Do <b>not</b> use the default values except Pub Date</li>
        <li>New entries in all text boxes except Pub Date are required</li>
      </ul></font>
    </div>
  </body>
</html>
```

Listing 17-1 Both form views—AllSections and ItemsOnly—have Toggle Task Pane Font Size buttons that execute the *ToggleFontSize* procedure, shown in Listing 17-1. For simplicity, the code changes the task pane's font size, not its text.

This code is a modified version of the HTML code from the section "Adding a Custom Help Task Pane," in Chapter 11.

```
Private Sub ToggleFontSize()
'Change the font size of the task pane from 1 to 2 or vice versa
   'Strong typing (Option Strict On) requires recasting types
   Try
      'Get the custom task pane and cast from TaskPane to HTMLTaskPane
      Dim htpCustom As HTMLTaskPane = _
         CType(thisXDocument.View.Window.TaskPanes(0), HTMLTaskPane)
      'Get the helptext div and cast from Object to HTMLDivElementClass
      Dim objDivHelp As HTMLDivElementClass = _
         CType(htpCustom.HTMLDocument.all.item("helptext"), _
         HTMLDivElementClass)
      'Get the original <div> text
      Dim strHTML As String = objDivHelp.innerHTML
      'Change the <font size=1> elment to <font size=2> or vice-versa
      If InStr(strHTML, "size=1") > 0 Then
         objDivHelp.innerHTML = Replace(strHTML, "size=1", "size=2")
      Else
         objDivHelp.innerHTML = Replace(strHTML, "size=2", "size=1")
      End If
   Catch excTask As Exception
      thisXDocument.UI.Alert(excTask.Message + excTask.StackTrace)
   End Try
End Sub
```

Listing 17-2 Code to toggle the task pane's font size.

Open Rss2EventsFinal.sln in Visual Studio, and press F5 to build and run the project. The preview window appears as shown in Figure 17-1. Click No to continue displaying the custom task pane, and click the Toggle Task Pane Font Size button to change the *size* attribute value to 2.

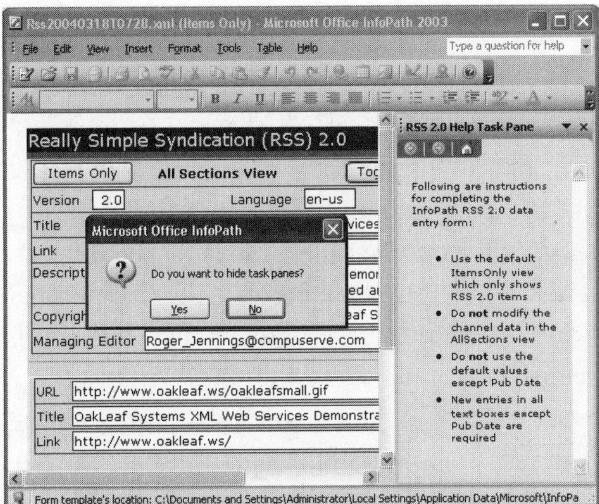

Figure 17-1 The Rss2EventsFinal project's opening view displays the default custom task pane with 1 as the font size.

The custom task pane is the first member of the *TaskPanes* collection, but the *TaskPane* type is read-only to prevent you from modifying the standard set of InfoPath task panes. The *TaskPane* interface exposes *TaskPaneType* and *Visible* properties only. You must cast the *TaskPanes(0)* member to the *HTMLTaskPane* type to expose the *HTMLDocument* property and get or set the HTML content of the entire task pane or, for this example, the *<div id="helptext">* *HTMLDivElementClass* member. Your custom HTML task pane code can contain cascading style sheets (CSS) to format the text and script to access InfoPath objects with the *window.external.Window.XDocument* object.

See Also **The topic "Custom Task Panes in the Information Lookup Developer Sample Form" in the InfoPath SDK release version describes how to use the *window.external.Window.XDocument* object. Search for *"Custom Task Panes"* (include the quotation marks), and double-click the first item in the Select Topic list.**

Testing for Required Digital Signatures

The Rss2EventsFinal project has two signed data blocks–*ChannelPlusItems* (cosign) and *Items* (countersign). In most cases, each data block should have at least one signature before the form is saved. You can't use declarative programming to test whether the blocks are signed, because the Data Validation feature of the Field Or Group Properties dialog box's Validation And Event Handlers tab is disabled for groups. Conditional formatting doesn't solve the problem, because the Conditional Formatting dialog box's operator list doesn't include an Is Signed item. Thus, you must write a handler for the appropriate event–usually *OnSaveRequest*–to test for missing signatures and give the user the choice of adding missing signatures, saving the form without them, or canceling the save operation. If the signatures are invalid, the user's choices are limited to correcting the invalid signature or canceling the save operation.

This section describes how to add handlers for the *OnSaveRequest* event and, for testing in preview mode, modify the *btnViewItems_OnClick* event. Listing 17-2 shows the code for the two event handlers. To complete this section's procedure, you must have a digital signing certificate. The section "Obtaining a Digital Signing Certificate," in Chapter 11, describes how to obtain a digital signature from a Microsoft Windows Server 2000 or later certificate server.

```
<InfoPathEventHandler(MatchPath:="btnViewItems", EventType:=InfoPathEvent-
Type.OnClick)> _
Public Sub btnViewItems_OnClick(ByVal e As DocActionEvent)
   If blnIsPreview Then
      'For preview testing; call from OnSaveRequest for a live form
      Dim blnCancel As Boolean = TestDigitalSignatures()
      thisXDocument.View.SwitchView("ItemsOnly")
   End If
   strViewName = " (Items Only)"
End Sub
<InfoPathEventHandler(EventType:=InfoPathEventType.OnSaveRequest)> _
Public Sub OnSaveRequest(ByVal e As SaveEvent)
   'e.IsCancelled = e.PerformSaveOperation
   'Invoke the function
   Dim blnCancel As Boolean = TestDigitalSignatures()
   e.IsCancelled = blnCancel
   If Not blnCancel Then
      'Save the file
      e.PerformSaveOperation()
   End If
   e.ReturnStatus = True
End Sub
```

Listing 17-3 Digital signature testing requires modifying one event handler and adding another.

Two handlers are required because preview mode disables the File, Save and File, Save As menu items. The *blnIsPreview* variable, whose value is set in the *OnSwitchView* event handler, determines which procedure calls the *TestDigitalSignatures* function. This function returns *True* if the user clicks the Cancel button of a *Condition* message box. The function has no data source or form design dependencies, so you can copy it directly into your projects.

▶ Add a custom *OnSaveRequest* event handler

1. **With the Rss2EventsFinal form opened from Visual Studio in the InfoPath Designer, choose Tools, Form Options to open the Form Options dialog box, and click the Open And Save tab.**
2. **Select the Save Using Custom Code check box, and click Edit, which adds an *OnSaveRequest* event-handling stub at the end of the FormCode.vb window if the event handler isn't present. In this case, the handler is present, so Visual Studio moves the insertion point to the end of the handler's last active statement.**
3. **Close the dialog box, and add the code shown in Listing 17-2 inside the *OnSaveRequest* event handler to handle File, Save and File, Save As operations. If you don't close the dialog box, Visual Studio won't build the project.**
4. **Choose Debug, Build Solution or press Ctrl+Shift+B to build the code; don't press F5 because a preview won't test your added code.**
5. **Select the Fill Out A Form task pane, open the Rss2EventsFinal form in data entry mode, add a few characters to the Title and Description text boxes, and choose File, Save or File, Save As to test your code.**

The *TestDigitalSignatures* function's code demonstrates use of the *SignedDataBlocks* collection and its members, the *Signatures* collection, the *Signature* object's *SignatureRelation* property, and the *Certificate* object's *IssuedTo*, *IssuedBy*, and *Status* properties. The function's code is too lengthy to reproduce here, so do the following to test and, optionally, step through the code.

▶ Test and explore the *TestDigitalSignatures* function

1. **With the Rss2EventsFinal FormCode.vb window open in Visual Studio, press F5 to build and run the form. Click Yes to close the message box.**
2. **Click Yes to hide the task panes, and click the Items Only button if the preview window opens in All Sections view. Otherwise, click All Sections and then Items Only. The initial digital signatures message opens, as shown here on the next page.**

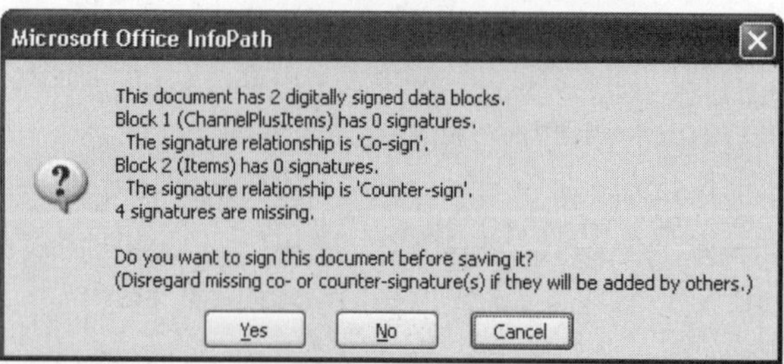

3. Click Yes in the message box to open the Digital Signatures dialog box, add a single signature to each block, and click All Sections and then Items Only to display a message similar to this (ignore messages about missing required values):

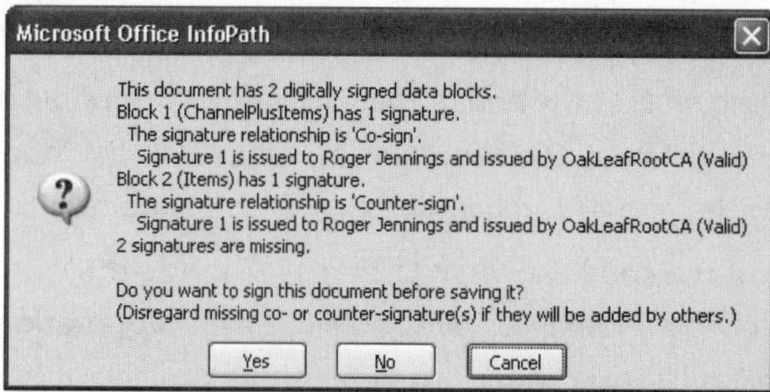

4. Click All Sections and Items Only, add a second copy of your signature to the ChannelPlusItems block, and click All Sections and Items Only again to display a message that cosigning a form with the same certificate is invalid, as shown here:

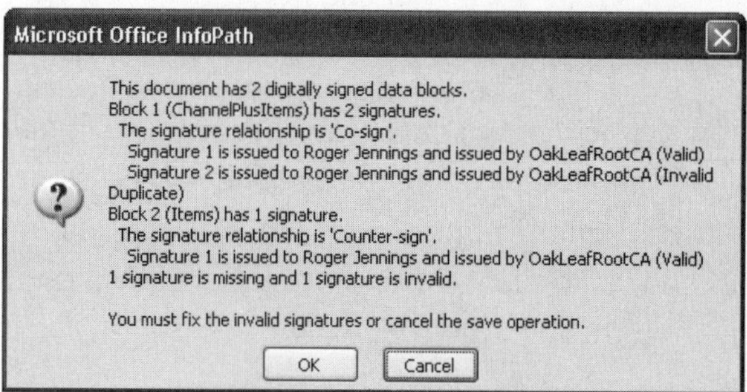

5. If you want to add your own digital signature to a previously signed form, close the preview window, reopen the InfoPath designer, choose Fill Out A Form, and click the On My Computer link to display the Open dialog box.
6. Navigate to the ...\Chapter17\Rss2EventsFinal\Rss2EventsFinal folder, double-click the sample Rss2*Date*T*Time*.xml form, which has one signature for each data block, and click OK to acknowledge the digital signing message.
7. Choose File, Save to display the message shown in step 4. Click Yes, and add your signature as the cosigner of the ChannelPlusItems message block.
8. Choose File, Save again to display a message similar to that shown here:

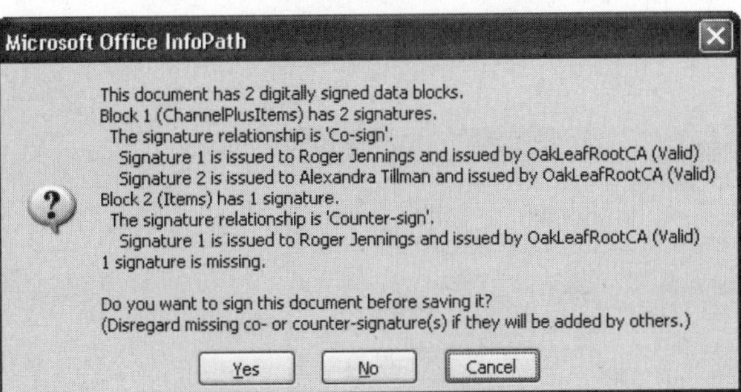

Working with the Rss2Production Project

The Rss2Production project, located in your C:\Microsoft Press\Introducing InfoPath 2003\Chapter17\Rss2Production folder, expands on the Rss2EventsFinal project by adding the following features:

- The AllSections view adds Docs, Generator, and multiple Category entries to the parent Channel element, as shown in Figure 17-2. The Save rss.xml button saves a modified copy of the current InfoPath data document to an rss.xml file at the location you specify. The modifications include removing the InfoPath processing instructions and altering the *namespace* attribute of the *<body>* element to conform to the RSS 2.0 specification.

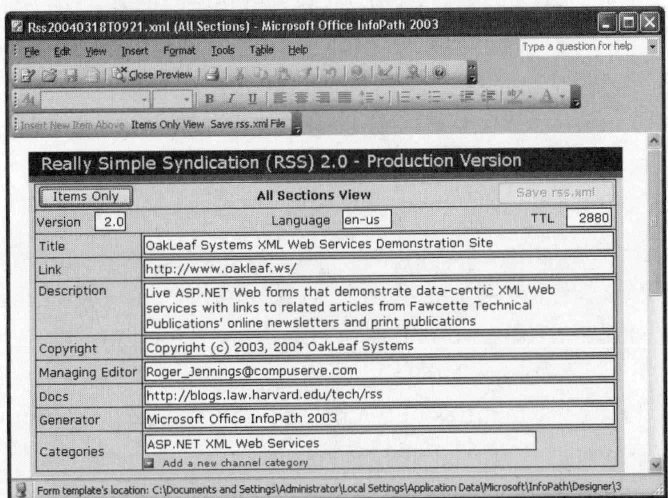

Figure 17-2 The Rss2Production form's All Sections view has added elements, a form toolbar, an Insert Item Above button, and two custom toolbar buttons that have Visual Basic event handlers for the *OnClick* event.

- The ItemsOnly view, shown in Figure 17-3, adds a GUID text box, an Is PermaLink check box, a Body rich text box, and multiple Categories elements.

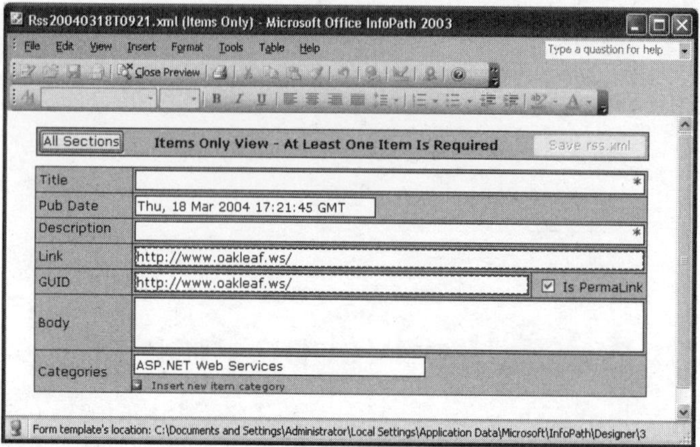

Figure 17-3 The ItemsOnly view is a subset of the AllSections view. You'll add a form toolbar similar to that of the AllSections view in the section "Adding a Custom Form Toolbar and Buttons," later in the chapter.

- An *OnAfterChange* event handler copies text that you enter in the item group's description field to the body field's rich text box. This feature accommodates RSS news reader/aggregator applications that substitute XHTML body text for unformatted description text in their display. Another event handler copies the link field value to the guid field automatically.
- Creating an rss.xml file also creates an rss-no_body.xml file—without the *<body>* element—that's validated by the original version of the XML schema for RSS 2.0 XML files. The current version of the rss-2_0.xsd schema doesn't support *<body>* elements. Both files are indented for readability.
- The Pub Date text box has a validation rule that uses a complex regular expression to test the pattern's conformance to the RSS 2.0 specification.

The Rss2Production project has all of the important elements that are required to produce RSS 2.0 files for Web content syndication. It's becoming a common practice to include XHTML-encoded full text of weblog items in *<body>* elements, so Rss2Production includes this capability. The following sections describe the event-handling code that implements the features of the preceding list. The project must run with full trust because saving rss.xml and rss-no_body.xml requires access to the user's or the Web server's file system.

Using an RSS 2.0 Schema to Create a Data Source

You can't add a useful XHTML *<body>* element to an RSS 2.0 data source that you generate with Jorgen Thelin's rss-2_0.xsd schema, because you can't add an element to the item choice group that the schema generates, and the Rich Text (XHTML) data type isn't available when you add the element to the list repeating group directly. The unmodified schema also generates a large number of option and repeating option groups, which you see when you open the sample ...\Chapter17\Rss2FromSchema\Rss2FromSchema.xsn template in design mode. Modifying the schema by changing *xs:choice* to *xs:sequence* groups and making a few other alterations solves the option groups problem and adds a body field with the *xs:string* datatype to the items group, as illustrated by the sample ...\Chapter17\Rss2FromSchema\Rss2FromModifiedSchema.xsn template.

You can remove InfoPath's restriction on altering the structure and data types of a data source created from an XML schema by making a change to the manifest.xsf file. To do so, extract the form files, close the template, and open manifest.xsf in Notepad. Locate the *<xsf:property name="editability" type="string" value="none"> </xsf:property>* element, change *none* to **partial**, and save the change. Open manifest.xsf in design mode, choose File, Save As, and overwrite the original template. The ...\Chapter17\Rss2FromSchema\Rss2FromEditableSchema folder contains a modified template and its form files.

The path of least resistance—and effort—in many cases of this type is to create the InfoPath data source from an XML document that has the required structure and real or simulated content and validates with the associated schema. (Rss2Production's data source is ...\Chapter17\Rss2FromSchema\Rss2NewDataSource.xml, which validates with the original rss-2_0.xsd schema, because the schema's *<xs:any ...>* elements permit adding undeclared fields and groups.) The final step is to specify the data types for non-string fields and default values, if applicable. The path of least resistance becomes the primrose path if the schema defines complex data types whose values are difficult or impossible to validate—or conditionally format—by declarative methods, validation event handlers, or both.

See Also **For more information about Jorgen Thelin's rss-2_0.xsd schema, visit his Web site, at www.thearchitect.co.uk/weblog/archives/2003/06/000187.html.**

Generating a Modified InfoPath Data Document

Some XML applications might require you to modify InfoPath's XML data document to suit a specific XML schema with a data structure, elements, or attributes that InfoPath doesn't support directly. An example is the item group's body field, which is an RSS 2.0 extension element that requires a *<body xmlns="http://www.w3.org/1999/xhtml">* element. InfoPath won't let you add *xmlns* as an attribute name, because it's an XML reserved word and the InfoPath team considers it invalid in this context. Thus, you must generate and save a modified file to work around RSS 2.0's use of this namespace to support RSS news reader/aggregator applications that recognize the *<body>* extension.

The *OnClick* event of the Save rss.xml buttons in both views calls the *SaveRssToFile* procedure, which creates the local rss-no_body.xml validation file and the production rss.xml file. The procedure's code requires adding a reference to the *System.Xml* namespace and adding *Imports System.Xml*, *Imports System.IO*, and *Imports System.Text* statements to simplify class references.

The code for *SaveRssToFile* is too lengthy to present here, so do the following to learn how the procedure works and how to debug a form connected to the INFOPATH.EXE process.

▶ Explore the *SaveRssToFile* procedure

1. Navigate to the C:\Microsoft Press\Introducing InfoPath 2003\Chapter17\Rss2Production\Rss2Production\bin\Debug folder, and open Rss2Production.xsn in design mode.
2. Choose Tools, Form Options to open the Form Options dialog box. Click the Security tab, clear the Automatically Determine Security Level Based On Form's Design (Recommended) check box, select the Full Trust option, select the Sign This Form check box to apply your default code signing certificate, and click OK.
3. Save your changes, and close InfoPath.
4. Double-click the Rss2Production.sln file in the ...\Chapter17\Rss2Production\Rss2Production folder to open the project in Visual Studio, and close the InfoPath design window. If the FormCode.vb window isn't visible, open it from Solution Explorer.
5. Open Windows Explorer and double-click ShortOakLeafSiteRss.xml in the same folder to open a form that has a single item element and start the INFOPATH.EXE process.
6. Return to Visual Studio's FormCode.vb window, and choose Tools, Debug Processes or press Ctrl+Alt+P to open the Processes dialog box. Double-click the INFOPATH.EXE process item to open the Attach To Process dialog box.
7. Select the Common Language Runtime check box, if it isn't selected, and click OK to close the dialog box. The Processes dialog box appears as shown here:

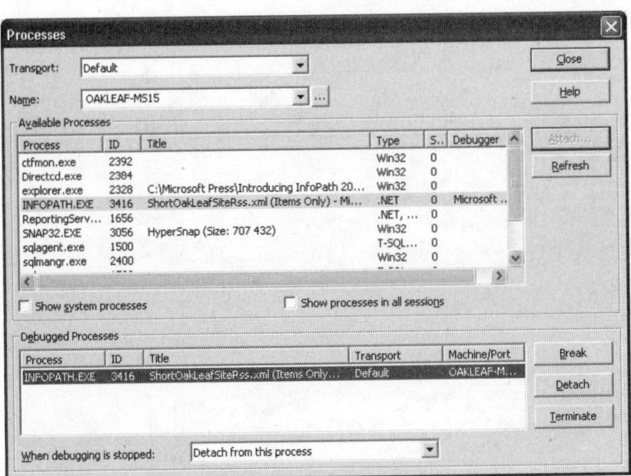

8. **Leave the remaining defaults, click Close to return to the FormCode.vb window, navigate to the *SaveRssToFile* procedure's *For intFile = 0 To 1* statement, and press F9 to set a breakpoint on the line.**
9. **Display the ShortOakLeafSiteRss form, and click the Save rss.xml button to activate Visual Studio and position the cursor on the breakpoint.**
10. **Pass the cursor over the last *strRSS =* statement to view the XML data with the processing instructions, white space, and unneeded attributes removed and the local XHTML namespace added to the *<body>* element.**
11. **Press F11 repeatedly to create a *StringBuilder* object that holds the formatted XML string for the rss-no_body.xml file, and create the *NameTable*, *XmlNameSpaceManager*, and *XmlParserContext* objects required to create a namespace-aware *XmlTextReader* object, which is a fast, forward-only reader for XML documents. The *Do While xtrRSS.Read* loop formats the document with carriage return/linefeed pairs and two-space indents per element level.**

See Also For more information about the *XmlTextReader* class, choose Help, Index, and type **XmlTextReader** in the Look For box, filtered by Visual Basic. Double-click the XmlTextReader Class entry, double-click Reading XML Data With XmlTextReader in the Index Results pane, and follow the topic's links. A namespace-aware *XmlTextReader* isn't required for this document, but one might be needed for documents with namespace-qualified elements.

12. **To check the current *StringBuilder* contents, open the Command Window, and type ? sbDoc.ToString.**
13. **Add a breakpoint on the *strDoc = sbDoc.ToString* statement, press F5 when you're tired of stepping through the first loop, press F11 once, and pass the mouse pointer over the statement to display the formatted text, as shown here. Notice that white space replaces the *<body>* element in this loop.**

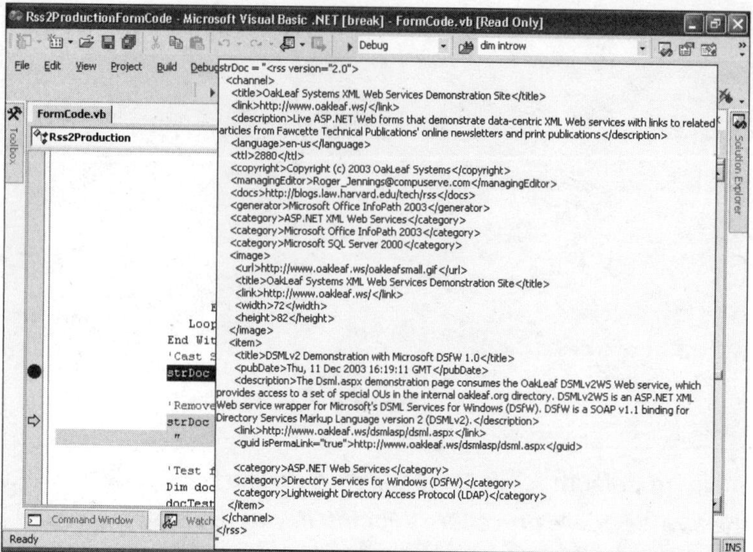

14. **Continue stepping through the two instructions that test the document for well-formedness by loading it into an *XmlDocument* object, and step into the *ValidateNoBodyDocument* procedure, which is the subject of the next section.**

The reasons for using the *System.Xml.XmlTextReader* object to generate the new document are the ability to return the *level* property value for indentation, faster execution speed, and a smaller memory footprint than a native *XmlDocument* or a wrapped *IXMLDOMDocument* object. Alternatively, you can apply an XSL transform from an .xsl file or replace the *StringBuilder* object with an *XmlTextWriter* object–either approach is a more complex undertaking.

Validating the XML of the rss-no_body Document

It's a good programming practice to validate XML documents against their schema before passing them to a workflow application or–for this example–a public Web site. InfoPath won't generate a document that violates its schema, which includes data validation rules, but variations you generate with code need validation. You can use the GotDotNet validating parser that's described in the section "Validating an XML Document Against an InfoPath Schema," in Chapter 3 for initial test purposes, but prudence dictates that every modified document should be validated before its use in a production environment. Listing 17-3 contains the code for the *ValidateNoBodyDocument* procedure and its *ValidationError* event handler, which validate the rss-no_body.xml file.

```
Private Sub ValidateNoBodyDocument(ByVal strDoc As String)
   'Validate the no <body> version against the RSS 2.0 schema
   Dim strRssSchema As String = strRssPath + "\rss-2_0.xsd"
   If File.Exists(strRssSchema) Then
      strErrors = ""
      'Create a schema collection and add the rss-2_0.xsd schema
      Dim xscRSS As New XmlSchemaCollection
      xscRSS.Add("", strRssSchema)
      'Create a StringReader, XmlTextReader, and XmlValidatingReader
      Dim srRSS As New StringReader(strDoc)
      Dim xtrRSS As New XmlTextReader(srRSS)
      Dim xvrRSS As New XmlValidatingReader(xtrRSS)
      With xvrRSS
         'Specify the validation type (XSD) and add the schema
         .ValidationType = ValidationType.Schema
         .Schemas.Add(xscRSS)
         'Specify a ValidationError event handler
         AddHandler .ValidationEventHandler, _
          AddressOf ValidationError
         While .Read
            'Process the document
         End While
         .Close()
      End With
   Else
      strErrors = "The schema file ('" + strRssSchema + _
        "') is missing. Can't validate the document."
   End If
End Sub

Private Sub ValidationError(ByVal sender As Object, _
ByVal args As ValidationEventArgs)
   'Event handler for intercepting validation errors
   strErrors += args.Message.ToString + vbCrLf
End Sub
```

Listing 17-4 Code to validating a document against the rss-2_0.xsd schema.

The *System.Xml.Schema* namespace provides an *XmlSchemaCollection* class to which you add the contents of one or more schema files, identified by their namespaces. This example uses a single schema, rss-2_0.xsd, for a document without a global namespace declaration. You use an *XmlValidatingReader* object, which is derived from the preceding section's *XmlTextReader* class. You specify the values of the *XmlValidatingReader* object's *ValidationType* and *Schema* properties and designate an event handler for exceptions raised by validation failures. As the *XmlValidatingReader* reads the document, elements or attributes that fail validation invoke the *ValidationError* event handler that you specify in the *Add Handler [xvrRSS].ValidationEventHandler, AddressOf ValidationError* statement. You must add the code for this event handler manually.

In Visual Studio, press F11 repeatedly to step through the code of the *ValidateNoBodyDocument* procedure. Add a breakpoint on the *If intFile = 1 Then* statement, and press F5 to continue.

Saving a Modified InfoPath Data Document as rss.xml

The remaining code of the *ValidateNoBodyDocument* procedure, shown in Listing 17-3, uses a *StreamWriter* object to save rss-no_body.xml in the first loop iteration and, if the user clicks Yes in the Confirm message box, saves rss.xml in the second iteration. The *Dim stwRSS As StreamWriter = New StreamWriter(strFile, False, Encoding.UTF8)* constructor statement specifies overwriting earlier versions of *strFile* without warning and using default UTF-8 encoding. You can simplify the statement by substituting *StreamWriter(strFile)*, which assigns the overwrite and UTF-8 defaults. The *stwRSS.Write(strDoc)* statement writes to the stream, *stwRSS.Flush* ensures that the full stream is written to disk, and *stwRSS.Close* closes *StreamWriter* and releases the lock on the file. (A production form wouldn't save rss-no_body.xml; the file is for debugging purposes only.)

Adding a Custom Form Toolbar and Buttons

Toolbar buttons and menus are useful for changing views or initiating tasks in a specified sequence. Users also appreciate toolbar buttons for tasks that might require scrolling the form to make form buttons visible. When users add new item elements to the form in AllSections view, the Items Only and Save rss.xml buttons might not be visible, depending on display resolution. The sample form's AllSections view has Insert New Item Above, Items Only View, and Save rss.xml File buttons. The form toolbar and Insert New Item Above buttons are defined in the Section Commands dialog box, which opens from the Repeating Section Properties dialog box.

The Items Only View and Save rss.xml File buttons are custom buttons that are defined by adding button definition elements to the appropriate view definition in manifest.xsf. The button definition includes the name of an event-handling procedure for the button's OnClick event. The following code in manifest.xsf defines the AllSections form toolbar and its three toolbar buttons.

```
<xsf:toolbar name="Form toolbar" caption="Form toolbar">
  <xsf:button action="xCollection::insertBefore" xmlToEdit="item_3"
    caption="Insert New Item Above" tooltip="Insert the latest
      item at the top of the list">
  </xsf:button>
  <xsf:button caption="Items Only View" name="btnItemsOnlyTB1">
  </xsf:button>
  <xsf:button caption="Save rss.xml File" name="btnSaveRssFileTB1">
  </xsf:button>
</xsf:toolbar>
```

Here's the basic event-handling code for the two custom toolbar buttons:

```
<InfoPathEventHandler(MatchPath:="btnSaveRssFileTB1",
   EventType:=InfoPathEventType.OnClick)> _
Public Sub btnSaveRssFileTB1_OnClick(ByVal e As DocActionEvent)
'Toolbar button on AllSections view
Call SaveRssToFile()
End Sub
<InfoPathEventHandler(MatchPath:="btnItemsOnlyTB1",
   EventType:=InfoPathEventType.OnClick)> _
 Public Sub btnItemsOnlyTB1_OnClick(ByVal e As DocActionEvent)
'Toolbar button on AllSections view
strViewName = " (Items Only)"
thisXDocument.View.SwitchView("ItemsOnly")
End Sub
```

If the button's name attribute value isn't identical to the event handler's MatchPath attribute value or the event handler isn't present, the preview window won't open when you press F5 to build and run the project. If you click the designer's Preview Form button, you receive an error message that displays the offending button's name.

To add a form toolbar and a set of buttons similar to the ItemsOnly view, follow these steps.

▶ Add a form toolbar and button in the designer

1. With the ItemsOnly view active in the InfoPath Designer, right-click the Repeating Section tab, and choose Properties from the shortcut menu to open its Properties dialog box.
2. Click the Modify button to open the Section Properties dialog box, and click Customize Commands to open the Section Commands dialog box.
3. Select Insert Above in the Action drop-down list, and select the Form Toolbar check box.
4. Type **Insert New Item Above** in the Command Name box, and type **Insert the latest item at the top of the list** in the ScreenTip box, as shown here:

5. Click OK three times to close the dialog boxes, and save your change.
6. Preview the form, click the repeating section's selection button to enable the toolbar button, and verify its operation.
7. Close the preview window, and close Visual Studio. You can't save form files when the project is open in Visual Studio.

▶ **Add two custom button definitions to manifest.xsf**

1. Navigate in Windows Explorer to the ...\Chapter17\Rss2Production\Rss2Production folder, make a backup copy of manifest.xsf, and open manifest.xsf in Notepad.
2. Search for the first *Form toolbar* instance, and copy the two custom button definition elements to the Clipboard.
3. Search for the next *Form toolbar* instance, which you added in step 5 of the preceding procedure, and paste the elements below the only button definition element.
4. Change *Items Only View* to **All Sections View**, *btnItemsOnlyTB1* to **btnAllSectionsTB2**, and *btnSaveRssFileTB1* to **btnSaveRssFileTB2**, as shown here:

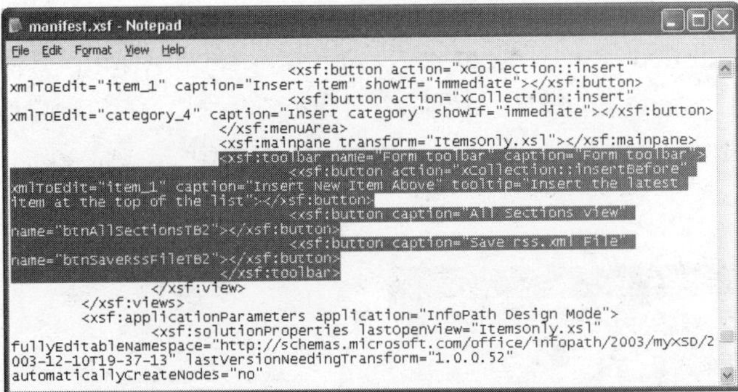

5. Save your changes, and reopen the Rss2Production.sln project in Visual Studio. If you receive an error message on opening the project, restore the backup copy of manifest.xsn, and repeats steps 2 through 4.
6. Copy and paste the *btnSaveRssFileTB1_OnClick* event handler below the original version, and change both instances of *btnSaveRssFileTB1* to **btnSaveRssFileTB2**.
7. Search for *btnViewAll*, copy and paste the *btnViewAll_OnClick* event handler below the original, change both instances of *btnViewAll* to **btnAllSectionsTB2**, and save your changes.
8. Press F5 to open a preview window. If the preview window doesn't open or displays an error message, open manifest.xsf, and verify that you completed steps 4 through 7 correctly. The ItemsOnly view with the repeating section selected appears as shown here:

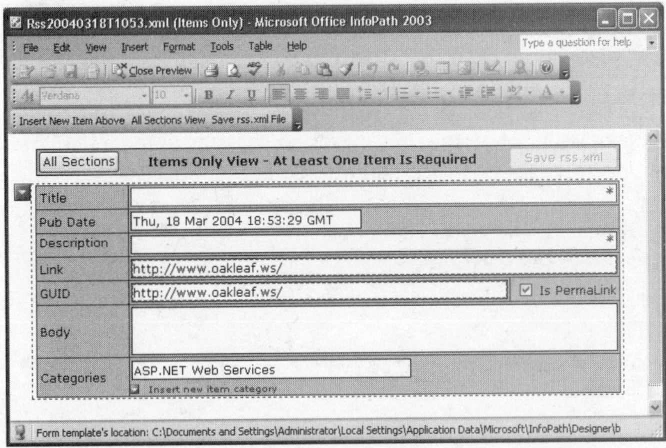

Using the *Errors* Collection

Conditional formatting disables the Save rss.xml form button if the form has data validation errors. You can't control the enabled state of a custom toolbar button with managed code or script, so users can save an invalid rss.xml file. The rss-2_0.xsd schema requires content only in the pubDate and link fields. If you don't test for errors and the user deletes all text box content in the item repeating group, a validation error message appears, as shown in Figure 17-4. If content required by the schema is present, but the title and description field are empty, the user can save the invalid data.

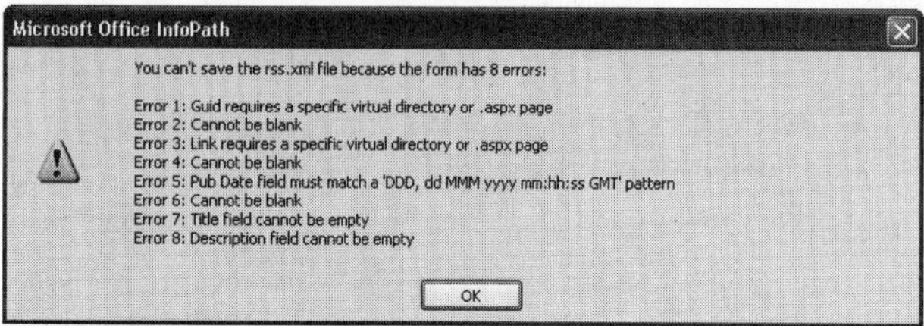

Figure 17-4 This validation error message appears when you attempt to save an rss.xml file with all content removed from the item repeating group.

InfoPath has an *Errors* collection that lets you detect data validation errors by testing for a nonzero value of the collection's *Count* property. The *TestFormForErrors* function, shown in Listing 17-4, tests for data validation errors and, if errors are present, displays an error message, such as that shown in Figure 17-5. Specifying custom data validation rules for required fields–rather than selecting the Cannot Be Blank check box–provides a more informative error message.

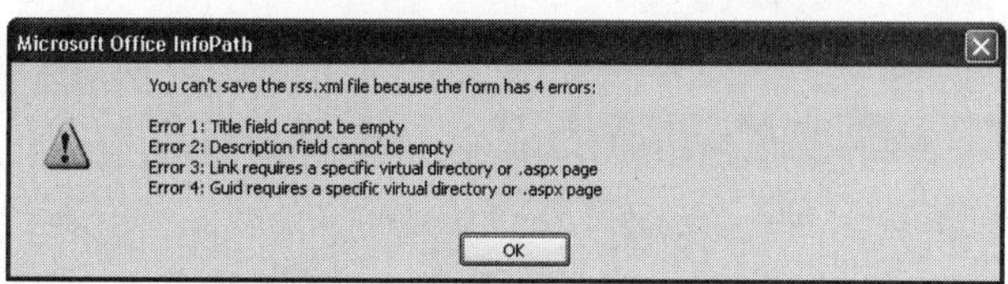

Figure 17-5 This error message appears when the user makes no changes to the default item section in the AllSections view and clicks the Save rss.xml button.

```
Private Function TestFormForErrors() As Boolean
   'Test for form errors: Return True if none, False if errors exist
   'This test is required for toolbar buttons only
   Try
      Dim intErrs As Integer
      Dim colErrors As ErrorsCollection = thisXDocument.Errors
      If colErrors.Count = 0 Then
         'Form is OK
         Return True
      Else
         'Display a detailed error alert
         Dim strMsg As String
         Dim intErr As Integer
         With colErrors
            strMsg = "You can't save the rss.xml file because " + _
               the form has " + .Count.ToString + " errors:" + _
               vbCrLf + vbCrLf
            'Loop runs in reverse due to the sequence of addition
```

```
            'of the validation rules for the fields
            For intErr = .Count - 1 To 0 Step -1
               strMsg += "Error " + (.Count - intErr).ToString + ": "
               strMsg += .Item(intErr).ShortErrorMessage + vbCrLf
            Next intErr
            thisXDocument.UI.Alert(strMsg)
         End With
         Return False
      End If
   Catch excErr As Exception
      thisXDocument.UI.Alert(excErr.Message + excErr.StackTrace)
   End Try
End Function
```

Listing 17-5 This function detects data validation errors.

The *ShortErrorMessage* value is the text you add to the Data Validation dialog box's Message box. Members of the *Errors* collection appear in the order of their addition to the manifest.xsf file; the title and description field's validation rules were added after the rules for the link and guid fields. Matching the error numbers to the sequence of the fields on the form requires the loop to display the last error first.

Copying Data Between Fields

If your forms have fields that contain duplicate information or values derived from other field data, you can minimize data entry time and typographic errors by copying the text from the source to destination fields. The Rss2Production form has two fields that usually contain the same data: body duplicates description, and guid duplicates item. The user adds HTML markup and additional formatted content to the copied body text. For this example, all Web site content is permanent, so the link and guid values are the same, and the isPermaLink field value is *true* by default.

Listing 17-5 shows the code for the description and link fields' *OnAfterChange* event handlers. Both procedures use the *parentNode* property to select the current *item* group and then copy the text to the appropriate node if it's empty or, for guid, if it contains the default value.

```
<InfoPathEventHandler(MatchPath:="/rss/channel/item/description",
EventType:=InfoPathEventType.OnAfterChange)> _
Public Sub item_description_OnAfterChange(ByVal e As DataDOMEvent)
   'Copy description to body if body is empty
   If e.IsUndoRedo Or e.Operation = "Delete" Then
         Return
   End If
   Dim strDescr As String = e.Source.nodeValue.ToString
   If strDescr <> "" Then
```

```
        'Update the body element
        Dim nodBody As IXMLDOMNode = _
         e.Source.parentNode.selectSingleNode("//body")
        If nodBody.text = "" Then
            nodBody.text = strDescr
        End If
        Exit Sub
    End If
End Sub

<InfoPathEventHandler(MatchPath:="/rss/channel/item/link",
EventType:=InfoPathEventType.OnAfterChange)> _
Public Sub item_link_OnAfterChange(ByVal e As DataDOMEvent)
    'Copy the link value to guid, if guid hasn't been updated
    If e.IsUndoRedo Or e.Operation = "Delete" Then
        Return
    End If
    Dim strLink As String = e.Source.nodeValue.ToString
    If strLink <> "http://www.oakleaf.ws/" And strLink <> "" Then
        'Update the guid element
        Dim nodGuid As IXMLDOMNode = _
         e.Source.parentNode.selectSingleNode("//guid")
        If nodGuid.text = "http://www.oakleaf.ws/" Then
            nodGuid.text = strLink
        End If
    End If
End Sub
```

Listing 17-6 Procedures for copying description and link fields.

Specifying a Form to Open in All Preview Windows

Choosing File, Preview, With Data File in the designer or Tools, Preview With Data File in Visual Studio opens a Choose Data File To Preview dialog box, from which you can navigate to and select an .xml file to open. When you're debugging a project that has required fields, such as Rss2Production, it's usually easier to type required values than to navigate from My Documents to the location of your test file.

InfoPath projects let you assign the test form to use in all project preview windows by specifying the file path and name in the Project Properties dialog box. To assign a test document as the default preview data file, follow these steps.

▶ Assign an InfoPath XML data document as the preview window default

1. **Open Solution Explorer, right-click the *ProjectName* node under the Solution node, and choose Properties from the shortcut menu to open the *ProjectName* Property Pages dialog box. (The *ProjectName* node appears in boldface, because it's the startup project.)**
2. **Click the button to the right of the Preview Data File Path box to open the Select Data File To Use For Preview dialog box, navigate to folder containing the test file, and double-click the file to assign to the project, as shown here:**

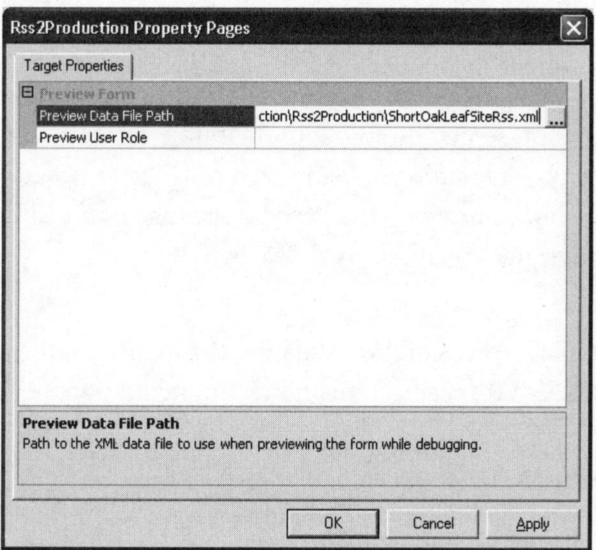

3. **Click OK to close the dialog box, and press F5 to open the preview window to verify that the preview window appears as expected with your test document.**

Selecting the ...\Chapter17\Rss2Production\Rss2Production\ShortOakLeaf-SiteRss.xml document assists testing regular expressions, which you'll do in the next section.

Validating Data with Complex Regular Expressions

The rss-2_0.xsd schema includes regular expression (pattern) tests for dates (pubDate and lastBuildDate) and e-mail addresses (managingEditor and webMaster). Following is the schema's definition of the tRfc822FormatDate type for a channel group's lastBuildDate and channel or item group's pubDate fields:

```
<xs:simpleType name="tRfc822FormatDate">
  <xs:annotation>
    <xs:documentation>A date-time displayed in RFC-822 format.
    </xs:documentation>
    <xs:documentation>Using the regexp definiton of rfc-822 date by
      Sam Ruby at http://www.intertwingly.net/blog/1360.html
    </xs:documentation>
  </xs:annotation>
  <xs:restriction base="xs:string">
    <xs:pattern value="(((Mon)|(Tue)|(Wed)|(Thu)|(Fri)|(Sat)|(Sun)), *)
?\d\d? +((Jan)|(Feb)|(Mar)|(Apr)|(May)|(Jun)|(Jul)|(Aug)|(Sep)|
      (Oct)|(Nov)|(Dec)) +\d\d(\d\d)? +\d\d:\d\d(:\d\d)?
      +(([+\-]?\d\d\d\d)|(UT)|(GMT)|(EST)|(EDT)|(CST)|
      (CDT)|(MST)|(MDT)|(PST)|(PDT)|\w)" />
  </xs:restriction>
</xs:simpleType>
```

The preceding pattern, which has line breaks added for readability, grants much more date formatting latitude than the RSS 2.0 specification permits. The expression permits omitting the day of the week, two-digit years are allowed, and seconds are optional. The time zone can be represented by a +/- four-digit time offset from GMT or any U.S. time zone. Boldface type identifies elements that must be removed to create a pattern that ensures conformance with the RSS 2.0 specification's RFC822-based date/time format. Although the specification allows two-digit years, it recommends four-digit years.

Following is the simplified regular expression for validating the item repeating group's pubDate values to the RSS 2.0 specification and recommendation:

```
(((Mon)|(Tue)|(Wed)|(Thu)|(Fri)|(Sat)|(Sun)), )\d\d?
+((Jan)|(Feb)|(Mar)|(Apr)|(May)|(Jun)|(Jul)|(Aug)|(Sep)|(Oct)|(Nov)|(Dec))
+\d\d\d\d? +\d\d:\d\d:\d\d? +(GMT)
```

Figure 17-6 shows the Data Entry Pattern dialog box displaying the first part of the expression and an example of a conforming entry.

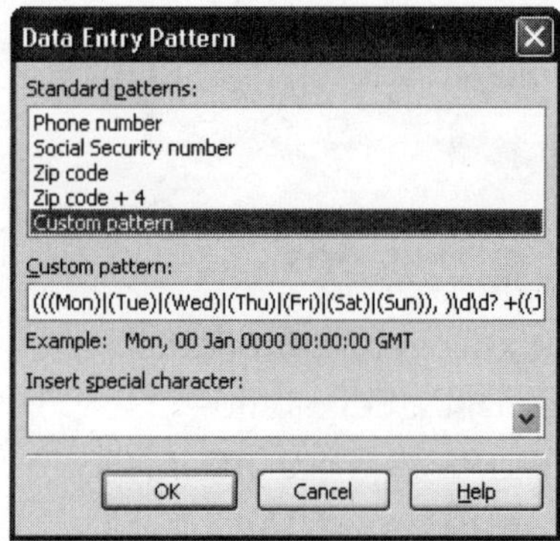

Figure 17-6 The Data Entry Pattern dialog box, which opens from the Data Validation or Conditional Formatting dialog box, displays an example of an entry that matches the pattern.

You can verify that the pattern works in an Rss2Production preview window by removing the day of the week, required digits of dates and times, or GMT and then pressing Tab. Typing invalid characters in any date element also causes a validation failure. The conditional formatting rules for the Save rss.xml button also include a pattern-matching test for the preceding regular expression.

The schema's pattern for e-mail addresses, which validates the managingEditor field, is shown here:

```
([a-zA-Z0-9_\-])([a-zA-Z0-9_\-\.]*)@
(\[((25[0-5]|2[0-4][0-9]|1[0-9][0-9]|[1-9][0-9]|[0-9])\.)
{3}|((([a-zA-Z0-9\-]+)\.)+))([a-zA-Z]{2,}|(25[0-5]|2[0-4][0-9]|
1[0-9][0-9]|[1-9][0-9]|[0-9])\])
```

This pattern permits combinations of letters and numbers, hyphens, and underscores in the name and a valid domain name as the address component. In this case, the Data Entry Pattern dialog box's example is somewhat misleading; open the Data Validation dialog box for the managingEditor field to see the example pattern: *–@[250.250.250.AA*.

See Also For more information about regular expressions, go to *msdn.microsoft.com*, type "Regular Expression Support" (include the quotation marks) in the Search For box, select the "Regular Expression Support in Microsoft Office System Smart Tags" topic, and click the link A Brief Introduction To Regular Expression Syntax. The .NET Regular Expression Repository at *www.3leaf.com/resources/articles/regex.aspx* has a regular expression tester and a tutorial that offers several useful patterns for validating form data. The rss-2_0.xsd schema's e-mail pattern is one of the site's sample regular expressions.

Displaying Running Sums in an Expression Box

One of the fundamental rules of database design is to eliminate storing in tables duplicate data or information that's calculated from database column values. Using the NorthwindCS database as an example, storing the extended net amount of an Order Details record in an Extended column requires updating the Extended value whenever the Quantity or Discount values change. Similarly, storing the sum of Extended values as the total order amount–less freight, taxes, and other charges–requires recalculating this value each time an Extended value changes or line items are added to or deleted from the order. The most common practice is to create views or stored procedures that provide calculated values. Views with calculated values aren't updatable.

The preceding rule doesn't apply to XML documents that you generate from databases because each document is a static representation of the column values at the time the document is created. Thus you can add to a basic InfoPath form fields that store calculated data. However, if you create your form's main data source from a database or Web service, you can't add calculated fields to the main data source, because the schema is locked. You must use expression boxes to display calculated values in database or Web service client forms.

The section "Calculating Values with the Expression Box," in Chapter 6, describes how to add an Extended Amount expression box to display net extended values.

Displaying a running sum of Extended Amount values with an expression box in the table footer is a more complex process. You add an expression box to the table footer, relocate and modify the *ViewName*.xsl file's expression box definition, and then add a function that calculates the running sum from the repeating table's element values and returns the value to the expression box. InfoPath doesn't offer a means for summing the values of the row's expression boxes.

Upgrading VBScript code to Visual Basic .NET

The original Microsoft sample form is one of the few examples that use VBScript rather than JScript. The InfoPath product team has a predilection for JScript and Visual C#, which undoubtedly has contributed to many VBScript, VBA, Visual Basic 6, and Visual Basic .NET programmers perceiving themselves as "second-class citizens." Most forms that use VBScript code will build in Visual Basic .NET with *Option Strict Off* and, in some cases, *Option Explicit Off* compiler directives. Build errors that appear in the Task List usually are easy to correct. The original VBScript code for the project, which is included in the project's FormCode.vb file, required only one minor change to compile with *Option Explicit On*.

The ExprBoxSumProject in the C:\Microsoft Press\Introducing InfoPath 2003\Chapter17\ExprBoxSums\ExprBoxSumProject folder is a simple running sum example. This project is an upgraded version of a sample form posted by Microsoft's Joel Alley in the *microsoft.public.infopath* newsgroup. The project sums an element and attribute value with an XPath expression to populate the row's expression box and generates a running sum in the table footer, as shown in Figure 17-7.

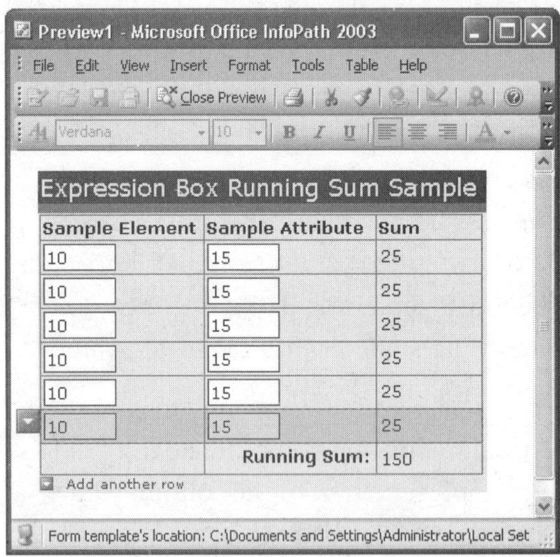

Figure 17-7 This form, which demonstrates calculating running sums of repeating table values, is an upgraded version of a Microsoft sample project from the InfoPath newsgroup.

Here are the basic steps for adding a running sum expression box to a table footer.

1. Add a table footer, if it's missing, and insert an expression box control under the column you want to sum.

2. Close the project, create a backup copy of *ViewName*.xsl file, and open *ViewName*.xsl in Notepad. Locate the <span> element that defines the expression box, cut the element to the Clipboard, and replace the element with an *<xsl:apply-templates match="groupName" mode="xd:preserve" />* instruction. If your form has a single group, substitute ".", which represents the data source's root element, for *"groupName"*. The *mode="xd:preserve"* attribute prevents InfoPath from deleting the element and its children when you make subsequent design changes to the form.
3. Add an *<xsl:template match="groupName" mode="xd:preserve" />* starting element, paste the code you cut below the element, and add an *</xsl:template>* closing element. In this case, you can't replace *"groupName"* with ".".
4. After the *<span ... />* element, add an *<xsl:value-of select="xdExtension:functionName(XPathPointerToTableRowDataSource)"/>* element that calls *functionName* with an *IXMLDOMNodeList* argument value that represents all nodes of *TableRowDataSource*. The *xdExtension:* prefix is required to call a script or managed code function.
5. Save the *ViewName*.xsl file, open the file in Internet Explorer to verify that it's well-formed, and close Internet Explorer and Notepad.
6. Reopen the project in Visual Studio, add the *Public Function functionName(ByVal objNodeSet As IXMLDOMNodeList) As dataType* stub, and write the code to iterate the rows and column values to generate the running sum.
7. Preview the form to test your work.

You can use the same approach to display in table footer cells averages or other values that you can't create with declarative XPath statements.

To test your XSLT editing skills, follow these steps to duplicate the ExprBoxSumProject's running sum expression box from a sample project without the expression box in the ...\Chapter17\ExprBoxSums\ExprBoxSumExercise folder.

▶ Add and test a running sum expression box

1. **Navigate to the ...\Chapter17\ExprBoxSums\ExprBoxSumExercise folder, and double-click ExprBoxSumProject.xsn to open the project and display the InfoPath designer.**
2. **Click the task pane's Controls link, and drag an Expression Box control to the repeating table's rightmost column. Leave the XPath box empty, and click OK to add the expression box.**

3. **Save your design change, close the project so that you can edit the view1.xsl file, make a backup copy of view1.xsl, and open view1.xsl in Notepad with Word Wrap enabled.**
4. **Search for the third and last instance of *xdExpressionBox*, which is associated with code similar to this:**

```
<div><span class="xdExpressionBox xdDataBindingUI" title=""
xd:CtrlId="CTRL9" xd:xctname="ExpressionBox" tabIndex="-1"
xd:disableEditing="yes" style="WIDTH: 100%"/>
</div>
```

   The second instance of *xdExpressionBox* is the table row's expression box. (The *xd:CtrlId* attribute value's number might differ.)

5. **Select the entire *<span ... />* element, and cut it to the Clipboard. Replace the code you deleted with the *<xsl:apply-templates match="." mode="xd:preserve" />* instruction. The *<div> ... </div>* element code appears as shown here:**

```
<div>
  <xsl:apply-templates select="." mode="xd:preserve"/>
</div>
```

   This instruction runs the template you add in the next few steps.

6. **Move to the end of the file. Immediately above the *</xsl:stylesheet>* element, add an *<xsl:template match="my:myFields" mode="xd:preserve" />* line, paste the code you cut below this line, add an ending *</xsl:template>* element, and indent the *<span ...>* element. The last few lines of the stylesheet appear as shown here:**

```
  </xsl:template>
  <xsl:template match="my:myFields" mode="xd:preserve">
    <span class="xdExpressionBox xdDataBindingUI" title="" _
      xd:CtrlId="CTRL9" xd:xctname="ExpressionBox" tabIndex="-1" _
      xd:disableEditing="yes" style="WIDTH: 100%"/>
</xsl:stylesheet>
  </xsl:template>
```

7. **Immediately after the *<span ... />* element, add an *<xsl:value-of select="xdExtension:testFunction(//my:sampleTable/my:sampleRow)"/>* element that calls *testFunction* with a *IXMLDOMNodeList* argument; *testFunction* calculates and returns the running sum as a *Double* value. Your template code now appears as shown here:**

```
<xsl:template match="my:myFields" mode="xd:preserve">
  <span class="xdExpressionBox xdDataBindingUI" title=""
  xd:CtrlId="CTRL8" xd:xctname="ExpressionBox" tabIndex="-1"
  xd:disableEditing="yes" style="WIDTH: 100%">
    <xsl:value-of
select="xdExtension:testFunction(//my:sampleTable/my:sampleRow)" />
  </span>
</xsl:template>
```

   The project includes the *testFunction* code, so you don't need to add it.

8. **Save your changes, return to Windows Explorer, and double-click view1.xsl to open it in Internet Explorer. Scroll to the end of the page to verify that your template is well-formed.**
9. **Close Internet Explorer and Notepad, and reopen the project. The form in design mode appears as shown here:**

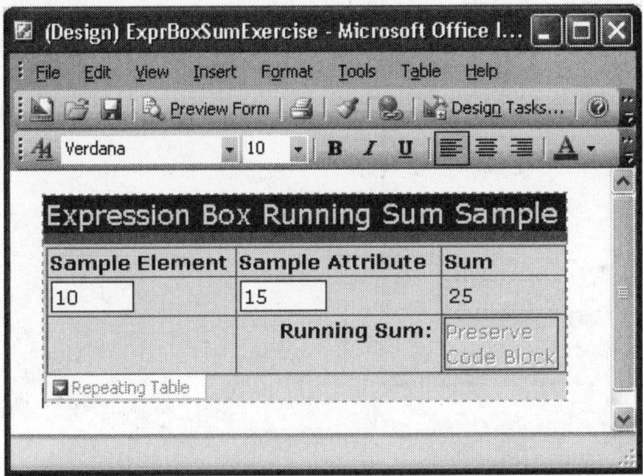

The Preserve Code Block control results from elements with the *mode="xd:preserve"* attribute you added in steps 5 and 6.

10. **Preview the form, and verify that the running sum value is correct.**

If you experience problems with the preceding procedure, use Notepad or Internet Explorer to compare your modifications to view1.xsl with the version in the ...\Chapter17\ExprBoxSums\ExprBoxSumProject folder.

Exploring the NWOrdersWSProject Web Service Client

The NWOrdersWSProject.sln solution in your C:\Program Files\Introducing InfoPath 2003\Chapter17\NWOrdersWS\NWOrdersWSProject folder is a major upgrade to the original NWOrdersWS Web service client that you developed in Chapter 14, "Designing InfoPath Web Service Clients." Figure 17-8 shows the upgraded version with an added Insert Order button and several enhancements to the OrderDetail repeating table. The original version, NWOrdersWS.xsn, is in the Chapter17\NWOrdersWS folder.

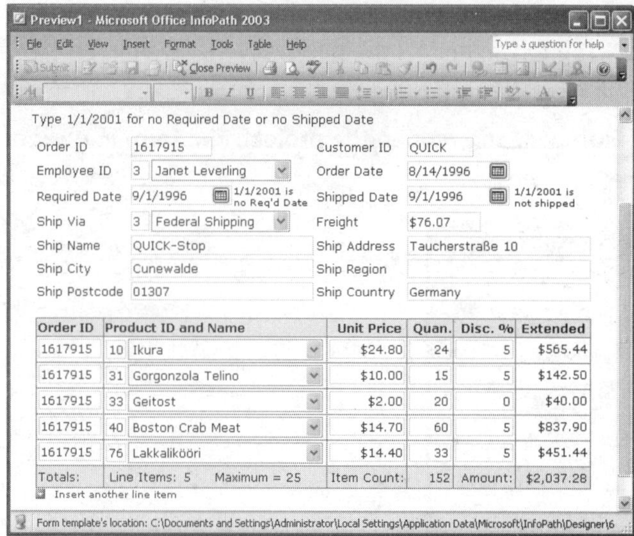

Figure 17-8 NWOrdersWSProject is an upgraded version of Chapter 14's NWOrdersWS template that adds the capability to insert a new order and adds new features to the OrderDetail repeating table.

Because NWOrdersWSProject has more than 500 lines of commented Visual Basic .NET code, reproducing the code here isn't practical. To get the most out of this section, open NWOrdersWSProject.sln, and examine the code. The sequence of event handlers, functions, and a procedure in the FormCode.vb window follows the order of this list of form features added by managed code:

- The *RequiredDate_OnAfterChange* and *ShippedDate_OnAfterChange* event handlers test RequiredDate and ShippedDate fields and substitute an arbitrary 2001-01-01T00:00:00 value for the Null *dateTime* value–0001-01-01T00:00:00.00000000-08:00 for Pacific Standard Time–returned by the Web service. The Web service recognizes January 1 of any year as a Null value.

- For new orders, the *OnContextChange* event handler automatically sets the RequiredDate value to a week after the OrderDate. The *OnContextChange* event fires when the user or code sets the focus to another bound control.
- The *RequiredDate_OnBeforeChange* event handler displays an error message if the user sets RequiredDate to less than five days after the OrderDate.
- The *ExtendedTotal* function displays in the repeating table's footer the running sum of extended net price. The function is a more complex version of the preceding section's *testFunction*. Open view1.xsl, and search for *xd:preserve* to view the changes made to the transform, which include right-aligning the expression box text.

- The *ProductID_OnBeforeChange* event handler tests for duplicate ProductID values that would violate the primary key constraint of the NorthwindCS database's Order Details table.
- The *ProductID_OnAfterChange* event handler inserts UnitPrice values for added or altered OrderDetail items. The third field of the GetProductsDetailed secondary data source supplies the UnitPrice value. This feature overcomes a major flaw in earlier versions of the Northwind Traders Order Entry and Editing forms–users were required to refer to a printed price list to add the UnitPrice value. A fourth data source field provides QuantityPerUnit (SKU) data, which you can use to populate a repeating table expression box.
- The *OrderDetail_OnBeforeChange* event handler tests for more than 25 line items per order, which is the maximum number the Web service accepts. This event handler demonstrates operations on all elements of the repeating OrderDetail group.
- The *UpdateOrInsertOrder* procedure provides the equivalent of the New Record feature, which InfoPath provides for database main data sources but not for Web service clients. Clicking the Insert Order button sets the OrderID value to 0, which the Web service recognizes as an insert request.
- InfoPath's submit process ignores the Web service's OrderID return value. To overcome this limitation, the *UpdateOrInsertOrder* procedure requeries the Web service to return the last-entered OrderID value after an insert operation. This value is subject to error in a very high volume order entry scenario, but it's unlikely that an InfoPath client would be used in this case.

NWOrdersWSProject.sln demonstrates that you can design and deploy a production-quality Web service client with InfoPath SP-1. You could implement all the preceding features with JScript or VBScript, but writing managed Visual Basic .NET or Visual C# code in Visual Studio .NET makes debugging much easier and enables advanced features that are very difficult or impossible to implement with script. As an example, you can write managed code in an *OnSubmitRequest* event handler for a Web service that requires SOAP headers. If you're an accomplished ASP.NET Web services programmer and have Web Services Enhancements (WSE) 2.0 installed, you can implement the WS-Security specification's digital signing feature, which eliminates the need to customize Web services to accommodate InfoPath form-level digital signatures and offers the added security of encrypted transmission. WSE 2.0 also lets you consume Web services that implement the WS-Addressing, WS-Policy, WS-SecurityPolicy, WS-Trust, and WS-SecureConversation specifications.

See Also For more information about WSE 2.0, go to *msdn.microsoft.com/webservices/*, and choose Building, Web Service Enhancements (WSE) from the menu. For the details of Microsoft's implementation of the WS-series specifications, visit *msdn.microsoft.com/webservices/understanding/advancedwebservices/*.

Creating Your Own NWOrdersWS Web Service

Relying on third-party Web services is chancy if the Web service publisher doesn't provide quality-of-service guarantees. The OakLeaf Demonstration Web site, which is connected to the Interned by a DSL line, has had 99.3 percent uptime for two years, but there's no guarantee that this level of service will continue indefinitely. Thus, there's the possibility that you won't be able to connect to the NWOrdersWS Web service at *www.oakleaf.ws/nwordersws/nwordersws.asmx*. Visual Studio .NET makes creating ASP.NET Web services a quick and easy process, so you might want to create a local ASP.NET Web service as a learning exercise, as well as for insurance against an inability to run the OakLeaf demonstration service.

To create the NWOrdersWS virtual directory for the local Web service, follow these steps.

▶ **Add an Internet Information Services (IIS) virtual directory**

1. Navigate to the \Inetpub\wwwroot folder, and add a new folder named **NWOrdersWS**. Alternatively, you can add the folder in step 4.
2. Open IIS Manager, right-click the Default Web Site node, and choose New, Virtual Directory from the shortcut menu to start the Virtual Directory Creation Wizard. Click Next.
3. In the Virtual Directory Alias dialog box, type **NWOrdersWS**, and click Next.
4. In the Web Site Content Directory dialog box, click Browse, navigate to and select the folder you created in step 1, click OK, and click Next.
5. Click Next to accept the default access permissions, and click Next and Finish to add the virtual directory and close the wizard.
6. Right-click the NWOrdersWS node, choose Properties from the shortcut menu to open the NWOrdersWS Properties dialog box, and click the Directory Security tab.
7. Click the Edit button in the Authentication And Access Control section to open the Authentication Methods dialog box. Select the Enable Anonymous Access check box (if it isn't selected), click OK twice to close dialog boxes and apply the change, and close IIS Manager.
8. If you have Windows SharePoint Services installed on your test server, use the SharePoint Central Administration tool to exclude the NWOrdersWS virtual directory from SharePoint management, as described in the note in the section "Obtaining a Digital Signing Certificate," in Chapter 11.

You must run the NWOrdersSP.sql Transact-SQL script to create the stored procedures for the main and secondary data sources. Substitute SQL Server 2000's sample Northwind database if you aren't running MSDE 2000 with the NorthwindCS database. You can't add the stored procedures as a group in the Stored Procedure box of an Access 2000 or later data project, so you must use the command-line osql.exe tool if you don't have SQL Server Query Analyzer installed. You also must change the Order Details table's Discount data type from *real* to **decimal**(4,3) to avoid rounding errors that affect the expression box's value.

To create the stored procedures with osql.exe and fix the Discount data type problem, follow these steps.

▶ Add stored procedures to NorthwindCS with the osql utility

1. Open a Command Prompt window, and navigate to the C:\Microsoft Press\Introducing InfoPath 2003\Chapter17\NWOrdersWS folder.
2. Type **osql -E -d NorthwindCS -i NWOrdersSP.sql**, and press Enter. This command uses Windows authentication for the local (default) SQL Server instance, specifies the NorthwindCS database, and runs the NWOrdersSP.sql script.
3. Type **quit**, and press Enter to exit osql. Close the Command Prompt window.
4. Start Access 2002 or later, open the sample NorthwindCS.adp project in your ...\Microsoft Office\Office{10|11}\Samples folder, and open the Order Details table in design view.
5. Change the data type of the Discount column to decimal, and set Precision to 4 and Scale to 3 to accommodate three decimal places, as shown here:

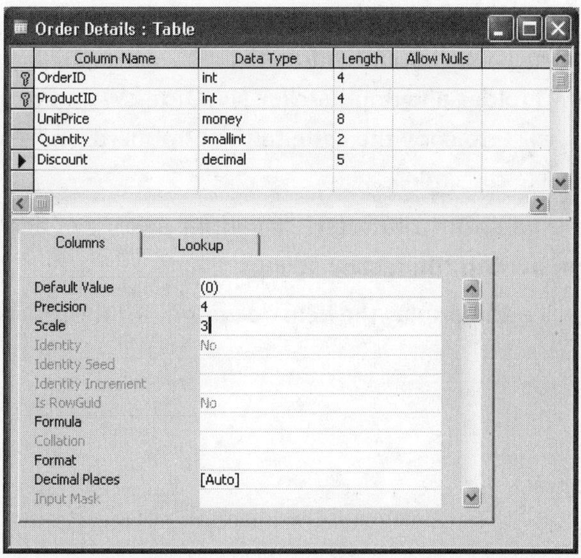

The Discount column inherited values with rounding errors from the Jet version. Rounding errors cause InfoPath expression boxes to display NaN (not a number) messages for some discount values instead of expected numeric values.

6. Close the Order Details: Table window, click Yes to save your changes, and click Yes in the Save window.
7. Click the Queries button, and verify that the four stored procedures—ipGetOrder, ipInsertDetail, ipInsertOrder, and ipUpdateOrder—are present in the list.
8. Double-click ipGetOrder, type a valid OrderID value—such as **11076**—in the Enter Parameter Value box, and click OK to display values for the order; Order Details values don't appear in the grid.

> **Caution**
> If you don't complete steps 5 and 6, invoking the *GetOrderSP* and *UpdateOrInsertOrderSP* Web methods throws an *Invalid OrderID value* SOAP exception. If you don't have Access 2002 or later, you must make this data type change with SQL Server Enterprise Manager.

In this section's final procedure, you'll create and test a local copy of the NWOrdersWS Web service with the NWOrdersWSLocal.xsn solution in the ...Chapter17\NWOrdersWS\NWOrdersWSLocal folder.

▶ **Create and test the NWOrdersWS Web service**

1. Open Visual Studio, and choose File, New, Project. Select Visual Basic Projects, click ASP.NET Web Service, change the Location text to http://localhost/**NWOrdersWS**, and click OK to create the project in the virtual directory folder.
2. Open Solution Explorer, and change Service1.asmx's name to **NWOrdersWS.asmx**. Right-click the node, and choose View Code from the shortcut menu to display the default Web service stub. Delete *all* code.
3. Navigate to the C:\Microsoft Press\Introducing InfoPath 2003\Chapter17\NWOrdersWS folder, and double-click NWOrdersWS.txt to open it in Notepad. Press Ctrl+A, Ctrl+C to copy the code to the Clipboard, and then return to Visual Studio and paste the code.
4. If the SQL Server sa account is password-protected, search for *pwd=* and add the password after the equal sign in both connection strings.
5. Press F5 to build the Web service and display the help document for the service, as shown here:

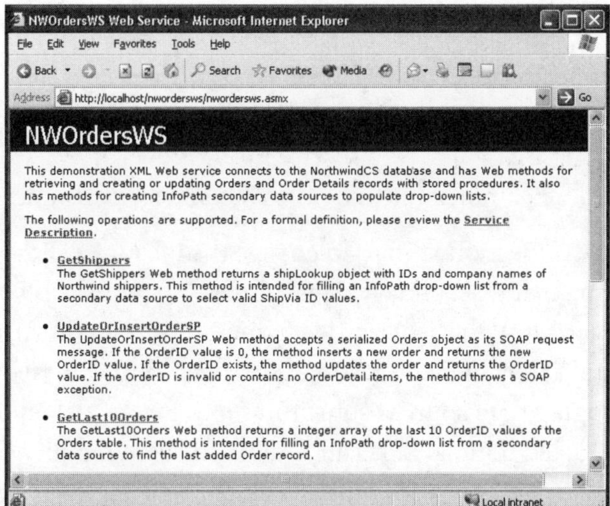

6. Verify the database connection by clicking each of the Get... method links to open the test page for the method and clicking Invoke to display the SOAP response message payload. The GetOrderSP method requires a valid OrderID parameter, as shown here:

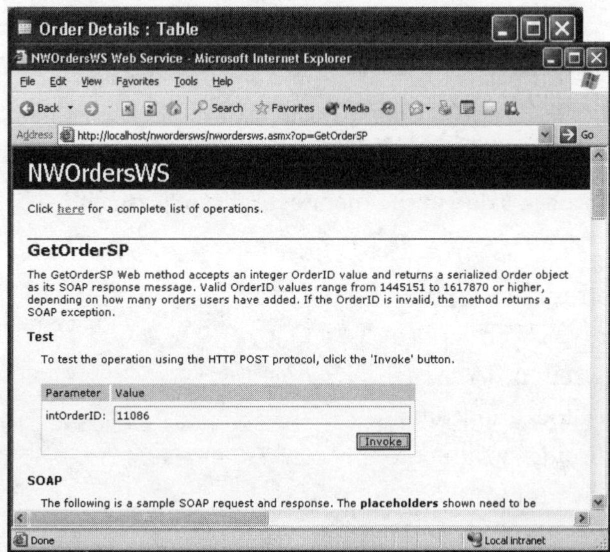

7. Open NWOrdersWSLocal.xsn from the ...Chapter17\NWOrdersWS\NWOrdersWSLocal folder and verify that the query, update, and insert operations behave as expected.

Changing the URL of a Web Service

It's a common practice to design and test new ASP.NET Web services on a local computer or development Web server and then migrate the service to a production server after testing. Changing the URL for a Web service in Windows or Web form clients is easy; the process is more complex for InfoPath Web service consumers.

InfoPath lets you use the Data Connection Wizard to change the location (URL) and the namespace of the form's main and secondary data sources. If you have several data sources, making these changes with the wizard is tedious and fraught with opportunity for generating fatal errors, which you don't discover until you save the changes to the template. Changing data sources substitutes *ns2:* for the default *s0:* namespace prefix in most extracted template files and InfoPath event-handler attributes, but not in the XPath expressions of code you write.

A faster and less error-prone approach is to make the required *serviceUrl*, *soapAction*, and *xmlns:s0* namespace changes to the project's manifest.xsf, .xml, and .xsl files directly. Here are the basic steps.

▶ **Make namespace changes directly in project files**

1. **Obtain the new *serviceUrl*, *soapAction*, and *xmlns:s0* namespace values from the *location*, *soapAction*, and *targetNamespace* values of the relocated service's Web Services Description Language (WSDL) document.**
2. **Replace the *serviceUrl* and *soapAction* values in the manifest.xsf file.**
3. **Replace the *xmlns:s0* namespace value in the manifest.xsf, .xml, .xsl, and FormCode.vb files.**

The following procedure requires creating the local version of the NWOrdersWS Web service, as described in the preceding section. To change the NWOrdersWS Web service location from *www.oakleaf.ws/nwordersws/nwordersws.asmx* to *localhost/nwordersws/nwordersws.asmx*, follow these steps.

> **Expediting the search and replace process**
> A multifile Notepad replacement—such as Just Great Software's EditPad Lite (free for non-commercial use) or EditPad Pro—speeds the replacement process. You can download either version from *www.editpadlite.com*.

▶ **Change the URL of a copy of NWOrdersWSProject**

1. **Create a copy of the NWOrdersWSProject folder in your ...\Chapter17\ NWOrdersWS folder, and rename the folder to NWOrdersWSTest or the like.**

2. Open Solution Explorer, right-click the NWOrdersWSProject node (immediately under the Solution node), and choose Set As StartUp Project from the shortcut menu.
3. Rename the solution file to **NWOrdersWSTest**, right-click the Solution node, and choose Save NWOrdersWSTest.sln.
4. Double-click FormCode.vb in Solution Explorer, press F5, verify that the preview works with the OakLeaf Web service, and then close the project. Optionally, remove NWOrdersWSProject.sln and NWOrdersWSProject.suo to avoid confusion with the source project.
5. Open *http://localhost/nworderws/nworderws.asmx?wsdl* in Internet Explorer, and note the *location*, *soapAction*, and *targetNamespace* attribute values.
6. If you're using a multifile editor, select manifest.xsf, FormCode.vb, and all .xsd, .xml, and .xsl files to edit simultaneously. Otherwise, skip to step 9.
7. For this example, replace *www.oakleaf.ws* with **localhost**.
8. Replace *oakleaf.ws* with **localhost**, and save all changes. (The sequence of steps 7 and 8 is important.) Skip the remaining steps.
9. If you're using Notepad, make the changes in steps 7 and 8 to manifest.xsf, and save the changes. (The manifest.xsf file is the only file that contains *serviceUrl* and *soapAction* values.)
10. Make the changes in step 8 to FormCode.vb, and to each .xsd, .xml, and .xsl file in your project.

▶ **Test the project and fix a potential OrderDate problem**

1. Reopen NWOrdersWSTest.sln, press F5 to build the project, and open the preview window.
2. Run a query with several of the last 10 orders, including those with non-Null ShipDate values.
3. If the Ship Date date picker value is today's date for all queries, perform the following steps. Otherwise, skip to step 8.
4. Close the preview window, and open InfoPath in design mode. Click the Data Source link, expand the Date Fields node, and right-click OrderDate and choose Properties from the shortcut menu to open its Properties dialog box.
5. Change the default value from *now()* to **1/1/2001**, click OK, and save your changes.
6. Add the following code immediately after the *Try* statement of the *OnContextChange* event handler:

```
Dim nodOrderDate As IXMLDOMNode = _
   e.XDocument.DOM.selectSingleNode("//s0:OrderDate")
If Not nodOrderDate Is Nothing Then
   If nodOrderDate.text = "2001-01-01T00:00:00" Then
      nodOrderDate.text = DateTime.Now.ToString("s")
   End If
End If
```

This code runs only when the form opens and solves a problem that can occur when you use a computed rather than a fixed default value for dates.

7. **Rerun the project, and verify that the Order Date values are correct.**
8. **Update and insert one or two orders to verify that the service behaves as expected.**

Chapter Summary

Adding managed Visual Basic .NET or Visual C# code event handlers and functions to InfoPath projects frees you from reliance on VBScript and JScript and lets you take full advantage of the .NET Framework 1.1. This chapter's example procedures incorporate managed code counterparts of several InfoPath SDK Developer Sample Forms. The examples require running the forms' code with full trust, which you enable with the .NET Framework 1.1 Configuration tool.

The Rss2EventsFinal.sln solution demonstrates how to use Visual Basic to change the contents of a custom task pane and test a form with signed data blocks for missing digital signatures. The Rss2Production.sln project is an upgraded version of Rss2EventsFinal.sln that adds several new fields and illustrates how to generate a production-quality, fully formatted rss.xml file that's validated by Jorgen Thelin's RSS 2.0 schema, which you can download from his Web site. This project also shows you how to add a form toolbar and create event handlers for custom toolbar buttons, detect errors before saving a file with a toolbar button, write a complex regular expression to validate RSS 2.0–compliant date/time values, and write event handlers to copy a field's content to another field.

The ExprBoxSumProject.sln solution shows you how to display in a footer expression box running sums of values calculated from field values of repeating table rows. The NWOrdersWSProject.sln Web service client project provides a more sophisticated running sum example. This project also explains how to write event-handling code that calculates and tests date values, prevents violation of a database table's primary key fields, adds values from a single secondary data source to two fields of a repeating table, inserts new database records, and emulates return values from Web service submit operations.

This book's final procedures show you how to create a local version of the NWOrdersWS ASP.NET Web service and change the URL for a Web service that's moved to a new location.

Here's hoping that you've enjoyed your introduction to Microsoft Office InfoPath 2003 SP-1. You're now ready to take full advantage of InfoPath SP-1's power, the .NET Framework 1.1's advanced features, and the Visual Basic .NET language to develop enterprise-level, XML-based forms.

Q&A

Does the *XDocument.Solution.URI* property value return a different path when you open a form from its .xsn file in the ...\bin\Debug or ...\bin\Release folder instead of from the InfoPath solution's folder?

Yes. When you open an existing form or create a new one from the .xsn file, *XDocument.Solution.URI* returns the well-formed path to the .xsn file. Open Rss2EventsFinal.xsn in the ...\Chapter17\Rss2EventsFinal\Rss2EventsFinal\bin\Release folder, create a new form, and choose File, Save As to verify that the file is saved in the correct folder.

Q. Must users change their .NET Framework 1.1 security level for InfoPath Form Templates to run fully trusted forms?

A. Not if the deployed form has been digitally signed or published as a custom-installed template. It's an uncommon practice to deploy a production form without signing the code, even if the form doesn't require full trust. The code signing certificate ensures that the form hasn't undergone unauthorized modifications. This assurance depends on users who carefully examine the signing certificate when they first open a new or modified form and don't automatically trust the publisher.

Q. Why do I need to resign a fully trusted form's template .xsn file after every build to test it with an XML data document?

A. Even if you don't change the form's design or managed code, building the form deletes and re-creates the .xsn file.

Q. Is there any limit to the number of text boxes or other controls I can populate with a single secondary data source?

A. The only limitation is the size of the secondary data source document, which affects the opening time of forms that receive data from Web services or stored procedures. If your data changes infrequently, you can add an Update Data Sources button to the form and write an event handler to query the database or Web service and write the data to a local XML file. In this case, your secondary data source must be an XML document that's not incorporated into the form as a resource file. You can add a receive-data Web method that reports the date of the last update to each secondary data source and compare the local XML file's modified date to determine whether a refresh operation is required.

On Your Own

Here are some advanced exercises to test your knowledge of the topics in this and the preceding two chapters:

1. Using the techniques you learned in the section "Setting Custom File Paths and Names," in Chapter 16, use the *XDocument.Solution.URI* property value, which returns the path and file name of the form's template, to set the form's Caption property to **NW** followed by the OrderID value and save documents as NW*OrderID*.xml.
2. Create a copy of the NWOrdersWSProject or NWOrdersWSLocal folder, and write an event handler to request and save the GetProductsDetailed Web method's response document file in the project folder. Optionally change the data source for the ProductID combo box to the XML file.
3. Add a Line Item number expression box to the repeating table of the copy you created. Hint: You can use the XPath *position* function or a counter to determine the item number.
4. Add an SKU expression box to the repeating table, and populate it with the SKU text of the GetProductsDetailed secondary data source. This process is similar to–but a bit trickier than–programming the running sum expression box.
5. Create a custom, formatted XML file that's identical to the payload of the SOAP response document of a query. Make *<GetOrderSPResult>* the root element, include all its child nodes, and change the root element name to **<Order>**.

Index

D

E

N

Q

R

S

U

X

Y

Z